Business and Administrative Communication

ELEVENTH EDITION

KITTY O. LOCKER
The Ohio State University

DONNA S. KIENZLER
Iowa State University

Mc
Graw
Hill
Education

BUSINESS AND ADMINISTRATIVE COMMUNICATION, ELEVENTH EDITION

Published by McGraw-Hill Education, 2 Penn Plaza, New York, NY 10121. Copyright © 2015 by McGraw-Hill Education. All rights reserved. Printed in the United States of America. Previous editions © 2013, 2010, and 2008. No part of this publication may be reproduced or distributed in any form or by any means, or stored in a database or retrieval system, without the prior written consent of McGraw-Hill Education, including, but not limited to, in any network or other electronic storage or transmission, or broadcast for distance learning.

Some ancillaries, including electronic and print components, may not be available to customers outside the United States.

This book is printed on acid-free paper.

3 4 5 6 7 8 9 DOW 21 20 19 18 17 16

ISBN   978-1-259-09565-8
MHID   1-259-09565-7

www.mhhe.com

To my beloved husband, Jim, and dearest friend Kitty.

A Debt of Gratitude

Kitty O. Locker was my closest friend and professional colleague. We met in graduate school and mentored each other throughout our careers. She devoted herself to making Business and Administrative Communication *a leading textbook, and I am proud to carry forward her tradition of excellence.*

Christopher Toth is a third person who has consistently contributed to the content and quality of Business and Administrative Communication (BAC). *Christopher began working on BAC with the 8th edition, researching content, writing many sidebars, developing new exercises, and selecting photos; he also wrote the Mosaic extended case (available online), and co-revised the Instructor's Manual and PowerPoint slides. He has continued to take a growing role in BAC. For the last two editions, in addition to helping with research and photographs, he has collaborated on text changes, updated the five chapters in the "Proposals and Reports" section plus the "Designing Documents" chapter, and written most of the ancillary materials.*

Christopher is an Assistant Professor at Grand Valley State University in Allendale, Michigan, where he teaches business communication, document design, professional writing, and visual rhetoric. His research interests are visual design, negative messages, technology concerns, and writing pedagogy. He consistently presents his research at the Association for Business Communication's annual conference. For that organization, he also serves as the chair of the Technology Board.

THE AUTHOR

Donna S. Kienzler is a Professor Emeritus of English at Iowa State University in Ames, Iowa, where she taught in the Rhetoric and Professional Communication program. She was the Director of Advanced Communication and oversaw more than 120 sections of business and technical communication annually. She was also an Assistant Director of the university's Center for Excellence in Learning and Teaching, where she taught classes, seminars, and workshops on pedagogy; directed graduate student programming; and directed the Preparing Future Faculty program, a career-training program for graduate students and postdoctoral fellows.

Her research focused on pedagogy and ethics. Her article with Helen Ewald, "Speech Act Theory and Business Communication Conventions," won an Association for Business Communication (ABC) Alpha Kappa Psi Foundation Award for distinguished publication in business communication. Her article with Carol David, "Towards an Emancipatory Pedagogy in Service Courses and User Departments," was part of a collection that won a National Council of Teachers of English (NCTE) Award for Excellence in Technical and Scientific Communication: Best Collection of Essays in Technical or Scientific Communication.

She has done consulting work for the Air Force, Tracor Consulting, Green Engineering, Northwestern Bell, Iowa Merit Employment, the Iowa Department of Transportation, the University of Missouri, and her local school district.

She is active in the Association for Business Communication (ABC), where she currently serves on the board of directors as well as on the Business Practices and the Teaching Practices Committees. She also served on ABC's Ad Hoc Committee on Professional Ethics, which developed a Professional Ethics Statement for the national organization.

In 2002, she received ABC's Meada Gibbs Outstanding Teacher Award.

BRIEF CONTENTS

Connect® + BAC = Effective Communicators

Business and Administrative Communication (BAC) is flexible, specific, interesting, comprehensive, and up-to-date. BAC uses a rhetorical emphasis of audience purpose, and context allowing communicators to shape their messages appropriately for all channels and purposes.

BAC conveys the best possible advice to students while Connect® Business Communication allows students to apply concepts and practice skills.

McGraw-Hill *Connect Business Communication*

Connect is an all-digital teaching and learning environment designed from the ground up to work with the way instructors and students think, teach, and learn. As a digital teaching, assignment, and assessment platform, *Connect* strengthens the link among faculty, students, and coursework, helping everyone accomplish more in less time.

LearnSmart Achieve: Excel in Your Writing *LearnSmart Achieve* is a revolutionary new learning system that combines a continually adaptive learning experience with important, rich, dynamic learning resources to help students learn the material, retain more knowledge and get better grades. Some student results can be found on the front inside cover of this text.

As a student progresses through *LearnSmart Achieve,* the program's continuously adaptive learning path adjusts to deliver just-in-time resources—instructional videos, simulations—catered to each student's needs. This model is designed to accelerate learning and strengthen memory recall.

LearnSmart Achieve for Business Communication develops or improves editing skills and empowers students to put responsible writing into practice. With interactive documentation tools, it helps students master the foundations of writing. Developed based on ethnographic qualitative and quantitative research, it addresses the needs of today's classrooms, both online and traditional.

Presentation Skills: Skill Practice Inside and Outside the Classroom *Connect's* presentation capture tool gives instructors the ability to evaluate presentations and students the freedom to practice their presentations anytime, and anywhere. With its fully customizable rubric, instructors can measure students' uploaded presentations against course outcome and give students specific feedback on where improvement is needed.

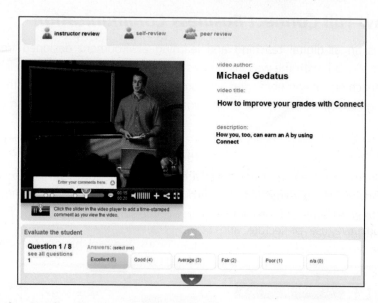

Interactive Applications: A Higher Level of Learning *Interactive Applications* for each chapter allow students to practice real business situations, stimulate critical thinking, and reinforce key concepts. Students receive immediate feedback and can track their progress in their own report. Detailed results let instructors see at a glance how each student performs and easily track the progress of every student in their course.

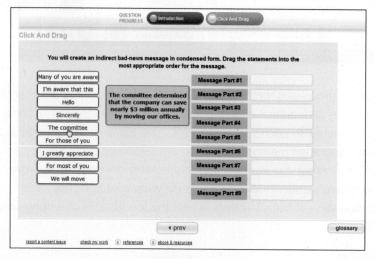

Connect Plus Business Communication   *Connect Plus Business Communication* gives students access to an integrated e-book, allowing for anytime, anywhere access to the textbook. With each homework problem directly mapped to the topic in the book, the student is only one click away from the textbook. The e-book also includes a powerful search function that allows students to quickly scan the entire book for relevant topics.

Efficient Administrative Capabilities   *Connect* offers you, the instructor, auto-gradable material in an effort to facilitate teaching and learning.

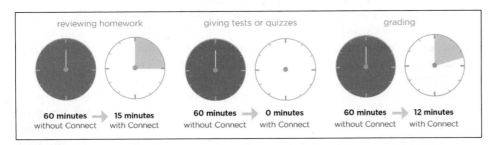

reviewing homework		giving tests or quizzes		grading	
60 minutes without Connect	**15 minutes** with Connect	**60 minutes** without Connect	**0 minutes** with Connect	**60 minutes** without Connect	**12 minutes** with Connect

Student Progress Tracking   *Connect* keeps instructors informed about how each student, section, and class is performing, allowing for more productive use of lecture and office hours. The progress tracking function enables instructors to:

- View scored work immediately and track individual or group performance with assignment and grade reports.
- Access an instant view of student or class performance relative to learning objectives.
- Collect data and generate reports required by many accreditation organizations, such as AACSB.

Connect and *LearnSmart* allow me to present course material to students in more ways than just the explanations they hear from me directly. Because of this, students are processing the material in new ways, requiring them to think. I now have more students asking questions in class because the more we think, the more we question.

Sharon Feaster, Instructor at Hinds Community College

What's New?

Many changes make the 11th edition even better. You will find new examples throughout the book. As you might expect, one of the biggest changes is even more emphasis on electronic communication and tools. In addition to an expanded Chapter 9, "Sharing Informative and Positive Messages with Appropriate Technology," almost every chapter now has its own technology section. You will also notice more learning objectives and chapter summaries organized around learning objectives. New end-of-chapter exercises include shorter cases to complement the extended case on the *BAC* website.

The 11th edition includes new communication advice from business figures such as Warren Buffett, Nate Silver, and Colin Powell; as well as new examples of communication practices from major businesses such as Amazon, Boeing, Campbell, Dairy Queen, IBM, J.C. Penney, Microsoft, Toyota, Yahoo, and Zappos.

New web resources, as well as coverage of new topics, such as why positive psychology is important for business, why trust is important for good communication, how our body language influences our own behavior, what communication skills big data demands, how to create infographics, and why etiquette is important are discussed.

Chapters offer new material from major business books, such as

- Dan Ariely, *Predictably Irrational: The Hidden Forces that Shape Our Decisions.*
- Marc Benioff and Karen Southwick, *Compassionate Capitalism: How Corporations Can Make Doing Good an Integral Part of Doing Well.*
- Jonah Berger, *Contagious: Why Things Catch On.*
- Clayton M. Christensen, James Allworth, and Karen Dillon, *How Will You Measure Your Life?*
- Frances Frei and Anne Morriss, *Uncommon Service: How to Win by Putting Customers at the Core of Your Business.*
- Daniel Kahneman, *Thinking, Fast and Slow.*
- Carol Loomis, ed. *Tap Dancing to Work: Warren Buffett on Practically Everything, 1966-2012: A Fortune Magazine Book.*
- Daniel H. Pink, *To Sell Is Human: The Surprising Truth about Moving Others.*
- Colin Powell with Tony Koltz, *It Worked for Me: In Life and Leadership.*
- Nate Silver, *The Signal and the Noise: Why So Many Predictions Fail—But Some Don't.*

Chapters also offer new information from leading business sources such as

- *Bloomberg Businessweek*
- *CNNMoney*
- *Fast Company*
- *Forbes*
- *Fortune*
- *Harvard Business Review*
- *Inc.*
- *Wall Street Journal*

Updates also come from leading metropolitan newspapers, including the *Los Angeles Times*, *New York Times*, and *Washington Post*, as well as too many websites to mention.

Every chapter has been revised to keep it up-to-date for instructors and interesting for students. Listed below are new or updated content and features.

Chapter 1: Succeeding in Business Communication

- Opens with the nearly $50 billion cost of miscommunication for Bank of America.
- Updates figures for USPS mail and electronic communication quantities.
- Places section on "Benefits of Good Communication Skills" first.
- Reinforces good communication as a quality that makes organizations desirable places to work.
- Includes new information on how good communication skills benefit individuals.
- Provides new examples of billion-dollar costs for poor communication.
- Updates list of executives who have lost their positions because of e-mail.
- Updates section on electronic communication.
- Provides sidebars on importance of good writing and reading skills at Amazon, Warren Buffett's advice on good business writing, and problem-solving advice from Nate Silver's *The Signal and the Noise*.

Chapter 2: Adapting Your Message to Your Audience

- Opens with the outreach to male audiences for formerly female-oriented products.
- Increases information on electronic channels and their different advantages.
- Summarizes Pew research on channel shifts and age and gender preferences for channels.
- Provides examples on topics such as creative uses of channels and the efficacy of audience benefits.
- Discusses customers not willing to pay for benefits they need.
- Presents sidebars on audiences for General Colin Powell, audience subgroups for Americans without health insurance, Wikipedia channel mending, customer texting, business cards as a channel, and a younger audience for Campbell soups.

Chapter 3: Building Goodwill

- Includes new sections on "Positive Psychology," what it is, how it uses you-attitude and goodwill, why business should care about it, and how companies can use it; "Trust," how it relates to the skills described in this chapter and why it is important for job success; and "Using Technology to Build Goodwill," how companies are successfully using electronic channels.
- Opens with department store Macy's efforts to offer merchandise appealing to specific minorities.
- Shows Microsoft using you-attitude in its relations with Chinese officials.

- Emphasizes the importance of you-attitude as a job skill that computers will not replace.
- Updates information on the makeup of the U.S. population showing the growing diversity of the workplace and the need to communicate with appropriate, unbiased language.
- Provides sidebars on airline goodwill, Progressive insurance goodwill, the positive/negative ratio for success in business, workplace thanks, inaccurate positive spin from movie studios, the perils of offensive advertising, and web accessibility.

Chapter 4: Navigating the Business Communication Environment

- Includes new sections on etiquette and big data.
- Opens with a description of grocery stores using nonverbal communication to create a sales environment.
- Provides additional information on and examples of ethics initiatives and the huge costs of ethics lapses.
- Presents additional criteria for ethical choices and action.
- Gives new web resources on ethics.
- Updates information on outsourcing, globalization, and corporate culture.
- Explains ways our body language influences our own behavior.
- Includes new material on networking, data security problems, electronic media invasions of privacy, and the innovation process. Also presents new material on big data: what it is, why it is important, how it is being used, and communication skills it demands.
- Provides new examples of firms working to keep a more positive work/family balance and to reduce their environmental impact.
- Explains the debate over telecommuting sparked by Yahoo's new CEO.
- Presents sidebars on communication ethics, job perks as part of corporate culture, exercise workstations, the role of serendipity in interpersonal communications, the hacking of the Sony networks, and data mining competitions.

Chapter 5: Planning, Composing, and Revising

- Opens with a $1.2 billion two-word phrase.
- Provides writing advice from professional writers Donald Murray and Anne Lamott.
- Elaborates on creating a rough draft.
- Presents style illustrations from Warren Buffett's 2012 letter to stockholders.
- Provides new examples of diction choices with profound implications.
- Includes information on technology that helps in giving and receiving feedback.
- Presents sidebars on *forecasting* vs. *predicting* earthquakes, bribery definitions, words for selling homes, the Internet's influence on conciseness, and proofreading errors.

Chapter 6: Designing Documents

- Includes new sections on using various software programs to create designs and on creating infographics.
- Opens with a description of how Morningstar, an investment firm, uses document design to communicate complicated ideas to customers.
- Presents new information on white space plus social media and conventions.
- Provides new examples, including before and after examples of Delta boarding passes, as well as an infographic example.
- Presents sidebars on useful design principles, the power of color, infographic resources, image/photo resources, and usability.gov.

Chapter 7: Communicating across Cultures

- Includes a new section on outsourcing as a major aspect of global business.
- Opens with an explanation of how the success of Dairy Queen in China came from its adaptations to local culture.
- Updates information on global business, local culture adaptations, and diversity in North America.
- Presents information on customs for business meetings in Brazil, China, Germany, India, Japan, Russia, and Saudi Arabia.
- Also includes new information on food at global business meetings, body language in different countries, writing to international audiences, and oral communication, including a new section on handling negatives.
- Presents sidebars on marketing for Hispanic audiences, nonverbal communication tips for China, the difficulty of translating brand names into other languages, and IBM's expansion in Africa.

Chapter 8: Working and Writing in Teams

- Provides a new section on technology for teams.
- Opens with the importance of teamwork for animators.
- Includes new information on leadership, brainstorming techniques, and conflict resolution, as well as the importance of team skills for hiring and job success. Also adds new material on technology for teams, including sections on technologies for meetings, scheduling and assignments, and collaboration.
- Presents sidebars on scorecards for teams; teamwork myths; a company that's all teams, no bosses; and Berkshire Hathaway's 2013 annual meeting.

Chapter 9: Sharing Informative and Positive Messages with Appropriate Technology

- Includes new sections on tablet technology and on the use of story in informative messages.
- Opens with an article on how the Cleveland Clinic is providing better information to patients.

- Includes new information on using communication technology, text messages, tweets, and other social media; also, content on e-mail etiquette and following up on e-mails.
- Updates examples—from sources as varied as text messages, tweets, the National Hurricane Center, banks, credit card contracts, Zappos, and Standard and Poor.
- Provides sidebars on teaching doctors communication skills, pilots and air controllers texting each other, using social media at work, small businesses preferring LinkedIn over Twitter, managing your e-mail inbox, International Finance Corporation using storytelling to help transfer information, and the CDC's zombie apocalypse campaign spreading information on disaster preparations.

Chapter 10: Delivering Negative Messages

- Includes a new section on using technology for negative messages.
- Opens with J.C. Penney's media apology to try to slow its drastic decline in revenue.
- Provides new information on the costs of mishandling negative communication, including the costs of withholding negative communication; handling negative communication from employees; dealing with criticism; and tone in oral communications (rudeness).
- Shows how to respond to some common oral negative situations.
- Discusses pros and cons of various technologies for handling negative situations.
- Presents sidebars on bad weather warnings; restoring goodwill at Delta Air Lines; Toyota's media blitz to recover from its massive recall; the difficulties of cross-cultural apologies; a successful apology for a product meltdown; negative communications from lawyers negatively influencing judges, juries, and settlements; and Progressive Insurance's media flop: "My Sister Paid Progressive Insurance to Defend Her Killer in Court."

Chapter 11: Crafting Persuasive Messages

- Includes new sections on using technology for persuasive messages and on explaining problem solutions.
- Opens with a persuasive letter from congressional representatives to Washington Redskins owner Dan Snyder asking him to change the name of his team and not use Native Americans as mascots.
- Bolsters support for the importance of persuasion in business communications.
- Presents new examples for using emotional appeals and adapting persuasion to organizational cultures.
- Offers new information on choice architecture, constraints on evidence, performance reviews, and pricing; as well as choosing the wrong kind of persuasion, controlling information for sales, and explaining why the belief in the efficacy of threats is so widespread.

- Provides sidebars on a water charity, the importance of simplifying information and navigation on the web, persuasion to lose weight, Nobel prize winner Daniel Kahneman on how to write a believable persuasive message, behavioral economics being used in India for safety and health issues, Obama presidential campaign e-mail subject lines, in-store persuasion, how to persuade people to buy your business book, distinctions between charities and businesses, and fund-raising etiquette.

Chapter 12: Building Résumés

- Includes a new section on innovation and résumés, including videos, social media résumés, and "prezumés."
- Opens with a discussion of former Yahoo CEO Scott Thompson losing his job because of résumé dishonesty and then highlights other famous people who recently lost their jobs because of résumé dishonesty.
- Expands information on the role of social media in the job search.
- Updates job changing information, the steps of a job hunt, the importance of the GPA.
- Adds information on how to organize for a job hunt, how new employees are being found, how employers are filling jobs through social media, how to job hunt while currently employed.
- Expands emphasis on the importance of the traditional résumé.
- Provides sidebars on electronic tools for organizing job hunt materials, résumé blunders, famous people who have worked at McDonald's, the value of "soft" skills, and overused buzzwords, as well as what employers want, how Coca-Cola hires, and how to clean up online footprints (the Grandma Test).

Chapter 13: Writing Job Application Letters

- Includes a new section on social networking and personal websites.
- Opens with two very different application letters, both widely circulated, for Wall Street jobs.
- Includes new information on e-mail application letters and managing social media while job hunting.
- Updates examples.
- Presents sidebars on career changes, phantom job ads, unconventional tactics, bad cover letter content, and good cover letter content.

Chapter 14: Interviewing, Writing Follow-Up Messages, and Succeeding in the Job

- Offers new sections on meal etiquette and long-term career strategy.
- Opens with a Twitter interview for Pizza Hut.
- Includes new information on campus interviews.
- Provides new tips on phone, video, and multiple interviews.
- Presents new sidebars on jobs at *Fortune's* best companies to work for, Amazon interviews, Elena Kagan's confirmation "interview," and interview bloopers.

Chapter 15: Researching Proposals and Reports

- Includes new sections on using technology, including social media, for research and using quotations.
- Opens with a discussion of the United Nations report on how children are affected by war.
- Provides new examples of plagiarism in the news and how businesses routinely use research and surveys.
- Includes new information on Google searches, problems with phone surveys, and phrasing survey questions.
- Presents new sidebars on plagiarism among high-ranking politicians, research with e-readers, and research on the Deepwater Horizon explosion causes.

Chapter 16: Creating Visuals and Data Displays

- Includes new sections on infographics and software programs for creating visuals and data displays.
- Opens with a discussion of Australian cigarette packaging.
- Offers new information on dynamic displays, cross-cultural color associations, accommodations for persons with color blindness, ethical concerns with photos.
- Provides new examples and figures.
- Presents sidebars on ads for two audiences in one, color and NHL penalties, a doctored photo of the Boston Marathon bombing, and smartphones and photographs.

Chapter 17: Writing Proposals and Progress Reports

- Includes new sections on brainstorming for proposals, proposal varieties, and proposals for businesses.
- Opens with a new banking proposal.
- Provides new information on using technology and organizing proposals for businesses.
- Presents sidebars on MBA business plan competitions, Airbus proposal contest, business plan resources, Boeing's Progress Report on 787 Dreamliner, and databases and librarians.

Chapter 18: Analyzing Information and Writing Reports

- Includes new sections on data selection and appendixes.
- Opens with Boeing's Environmental Report.
- Provides new information on technology aids, especially for using time efficiently and auto-generating a table of contents.
- Presents sidebars on spreadsheet errors; hard-to-quantify sports participation data; the Feltron, an annual report on a life; cost-of-living comparison patterns; charity data; and a report on U.S. health.

Chapter 19: Making Oral Presentations

- Includes new sections on creating a Prezi and practicing presentations.
- Opens with Steve Jobs as orator.
- Includes new information on content choices, demonstrations, presentation openings, PowerPoint, other types of presentation software, backchannels and Twitter, and handling questions.
- Presents new sidebars on charisma, U.S. Army's spaghetti slide, audience perception of voices, handling tough questions, and slide sharing websites.

Retained Features

BAC Is Flexible

Choose the chapters and exercises that best fit your needs. Choose from in-class exercises, messages to revise, problems with hints, and cases presented as they'd arise in the workplace. Many problems offer several options: small group discussions, individual writing, group writing, or oral presentations.

BAC Is Specific

BAC provides specific strategies, specific guidelines, and specific examples, including annotated examples and paired good and bad examples. *BAC* takes the mystery out of creating effective messages.

BAC Is Interesting

Anecdotes from a variety of fields show business communication at work. The lively side columns from a host of sources provide insights into the workplace.

BAC Is Comprehensive

BAC includes international communication, communicating across cultures in this country, ethics, collaborative writing, organizational cultures, visuals and data displays, and technology as well as traditional concerns such as style and organization. Assignments offer practice dealing with international audiences or coping with ethical dilemmas. Analyses of sample problems prepare students to succeed in assignments.

BAC Is Up-to-Date

The 11th edition of BAC incorporates the latest research and practice so that you stay on the cutting edge.

Chapter Pedagogy

Chapter Outline and Learning Objectives

Each chapter begins with a chapter outline and learning objectives to guide students as they study. The chapter summary is organized by learning objectives and followed by learning objective review questions.

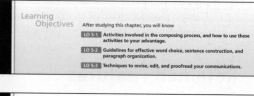

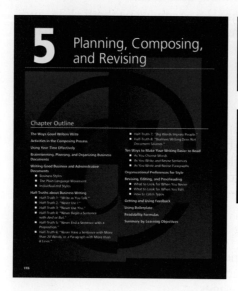

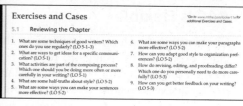

Business Communication in the News

Each chapter is introduced with a current news article relevant to the chapter's concepts. These opening articles set the stage for the chapter's content and allow students a glimpse at how the material applies in the business world.

Wealth of Sidebar Examples

These novel and interesting examples effectively enhance student understanding of key concepts. Featured in the margins of every chapter, these sidebars cover topic areas that include International, Legal/Ethical, Just for Fun, Technology, Web, and On the Job. In addition, gold stars identify "classic" sidebars.

Full-Page Sample Documents

A variety of visual examples featuring full-sized letters, e-mails, reports, and résumés are presented in the text. These examples include the authors' "handwritten" annotations, explaining communication miscues, while offering suggestions for improvement.

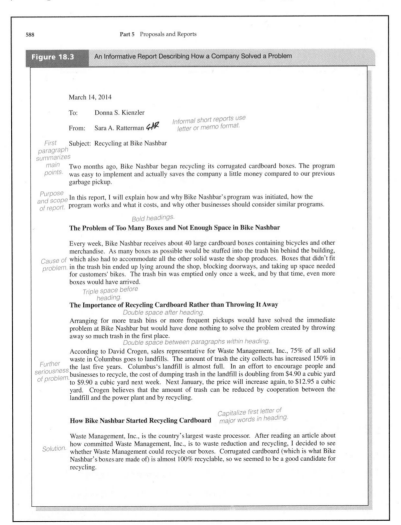

Good and Bad Examples

Paired effective and ineffective communication examples are presented so students can pinpoint better ways to phrase messages to help improve their communication skills. Commentaries in red and blue inks indicate poor or good methods of message communication and allow for easy comparison.

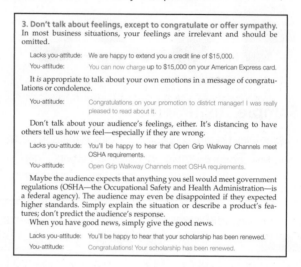

Checklists

Checklists for important messages appear throughout the book. These helpful lists serve as a handy reference guide of items to keep in mind when composing and editing messages.

Exercises and Cases

These hands-on exercises are flexible and can be used as in-class discussions or as individual and group assignments. These workplace exercises allow students to assume a role or perform a task in a variety of realistic business scenarios. Helpful "hints" provide structure and guidance to students for them to complete the exercises.

Teaching Support

Instructor Library

Connect's instructor library serves as a one-stop, secure site for essential course materials, allowing you to save prep time before class. The instructor resources found in the library include:

Instructor Manual   The Instructor's Manual, which contains

- **Answers to all exercises,** an overview and difficulty rating for each problem, and, for several of the problems in the book, a detailed analysis, discussion questions, and a good solution.

- **Additional exercises and cases** for diagnostic and readiness tests, grammar and style, and for letters, memos, and reports.

- **Lesson plans and class activities for each chapter.** You'll find discussion guides, activities to reinforce chapter materials and prepare students for assignments, and handouts for group work, peer editing, and other activities.

- **Sample syllabi** for courses with different emphases and approaches.

Test Bank   The Test Bank contains approximately 1,400 test items with answers. Each is tagged with learning objective, level of difficulty (corresponding to Bloom's taxonomy of educational objectives), and AACSB standards.

EZ Test Online   McGraw-Hill's EZ Test Online is a flexible and easy-to-use electronic testing program. The program allows instructors to create tests from book-specific items, accommodates a wide range of question types, and enables instructors to even add their own questions. Multiple versions of a test can be created, and any test can be exported for use with course management systems such as WebCT and Blackboard or with any other course management system. EZ Test Online is accessible to busy instructors virtually anywhere via the web, and the program eliminates the need to install test software. For more information about EZ Test Online, please see the website at **www.eztestonline.com**.

PowerPoint®   PowerPoint® presentations with lecture notes, graphics, and figures from the book to further explain concepts from the text.

Management Asset Gallery   McGraw-Hill is excited to provide a one-stop shop for our wealth of assets, making it quick and easy for instructors to locate specific materials to enhance their course.

All of the following can be accessed within the Management Asset Gallery:

Manager's Hot Seat—This interactive, video-based application puts students in the manager's hot seat, builds critical thinking and decision-making skills, and allows students to apply concepts to real managerial challenges. Students watch as 15 real managers apply their years of experience when confronting unscripted issues such as bullying in the workplace, cyber loafing, globalization, intergenerational work conflicts, workplace violence, and leadership versus management.

Self-Assessment Gallery—Unique among publisher-provided self-assessments, our 23 self-assessments give students background information to ensure they understand the purpose of the assessment. Students test their values, beliefs, skills, and interests in a wide variety of areas, allowing them to personally apply chapter content to their own lives and careers.

Every self-assessment is supported with PowerPoints and an instructor manual in the Management Asset Gallery, making it easy for the instructor to create an engaging classroom discussion surrounding the assessments.

Online Learning Center (OLC)

A limited set of student study tools, as well as all instructor resources can also be accessed on the following password protected website: **www.mhhe.com/locker11e**.

McGraw-Hill Customer Experience Group Contact Information

At McGraw-Hill, we understand that getting the most from new technology can be challenging. That's why our services don't stop after you purchase our products. You can e-mail our product specialists 24 hours a day to get product training online. Or you can search our knowledge bank of Frequently Asked Questions on our support website. For customer support, call **800-331-5094,** or visit **www.mhhe.com/support**. One of our technical support analysts will be able to assist you in a timely fashion.

Course Design and Delivery

Create

Craft your teaching resources to match the way you teach! With McGraw-Hill Create, **www.mcgrawhillcreate.com**, you can easily rearrange chapters, combine material from other content sources, and quickly upload content you have written, like your course syllabus or teaching notes. Find the content you need in Create by searching through thousands of leading McGraw-Hill textbooks. Arrange your book to fit your teaching style. Create even allows you to personalize your book's appearance by selecting the cover and adding your name, school, and course information. Order a Create book and you'll receive a complimentary print review copy in three to five business days or a complimentary electronic review copy (eComp) via e-mail in about one hour. Go to **www.mcgrawhillcreate.com** today and register. Experience how McGraw-Hill Create empowers you to teach *your* students *your* way.

E-Book Option

E-books are an innovative way for students to save money and to "go green." McGraw-Hill e-books are typically 40% off the bookstore price. Students have this choice between an online and a downloadable CourseSmart e-book.

Through CourseSmart, students have the flexibility to access an exact replica of their textbook from any computer that has Internet service, without plug-ins or special software, via the online version or to create a library of books on their hard drive via the downloadable version. Access to the CourseSmart e-books lasts for one year.

Features: CourseSmart e-books allow students to highlight, take notes, organize notes, and share the notes with other CourseSmart users. Students can also search for terms across all e-books in their purchased CourseSmart library. CourseSmart e-books can be printed (five pages at a time).

Visit **www.coursesmart.com** for more information and to purchase access to our e-books. CourseSmart allows students to try one chapter of the e-book, free of charge, before purchase.

Binder-Ready Loose-Leaf Text

This full-featured text is provided as an option to the price-sensitive student. It is a four-color text that's three-hole punched and made available at a discount to students. It is also available in a package with *Connect Plus.*

Tegrity Campus

Tegrity makes class time available 24/7 by automatically capturing every lecture in a searchable format for students to review when they study and complete assignments. With a simple one-click start-and-stop process, you capture all computer screens and corresponding audio. Students can replay any part of any class with easy-to-use browser-based viewing on a PC or Mac. Educators know that the more students can see, hear, and experience class resources, the better they learn. In fact, studies prove it. With patented Tegrity "search anything" technology, students instantly recall key class moments for replay online, or on iPods and mobile devices. Instructors can help turn all their students' study time into learning moments immediately supported by their lecture. To learn more about Tegrity, watch a two-minute Flash demo at http://tegritycampus.mhhe.com.

Blackboard® Partnership

McGraw-Hill and Blackboard have teamed up to simplify your life. Now you and your students can access *Connect* and *Create* right from within your Blackboard course—all with one single sign-on. The grade books are seamless, so when a student completes an integrated *Connect* assignment, the grade for that assignment automatically (and instantly) feeds your Blackboard grade center. Learn more at www.domorenow.com.

McGraw-Hill Campus™

McGraw-Hill Campus is a new one-stop teaching and learning experience available to users of any learning management system.

This institutional service allows faculty and students to enjoy single sign-on (SSO) access to all McGraw-Hill materials, including the award-winning McGraw-Hill *Connect* platform, from directly within the institution's website. With McGraw-Hill Campus, faculty receive instant access to teaching materials (e.g., e-textbooks, test banks, PowerPoint slides, learning objects, etc.), allowing them to browse, search, and use any instructor ancillary content in our vast library at no additional cost to instructor or students. In addition, students enjoy SSO access to a variety of free content and subscription-based products (e.g., McGraw-Hill *Connect*). With McGraw-Hill Campus enabled, faculty and students will never need to create another account to access McGraw-Hill products and services. Learn more at www.mhcampus.com.

Assurance of Learning Ready

Many educational institutions today are focused on the notion of *assurance of learning*, an important element of some accreditation standards. **Business and Administrative Communication** is designed specifically to support your assurance of learning initiatives with a simple, yet powerful solution. Each test bank question for **Business and Administrative Communication** maps to a specific chapter learning objective listed in the text. You can use our test bank software, EZ Test and EZ Test

Online, or *Connect* **Business Communication** to easily query for learning outcomes/objectives that directly relate to the learning objectives for your course. You can then use the reporting features of EZ Test to aggregate student results in similar fashion, making the collection and presentation of assurance of learning data simple and easy.

AACSB Tagging

McGraw-Hill is a proud corporate member of AACSB International. Understanding the importance and value of AACSB accreditation, this text recognizes the curricula guidelines detailed in the AACSB standards for business accreditation by connecting selected questions in the test bank to the six general knowledge and skill guidelines in the AACSB standards.

The statements contained in this text are provided only as a guide for the users of this textbook. The AACSB leaves content coverage and assessment within the purview of individual schools, the mission of the school, and the faculty. While **Business and Administrative Communication** and the teaching package make no claim of any specific AACSB qualification or evaluation, we have within **Business and Administrative Communication** labeled selected questions according to the six general knowledge and skills areas.

ACKNOWLEDGMENTS

All writing is in some sense collaborative. This book in particular builds upon the ideas and advice of teachers, students, and researchers. The people who share their ideas in conferences and publications enrich not only this book but also business communication as a field.

Many people reviewed the 11th edition, suggesting what to change and what to keep. We thank all of these reviewers for their attention to detail and their promptness!

Eve Ash, *Oklahoma State University Tulsa*

Tracy Austin, *Sam Houston State University*

Sarah Bleakney, *Georgia Institute of Technology*

Yvonne Block, *College of Lake County*

Nicole Buzzetto-More, *University of Maryland Eastern Shore*

Rosemarie Cramer, *Community College of Baltimore County*

Tena Crews, *University of South Carolina*

Yvette Essounga-Njan, *Fayetteville State University*

Cynthia Houlden, *University of Nebraska–Kearney*

Paul Lewellan, *Augustana College*

Joyce Lopez, *Missouri State University*

Carol Meyer, *American Public University*

Tanya Patrick, *Clackamas Community College*

Kara Romance, *Indiana University of Pennsylvania*

Tim Rowe, *SUNY Fredonia*

Bobbie Schnepf, *South Central Louisiana Technical College–River Parishes*

Stacey Short, *Northern Illinois University*

Chris Ziemnowicz, *University of North Carolina at Pembroke*

In addition, the book continues to benefit from people who advised me on earlier editions:

Mark Alexander, *Indiana Wesleyan University*

Bill Allen, *University of LaVerne*

Vanessa Arnold, *University of Mississippi*

Lynn Ashford, *Alabama State University*

Jean Baird, *Brigham Young University–Idaho*

Lenette Baker, *Valencia Community College*

Dennis Barbour, *Purdue University–Calumet*

Laura Barelman, *Wayne State College*

Fiona Barnes, *University of Florida*

Jan Barton-Zimerman, *University of Nebraska–Kearney*

Jaye Bausser, *Indiana University–Purdue University at Fort Wayne*

Sallye Benoit, *Nicholls State University*

Michael Benton, *Bluegrass Community and Technology College*

Raymond W. Beswick, *formerly of Synerude, Ltd.*

Carole Bhakar, *The University of Manitoba*

Cathie Bishop, *Parkland College*

Randi Meryl Blank, *Indiana University*

Yvonne Block, *College of Lake County*

Bennis Blue, *Virginia State University*

John Boehm, *Iowa State University*

Maureen S. Bogdanowicz, *Kapi'olani Community College*

Kendra S. Boggess, *Concord College*

Melanie Bookout, *Greenville Technical College*

Christy Ann Borack, *California State University–Fullerton; Orange Coast College–Costa Mesa*

Mary Young Bowers, *Northern Arizona University*

Charles P. Bretan, *Northwood University*

Paula Brown, *Northern Illinois University*

Vincent Brown, *Battelle Memorial Institute*

William Brunkan, *Augustana College*

John Bryan, *University of Cincinnati*

Phyllis Bunn, *Delta State University*

Trudy Burge, *University of Nebraska–Lincoln*

Janice Burke, *South Suburban College of Cook County*

Nicole Buzzetto-More, *University of Maryland–East Shore*

Robert Callahan, *The University of Texas–San Antonio*

Andrew Cantrell, *University of Illinois*

Danny Cantrell, *West Virginia State College*

Peter Cardon, *University of South Carolina*

Susan Carlson

John Carr, *The Ohio State University*

Kathy Casto

Marilyn Chalupa, *Ball State University*

Kelly Chaney, *Southern Illinois University–Carbondale*

Jay Christiansen, *California State University–Northridge*

Lynda Clark, *Maple Woods Community College*

Robert Cohn, *Long Island University*

Brendan G. Coleman, *Mankato State University*

Andrea Compton, *St. Charles Community College*

John Cooper, *University of Kentucky*

Donna Cox, *Monroe Community College*

Christine Leigh Cranford, *East Carolina University*

Tena Crews, *State University of West Georgia*

Smiljka Cubelic, *Indiana University–South Bend*

Carla Dando, *Idaho State University*

Aparajita De, *University of Maryland–College Park*

Susan H. Delagrange, *The Ohio State University*

Mark DelMaramo, *Thiel College*

Moira E. W. Dempsey, *Oregon State University*

Gladys DeVane, *Indiana University*

Linda Di Desidero, *University of Maryland–University College*

Veronica Dufresne, *Finger Lakes Community College*

Jose A. Duran, *Riverside Community College*

Dorothy J. Dykman, *Point Loma Nazarene College*

Marilyn Easter, *San Jose State University*

Anna Easton, *Indiana University*

Donna Everett, *Morehead State University*

Joyce Ezrow, *Ann Arundel Community College*

Susan Fiechtner, *Texas A&M University*

Susan Finnerty, *John Carroll University*

Bartlett Finney, *Park University–Parkville*

Mary Ann Firmin, *Oregon State University*

Melissa Fish, *American River College*

W. Clark Ford, *Middle Tennessee State University*

Louisa Fordyce, *Westmoreland County Community College*

Paula J. Foster, *Foster Communication*

Mildred Franceschi, *Valencia Community College–West Camp*

Linda Fraser, *California State University–Fullerton*

Silvia Fuduric, *Wayne State University*

Lynda Fuller, *Wilmington University*

Robert D. Gieselman, *University of Illinois*

Cheryl Glenn, *Pennsylvania State University*

Wade Graves, *Grayson County College*

Mary Greene, *Prince George's Community College*

Jane Greer

Daryl Grider, *West Virginia State College*

Peter Hadorn, *Virginia Commonwealth University*

Ed Hagar, *Belhaven College*

Elaine Hage, *Forsythe Technical Community College*

Barbara Hagler, *Southern Illinois University*

Robert Haight, *Kalamazoo Valley Community College*

Mark Hama, *Angelo State University*

Les Hanson, *Red River Community College–Canada*

Kathy Harris, *Northwestern State University*

Mark Harstein, *University of Illinois*

Maxine Hart, *Baylor University*

Vincent Hartigan, *New Mexico State University*

David Hawes, *Owens Community College*

Charles Hebert, *The University of South Carolina*

Tanya Henderson, *Howard University*

Ruth Ann Hendrickson

Paulette Henry, *Howard University*

Deborah Herz, *Salve Regina University*

Kathy Hill, *Sam Houston State University*

Robert Hill, *University of LaVerne*

Kenneth Hoffman, *Emporia State University*

Elizabeth Hoger, *Western Michigan University*

Carole A. Holden, *County College of Morris*

Carlton Holte, *California State University–Sacramento*

Glenda Hudson, *California State University–Bakersfield*

Elizabeth Huettman, *Cornell University*

Melissa Ianetta, *University of Southern Indiana*

Susan Isaacs, *Community College of Philadelphia*

Daphne A. Jameson, *Cornell University*

Elizabeth Jenkins, *Pennsylvania State University*

Carolyn Jewell, *Fayetteville State University*

Lee Jones, *Shorter College*

Paula R. Kaiser, *University of North Carolina–Greensboro*

Jeremy Kemp, *San Jose State University*

Robert W. Key, *University of Phoenix*

Joy Kidwell, *Oregon State University*

Susan E. Kiner, *Cornell University*

Lisa Klein, *The Ohio State University*

Gary Kohut, *University of North Carolina–Charlotte*

Sarah McClure Kolk, *Hope College*

Patti Koluda, *Yakima Valley Community College*

Keith Kroll, *Kalamazoo Valley Community College*

Milton Kukon, *Southern Vermont College*

Linda M. LaDuc, *University of Massachusetts–Amherst*

Suzanne Lambert, *Broward Community College*

Jamie Strauss Larsen, *North Carolina State University*

Newton Lassiter, *Florida Atlantic University*

Barry Lawler, *Oregon State University*

Sally Lawrence, *East Carolina University*

Cheryl Ann Laws, *City University*

Gordon Lee, *University of Tennessee*

Paul Lewellan, *Augustana College*

Kathy Lewis-Adler, *University of North Alabama*

Luchen Li, *Iowa State University*

Barbara Limbach, *Chadron State College*

Bobbi Looney, *Black Hills State University*

Dana Loewy, *California State University–Fullerton*

Andrea A. Lunsford, *Stanford University*

Catherine Macdermott, *Saint Edwards University*

Elizabeth Macdonald, *Thunderbird Graduate School of International Management*

John T. Maguire, *University of Illinois*

Michael D. Mahler, *Montana State University*

Margaret Mahoney, *Iowa State University*

Gianna Marsella

Pamela L. Martin, *The Ohio State University*

Iris Washburn Mauney, *High Point College*

Patricia McClure, *West Virginia State College*

Kelly McCormick-Sullivan, *Saint John Fisher College*

Nancie McCoy-Burns, *University of Idaho*

Brian R. McGee, *Texas Tech University*

Virginia Melvin, *Southwest Tennessee Community College*

Yvonne Merrill, *University of Arizona*

Julia R. Meyers, *North Carolina State University*

Julianne Michalenko, *Robert Morris University*

Paul Miller, *Davidson College*

Scott Miller

Danielle Mitchell, *Pennsylvania State University–Fayette*

Karl Mitchell, *Queens College–CUNY*

Mialisa Moline, *University of Wisconsin–River Falls*

Jayne Moneysmith, *Kent State University–Stark*

Josef Moorehead, *California State University–Sacramento*

Gregory Morin, *University of Nebraska–Omaha*

Evelyn Morris, *Mesa Community College*

Rodger Glenn Morrison, *Troy University*

Frederick K. Moss, *University of Wisconsin–Waukesha*

Andrea Muldoon, *University of Wisconsin–Stout*

Anne Nail, *Amarillo College*

Frank P. Nemecek, *Jr., Wayne State University*

Cheryl Noll, *Eastern Illinois University*

Nancy Nygaard, *University of Wisconsin–Milwaukee*

Robert Von der Osten, *Ferris State University*

Carole Clark Papper

Greg Pauley, *Moberly Area Community College*

Jean E. Perry, *University of Southern California*

Linda N. Peters, *University of West Florida*

Florence M. Petrofes, *University of Texas–El Paso*

Melinda Phillabaum, *IUPUI–Indianapolis*

Evelyn M. Pierce, *Carnegie Mellon University*

Cathy Pleska, *West Virginia State College*

Susan Plutsky, *California State University–Northridge*

Virginia Polanski, *Stonehill College*

Janet Kay Porter, *Leeward Community College*

Susan Prenzlow, *Minnesota State University–Mankato*

Brenda Price, *Bucks County Community College*

Brenner Pugh, *Virginia Commonwealth University*

David Ramsey, *Southeastern Louisiana University*

Greg Rapp, *Portland Community College*

Kathryn C. Rentz, *University of Cincinnati*

Janetta Ritter, *Garland County Community College*

Naomi Ritter, *Indiana University*

Jeanette Ritzenthaler, *New Hampshire College*

Betty Jane Robbins, *University of Oklahoma*

Cassie Rockwell, *Santa Monica College*

Ralph Roberts, *University of West Florida*

Carol Roever, *Missouri Western State College*

Alisha Rohde

Deborah Roper, *California State University–Dominguez Hills*

Mary Jane Ryals, *Florida State University*

Mary Saga, *University of Alaska–Fairbanks*

Betty Schroeder, *Northern Illinois University*

Nancy Schullery, *Western Michigan University*

Kelly Searsmith, *University of Illinois*

Sherry Sherrill, *Forsythe Technical Community College*

Frank Smith, *Harper College*

Pamela Smith, *Florida Atlantic University*

Don Soucy

Helen W. Spain, *Wake Technical Community College*

Valarie Spiser-Albert, *University of Texas–San Antonio*

Janet Starnes, *University of Texas–Austin*

Natalie Stillman-Webb, *University of Utah–Salt Lake City*

Ron Stone, *DeVry University*

Bruce Todd Strom, *University of Indianapolis*

Judith A. Swartley, *Lehigh University*

Christine Tachick, *University of Wisconsin–Milwaukee*

Mel Tarnowski, *Macomb Community College*

Bette Tetreault, *Dalhousie University*

Barbara Z. Thaden, *St. Augustine's College*

Lori Townsend, *Niagara County Community College–Sanborn*

Linda Travis, *Ferris State University*

Lisa Tyler, *Sinclair Community College*

Donna Vasa, *University of Nebraska–Lincoln*

David A. Victor, *Eastern Michigan University*

Catherine Waitinas, *University of Illinois–Champaign-Urbana*

Vicky Waldroupe, *Tusculum College*

Randall Waller, *Baylor University*

George Walters, *Emporia State University*

Jie Wang, *University of Illinois–Chicago*

Craig Warren, *Pennsylvania State–Erie Behrend College*

Linda Weavil, *Elon College*

Judy West, *University of Tennessee–Chattanooga*

Paula Weston

Gail S. Widner, *University of South Carolina*

Rebecca Wiggenhorn, *Clark State Community College*

Andrea Williams

Paula Williams, *Arkansas Northeastern College*

Marsha Daigle Williamson, *Spring Arbor University*

Bennie Wilson, *University of Texas–San Antonio*

Rosemary Wilson, *Washtenaw Community College*

Janet Winter, *Central Missouri State University*

Annette Wyandotte, *Indiana University Southeast*

Bonnie Thames Yarbrough, *University of North Carolina–Greensboro*

Sherilyn K. Zeigler, *Hawaii Pacific University*

I'm pleased to know that the book has worked so well for so many people and appreciative of suggestions for ways to make it even more useful in this edition. I especially want to thank the students who have allowed me to use their letters and memos, whether or not they allowed me to use their real names in the text.

I am grateful to all the businesspeople who have contributed. The companies where I have done research and consulting work have given me insights into the problems and procedures of business and administrative communication. Special acknowledgment is due Joseph T. Ryerson & Son, Inc., where Kitty created the Writing Skills program that ultimately became the first draft of this book. And I thank the organizations that permitted McGraw-Hill/Irwin to reproduce their documents in this book and in the ancillaries.

Special thanks go to three assistants. Jackie Hoermann, an Iowa State University graduate student, performed research wonders, checked all citations, wrote some sidebars, and sorted reams of material into useful bundles. Danica Schieber, another Iowa State University graduate student, wrote new exercises. Jacob Rawlins, an assistant professor in the College of Business at the University of Louisville, wrote all of the Newsworthy Communications and updated Chapter 8, "Working and Writing in Teams," as well as the three chapters of the job unit: "Building Résumés," "Writing Job Application Letters," and "Interviewing, Writing Follow-Up Messages, and Succeeding in the Job."

The publisher, McGraw-Hill/Irwin, provided strong editorial and staff support. I wish to thank Anke Weekes for editorial help, Kelly Pekelder for caring so much, as well as Diane Nowaczyk, Debra Kubiak, and Susan Lombardi for the appearance of the book and website. Further thanks go to Sarah Evertson for finding such wonderful photos and Rebecca Lazure for her great support and triage abilities while guiding *BAC* through production, and Michael Gedatus and Elizabeth Steiner for their marketing abilities.

And, finally, I thank my husband, Jim, who provided support, research, editorial assistance, proofreading, and major formatting work.

Continuing the Conversation

This edition incorporates the feedback I've received from instructors who used earlier editions. Tell me about your own success stories teaching *Business and Administrative Communication*. I look forward to hearing from you!

Donna S. Kienzler
kienzlerd@yahoo.com

CONTENTS

PART ONE

The Building Blocks of Effective Messages

PART TWO

The Communication Process

PART THREE

Basic Business Messages

PART FOUR

The Job Hunt

PART FIVE
Proposals and Reports

17 Writing Proposals and Progress Reports 550

18 Analyzing Information and Writing Reports 574

19 Making Oral Presentations 620

Appendixes

Business and Administrative Communication

How to Use This Book

- Chapter outlines, learning objectives, and headings all provide previews of the contents. They can give you hooks on which to hang the information you are reading.
- Examples of written documents provide illustrations of effective and ineffective communications. Comments in red ink highlight problems; those in blue ink note effective practices.
- Terminology is defined in the glossary at the end of the book.
- Sidebars provide workplace examples of ideas discussed in the text. They are categorized for you by the icons that appear beside them. A gold star with any icon signifies a classic example.
  - On-the-job examples have briefcase icons.
  - Ethics and legal examples have gavel icons.
  - Websites have an @ sign.
  - Technology examples have smartphone icons.
  - International examples have globe icons.
  - Fun examples have balloon icons.
- Chapter summaries at the end of each chapter, and review questions at the beginning of each set of chapter exercises, help you review the chapters for retention.

1 Succeeding in Business Communication

Chapter Outline

NEWSWORTHY COMMUNICATION

Costly Miscommunications: Approaching $50 Billion for Bank of America

Poorly done business communications can have global consequences, as well as huge penalties. Deceptive communications about mortgages played a significant role in the financial crisis of 2008 and the ensuing global recession. Bank of America became a large player in the debacle when it bought Countrywide Financial, a major mortgage company involved in the foreclosure furor.

BofA's costs relating to the mortgage fiasco are approaching $50 billion. These include

- A $1.3 billion settlement with Fannie Mae.
- An $11.8 billion payment as its share of a $25 billion settlement with four other mortgage servicers for mortgage abuses, including business communication abuses such as deceptive loan practices, improper documentation, and false statements about foreclosure reviews.
- An $8.5 billion agreement with bondholders.
- Billions of dollars to defend itself against lawsuits claiming Countrywide was dishonest about the quality of its mortgage securities.

In addition, BofA settled for $2.43 billion a lawsuit accusing the bank of making misleading statements to investors about its Merrill Lynch acquisition.

Sources: Shayndi Raice, Nick Timiraos, and Dan Fitzpatrick, "Big Banks Settle Mortgage Hangover," *Wall Street Journal*, January 8, 2013, A1–2; and Dan Fitzpatrick, Christian Berthelsen, and Robin Sidel, "BofA Takes New Crisis-Era Hit," *Wall Street Journal*, September 29, 2012, http://online.wsj.com/article/SB10000872396390443843904578024110468736042.html.

After studying this chapter, you will know

LO 1-1 What the benefits of good communication are.

LO 1-2 Why you need to be able to communicate well.

LO 1-3 What the costs of communication are.

LO 1-4 What the costs of poor communication are.

LO 1-5 What the basic criteria for effective messages are.

LO 1-6 What role conventions play in business communication.

LO 1-7 How to solve business communication problems.

Communication Is Key to Pay

How can you make more money at your job?

The number one way, according to the *Wall Street Journal*, is to "listen to your boss." Specifically, do the work your boss wants done, follow directions, work hard, and let your boss know what you have accomplished. Employees who follow this method collect raises at a rate of 9.9%, while average performers receive 3.6% and poor performers get 1.3%, according to one survey.

Just as important is to make sure you ask your manager to define expectations. Don't assume you know what your manager wants. Make sure you understand what your manager considers an outstanding performance in your position.

Adapted from Perri Capell, "10 Ways to Get the Most Pay out of Your Job," *Wall Street Journal*, September 18, 2006, R1.

Communication is a vital part of business. As you will see in this and later chapters, missteps in handling business communications can cost organizations millions, and even billions, of dollars.

The amount of business communication is staggering. The U.S. Postal Service processed 160 billion pieces of mail in 2012, more than half of which were business communications. Advertising mail accounted for 79.5 billion pieces; first-class mail accounted for 68.7 billion,[1] many of which were business communications such as bills and insurance documents. When you consider that most of your business communications are electronic or oral, you can start to imagine the staggering number of business communications that people compose, hear, and read.

More and more, communications—both professional and personal—are moving to electronic media.

- According to the *Harvard Business Review,* "In the past decade the world has gone from a total of 12 billion emails a day to 247 billion."[2]

- The Radicati Group, a technology market research firm, estimates that employees send and receive 110 e-mails a day.[3]

- CTIA-The Wireless Association says Americans sent 2.2 trillion text messages in 2012. That averages out to 19 text messages daily per person.[4]

- In October 2012, Facebook passed 1 billion monthly users; in November 2012 Twitter passed 200 million monthly users.[5]

Business depends on communication. People must communicate to plan products and services; hire, train, and motivate workers; coordinate manufacturing and delivery; persuade customers to buy; and bill them for the sale. Indeed, for many businesses and nonprofit and government organizations, the "product" is information or services rather than something tangible. Information and services are created and delivered by communication. In every organization, communication is the way people get work done.

Communication takes many forms: face-to-face or phone conversations, informal meetings, presentations, e-mail messages, letters, memos, reports, blogs, tweets, text messaging, social media, and websites. All of these methods are forms of **verbal communication,** or communication that uses words. **Nonverbal communication** does not use words. Pictures, computer graphics, and company logos are nonverbal. Interpersonal nonverbal signals include how people sit at meetings, how large offices are, and how long someone keeps a visitor waiting.

Benefits of Good Communication Skills   LO 1-1

Good communication is worth every minute it takes and every penny it costs. A study of 335 U.S. and Canadian companies with an average of 13,000 employees each and median annual revenues of $1.8 billion found those companies that best communicated with their employees enjoyed "greater employee engagement and commitment, higher retention and productivity, and—ultimately—better financial performance. . . .

- They boasted a 19.4% higher market premium (the degree to which the company's market value exceeds the cost of its assets).

- They were 4.5 times more likely to report high levels of employee engagement.

- They were 20% more likely to report lower turnover rates."[6]

A major quality shared by companies at the top of Glassdoor.com's annual list of best places to work is good communication. This list is compiled from the survey responses of anonymous employees. Even companies laying off employees can rank high on the list if they communicate well. United Space Alliance was fourteenth on the 2012 list, even though it had been laying off thousands since 2009, because of its "good job of explaining and communicating throughout the layoffs."[7]

Good communication skills will also benefit you. You may have wonderful ideas for your workplace, but unless you can communicate them to the relevant people, they will get you nowhere. In fact, many experts call communication skills—the ability to persuade, explain complex material, and adapt information to particular audiences—one of the most crucial skills of the new workplace, and a skill that is unlikely to be replaced by a computer.

Even in your first job, you'll communicate. You'll listen to instructions; you'll ask questions; you may solve problems with other workers in teams. Even entry-level jobs require high-level skills in reasoning, mathematics, and communicating. As a result, communication ability consistently ranks first among the qualities that employers look for in college graduates.[8] Warren Buffett, chairman of Berkshire Hathaway and ranked among the world's wealthiest people, told Columbia Business School students that they could increase their value 50% by learning communication skills, and that many of them did not yet have those skills.[9]

As more people compete for fewer jobs, the ones who will build successful careers are those who can communicate well with customers and colleagues. Robert O. Best, chief information officer of UnumProvident, an insurance corporation, cautioned, "You used to be able to get away with being a technical nerd. . . . Those days are over."[10]

The National Commission on Writing surveyed 120 major corporations, employing nearly 8 million workers. Almost 70% of respondents said that at least two-thirds of their employees have specific writing responsibilities included in their position descriptions. These writing responsibilities include:

- E-mail (100% of employees).

- Presentations with visuals, such as PowerPoint slides (100%).

- Memos and correspondence (70%).

- Formal reports (62%).

- Technical reports (59%).

Respondents also noted that communication functions were least likely to be outsourced.[11]

Because communication skills are so important, good communicators earn more. Research has shown that among people with two- or four-year degrees, workers in the top 20% of writing ability earn, on average, more than three times as much as workers whose writing falls into the worst 20%.[12] Jeffrey Gitomer, business consultant and author of best-selling business books, says there are three secrets to getting known in the business world; all of them are communication skills: writing, e-zining (he reaches over 130,000 subscribers each week), and speaking. He states, "Writing leads to wealth."[13]

"I'll Never Have to Write Because . . ."   LO 1-2

Despite the frequency of on-the-job writing and the importance of overall communication skills, college graduates seem to be lacking the necessary writing skills as they enter the workforce. A survey of employers conducted on behalf of the Association of American Colleges and Universities found that writing was one of the weakest skills of college graduates.[14] In another large survey, respondents noted that a lack of "effective business communication skills appears to be a major stumbling block among new [job] entrants—even at the college level."[15]

Some students think that an administrative assistant will do their writing, that they can use form letters if they do have to write, that only technical skills matter, or that they'll call or text rather than write. Each of these claims is fundamentally flawed.

Claim 1:   An administrative assistant will do all my writing.

Reality: Because of automation and restructuring, job responsibilities in offices have changed. Today, many offices do not have typing pools. Most secretaries have become administrative assistants with their own complex tasks such as training, research, and database management for several managers. Managers are likely to take care of their own writing, data entry, and phone calls.

Claim 2:   I'll use form letters or templates when I need to write.

Reality: A form letter is designed to cover only routine situations, many of which are computerized or outsourced, Also, the higher you rise, the more frequently you'll face situations that aren't routine, that demand creative solutions.

Claim 3:   I'm being hired as an accountant, not a writer.

Reality: Almost every entry-level professional or managerial job requires you to write e-mail messages, speak to small groups, write documents, and present your work for annual reviews. People who do these things well are likely to be promoted beyond the entry level. Employees in jobs as diverse as firefighters, security professionals, and construction project managers are all being told to polish their writing and speaking skills.[16]

Claim 4:   I'll just pick up the phone.

Reality: Important phone calls require follow-up letters or e-mails. People in organizations put things in writing to make themselves visible, to create a record, to convey complex data, to make things convenient for the reader, to save money, and to convey their own messages more effectively. "If it isn't in writing, it didn't happen" is a maxim at many companies. Writing is an essential way to record agreements, to make yourself visible, and to let your accomplishments be known.

Communicating on the Job

Communication—oral, nonverbal, and written—goes to both internal and external audiences. **Internal audiences** are other people in the same organization: subordinates, superiors, peers. **External audiences** are people outside the organization: customers, suppliers, distributors, unions, stockholders, potential employees, trade associations, special interest groups, government agencies, the press, and the general public.

People in organizations produce a large variety of documents. Figures 1.1 and 1.2 list a few of the specific documents produced at Ryerson, a company

Figure 1.1	Internal Documents Produced in One Organization	
Document	**Description of document**	**Purpose(s) of document**
Transmittal	Memo accompanying document, telling why it's being forwarded to the receiver	Inform; persuade reader to read document; build image and goodwill
Monthly or quarterly report	Report summarizing profitability, productivity, and problems during period. Used to plan activity for next month or quarter	Inform; build image and goodwill (report is accurate, complete; writer understands company)
Policy and procedure bulletin	Statement of company policies and instructions (e.g., how to enter orders, how to run fire drills)	Inform; build image and goodwill (procedures are reasonable)
Request to deviate from policy and procedure bulletin	Persuasive message arguing that another approach is better for a specific situation than the standard approach	Persuade; build image and goodwill (request is reasonable; writer seeks good of company)
Performance appraisal	Evaluation of an employee's performance	Inform; persuade employee to improve
Memo of congratulations	Congratulations to employees who have won awards, been promoted	Build goodwill

Figure 1.2	External Documents Produced in One Organization	
Document	**Description of document**	**Purpose(s) of document**
Quotation	Letter giving price for a specific product or service	Inform; build goodwill (price is reasonable)
Claims adjustment	Letter granting or denying customer request to be given credit for defective goods or service	Inform; build goodwill
Job description	Description of qualifications and duties of job. Used for performance appraisals, salaries, and hiring	Inform; persuade good candidates to apply; build goodwill (job duties match level, pay)
10-K report	Report filed with the Securities and Exchange Commission detailing financial information	Inform
Annual report	Report to stockholders summarizing financial information for year	Inform; persuade stockholders to retain stock and others to buy; build goodwill (company is a good corporate citizen)
Thank-you letter	Letter to suppliers, customers, or other people who have helped individuals or the company	Build goodwill

Business communication involves paper documents, electronic communications, and interpersonal abilities.

that fabricates and sells steel, aluminum, other metals, and plastics to a wide variety of industrial clients and has sales offices across the United States, Canada, and China.

All of the documents in Figures 1.1 and 1.2 have one or more of the three basic purposes of organizational writing: to inform, to request or persuade, and to build goodwill. In fact, most messages have multiple purposes. When you answer a question, for instance, you're informing, but you also want to build goodwill by suggesting that you're competent and perceptive and that your answer is correct and complete.

The Cost of Communication   LO 1-3

Writing costs money. The annual Social Security statements cost $70 million a year to mail, even with huge economies of scale.[17] The cost does not include employee time in the writing and processing, a major expense.

Document cycling processes also increase costs. In many organizations, all external documents must be approved before they go out. A major document may **cycle** from writer to superior to writer to another superior to writer again 10 or more times before final approval. Longer documents can involve large teams of people and take months to write.

Large organizations handle so much paper that even small changes to their communication practices amount to millions of dollars. Xerox Global Services Europe touts contractual annual savings of up to 1 million euros for organizations with 4,000 or more employees who switch to its printing services.[18]

Another significant cost of communication is e-mail storage. In addition to the exponential increase in frequency, e-mails are also growing in size. Many more of them also come with attachments. And businesses are storing much of this huge load on their servers. But the cost of the hardware is only some of the storage cost; a larger cost is administering and maintaining the archives. These costs include downtime when storage systems crash and time spent retrieving lost or corrupted messages.[19]

Costs of Poor Communication   LO 1-4

Poor communication can cost billions of dollars.

- Hurricane Katrina caused billions of dollars of damage—damage that was worsened by horrendous miscommunications between federal, state, and private relief organizations (see the sidebar "Hurricane Katrina Storms Communication Lines" on the next page).

- The space industry has had billion-dollar mistakes—mistakes where miscommunications were major contributing factors as confirmed by official government investigations (see sidebars on pages 10 and 12).

- Internal and external communication problems contributed greatly to delays in Boeing's 787 Dreamliner, delays that cost Boeing billions in penalties and caused some customers to switch their orders to Airbus.[20]

■ From figures provided by the members of the Business Roundtable, the National Commission on Writing calculated the annual private-sector costs of writing training at $3.1 billion.[21] These figures do not include the retail and wholesale trade businesses.

■ GlaxoSmithKline was fined $3 billion, the largest payment ever by a drug company, for failing to communicate accurately safety data on some of its popular drugs and for misdirecting the use of others.[22]

■ British Petroleum agreed to a $4 billion fine for its role in the Gulf of Mexico oil spill. That sum is in addition to the $36.5 billion BP had already spent, or committed to spend, in additional fines, cleanup costs, and settlements to individuals and businesses. According to the presidential commission, inadequate communication among British Petroleum, Halliburton, and Transocean, as well as within their own companies, was a contributing factor in BP's massive oil spill, which caused extensive damage, as well as fatalities, in the Gulf of Mexico.[23]

Costs of poor communication are not just financial. People died in the explosion of the Columbia space shuttle and British Petroleum's oil well. In the aftermath of Hurricane Katrina, inaccurate media reports of looting convinced some residents to stay to protect their property instead of evacuating; false reports of shootings at helicopters resulted in some states refusing to send trained emergency workers.

Not all communication costs are so dramatic, however. When communication isn't as good as it could be, you and your organization pay a price in wasted time, wasted effort, lost goodwill, and legal problems.

Wasted Time

Bad writing takes longer to read as we struggle to understand what we're reading. How quickly we can comprehend written material is determined by the difficulty of the subject matter and by the document's organization and writing style.

Second, bad writing needs to be rewritten. Poorly written documents frequently cycle to others for help, thus wasting time of people other than the original writer.

Third, ineffective communication may obscure ideas so that discussions and decisions are needlessly drawn out.

Fourth, unclear or incomplete messages may require the receiver to gather more information. Some receivers may

Communication failures increased the damage caused by Hurricane Katrina.

Hurricane Katrina Storms Communication Lines

Hurricane Katrina caused massive destruction to the Gulf Coast. During the storm, communication failures among local, state, and federal officials left their own harm.

The main communication problems included these issues:

■ Lack of communication among responding organizations: The Federal Emergency Management Agency (FEMA) claimed it was days before the relief agency knew about the thousands of people stranded in the New Orleans Convention Center.

■ Incompatible communication systems: The lack of coordination and communication caused by these systems put even more lives at risk by delaying assistance where it was most needed. Some rescuers in helicopters were unable to communicate with rescuers in boats. Some National Guard units actually used runners to communicate.

■ Inconsistent messages: State and local agency teams received conflicting messages, which led to confusion.

The massive communication problems led to an entire chapter on communication in the U.S. House of Representatives report on the Hurricane Katrina disaster.

Adapted from U.S. House of Representatives, *A Failure of Initiative: Final Report of the Select Bipartisan Committee to Investigate the Preparation for and Response to Hurricane Katrina*, 109th Cong., 2d sess. (Washington, DC, February 15, 2006), http://www.gpoaccess.gov/katrinareport/mainreport.pdf.

not bother to do so, leading to wrong decisions or a refusal to act.

Wasted Efforts

Ineffective messages don't get results. A receiver who has to guess what the sender means may guess wrong. A reader who finds a letter or e-mail unconvincing or insulting simply won't do what the message asks.

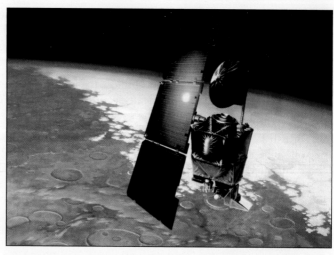

When the *Mars Climate Orbiter* spacecraft crashed as a result of poor communication, the United States lost a $125 million satellite and years of effort. See sidebar on this page.

> Per our conversation, enclosed are two copies of the above-mentioned invoice. Please review and advise. Sincerely, . . .

One company sent out past-due bills with the following language:

The company wanted money, not advice, but it didn't say so. The company had to write third and fourth reminders. It waited for its money, lost interest on it—and kept writing letters.

Lost Goodwill

Whatever the literal content of the words, every communication serves either to build or to undermine the image the audience has of the communicator.

Part of building a good image is taking the time to write correctly. Even organizations that have adopted casual dress still expect writing to appear professional and to be free from typos and grammatical errors.

Messages can also create a poor image because of poor audience analysis and inappropriate style. The form letter printed in Figure 1.3 failed because it was stuffy and selfish. The comments in red show specific problems with the letter:

- **The language is stiff and legalistic.**   Note the sexist "Gentlemen:" and obsolete "Please be advised," and "herein."

- **The tone is selfish.**   The letter is written from the writer's point of view; there are no benefits for the reader. (The writer says there are, but without a shred of evidence, the claim isn't convincing.)

- **The main point is buried**   in the middle of the long first paragraph. The middle is the least emphatic part of a paragraph.

- **The request is vague.**   How many references does the supplier want? Are only vendor references OK, or would other credit references, such as banks, work too? Is the name of the reference enough, or is it necessary also to specify the line of credit, the average balance, the current balance, the years credit has been established, or other information? What "additional financial information" does the supplier want? Annual reports? Bank balance? Tax returns? The request sounds like an invasion of privacy, not a reasonable business practice.

■ **Words are misused** (*herein* for *therein*), suggesting either an ignorant writer or one who doesn't care enough about the subject and the reader to use the right word.

You will learn more about tone in Chapter 3 and language in Chapter 5.

Legal Problems

Poor communication choices can lead to legal problems for individuals and organizations. The news is full of examples. Papa John's pizza was hit with a quarter billion dollar lawsuit for text advertisements that customers claimed were spam.[24] Capital One Financial, the large credit card company, agreed to pay $210 million to settle allegations that its call center pressured customers into buying credit-protection products such as credit monitoring.[25]

Individual communications can also have legal consequences. Steamy text messages revealed an affair between Detroit Mayor Kwame Kilpatrick and one of his aides; both the messages and the affair contradicted testimony the mayor had given under oath. Consequences included loss of office, jail time, and a $1 million fine.

| Figure 1.3 | A Form Letter That Annoyed Customers |

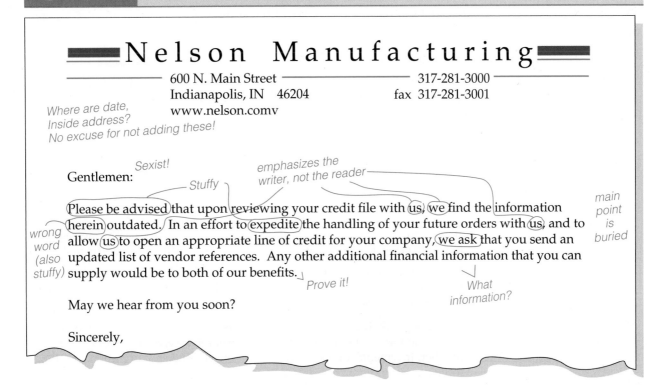

U.S. Representative Mark Foley of Florida resigned after his instant messages to House pages were published. E-mails have helped bring about the fall of many executives, including

- Senior Enron executives.
- Boeing CEO Harry Stonecipher.
- Hewlett-Packard Chairperson Patricia Dunn.
- Walmart Vice Presidents Julie Roehm and Sean Womack.
- South Carolina Governor Mark Sanford.
- CIA Director David Petraeus.

One San Francisco law firm says 70% of its routine evidence now comes from e-mails.[26]

In particular, letters, memos, e-mails, and instant messages create legal obligations for organizations. When a lawsuit is filed against an organization, the lawyers for the plaintiffs have the right to subpoena documents written by employees of the organization. These documents may then be used as evidence, for instance, that an employer fired an employee without adequate notice or that a company knew about a safety defect but did nothing to correct it.

These documents may also be used as evidence in contexts the writer did not intend. This means a careless writer can create obligations that the organization does not mean to assume. For instance, a letter from a manager telling scouts they may not visit a factory floor because it is too dangerous could be used in a worker's compensation suit.[27]

Careful writers and speakers think about the larger social context in which their words may appear. What might those words mean to other people in the field? What might they mean to a judge and jury?

Basic Criteria for Effective Messages   LO 1-5

Good business and administrative communication meets five basic criteria: it's clear, complete, and correct; it saves the audience's time; and it builds goodwill.

- **It's clear.**   The meaning the audience gets is the meaning the communicator intended. The audience doesn't have to guess.

- **It's complete.**   All of the audience questions are answered. The audience has enough information to evaluate the message and act on it.

- **It's correct.**   All of the information in the message is accurate. The message is free from errors in spelling, grammar, word choice, and sentence structure.

- **It saves the audience's time.**   The style, organization, and visual or aural impact of the message help the audience read or hear, understand, and act on the information as quickly as possible.

- **It builds goodwill.**   The message presents a positive image of the communicator and his or her organization. It treats the receiver as a person, not a number. It cements a good relationship between the communicator and the receiver.

Whether a message meets these five criteria depends on the interactions among the communicator, the audience, the purposes of the message, and the situation. No single set of words will work in all possible situations.

Using Technology for Communication

Electronic communications continue to play an ever-increasing role in both business and personal contexts. At home, Americans still use TV more than any other media: almost 145 hours a month. They also spend about 28 hours a month on the Internet; the largest chunk of that time is for social networking.[28]

In the office, more and more communication is done through media such as e-mail and texts. The business world continually embraces all forms of technology that help increase productivity and save money. Almost all office employees are expected to know how to navigate through the web and to use word processing, e-mail, spreadsheet, database, and presentation software. Newer forms of technology, especially social media such as Facebook, Twitter, and texting, are also becoming prominent in business offices. Chapter 2 discusses communication channels in more detail. Chapter 9 discusses how to use various communication technologies effectively.

Following Conventions `LO 1-6`

Conventions are widely accepted practices you routinely encounter. Common business communications have conventions. These conventions help people recognize, produce, and interpret different kinds of communications. Each chapter in this textbook presents conventions of traditional business documents. For example, Chapter 13 discusses conventions of job application letters, and Chapter 19 talks about conventions of delivering oral presentations.

Conventions change over time. Consider how the conventions governing movies and television have changed just during your lifetime, allowing more explicit sex and violence. Similarly, conventions change in business. Paper memos have mostly given way to e-mails, and some e-mails are being replaced by text messaging.

The key to using conventions effectively, despite their changing nature, is to remember that they always need to fit the rhetorical situation—they always need to be adjusted for the particular audience, context, and purpose. For instance, Chapter 10 provides guidelines on constructing negative messages. However, you will need to adapt these guidelines based on the way your organization presents its negative messages. Some organizations will use a more formal tone than others; some present negative news bluntly, while others ease into it more gently.

Since every organization will be unique in the conventions they follow, the information presented in this text will provide a basic understanding of common elements for particular genres. You will always need to adjust the basics for your particular needs.

The best way to learn conventions in a particular workplace is to see what other workers are doing. How do they communicate with each other? Do their practices change when they communicate with superiors? What kinds of letters and e-mails do they send? How much do they e-mail? What tone is preferred? Close observation will help your communications fit the conventions of your employer.

Understanding and Analyzing Business Communication Situations

The best communicators are conscious of the context in which they communicate; they're aware of options.

Warren Buffett on Good Business Writing

"For more than forty years, I've studied the documents that public companies file. Too often, I've been unable to decipher just what is being said or, worse yet, had to conclude that nothing was being said. . . .

"There are several possible explanations as to why I and others sometimes stumble over an accounting note or indenture description. Maybe we simply don't have the technical knowledge to grasp what the writer wishes to convey. Or perhaps the writer doesn't understand what he or she is talking about. In some cases, moreover, I suspect that a less-than-scrupulous issuer doesn't want us to understand a subject it feels legally obligated to touch upon.

"Perhaps the most common problem, however, is that a well-intentioned and informed writer simply fails to get the message across to an intelligent, interested reader. In that case, stilted jargon and complex constructions are usually the villains. . . .

"One unoriginal but useful tip: Write with a specific person in mind. When writing Berkshire Hathaway's annual report, I pretend that I'm talking to my sisters. . . . Though highly intelligent, they are not experts in accounting or finance. They will understand plain English, but jargon may puzzle them. My goal is simply to give them the information I would wish them to supply me if our positions were reversed. . . .

"No sibling to write to? Borrow mine: Just begin with 'Dear Doris and Bertie.'"

Quoted from Warren Buffett, Preface to *A Plain English Handbook: How to Create Clear SEC Disclosure Documents,* by the Office of Investor Education and Assistance (Washington, DC: U.S. Securities and Exchange Commission, 1998), 1–2, http://www.sec.gov/pdf/handbook.pdf.

Ask yourself the following questions:

- **What's at stake—to whom?**   Think not only about your own needs but also about the concerns your boss and your audience will have. Your message will be most effective if you think of the entire organizational context—and the larger context of shareholders, customers, and regulators. When the stakes are high, you'll need to take into account people's feelings as well as objective facts.

- **Should you send a message?**   Sometimes, especially when you're new on the job, silence is the most tactful response. But be alert for opportunities to learn, to influence, to make your case.

- **What channel should you use?**   Paper documents and presentations are formal and give you considerable control over the message. E-mail, texting, tweeting, phone calls, and stopping by someone's office are less formal. Oral channels are better for group decision making, allow misunderstandings to be cleared up more quickly, and seem more personal. Sometimes you may need more than one message, in more than one channel.

- **What should you say?**   Content for a message may not be obvious. How detailed should you be? Should you repeat information that the audience already knows? The answers will depend on the kind of message, your purposes, audiences, and the corporate culture. And you'll have to figure these things out for yourself, without detailed instructions.

- **How should you say it?**   How you arrange your ideas—what comes first, second, and last—and the words you use shape the audience's response to what you say.

How to Solve Business Communication Problems   LO 1-7

When you're faced with a business communication problem, you need to develop a solution that will both solve the organization's problem and meet the psychological needs of the people involved. The strategies in this section will help you solve the problems in this book. Almost all of these strategies can also be applied to problems you encounter on the job. Use this process to create good messages:

- Gather knowledge and brainstorm solutions.

- Answer the five questions for analysis in Figure 1.4.

- Organize your information to fit your audiences, your purposes, and the context.

- Make your document visually inviting.

- Revise your draft to create a friendly, businesslike, positive style.

- Edit your draft for standard spelling, punctuation, and grammar; double-check names and numbers.

- Use the response you get to plan future messages.

Gather Knowledge and Brainstorm Solutions.

Problem solving usually starts by gathering knowledge. What are the facts? What can you infer from the information you're given? What additional information might be helpful? Where could you get it? What emotional complexities

Figure 1.4	Questions for Analysis

1. Who is (are) your audience(s)?
2. What are your purposes in communicating?
3. What information must your message include?
4. How can you build support for your position? What reasons or benefits will your audience find convincing?
5. What aspects of the total situation may be relevant?

are involved? This information will usually start to suggest some solutions, and you should brainstorm other solutions. In all but the very simplest problems, there are multiple possible solutions. The first one you think of may not be best. Consciously develop several solutions. Then measure them against your audience and purposes: Which solution is likely to work best?

You will learn more about gathering knowledge in Chapter 15 and more about brainstorming in Chapter 8.

Answer the Five Questions for Analysis.

The five questions in Figure 1.4 help you analyze your audience(s), purpose(s), and the organizational context.

1. Who Is (Are) Your Audience(s)?   What audience characteristics are relevant for this particular message? If you are writing or speaking to more than one person, how do the people in your audience differ? How much does your audience know about your topic? How will they respond to your message? What objections might they have?

Some characteristics of your audience will be irrelevant; focus on ones that matter *for this message*. Whenever you address several people or a group, try to identify the economic, cultural, or situational differences that may affect how various subgroups may respond to what you have to say. For a more complete audience analysis, see the questions in Chapter 2.

2. What Are Your Purposes in Communicating?   What must this message do to meet the organization's needs? What must it do to meet your own needs? What do you want your audience to do? To think or feel? List all your purposes, major and minor.

Even in a simple message, you may have several related purposes: to announce a new policy, to make the audience aware of the policy's provisions and requirements, and to have them feel that the policy is a good one, that the organization cares about its employees, and that you are a competent communicator and manager.

3. What Information Must Your Message Include?   Make a list of the points that must be included; check your draft to make sure you include them all. To include information without emphasizing it, put it in the middle of a paragraph or document and present it as briefly as possible.

4. How Can You Build Support for Your Position? What Reasons or Benefits Will Your Audience Find Convincing?   Brainstorm to develop reasons for your decision, the logic behind your argument, and possible benefits to the audience if they do as you ask. Reasons and audience benefits do not have to be monetary. Making the audience's job easier or more pleasant is a good benefit. In an informative or persuasive message, identify multiple audience benefits. In your message, use those that you can develop most easily and effectively.

Be sure the benefits are adapted to your audience. Many people do not identify closely with their organizations; the fact that the organization benefits from a policy will help the individual only if the saving or profit is passed directly on to the employees. Instead, savings and profits are often eaten up by returns to stockholders, bonuses to executives, and investments in plants and equipment or in research and development.

5. What Aspects of the Total Situation May Be Relevant?

Should you consider the economy? The time of year? Morale in the organization? Any special circumstances? The organization may be prosperous or going through hard times; it may have just been reorganized or may be stable. All these different situations will affect what you say and how you say it.

Think about the news, the economy, the weather. Think about the general business and regulatory climate, especially as it affects the organization specified in the problem. Use the real world as much as possible. Think about interest rates, business conditions, and the economy. Is the industry doing well? Is the government agency enjoying general support? Think about the time of year. If it's fall when you write, is your business in a seasonal slowdown after a busy summer? Gearing up for the Christmas shopping rush? Or going along at a steady pace unaffected by seasons?

To answer these questions, draw on your experience, your courses, and your common sense. Read the *Wall Street Journal* or look at a company's website. Sometimes you may even want to phone a local businessperson to get information.

Organize Your Information to Fit Your Audiences, Your Purposes, and the Situation.

You'll learn different psychological patterns of organization in Chapters 9 through 11. For now, remember these three basic principles:

- Put good news first.

- In general, put the main point or question first. In the subject line or first paragraph, make it clear that you're writing about something that is important to the reader.

- Disregard the above point and approach the subject indirectly when you must persuade a reluctant audience.

Make Your Document Visually Inviting.

A well-designed document is easier to read and builds goodwill. To make a document visually attractive

- Use subject lines to orient the reader quickly.

- Use headings to group related ideas.

- Use lists and indented sections to emphasize subpoints and examples.

- Number points that must be followed in sequence.

- Use short paragraphs—usually eight typed lines or fewer.

If you plan these design elements before you begin composing, you'll save time and the final document will probably be better.

The best medium for a document depends on how it will be used. For example, a document that will be updated frequently may need to be on a website so the reader can easily obtain the most current information. Chapters 6 and 16 will provide more information on the design of documents and visuals.

Revise Your Draft to Create a Friendly, Businesslike, Positive Style.

In addition to being an organizational member or a consumer, your audience has feelings just as you do. Communication that keeps the audience in mind uses **you-attitude** (see Chapter 3). Read your message as if you were in your audience's shoes. How would you feel if *you* received it?

Good business and administrative communication is both friendly and businesslike. If you're too stiff, you put extra distance between your audience and yourself. If you try to be too chummy, you'll sound unprofessional. When you communicate with strangers, use simple, everyday words and make your message as personal and friendly as possible. When you write to friends, remember that your message may be read by people you've never even heard of: avoid slang, clichés, and "in" jokes.

Sometimes you must mention limitations, drawbacks, or other negative elements, but don't dwell on them. People will respond better to you and your organization if you seem confident. Expect success, not failure. If you don't believe that what you're writing about is a good idea, why should they?

You emphasize the positive when you

- Put positive information first, give it more space or time, or set it off visually in an indented list.

- Eliminate negative words whenever possible.

- Focus on what is possible, not what is impossible.

Edit Your Draft for Standard English; Double-Check Names and Numbers.

Businesspeople care about correctness in spelling, grammar, and punctuation. If your grasp of mechanics is fuzzy, if standard English is not your native dialect, or if English is not your native language, you'll need to memorize rules and perhaps find a good book or a tutor to help you. Even software spelling and grammar checkers require the writer to make decisions. If you know how to write correctly but rarely take the time to do so, now is the time to begin to edit and proofread to eliminate careless errors. Correctness in usage, punctuation, and grammar is covered in Appendix B.

Always proofread your document before you send it out. Double-check the reader's name, any numbers, and the first and last paragraphs. Chapter 5 will provide more tips on revising and editing communication.

Use the Response You Get to Plan Future Messages.

Evaluate the **feedback,** or response, you get. The real test of any message is "Did you get what you wanted, when you wanted it?" If the answer is *no,* then the message has failed—even if the grammar is perfect, the words elegant, the

Succeeding against the Odds

I developed my communication skills as a technique of survival. I was born in poverty and spent two years on the welfare rolls, and I learned early that I had to communicate or die. And so I talked my way out of poverty—I communicated my way to the top. . . .

I read and re-read books on self-improvement, success, and communication. The most important lesson I learned from these books is what I call "other focusing." This means, among other things, that if we want to communicate with employees, managers, and even competitors we must ask ourselves not what we want but what they want.

This rule made me a millionaire. For the only way I got to where I am today was by persuading thousands of blacks and whites, some of whom were very prejudiced, that the only way they could get what they wanted was by helping me get what I wanted. All the law and prophecy of communication theory can be found in that formula.

John H. Johnson, owner and publisher of *Ebony* magazine, quoted in Gloria Gordon, "EXCEL Award Winner John H. Johnson Communicates Success," *IABC Communication World* 6, no. 6 (May 1989): 18–19.

approach creative, the document stunningly attractive. If the message fails, you need to find out why.

Analyze your successes, too. You want to know *why* your message worked. There has to be a reason, and if you can find what it is, you'll be more successful more often.

Summary by Learning Objectives

LO 1-1   What the benefits of good communication are.

Communication helps organizations and the people in them achieve their goals. People put things in writing to create a record, to convey complex data, to make things convenient for the reader, to save money, and to convey their own messages more effectively.

LO 1-2   Why you need to be able to communicate well.

- The three basic purposes of business and administrative communication are to inform, to request or persuade, and to build goodwill. Most messages have more than one purpose.
- The ability to write and speak well becomes increasingly important as you rise in an organization.

LO 1-3   What the costs of communication are.

Common communication costs include writing time, document cycling, printing, mailing, and electronic storage of copies.

LO 1-4   What the costs of poor communication are.

Poor writing wastes time, wastes effort, and jeopardizes goodwill.

LO 1-5   What the basic criteria for effective messages are.

Good business and administrative writing meets five basic criteria: it's clear, complete, and correct; it saves the reader's time; and it builds goodwill.

LO 1-6   What role conventions play in business communication.

Common business communications have conventions, as do organizations. Business communicators need to know how to adjust conventions to fit a particular audience, context, and purpose.

LO 1-7   How to solve business communication problems.

- To evaluate a specific document, we must know the interactions among the writer, the reader(s), the purposes of the message, and the context. No single set of words will work for all readers in all situations.
- To understand business communication situations, ask the following questions:
  - What's at stake—to whom?
  - Should you send a message?
  - What channel should you use?
  - What should you say?
  - How should you say it?
- The following process helps create effective messages:
  - Gather knowledge and brainstorm solutions.
  - Answer the analysis questions in Figure 1.4.
  - Organize your information to fit your audiences, your purposes, and the context.
  - Make your document visually inviting.
  - Revise your draft to create a friendly, businesslike, positive style.
  - Edit your draft for standard English; double-check names and numbers.
  - Use the response you get to plan future messages.

Continuing Case

The All-Weather Case, set in an HR department in a manufacturing company, extends through all 19 chapters and is available at www.mhhe.com/locker11e. The portion for this chapter introduces some of the employees in the department and asks students what they would include in a presentation on the importance of business communication skills.

Exercises and Cases

*Go to www.mhhe.com/locker11e for additional Exercises and Cases.

1.1 Reviewing the Chapter

1. Why do businesses need to be able to communicate well? (LO 1-1)
2. Why do you need to be able to communicate well? (LO 1-1)
3. What are some flawed assumptions about workplace communication? What is the reality for each myth? (LO 1-2)
4. What are the costs of communication? (LO 1-3)
5. What are the costs of poor communication? (LO 1-4)
6. What are the basic criteria for effective messages? (LO 1-5)
7. What role do conventions play in business communication? (LO 1-6)
8. What are the components of a good problem-solving method for business communication opportunities? (LO 1-7)

1.2 Assessing Your Punctuation and Grammar Skills

To help you see where you need to improve in grammar and punctuation, take the Diagnostic Test, B.1, Appendix B.

1.3 Messages for Discussion I—Asking for a Class

The following are e-mails from various students to Dr. Violet Sands, who is a professor in the English Department. These students are wondering if Dr. Sands would let them register for her already-full class (English 320: Business Communication). Each e-mail shows a different way a student could make a request of Dr. Sands. How well does each message meet the needs of the reader and the writer? Is the message clear, complete, and correct?

1.

Hi Violet,

My name is Jake and I was wondering if you had any extra seats in your English 320 class. See, I'm a senior and I really need to take your class so I can graduate. I don't know what else to do. I didn't take it last year cuz I really didn't want to.

I'm desperate. Help me out.

Jake

2.

Hello Sands,

I'm sorry to bother you, but I really, really need to get into your English 320 class. My advisor totally screwed up my schedule and I didn't know I needed to take this class. It's so weird because I shouldn't have to take this class anyway, but whatever. So, if you could just add me into your class, that would be great.

Thanks,

Ally

3.

Dr. Sands,

Good morning. I hate to e-mail you right before the semester begins, but I have a request. When I tried to register for your Eng 320 course the website stated the course was full. I was wondering if I could possibly be put on a list to add the course just in case someone drops it? I am very interested in this course and would love to take it this semester if at all possible.

Thank you so much for your time,

Christine

4.

> Dear Dr. Sands,
>
> Do u have anymore seats open in your class? I think its 302 or 320 or something like that. Anyways, it would be cool if you would let me into the class. Sorry for e-mailing right at the last minute, but I didn't know what else to do.
>
> You are the best,
>
> Andrew

1.4   Messages for Discussion II—Responding to Rumors

The Acme Corporation has been planning to acquire Best Products, and Acme employees are worried about how the acquisition will affect them. Ed Zeplin, Acme's human resource manager, has been visiting the Acme chat sites and sees a dramatic rise in the number of messages spreading rumors about layoffs. Most of the rumors are false.

The following messages are possible responses that Ed can post to the chat sites. How well does each message meet the needs of the reader, the writer, and the organization? Is the message clear, complete, and correct? Does it save the reader's time? Does it build goodwill?

1.

> It Will Be Great!
>
> Author: L. Ed Zeplin, HR
>
> Date: Tuesday, May 23
>
> I am happy to tell you that the HR news is good. Two months ago, the CEO told me about the merger, and I have been preparing a human resource plan ever since.
>
> I want you to know about this because morale has been bad, and it shouldn't be. You really should wait for the official announcements, and you'll see that the staffing needs will remain strong. My department has been under a lot of pressure, but if you'll be patient, we'll explain everything—the staffing, the compensation.
>
> Our plan should be ready by Monday, and then if you have any questions, just contact your HR rep.

2.

> HR Staffing
>
> Author: HR Boss
>
> Date: Tuesday, May 23
>
> The rumors are false. Just ask anyone in HR. There will be no layoffs.

3.

> Don't Believe the Rumors
>
> Author: lezeplin@acme.com
>
> Date: Tuesday, May 23
>
> Acme has 475 employees, and Best Products has 132 employees. Our human resource plan for next year calls for 625 employees. If you do the math, you can see that there will be no layoffs. Rather, we will be hiring 18 employees. Of course, as we consolidate operations with Best, there will be some redeployments. However,

our plan indicates that we will be able to retain our current staff. All employees are valued at Acme, as our current benefits package testifies.

Our HR plan is based on the best analytic techniques and a business forecast by a top consulting firm. If you're an employee, you should review our business plan, at the Our Goals page on Acme's intranet. Everyone should read Acme's mission statement on our home page, www.acme.com/homepage.html.

4.

Layoff Rumors Do Acme a Disservice

Author: Zeplin in HR

Date: Tuesday, 23 May

If you come here to get your company information, you aren't getting the straight story. The people posting to this discussion board are spreading false rumors, not the truth. If you want to know the truth about Acme, ask the people who have access to the information.

As HR manager, I can assure you we won't be laying off employees after the merger with Best Products. I'm the one who approves the staffing plan, so I should know. If people would ask me, instead of reading the negative, whining lies at this site, they would know the facts, too.

If people really cared about job security, they would be working and exceeding their goals, rather than wasting their time in rumor-mongering on message boards. Hard work: that's the key to success!

5.

The True Story about Lay-Offs

Author: lezeplin@acme.com

Date: Tuesday, 23 May

Whenever there is a merger or acquisition, rumors fly. It's human nature to turn to rumors when a situation seems uncertain. The case of Acme acquiring Best Products is no exception, so I'm not surprised to see rumors about layoffs posted on this message board.

Have no fear! I am working closely with our CEO and with the CEO and human resource manager at Best Products, and we all agree that our current staff is a valuable asset to Acme, to Best, and to our combined companies in the future. We have no plans to lay off any of our valued people. I will continue monitoring this message board and will post messages as I am able to disclose more details about our staffing plans. In the meantime, employees should watch for official information in the company newsletter and on our intranet.

We care about our people! If employees ever have questions about our plans and policies, they should contact me directly.

L. Ed Zeplin, HR Manager

1.5   Discussing Communication Barriers

With a small group, discuss some of the communication barriers you have witnessed in the workplace or classroom. What confuses audiences? What upsets them? What creates ill will? What causes loss of interest? Try to pinpoint exactly how the communication broke down. How closely do the problems you've identified coincide with the content from Chapter 1?

1.6   Identifying Poor Communicators

Almost everyone has come in contact with someone who is a poor communicator. With a small group, discuss some of your experiences with poor communicators either in the workplace or in the classroom. Why was the communicator ineffective? What would have made communication clearer? After your discussion, develop a list of poor communication traits and what can be done to overcome them.

1.7   Identifying Changing Conventions

This chapter talks about the need to be aware of conventions and how they shift with time. What are some changing classroom communication conventions you have observed in your classes? What are some changing communication conventions you have observed at your workplace, or those of your family and friends? With a small group, discuss your examples.

1.8   Understanding the Role of Communication in Your Organization

Interview your work supervisor to learn about the kinds and purposes of communication in your organization. Your questions could include the following:

■ What kinds of communication (e.g., e-mails, presentations) are most important in this organization?
■ What communications do you create? Are they designed to inform, to persuade, to build goodwill—or to do a combination?
■ What communications do you receive? Are they designed to inform, to persuade, to build goodwill—or to do a combination?
■ Who are your most important audiences within the organization?

■ Who are your most important external audiences?
■ What are the challenges of communicating in this organization?
■ What kinds of documents and presentations does the organization prefer?

As your instructor directs,

a. Share your results with a small group of students.
b. Present your results in an e-mail to your instructor.
c. Join with a group of students to make a group presentation to the class.
d. Post your results online to the class.

1.9   Introducing Yourself to Your Instructor

Write an e-mail (at least 1½ pages long if printed) introducing yourself to your instructor. (See Appendix A for examples of e-mail format.) Include the following topics:

Background: Where did you grow up? What have you done in terms of school, extracurricular activities, jobs, and family life?

Interests: What are you interested in? What do you like to do? What do you like to think about and talk about?

Academics: What courses have you liked the best in school? Why? What life skills have you gained? How do you hope to use them? What do you hope to gain from this course?

Achievements: What achievements have given you the greatest personal satisfaction? List at least five.

Include things that gave *you* a real sense of accomplishment and pride, whether or not they're the sort of thing you'd list on a résumé.

Goals: What do you hope to accomplish this term? Where would you like to be professionally and personally five years from now?

Use appropriate headings and a conversational writing style; check your draft to polish the style and edit for mechanical and grammatical correctness. A good e-mail will enable your instructor to see you as an individual. Use specific details to make your writing vivid and interesting. Remember that one of your purposes is to interest your reader!

1.10 Introducing Yourself to Your Collaborative Writing Group

Write an e-mail (at least 1½ pages long if printed) introducing yourself to the other students in your collaborative writing group. (See Appendix A for examples of e-mail format.) Include the following topics:

Background: What is your major? What special areas of knowledge do you have? What have you done in terms of school, extracurricular activities, jobs, and family life?

Previous experience in groups: What groups have you worked in before? Are you usually a leader, a follower, or a bit of both? Are you interested in a quality product? In maintaining harmony in the group? In working efficiently? What do you like most about working in groups? What do you like least?

Work and composing style: Do you like to talk out ideas while they're in a rough stage or work them out on paper before you discuss them? Would you rather have a complete outline before you start writing or just a general idea? Do you want to have a detailed schedule of everything that has to be done and who will do it, or would you rather "go with the flow"? Do you work best under pressure, or do you want to have assignments ready well before the due date?

Areas of expertise: What can you contribute to the group in terms of knowledge and skills? Are you good at brainstorming ideas? Researching? Designing charts? Writing? Editing? Word processing? Managing the flow of work? Maintaining group cohesion?

Goals for collaborative assignments: What do you hope to accomplish this term? Where does this course fit into your priorities?

Use appropriate headings and a conversational writing style; edit your final draft for mechanical and grammatical correctness. A good e-mail will enable others in your group to see you as an individual. Use details to make your writing vivid and interesting. Remember that one of your purposes is to make your readers look forward to working with you!

1.11 Describing Your Writing Experiences and Goals

Write an e-mail (at least 1½ pages long if printed) to your instructor describing the experiences you've had writing and what you'd like to learn about writing during this course. (See Appendix A for examples of e-mail format.) Answer several of the following questions:

- What memories do you have of writing? What made writing fun or frightening in the past?
- What have you been taught about writing? List the topics, rules, and advice you remember.
- What kinds of writing have you done in school? How long have the papers been?
- How has your school writing been evaluated? Did the instructor mark or comment on mechanics and grammar? Style? Organization? Logic? Content? Audience analysis and adaptation? Have you gotten extended comments on your papers? Have instructors in different classes had the same standards, or have you changed aspects of your writing for different classes?
- What voluntary writing have you done—journals, poems, stories, essays? Has this writing been just for you, or has some of it been shared or published?
- Have you ever written on a job or in a student or volunteer organization? Have you ever edited other people's writing? What have these experiences led you to think about real-world writing?
- What do you see as your current strengths and weaknesses in writing skills? What skills do you think you'll need in the future? What kinds of writing do you expect to do after you graduate?

Use appropriate headings and a conversational writing style; edit your final draft for mechanical and grammatical correctness.

Notes

1. United States Postal Service, "Postal Facts 2013," https://about.usps.com/who-we-are/postal-facts/welcome.htm#H2.
2. Cathy Davidson, "Dividing Attention Deliberately," *Harvard Business Review* 90, no. 1–2 (January–February 2012): 142.
3. Ellen Lee, "How to (Finally!) Manage Your Email [sic]," CNBC, November 22, 2012, http://www.usatoday.com/story/tech/2012/11/22/manage-email/1704111/.
4. Peter Svensson, "More Thumbs Relax as Texting Declines in US," *Des Moines Register,* May 4, 2013, 4A.
5. "Internet 2012 in Numbers," *Royal Pingdom,* January 16, 2013, http://royal.pingdom.com/2013/01/16/internet-2012-in-numbers/.
6. Eric Krell, "The Unintended Word," *HRMagazine* 51, no. 8 (2006): 52.
7. Kelly Eggers, "The Best Places to Work in 2012," *FINS Sales & Marketing,* December 14, 2011, http://sales-jobs

.fins.com/Articles/SBB0001424052970204026804577098380172987416/The-Best-Places-to-Work-in-2012.

8. National Association of Colleges and Employers, "Top 10 Skills for Job Candidates," April 3, 2013, http://www.naceweb.org/Publications/Spotlight_Online/2013/0403/Top_10_Skills_for_Job_Candidates.aspx.

9. Alex Crippen, "Warren Buffett's $100,000 Offer and $500,000 Advice for Columbia Business School Students," CNBC, November 12, 2009, http://www.cnbc.com/id/33891448/Warren_Buffett_s_100_000_Offer_and_500_000_Advice_for_Columbia_Business_School_Students.

10. Peter Coy, "The Future of Work," *BusinessWeek*, March 22, 2004, 50.

11. The National Commission on Writing for America's Families, Schools, and Colleges, "Writing: A Ticket to Work . . . or a Ticket Out: A Survey of Business Leaders," *College Board* (2004), 7–8.

12. Anne Fisher, "The High Cost of Living and Not Writing Well," *Fortune*, December 7, 1998, 244.

13. Jeffrey Gitomer, *Jeffrey Gitomer's Little Black Book of Connections: 6.5 Assets for Networking Your Way to Rich Relationships* (Austin, TX: Bard Press, 2006), 128–31.

14. Peter D. Hart Research Associate, Inc., *How Should Colleges Assess and Improve Student Learning? Employers' Views on the Accountability Challenge: A Survey of Employers Conducted on Behalf of the Association of American Colleges and Universities* (Washington, DC: The Association of American Colleges and Universities, 2008), 3.

15. The Conference Board et al., *Are They Really Ready to Work? Employers' Perspectives on the Basic Knowledge and Applied Skills of New Entrants to the 21st Century U.S. Workforce*, accessed April 10, 2013, http://www.conference-board.org/pdf_free/BED-06-workforce.pdf.

16. Tom DeMint, "So You Want to be Promoted," *Fire Engineering* 159, no. 7 (2006); Karen M. Kroll, "Mapping Your Career," *PM Network* 19, no. 11 (2005): 28; and Jeff Snyder, "Recruiter: What It Takes," *Security* 43, no. 11 (2006): 70.

17. Emily Brandon, "Social Security Statements Now Available Online," *USNews Money*, May 1, 2012, http://money.usnews.com/money/blogs/planning-to-retire/2012/05/01/social-security-statements-now-available-online.

18. Xerox, *The Optimum Office: How to Achieve Immediate and Guaranteed Cost Savings via a Managed Print Service*, April 2009, http://www.xerox.com/downloads/gbr/en/x/XGS_Optimum_Office_en.pdf.

19. Pui-Wing Tam, "Cutting Files Down to Size: New Approaches Tackle Surplus of Data," *Wall Street Journal*, May 8, 2007, B4.

20. Peter Sanders, "Boeing Has New Delay for Dreamliner," *Wall Street Journal*, August 28, 2010, B6.

21. The National Commission on Writing for America's Families, Schools, and Colleges, "Writing: A Ticket to Work . . . or a Ticket Out: A Survey of Business Leaders," 29.

22. Charles Riley and Emily Jane Fox, "GlaxoSmithKline in $3 Billion Fraud Settlement," CNNMoney.com, July 2, 2012, http://money.cnn.com/2012/07/02/news/companies/GlaxoSmithKline-settlement/index.htm.

23. Selina Williams, "For BP, the Cleanup Isn't Entirely Over," *Wall Street Journal*, February 4, 2013, B2.

24. Olivia Smith, "Papa John's Faces $250 Million Spam Lawsuit," *CNNMoney*, November 13, 2012, http://money.cnn.com/2012/11/13/technology/mobile/papa-johns/index.html?iid=obinsite.

25. Matthias Rieker, Andrew R. Johnson, and Alan Zibel, "Capital One Dealt Fine for Pitch to Customers," *Wall Street Journal*, July 19, 2012, C1.

26. Stephen Baker, "A Painful Lesson: E-mail Is Forever," *BusinessWeek*, March 21, 2005, 36; Gary McWilliams, "Wal-Mart Details Roehm Firing," *Wall Street Journal*, March 21, 2007, B11; Peter Waldman and Don Clark, "California Charges Dunn, 4 Others in H-P Scandal; Action Sends Strong Message to Business about Privacy; Precedents for the Web Age?" *Wall Street Journal*, October 5, 2006, A1; and "Will 'Love Factor' Help Make S. C.'s Sanford More Forgivable?" *Des Moines Register*, June 29, 2009, 12A.

27. Elizabeth A. McCord, "The Business Writer, the Law, and Routine Business Communication: A Legal and Rhetorical Analysis," *Journal of Business and Technical Communication* 5, no. 3 (1991): 173–99.

28. Sarah Perez, "Nielsen: TV Still King in Media Consumption; Only 16 Percent of TV Homes Have Tablets," *Techcrunch*, January 7, 2013, http://techcrunch.com/2013/01/07/nielsen-tv-still-king-in-media-consumption-only-16-percent-of-tv-homes-have-tablets/.

2

Adapting Your Message to Your Audience

Chapter Outline

NEWSWORTHY COMMUNICATION

Making It Manly

Marketing products to make men look younger and fitter can be tricky. Although American men feel increasing pressure to pay attention to their appearances, they don't want to admit they are dieting or using cosmetics. And men certainly don't want to use any product made for women. That's why some brands, including Dove, Weight Watchers, Spanx, and Dr Pepper, target some products specifically to men through carefully crafted advertising.

■ In 2010, Dove launched a line of shower gels for men with advertisements that used the musical theme from "The Lone Ranger." The announcer's voice made it clear that the gels were designed for tough men to care for their skin.

■ Weight Watchers, which has always used female celebrities to sell its program, attracted men with new commercials featuring ordinary guys doing manly things—and losing weight.

■ Spanx changed its packaging and wording to emphasize that its girdle product could make men "feel powerful and strong."

■ Dr Pepper went even further by playfully marketing its new 10-calorie diet soda as "not for women."

Although some groups have complained about sexism in these ads, the goal of the marketing is to reach a new audience by understanding its motivations and desires. And it seems to be working. Each of the companies reports a marked increase in male customers because of advertising that appeals to them. As James Harris, one new Dove customer, said, "If it's for men, I'll use it. If it's for women, I won't."

Source: "Marlboro Man Meets Moisturizer," *Des Moines Register*, October 30, 2011, 2D.

Learning Objectives

After studying this chapter, you will know

LO 2-1 How to identify your audience.

LO 2-2 Ways to analyze different kinds of audiences.

LO 2-3 How to choose channels to reach your audience.

LO 2-4 How to adapt your message to your audience.

LO 2-5 How to characterize good audience benefits.

LO 2-6 How to create audience benefits.

LO 2-7 How to communicate with multiple audiences.

Audiences for a General

Colin Powell, four-star general and former secretary of state, identified five audiences for his press conferences:

- Reporters.
- Americans listening and watching.
- Political and military leaders, plus their fellow citizens, in other countries.
- The enemy.
- American troops.

He advised speakers to talk "through" the reporter, although respectfully, to the audiences that mattered most.

Adapted from Colin Powell with Tony Koltz, *It Worked for Me: In Life and Leadership* (New York: Harper, 2012), 130–31.

Knowing who you're talking to is fundamental to the success of any message. You need to identify your audiences, understand their motivations, and know how to reach them.

Identifying Your Audiences   LO 2-1

The first step in analyzing your audience is to decide who your audience is. Organizational messages have multiple audiences:

1. A **gatekeeper** has the power to stop your message instead of sending it on to other audiences. The gatekeeper therefore controls whether your message even gets to the primary audience. Sometimes the supervisor who assigns the message is the gatekeeper; sometimes the gatekeeper is higher in the organization. In some cases, gatekeepers may exist outside the organization.

2. The **primary audience** decides whether to accept your recommendations or acts on the basis of your message. You must reach the primary audience to fulfill your purposes in any message.

3. The **secondary audience** may be asked to comment on your message or to implement your ideas after they've been approved. Secondary audiences also include lawyers who may use your message—perhaps years later—as evidence of your organization's culture and practices.

4. An **auxiliary audience** may encounter your message but will not have to interact with it. This audience includes the "read-only" people.

5. A **watchdog audience,** though it does not have the power to stop the message and will not act directly on it, has political, social, or economic power. The watchdog pays close attention to the transaction between you and the primary audience and may base future actions on its evaluation of your message.

As the following examples show, one person can be part of two audiences. Frequently, a supervisor is both the primary audience and the gatekeeper.

Dawn is an assistant account executive in an ad agency. Her boss asks her to write a proposal for a marketing plan for a new product the agency's client is introducing. Her primary audience is the executive committee of the client company, who will decide whether to adopt the plan. The secondary audience includes the marketing staff of the client company, who will be asked for comments on the plan, as well as the artists, writers, and media buyers who will carry out details of the plan if it is adopted. Her boss, who must approve the plan before it is submitted to the client, is the gatekeeper. Her office colleagues who read her plan are her auxiliary audience.

Joe works in the information technology department of a large financial institution. He must write an e-mail explaining a major software change. His boss is the gatekeeper; the software users in various departments are the primary audience. The secondary audience includes the tech people who will be helping the primary audience install and adjust to the new software. The auxiliary audience includes department program assistants who forward the e-mail to appropriate people in each department. A watchdog audience is the board of directors.

Analyzing Your Audience LO 2-2

The most important tools in audience analysis are common sense and empathy. **Empathy** is the ability to put yourself in someone else's shoes, to feel with that person. Use what you know about people and about organizations to predict likely responses.

Analyzing Individuals

When you write or speak to people in your own organization and in other organizations you work closely with, you may be able to analyze your audience as individuals. You may already know them, or can probably get additional information easily. You may learn that one manager may dislike phone calls, so you will know to write your request in an e-mail. Another manager may have a reputation for denying requests made on a Friday, so you will know to get yours in earlier.

A useful schema for analyzing people is the **Myers-Briggs Type Indicator.**® This instrument uses four pairs of dichotomies to identify ways that people differ.[1] The Extraversion (the Myers-Briggs term) Introversion dichotomy measures how individuals prefer to focus their attention and get energy. Extraverted types are energized by interacting with other people. Introverted types get their energy from within.

The other three dichotomies in Myers-Briggs® typology are Sensing-Intuition, Thinking-Feeling, and Judging-Perceiving. The Sensing-Intuition dichotomy measures the way an individual prefers to take in information. Sensing types gather information through their senses, preferring what is real and tangible. Intuitive types prefer to gather information by looking at the big picture, focusing on the relationships and connections between facts.

The Thinking-Feeling dichotomy measures the way an individual makes decisions. Thinking types prefer to use thinking in decision making to consider the logical consequences of a choice or action. Feeling types make decisions based on the impact to people, considering what is important to them and to others involved.

The Judging-Perceiving dichotomy measures how individuals orient themselves to the external world. Judging types like to live in a planned, orderly way, seeking closure. Perceiving types prefer to live in a flexible, spontaneous way, enjoying possibilities.

The descriptors on each of the scales' dichotomies represent a preference, just as we have a preference for using either our right or our left hand to write. If necessary, we can use the opposite style, but we have less practice in it and use it less easily.

You can find your own personality type by taking the Myers-Briggs Type Indicator® instrument at your college's counseling center or student services office. Some businesses administer the Myers-Briggs Type Indicator® instrument to all employees to assist with team building and/or personal growth and development.

Reading Levels

One of the most relevant demographic measures for writers is the audience's literacy level. Unfortunately, even in advanced economies you have to ask how well your audience can read and put information to use. In the United States, the answer may be "not very well."

The National Assessment of Adult Literacy (NAAL), conducted by the U.S. Department of Education, found that 14% of adults had difficulty reading well enough to follow simple instructions (such as when to take medication), 12% struggled to use simple forms (deciding where to sign their name on a form), and 22% had trouble working with numbers (simple addition tasks). NAAL also found that 5% of adults were nonliterate—their language skills weren't strong enough to participate in the assessment.

Overall, that translates into 30 million adults in the United States with "below basic" reading and comprehension levels, and another 63 million with only "basic" literacy levels. For business writers, this poses a challenge. When composing a message for a broad audience of employees or customers, you may have to use short sentences, simple words, and clarifying graphics. What other techniques might you use to ensure that audiences with lower literacy levels can understand and use your message?

Adapted from Mark Kutner, Elizabeth Greenberg, and Justin Baer, "National Assessment of Adult Literacy (NAAL): A First Look at the Literacy of America's Adults in the 21st Century," American Institutes for Research, National Center for Education Statistics, U.S. Department of Education, 2006, http://nces.ed.gov/NAAL/PDF/2006470.PDF; and Alan M. Lesgold and Melissa Welch-Ross, Eds. *Improving Adult Literacy Instruction: Options for Practice and Research* (Washington, DC: National Research Council, 2012).

As Figure 2.1 suggests, you'll be most persuasive if you play to your audience's strengths. Indeed, many of the general principles of business communication appeal to the types most common among managers. Putting the main point up front satisfies the needs of judging types, and some 75% of U.S. managers are judging. Giving logical reasons satisfies the needs of the nearly 80% of U.S. managers who are thinking types.[2]

Analyzing Members of Groups

In many organizational situations, you'll analyze your audience not as individuals but as members of a group: "taxpayers who must be notified that they owe more income tax," "customers who use our accounting services," or "employees with small children." Focus on what group members have in common. Although generalizations won't be true for all members of the group, generalization is necessary when you must appeal to a large group of people with one message. In some cases, no research is necessary: it's easy to guess the attitudes of people who must be told they owe more taxes. In other cases, databases may yield useful information. In still other cases, you may want to do original research.

Demographic Characteristics Databases enable you to map demographic and psychographic profiles of customers or employees. **Demographic**

Figure 2.1	Using Personalities in Communication	
If your audience is	**Use this strategy**	**Because**
Extraverting	Try out ideas orally.	Extraverts like to develop ideas by talking; they are energized by people.
Introverting	Communicate in writing so the audience can think about your message before responding.	Introverts like to think before they communicate. Written messages give them their thinking time.
Sensing	Present all of the needed facts, and get them right. Present your reasoning step-by-step. Stress practicalities.	Sensing people are good at facts and expect others to be, also. They trust their own experience more than someone else's account.
Intuiting	Focus on the big picture and underlying patterns first. Save details for later. Use metaphors and analogies in explanations. Stress innovation.	Intuitive people like new possibilities and innovation; they enjoy problem solving and creative endeavors. They can be impatient with details, routine, and repetition.
Thinking	Use logic and principles of consistency and fairness rather than emotion or personal circumstances.	Thinking people make decisions based on logic and abstract principles. They are often uncomfortable with emotion or personal revelations.
Feeling	Stress positives. Show how your ideas value the people needs of the organization. Use tactful language.	Feeling people care about other people and their feelings. They are empathetic and desire harmony.
Judging	Make your communications very organized. Provide all needed information. Follow company procedures. Schedule work in advance; provide time frames for various tasks.	Judging people are eager to make decisions, so they may not seek out additional information. They prefer a structured, orderly work life.
Perceiving	Provide alternatives. Ask for action or a decision by a specific date.	Perceiving people like to gather lots of information before making decisions, and they like to keep all options open as long as possible.

Source: Gordon Lawrence, *People Types and Tiger Stripes: Using Psychological Type to Help Students Discover Their Unique Potential,* 4th ed. (Gainesville, FL: CAPT, Inc., 2009). Used with permission.

Group membership sometimes gives clues about your audience.

One Huge Audience

Baby boomers number 76 million and account for about half of total U.S. consumer spending. They are expected to spend an additional $50 billion over the next decade. So businesses are subtly beginning to accommodate the needs of this major audience.

Subtle is a key word: boomers do not like to be reminded that they are aging. For instance, many boomers dislike having people talk slowly to them, so ADT Security Services trains new operators to talk quickly and get to the point. CVS stores have installed carpeting to reduce slipping. Arm & Hammer sharpened the color contrast on its cat litter packaging and increased font size 20%.

Euphemisms abound. ADT's medical-alert systems are now "companion services"; bathroom-fixture manufacturer Kohler has "belay" bars instead of grab bars for showers; and Kimberly-Clark's Depends are sometimes labeled as underwear. Small packages of Depends look like underwear and hang on hooks rather than being stacked on shelves like diapers.

Adapted from Ellen Byron, "How to Market to an Aging Boomer: Flattery, Suberfuge, and Euphemism," *Wall Street Journal*, February 5, 2011, A1.

characteristics are measurable features that can be counted objectively: age, sex, race, religion, education level, income, and so on.

Sometimes demographic information is irrelevant; sometimes it's important. Does education matter? The fact that the reader has a degree from Eastern State rather than from Harvard may not matter, but how much the reader knows about accounting may. Does family structure matter? Sometimes. Some hotels and resorts offer family packages that include babysitting, multiple bedrooms, and children's activities.

Age certainly matters. One aspect of age that gets much press is the differences between generations in the office. Many older people believe younger workers have a sense of entitlement, that they expect great opportunities and perks without working for them. On the other hand, many younger workers see their older colleagues as rigid and hostile. Figure 2.2 shows some of the frequently mentioned differences between baby boomers and millennials. While awareness of generational differences may help in some communication situations, such lists are also a good place to attach mental warnings against stereotypes. Plenty of baby boomers also like frequent positive feedback, and almost everyone likes a chance to make a difference.

For most companies, income is a major demographic characteristic. In 2011, Walmart quietly returned to its "everyday low prices" after experimenting with low-priced sale products balanced by slightly higher prices elsewhere. The new pricing had not appealed to Walmart's financially strapped customers. The chain also returned guns and fishing equipment to the shelves of many of its stores in an attempt to attract more male customers.[3]

Location is yet another major demographic characteristic. You can probably think of many differences between regional audiences, or urban/rural audiences, in the United States. See Chapter 7 for more information on cross-cultural audiences.

Psychographic Characteristics **Psychographic characteristics** are qualitative rather than quantitative: values, beliefs, goals, and lifestyles. Knowing what your audience finds important allows you to choose information and benefits that the audience will find persuasive.

Figure 2.2	Some Generational Differences in the Office	
	Baby Boomers	**Generation X and Millennials**
Birth dates	1946–1964	1965 and on
Work ethic	Long hours in office	Flexible hours in office
	Respect corporate confidentiality	Apt to blog or tweet corporate negatives
	Long-term commitment to company	Expectation of multiple employers
Values	Hard work	Work–life balance
	Consistency	Flexibility
	Privacy	Sharing
	Hierarchy	Social equality, autonomy
	Clearly defined roles	Variety of challenges
	Confident in proven abilities	Overconfidence in abilities
	Serious about work	Want work to be fun
Preferred channels	Face-to-face, e-mail	Texting, social networks
Motivators	Duty to company	What's in it for them; want important tasks
Communication style	Through channels and hierarchy; accept annual evaluation	Freely offer opinions, both laterally and upward; want great amounts of attention and praise; want faster feedback
Decorum	Follow basic business decorum	May need to be reminded about basic business decorum

Sources: "Millennials, Gen X and Baby Boomers: Who's Working at Your Company and What Do They Think about Ethics?" Ethics Resource Center, 2010, http://ethics.org/files/u5/Gen-Diff.pdf; and Jen Wieczner, "10 Things Millennials Won't Tell You," *Market Watch,* June 24, 2013, http://finance.yahoo.com/news/10-things-millennials-won-t-113327583.html?page=all.

Marketing companies are combining consumers' web surfing records with personal off-line data from sources such as the Census Bureau, consumer research firms such as Nielsen, credit card and shopping histories, and real estate and motor vehicle records. The combined data allow marketers to reach narrowly defined audiences.

Analyzing the Organizational Culture and the Discourse Community

Be sensitive to the culture in which your audiences work and the discourse community of which they are a part. **Organizational culture** is a set of values, attitudes, and philosophies. An organization's culture is revealed verbally in the organization's myths, stories, and heroes, as well as in documents such as employee manuals. It is revealed nonverbally through means such as dress codes, behavior standards, or the allocation of space, money, and power. A **discourse community** is a group of people who share assumptions about what channels, formats, and styles to use for communication, what topics to discuss and how to discuss them, and what constitutes evidence.

In an organization that values equality and individualism, you can write directly to the CEO and address him or her as a colleague. In other companies, you'd be expected to follow a chain of command. Some organizations prize short messages; some expect long, thorough documents. Messages that are consistent with the organization's culture have a greater chance of succeeding.

Some companies are beginning to accept visible body art and long hair in traditional workplace cultures.

You can begin to analyze an organization's culture by asking the following questions:

- Is the organization tall or flat? Are there lots of levels between the CEO and the lowest worker, or only a few?

- How do people get ahead? Are the organization's rewards based on seniority, education, being well-liked, saving money, or serving customers? Are rewards available only to a few top people, or is everyone expected to succeed?

- Does the organization value diversity or homogeneity? Does it value independence and creativity or being a team player and following orders?

- What stories do people tell? Who are the organization's heroes and villains?

- How important are friendship and sociability? To what extent do workers agree on goals, and how intently do they pursue them?

- How formal are behavior, language, and dress?

- What does the work space look like? Do employees work in offices, cubicles, or large rooms?

- What are the organization's goals? Making money? Serving customers and clients? Advancing knowledge? Contributing to the community?

To analyze an organization's discourse community, ask the following questions:

- What media, formats, and styles are preferred for communication?

- What do people talk about? What topics are not discussed?

- What kind of and how much evidence is needed to be convincing?

Choosing Channels to Reach Your Audience LO 2-3

A communication **channel** is the means by which you convey your message. Communication channels vary in speed, accuracy of transmission, cost, number of messages carried, number of people reached, efficiency, and ability to promote goodwill.

Electronic channel usage is growing phenomenally. In 2012, there were

- 2.4 billion Internet users, globally.

- 634 million websites.

- 1.2 trillion searches on Google.

- 144 billion e-mails per day, globally.

- 89 billion e-mails sent and received daily by businesses.[4]

Evolving channels can have enormous impacts on businesses. Websites such as Amazon have helped put bookstores and electronics stores out of business. Whole chains such as Best Buy and RadioShack are fighting for existence.[5]

Depending on the audience, your purposes, and the situation, one channel may be better than another. Marketers frequently use both the Internet and television because they believe the two channels do different things. The Internet excels at selling when customers know what they want, such as a book or airline ticket; television is good at getting people to want to buy something and then remembering to do so.[6] Procter & Gamble has a website, BeingGirl .com, where girls can share experiences and questions about feminine hygiene products. P&G says this channel is four times more effective, dollar for dollar, than television commercials.[7]

A written message makes it easier to

- Present extensive or complex data.

- Present many specific details.

- Minimize undesirable emotions.

- Track details and agreements.

Oral messages make it easier to

- Use emotion to help persuade the audience.

- Focus the audience's attention on specific points.

- Resolve conflicts and build consensus.

- Modify plans.

- Get immediate action or response.

Choosing the right channel can be tricky sometimes. As Hurricane Katrina approached the Gulf Coast, the National Hurricane Center found its electronic communications about the looming wallop were not enough; officials at the center then phoned Gulf Coast mayors and governors to hasten disaster preparations.[8]

Even in the office, you will have to decide if your message will be more effective as an e-mail, text message, phone call, visit, or sticky note posted on a colleague's computer. In nonstandard situations, choosing a channel can be challenging.

- If you are the head of a small, nonprofit literacy agency that helps adults learn to read, how do you reach your clients? You cannot afford TV ads, and they cannot read print channels such as flyers.

- If you are a safety officer for a manufacturer, how do you send out product recall notifications? How many people file the contact-information cards when they purchase an item?

- If you are the benefits manager in a large manufacturing plant, how will you get information about your new benefits plan out to the thousand people on the floor? They don't use computers at work and may not have computer access at home.

Businesses are becoming savvier about using the array of channels. Ad money has been moving out of print and TV channels and into online advertising, which topped $39.5 billion in 2012.[9]

Businesses use Facebook, Twitter, YouTube, and Flickr to highlight new products and services. Many companies have interactive websites and forums where customers can get product information and chat about products; Amazon is a prime example. Manufacturers give perks to bloggers to talk about their products. Police departments are posting pictures of wanted people on Pinterest. Nonprofits advertise events, connect with volunteers, and schedule volunteer service on their Facebook pages. And all that social network communication can now be mined by software that performs semantic analyses, providing feedback to advertisers about both products and audiences.

M&M candies offer a sweet communication channel to organizations.

Even traditional paper channels are moving online. Publishers are making their travel books into e-books and cell phone apps. Magazines and newspapers are expanding from paper copies to include electronic copies as well as blogs, podcasts, and chat rooms as more people receive their news on mobile platforms and social networking sites. In fact, Warren Buffett warned the *Washington Post*, on whose board he served, that the paper-only model would no longer work.[10]

According to the Pew Research Center for the People & the Press, in the past 20 years, the percentage of Americans who regularly

- Watch local TV news has dropped from about 80% to 48%.

- Watch evening network news has dropped from 60% to 27%.

- Regularly read a daily newspaper has dropped from almost 60% to 38%.[11]

A Wicked Wiki Problem

What should you do if someone has written something harmful on your company's Wikipedia page? Do not ignore it, because often customers, journalists, and even new hires frequently go to Wikipedia to glean basic information about a company or product. Yet 60% of Wikipedia's pages contain factual errors.

Ryan Holiday, author of *Trust Me, I'm Lying: Confessions of a Media Manipulator,* gives these suggestions:

- "Be notable enough for a page." Seek coverage from reliable, independent sources.

- "Do not blindly edit your page." Learn the practices of the Wikipedia editorial community. Try posting your thoughts (and reliable, independent sources to back them) on the discussion section of the page instead of rushing in and trying to edit the page yourself.

- "Fight fire with fire." The author advises companies to carefully control their own page, but edit only the parts that are not factual.

Adapted from Ryan Holiday, "How to Solve Your Wikipedia Problem. (Yes, You Have One.)," CNN Money, August 14, 2012, http://management .fortune.cnn.com/2012/08/14/ wikipedia-reputation- manage-/?iid=SF_SB_LN.

Market research firm Claritas, Inc., combines demographic and psychographic data to identify 66 lifestyle segments, including "Young Digerati" (tech-savvy young adults), "Close-In Couples" (older, African-American couples), and "Blue-Chip Blues" (young families with well-paying blue-collar jobs). PRIZM is a trademark or registered trademark of The Nielsen Company (US), LLC.

Prime-time television viewing in general is declining, as people turn to DVRs, streaming, and video on demand; prime-time ads are also losing some of their appeal for companies.[12]

Preferred channels reflect age categories. Americans 50 and older prefer traditional channels—television, radio, and print newspapers. Americans under 30 prefer digital sources. Comedy news shows such as *The Daily Show with Jon Stewart* and *The Colbert Report* attract younger audiences; cable talk shows, such as *The O'Reilly Factor* and *Hannity*, attract viewers 65 and older.[13]

Some channels also reflect gender difference. Audiences for business publication such as the *Wall Street Journal*, *Economist*, and *Bloomberg Businessweek* are over 70% male, while audiences for daytime talk shows such as Ellen DeGeneres's show and *The View* are over 70% female.[14]

Creative uses of channels are appearing everywhere (for more on electronic channels, see Chapter 9):

- Ads are appearing on subway tunnels, fire hydrants, grocery checkout conveyors, sidewalks, toilet stall doors, and cardboard shirt hangers used by cleaners.[15]

- Toy maker Mattel used Facebook, Twitter, and a series of eight webisodes to celebrate the 50th birthday of Ken, Barbie's boyfriend. The webisodes allowed Mattel to extend the audience to teenagers and adults who have an emotional tie with the toy and may be collectors.[16]

- CBS used 35 million eggs printed with show logos and related puns; they called the endeavor "egg-vertising."[17]

- The USA Network used 50,000 $1 bills bearing stickers for one of its miniseries.[18]

- Scientists are using computer games to enlist the help of nonscientists. EyeWire enlists players to map neural connections in the eye; Foldit enlists players to help solve the question of how proteins fold.[19]

- Vienna, Austria, raised money for the main public library with a phone sex hotline. Pay by the minute and you got to hear a famous Austrian actress reading passages from the library's collection of erotic fiction from the eighteenth through the twentieth centuries.[20]

Using Audience Analysis to Adapt Your Message LO 2-4

Zeroing in on the right audience with the right message is frequently a formula for success. If you know your audience well and if you use words well, much of your audience analysis and adaptation will be unconscious. If you don't know your audience or if the message is very important, take the time to analyze your audience formally and to revise your message with your analysis in mind. Remember that audiences change, sometimes drastically, over time. Just think how much college students have changed since your parents' generation went to college. The questions in Figure 2.3 will help guide a careful audience analysis.

As you answer these questions for a specific audience, think about the organizational culture in which the person works. At every point, your audience's reaction is affected not only by his or her personal feelings and preferences but also by the political environment of the organization, the economy, and current events.

1. How Will the Audience Initially React to the Message?

a. **Will the audience see this message as important?** Audiences will read and act on messages they see as important to their own careers; they may ignore messages that seem unimportant to them.

When the audience may see your message as unimportant, you need to

- Use a subject line or first paragraph that shows your reader this message is important and relevant.

- Make the action as easy as possible.

- Suggest a realistic deadline for action.

- Keep the message as short as possible.

b. **How will the fact that the message is from you affect the audience's reaction?** The audience's experience with you and your organization shapes the response to this new message. Someone who thinks well of you and your organization will be prepared to receive your message favorably; someone who thinks poorly of you and the organization will be quick to find fault with what you say and the way you say it.

Figure 2.3	Analyzing Your Audience

These questions will help you analyze your audience:

1. How will the audience initially react to the message?
2. How much information does the audience need?
3. What obstacles must you overcome?
4. What positive aspects can you emphasize?
5. What are the audience's expectations about the appropriate language, content, and organization of messages?
6. How will the audience use the document?

A Zappos Channel

[According to Tony Hsieh, founder and CEO of Zappos, the popular Internet footwear business], "There's a lot of buzz these days about 'social media' and 'integration marketing.' As unsexy and low-tech as it may sound, our belief is that the telephone is one of the best branding devices out there. You have the customer's undivided attention for five to ten minutes, and if you get the interaction right, what we've found is that the customer remembers the experience for a very long time and tells his or her friends about it.

. . .

"At Zappos, we don't measure call times (our longest phone call was almost six hours long!). . . . We don't have scripts because we trust our employees to use their best judgment when dealing with each and every customer. . . . We're trying to build a lifelong relationship with each customer one phone call at a time."

Quoted from Tony Hsieh, *Delivering Happiness: A Path to Profits, Passion, and Purpose* (New York: Business Plus, 2010), 143–45. With permission from Central Grand Publishing.

When your audience has negative feelings about your organization, your position, or you personally, you need to

- Make a special effort to avoid phrases that could seem condescending, arrogant, rude, hostile, or uncaring.
- Use positive emphasis (see Chapter 3) to counteract the natural tendency to sound defensive.
- Develop logic and benefits fully.

2. How Much Information Does the Audience Need?

a. **How much does the audience already know about this subject?** It's easy to overestimate the knowledge an audience has. People outside your own immediate unit may not really know what it is you do. Even people who once worked in your unit may have forgotten specific details now that their daily work is in management. People outside your organization won't know how *your* organization does things.

   When some of your information is new to the audience, you need to

- Make a special effort to be clear. Define terms, explain concepts, use examples, avoid acronyms.
- Link new information to old information that the audience already knows.
- Use paragraphs and headings to break up new information into related chunks so that the information is easier to digest.
- Test a draft of your document with your reader or a subset of your intended audience to see whether the audience can understand and use what you've written.

b. **Does the audience's knowledge need to be updated or corrected?** Our personal experience guides our expectations and actions, but sometimes needs to be corrected. If you're trying to change someone's understanding of something, you need to

- Acknowledge the audience's initial understanding early in the message.
- Use examples, statistics, or other evidence to show the need for the change, or to show that the audience's experience is not universal.
- Allow the audience to save face by suggesting that changed circumstances call for new attitudes or action.

c. **What aspects of the subject does the audience need to be aware of to appreciate your points?** When the audience must think of background or old information to appreciate your points, you can

- Preface information with "As you know" or "As you may remember" to avoid suggesting that you think the audience does not know what you're saying.
- Put old or obvious information in a subordinate clause.

3. What Obstacles Must You Overcome?

a. **Is your audience opposed to what you have to say?** People who have already made up their minds are highly resistant to change. When the audience will oppose what you have to say, you need to

- Start your message with any areas of agreement or common ground that you share with your audience.

- Make a special effort to be clear and unambiguous. Points that might be clear to a neutral audience can be misinterpreted by someone opposed to the message.

- Make a special effort to avoid statements that will anger the audience.

- Limit your statement or request to the smallest possible area. If parts of your message could be delivered later, postpone them.

- Show that your solution is the best solution currently available, even though it isn't perfect.

b. **Will it be easy for the audience to do as you ask?** Everyone has a set of ideas and habits and a mental self-image. If we're asked to do something that violates any of those, we first have to be persuaded to change our attitudes or habits or self-image—a change we're reluctant to make.

   When your request is time-consuming, complicated, or physically or psychologically difficult, you need to

- Make the action as easy as possible.

- Break down complex actions into a list, so the audience can check off each step as it is completed. This list will also help ensure complete responses.

- Show that what you ask is consistent with some aspect of what the audience believes.

- Show how the audience (not just you or your organization) will benefit when the action is completed.

4. What Positive Aspects Can You Emphasize?

a. **From the audience's point of view, what are the benefits of your message?** Benefits help persuade the audience that your ideas are good ones. Make the most of the good points inherent in the message you want to convey.

- Put good news first.
- Use audience benefits that go beyond the basic good news.

b. **What experiences, interests, goals, and values do you share with the audience?** A sense of solidarity with someone can be an even more powerful reason to agree than the content of the message itself. When everyone in your audience shares the same experiences, interests, goals, and values, you can

Business Cards Have Gone High-Tech

Does your business card represent you well? The business card is one of the best channels to share necessary contact information—like your name, company, e-mail, website, and social media information.

Many innovative companies and individuals are turning to high-tech means to make their business cards stand out from the crowd. Some creative ideas include

- Cards that resemble hotel key cards.
- Cards that have USB connections or QR codes that can be read by smartphones.
- Cards that are little Lego figures with contact information stamped upon them (for a product manager at Lego).
- Cards that resemble profiles from social media.

Using or creating an unusual business card may be a creative way to get noticed.

Adapted from Katherine Rosman, "Business Cards Do High-Tech Work," *Wall Street Journal*, October 18, 2012, D1.

■ Consider using a vivid anecdote to remind the audience of what you share. The details of the anecdote should be interesting or new; otherwise, you may seem to be lecturing the audience.

■ Use a salutation and close that remind the audience of their membership in this formal or informal group.

5. What Are the Audience's Expectations about the Appropriate Language, Content, and Organization of Messages?

a. **What style of writing does the audience prefer?** Good writers adapt their style to suit the reader's preferences. A reader who sees contractions as too informal needs a different style from one who sees traditional business writing as too stuffy. As you write,

■ Use what you know about your reader to choose a more or less formal, more or less friendly style.

■ Use the reader's first name in the salutation only if both of you are comfortable with a first-name basis.

b. **Are there hot buttons or "red flag" words that may create an immediate negative response?** You don't have time to convince the audience that a term is broader or more neutral than his or her understanding. When you need agreement or approval, you should

■ Avoid terms that carry emotional charges for many people: for example, *criminal, un-American, feminist, fundamentalist, liberal.*

■ Use your previous experience with individuals to replace any terms that have particular negative meanings for them.

c. **How much detail does the audience want?** A message that does not give the audience the desired amount or kind of detail may fail. Sometimes you can ask your audience how much detail they want. When you write to people you do not know well, you can

■ Provide all the detail needed to understand and act on your message.

■ Group chunks of information under headings so that readers can go directly to the parts of the message they find most interesting and relevant.

■ Be sure that a shorter-than-usual document covers the essential points; be sure that a longer-than-usual document is free from wordiness and repetition.

d. **Does the audience prefer a direct or indirect organization?** Individual personality or cultural background may lead someone to prefer a particular kind of structure. You'll be more effective if you use the structure and organization your audience prefers.

6. How Will the Audience Use the Document?

a. **Under what physical conditions will the audience use the document?**
Reading a document in a quiet office calls for no special care. But suppose
the audience will be reading your message on the train commuting home
or on a ladder as he or she attempts to follow instructions. Then the physical preparation of the document can make it easier or harder to use.

When the reader will use your document outside an office,

- Use lots of white space.

- Make the document small enough to hold in one hand.

- Number items so readers can find their place after an interruption.

b. **Will the audience use the document as a general reference? As a specific guide?** Understanding how your audience will use the document will
enable you to choose the best pattern of organization and the best level of
detail.

If the document will serve as a general reference,

- Use a specific subject line to aid in filing and retrieval. If the document is
online, consider using several key words to make it easy to find the document
in a database search program.

- Use headings within the document so that readers can skim it.

- Give the office as well as the person to contact so that the reader can get in
touch with the appropriate person some time from now.

- Spell out details that may be obvious now but might be forgotten in a year.

If the document will be a detailed guide or contain instructions,

- Check to be sure that all the steps are in chronological order.

- Number steps so that readers can easily see which steps they've completed.

- Group steps into five to seven categories if there are many individual steps.

- Put any warnings at the beginning of the document; then repeat them just
before the specific step to which they apply.

Audience Analysis Works

Audience analysis is a powerful tool. Amazon.com tracks users' online histories to make suggestions on items they might like. PetFlow carved out a niche
in the pet supply business by delivering pet food ordered online. The company's audience consists mostly of women, who were tired of lugging home
heavy bags of pet food.[21]

Nintendo believes that much of its success is extending its concept of audience. An important part of its audience is hard-core gamers, a very vocal
group—they love to blog. But if Nintendo listened just to them, they would be

---

**Audience Is Not a
Mystery for Her**

Every year, mys-
tery writer Mary Higgins
Clark sells 3.7 million copies of
her books; in fact, she has sold
over 100 million copies in the
United States alone.

Perhaps the biggest factor in
her success is her careful audience analysis; she gives her
audience what they want. In
her case, this means intelligent
women in danger who unravel
sinister plots and often help
engineer their own escapes. Her
heroines tend to be self-made
professionals.

Because her novels are
always "G-rated" (no cursing,
no living together before marriage, no explicit depictions of
violence), they are a favorite of
mother–daughter book clubs
and sell heavily for Mother's Day,
the third biggest book-selling
holiday of the year (Father's Day
and Christmas are bigger).

Adapted from Alexandra Alter, "The
Case of the Best-Selling Author:
How a Former Pan-Am Stewardess
Has Stayed at the Top of
the Publishing Game Since
1975," *Wall Street Journal*,
March 25, 2011, D1.

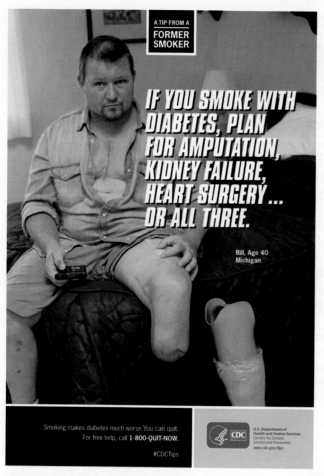

IF YOU SMOKE WITH DIABETES, PLAN FOR AMPUTATION, KIDNEY FAILURE, HEART SURGERY ... OR ALL THREE.

Bill, Age 40
Michigan

Smoking makes diabetes much worse. You can quit.
For free help, call **1-800-QUIT-NOW**.

#CDCTips

U.S. Department of
Health and Human Services
Centers for Disease
Control and Prevention
www.cdc.gov/tips

This medical message is targeted to a specific audience: smokers with diabetes.

the only audience Nintendo had. Instead, Nintendo extended its audience by creating the Wii, a new system that the hard-core gamers had not imagined and one that is collecting new users who never imagined owning a system.[22] With the introduction of Wii Fit, Nintendo expanded its audience to more women and even senior citizens.

Tesco PLC, Britain's largest retailer, signs up customers for its Clubcard. The card gives customers discounts, and it gives Tesco audience data. When Tesco added Asian herbs and ethnic foods in Indian and Pakistani neighborhoods, the data showed the products were also popular with affluent white customers, so Tesco expanded the rollout. When customers buy diapers the first time, they get coupons for usual baby products such as wipes and toys. They also get coupons for beer, because the data show that new fathers buy more beer.[23]

Characteristics of Good Audience Benefits LO 2-5

Use your analysis of your audience to create effective **audience benefits,** advantages that the audience gets by using your services, buying your products, following your policies, or adopting your ideas. In informative messages, benefits give reasons to comply with the information you announce and suggest that the information is good. In persuasive messages, benefits give reasons to act and help overcome audience resistance. Negative messages do not use benefits.

Good benefits meet four criteria. Each of these criteria suggests a technique for writing good benefits.

1. Adapt Benefits to the Audience.

When you write to different audiences, you may need to stress different benefits. Suppose that you manufacture a product and want to persuade dealers to carry it. The features you may cite in ads directed toward customers—stylish colors, sleek lines, convenience, durability, good price—won't convince dealers. Shelf space is at a premium, and no dealer carries all the models of all the brands available for any given product. Why should the dealer stock your product? To be persuasive, talk about the features that are benefits from the dealer's point of view: turnover, profit margin, the national advertising campaign that will build customer awareness and interest, the special store displays you offer that will draw attention to the product.

2. Stress Intrinsic as Well as Extrinsic Motivators.

Intrinsic motivators come automatically from using a product or doing something. **Extrinsic motivators** are "added on." Someone in power decides to give them; they do not necessarily come from using the product or doing the action. Figure 2.4 gives examples of extrinsic and intrinsic motivators for three activities.

Figure 2.4	Extrinsic and Intrinsic Motivators	
Activity	**Extrinsic Motivator**	**Intrinsic Motivator**
Making a sale	Getting a commission	Pleasure in convincing someone; pride in using your talents to think of a strategy and execute it
Turning in a suggestion to a company suggestion system	Getting a monetary reward when the suggestion is implemented	Solving a problem at work; making the work environment a little more pleasant
Writing a report that solves an organizational problem	Getting praise, a good performance appraisal, and maybe a raise	Pleasure in having an effect on an organization; pride in using your skills to solve problems; solving the problem itself

Intrinsic motivators or benefits are better than extrinsic motivators for two reasons:

- There just aren't enough extrinsic motivators for everything you want people to do. You can't give a prize to every customer every time he or she places an order or to every subordinate who does what he or she is supposed to do.

- Research shows that extrinsic motivators may actually make people *less* satisfied with the products they buy or the procedures they follow.

In a groundbreaking study of professional employees, Frederick Herzberg found that the things people said they liked about their jobs were all intrinsic motivators—pride in achievement, an enjoyment of the work itself, responsibility. Extrinsic motivators—pay, company policy—were sometimes mentioned as things people disliked, but they were never cited as things that motivated or satisfied them. People who made a lot of money still did not mention salary as a good point about the job or the organization.[24]

3. Prove Benefits with Clear Logic and Explain Them in Adequate Detail.

An audience benefit is a claim or assertion that the audience will benefit if they do something. Convincing the audience, therefore, involves two steps: making sure the benefit really will occur, and explaining it to the audience.

If the logic behind a claimed benefit is faulty or inaccurate, there's no way to make that particular benefit convincing. Revise the benefit to make it logical.

Faulty logic:	Moving your account information into Excel will save you time.
Analysis:	If you have not used Excel before, in the short run it will probably take you longer to work with your account information using Excel. You may have been pretty good with your old system!
Revised benefit:	Moving your account information into Excel will allow you to prepare your monthly budget pages with a few clicks of a button.

If the logic is sound, making that logic evident to the audience is a matter of providing enough evidence and showing how the evidence proves the claim that there will be a benefit. Always provide enough detail to be vivid and concrete. You'll need more detail in the following situations:

- The audience may not have thought of the benefit before.

- The benefit depends on the difference between the long run and the short run.

- The audience will be hard to persuade, and you need detail to make the benefit vivid and emotionally convincing.

The apparel industry, which is actively seeking a middle-aged and baby boomer audience, is using details to attract them. Slacks may offer slimming panels, and jeans may offer stretch waists and room for padded hips and thighs. Tops may cover upper arms. The potential market is huge. Women's apparel sales are over $100 billion annually, and women over 35 account for over half of those sales.[25]

Sometimes customers are willing to pay more for a product with desired benefits. Starbucks charges a high price for coffee, but lets you linger for hours at your table. However, customers are not always willing to pay for benefits they like or even need. Bank attempts to charge for using tellers often fail miserably. Customers resent paying to talk to someone about their own money, even when most would be better off economically paying per teller visit rather than paying for everyone's visits through some other fee or lower interest rates.[26]

4. Phrase Benefits in You-Attitude.

If benefits aren't worded with you-attitude (see Chapter 3), they'll sound selfish and won't be as effective as they could be. It doesn't matter how you phrase benefits while you're brainstorming and developing them, but in your final draft, check to be sure that you've used you-attitude.

Lacks you-attitude:	We have the lowest prices in town.
You-attitude:	At Havlichek Cars, you get the best deal in town.

Identifying and Developing Audience Benefits LO 2-6

Brainstorm lots of benefits—perhaps twice as many as you'll need. Then you can choose the ones that are most effective for your audience, or that you can develop most easily. The first benefit you think of may not be the best.

Sometimes benefits will be easy to think of and to explain. When they are harder to identify or to develop, use the following steps to identify and then develop good benefits.

1. Identify the Needs, Wants, and Feelings that May Motivate Your Audience.

All of us have basic needs, and most of us supplement those needs with possessions or intangibles we want. We need enough food to satisfy nutritional needs, but we may want our diet to make us look sexy. We need basic shelter, but we may want our homes to be cozy, luxurious, or green. And our needs and wants are strongly influenced by our feelings. We may feel safer in a more expensive car, even though research does not show that car as being safer than cheaper models.

2. Identify the Objective Features of Your Product or Policy that Could Meet the Needs You've Identified.

Sometimes just listing the audience's needs makes it obvious which feature meets a given need. Sometimes several features together meet the need. Try to think of all of them.

Suppose that you want to persuade people to come to the restaurant you manage. It's true that everybody needs to eat, but telling people they can satisfy their hunger needs won't persuade them to come to your restaurant rather than going somewhere else or eating at home. Depending on what features your restaurant offered, you could appeal to one or more of the following subgroups:

Subgroup	Features to meet the subgroup's needs
People who work outside the home	A quick lunch; a relaxing place to take clients or colleagues
Parents with small children	High chairs, children's menus, and toys to keep the kids entertained while they wait for their order
People who eat out a lot	Variety both in food and in decor
People on tight budgets	Economical food; a place where they don't need to tip (cafeteria or fast food)
People on special diets	Low-sodium and low-carb dishes; vegetarian food; kosher food
People to whom eating out is part of an evening's entertainment	Music or a floor show; elegant surroundings; reservations so they can get to a show or event after dinner; late hours so they can come to dinner after a show or game

Whenever you're communicating with customers or clients about features that are not unique to your organization, it's wise to present both benefits of the features themselves and benefits of dealing with your company. If you talk about the benefits of the new healthy choices in children's menus but don't mention your own revised menu, people may go somewhere else!

3. Show How the Audience Can Meet Their Needs with the Features of the Policy or Product.

Features alone rarely motivate people. Instead, link the feature to the audience's needs—and provide details to make the benefit vivid.

Weak: You get quick service.

Better: If you only have an hour for lunch, try our Business Buffet. Within minutes, you can choose from a variety of main dishes, vegetables, and a make-your-own-sandwich-and-salad bar. You'll have a lunch that's as light or filling as you want, with time to enjoy it—and still be back to the office on time.

Audience Benefits Work

Appropriate audience benefits work so well that organizations spend much time and money identifying them and then developing them.

- Hotels study which benefits are worth the money, and which are not. Holiday Inn keeps restaurants and bars in all its hotels, even though they are not money makers, but does not have bellhops. Staybridge Suites cleans less often but has "Sundowner receptions," which give guests a free meal and a chance to socialize.[27]

- The reviewing site Yelp offers its best reviewers exclusive social events ranging from museum cocktail parties to Mardi Gras parties. These elite reviewers, who continue to write reviews to maintain their status, produce about 100 more reviews than non-elite reviewers and about 25% of Yelp's reviews.[28]

- American Express maintains Connectodex, a social network for holders of its OPEN credit cards (for small-business owners). More than 15,000 small businesses have joined. Members, who post profiles, list services and needs, and make business connections, say they prefer Connectodex to LinkedIn because the small businesses with which they connect have been vetted by American Express.[29] American Express benefits because the service has significantly reduced customer churn.

- To fight online purchasing, many retail chains offer loyalty programs that offer buyers rewards such as coupons, free purchases, or money back. Some chains offer buyers an elite status: bigger spenders get better rewards, but the status lasts only one year to encourage continual shopping.

- Automakers know that brand loyalty is money in the bank. In addition to purchase "loyalty" discounts, many are now turning to service to reward—and keep—customers. General Motors offers the "GM Preferred Owner" program. Those customers get credits for having their cars serviced at the dealership, credits which count toward discounts on repair work or new vehicles. BMW offers its buyers four years of free maintenance, years that give dealers time to nurture relationships with customers.[30]

Remember that audience benefits must be appropriate for the audience before they work. Tylenol tried a new ad campaign that said, "We put our love into Tylenol." Upset customers who remembered the Tylenol cyanide poisonings wrote in saying they didn't want anyone putting anything into their Tylenol.[31]

Sometimes it is hard to know what your audience wants. A classic example is "feature creep" in electronic goods. Unfortunately, consumers seem to want lots of features in their electronics when they buy them, but then become frustrated trying to use them and return the devices. In the United States, product returns cost more than $100 billion.[32] Research has shown that over half the wares are in complete working order; consumers just cannot operate them.[33]

Writing or Speaking to Multiple Audiences with Different Needs   LO 2-7

Many business and administrative messages go not to a single person but to a larger audience. When the members of your audience share the same interests and the same level of knowledge, you can use the principles outlined above for individual readers or for members of homogeneous groups. But often different members of the audience have different needs.

Researcher Rachel Spilka has shown that talking to readers both inside and outside the organization helped corporate engineers adapt their documents successfully. Talking to readers and reviewers helped writers involve readers in the planning process, understand the social and political relationships among readers, and negotiate conflicts orally rather than depending solely on the document. These writers were then able to think about content as well as about organization and style, appeal to common grounds (such as reducing waste or increasing productivity) that multiple readers shared, and reduce the number of revisions needed before documents were approved.[34]

When it is not possible to meet everyone's needs, meet the needs of gatekeepers and decision makers first. Figure 2.5 offers strategies for creating documents for multiple audiences.

Although you will probably use different styles, and sometimes include different content, when communicating with multiple audiences, you need to keep your core message consistent. Engineers might need more technical information than managers, but the core messages they receive should not be conflicting in any way.

Figure 2.5	Strategies for Documents with Multiple Audiences

Content and number of details

- Provide an overview or executive summary for readers who want just the main points.
- In the body of the document, provide enough detail for decision makers and for anyone else who could veto your proposal.
- If the decision makers don't need details that other audiences will want, provide those details in appendixes—statistical tabulations, earlier reports, and so forth.

Organization

- Use headings and a table of contents so readers can turn to the portions that interest them.
- Organize your message based on the decision makers' attitudes toward it.

Level of formality

- Avoid personal pronouns. *You* ceases to have a specific meaning when several different audiences use a document.
- If both internal and external audiences will use a document, use a slightly more formal style than you would in an internal document.
- Use a more formal style when you write to international audiences.

Technical level

- In the body of the document, assume the degree of knowledge that decision makers will have.
- Put background and explanatory information under separate headings. Then readers can use the headings and the table of contents to read or skip these sections, as their knowledge dictates.
- If decision makers will have more knowledge than other audiences, provide a glossary of terms. Early in the document, let readers know that the glossary exists.

Summary by Learning Objectives

LO 2-1 How to identify your audience.

The primary audience will make a decision or act on the basis of your message. The secondary audience may be asked by the primary audience to comment on your message or to implement your ideas after they've been approved. The auxiliary audience encounters the message but does not have to interact with it. A gatekeeper controls whether the message gets to the primary audience.

A watchdog audience has political, social, or economic power and may base future actions on its evaluation of your message.

LO 2-2 Ways to analyze different kinds of audiences.

The most important tools in audience analysis are common sense and empathy. The Myers-Briggs Type Indicator can help you analyze individuals.

Demographic and psychographic characteristics can help you analyze groups.

LO 2-3 **How to choose channels to reach your audience.**

A communication channel is the means by which you convey your message to your audience. Different channels have different strengths and weaknesses, which need to be matched to the audience.

LO 2-4 **How to adapt your message to your audience.**

The following questions help guide a careful audience analysis:

- What will the audience's initial reaction be to the message?
- How much information does the audience need?
- What obstacles must you overcome?
- What positive aspects can you emphasize?
- What expectations does the audience have about the appropriate language, contents, and organization of messages?
- How will the audience use the document?

LO 2-5 **How to characterize good audience benefits.**

Audience benefits are advantages that the audience gets by using your services, buying your products, following your policies, or adopting your ideas. Benefits can exist for policies and ideas as well as for goods and services.

Good benefits are adapted to the audience, based on intrinsic rather than extrinsic motivators, supported by clear logic, explained in adequate detail, and phrased in you-attitude. Extrinsic benefits simply aren't available to reward every desired behavior; further, they reduce the satisfaction in doing something for its own sake.

LO 2-6 **How to create audience benefits.**

To create audience benefits,

- Identify the feelings, fears, and needs that may motivate your audience.
- Identify the features of your product or policy that could meet the needs you've identified.
- Show how the audience can meet their needs with the features of the policy or product.

LO 2-7 **How to communicate with multiple audiences.**

When you write to multiple audiences, use the primary audience to determine level of detail, organization, level of formality, and use of technical terms and theory.

Continuing Case

The All-Weather Case, set in an HR department in a manufacturing company, extends through all 19 chapters and is available at www.mhhe.com/locker11e. The portion for this chapter asks students to prepare an audience analysis for an in-house presentation.

Exercises and Cases

2.1   Reviewing the Chapter

Go to www.mhhe.com/locker11e for additional Exercises and Cases.

1. Who are the five different audiences your message may need to address? (LO 2-1)
2. What are some characteristics to consider when analyzing individuals? (LO 2-2)
3. What are some characteristics to consider when analyzing groups? (LO 2-2)
4. What are some questions to consider when analyzing organizational culture? (LO 2-2)
5. What is a discourse community? Why will discourse communities be important in your career? (LO 2-2)
6. What are standard business communication channels? (LO 2-3)

7. What kinds of electronic channels seem most useful to you? Why? (LO 2-3)
8. What are considerations to keep in mind when selecting channels? (LO 2-3)
9. What are 12 questions to ask when considering how to adapt your message to your audience? (LO 2-4)
10. What are four characteristics of good audience benefits? (LO 2-5)
11. What are three ways to identify and develop audience benefits? (LO 2-6)
12. What are considerations to keep in mind when addressing multiple audiences? (LO 2-7)

2.2   Reviewing Grammar

Good audience analysis requires careful use of pronouns. Review your skills with pronoun usage by doing grammar exercise B.5, Appendix B.

2.3   Identifying Audiences: I

In each of the following situations, label the audiences as gatekeeper, primary, secondary, auxiliary, or watchdog audiences (all audiences may not be in each scenario):

1. Kent, Carol, and Jose are planning to start a website design business. However, before they can get started, they need money. They have developed a business plan and are getting ready to seek funds from financial institutions for starting their small business.
2. Barbara's boss asked her to write a direct-mail letter to potential customers about the advantages of becoming a preferred member of their agency's travel club. The letter will go to all customers of the agency who are more than 65 years old.
3. Paul works for the mayor's office in a big city. As part of a citywide cost-cutting measure, a blue-ribbon panel has recommended requiring employees who work more than 40 hours in a week to take compensatory time off rather than being paid overtime. The only exceptions will be the police and fire departments. The mayor asks Paul to prepare a proposal for the city council, which will vote on whether to implement the change. Before they vote, council members will hear from (1) citizens, who will have an opportunity to read the proposal and communicate their opinions to the city council; (2) mayors' offices in other cities, who may be asked about their experiences; (3) union representatives, who may be concerned about the reduction in income that will occur if the proposal is implemented; (4) department heads, whose ability to schedule work might be limited if the proposal passes; and (5) the blue-ribbon panel and good-government lobbying groups. Council members come up for reelection in six months.
4. Sharon, Steven's boss at Bigster Corporation, has asked him to write an e-mail for everyone in her division, informing them of HR's new mandatory training sessions on new government regulations affecting Bigster's services.

2.4   Identifying Audiences: II

Reread the first sidebar in this chapter, "Audiences for a General," and answer the following questions:

1. Who would be Powell's gatekeeper, primary, secondary, auxiliary, and watchdog audiences?
2. What potential conflicts can you imagine among his audiences involving expectations for press conferences?

Discuss your answers in small groups.

2.5   Analyzing Multiple Audiences

Like most major corporations, the U.S. Census Bureau has multiple, conflicting audiences, among them the president, Congress, press, state governments, citizens (both as providers and users of data), statisticians, and researchers.

- For the bureau, who might serve as gatekeeper, primary, secondary, auxiliary, and watchdog audiences?
- What kinds of conflicting goals might these audiences have?
- What would be appropriate benefits for each type of audience?
- What kinds of categories might the bureau create for its largest audience (citizens)?
- How do some of the posters at the website below differ for different audiences? "In-Language Fact Sheets, Posters and Key Dates," U.S. Census Bureau, http://www.census.gov/2010census/partners/materials/inlangfacts.php#arabic

2.6   Choosing a Channel to Reach a Specific Audience

Suppose your organization wants to target a product, service, or program for each of the following audiences. What would be the best channel(s) to reach that group in your city? To what extent would that channel reach all group members?

1. Parents of autistic children.
2. Ballroom dancers.
3. Nontraditional college students.
4. Parents whose children play basketball.
5. People who are blind.
6. Mothers who are vegan.
7. People who are interested in improvisation.
8. Dog owners.

2.7   Identifying and Developing Audience Benefits

Listed here are several things an organization might like its employees to do:

1. Write fewer e-mails.
2. Volunteer at a local food pantry.
3. Volunteer to recruit interns at a job fair.
4. Attend team-building activities every other Friday afternoon.
5. Attend HR seminars on health policy changes.

As your instructor directs,

a. Identify the motives or needs that might be met by each of the activities.
b. Develop each need or motive as an audience benefit in a full paragraph. Use additional paragraphs for the other needs met by the activity. Remember to use you-attitude!

2.8   Identifying Objections and Audience Benefits

Think of an organization you know something about, and answer the following questions for it:

1. Your organization is thinking about developing a knowledge management system that requires workers to input their knowledge and experience in their job functions into the organizational database. What benefits could the knowledge management system offer your organization? What drawbacks are there? Who would be the easiest to convince? Who would be the hardest?
2. New telephone software would efficiently replace your organization's long-standing human phone operator who has been a perennial welcoming voice to incoming callers. What objections might people in your organization have to replacing the operator? What benefits might your organization receive? Who would be easiest to convince? Who would be the hardest?
3. Your organization is thinking of outsourcing one of its primary products to a manufacturer in another country where the product can be made more cost-efficiently. What fears or objections might people have? What benefits might your organization receive? Who would be easiest to convince? Who would be hardest?

As your instructor directs,

a. Share your answers orally with a small group of students.
b. Present your answers in an oral presentation to the class.
c. Write a paragraph developing the best audience benefit you identified. Remember to use you-attitude.

2.9   Analyzing Benefits for Multiple Audiences

The U.S. Census Bureau lists these benefits from cooperating with the census:

"Census information affects the numbers of seats your state occupies in the U.S. House of Representatives. And people from many walks of life use census data to advocate for causes, rescue disaster victims, prevent diseases, research markets, locate pools of skilled workers and more.

"When you do the math, it's easy to see what an accurate count of residents can do for your community. Better infrastructure. More services. A brighter tomorrow for everyone. In fact, the information the census collects helps to determine how more than $400 billion of federal funding each year is spent on infrastructure and services like:

- Hospitals

- Job training centers

- Schools

- Senior centers

- Bridges, tunnels and other public works projects

- Emergency services"[35]

How well do these benefits meet the four characteristics of good audience benefits discussed in this chapter?

2.10   Addressing Your Audience's Need for Information

"Tell me about yourself."

This may be the most popular opening question of job interviews, but it's also a question that you'll encounter in nearly any social situation when you meet someone new. Although the question may be the same, the answer you give will change based upon the rhetorical situation: the audience, purpose, and context of the question.

For each of the following situations in a–g, ask yourself these questions to help create a good response:

1. How will the audience react to your answer? Will the audience see the message as important? What information will you need to include in your answer to keep their attention?

2. How will the audience use your answer? Why is the audience asking the question? What information is relevant to the audience and what information can you leave out?

3. How much information does the audience need? What information do they already know about you? What level of detail do they need?

4. What are the audience's expectations about your answer? What are the appropriate word choices and tone for your answer? What topics should you avoid (at least for now)?

5. What are the physical conditions that will affect your answer? Where are you (e.g., outside, in a noisy room, on the phone)? How much time do you have to give your response?

Write your response to the statement "Tell me about yourself." Assume that the question is being asked by

a. A recruiter at a career fair in your university's auditorium.

b. A recruiter in a job interview in a small interview or conference room.

c. An attractive male or female at a popular weekend nightspot.

d. Your instructor on the first day of class.

e. Your new roommate on your first day in the dormitory.

f. A new co-worker on your first day at a new job.

g. A new co-worker on your first day volunteering at your local food pantry.

2.11   Analyzing Individuals

Read about the Myers-Briggs Type Indicator on page 29. On the web, take one of the free tests similar to the Myers-Briggs. Read about your personality type and consider how accurate the description may be. Print your results.

As your instructor directs,

a. Share your results orally with a small group of students and discuss how accurately the type indicator describes you. Identify some of the differences among your personality types and consider how the differences would affect efforts to collaborate on projects.

b. Identify other students in the classroom with the same combination of personality traits. Create a brief oral presentation to the class that describes your type indicator and explains how the pros and cons of your personality will affect group dynamics in collaborative work.

c. Write a brief e-mail to your instructor describing your results, assessing how well the results reflect your personality, and suggesting how your personality traits might affect your work in class and in the workplace.

2.12   Getting Customer Feedback

Smart businesses want to know what their customers and clients are saying about their products and services. Many websites can help them do so.

Check some of the common sites for customer comments. Here is a list to get you started:

http://www.amazon.com

http://www.angieslist.com

http://getsatisfaction.com

http://www.my3cents.com

http://www.suggestionbox.com

http://www.thesqueakywheel.com

http://www.yelp.com

What does each site do? What are good features of each site? What are drawbacks?

As your instructor directs,

a. Discuss your findings in an e-mail to your instructor.

b. Share your findings in small groups.

c. As a group, make a presentation to your classmates.

2.13   Evaluating a New Channel

To combat software piracy, Microsoft tried an unusual communication channel. A new software update turned screens black on computers using pirated software; the update also posted a message to switch to legitimate software copies. The update did not prevent people from using their machines, and they could manually change their wallpaper back to its previous design. But the black screen returned every 60 minutes. Microsoft said there was little protest except in China, where ironically the software piracy problem is greatest.[36]

In small groups, discuss this practice.

1. What do you think of this channel?

2. Is it ethical?

3. Do you think it helped or hurt Microsoft profits in China?

4. How do you think receivers of the black screen reacted?

As your instructor directs,

a. Post your findings electronically to share with the class.

b. Present your findings in an e-mail to your instructor.

c. Present your findings in an oral presentation to the class.

2.14   Discussing Ethics

1. What do you think about the practice of companies giving perks such as free samples to bloggers to discuss their products? Does your opinion change according to the expense of the perk (free tissues versus tablet computers, for instance)? How can you tell if bloggers have been influenced by the companies whose products they discuss?

2. What do you think about the practice of law firms using social media to find plaintiffs? Is it any worse to use social media than print or TV ads? Why? Look at some of the sites provided by law firms. Try http://www.oil-rig-explosions.com/; http://www.consumerwarningnetwork.com/; http://www.sokolovelaw.com/legal-help/dangerous-drugs/birth-control.

How persuasive is the content?

3. What do you think about the practice of tracking consumers' Internet surfing and selling the information to marketers? Does the tracking seem more intrusive when it is combined with off-line records such as shopping and credit card records?

4. What do you think about the practice of companies asking their employees to take health screenings and then giving them hundreds of dollars off their health insurance if they do so? What benefits do you see for employees? Drawbacks? Is this just a way to penalize employees who refuse by making them pay more for health insurance?

2.15   Banking on Multiple Audiences

Bruce Murphy, an executive at KeyBank, tackled a new problem: how to extend banking services to a new audience—people who use banks intermittently or not at all. It is a large group, estimated at 73 million people. Together, they spend an estimated $11 billion in fees at places such as check-cashing outlets, money-wire companies, and paycheck lenders (companies offering cash advances on future paychecks).

However, they are a tough audience. Many of them have a deep distrust of banks or believe banks will not serve them. Murphy also faced another tough audience: bank managers who feared attracting forgeries and other bad checks and thus losing money. One manager actually said, "Are you crazy? These are the very people we're trying to keep out of the bank!"

To attract the new customers, KeyBank cashes payroll and government checks for a 1.5% fee, well below the 2.44% average for check-cashing outlets. The bank also started offering free financial education classes. In fact, the bank even has a program to help people with a history of bounced checks to clear their records by paying restitution and taking the financial education class.

The program is growing, both among check-cashing clients and branches offering the services, to the satisfaction of both audiences.[37]

- What are some other businesses that could expand services to underserved populations?
- What services would they offer?
- What problems would they encounter?
- What audience appeals could they use to attract clients or customers?

2.16   Announcing a Tuition Reimbursement Program

Assume your organization is considering reimbursing workers for tuition and fees for job-related courses. As director of education and training, you will present to company executives a review of pros and cons for the program. To prepare, you have composed a list of questions you know they may have. Pick a specific organization that you know something about, and answer the following questions about it.

1. What do people do on the job? What courses or degrees could help them do their current jobs even better?
2. How much education do people already have? How do they feel about formal schooling?
3. How busy are employees? Will most have time to take classes and study in addition to working 40 hours a week (or more)?
4. Is it realistic to think that people who get more education would get higher salaries? Or is money for increases limited? Is it reasonable to think that most

people could be promoted? Or does the organization have many more low-level than high-level jobs?
5. How much loyalty do employees have to this particular organization? Is it "just a job," or do they care about the welfare of the organization?
6. How competitive is the job market? How easy is it for the organization to find and retain qualified employees?
7. Is the knowledge needed for the job changing, or is knowledge learned 5 or 10 years ago still up-to-date?
8. How competitive is the economic market? Is this company doing well financially? Can its customers or clients easily go somewhere else? Is it a government agency dependent on tax dollars for funding? What about the current situation makes this an especially good time to hone the skills of the employees you have?
9. Do you support the program? Why or why not?

2.17   Crafting a Letter for a Particular Audience

Your supervisor at a fitness center wants to increase the organization's membership and has asked you to write a letter to the three primary population segments in your town: retirees, college students, and working professionals with families. Using the following fitness benefits your supervisor gave you to help you get started, write a version of a letter targeted at each of the three audiences.

1. Become a member with no sign-up fees.
2. Attend free nutrition classes to help with weight control and optimal fitness.

3. Attend any of our many fitness classes, scheduled for your convenience.
4. Enjoy the new zero-entry indoor/outdoor pool with lap lanes.
5. Use the large selection of free weights and exercise machines.
6. Lose weight and feel your healthiest with a personal trainer, who will guide you toward your fitness goals.

Remember these benefits were just to get you started; you are expected to come up with more on your own.

2.18   Analyzing Your Co-Workers

What do your co-workers do? What hassles and challenges do they face? To what extent do their lives outside work affect their responses to work situations? What do your co-workers value? What are their pet peeves? How committed are they to organizational goals? How satisfying do they find their jobs? Are the people you work with quite similar to each other, or do they differ from each other? How?

As your instructor directs,

a. Share your answers orally with a small group of students.

b. Present your answers in an oral presentation to the class.

c. Present your answers in an e-mail to your instructor.

d. Share your answers with a small group of students and write a joint e-mail reporting the similarities and differences you found.

2.19   Analyzing the Audiences of Noncommercial Web Pages

Analyze the implied audiences of two web pages of two noncommercial organizations with the same purpose (combating hunger, improving health, influencing the political process, etc.). You could pick the home pages of the national organization and a local affiliate, or the home pages of two separate organizations working toward the same general goal.

1. Do the pages work equally well for surfers and for people who have reached the page deliberately?

2. Possible audiences include current and potential volunteers, donors, clients, and employees. Do the pages provide material for each audience? Is the material useful? Complete? Up-to-date? Does new material encourage people to return?

3. What assumptions about audiences do content and visuals suggest?

4. Can you think of ways that the pages could better serve their audiences?

As your instructor directs,

a. Share your results orally with a small group of students.

b. Present your results orally to the class.

c. Present your results in an e-mail to your instructor. Attach copies of the home pages.

d. Share your results with a small group of students, and write a joint e-mail reporting the similarities and differences you found.

e. Post your results in an e-mail message to the class. Provide links to the two web pages.

2.20   Analyzing a Discourse Community

Analyze the way a group you are part of uses language. Possible groups include

1. Work teams.

2. Sports teams.

3. Sororities, fraternities, and other social groups.

4. Churches, mosques, synagogues, and temples.

5. Geographic or ethnic groups.

6. Groups of friends.

Questions to ask include the following:

1. What specialized terms might not be known to outsiders?

2. What topics do members talk or write about? What topics are considered unimportant or improper?

3. What channels do members use to convey messages?

4. What forms of language do members use to build goodwill? To demonstrate competence or superiority?

5. What strategies or kinds of proof are convincing to members?

6. What formats, conventions, or rules do members expect messages to follow?

7. What are some nonverbal ways members communicate?

As your instructor directs,

a. Share your results orally with a small group of students.

b. Present your results in an oral presentation to the class.

c. Present your results in an e-mail to your instructor.

d. Share your results with a small group of students, and write a joint e-mail reporting the similarities and differences you found.

Notes

1. Isabel Briggs Myers, *Introduction to Type* (Palo Alto, CA: Consulting Psychologists Press, 1980). The material in this section follows Myers's paper.
2. Isabel Briggs Myers and Mary H. McCaulley, *Manual: A Guide to the Development and Use of the Myers-Briggs Type Indicato*r (Palo Alto, CA: Consulting Psychologists Press, 1985), 248–51.
3. Miguel Bustillo, "Wal-Mart Adds Guns Alongside Butter," *Wall Street Journal,* April 28, 2011, B1; and Karen Talley and Shelly Banjo, "With More on Shelves, Wal-Mart Profit Rises," *Wall Street Journal,* May 18, 2012, B3.
4. "Internet 2012 in Numbers," Royal Pingdom, January 16, 2013, http://royal.pingdom.com/2013/01/16/internet-2012-in-numbers/; and Sara Radicati, ed., "Email Market, 2012–2016—Executive Summary," The Radicati Group, accessed May 4, 2013, http://www.radicati.com/wp/wp-content/uploads/2012/10/Email-Market-2012-2016-Executive-Summary.pdf.
5. Ann Zimmerman, "Can Electronics Stores Survive?" *Wall Street Journal,* August 31, 2012, B1.
6. Jessica E. Vascellaro and Sam Schechner, "TV Lures Ads but Viewers Drop Out," *Wall Street Journal,* September 21, 2011, B1.
7. Frances Frei and Anne Morriss, *Uncommon Service: How to Win by Putting Customers at the Core of Your Business* (Boston: Harvard Business Review Press, 2012), 152.
8. Nate Silver, *The Signal and the Noise: Why So Many Predictions Fail—But Some Don't* (New York: Penguin, 2012), 139-40.
9. "Statistics and Facts on Online Advertising in the U.S.," *Statista,* accessed March 6, 2013, http://www.statista.com/topics/1176/online-advertising/.
10. Marc Gunther, "Hard News," *Fortune,* August 6, 2007, 82.
11. Pew Research Center for the People & the Press, "In Changing News Landscape, Even Television Is Vulnerable: Trends in News Consumption: 1991–2012," September 27, 2012, http://www.people-press.org/files/legacy-pdf/2012%20News%20Consumption%20Report.pdf.
12. Christopher S. Stewart, "King of TV for Now, CBS Girds for Digital Battle," *Wall Street Journal,* November 30, 2012, A1.
13. Pew Research Center for the People & the Press, "In Changing News Landscape, Even Television is Vulnerable."
14. Ibid.
15. Suzanne Vranica, "Hanger Ads Ensure Message Gets Home," *Wall Street Journal,* March 12, 2007, B4; and Curtis Peters, "Your Ad Here: As Marketers Fight for Consumer Eyeballs, Everything Has Become a Billboard," *Bloomberg Businessweek,* August 6, 2012, 73.
16. Elizabeth Olson, "The Ken Doll Turns 50, and Wins a New Face," *New York Times,* March 21, 2011, http://www.nytimes.com/2011/03/22/business/media/22adco.html.
17. Peters, "Your Ad Here."
18. Ibid.
19. Joe Palca, "Wanna Play? Computer Gamers Help Push Frontier of Brain Research," *NPR,* March 5, 2013, http://www.npr.org/2013/03/05/173435599/wanna-play-computer-gamers-help-push-frontier-of-brain-research?ft=1&f=1001.
20. "Steamy Hot Line Raises Pulses, Library Funds," *Des Moines Register,* May 9, 2007, 4A.
21. Elaine Pofeldt, "David vs. Goliath," *Fortune,* July 4, 2011, 30.
22. Lev Grossman, "A Game for All Ages," *Time,* May 15, 2006, 39.
23. Cecilie Rohwedder, "Store of Knowledge: No. 1 Retailer in Britain Uses 'Clubcard' to Thwart Wal-Mart: Data from Loyalty Program Help Tesco Tailor Products as It Resists U.S. Invader," *Wall Street Journal,* June 6, 2006, A1.
24. Frederick Herzberg, "One More Time: How Do You Motivate Employees?" *Harvard Business Review* 65, no. 5 (1987), 109–20.
25. Teri Agins, "Over-40 Finds a Muse," *Wall Street Journal,* December 6, 2008, W4.
26. Frei and Morriss, *Uncommon Service,* 57–58.
27. Ryan Chittum, "Price Points: Good Customer Service Costs Money. Some Expenses Are Worth It—and Some Aren't," *Wall Street Journal,* October 30, 2006, R7.
28. Mikotaj Jan Piskorski, "Social Strategies That Work," *Harvard Business Review* 90, no. 11 (November 2012): 119.
29. Ibid.
30. Joseph B. White, "How Auto Makers Keep You Coming Back," *Wall Street Journal,* January 23, 2013, D3.
31. Richard M. Smith, "Stay True to Your Brand: Ad Guru Rance Crain Says the Rules Are Eternal," *Newsweek,* May 5, 2008, E18.
32. James Surowiecki, "The Financial Page Feature Presentation," *The New Yorker,* May 28, 2007, 28.
33. Reuters, "Scientist: Complexity Causes 50% of Product Returns," *Computer World,* May 6, 2006, http://www.computerworld.com/s/article/109254/Scientist_Complexity_causes_50_of_product_returns.
34. Rachael Spilka, "Orality and Literacy in the Workplace: Process- and Text-Based Strategies for Multiple Audience Adaptation," *Journal of Business and Technical Communication* 4, no. 1 (1990): 44–67.
35. Quoted from "Why It's Important," U.S. Census Bureau: United States Census 2010, accessed March 6, 2013, http://www.census.gov/2010census/about/why-important.php.
36. Loretta Chao and Juliet Ye, "Microsoft Tactic Raises Hackles in China: In Antipiracy Move, Software Update Turns Screens Black and Urges Users to Buy Legal Windows Copies," *Wall Street Journal,* October 23, 2008, B4.
37. Ann Carrns, "Banks Court a New Client: The Low-Income Earner: KeyCorp Experiments with Check Cashing," *Wall Street Journal,* March 16, 2007, A1, A14.

3

Building Goodwill

Chapter Outline

NEWSWORTHY COMMUNICATION

Diversifying Macy's

An important aspect of building goodwill is increasing inclusiveness. Such an increase is not only ethical, but also good business. The Hispanic population, for instance, is the fastest growing in the United States.

Macy's department store knows that more than half of its potential customers in its largest urban markets are minorities, so the chain has designed a new training program as an opportunity for minority vendors to sell their products in Macy's stores. The program instructs participants in the business of large-store retail.

Macy's has agreed to order from some of its new graduates. New products include cosmetics targeted at African-American and polyethnic women, dresses targeted primarily for Hispanic women, and sexy plus-size swimsuits for larger women.

Macy's is trying to reach out to their minority shoppers, as the chain has been receiving more requests for specialized items for minority groups. According to the University of Georgia's Selig Center for Economic Growth, by 2015, Hispanic shoppers will spend $1.5 trillion on goods and services, black shoppers $1.2 trillion, and Asian shoppers $775 billion. Macy's stores hope to be a big part of that expanding market.

Source: Cotton Timberlake, "At Macy's, the Many Colors of Cash," *Bloomberg Businessweek*, January 16, 2012, 21–22.

Learning Objectives

After studying this chapter, you will know how to

LO 3-1 Create you-attitude.

LO 3-2 Create positive emphasis.

LO 3-3 Improve tone in business communications.

LO 3-4 Reduce bias in business communications.

Airline Goodwill

Southwest Airlines is known for fun, caring flight attendants who joke, sing, and generally try to entertain and please customers.

Another airline known for goodwill is Alaska Airlines. It gives its agents the power to find solutions for customers left behind for any reason. One regional manager reported receiving a call from a customer he had helped five years ago. The man's grandchild had just gone into cardiac arrest, and he needed a flight from Honolulu to Seattle. He had found all flights full, but the agent found him a flight right away. Goodwill efforts like this have given Alaska Airlines top ratings and many awards.

Adapted from Gretchen Spreitzer and Christine Porath, "Creating Sustainable Performance," *Harvard Business Review* 90, no. 1–2 (January–February 2012): 95.

Goodwill eases the challenges of business and administration. Companies have long been aware that treating customers well pays off in more sales and higher profits. Today we work in a service economy: the majority of jobs are in service, where goodwill is even more important.[1]

- Amazon's corporate mission says, "We seek to be Earth's most customer-centric company for four primary customer sets: consumers, sellers, enterprises, and content creators." Jeff Bezos, Amazon's founder and CEO, has a video on YouTube titled "Everything I Know." It has three points: obsess over customers, invent on behalf of customers, and think long term, because doing so allows you to serve customers better.[2]

- Tony Hsieh built Zappos around customer service, including a service attitude toward vendors.

- A study by Vanderbilt University found that a portfolio of companies whose ACSI (American Consumer Satisfaction Index) scores were above the national average far outperformed the market. Over a 10-year period, the portfolio gained 212%; the Standard & Poor's 500 stock index rose 105% over the same period.[3]

Goodwill is important internally as well as externally. More and more organizations are realizing that treating employees well is financially wise as well as ethically sound. Happy employees result in less staff turnover, thus reducing hiring and training costs. A University of Pennsylvania study of 3,000 companies found that investing 10% of revenue on capital improvement boosted company productivity 3.9%, but spending the money on employees increased productivity 8.5%, or more than twice as much.[4] The QuikTrip chain invests heavily in employees, offering them better pay, benefits, training, and schedules than competitors do. That investment pays off: QuikTrip's sales per labor hour are 66% higher than average for convenience store chains.[5]

You-attitude, positive emphasis, trust, and bias-free language are four ways to help build goodwill. All four help you achieve your purposes and make your messages friendlier, more persuasive, more professional, and more humane. They suggest that you care not just about money but also about the needs and interests of your customers, employees, and fellow citizens.

You-Attitude   LO 3-1

You-attitude is a communication style that looks at things from the audience's point of view, emphasizing what the audience wants or needs to know, respecting the audience's intelligence, and protecting the audience's ego.

For years Microsoft fought lax enforcement of intellectual property laws in China. The software company finally started making progress when it looked at the problem from the Chinese point of view. Government officials were ignoring the problem because many of their people made a living from illegal copies and because Microsoft prices put the products beyond the reach of most citizens. With this new perspective, Microsoft began creating jobs in China and lowering the prices of its products—in return for better law enforcement.[6]

How to Create You-Attitude

Expressing what you want to say with you-attitude is a crucial step in communicating your concern to your audience. In fact, pundits such as Daniel Pink and Thomas Friedman consider it one of the major skills that computers and outsourcing will not replace in the near future. Pink notes, for instance, that software and websites have replaced much routine legal work; legal researchers in other countries do much work for American law firms. Pink asks, "So which lawyers will remain? Those who can empathize with their clients and understand their true needs."[7]

To apply you-attitude on a sentence level, use the following techniques:

1. Talk about the audience, not about yourself.
2. Refer specifically to the customer's request or order.
3. Don't talk about feelings, except to congratulate or offer sympathy.
4. In positive situations, use *you* more often than *I*. Use *we* when it includes the audience.
5. In negative situations, avoid the word *you*. Protect the audience's ego. Use passive verbs and impersonal expressions to avoid assigning blame.

Revisions for you-attitude do not change the basic meaning of the sentence. However, revising for you-attitude often makes sentences longer because the revision is more specific and has more information. Long sentences need not be wordy. **Wordiness** means having more words than the meaning requires. We can add information and still keep the writing concise.

1. Talk about the audience, not about yourself.   Your audience wants to know how they benefit or are affected. When you provide this information, you make your message more complete and more interesting.

Lacks you-attitude:	We have negotiated an agreement with Apex Rent-a-Car that gives you a discount on rental cars.
You-attitude:	As a Sunstrand employee, you can now get a 20% discount when you rent a car from Apex.

2. Refer specifically to the customer's request or order.   A specific referral, rather than a generic *your order* or *your policy,* helps show that your customer

Customer Service Becoming Popular with Businesses

More companies are improving customer service to increase both sales and market share.

Walgreens is training pharmacists to work more closely with patients with chronic illnesses such as diabetes. Pharmacists are replacing their normal 3- to 5-minute meetings with regular 20- to 45-minute patient meetings to help them manage their disease.

American Express is training call-center agents to focus on building customer loyalty rather than processing the call quickly.

Even Comcast, which has had well-publicized problems with customer service, is giving its 24,000 call-center agents additional training.

Adapted from Dana Mattioli, "Customer Service as a Growth Engine," *Wall Street Journal*, June 7, 2010, B6.

is important to you. If your customer is an individual or a small business, it's friendly to specify the content of the order. If you're dealing with a company with which you do a great deal of business, give the invoice or purchase order number.

Lacks you-attitude:	Your order . . .
You-attitude (to individual):	The desk chair you ordered . . .
You-attitude (to a large store):	Your invoice #783329 . . .

3. Don't talk about feelings, except to congratulate or offer sympathy.
In most business situations, your feelings are irrelevant and should be omitted.

Lacks you-attitude:	We are happy to extend you a credit line of $15,000.
You-attitude:	You can now charge up to $15,000 on your American Express card.

It *is* appropriate to talk about your own emotions in a message of congratulations or condolence.

You-attitude:	Congratulations on your promotion to district manager! I was really pleased to read about it.

Don't talk about your audience's feelings, either. It's distancing to have others tell us how we feel—especially if they are wrong.

Lacks you-attitude:	You'll be happy to hear that Open Grip Walkway Channels meet OSHA requirements.
You-attitude:	Open Grip Walkway Channels meet OSHA requirements.

Maybe the audience expects that anything you sell would meet government regulations (OSHA—the Occupational Safety and Health Administration—is a federal agency). The audience may even be disappointed if they expected higher standards. Simply explain the situation or describe a product's features; don't predict the audience's response.

When you have good news, simply give the good news.

Lacks you-attitude:	You'll be happy to hear that your scholarship has been renewed.
You-attitude:	Congratulations! Your scholarship has been renewed.

4. In positive situations, use *you* more often than *I*. Use *we* when it includes the audience.
Talk about the audience, not you or your company.

Lacks you-attitude:	We provide health insurance to all employees.
You-attitude:	You receive health insurance as a full-time Procter & Gamble employee.

Most readers are tolerant of the word *I* in e-mail messages, which seem like conversation. But edit paper documents to use *I* rarely if at all. *I* suggests that you're concerned about personal issues, not about the organization's problems, needs, and opportunities. *We* works well when it includes the reader. Avoid *we* if it excludes the reader (as it would in a letter to a customer or supplier or as it might in an e-mail about what *we* in management want *you* to do).

5. In negative situations, avoid the word *you*. Protect your audience's ego. Use passive verbs and impersonal expressions to avoid assigning blame.   When you report bad news or limitations, use a noun for a group of which your audience is a part instead of *you* so people don't feel that they're singled out for bad news.

Lacks you-attitude:	You must get approval from the director before you publish any articles or memoirs based on your work in the agency.
You-attitude:	Agency personnel must get approval from the director to publish any articles or memoirs based on their work at the agency.

Use passive verbs and impersonal expressions to avoid blaming people. **Passive verbs** describe the action performed on something, without necessarily saying who did it. (See Chapter 5 for a full discussion of passive verbs.) In most cases, active verbs are better. But when your audience is at fault, passive verbs may be useful to avoid assigning blame.

Impersonal expressions omit people and talk only about things. Normally, communication is most lively when it's about people—and most interesting to audiences when it's about them. When you have to report a mistake or bad news, however, you can protect your audience's ego by using an impersonal expression, one in which things, not people, do the acting.

Lacks you-attitude:	You made no allowance for inflation in your estimate.
You-attitude (passive):	No allowance for inflation has been made in this estimate.
You-attitude (impersonal):	This estimate makes no allowance for inflation.

A purist might say that impersonal expressions are illogical: An estimate, for example, is inanimate and can't "make" anything. In the pragmatic world of business writing, however, impersonal expressions help you convey criticism tactfully.

You-Attitude beyond the Sentence Level

Good messages apply you-attitude beyond the sentence level by using content and organization as well as style to build goodwill.

To create goodwill with content,

- Be complete. When you have lots of information to give, consider putting some details in an appendix, which may be read later.

- Anticipate and answer questions your audience is likely to have.

- Show why information your audience didn't ask for is important.

- Show your audience how the subject of your message affects them.

To organize information to build goodwill,

- Put information your audience is most interested in first.

- Arrange information to meet your audience's needs, not yours.

- Use headings and lists so readers can find key points quickly.

You-Attitude with International Audiences

When you communicate with international audiences, look at the world from their point of view.

The United States is in the middle of most of the maps sold in the United States. It isn't in the middle of maps sold elsewhere in the world.

The United States clings to a measurement system that has been abandoned by most of the world. When you write for international audiences, use the metric system.

Even pronouns and direction words need attention. *We* may not feel inclusive to readers with different assumptions and backgrounds. *Here* won't mean the same thing to a reader in Bonn as it does to one in Boulder.

Figure 3.1 | An E-mail Lacking You-Attitude

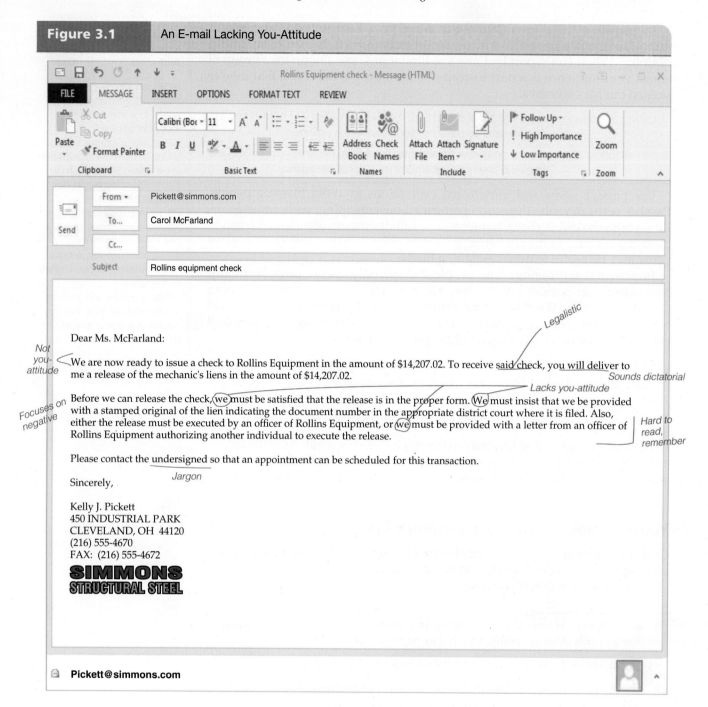

Consider the e-mail in Figure 3.1. As the red marginal notes indicate, many individual sentences in this message lack you-attitude. Fixing individual sentences could improve the e-mail. However, it really needs to be totally rewritten.

Figure 3.2 shows a possible revision of this e-mail. The revision is clearer, easier to read, and friendlier.

Positive Emphasis LO 3-2

With some bad news—announcements of layoffs, product defects and recalls, salary cuts—straightforward negatives build credibility. (See Chapter 10 on how to present bad news.) Sometimes negatives are needed to make people

Figure 3.2	An E-mail Revised to Improve You-Attitude

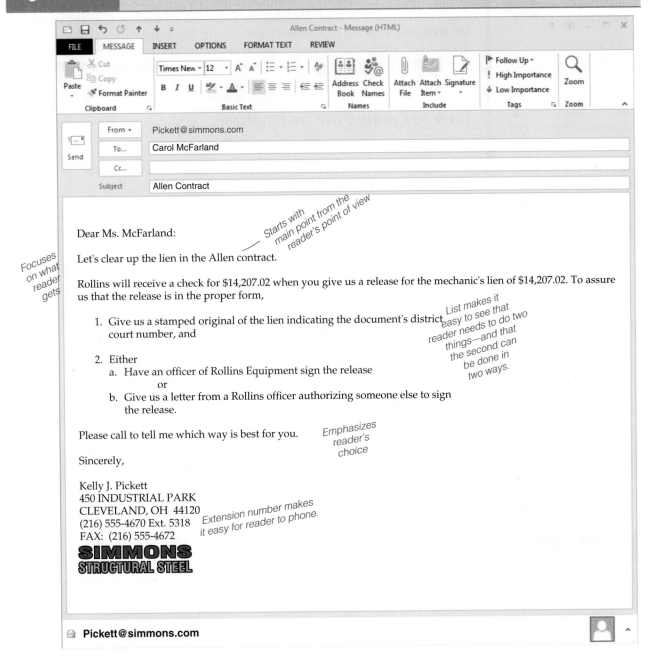

Dear Ms. McFarland:

Starts with main point from the reader's point of view

Let's clear up the lien in the Allen contract.

Focuses on what reader gets

Rollins will receive a check for $14,207.02 when you give us a release for the mechanic's lien of $14,207.02. To assure us that the release is in the proper form,

1. Give us a stamped original of the lien indicating the document's district court number, and

2. Either
   a. Have an officer of Rollins Equipment sign the release
      or
   b. Give us a letter from a Rollins officer authorizing someone else to sign the release.

List makes it easy to see that reader needs to do two things—and that the second can be done in two ways.

Please call to tell me which way is best for you. *Emphasizes reader's choice*

Sincerely,

Kelly J. Pickett
450 INDUSTRIAL PARK
CLEVELAND, OH 44120
(216) 555-4670 Ext. 5318 *Extension number makes it easy for reader to phone.*
FAX: (216) 555-4672

SIMMONS STRUCTURAL STEEL

Pickett@simmons.com

---

take a problem seriously. In some messages, such as disciplinary notices and negative performance appraisals, one of your purposes is to make the problem clear. Even here, avoid insults or attacks on your audience's integrity or sanity.

In most situations, however, it's better to be positive. Researchers have found that businesspeople responded more positively to positive than to negative language and were more likely to say they would act on a positively worded request.[8] In groundbreaking research for Met Life, Martin Seligman found that optimistic salespeople sold 37% more insurance than pessimistic colleagues. As a result, Met Life began hiring optimists even when they failed to meet the company's other criteria. These "unqualified" optimists outsold pessimists 21% in their first year and 57% in the next.[9]

Positive emphasis is a way of looking at things. Is the bottle half empty or half full? You can create positive emphasis with the words, information, organization, and layout you choose. "Part-time" may be a negative phrase for someone seeking full-time employment, but it may be a positive phrase for college students seeking limited work hours while they pursue their education. It may become even more positive if connected with flexible hours.

How to Create Positive Emphasis

Create positive emphasis by using the following techniques:

1. Avoid negative words and words with negative connotations.
2. Beware of hidden negatives.
3. Focus on what the audience can do rather than on limitations.
4. Justify negative information by giving a reason or linking it to an audience benefit.
5. Put the negative information in the middle and present it compactly.

Choose the technique that produces the clearest, most accurate communication.

1. Avoid negative words and words with negative connotations. Figure 3.3 lists some common negative words. If you find similar words in a draft, try to substitute a more positive word. When you must use a negative, use the least negative term that will convey your meaning:

Negative:	We have failed to finish taking inventory.
Better:	We haven't finished taking inventory.
Still better:	We will be finished taking inventory Friday.
Negative:	If you can't understand this explanation, feel free to call me.
Better:	If you have further questions, just call me.
Still better:	Omit the sentence.

Figure 3.3	Negative Words to Avoid

afraid	impossible	**Some dis- words:**	**Many un- words:**
anxious	lacking	disapprove	unclear
avoid	loss	dishonest	unfair
bad	neglect	dissatisfied	unfortunate
careless	never		unfortunately
damage	no		unpleasant
delay	not	**Many in- words:**	unreasonable
delinquent	objection	inadequate	unreliable
deny	problem	incomplete	unsure
difficulty	reject	inconvenient	
eliminate	sorry	insincere	
error	terrible	injury	
except	trivial		
fail	trouble		
fault	wait	**Some mis- words:**	
fear	weakness	misfortune	
hesitate	worry	missing	
ignorant	wrong	mistake	
ignore			

Omit double negatives.

Negative:	Never fail to back up your documents.
Better:	Always back up your documents.

When you must use a negative term, use the least negative word that is accurate.

Negative:	Your balance of $835 is delinquent.
Better:	Your balance of $835 is past due.

Getting rid of negatives has the added benefit of making what you write easier to understand. Sentences with three or more negatives are hard to interpret correctly.[10]

2. Beware of hidden negatives.

Some words are not negative in themselves but become negative in context. *But* and *however* indicate a shift, so, after a positive statement, they are negative. *I hope* and *I trust that* suggest that you aren't sure. *Patience* may sound like a virtue, but it is a necessary virtue only when things are slow. Even positives about a service or product may backfire if they suggest that in the past the service or product was bad.

Negative:	I hope this is the information you wanted. [Implication: I'm not sure.]
Better:	Enclosed is a brochure about road repairs scheduled for 2014.
Still better:	The brochure contains a list of all roads and bridges scheduled for repair during 2014, specific dates when work will start, and alternate routes.
Negative:	Please be patient as we switch to the automated system. [Implication: You can expect problems.]
Better:	If you have questions during our transition to the automated system, please call Melissa Morgan.
Still better:	You'll be able to get information instantly about any house on the market when the automated system is in place. If you have questions during the transition, please call Melissa Morgan.
Negative:	Now Crispy Crunch tastes better. [Implication: it used to taste terrible.]
Better:	Now Crispy Crunch tastes even better.

Removing negatives does not mean being arrogant or pushy.

Negative:	I hope that you are satisfied enough to place future orders.
Arrogant:	I look forward to receiving all of your future business.
Better:	Whenever you need computer chips, a call to Mercury is all it takes for fast service.

When you eliminate negative words, be sure to maintain accuracy. Words that are exact opposites will usually not be accurate. Instead, use specifics to be both positive and accurate.

Negative:	The exercycle is not guaranteed for life.
Not true:	The exercycle is guaranteed for life.
True:	The exercycle is guaranteed for 10 years.

Legal phrases also have negative connotations for most readers and should be avoided whenever possible.

3. Focus on what the audience can do rather than on limitations.

When there are limits, or some options are closed, focus on the alternatives that remain.

Thanks a Lot at Work

Typically, people do not tend to show gratitude in the workplace, even though research suggests they should. According to a study by the Society for Human Resource Management (SHRM), showing appreciation for workers cuts turnover and increases profit.

So, is showing appreciation that big of a deal? Apparently so. Some bosses fear employees will then take advantage of them. Others worry about embarrassing themselves or the employee. Still others think they show their appreciation with a paycheck.

Asking employees how they want feedback, including expressions of gratitude, is a good approach. One supervisor who was going to praise an employee in front of supervisors discovered that action would be embarrassing for the employee; instead, the employee asked to use the boss's executive parking spot for a day.

Adapted from Sue Shellenbarger, "Showing Appreciation at the Office? No, Thanks," *Wall Street Journal,* November 12, 2012, D3.

Negative:	We will not allow you to charge more than $5,000 on your Visa account.
Better:	You can charge $5,000 on your new Visa card.
or:	Your new Visa card gives you $5,000 in credit that you can use at thousands of stores nationwide.

As you focus on what will happen, check for **you-attitude.** In the previous example, "We will allow you to charge $5,000" would be positive, but it lacks you-attitude.

When you have a benefit and a requirement the audience must meet to get the benefit, the sentence is usually more positive if you put the benefit first.

| Negative: | You will not qualify for the student membership rate of $55 a year unless you are a full-time student. |
| Better: | You get all the benefits of membership for only $55 a year if you're a full-time student. |

4. Justify negative information by giving a reason or linking it to an audience benefit.
A reason can help your audience see that the information is necessary; a benefit can suggest that the negative aspect is outweighed by positive factors. Be careful, however, to make the logic behind your reason clear and to leave no loopholes.

| Negative: | We cannot sell individual pastel sets. |
| Loophole: | To keep down packaging costs and to help you save on shipping and handling costs, we sell pastel sets in packages of 12. |

Suppose the customer says, "I'll pay the extra shipping and handling. Send me six." If you truly sell only in packages of 12, you need to say so:

| Better: | To keep down packaging costs and to help customers save on shipping and handling costs, we sell pastel sets only in packages of 12. |

If you link the negative element to a benefit, be sure it is a benefit your audience will acknowledge. Avoid telling people that you're doing things "for their own good." They may have a different notion of what their own good is. You may think you're doing customers a favor by limiting their credit so they don't get in over their heads and go bankrupt. They may think they'd be better off with more credit so they could expand in hopes of making more sales and more profits.

5. Put the negative information in the middle and present it compactly.
Put negatives at the beginning or end only if you want to emphasize the negative. To de-emphasize a written negative, put it in the middle of a paragraph rather than in the first or last sentence and in the middle of the message rather than in the first or last paragraphs.

When a letter or memo runs several pages, remember that the bottom of the first page is also a position of emphasis, even if it is in the middle of a paragraph, because of the extra white space of the bottom margin. (The first page gets more attention because it is on top and the reader's eye may catch lines of the message even when he or she isn't consciously reading it; the tops and bottoms of subsequent pages don't get this extra attention.) If possible, avoid placing negative information at the bottom of the first page.

Giving a topic lots of space emphasizes it. Therefore, you can de-emphasize negative information by giving it as little space as possible. Give negative information only once in your message. Don't list negatives with bulleted or numbered lists. These lists take space and emphasize material.

How to Check Positive Emphasis

All five of the strategies listed above help create positive emphasis. However, you should always check to see that the positive emphasis is appropriate, sincere, and realistic.

As you read at the beginning of this section, positive emphasis is not always **appropriate.** Some bad news is so serious that presenting it with a positive tone is insensitive, if not unethical. Layoffs, salary cuts, and product defects are all topics in this category.

Some positive emphasis is so overdone that it no longer seems **sincere.** The used-car sales rep selling a rusting auto is one stereotype of insincerity. A more common example for most businesspeople is the employee who gushes praise through gritted teeth over your promotion. Most of us have experienced something similar, and we know how easy it is to see through the insincerity.

Positive emphasis can also be so overdone that it clouds the reality of the situation. If your company has two finalists for a sales award, and only one award, the loser does not have second place, which implies a second award. On the other hand, if all sales reps win the same award, top performers will feel unappreciated. Too much praise can also make mediocre employees think they are doing great. Keep your communications **realistic.**

Restraint can help make positive emphasis more effective. Conductor Otto Klemperer was known for not praising his orchestra. One day, pleased with a particularly good rehearsal, he spoke a brusque "good." His stunned musicians broke into spontaneous applause. Klemperer rapped his baton on his music stand to silence them and said, "Not *that* good."[11]

Positive Psychology

Positive psychology is a branch of psychology that studies how to help people thrive. Its goal is to increase thriving, also called flourishing, well-being, and happiness. This goal connects closely with goodwill, you-attitude, and positive tone, all of which help employee happiness. A workplace that looks at its culture from its employees' perspectives, a culture where praise and goodwill are part of daily communications, will help increase thriving in employees. According to the *Harvard Business Review,* which devoted an entire issue to positive psychology, research from various fields "makes the link between a thriving workforce and better business performance absolutely clear."[12] Even Federal Reserve Chairman Ben Bernanke has called happiness an important gauge for measuring economic progress.[13]

Negative information can cause an intense reaction.
© Tribune Media Services, Inc. All Rights Reserved. Reprinted with permission.

Why should companies care if their employees are happy? Happy employees help improve corporate profits, as well as other corporate goals:

- A University of Michigan study found that thriving employees had 125% less burnout, 46% more job satisfaction, and 32% more commitment to the company than their peers who weren't thriving. They also had 16% better performance, according to their managers. These findings were true across industries and job types.[14]

- A University of Illinois meta-analysis of 225 studies found that happy employees are 31% more productive, have 37% higher sales, and are three times more creative than unhappy ones.[15]

- Researchers studying a retail chain found that stores with thriving employees earned $21 more per square foot of retail space than the other stores, resulting in $32 million additional profit for the chain.[16]

Thriving employees also are healthier and more energetic, go beyond the call of duty, and attract other good workers.[17]

How do organizations boost happiness among their employees? One major way is to provide meaningful, challenging work with a variety of tasks. Allow employees to continue to learn on the job and to make decisions that affect their work.[18] Use you-attitude to help all employees see that what they do daily makes a difference.

Another major way to boost happiness is to facilitate social support. Social factors such as teamwork or mentoring, plus environmental factors such as break rooms and exercise areas, help enhance social connections among workers. Social support doesn't have to be time consuming. One large health care provider with 11,000 employees instituted a 10/5 rule to increase social support for both employees and patients. Anyone within 10 feet of another person had to make eye contact and smile; anyone within 5 feet had to say hello. Adopting this rule led to an increase in patient satisfaction and significant improvement in medical practice provider scores.[19]

On the job, as well as in individual lives, the frequency of positive experiences is a better predictor of happiness than the intensity of such experiences. Job happiness may depend more on daily experiences, such as interesting work projects, pleasant interactions with colleagues, and positive feedback from managers, than with big-ticket items such as salary and job title.[20]

Tone, Power, and Politeness   LO 3-3

Tone is the implied attitude of the communicator toward the audience. If the words of a document seem condescending or rude, tone is a problem. Norms for politeness are cultural and generational; they also vary from office to office.

Tone is tricky because it interacts with context and power. Language that is acceptable within one group may be unacceptable if used by someone outside the group. Words that might seem friendly from a superior to a subordinate may seem uppity if used by the subordinate to the superior. Similarly, words that may be neutral among peers may be seen as negative if sent by a superior to subordinate.

Using the proper tone with employees can have huge economic impact for a business. Disgruntled employees are suing more than ever before, and disputes over wages or hours frequently can be brought as class action suits, making them even more expensive.[21]

The desirable tone for business writing is businesslike but not stiff, friendly but not phony, confident but not arrogant, polite but not groveling. Several guidelines will help you achieve the tone you want.

Use Courtesy Titles for People You Don't Know Well

Most U.S. organizations use first names for everyone, whatever their age or rank. But many people don't like being called by their first names by people they don't know or by someone much younger. When you talk or write to people outside your organization, use first names only if you've established a personal relationship. If you don't know someone well, use a courtesy title (discussed later in this chapter).

Be Aware of the Power Implications of the Words You Use

"Thank you for your cooperation" is generous coming from a superior to a subordinate; it's not appropriate in a message to your superior. Different ways of asking for action carry different levels of politeness.[22]

Order: (lowest politeness)	Turn in your time card by Monday.
Polite order: (midlevel politeness)	Please turn in your time card by Monday.
Indirect request: (higher politeness)	Time cards should be turned in by Monday.
Question: (highest politeness)	Would you be able to turn in your time card by Monday?

Higher levels of politeness may be unclear. In some cases, a question may seem like a request for information to which it's acceptable to answer, "No, I can't." In other cases, it will be an order, simply phrased in polite terms.

You need more politeness if you're asking for something that will inconvenience the audience and help you more than the person who does the action. Generally, you need less politeness when you're asking for something small, routine, or to the audience's benefit. Some discourse communities, however, prefer that even small requests be made politely.

Trust

Financial crises, Internet scams, and shoddy goods and services have all contributed to a lack of trust of the commercial world. Trust is a vital element in goodwill, and it is necessary on the personal level as well as the corporate level. Robert Hurley, author of *The Decision to Trust: How Leaders Can Create High Trust Companies,* says, "Trust comes from delivering every day on what you promise—as a manager, an employee, and a company. It involves constant teamwork, communication and collaboration."[23]

A large part of trust comes from honesty and ethics. But by themselves, these qualities are not enough. As Hurley notes, trust is also delivering on our commitments. This delivery is important for you when you start a new job and then move up the organizational rungs. Do you do what you are expected to do? What you say you will do? Or do you say yes to more than you can possibly deliver? Honoring commitments is also important for the organization: does it deliver the expected quality and quantity of goods and services in a timely fashion?

Trust also comes from the goodwill communication skills described in this chapter, and especially from skill with you-attitude. Are you good at discerning the interests of others, and fulfilling or promoting those interests fairly and ethically?

Clear, open, and timely communication helps build and maintain trust.

Using Technology to Build Goodwill

Most organizations use a variety of technology-based communications to create and sustain goodwill with their customers, clients, and employees. (See Chapter 9 for a full discussion of communication technologies.) Companies have long used technologies such as electronic newsletters for employees and e-mail addresses where customers could ask questions.

Now most organizations also have websites and Facebook pages featuring new products and services, tips on using products and services, and customer forums. Toy companies offer creative ways to use their products. News organizations use blogs to provide commentary. Many companies use Facebook to enter into dialogues with customers, Twitter to solve customer complaints quickly, or YouTube clips to offer instructions, or even humorous content about their products and services. In 2013, even the staid Securities and Exchange Commission started allowing corporate news postings on Twitter and corporate Facebook sites, as long as companies have informed their investors which channels will be used.[24]

Many companies are getting creative in their efforts to use technology to increase goodwill.

- Charmin launched its SitOrSquat app that helps people find a nearby public restroom, and then allows them to rate it for cleanliness. They also created the hashtag #tweetfromtheseat.[25]

- Energy drink Red Bull, sponsor of extreme sports, broadcast on YouTube Felix Baumgartner's enormous skydive that broke the sound barrier.[26]

- April Fools' Day traditionally finds jokes on social media. Past jokes include an Ikea self-assembly lawn mower, posted on Facebook; glass-bottomed airplanes for a new flying experience, posted on Virgin Atlantic Airways' founder Richard Branson's blog; and an announcement by Twitter that it was banishing vowels unless users paid a fee.[27]

As one advertising consultant says, "If you can give someone a laugh, you can create good will for your brand."[28]

Reducing Bias in Business Communication   LO 3-4

The makeup of the U.S. population is changing. According to the U.S. Census Bureau,

- Women outnumber men.

- More women than men are attaining associate, bachelor's, and master's degrees.

- For people 16 and older, more women (41.7%) than men (35.11%) work in management, professional, and related occupations.

- The Hispanic population is the fastest growing in the country; it numbered 50.5 million in the 2010 census. Four states (California, Hawaii, New Mexico, and Texas) plus the District of Columbia have a "majority-minority" population, where more than 50% are part of a minority group.

- Projections show non-Hispanic whites becoming a minority soon after 2040.

- The number of people 65 and older is also growing; that population now numbers over 41 million, and 6.5 million of them are still in the workforce.[29]

These figures highlight the growing diversity of the workplace and the need to communicate with appropriate, unbiased language.

Bias-free language is language that does not discriminate against people on the basis of sex, physical condition, race, ethnicity, age, religion, or any other category. It includes all audience members, helps to sustain goodwill, is fair and friendly, and complies with the law.

Check to be sure that your language is bias-free. Doing so is ethical; it can also avoid major problems and lawsuits.

■ Josef Ackermann, chief executive of Deutsche Bank, was mocked in the international news when he said at a news conference that including women on the bank's all-male executive board would make it "more colorful and prettier too." The publicity added to mistrust of the bank at an awkward time when it was lobbying to dissuade German policy makers from imposing restrictions.[30]

■ Conservative advice expert Dr. Laura Schlessinger resigned abruptly from her syndicated radio show after a controversy arising from her multiple use of a racial epithet while talking to an African American caller.

■ Famous radio personality Don Imus was fired by CBS after making racist comments about the Rutgers University women's basketball team.

Making Language Nonsexist

Nonsexist language treats both sexes neutrally. Check to be sure your messages are free from sexism in four areas: job titles, courtesy titles and names, pronouns, and other words and phrases.

Job Titles   Use neutral titles that do not imply a job is held only by men or only by women. Many job titles are already neutral: *accountant, banker, doctor, engineer, inspector, manager, nurse, pilot, secretary, technician,* to name a few. Other titles reflect gender stereotypes and need to be changed.

Instead of	Use
Businessman	A specific title: executive, accountant, department head, owner of a small business, men and women in business, businessperson
Chairman	Chair, chairperson, moderator
Fireman	Firefighter
Foreman	Supervisor
Mailman	Mail carrier
Salesman	Salesperson, sales representative
Waitress	Server
Woman lawyer	Lawyer
Workman	Worker, employee. Or use a specific title: crane operator, bricklayer, etc.

Courtesy Titles and Names   E-mails to people you know normally do not use courtesy titles. However, letters and e-mails to people with whom you have a more formal relationship require courtesy titles in the salutation *unless* you're on a first-name basis with your reader. (See Appendix A for examples of e-mail and letter formats.)

When you know your reader's name and gender, use courtesy titles that do not indicate marital status: *Mr.* for men and *Ms.* for women. *Ms.* is particularly useful

Women in the Workplace

In 2011 the White House released a comprehensive report on the status of U.S. women; it was the first update in nearly 50 years. Drawn from federal statistics, the report highlights women's changing roles, showing a shift toward education and employment. Women caught up with men in college attendance; in fact, younger women are more likely than younger men to obtain a college degree. And more women go on to graduate school than do men. Women are also flocking to the workplace; the number of women age 20 or older working outside the home doubled over the period covered by the report.

These gains, however, have not carried over into wage equity: in 2009 women still earned only about 75 percent of what their male counterparts earned. Women also continue to fill a major share of administrative jobs, but lag behind men in pursuing higher-paying science- and math-oriented careers. The report also points out that U.S. single-parent families are still headed predominantly by women, resulting in more women than men living below the poverty line.

Adapted from "White House Releases First Comprehensive Federal Report on the Status of American Women in Almost 50 Years," press release, White House, March 1, 2011, http://www.whitehouse.gov/the-press-office/2011/03/01/white-house-releases-first-comprehensive-federal-report-status-american-.

when you do not know what a woman's marital status is. However, even when you happen to know that a woman is married or single, you still use *Ms.* unless you know that she prefers another title. There are, however, two exceptions:

1. If the woman has a professional title, use that title if you would use it for a man.
   Dr. Kristen Sorenson is our new company physician.
   The Rev. Elizabeth Townsley gave the invocation.
2. If the woman prefers to be addressed as *Mrs.* or *Miss,* use the title she prefers rather than Ms. (You-attitude takes precedence over nonsexist language: address the reader as she—or he—prefers to be addressed.) To find out if a woman prefers a traditional title,

---

- Check the signature block in previous correspondence. If a woman types her name as *(Miss) Elaine Anderson* or *(Mrs.) Kay Royster,* use the title she designates.

- Notice the title a woman uses in introducing herself on the phone. If she says, "This is Robin Stine," use Ms. when you write to her. If she says, "I'm Mrs. Stine," use the title she specifies.

- When you're writing job letters or crucial correspondence, call the company and ask the receptionist which title your reader prefers.

In addition to using parallel courtesy titles, use parallel forms for names.

Not Parallel	Parallel
Members of the committee will be Mr. Jones, Mr. Yacone, and Lisa.	Members of the committee will be Mr. Jones, Mr. Yacone, and Ms. Melton.
	or
	Members of the committee will be Irving, Ted, and Lisa.

When you know your reader's name but not the gender, either

- Call the company and ask the receptionist, or

- Use the reader's full name in the salutation:
  Dear Chris Crowell:
  Dear J. C. Meath:

When you know neither the reader's name nor gender, you have three options:

- Omit the salutation and use a subject line in its place. (See Figure A.2, Simplified Format.)
  SUBJECT: RECOMMENDATION FOR BEN WANDELL

- Use the reader's position or job title:
  Dear Loan Officer:
  Dear Registrar:

- Use a general group to which your reader belongs:
  Dear Investor:
  Dear Admissions Committee:

Pronouns   When you refer to a specific person, use the appropriate gender pronouns:

> In his speech, John Jones said…
>
> In her speech, Judy Jones said…

When you are referring not to a specific person but to anyone who may be in a given job or position, traditional gender pronouns are sexist.

> Sexist: a. Each supervisor must certify that the time sheet for his department is correct.
>
> Sexist: b. When the nurse fills out the accident report form, she should send one copy to the Central Division Office.

Business communication uses four ways to eliminate sexist generic pronouns: use plurals, use second-person *you,* revise the sentence to omit the pronoun, or use pronoun pairs. Whenever you have a choice of two or more ways to make a phrase or sentence nonsexist, choose the alternative that is the smoothest and least conspicuous.

The following examples use these methods to revise sentences *a* and *b* above.

1. Use plural nouns and pronouns.

> Nonsexist: a. Supervisors must certify that the time sheets for their departments are correct.

Note: When you use plural nouns and pronouns, other words in the sentence may need to be made plural too. In the example above, plural supervisors have plural time sheets and departments.

Avoid mixing singular nouns and plural pronouns.

> Nonsexist but lacks agreement: b. When the nurse fills out the accident report, they should send one copy to the Central Division Office.

Because *nurse* is singular, it is incorrect to use the plural *they* to refer to it. The resulting lack of agreement is acceptable orally but is not yet acceptable in writing. Instead, use one of the other ways to make the sentence nonsexist.

2. Use *you.*

> Nonsexist: a. You must certify that the time sheet for your department is correct.
>
> Nonsexist: b. When you fill out an accident report form, send one copy to the Central Division Office.

You is particularly good for instructions and statements of the responsibilities of someone in a given position.

3. Substitute an article (*a, an,* or *the*) for the pronoun, or revise the sentence so that the pronoun is unnecessary.

> Nonsexist: a. The supervisor must certify that the time sheet for the department is correct.
>
> Nonsexist: b. The nurse will
>
>> 1. Fill out the accident report form.
>>
>> 2. Send one copy of the form to the Central Division Office.

4. When you must focus on the action of an individual, use pronoun pairs.

> Nonsexist: a. The supervisor must certify that the time sheet for his or her department is correct.
>
> Nonsexist: b. When the nurse fills out the accident report form, he or she should send one copy to the Central Division Office.

Avoiding Offense

Biased or offensive language and images detract from your overall message; they also cause companies expensive trouble. In one 2013 month alone, several companies had to pull advertising and apologize for the content.

- General Motors had to retract a television ad for the new Chevy Trax because it featured a song recorded in 1938 that included offensive lyrics about Asians.

- PepsiCo took down an online advertising campaign for Mountain Dew that showed a talking goat beating up a woman, running from police, and appearing in a police lineup with several black men.

- Hyundai apologized for an online ad for a new vehicle that emits only water vapor. The ad showed a man attempting to commit suicide unsuccessfully by inhaling the Hyundai's harmless emissions.

While advertising needs to catch attention, using racist, sexist, or offensive language and images grabs the wrong kind of attention. Focusing instead on building goodwill with all elements of your audience will help you have more success in your communication.

Kevin Fallon, "GM Is Racist, Pepsi Is Sexist & More in the Week in Offensive Ads," *The Daily Beast,* May 2, 2013, http://www.thedaily-beast.com/articles/2013/05/02/gm-is-racist-pepsi-is-sexist-more-in-the-week-in-offensive-ads-video.html.

Other Words and Phrases   If you find any terms similar to those in the first column in Figure 3.4 in your messages or your company's documents, replace them with terms similar to those in the second column.

Not every word containing *man* is sexist. For example, *manager* is not sexist. The word comes from the Latin *manus* meaning *hand;* it has nothing to do with maleness.

Avoid terms that assume that everyone is married or is heterosexual.

Biased: You and your husband or wife are cordially invited to the reception.

Better: You and your guest are cordially invited to the reception.

Making Language Nonracist and Nonageist

Language is **nonracist** and **non-ageist** when it treats all races and ages fairly, avoiding negative stereotypes of any group. Use the following guidelines to check for bias in documents you write or edit.

Give someone's race or age only if it is relevant to your story. When you do mention these characteristics, give them for everyone in your story—not just the non-Caucasian, non-young-to-middle-aged adults you mention.

Refer to a group by the term it prefers. As preferences change, change your usage. Fifty years ago, *Negro* was preferred as a more dignified term than *colored* for African Americans. As times changed, *black* and *African American* replaced it. Gallup polls show that the majority of black Americans (about 60%) have no preference between the two terms. However, among those who do care, polls show a slight trend toward African American.[31]

Oriental has now been replaced by *Asian.*

The term *Latino* is the most acceptable group term to refer to Mexican Americans, Cuban Americans, Puerto Ricans, Dominicans, Brazilianos, and other people with Central and Latin American backgrounds. (*Latina* is the term for an individual woman.) Better still is to refer to the precise group. The differences among various Latino groups are at least as great as the differences among Italian Americans, Irish Americans, Armenian Americans, and others descended from various European groups.

Baby boomers, older people, and *mature customers* are more generally accepted terms than *senior citizens* or *golden agers.*

Avoid terms that suggest competent people are unusual. The statement "She is an intelligent purple woman" suggests the writer expects most purple

Figure 3.4	Getting Rid of Sexist Terms and Phrases	
Instead of	**Use**	**Because**
The girl at the front desk	The woman's name or job title: "Ms. Browning," "Rosa," "the receptionist"	Call female employees *women* just as you call male employees *men.* When you talk about a specific woman, use her name, just as you use a man's name to talk about a specific man.
The ladies on our staff	The women on our staff	Use parallel terms for males and females. Therefore, use *ladies* only if you refer to the males on your staff as *gentlemen.* Few businesses do, since social distinctions are rarely at issue.
Manpower	Personnel	The power in business today comes from both women and men.
Manhours	Hours or worker hours	
Manning	Staffing	
Managers and their wives	Managers and their guests	Managers may be female; not everyone is married.

Organizations are making their business sites more accommodating to people with disabilities.

women to be stupid. "He is an asset to his race" suggests excellence in the race is rare. "He is a spry 70-year-old" suggests the writer thinks anyone that old has mobility issues.

Talking about People with Disabilities and Diseases

A disability is a physical, mental, sensory, or emotional impairment that interferes with the major tasks of daily living. According to the U.S. Census Bureau, 19% of Americans currently have a disability; of those, about 71% who were 21 to 64 years old and had a "nonsevere disability" were employed.[32] The number of people with disabilities will rise as the population ages.

To keep trained workers, more and more companies are making disability accommodations such as telecommuting, flexible hours, work shift changes, and assignment changes.

When talking about people with disabilities, use **people-first language** to focus on the person, not the condition. People-first language names the person first, then adds the condition. Use it instead of the traditional noun phrases that imply the condition defines the person. In 2010, President Obama signed Rosa's Law, which replaces "mentally retarded" with "an individual with an intellectual disability," in most federal statutes.[33]

Instead of	Use	Because
The mentally retarded	People with an intellectual disability	The condition does not define the person or his or her potential.
Cancer patients	People being treated for cancer	

Avoid negative terms, unless the audience prefers them. You-attitude takes precedence over positive emphasis: use the term a group prefers. People who lost their hearing as infants, children, or young adults often prefer to be called *deaf*, or *Deaf* in recognition of Deafness as a culture. But people who lose their hearing as older adults often prefer to be called *hard of hearing*, even when their hearing loss is just as great as that of someone who identifies him- or herself as part of the Deaf culture.

Using the right term requires keeping up with changing preferences. If your target audience is smaller than the whole group, use the term preferred by that audience, even if the group as a whole prefers another term.

Some negative terms, however, are never appropriate. Negative terms such as *afflicted*, *suffering from*, and *struck down* also suggest an outdated view of any illness as a sign of divine punishment.

Instead of	Use	Because
Confined to a wheelchair	Uses a wheelchair	Wheelchairs enable people to escape confinement.
AIDS victim	Person with AIDS	Someone can have a disease without being victimized by it.
Abnormal	Atypical	People with disabilities are atypical but not necessarily abnormal.

Choosing Bias-Free Photos and Illustrations

When you produce a document with photographs or illustrations, check the visuals for possible bias. Do they show people of both sexes and all races? Is there a sprinkling of various kinds of people (younger and older, people using wheelchairs, etc.)? It's OK to have individual pictures that have just one sex or one race; the photos as a whole do not need to show exactly 50% men and 50% women. But the general impression should suggest that diversity is welcome and normal.

Check relationships and authority figures as well as numbers. If all the men appear in business suits and the women in jeans, the pictures are sexist even if an equal number of men and women are pictured. If the only non-whites pictured are factory workers, the photos support racism even when an equal number of people from each race are shown. The 2013 *Sports Illustrated* swimsuit issue aroused controversy for its use of natives as "props" and laborers.[34]

Summary by Learning Objectives

LO 3-1   Create you-attitude.

You-attitude is a style of communication that looks at things from the audience's point of view, emphasizing what the audience wants to know, respecting the audience's intelligence, and protecting the audience's ego. To create you-attitude

1. Talk about the audience, not about yourself.

2. Refer to the audience's request or order specifically.

3. Don't talk about feelings except to congratulate or offer sympathy.

4. In positive situations, use *you* more often than *I*. Use *we* when it includes the audience.

5. In negative situations, avoid the word *you*. Protect the audience's ego. Use passive verbs and impersonal expressions to avoid assigning blame.

Apply you-attitude beyond the sentence level by using organization and content as well as style to build goodwill.

LO 3-2 **Create positive emphasis.**

Positive emphasis means focusing on the positive rather than the negative aspects of a situation. To create positive tone

1. Avoid negative words and words with negative connotations.
2. Beware of hidden negatives.
3. Focus on what the audience can do rather than on limitations.
4. Justify negative information by giving a reason or linking it to an audience benefit.
5. Put the negative information in the middle and present it compactly.

Check to see that your positive emphasis is appropriate, sincere, and clear.

Studies in positive psychology show that using goodwill within the organization leads to increases in well-being for employees and better business performance.

Many companies are using social media such as Twitter, Facebook, and YouTube to increase positive emphasis and goodwill.

LO 3-3 **Improve tone in business communications.**

The desirable tone for business communication is businesslike but not stiff, friendly but not phony, confident but not arrogant, polite but not groveling.

LO 3-4 **Reduce bias in business communications.**

Bias-free language is fair and friendly; it complies with the law. It includes all members of your audience; it helps sustain goodwill.

■ Check to be sure your language is nonsexist, nonracist, and nonageist.

■ Communication should be free from sexism in four areas: job titles, courtesy titles and names, pronouns, and other words and phrases.

■ *Ms.* is the nonsexist courtesy title for women. Whether or not you know a woman's marital status, use *Ms.* unless the woman has a professional title or unless you know she prefers a traditional title.

■ Four ways to make pronouns nonsexist are to use plurals, to use *you*, to revise the sentence to omit the pronoun, and to use pronoun pairs.

■ When you talk about people with disabilities or diseases, use the term they prefer.

■ When you produce newsletters or other documents with photos and illustrations, picture a sampling of the whole population, not just part of it.

Continuing Case

The All-Weather Case, set in an HR department in a manufacturing company, extends through all 19 chapters and is available at www.mhhe.com/locker11e. The portion for this chapter asks students to revise a message to increase you-attitude, positive tone, and goodwill.

Exercises and Cases

*Go to www.mhhe.com/locker11e for additional Exercises and Cases.

3.1 Reviewing the Chapter

1. What are five ways to create you-attitude? (LO 3-1)
2. What are five ways to create positive emphasis? (LO 3-2)
3. How can you improve the tone of business messages? (LO 3-3)
4. What are different categories to keep in mind when you are trying to reduce bias in business messages? (LO 3-4)
5. What techniques can you use when you are trying to reduce bias in business messages? (LO 3-4)

3.2 Evaluating the Ethics of Positive Emphasis

The first term in each pair is negative; the second is a positive term that is sometimes substituted for it. Which of the positive terms seem ethical? Which seem unethical? Briefly explain your choices.

cost	investment	nervousness	adrenaline
second mortgage	home equity loan	problem	challenge
tax	user fee	price increase	price change
		for-profit hospital	tax-paying hospital
		used car	pre-owned car
		credit card fees	usage charges

3.3 Eliminating Negative Words and Words with Negative Connotations

Revise each of the following sentences to replace negative words with positive ones. Be sure to keep the meaning of the original sentence.

1. You will lose the account if you make a mistake and the customer is dissatisfied.
2. Avoid errors on customer reports by carefully proofreading.
3. Your account, #82654, is delinquent. If you neglect to pay this balance, your account will be sent to collections.
4. When you write a report, do not make claims that you cannot support with evidence.
5. Don't drop in without an appointment. Your counselor or caseworker may be unavailable.
6. I am anxious to discuss my qualifications in an interview.

3.4 Focusing on the Positive

Revise each of the following sentences to focus on the options that remain, not those that are closed off.

1. Applications that are postmarked after January 15 will not be accepted.
2. All new employees will not be able to receive benefits for 90 days.
3. I will not be available by phone on Saturdays and Sundays.
4. Overtime cannot be processed without the supervisor's signature.
5. Travel reimbursement forms will only be processed at the end of the month.

3.5 Identifying Hidden Negatives

Identify the hidden negatives in the following sentences and revise to eliminate them. In some cases, you may need to add information to revise the sentence effectively.

1. The seminar will help you become a better manager.
2. Thank you for the confidence you have shown in us by ordering one of our products. It will be shipped to you soon.
3. This publication is designed to explain how your company can start a recycling program.
4. I hope you find the information in this brochure beneficial to you and a valuable reference as you plan your move.
5. In thinking about your role in our group, I remember two occasions where you contributed something.
6. [In job letter] This job in customer service is so good for me; I am so ready to take on responsibility.

3.6 Improving You-Attitude and Positive Emphasis

Revise these sentences to improve you-attitude and positive emphasis. Eliminate any awkward phrasing. In some cases, you may need to add information to revise the sentence effectively.

1. You'll be happy to learn that the cost of tuition will not rise next year.
2. Although I was only an intern and didn't actually make presentations to major clients, I was required to prepare PowerPoint slides for the meetings and to answer some of the clients' questions.
3. At DiYanni Homes we have more than 30 plans that we will personalize just for you.

4. Please notify HR of your bank change as soon as possible to prevent a disruption of your direct deposit.

5. I'm sorry you were worried. You did not miss the deadline for signing up for a flexible medical spending account.

6. You will be happy to hear that our cell phone plan does not charge you for incoming calls.

7. The employee discount may only be used for purchases for your own use or for gifts; you may not buy items for resale. To prevent any abuse of the discount privilege, you may be asked to justify your purchase.

8. I apologize for my delay in answering your inquiry. The problem was that I had to check with our suppliers to see whether we could provide the item in the quantity you say you want. We can.

9. If you mailed a check with your order, as you claim, we failed to receive it.

10. This job sounds perfect for me.

3.7   Eliminating Biased Language

Explain the source of bias in each of the following, and revise to remove the bias.

1. Mr. Brady, Mr. Barnes, and the new intern, Jodi, will represent our company at the job fair.

2. All sales associates and their wives are invited for cocktails.

3. Although he is blind, Mr. Morin is an excellent group leader.

4. Please join us for the company potluck! Ladies, please bring a main dish. Men, please bring chips and dip (store bought is fine).

5. Lee Torsad
Pacific Perspectives
6300 West Coronado Blvd.
Los Angles, CA
Dear Sir:

6. Please stop by and say "hi" to our new IT guy. Be very polite; he is oriental.

7. I would prefer if you hired a female secretary; women are typically friendlier than men.

8. Please do not use the side elevator, because it is reserved for people who can't walk.

9. Sue Corcoran celebrates her 50th birthday today. Stop by her cubicle at noon to get a piece of cake and to help us sing "The Old Grey Mare Just Ain't What She Used to Be."

10. Because older customers tend to be really picky, we will need to give a lot of details in our ads.

3.8   Analyzing You-Attitude

This book gives examples of occasions when you-attitude is inappropriate. What are some other examples? Why are they inappropriate? How would you fix them?

3.9   Analyzing Goodwill Ethics: I

A study by a law professor shows that credit card companies make offers to people fresh out of bankruptcy. In the study of 341 families, almost 100% received credit card offers within a year after completing bankruptcy proceedings, and 87% of those offers mentioned the bankruptcy proceedings. In fact, 20% of the offers came from companies the family had owed before the bankruptcy.[35]

In small groups, discuss whether you think this practice is ethical. Why or why not? What reasons exist for not offering new credit to people who have just gone through bankruptcy? Why might such people need new credit cards?

3.10   Analyzing Goodwill Ethics: II

Women-only networking events for employees and clients are occurring at some companies. Including activities such as spa retreats, boutique shopping, and cooking demonstrations, they are organized by women who want to network with female clients in their own way—at least some of the time.

How do you feel about women-only events? Are they ethical? Are they just as exclusionary as the traditional ball games or steak-and-cigar dinners have been for men? What about women who have male clients and vice versa?

3.11   Analyzing a Form Letter

Analyze the following form letter.

Is it a goodwill message?

Where does it show you-attitude? Where does it need more you-attitude?

Evaluate the use of positive tone.

What is your overall impression of the letter?

Debbie Harrington
1436 Gooden Road
Lincoln, NE 54367

THE FOLLOWING INFORMATION IS TIME SENSITIVE; PLEASE REVIEW CAREFULLY

James Honda of Lincoln has partnered with Automobile Resellers, Inc., to replenish drastically reduced vehicle inventories. James Honda of Lincoln is in need of a number of high-demand pre-owned vehicles and records indicate that you may own one of these vehicles. Your 2009 Honda Civic has been classified as a high-demand vehicle. The purpose of this letter is to request the opportunity to BUY BACK your vehicle for perhaps more than you thought possible.

Bring this letter for admittance to this event. Simply present it to a dealership representative who will assist you in this BUY BACK process. Also, you may have won up to $20,000. To see if your claim number is a guaranteed cash prize winner, simply visit James Honda of Lincoln on the event date and claim your prize.

During this exciting event, James Honda of Lincoln has agreed to aggressively price its entire inventory of new and pre-owned cars, trucks, vans, and sport utilities. With rates as low as 0% and rebates up to $5,000, we are confident that you can upgrade your 2009 Honda Civic and in many cases reduce your current monthly payment with little out-of-pocket expense.

Due to the nature of this event it will not be advertised to the general public. Your status as a customer as well as your possession of a high-demand vehicle entitles you to attend this exciting event.

Appointments are recommended due to the anticipated response of this event. To schedule an appointment or if you are unable to attend on the below event date, please contact James Honda of Lincoln toll-free at 800.123.4567.

EVENT DATE:
Saturday, Nov 21st—9:00 a.m. to 6:00 p.m.

EVENT SITE:
JAMES HONDA OF LINCOLN
220 Kitty Hawk
Lincoln, NE 54367

As your instructor directs,

a. Share your findings orally with a small group of students.

b. Share your findings orally with the class.

c. Post your findings in an e-mail to the class.

d. Summarize your findings in an e-mail to your instructor.

3.12   Revising a Form Letter

Revise this form letter to improve positive tone and you-attitude (and to catch spelling and punctuation errors):

> Dear customer,
>
> We wish you a Happy New Year from Happy Catalog. Its been awhile since we heard from you. We have a special offer to welcome you back.
>
> Our customers are the focus of what we do. All of our efforts center on exceeding our customer expectations.
>
> Happy Catalog stands behind everything we sell, as we have since 1986. No matter what your problem with anything we sell, we will fix it. We will provide you with even better service, tailored to meet you needs and guaranteed to offer more of the helpful, unique and hard to find merchandise we're known for. Whether you choose to shop by phone, mail, or e-mail us, we promise to continually improve our process to better serve you. If you have been disappointed in any way, please accept our sincerest apology.
>
> We have a special offer, exclusively for you, to welcome you back. When you use the enclosed coupon, you'll save 20% on any order, regardless of order size. Hurry, this offer will expire the beginning of February.
>
> Welcome back! Thank you for your business.
>
> Sincerly,
> I. M. President
> Happy Catalog.

3.13   Advising a Hasty Subordinate

Three days ago, one of your subordinates forwarded to everyone in the office a bit of e-mail humor he'd received from a friend. Titled "You know you're Southern when…," the message poked fun at Southern speech, attitudes, and lifestyles. Today you get this message from your subordinate:

> Subject: Should I Apologize?
>
> I'm getting flamed left and right because of the Southern message. I thought it was funny, but some people just can't take a joke. So far I've tried not to respond to the flames, figuring that would just make things worse. But now I'm wondering if I should apologize. What do you think?

Answer the message.

3.14   Responding to a Complaint

You're the director of corporate communications; the employee newsletter is produced by your office. Today you receive this e-mail message from Tonya Freira:

> Subject: Complaint
>
> The section on the back of the employee newsletter referred to Mindy Kelso and me as "the girls at the front desk." We are not "girls," and we don't see why our gender was even pointed out in the first place. We are customer service representatives and would like to be referred to that way.

Write a response to Tonya Freira. Also, draft a message to your staff, reminding them to edit newsletter stories as well as external documents to replace biased language.

3.15   Evaluating Bias in Visuals

Evaluate the portrayals of people in one of the following:

- Ads in one issue of a business magazine.
- A company's annual report.
- A company's web page.

Do the visuals show people of both sexes and all races? Is there a sprinkling of people of various ages and physical conditions? What do the visuals suggest about who has power?

As your instructor directs,

a. Share your findings orally with a small group of students.
b. Post your findings in an e-mail to the class.
c. Summarize your findings in an e-mail to your instructor.
d. Present your findings in an oral presentation to the class.
e. Join with a small group of students to create a written report about your combined findings.

3.16   Revising an E-mail for Positive Tone

Revise the following e-mail to improve positive tone.

TO: All Staff

SUBJECT: Decorating Your Work Area

With the arrival of the holiday season, employees who wish to decorate their work areas should do so only with great caution. Don't do something stupid that might burn down the entire office. If you wish to decorate, don't forget the following guidelines:

1. If using decorative lights, don't place them in obstructive places.
2. Do not overload your workstation with decorations that will interfere with your daily duties.
3. Don't forget to turn off and/or unplug all lights at the end of your workday.
4. Do not use hot lights; they can burn your countertop so it is imperative that everyone take care in selecting your lights.
5. Do not use decorations which will offend people of other religions.
6. Absolutely no candles are allowed.

Don't forget these guidelines, and we'll have a great holiday season. Thank you for your cooperation.

3.17   Dealing with Negative Clients

An executive at one of your largest client companies is known for his negative attitude. He is feared for his sharp tongue and scathing attacks, and he bullies everyone. Everyone you know, including yourself, is afraid of him. Unfortunately, he is also the one who decides whether or not you get your annual contract. Your contract is up for renewal, and you have some new services you think his company would like.

In small groups, discuss at least four ways to handle Mr. Bully. Write up your two best to share with the whole class. Also write up the reasons you think these two approaches will work. Share your two approaches with the whole class, as a short oral presentation or online.

As a class, select the two best approaches from those offered by the small groups. Discuss your criteria for selection and rejection.

3.18   Writing Business Thank-You Notes

Some businesses make a practice of sending goodwill messages to some of their customers.

Pick a business you patronize that might logically send some thank-you notes. Write a suitable note and design a tasteful visual for it. In a separate document, write an e-mail to your instructor explaining your design and content decisions.

Questions you might want to consider:

- Who is your audience? Will you write to everyone? Will you target big spenders? Trendsetters? People who might become long-term customers? How will you identify your categories?
- What tone did you select? What words and phrases help produce that tone? What words and phrases did you avoid? What diction choices did you make to convey sincerity?
- What content did you choose? Why? What content choices did you discard?
- What design features did you choose? Why? What design features did you discard?

3.19   Evaluating You-Attitude and Positive Emphasis in University Websites

As they plan their college visits, many students begin by visiting university websites. Imagine you are a high school senior and a prospective student. Go to the "Prospective Students" part of your school's website and read about housing, course offerings, and student life. Evaluate the information you find for you-attitude and positive emphasis. Compare the text for prospective students with the text on several sites targeted for current students. Does the tone change? In what ways? What information increases or decreases you-attitude?

Now visit the website of another university. Review the same type of information for prospective students and compare it to that of your own school. Which school does a better job? Why?

As your instructor directs,

a. Share your findings orally with a small group of students.
b. Share your findings orally with the class.
c. Post your findings in an e-mail to the class.
d. Summarize your findings in an e-mail to your instructor.

3.20   Revising a "Goodwill Disaster"

Li, an intern at All-Weather, a window manufacturer, has been asked to write a letter to a recent young customer asking him if some new engineers can tour his gallery to see the products in use. Here is his draft:

Dear Mr. Mason,
Executive Director,
Iconic Art Gallery, St. Paul, MN

You must be glad that you chose All-Weather's energy efficient bow windows, horizontal sliders, and fiberglass doors for your art gallery. As everyone who is anyone knows, we offer the finest quality wood, vinyl, aluminum, steel, and fiberglass composite windows and doors you can find in the US of A. As you also know, our customer service representatives are ready to assist you 24/7 (and more!) with any installation or maintenance needs you may have (even if it's your responsibility or fault, I might add). After doing so much for an important customer such as you, we have a small favor to ask of you, which we're sure you will not deny us. We just hired some new engineers who will join our manufacturing division to continue to make the fine products that we make. Unfortunately, they have never seen how our finished products look outside or inside actual homes or offices. (On a personal note, I confess I don't know what they can learn from one visit to a home or an office.) Our VP (Manufacturing), an asset to All-Weather, says that we should send these engineers out on a field visit. And he should know, shouldn't he, being the VP and all? That is why I'm writing to you (the pleasure is mine, though).

These fresh minds need exposure to actual conditions in actual markets. We think that if they visit your art gallery, they will see how our products are helping you get results your art gallery could never dream of before. If you don't believe me, take a peek inside your exhibits room, whose space seems to have expanded thanks to our bow window that you have installed. I myself remember what a cramped-looking room it was before. No, I'm not asking you to share your admission fees with us, though free exhibition tickets wouldn't hurt (I'm kidding, sir). Also, you should perhaps buy more windows and doors from us (and attract more visitors as a result!). Also, don't forget to mention us favorably to your patrons.

Oh, and by the way, will you please let us know the day and time suitable to you when we might send those engineers to your art gallery? Our orientation program begins in three weeks time. Looking forward to your prompt acceptance of our request (with or without free exhibition tickets).

Sincerely,
Li

Li was trying for a breezy tone that he thought appropriate for a young art gallery owner but obviously went overboard.

Based on your reading of Chapter 3, complete the following tasks:

- List problems in Li's draft.
- Prepare another list of changes that would improve the draft. Be specific in your suggestions. For instance, it's insufficient to say "more you-attitude" or "more politeness." Point to places in the draft where these strategies might be useful. Also, rephrase relevant sentences or paragraphs for more you-attitude or more politeness, whichever is the case.

- What is the primary purpose of the letter? The secondary purpose?
- Revise the draft.

Notes

1. Frances Frei and Anne Morriss, *Uncommon Service: How to Win by Putting Customers at the Core of Your Business* (Boston: Harvard Business Review Press, 2012), 1.
2. "Amazon Investor Relations," Amazon.com, May 6, 2013, http://phx.corporate-ir.net/phoenix.zhtml?c=97664&p=irol-irhome; and "Video from Jeff Bezos about Amazon and Zappos," YouTube video, July 22, 2009, http://www.youtube.com/watch?v=-hxX_Q5CnaA.
3. Aaron Pressman, "When Service Means Survival," *Businessweek*, March 2, 2009, 62.
4. John A. Byrne, "How to Lead Now: Getting Extraordinary Performance When You Can't Pay for It," *Fast Company*, August 2003, 65.
5. Zeynep Ton, "Why 'Good Jobs' Are Good for Retailers," *Harvard Business Review* 90, no. 1–2 (January–February 2012): 125–31.
6. Pino G. Audia, "Train Your People to Take Others' Perspectives," *Harvard Business Review* 90, no. 10 (November 2012): 28.
7. Daniel H. Pink, *A Whole New Mind: Why Right-Brainers Will Rule the Future* (New York: Riverhead Books, 2006), 165.
8. Annette N. Shelby and N. Lamar Reinsch, "Positive Emphasis and You-Attitude: An Empirical Study," *Journal of Business Communication* 32, no. 4 (1995): 303–27.
9. Martin E. P. Seligman, *Learned Optimism: How to Change Your Mind and Your Life*, 2nd ed. (New York: Pocket Books, 1998), 96–107.
10. Mark A. Sherman, "Adjectival Negation and Comprehension of Multiply Negated Sentences," *Journal of Verbal Learning and Verbal Behavior* 15 (1976):143–57.
11. Jeffrey Zaslow, "In Praise of Less Praise," *Wall Street Journal*, May 3, 2007, D1.
12. "The Happiness Factor," *Harvard Business Review* 90, no. 1–2 (January–February 2012): 77.
13. "How Happy Are You? That Could Be Key to Measuring Economic Progress," *NJ.com*, August 7, 2012, http://www.nj.com/news/index.ssf/2012/08/how_happy_are_you_that_could_b.html.
14. Gretchen Spreitzer and Christine Porath, "Creating Sustainable Performance: If You Give Your Employees the Chance to Learn and Grow, They'll Thrive—and So Will Your Organization," *Harvard Business Review* 90, no. 1–2 (January–February 2012): 94.
15. Shawn Achor, "Positive Intelligence: Three Ways Individuals Can Cultivate Their Own Sense of Well-Being and Set Themselves Up To Succeed," *Harvard Business Review* 90, no. 1–2 (January–February 2012): 102.
16. Ibid.
17. Spreitzer and Porath, "Creating Sustainable Performance," 93.
18. Clayton M. Christensen, James Allworth, and Karen Dillon, *How Will You Measure Your Life?* (New York: Harper Business, 2012), 34.
19. Achor, "Positive Intelligence," 100–02.

20. Matthew Killingsworth, "The Future of Happiness Research," *Harvard Business Review* 90, no. 1–2 (January–February 2012): 89.

21. Stephen C. Dillard, "Litigation Nation," *Wall Street Journal,* November 25, 2006, A9.

22. Margaret Baker Graham and Carol David, "Power and Politeness: Administrative Writing in an 'Organized Anarchy,'" *Journal of Business and Technical Communication* 10, no. 1 (1996): 5–27.

23. Robert Hurley, "Trust Me," *Wall Street Journal,* October 24, 2011, R4.

24. Jessica Holzer and Greg Bensinger, "SEC Embraces Social Media: New Way to Make Disclosures Gets Go-Ahead if Investors Are Told Where to Look," *Wall Street Journal,* April 3, 2013, A1.

25. Danielle Sacks, "Can You Hear Me Now?: The Art of Dialogue," *Fast Company,* February 2013, 37–43.

26. Ibid.

27. Bruce Horovitz, "Bacon Mouthwash? April Fools' Marketing Jokes Go Viral," *USA Today,* April 1, 2013, http://www.usatoday.com/story/money/business/2013/04/01/april-fools-day-pranks-scope-virgin-atlantic-ikea/2042451/.

28. Ibid.

29. "Women's History Month: March 2013," U.S. Census Bureau Newsroom, February 7, 2013, http://www.census.gov/newsroom/releases/archives/facts_for_features_special_editions/cb13-ff04.html; "2010 Census Shows America's Diversity," U.S. Census Bureau Newsroom, March 24, 2011, http://www.census.gov/2010census/news/releases/operations/cb11-cn125.html; "Rise of Latino Population Blurs US Racial Lines," Associated Press, May 17, 2013, http://www.npr.org/templates/story/story.php?storyId=174546756; and "Older Americans Month: May 2013," U.S. Census Bureau Newsroom, March 7, 2013, http://www.census.gov/newsroom/releases/archives/facts_for_features_special_editions/cb13-ff07.html.

30. Laura Stevens, "German CEO's Remark on Women Draws Fire," *Wall Street Journal,* February 8, 2011, A9.

31. Frank Newport, "Black or African American?" Gallup, September 28, 2007, http://www.gallup.com/poll/28816/black-african-american.aspx.

32. "20th Anniversary of Americans with Disabilities Act: July 26," U.S. Census Bureau Newsroom, May 26, 2010, http://www.census.gov/newsroom/releases/archives/facts_for_features_special_editions/cb10-ff13.html.

33. Clark Ansberry, "Erasing a Hurtful Label from the Books," *Wall Street Journal,* November 30, 2010, A6.

34. Ann Oldenburg, "'SI' Swimsuit Issue Courts Controversy," *USA Today,* February 14, 2013, http://www.usatoday.com/story/life/people/2013/02/14/sports-illustrated-kate-upton-swimsuit-prop-controversy/1920311/.

35. Marie Beaudette, "Study: Credit Card Offers Flood Once-Bankrupt Consumers," *Des Moines Register,* August 10, 2007, 6D.

4 Navigating the Business Communication Environment

Chapter Outline

Ethics

Corporate Culture

Interpersonal Communication
- Listening
- Conversational Style
- Nonverbal Communication
- Etiquette
- Networking

Time Management
- Techniques
- Multitasking

Trends in Business Communication
- Data Security
- Electronic Privacy
- Customer Service
- Work/Family Balance
- Environmental Concern
- Globalization and Outsourcing
- Diversity
- Teamwork
- Job Flexibility
- Innovation and Entrepreneurship
- Big Data
- Rapid Rate of Change

Summary by Learning Objectives

NEWSWORTHY COMMUNICATION

Creating a Fresh Environment

The nonverbal communication in a business environment affects what people think and do, even in grocery stores.

Traditionally, grocery stores have been arranged around the typical person's shopping list, with quickly bought items in the front of the store, produce on the side, and meat and dairy in the back. But as more consumers seek fresh and organic items, grocery stores are changing their organizational strategies.

One major change is including packaged goods in the produce section. Researchers have found that when items such as boxed pasta or bottled juice are on the same shelves as fresh fruits and vegetables, consumers believe those items are fresher and higher in quality.

Grocery stores are building on the "halo effect" of fresh produce by making produce sections larger, including more packaged items with the produce, and redesigning the produce sections to be more appealing to customers.

Some food companies, such as Kraft Foods, are pushing retailers to change other parts of the stores, as well. Kraft believes items such as cheese and milk should be closer to the produce to communicate that those items are also farm fresh.

The design and arrangement of products in grocery stores can have a huge impact on consumers' perceptions and their purchasing decisions. Creating the right business environment takes time and attention to both verbal and nonverbal forms of communication.

Source: Sarah Nassauer, "A Food Fight in the Produce Aisle," *Wall Street Journal*, October 20, 2011, D1.

Learning Objectives

After studying this chapter, you will know

LO 4-1 Why ethics is so important in business communication.

LO 4-2 How corporate culture impacts the business environment.

LO 4-3 Why interpersonal communication is important.

LO 4-4 How to use your time more efficiently.

LO 4-5 What the trends in business communication are.

In addition to adapting to audiences and building goodwill, business communications are heavily influenced by the environments in which they are created and interpreted. Part of this environment is shaped by national culture, such as the growing concern about business ethics, and part is shaped by corporate culture. Part is shaped by individual behaviors, such as those involved in interpersonal communication. A final part is shaped by widespread trends, such as globalization or the green movement. Technology and information overload, which are perhaps the largest of these trends, are discussed extensively in Chapter 9, along with effective ways to deal with them.

Ethics **LO 4-1**

With the official recognition of a serious worldwide recession, along with the subprime mortgage debacle, ethics concerns have become a major part of the business environment. Financial giants such as AIG, Bear Stearns, Lehman Brothers, Merrill Lynch, Wachovia, and Washington Mutual had to be bailed out or went bankrupt. Banks, corporate officials, and rating agencies all were accused of unethical behavior. The Securities and Exchange Commission (SEC) charged Goldman Sachs with fraud on securities linked to subprime mortgages; the firm settled out of court for more than half a billion dollars.

In a much larger lawsuit, Credit Suisse was sued for $11.2 billion in losses from bundled mortgage securities. According to New York's attorney general, Credit Suisse "kept its investors in the dark about the inadequacy of its review procedures and defects in the loans," a major lapse in business communication. The bank was also accused of misrepresenting information in its SEC filings regarding when problem loans would be repurchased.[1]

Ethics breaches have cost other organizations millions and even billions of dollars.

- GlaxoSmithKline incurred a $3 billion fine for failing to report drug safety data. Previously the company had pleaded guilty to charges that it knowingly sold adulterated drugs, including the antidepressant Paxil, and paid fines of $750 million.[2]

- Visa and MasterCard, plus the banks that issue their credit cards, settled for $7.25 billion over fixing card fees.[3]

- British bank HSBC set aside more than $2 billion to cover fines and lawsuits in a money laundering case.[4]

Warren Buffett on Ethics

In a letter to Berkshire Hathaway directors, Chairman and CEO Warren Buffett says this about ethics:

"We *must* continue to measure every act against not only what is legal but also what we would be happy to have written about on the front page of a national newspaper in an article written by an unfriendly but intelligent reporter.

"Sometimes your associates will say, 'Everybody else is doing it.' This rationale is almost always a bad one if it is the main justification for a business action. It is totally unacceptable when evaluating a moral decision. Whenever somebody offers that phrase as a rationale, in effect they are saying that they can't come up with a *good* reason. If anyone offers this explanation, tell them to try using it with a reporter or a judge and see how far it gets them.

"…It's very likely that if a given course of action evokes hesitation *per se*, it's too close to the line and should be abandoned. There's plenty of money to be made in the center of the court. If it's questionable whether some action is close to the line, just assume it is outside and forget it."

Quoted from Richard. J. Connors, ed., *Warren Buffett on Business: Principles from the Sage of Omaha* (Hoboken, NJ: Wiley, 2010), 210. The material is copyrighted and used with permission of the author.

■ Siemens settled with the government for $800 million in a bribery case; the document review alone cost an additional $100 million.[5]

■ In 2013, the credit-rating agency Standard & Poor's was sued by the U.S. government for $5 billion; the suit alleged the agency inflated credit ratings for bundled mortgage securities.[6]

Billionaires fell as well. Bernie Madoff was sentenced to prison in what may have been the biggest Ponzi scheme in history, one that defrauded thousands of investors of billions of dollars. Hedge-fund manager Raj Rajaratnam was convicted of securities fraud and conspiracy in the biggest insider-trading case to that time.[7]

The Ethics Resource Center, America's oldest nonprofit organization devoted to ethical practice, reported in its 2011 National Business Ethics Survey, that 45% of employees surveyed personally witnessed unethical or illegal behavior; 35% of those witnesses did not report it. The most frequent misconducts were misuse of company time, abusive behavior, lying, company resource abuse, violating company Internet use policies, discrimination, conflicts of interest, inappropriate social networking, health or safety violations, stealing, falsifying time reports, benefits violations, and sexual harassment.[8]

Some common reasons for not reporting ethical misconduct are the following: it's standard practice here, it's not a big deal, it's not my responsibility (a particularly common reason for junior employees), and I want to be loyal to my colleagues/manager/company (stated negatively, this reason is "fear of consequences").[9]

On the other side of the coin, positive ethical efforts are also getting attention. The United Nations Global Compact, "the world's largest corporate citizenship and sustainability initiative," focuses on human rights, labor, environment, and anticorruption measures. More than 7,000 businesses in 145 countries participate.[10] The Clinton Global Initiative has brought together 150 heads of state, 20 Nobel laureates, and hundreds of CEOs, who collectively have committed $63 billion. This money has already impacted the lives of 400 million people in 180 countries.[11]

Other organizations and people also promote ethical efforts:

■ The Bill & Melinda Gates Foundation received new attention when Warren Buffett announced his transfer of billions of dollars to it. The three philanthropists have attracted still more attention with their efforts to convince other billionaires to pledge the majority of their wealth to philanthropy. The list of those who have made the pledge is posted at givingpledge.org; it included 105 pledgers in Spring 2013.

■ Google has created Google.org "to help address global challenges." It focuses on problems where Google's "core capabilities" are most useful, such as creating the Google Person Finder, to help people connect after major disasters, and the Flu and Dengue Trends, which provide early warning of possible outbreaks.[12]

■ Robin Hood, a venture philanthropy, "robs" the rich (its board members cover all costs, so 100% of money donated goes to fund programs) to help the poor in New York City. In the past 20 years, it has distributed over $1 billion.[13]

■ Merck provides its drug Mectizan "free of charge and in perpetuity" to treat river blindness worldwide. Its donations reach more than 60 million people a year in 33 countries.[14]

Egg-semplary Communication Ethics?

Scientists at a university diagnostic lab faced an ethical communication problem. Four months before a large salmonella outbreak involving eggs, they were aware that hens at a huge egg-producing business were infected with salmonella.

They reported their findings to the producer requesting the testing. However, because of the lab's confidentiality policy, they were unable to report the presence of salmonella to authorities (salmonella was not a disease that legally had to be reported). What followed was the sickening of 60,000 consumers and the recall of 550 million eggs.

Scientists who worked at the lab told the press later that owners would no longer get their animals tested if the lab lacked the confidentiality policy. They noted that the lab's policy was similar to laboratory/patient policies in human medicine. Under the confidentiality agreements between the lab and people whose animals were tested, going to the authorities would have been unethical and probably would have resulted in firings.

What would you have done in their situation?

Adapted from Hannah Furfaro, "ISU Egg Researchers Discuss Their Role in 2010 Recall," *Ames Tribune*, June 6, 2012, A1; and Ryan J. Foley, "ISU Lab Warned of Salmonella in Eggs," *Ames Tribune*, June 5, 2012, A1.

Figure 4.1	Business Ethics Resources on the Web
http://www.ethicsweb.ca/resources/business	
http://www.scu.edu/ethics/practicing/focusareas/business/	
http://www.businessethicsresources.com/	
http://www.ethics.org	
http://www.ethicsweb.ca/resources/business/codes.html	

While many tech companies invest in computers and computer support for schools, in 1994 IBM launched a new program, Reinventing Education, in the hopes of bringing about some systemic improvements in pedagogy. IBM has invested over $75 million in this philanthropic endeavor. In addition to the schools involved, IBM profited from the program as well; 45 patents or patent applications resulted from the work as IBM learned new ways to apply technology to tackle huge, complex issues.[15]

Business ethics includes far more than corporate greed, international pacts, and philanthropy, of course. Much of business ethics involves routine practices, and many of these practices involve communication. How can we make our contracts with our clients and suppliers easier to understand? How can we best communicate with our employees? How much should our hospital disclose about infection rates?

Many basic, daily communication decisions involve an ethics component. Am I including all the information my audience needs? Am I expressing it in ways they will understand? Am I putting it in a format that helps my audience grasp it quickly? Am I including information for all segments of my audience? Am I taking information from other sources accurately? Am I acknowledging my sources? Figure 4.1 lists some web resources that deal with business ethics.

Figure 4.2 elaborates on ethical components of communication. As it suggests, language, graphics, and document design—basic parts of any business document—can be ethical or manipulative. Persuading and gaining compliance—activities at the heart of business and organizational life—can be done with respect or contempt for customers, co-workers, and subordinates.

In these days of instant communication, you, like the organization in which you work, must always act in an ethical manner. Consequences for not doing so are becoming more common as disgruntled colleagues/employees now have ample means for whistle-blowing.

There are also positive reasons for ethical behavior. In addition to moral reasons, there are business ones. As the Ethics Resource Center notes, customers and employees are attracted to ethical businesses. Rosabeth Moss Kanter, a professor at Harvard Business School, argues in her book, *SuperCorp: How Vanguard Companies Create Innovation, Profits, Growth, and Social Good*, that companies desiring to do good have a competitive advantage. In fact, a benevolent viewpoint provides a wider view of society and thus awareness of new opportunities for growth and innovation by solving the problems of unmet needs.

Many religions and philosophers have offered advice on how to be ethical. Some of the more familiar advice is the Golden Rule (do unto others as you would have them do unto you) and the utilitarian principle that an action should produce the greatest happiness for the greatest number of people. Business leaders have also given advice. Warren Buffett has offered the newspaper criterion: how would you feel if your actions were on the front page of a national newspaper? (For more Buffett guidelines, see the sidebar on page 88.)

Figure 4.2	Ethical Issues in Business Communications	
Manner of conveying the message	**Qualities of the message**	**Larger organizational context of the message**
• Is the language clear to the audience? Does it respect the audience? • Do the words balance the organization's right to present its best case with its responsibility to present its message honestly? • Do graphics help the audience understand? Or are graphics used to distract or confuse? • Does the design of the document make reading easy? Does document design attempt to make readers skip key points?	• Is the message an ethical one that is honest and sensitive to all stakeholders? • Have interested parties been able to provide input? • Does the audience get all the information it needs to make a good decision or is information withheld? • Is information communicated so the audience can grasp it or are data "dumped" without any context? • Are the arguments logical? Are they supported with adequate evidence? • Are the emotional appeals used fairly? Do they supplement logic rather than substitute for it? • Does the organizational pattern lead the audience without undue manipulation? • Does the message use good sources? Are the sources used honestly? Are they documented?	• How does the organization treat its employees? How do employees treat each other? • How sensitive is the organization to stakeholders such as the people who live near its factories, stores, or offices and to the general public? • Does the organization support employees' efforts to be honest, fair, and ethical? • Do the organization's actions in making products, buying supplies, and marketing goods and services stand up to ethical scrutiny? • Is the organization a good corporate citizen, helpful rather than harmful to the community in which it exists? • Are the organization's products or services a good use of scarce resources?

Tony Hsieh, the founder and CEO of Zappos, offers this useful ethics guideline:

> As a guiding principle in life for anything I do, I try to ask myself, *What would happen if everyone in the world acted in the same way? What would the world look like? What would the net effect be on the overall happiness in the world?* [Hsieh's italics]

> This thought experiment has been useful to me when thinking about whether to share how we do things at Zappos, or whether to get upset at the waitress who accidentally got my order wrong, or whether to hold the door open for a stranger who's a slightly inconvenient distance away.

> The same questions are just as important for deciding what not to do, even if not doing anything is the default choice.[16]

A widely used system by philosopher Michael Davis for ethical decision making offers these tests for options in an ethical dilemma:

- **Harm:** Does this option do less harm than any other?

- **Publicity:** Would I want my choice of this option published in the news?

- **Defensibility:** Could I defend my choice of this option before a congressional committee or a committee of my peers?

- **Self-application:** Would I still think this choice good if I were one of those adversely affected by it?

Rule 34: Don't Plagiarize

"Do not plagiarize" should have been included in *Unwritten Rules of Management,* the book by William Swanson, CEO of Raytheon. In 2004, Raytheon gave employees free copies of the book, which contained 33 rules. The book quickly became widely read by professionals and executives because of its humorous approach. However, an engineer at Hewlett-Packard discovered that 13 of the rules had been previously published by W. J. King in his 1944 bestseller, *The Unwritten Laws of Engineering.* Further findings uncovered that the additional rules were obtained from Defense Secretary Donald Rumsfeld and humor editorial writer Dave Barry.

Swanson apologized for the mistake, which, he states, began when he asked employees to create a presentation from a file. The presentation was a great hit, which led to the creation of the 33 rules—one for each year he worked for Raytheon. Unfortunately, the rules were not original and the sources were not properly cited.

How can you avoid plagiarism?

Adapted from Lisa Takeuchi Cullen, "Rule No. 1: Don't Copy," *Time,* May 15, 2006, 41.

■ Colleagues: What do my colleagues say when I suggest this option as my solution?

■ Profession: What might my profession's governing body or ethics committee say about this option?

■ Organization: What does the company's ethics officer or legal counsel say about this option?[17]

Corporate Culture LO 4-2

Another strong influence on the business environment is corporate culture (see Chapter 2 for ways to analyze corporate culture). Corporate cultures vary widely. They range from formal—with individual offices, jackets, and hierarchical lines of command—to informal—with open office space, casual attire, and individually empowered workers. Characteristics of popular corporate cultures include flexible work arrangements, profit sharing, information sharing, good training, health insurance, and wellness programs.

Both large and small companies get positive publicity for their corporate cultures.

■ Google is known for company gyms, well-stocked snack rooms, restaurants, and casual work attire.

■ Ogilvy & Mather's Canton, China, office has a carnival theme to remind employees of the company's mission to "stay fresh." The décor includes a full-size carousel, carousel horses throughout the office, circus lights, and a fake Ferris wheel, whose carriages serve as small meeting rooms.[18]

■ Dealer.com offers subsidized meals at its café, with organic and locally grown food, wellness seminars on exercise and stress management, chair massages, bike rentals, tennis and basketball courts, fitness center, and half-price ski passes. The company supports its sports teams, including softball, volleyball, soccer, bowling, and dragon-boat racing.[19]

Two companies in the same field may have very different cultures. When Procter & Gamble bought Gillette, the company expected a smooth marriage between the world's number one toothbrush, Oral-B, and the world's number two toothpaste, Crest. But cultural differences caused problems. Gillette employees found P&G's culture rigid, its decision making slow. Gillette employees also had to learn P&G's famous acronyms, such as CIB (consumer is boss) and FMOT (first moment of truth, when consumers notice the product). P&G people sent memos, Gillette people called meetings.[20]

Some employees use exercise balls as desk chairs. The balls require employees to use core muscles to maintain posture. Employees say they are also fun because they can bounce.

Wise companies also use effective corporate cultures to retain hourly workers. Hotels lose two-thirds of their hourly workers annually, according to hotel survey firm Market Metrix. Each departure costs midrange hotels about $5,000 in lost productivity, recruiting, and training. But Joie de Vivre Hospitality has a turnover rate that is half the industry average. The CEO attributes the low rate to a corporate culture that listens to employees, enacts some of their suggestions, and tries to make work fun. In addition to awards, the company sponsors parties, annual retreats, and regularly scheduled dinners. It also offers free classes on subjects such as Microsoft Excel and English as a second language.[21]

Corporate culture is at the heart of the customer service focus at Zappos, the Internet footwear retailer. The company nurtures a touch of weirdness to make work more fun. That same touch of weirdness also encourages innovation. To increase serendipitous interactions, all employees enter and exit through the reception area, not other building doors. Logging in to the company computer requires completing the short multiple-choice test to name the randomly selected employee whose picture is displayed.[22] Tours of corporate offices are always unique, because teams are always changing their décor:

> You might find a popcorn machine or a coffee machine dressed up as a robot in our lobby. As you passed through different departments, you might find an aisle of cowbells…, a makeshift bowling alley…, employees dressed up as pirates, employees karaokeing, a nap room, a petting zoo, or a hot dog social. You might see a parade pass by because one of our departments decided that it was the perfect day to celebrate Oktoberfest.[23]

Interpersonal Communication   LO 4-3

Within the corporate environment, interpersonal communication skill is one major reason some people are more likely to be successful than others. Much important communication occurs in hallways, at the coffee machine, and in break rooms. Successful professionals communicate well with different categories of people—co-workers, bosses, clients—in a variety of settings. To do so, they cultivate skills in diverse areas such as listening, conversation, nonverbal communication, and networking. They also practice skills in conflict resolution and teamwork (see Chapter 8 for a discussion of these latter two skills).

These skills are part of what Daniel Goleman has widely popularized as emotional intelligence in his books on the subject. He presents much evidence to show that while intelligence and expertise are necessary to climb to the top in organizations, once at the top, emotional intelligence, not IQ, predicts the star leaders.[24]

Listening

Listening is crucial to building trust. However, listening on the job may be more difficult than listening in class. Many classroom lectures are well organized, with signposts and repetition of key points to help hearers follow. But conversations usually wander. A key point about when a report is due may be sandwiched among statements about other due dates for other projects.

In a classroom you're listening primarily for information. In interchanges with co-workers, you need to listen for feelings, too. Feelings such as being rejected or overworked need to be dealt with as they arise. But you can't deal with a feeling unless you are aware of it.

Listening errors also can result from being distracted by your own emotional response, especially when the topic is controversial. Listeners have to be aware of their emotional responses so they can clarify the speaker's intent

---

Thoughtful Perks

As part of their corporate culture, some companies have thoughtful perks:

- On-site day care and after-school care.
- Fitness center and pool.
- On-site laundry pickup and delivery.
- Free lunches and snacks.
- Unlimited paid vacation.

Worker-cise

In a new furniture trend in corporate culture, many new workstations have been designed to help employees exercise on the job. Some popular new products are workstations that are connected to a treadmill, allowing people to walk or run while working, and giant balls that employees must balance on while sitting at their desks.

However, "active workstations" may be hurting productivity and may even cause issues of hygiene, etiquette, and liability. A study by the Mayo Clinic showed that medical transcriptionists slowed down by 16% if they typed while walking instead of sitting. A similar study by the University of Tennessee found that fine motor skills decreased by 11% while walking on a treadmill.

The University of Kentucky put together rules for using active workstations. The rules suggested that users wear proper shoes to walk in, walk slowly (less than 2 miles per hour), muffle the noise of the treadmills, practice good hygiene, and keep a traditional desk and chair.

Adapted from Jen Wieczner, "Falling Down on the Job?" *Wall Street Journal,* January 29, 2013, D1–D2.

and also allow time for cooling off, if necessary. A you-attitude is as helpful for listening as it is for writing. Listening is more effective if the listener focuses more on understanding than on formulating a reply. Thinking about your own response too often causes you to miss important information.

Some listening errors also happen because the hearer wasn't paying enough attention to a key point. Be aware of points you need to know and listen for them.

Inattention and emotions can cause listeners to misinterpret a speaker. To reduce listening errors caused by misinterpretation,

- Paraphrase what the speaker has said, giving him or her a chance to correct your understanding.

- At the end of the conversation, check your understanding with the other person. Especially check who does what next.

- After the conversation, write down key points that affect deadlines or how work will be evaluated. Sometimes these key points need to be confirmed in an e-mail.

- Don't ignore instructions you think are unnecessary. Before you do something else, check with the order giver to see if there is a reason for the instruction.

- Consider the other person's background and experiences. Why is this point important to the speaker? What might he or she mean by it?

Listening to people is an indication that you're taking them seriously. **Acknowledgment responses**—nods, *uh huhs*, smiles, frowns—help carry the message that you're listening. However, remember that listening responses vary in different cultures.

In **active listening,** receivers actively demonstrate that they've understood a speaker by feeding back the literal meaning, the emotional content, or both. These strategies create active responses:

- Paraphrase the content. Feed back the meaning in your own words.

- Identify the feelings you think you hear.

- Ask for information or clarification.

- Offer to help. ("What can I do to help?")

When dealing with problems, instead of acknowledging what the other person says, many of us immediately respond in a way that analyzes or attempts to solve or dismiss the problem. People with problems need first of all to know that we hear that they're having a rough time. Figure 4.3 lists some responses that block communication.[25] Ordering and threatening both tell the other person that the speaker doesn't want to hear what he or she has to say. Preaching attacks the other person. Minimizing the problem suggests the other person's concern is misplaced. It can even attack the other person's competency by suggesting that other people are coping just fine with bigger problems. Even advising shuts off discussion. Giving a quick answer minimizes the pain the person feels and puts him or her down for not seeing (what is to us) the obvious answer. Even if it is a good answer from an objective point of view, the other person may not be ready to hear it. And too often, the off-the-top-of-the-head solution doesn't address the real problem.

Figure 4.3	Blocking Responses versus Active Listening

Blocking response	Possible active response
Ordering, threatening	**Paraphrasing content**
"I don't care how you do it. Just get that report on my desk by Friday."	"You're saying that you don't have time to finish the report by Friday."
Preaching, criticizing	**Mirroring feelings**
"You should know better than to air the department's problems in a general meeting."	"It sounds like the department's problems really bother you."
Minimizing the problem	**Asking for information or clarification**
"You think *that's* bad. You should see what *I* have to do this week."	"What parts of the problem seem most difficult to solve?"
Advising	**Offering to help solve the problem together**
"Well, why don't you try listing everything you have to do and seeing which items are most important?"	"Is there anything I could do that would help?"

Active listening takes time and energy. Even people who are skilled active listeners can't do it all the time. Active listening can reduce the conflict that results from miscommunication, but it alone cannot reduce the conflict that comes when two people want apparently inconsistent things or when one person wants to change someone else.

Conversational Style

Deborah Tannen, a linguist who specializes in gender discourse, uses the term **conversational style** to denote our conversational patterns and the meaning we give to them: the way we show interest, politeness, appropriateness.[26] Your answers to the following questions help reveal your own conversational style:

- How long a pause tells you that it's your turn to speak?

- Do you see interruption as rude? Or do you say things while other people are still talking to show that you're interested and to encourage them to say more?

- Do you show interest by asking lots of questions? Or do you see questions as intrusive and wait for people to volunteer whatever they have to say?

Tannen concludes that the following features characterize her own conversational style:

Fast rate of speech.
Fast rate of turn-taking.
Persistence—if a turn is not acknowledged, try again.
Preference for personal stories.
Tolerance of, preference for simultaneous speech.
Abrupt topic shifting.

Different conversational styles are not necessarily good or bad, but people with different conversational styles may feel uncomfortable without knowing why. A subordinate who talks quickly may be frustrated by a boss who speaks

Serendipitous Interpersonal Communication

Some organizations are thinking of new ways to get their employees to meet each other. They hope these chance encounters will encourage creativity, collaboration, and innovation.

Some companies use architectural features, such as crowded break rooms that cause employees to literally bump into each other or centralized bathrooms. Others use creative features, like trivia games in elevators, to get employees talking to each other.

Efforts don't have to cost a lot of money. National Public Radio holds "Serendipity Days," during which employees—from departments as disparate as HR, news, and engineering—meet to think of new projects. At marketing agency CTP, employees swap offices and desks in the summer to foster cross-departmental interactions.

Adapted from Rachel Emma Silverman, "The Science of Serendipity in the Workplace," *Wall Street Journal*, May 1, 2013, B6.

Interpersonal Skills for Doctors

The risk of being sued for medical malpractice lies not so much with training, credentials, or even the number of mistakes made. Rather, it depends on doctors' interpersonal skills. Again and again, patients in malpractice suits say they were rushed, ignored, or treated like objects.

A study of surgeons showed that those who had never been sued

- Made orienting comments at visits, so patients knew what was going to happen and when it was best to ask questions.

- Practiced active listening ("Tell me more about that").

- Laughed and were funny during visits.

The difference was all in how they talked to their patients; there was no difference in amount or quality of information.

Adapted from Malcolm Gladwell, *Blink: The Power of Thinking without Thinking* (New York: Back Bay Books, 2007), 40–43.

slowly. People who talk more slowly may feel shut out of a conversation with people who talk more quickly. Someone who has learned to make requests directly ("Please pass the salt") may be annoyed by someone who uses indirect requests ("This casserole needs some salt").

In the workplace, conflicts may arise because of differences in conversational style. If people see direct questions as criticizing or accusing, they may see an ordinary question ("Will that report be ready Friday?") as a criticism of their progress. One supervisor might mean the question simply as a request for information. Another supervisor might use the question to mean "I want that report Friday."

Researchers Daniel N. Maltz and Ruth A. Borker believe that differences in conversational style (see Figure 4.4) may be responsible for the miscommunication that often occurs in **male–female conversations.** Certainly conversational style is not the same for all men and for all women, but research has found several common patterns in the U.S. cultures studied.[27] For example, researchers have found that women are much more likely to nod and to say *yes* or *mm hmm* than men are.[28] Maltz and Borker hypothesize that to women, these symbols mean simply "I'm listening; go on." Men, on the other hand, may decode these symbols as "I agree" or at least "I follow what you're saying so far." A man who receives nods and *mms* from a woman may feel that she is inconsistent and unpredictable if she then disagrees with him. A woman may feel that a man who doesn't provide any feedback isn't listening to her.

Research has also shown that in the United States men tend to interrupt more than women; women tend to wait for a pause in the discussion before speaking. When former Secretary of State Madeleine Albright was asked to give advice to professional women hoping to rise in the ranks, she replied, "Learn to interrupt."[29]

Figure 4.4	Different Conversational Styles	
	Debating	**Relating**
Interpretation of questions	See questions as requests for information.	See questions as way to show interest and keep a conversation flowing.
Relation of new comment to what last speaker said	Do not require new comment to relate explicitly to last speaker's comment. Ignoring previous comment is one strategy for taking control.	Expect new comments to acknowledge the last speaker's comment and relate directly to it.
View of interrupting	See interrupting as one way to organize the flow of conversation.	See interrupting as disruptive to a conversation.
View of indirectness	Appreciate directness	See indirectness as maintaining camaraderie, as giving other people choice in a conversation.
Definition of topics	Tend to announce topics directly. Interpret statements about side issues as effort to change the topic.	Tend to define topics gradually, progressively. Interpret statements about side issues as effort to shape, expand, or limit the topic.
Response to someone who shares a problem	Offer advice, solutions.	Offer solidarity, reassurance. Share troubles to establish sense of community.

Source: Based on Deborah Tannen, *That's Not What I Meant!: How Conversational Style Makes or Breaks Relationships,* Rei Rep ed. (New York: Harper Perennial, 2011).

Nonverbal Communication

Nonverbal communication—communication that doesn't use words—occurs all the time. Smiles, frowns, office décor, who sits where at a meeting, the size of an office, how long someone keeps a visitor waiting—all these communicate pleasure or anger, friendliness or distance, power and status.

Researchers have begun to study a category of nonverbal communication called **social signals**—tone of voice, gestures, proximity to others, facial expressions—as keys to business success. Researchers can study these signals in individuals and then predict accurately who will win raises or business plan contests. The more successful people are more energetic and positive. They do talk more, but they also listen more, drawing other people out.[30]

Most of the time we are no more conscious of interpreting nonverbal signals than we are conscious of breathing. Yet nonverbal signals can be misinterpreted just as easily as can verbal symbols (words). And the misunderstandings can be harder to clear up because people may not be aware of the nonverbal cues that led them to assume they aren't liked, respected, or approved.

Learning about nonverbal language can help us project the image we want to present and make us more aware of the signals we are interpreting. However, even within a single culture, a nonverbal symbol may have more than one meaning.

In the business world, two sets of nonverbal signals are particularly important: spatial cues and body language.

Spatial Cues   In the United States, the size, placement, and privacy of one's office connotes status. Large corner offices have the highest status. An individual office with a door that closes connotes more status than a desk in a common area. Windows also may matter. An office with a window may connote more status than one without.

People who don't know each other well may feel more comfortable with each other if a piece of furniture separates them. For example, a group may work better sitting around a table than just sitting in a circle. Desks can be used as barricades to protect oneself from other people.

Liar Detection

Although not infallible, these are signs of lying:

Body language: Physical cues such as sweating and fidgeting may be telling.

Details: False stories often lack details. Pushing for details increases chances the liar may slip up.

Unpleasantness: Liars are less cooperative, pleasant, and friendly than truth tellers. They also make more negative statements and complaints.

Eye contact: Failure to make eye contact is often a sign of lying.

Stress signs: Dilated pupils and a rise in voice pitch may be present.

Pauses: Most liars will have pauses in their stories as they make them up.

Inconsistencies: Ask suspected liars to repeat their stories; listen for inconsistencies.

Adapted from Elisabeth Eaves, "Ten Ways to Tell if Someone Is Lying to You," *Forbes,* July 22, 2010, http://www.forbes.com/2006/11/02/tech-cx_ee_technology_liar_slide.html.

(a) (left) "THE REAL THING: A real smile involves the whole face, not just the mouth. While muscles pull the corners of the mouth up (1), an involuntary nerve causes the upper eyefold (2) to relax."(b) (right) "THE SOCIAL SMILE: When faking, the lips are pulled straight across (3). Though this creates cheek folds (4) similar to those of a real smile, the lack of eye crinkles (5) is a dead giveaway."

Quoted from Andy Raskin, "A Face Any Business Can Trust," *Business 2.0* 4, no. 11 (December 2003): 60.

Authoritative Body Language

Carol Kinsey Goman, author of *The Silent Language of Leaders: How Body Language Can Help—or Hurt—How You Lead*, offers these tips to increase your image of authority:

- Keep your head straight up. Head tilts show concern or interest for individuals, but may be processed as submission signals in power situations.

- Expand your space. Stand tall, spread your elbows a little, widen your stance, and spread your materials on the table at the next meeting. Authority is demonstrated through height and space.

- Use the tonal arc, in which your voice rises in pitch through a sentence but drops back down at the end. Ending on a higher pitch often indicates uncertainty or a need for approval.

- Look serious when the subject is serious. Smiles are frequently inappropriate in power situations.

- Do not nod to express listening or engagement; nodding undercuts authority.

- Minimize movements, especially gestures.

- Have a firm handshake.

Adapted from Carol Kinsey Goman, "10 Common Body Language Traps for Women in the Workplace," *On Leadership* (blog), *Washington Post*, May 2, 2011, http://www.washingtonpost .com/blogs/on-leadership/ post/10-common-body-language- traps-for-women-in-the- workplace/2011/03/03/ AFl0GFbF_blog.html.

Body Language   Our body language communicates to other people much about our feelings. Our facial expressions, eye contact, gestures, posture, and body positions all telegraph information about us. In the United States, **open body positions** include leaning forward with uncrossed arms and legs, with the arms away from the body. **Closed** or **defensive body positions** include leaning back, sometimes with both hands behind the head, arms and legs crossed or close together, or hands in pockets. As the labels imply, open positions suggest that people are accepting and open to new ideas. Closed positions suggest that people are physically or psychologically uncomfortable, that they are defending themselves and shutting other people out.

People who cross their arms or legs often claim that they do so only because the position is more comfortable. But notice your own body the next time you're in a perfectly comfortable discussion with a good friend. You'll probably find that you naturally assume open body positions. The fact that so many people in organizational settings adopt closed positions may indicate that many people feel at least slightly uncomfortable in school and on the job.

Some nonverbal communications appear to be made and interpreted unconsciously by many people. Researchers at MIT are showing that when we get excited about something, we have more nervous energy. Another such signal is fluency, or consistency. Consistency in motions (such as in surgery) or tone (speech) tells us who is expert, or at least well practiced. Such signals are hard to fake, which may explain their influence.[31]

Body language is complicated by the fact that nonverbal signs may have more than one meaning. A frown may signal displeasure or concentration. A stiff posture that usually means your co-worker is upset may today just be a sign of sore back muscles.

Our own body language can even influence us. Smiling, even when we don't want to, can make us feel better about what we are doing. Uncrossing

Body language can give big clues about our attitudes.

folded arms (a common sign of resistance) to accept a cup of coffee, business card, or paper copy of a document can make us less resistant to the other person. Standing tall or assuming an expansive posture can make us feel more confident.[32]

Misunderstandings are even more common when people communicate with people from other cultures or other countries. Knowing something about other cultures may help you realize that a subordinate who doesn't meet your eye may be showing respect rather than dishonesty. But it's impossible to memorize every meaning that every nonverbal sign has in every culture. And in a multicultural workforce, you may not know whether someone retains the meanings of his or her ancestors or has adopted the dominant U.S. meanings. The best solution is to ask for clarification.

Etiquette

Some people falsely think that etiquette consists of a bunch of stuffy old-fashioned rules. They are wrong. Good manners mean treating people with respect. In the office that means respecting people's space by not peering over their cubicle wall, not handling their stuff, and never borrowing anything from them without asking. In open offices it means lowering your voice on conversations and phone calls so the whole office doesn't have to hear. It also means not sneaking up on people using headphones. In the break room, it means sharing limited spaces such as refrigerators, making a new pot of coffee when you take the last cup, and cleaning up your messes.

Good manners include saying *please, thank you,* and *you're welcome.* They include making customers feel welcome and standing up to greet newcomers. They include returning shared equipment promptly and filling the printer with paper when you empty it.

For most people, the biggest etiquette breach in the workplace involves misuse of technology. Set your cell phone on vibrate. Refrain from texting during meetings. In fact, don't multitask when you are engaged in any interpersonal communications. When you do so, you are sending a clear message to other people that they are not as important as your phone messages, e-mail, or websites. This restriction also applies when you are on the phone; most people can tell if you are multitasking.

Networking

A much underappreciated skill in the business environment is **networking,** the ability to connect with many different kinds of people. Most of us can relate to the people in our immediate work group, although even there differences in ability to connect impact performance. But true networking is creating connections with still more people. It involves creating connections before they are needed, creating diverse connections in widely spread areas, knowing which people to turn to when you need additional expertise, knowing people outside the company.

Good networkers know who will help them cut through red tape, who can find an emergency supplier, who will take on extra work in a crisis. Informal conversations, about yesterday's game and Li's photography exhibit as well as what's happening at work, connect them with the **grapevine,** an informal source of company information. Participation in civic, school, religious, and professional organizations connects them to a larger environment. They attend conferences, trade shows, fund-raisers, and community events. They use social networking sites such as LinkedIn (see Chapter 9 for more on electronic networks).

Gossip Networking

Although it has a tarnished reputation, gossip can benefit both individuals and organizations, research shows. Gossiping is a form of networking. According to Joe Labianca, a professor at the University of Kentucky's Center for Research on Social Networks in Business, the more workers gossip, the better their understanding of the work environment and the higher their peers rate their influence. Gossip disseminates valuable information about workers, such as who doesn't do their share or who is impossible to work with.

And guess what? Managers gossip, too. In fact, they may have more "gossip partners" than nonmanagers.

Adapted from Giuseppe Labianca, "It's Not 'Unprofessional' to Gossip at Work," *Harvard Business Review* 88, no. 9 (September 2010): 29.

Networking becomes even more important as you climb the corporate ladder. Good managers interact with their employees continually, not just when they need something. They listen to lunchroom conversations; they chat with employees over coffee.

Much research shows that networking is crucial to job success. In *Emotional Intelligence,* Daniel Goleman tells of research in a division at Bell Labs to determine what made the star performers in the division. Everyone in the division had a high academic IQ, which meant that IQ was not a good predictor of job productivity (although academic knowledge and IQ are good predictors of success on earlier career ladder rungs). But networking skill was a good predictor. The stars put effort into developing their network, and they cultivated relationships in that network *before* they were needed.[33]

Goleman identifies three different kinds of workplace networks: conversational (who talks to whom), expertise (who can be turned to for advice), and trust (who can be trusted with sensitive information such as gripes). Unsurprisingly, the stars of an organization are often heavily networked in all three varieties.[34]

Good networkers share certain interpersonal communication behaviors.

- Use you-attitude to see things from the other person's perspective.

- Actively seek ways to help other people.

- Adapt their behavior and attitude to the people around them.

- Subtly mirror the postures, behaviors, and emotional states of people near them.

- Share some personal and emotional information about themselves, a sharing that helps build trust.

- Capitalize on the benefits of physical proximity—trading some phone calls for actual office visits, attending both informal and formal gatherings.

- Understand the importance of connecting with people outside their own social and professional circles.

One study showed that people with these skills penetrated the center of their workplace network in just 18 months; people lacking in these skills took 13 years.[35]

Time Management   `LO 4-4`

As your work environment becomes more complex, with multiple networks, responsibilities, and projects, good time management becomes crucial. The ever-increasing number of messages that must be answered as well as the distractions and interruptions that are part of open-plan offices all add to time problems. Although much time management advice sounds like common sense, it is amazing the number of people who do not follow it.

Techniques

Probably the most important time management technique is to prioritize the demands on your time, and make sure you spend the majority of your time on the most important demands. If your career success depends on producing reports, news articles, and press releases about company business, then that is what you need to spend the majority of your time doing.

Figure 4.5	Stephen Covey's Time Management Matrix. Covey advises putting significant time into quadrant II.

	Urgent	Not Urgent
Important	I ACTIVITIES: Crises Pressing problems Deadline-driven projects	II ACTIVITIES: Prevention, PC activities Relationship building Recognizing new opportunities Planning, recreation
Not Important	III ACTIVITIES: Interruptions, some calls Some mail, some reports Some meetings Proximate, pressing matters Popular activities	IV ACTIVITIES: Trivia, busy work Some mail Some phone calls Time wasters Pleasant activities

Source: Stephen R. Covey, *The 7 Habits of Highly Effective People: Restoring the Character* (New York: Free Press, 2004), 150–54. Reprinted with permission of the author.

Randy Pausch, in his highly popular video and book *The Last Lecture,* makes this point about prioritizing most eloquently. His lecture is a moving reminder to make time for friends and family. His colleagues noted that he would regularly tell his students they could always make more money later, but they could never make more time.[36]

In *The 7 Habits of Highly Effective People,* a book which remained on the best-seller list for over two decades, Stephen Covey presents a useful time management matrix that sorts activities by urgency and importance (see Figure 4.5). Obviously we should focus our time on important, urgent activities, but Covey also advises putting significant time into quadrant II, important but nonurgent activities, which he calls the heart of effective management. Quadrant II activities include networking, planning, and preparing.[37]

Figure 4.6 offers other common tips for time management.

Figure 4.6	Time Management Tips

- Keep lists—both daily and long term. Prioritize items on your list.

- Ask yourself where you want to be in three or five years and work accordingly.

- Do large, important tasks first, and then fill in around them with smaller tasks.

- Break large tasks into small ones. Remember that you do not always have to work sequentially. If you have been putting off a report because you cannot decide how to write its introduction, start with the conclusions or some other part that is easy for you to write.

- Find blocks of time: Set your phone to voice mail, ignore e-mail, avoid the break room, move discretionary meetings. Put these blocks at your most productive time; save e-mail and meetings for less productive times.

- Avoid time sinks: some people, long phone conversations, constant e-mail checks.

- Decide at the end of today's work session what you will do in tomorrow's session, and set yourself up to do it. Find the necessary file; look up the specifications for that proposal.

- At the end of the week, evaluate what you didn't get done. Should you have done it for promotion, goodwill, ethics?

Multitasking

Many workers believe they can manage some of their time-crunch problems by multitasking. Unfortunately, decades of research on the subject show that this is a false belief. It is particularly false when long-term learning or communication tasks are involved.[38] Just think of all the e-mails that get sent to unintended audiences while the writer is multitasking, or all the phone calls for which the caller, busy multitasking, forgets who is being called or why in the short time between dialing and pickup.

Research shows that when we think we are multitasking, we are really switching back and forth between tasks. And there is always a start-up delay involved in returning to a previous task, no matter how brief the delay. These delays may make it faster to do the tasks sequentially, in which case we will probably do them better, too. In fact, some research shows it can take up to 50% longer to multitask.[39] Other research shows that multitasking hurts overall attention and memory, even when not multitasking.[40]

When we return to a task following an interruption—either from someone else, like a phone call, or from ourselves, like a visit to Facebook—it may take us more than 20 minutes to get back into the original task.[41] Sometimes, we do not get back to the task correctly. Pilots who are interrupted in their preflight checklist may miss an item when they return to it. One crash, in which 153 people died, has been blamed on an error resulting from such an interruption.[42]

Some companies are allowing employees to schedule three to four hours a week for focused work. During that time, employees are allowed to ignore e-mails, phone calls, and meetings except for urgent matters.

Trends in Business Communication   LO 4-5

Both business and business communication are constantly changing. One of the biggest changes for most people is the shift to electronic communications. This all-encompassing trend is the subject of Chapter 9. Related to this shift are trends in data security and electronic privacy. Other trends are customer service, work/family balance, environmental concern, globalization and outsourcing, diversity, teamwork, job flexibility, innovation and entrepreneurship, and big data. As this list of trends suggests, rapid change itself is another major trend in the business environment.

Data Security

As business communication becomes increasingly electronic, concerns about data theft mushroom. Just as individuals take steps—like not providing important identification numbers by e-mail—to prevent identity theft, organizations take steps to protect their data. The need for them to do so becomes always more urgent as hackers continue to produce more sophisticated software.

- Names, birthdates, and possibly credit card numbers for 77 million people were stolen from Sony.

- 12 million Apple IDs were stolen from the laptop of an FBI agent.

- 6 million passwords were stolen from LinkedIn, which was using an outdated form of cryptography.

- Hackers gained access to 3.6 million state tax returns in South Carolina.[43]

Not all hacking attacks are to gain individuals' data. The Department of Homeland Security reported almost 200 serious attacks on power, water, and other utilities in 2012.[44]

Hackers are not responsible for all the lost data. Lost or stolen laptops and smartphones containing sensitive data also add to the problem. Flash drives, because of their small size, are an even bigger problem. Corporate security measures may include bans on personal electronic devices. Some companies are even disabling extra USB connections to ensure employees cannot attach these devices. Others are performing random checks of laptops to look for unauthorized or unsecured files and using scans of fingerprints, eyes, or faces to limit and track access to specific computers.[45]

Data security problems affect individuals, too. When hackers get names and e-mail addresses, they can send **phishing messages,** e-mails that try to lure receivers to send sensitive information. When hackers can connect the names and addresses to actual firms the readers use, such as banks and stores, the phishing e-mails look so official that even executives and professionals are convinced to respond.

Electronic Privacy

As organizations respond to growing security concerns, their efforts often encroach on workers' privacy. Organizations are monitoring many different kinds of electronic interactions. According to a survey by the American Management Association of 304 companies,

- 73% store and review e-mail.
- 66% monitor Internet usage.
- 65% block inappropriate websites.
- 48% use video surveillance.
- 45% record time spent on phone and numbers dialed.
- 43% store and review computer files.[46]

The same study also showed that 45% track keystrokes (and time spent at the computer). Because of findings from such monitoring, some companies are blocking access to particular websites, especially Facebook, YouTube, sports and online shopping sites. Many organizations claim that heavy usage of these sites slows company communications such as file transfers and e-mail.

Other surveillance techniques use GPS (global positioning system) chips to monitor locations of company vehicles, as well as arrival and departure times at job sites. Records from E-ZPass, the electronic toll collection system, are being used in courts as proof of infidelity. Workers may tell their spouses they are in a meeting, but E-ZPass has a record of where and when their vehicle entered or exited that day.[47] Cell phones and computers give approximate location signals that are accurate enough to help law enforcement officials locate suspects.

The division between corporate data security and personal privacy has become increasingly complex and blurry. Corporate surveillance does not necessarily stop when employees leave their offices or cars. It can continue to the company parking areas and even employees' homes. Companies such as Google, Delta Air Lines, and even Burger King have fired workers for content on their personal blogs. Although many workers believe their blogs are

Hack Attack

The Sony networks were hacked in April 2011, compromising 100 million accounts, exposing customer credit card numbers, and forcing Sony to shut down the networks for a month until the damage was repaired. It was the second-largest data breach in the United States.

Unlike other companies, Sony had taken hackers to court and threatened others with lawsuits. Other technical companies have been trying to make a truce with hackers: Google pays hackers who discover bugs; Microsoft permits hackers to unlock its Kinect gaming system.

While the company did not know who attacked the system, the following message was left by the hackers: "We are legion." That phrase is the motto of Anonymous, the hacker collective.

Adapted from Michael Riley and Ashlee Vance, "Sony: The Company That Kicked the Hornet's Nest," *Bloomberg Businessweek,* May 16, 2011, 35–36.

protected by the First Amendment, in most states companies can fire employees for almost any reason except discrimination.[48]

A survey by the American Management Association found that over a quarter of companies fired employees for e-mail misuse.[49] New technologies make it increasingly easy for companies—and lawyers—to track employees. "E-discovery" software can aid searchers in sorting millions of documents and e-mails in just days to find relevant ones for court cases. They go far beyond finding specific words and terms. In some of the best, if you search for "dog," you will also find documents with "man's best friends" and even the notion of "walk." Other programs can find concepts rather than just key words. Still others look at activities—who did what when, who talked to whom—to extract patterns. They find anomalies, such as switching media from e-mail to phone or a face-to-face communication, or when a document is edited an unusual number of times by unusual people.[50]

Other media are also connected with privacy issues.

- Google has begun combining user data from web searches, Gmail messages, Google + postings, YouTube viewings, and Android phone data to make comprehensive user profiles.[51]

- E-books allow sellers to track not only which books you buy, but how often you open them, how many hours you spend reading them, how far you get in them, and what you underline in them.[52]

- Some Twitter users have found the hard way that their messages are not private. Paul Chambers lost his job and was convicted of threatening to blow up an airport after sending a joking tweet to his friends.[53]

- Detroit Mayor Kwame Kilpatrick was charged with perjury and forced to resign after text messages he sent were used against him by prosecutors.

- Officials investigating the Boston Marathon bombing used photos from private cell phones, as well as security cameras, to identify the bombers.

- Employees have also been fired for posting on their personal Facebook site disparaging comments about their employers.

- Even "old" technology can threaten privacy. Illinois Governor Rod Blagojevich was impeached on the basis of taped phone conversations.

Although more individuals are starting to sue over their firings, and a few are winning, the legal scale is still weighted in favor of employers. In 2010 the Supreme Court ruled that searches on work equipment are reasonable and not a violation of Fourth Amendment rights.

Some companies help individuals protect their privacy by offering services that delete messages and documents from multiple phones at a set time. Users can set an expiration time for their messages, which will be used to delete the messages from their own phones, the recipients' phones, and the messaging service's computer servers.[54] Other companies, for example, allow users to choose what kinds of ads they will see or to opt out. Companies such as Microsoft and Mozilla are beginning to include do-not-track features in their popular Internet browsers, to keep advertisers and others from monitoring online habits.[55]

In 2009, the Federal Trade Commission (FTC) endorsed industry self-regulation to protect consumer privacy. Websites and companies that collect consumer data such as searches performed and websites visited are to (1) clearly notify consumers that they do so, (2) provide an easy way to opt out, (3) protect the data, and (4) limit its retention, but breaches of these guidelines continue to occur.[56] Recently Facebook settled with the FTC about privacy changes deemed "unfair and deceptive." The settlement included privacy audits for 20 years.[57]

A highly publicized study by the *Wall Street Journal* of the 50 most popular websites in the United States found that those sites installed 3,180 tracking files on the test computer. Twelve sites, including Dictionary.com, Comcast.net, and MSN.com, installed more than 100 tracking tools each. Some tracking files could track sensitive health and financial data; other files could transmit keystrokes; still other files could reattach trackers that a person deleted. Apps on smartphones are performing similar trackings.[58]

Customer Service

One effect of the recession was to push more businesses into focusing on their customer service. Amazon, for instance, is well known for its mission to be "Earth's most customer centric company." But it is far from alone. Customer satisfaction is increasingly important for all businesses; in fact, it is a leading indicator of financial success.[59] Companies with higher scores on the American Customer Satisfaction Index (ACSI) tend to see better sales and stock performance than do companies with lower scores.[60] In an age where unhappy customers can share their experiences with thousands on social media, focusing on customer satisfaction is vital.

Improving customer service doesn't always mean spending extra money. Companies are learning to cross-train employees, so they can fill in where needed. Other companies are giving extra attention to their best customers to keep them loyal. Walgreens is training its pharmacists to work more closely with patients with chronic illnesses such as diabetes.[61] A tried and true way of improving customer service is increasing the oral communication skills of sales reps and customer service agents. See Chapter 3 for more on customer service.

Work/Family Balance

In addition to improving customer satisfaction, businesses are also focusing on their own employees. To reduce turnover, and increase employee satisfaction, companies are trying to be more family friendly by providing flextime, telecommuting, time off for family needs, and extended breaks for caregiving. Deloitte has initiated a program bringing teams together to decide schedules, including telecommuting, flextime, and compressed workweeks. Ernst & Young pays for some child care costs incurred from travel or overtime work. Procter & Gamble allows all office employees to shift their workday up to two hours earlier or later.[62]

At times, employees find ways other than physical presence to demonstrate their commitment and enthusiasm for organizational goals. Thanks to technology advances, employees can use laptops, e-mail, or cell phones to do work at any time, including weekends and evenings. The downside of this trend is that sometimes work and family life are not so much balanced as blurred.

Some employees are also expected to conduct business 24 hours a day because of different time zones of workplaces. The flexibility of employees is necessary in an age of downsizing and globalization, but it means that families are being impacted.

Many organizations promote virtual offices, which allow employees to work from home.

The issue of work/life balance leapt into the news when Yahoo's CEO notified employees that they were no longer allowed to work from home. An internal memo explained,

> To become the absolute best place to work, communication and collaboration will be important, so we need to be working side-by-side. That is why it is critical that we are all present in our offices. Some of the best decisions and insights come from hallway and cafeteria discussions, meeting new people, and impromptu team meetings.[63]

After some expressions of outrage, business articles started noting that Yahoo had a corporate culture problem for both office workers and telecommuters. The CEO found empty parking lots and office floors during work hours. Too few telecommuters were logging into the company's system.[64]

The debate over telecommuting has been ongoing. Proponents point out that home environments can provide quiet, uninterrupted time for concentrated thought. Opponents note that working at home invites misbehaviors such as doing private tasks on company time and makes successful collaborative work harder. Both sides generally agree that telecommuting involves trust (an established record of productivity) and specific outcomes. One final caveat: a Stanford University study showed that home workers were 50% less likely to get promoted than office workers.[65]

Most of the studies of telecommuting are self-reported studies. The only scientific study with randomized groups was in a Chinese travel company where half of the employees' earnings was based on call and order volume.[66]

Environmental Concern

As climate change becomes an issue of increasing concern, more and more companies are trying to soften their environmental impact. They do so for a variety of reasons in addition to environmental concerns. Sometimes such awareness saves money; sometimes executives hope it will create favorable publicity for the company or counterbalance negative publicity.

Many marketing experts say that green advertising is now just standard operating procedure.[67] Environmental activist groups such as Greenpeace and Friends of the Earth go even further. These groups have sharply and publicly criticized some large companies for exaggerating their commitment to the environment. One study claims that 95% of the "green" products it examined made claims that were lies, unsupported by proof, or couched in meaningless language ("all-natural").[68]

Various research studies show that token environmental efforts negatively affect public opinion.[69] But there is nothing "token" in the environmental efforts of some major companies. For instance, Levi Strauss is trying to reduce its environmental impact in everything it does, including asking its customers to wash their jeans less often. PepsiCo is working to limit its own water use; it is also working to help conserve water in communities around the world. In spring 2013 it announced it had met its goal of helping provide access to safe water for 3 million people in developing countries and had set a new goal of helping an addition 3 million by 2016.[70]

Globalization and Outsourcing

In the global economy, importing and exporting are just a start. More and more companies have offices, stores, and factories around the world.

- McDonald's serves food in over 119 countries on six continents.[71]
- UPS serves more than 220 countries and territories.[72]
- Coca-Cola sells its beverages in more than 200 countries.[73]
- Walmart has 6,155 stores outside the continental United States, including ones in Central America, South America, Africa, Europe, and Asia.[74]

The site of the store, factory, or office may not be the site of all the jobs. A data center in Washington can support many workers in India as businesses are outsourcing domestically and globally. **Outsourcing** means going outside the company for products and services that once were produced by the company's employees. Companies may outsource work such as technology services, customer service, tax services, legal services, accounting services, benefit communications, manufacturing, and marketing. Outsourcing is often a win–win solution: the company saves money or gets better service, and the outsourcers make a profit. In *The World Is Flat*, Thomas Friedman says, "The accountant who wants to stay in business in America will be the one who focuses on designing creative, complex strategies.... It means having quality-time discussions with clients."[75] He sees the work of the future as customization, innovation, service, and problem solving.[76]

All the challenges of communicating in one culture and country increase exponentially when people communicate across cultures and countries. Succeeding in a global market requires **intercultural competence,** the ability to communicate sensitively with people from other cultures and countries, based on an understanding of cultural differences. To learn more about international communication, see Chapter 7.

Many businesses, such as McDonald's, now serve food in Asian countries.

Diversity

Women, people of color, and immigrants have always been part of the U.S. workforce. But for most of this country's history, they were relegated to clerical, domestic, or menial jobs. Now, U.S. businesses realize that barriers to promotion hurt the bottom line as well as individuals. Success depends on using the brains and commitment as well as the hands and muscles of every worker.

In the past decade, we have also become aware of other sources of diversity beyond those of gender, race, and country of origin: age, religion, class, regional differences, sexual orientation, and physical disabilities are now areas of diversity. Helping each worker reach his or her potential requires more flexibility from managers as well as more knowledge about intercultural communication. And it's crucial to help workers from different backgrounds understand each other—especially in today's global economy. To learn more about diversity and the workforce, read Chapter 7.

Teamwork

More and more companies are getting work done through teams. Teamwork brings together people's varying strengths and talents to solve problems and make decisions. Often, teams are cross-functional (drawing from different jobs or functions) or cross-cultural (including people from different nations or cultural groups served by the company).

Teams, including cross-functional teams, helped Sarasota Memorial Hospital resolve major problems with customer and employee satisfaction. For example, team members from the emergency room recorded every step in the process from pulling into the parking lot through decisions about patient care, and then they eliminated unnecessary steps. The ER team then worked with the laboratory staff to improve the process of getting test results. At Michelin, the French tire maker, teams bring together people from the United States and Europe. The exchange between the two continents helps employees on both sides of the Atlantic understand each other's perspectives and needs.[77]

Increasing emphasis on teamwork is a major reason given by organizations such as AT&T, Intel, Hewlett-Packard, and the U.S. Interior Department for calling telecommuting workers back to the office.[78] To learn more about working in teams, see Chapter 8.

Job Flexibility

In traditional jobs, people did what they were told to do. But today, jobs that are routine can readily be done in other countries at lower cost. Many U.S. jobs have already been subject to such "offshoring," and more are sure to follow. The work that remains in the United States is more likely to be complex work requiring innovation, flexibility, and adaptation to new learning.

Today's workers do whatever needs to be done, based on the needs of customers, colleagues, and anyone else who depends on their work. They help team members finish individual work; they assist office mates with pressing deadlines. They are resourceful: they know how to find information and solution ideas. They work extra hours when the task demands it. They are ready to change positions and even locations when asked to do so. They need new skill sets even when they don't change jobs.

At Sarasota Memorial Hospital, food service workers do more than bring food to patients; they open containers, resolve problems with meals, help patients read their menus, and adjust orders to meet patients' preferences. This attentiveness not only serves the patients, but it also is part of a team-spirited approach to patient care that in this case frees nurses to do other work.[79] The experience at Sarasota Memorial is backed up by research suggesting the most effective workers don't see work as assigned tasks. Instead, they define their own goals based on the needs of customers and clients.[80]

Your parents may have worked for the same company all their lives. You may do that, too, but you have to be prepared to job-hunt throughout your career. That means continuing to learn—keeping up with new technologies, new economic and political realities, new ways of interacting with people.

Innovation and Entrepreneurship

As global competition increases, and industrial milieus change ever more quickly, innovation becomes more and more important. Xerox was known for photocopiers, but with paperless offices, the company had to change. Now Xerox offers new services, such as managing E-ZPass and red-light camera systems for many states.[81]

Researchers say that innovation/creativity is a process that can be learned. Ideo, the world-famous design firm with hundreds of design awards, says the first step is empathy, or you-attitude, with customers, both internal and external ones. This empathy is gained by getting out of the office and mingling with the users of your products and services.[82]

The next step is to generate ideas, lots of ideas, and to keep track of those ideas. Idea generation is most effective when individuals draw upon a large volume of diverse ideas and when organizations bring together a diverse group of people. The best problem solutions frequently come from combining existing ideas and from people who know enough to understand the problem but who are not in the specific area of the problem.[83] Websites such as InnoCentive allow organizations to find problem solutions through crowdsourcing; 74% of the public challenges (organizations can limit the challenges to specific sets of people, such as a group of employees) on InnoCentive pay cash awards to solvers.[84]

After the ideas comes feedback, phrased in positive tone. The chairman of Ideo recommends starting with "I like..." and then moving on to "I wish...."

Once these ideas have coalesced into a concrete plan, it is time to take the first step to making the idea a reality. Experts suggesting plunging in with a small step that can be tackled immediately.[85]

One Ideo client, the giant health care provider Kaiser Permanente, now has its own innovation center that follows the Ideo way. That center tackled the all-too-common problem of medication errors, which harm more than 1.5 million people in the United States each year. A team shadowed doctors, nurses, and pharmacists as they prescribed, administered, and filled medications. They made videos; they kept journals. And they discovered that interruptions were the cause of most errors. So the team brainstormed solutions, including "Leave Me Alone!" aprons and red "Do Not Cross!" lines in front of medication stations. The program has reduced interruptions by 50%.[86]

Many other companies also rely on all employees for suggestions. A classic article in the *Harvard Business Review* made famous the examples of 3M (where researchers can spend 15% of their time on ideas that don't need management approval), Thermo Electron (where managers can "spin out" promising new businesses), and Xerox (where employees write business proposals competing for corporate funds to develop new technologies).[87] Google is famous for its 20% rule: technical employees can spend about 20% of their time on projects outside their main job, and even their managers cannot remove that free margin.[88]

The spirit of innovation is inspiring some workers to start their own businesses. The U.S. Census Bureau counted 21.4 million nonemployer businesses (self-employed workers without employees).[89] In fact, these businesses are the majority of all U.S. businesses. These entrepreneurs have to handle all the communication in the business: writing business plans; making presentations to venture capitalists; drafting surveys; responding to customer complaints; and marketing the product or service.

Big Data

One of the forces driving innovation in some companies is big data. **Big data** is the term for the enormous amount of data generated by our electronic communications—e-mails, texts, instant messages, tweets, apps, web searches, Facebook postings, and GPS signals from phones. The amount is measured in petabytes (one quadrillion bytes, or "the equivalent of about 20 million filing cabinets' worth of text") and exabytes (one billion gigabytes).[90] As of 2012, each day sees the creation of about 2.5 exabytes of data; the volume is doubling about every 40 months. Experts estimate that only about 0.5% of this data is analyzed.[91]

Some of the uses of this data are well known: game developers use it to add more attractive features, Amazon uses it to steer us to other purchases we might like, Google uses it to help us find websites and to help advertisers find us, shipping firms use data from truck sensors to shorten routes and cut gas consumption. But the extent of usage is less well known. By monitoring billions of searches (for items such as cough medicine), Google is faster at predicting locations of flu outbreaks than the Center for Disease Control.[92] Inter-Continental Hotels used its data to launch a new marketing campaign with over 1,500 different customized messages.[93] Walmart is estimated to collect more than 2.5 petabytes of data hourly from customer transactions.[94]

To use big data effectively, organizations need to have specific goals in mind; they cannot just randomly collect and analyze data. They also need personnel who can find patterns in large data sets and translate those patterns into useful information for managers, who will act on the data. Finally, they need employees who are adept at understanding visuals and data displays (see Chapter 16).

Data Mining Competitions

Kaggle was created to provide data mining competitions for those who enjoy working on solving data problems. An organization will give Kaggle the problem or question it wants answered, the necessary data set, and the prize for the winning person or group.

Companies that have hired Kaggle to run these competitions have included Deloitte, Ford, and Microsoft. Participants may include "geeks" from places like IBM and MIT, but participants from other fields, such as archeology and glaciology, also compete.

A few of the data competitions that Kaggle hosted were from

- Wikipedia for predicting the number of edits an editor will make.

- The Australian government for predicting traffic over the next 24 hours.

- Allstate for improved models to price automobile insurance.

Each of these competitions offered a $10,000 prize, but smaller companies with smaller prizes also post on Kaggle.

The largest prize offered is from the Heritage Provider Network: $3 million will be given to the person who can most accurately predict which patients will be admitted to a hospital within a year based upon past insurance data.

Adapted from Ashlee Vance, "Fight Club for Geeks," *Bloomberg Businessweek*, January 9–15, 2012, 37–38.

Rapid Rate of Change

As any employee who has watched his or her job shift can testify, change—even change for the better—is stressful. Even when change promises improvements, people have to work to learn new skills, new habits, and new attitudes.

Rapid change means that no college course or executive MBA program can teach you everything you need to know for the rest of your working life. You'll need to stay abreast of professional changes by reading trade journals as well as professional websites and blogs, participating in professional Listservs, and attending professional events. Take advantage of your company's training courses and materials; volunteer for jobs that will help you gain new skills and knowledge. Pay particular attention to your communication skills; they become even more important as you advance up your career ladder. A survey of 1,400 financial executives found that 75% considered oral, written, and interpersonal skills even more important for finance professionals now than they were just a few years ago.[95]

The skills you polish along the way can stand you in good stead for the rest of your life: critical thinking, computer savvy, problem solving, and the ability to write, speak, and work well with other people are vital in most jobs. It's almost a cliché, but it is still true: the most important knowledge you gain in college is how to learn.

Summary by Learning Objectives

LO 4-1   Why ethics is so important in business communication.

The economic news continues to create concern over lapses in business ethics. On the other hand, positive ethical efforts are also increasing.

LO 4-2   How corporate culture impacts the business environment.

Corporate cultures range from informal to formal and impact such widely diverse areas as worker performance and sales.

LO 4-3   Why interpersonal communication is important.

Interpersonal communication includes such areas as listening, conversational style, body language, etiquette, and networking. Its importance in career success is receiving new recognition.

LO 4-4   How to use your time more efficiently.

Time management skills are also crucial to job success. Probably the most important time management technique is to prioritize the demands on your time, and make sure you spend the majority of your time on the most important demands.

Decades of research on multitasking show that it does not increase job performance and may actually hinder it.

LO 4-5   What the trends in business communication are.

Twelve trends in business, government, and non-profit organizations affect business and administrative communication: data security, electronic privacy, customer service, work/family balance, environmental concern, globalization and outsourcing, diversity, teamwork, job flexibility, innovation and entrepreneurship, big data, and rapid change.

Continuing Case

The All-Weather Case, set in an HR department in a manufacturing company, extends through all 19 chapters and is available at www.mhhe.com/locker11e. The portion for this chapter asks students to create a message introducing a change in the problem-solving environment at the company.

Exercises and Cases

Go to www.mhhe.com/locker11e *for additional Exercises and Cases.*

4.1   Reviewing the Chapter

1. What are some positive ethical efforts that are getting attention? (LO 4-1)
2. What are some ethical components of communication? (LO 4-1)
3. What are some elements of corporate culture? How do they affect business? (LO 4-2)
4. What are some ways to improve interpersonal communication? (LO 4-3)

5. What are some communication signals you might receive from specific body language cues? (LO 4-3)
6. What are some ways to manage your time more efficiently? (LO 4-4)
7. What are 12 trends in business communication? What do these trends mean for you? (LO 4-5)
8. What are some electronic privacy issues that could affect you at your workplace? (LO 4-5)

4.2   Protecting Privacy Online

As companies demand ever more accurate audiences to whom they can pitch their products and services, the debate over online tracking versus privacy continues.

1. Working in small groups, discuss some of the challenges you see to protecting your privacy on the Internet.

   - Should companies be allowed to track your online activity? Is it OK if they notify you they are tracking you? Do you like targeted placement ads, similar to Google's recommendations for you? Where do you find a balance between allowing Internet sites to use your information to provide better service and protecting your privacy?
   - Are employers justified in monitoring employees' e-mail, Twitter, and Internet usage on company machines?
   - Are employers justified in monitoring employees' Facebook accounts? Do you think it

is fair when employees get fired for comments they post on their Facebook site?
   - What do you think of companies such as Google tracking searches to produce sites like Google Flu Trends, which shows where people are getting sick during flu season?

2. The Federal Trade Commission is considering a "Do Not Track" option. Like the Do Not Call Registry, it would offer consumers a way to avoid some electronic marketing. See http://www.ftc.gov/opa/reporter/privacy/donottrack.shtml for more information. If such an option becomes available, would you use it? Suppose that big websites such as Google or Facebook started dropping Do Not Track customers. How would that action influence your opinion? Write an e-mail to your instructor explaining your decision.

4.3   Following Trends in Business Communication

Pick three of the trends discussed in this chapter and explain how they have impacted business communications in an organization where you—or a friend or family member—have worked.

As your instructor directs,
a. Share your information in small groups.
b. Present your group findings to your classmates.
c. Post your information online for your classmates.

4.4   Applying Ethics Guidelines

Reread the ethics guidelines by Warren Buffett ("Warren Buffett on Ethics," page 88) and Tony Hsieh (page 91). In small groups, apply them to some business ethics situations currently in the news or occurring in your discipline.

   - How would the situations be handled by Buffett? Hsieh?
   - Do you approve of those solutions?
   - Do you find one statement more helpful than the other? Why?

4.5   Making Ethical Choices

Indicate whether you consider each of the following actions ethical, unethical, or a gray area. Which of the actions would you do? Which would you feel uncomfortable doing? Which would you refuse to do?

Discuss your answers with a small group of classmates. In what ways did knowing you would share with a group change your answers?

1. Taking home office supplies (e.g., pens, markers, calculators, etc.) for personal use.
2. Inflating your evaluation of a subordinate because you know that only people ranked *excellent* will get pay raises.
3. Making personal long-distance calls on the company phone.
4. Updating your Facebook page and visiting the pages of friends during business hours.
5. Writing a feasibility report about a new product and de-emphasizing test results that show it could cause cancer.
6. Coming in to the office in the evening to use the company's computer for personal projects.
7. Designing an ad campaign for a cigarette brand.
8. Working as an accountant for a company that makes or advertises cigarettes.
9. Working as a manager in a company that exploits its nonunionized hourly workers.
10. Writing copy for a company's annual report hiding or minimizing the fact that the company pollutes the environment.
11. "Padding" your expense account by putting on it charges you did not pay for.
12. Telling a job candidate that the company "usually" grants cost-of-living raises every six months, even though you know that the company is losing money and plans to cancel cost-of-living raises for the next year.
13. Laughing at the racist or sexist jokes a client makes, even though you find them offensive.
14. Reading the *Wall Street Journal* on company time.

4.6   Analyzing Business Ethics

New Oriental Education & Technology Group offers Chinese students intensive courses to prepare for SAT, GRE, and TOEFL exams. The object of the courses is to enable the students to achieve scores that will get them into American colleges and universities. The courses provide traditional prep help, such as cramming vocabulary words, but they also offer more controversial techniques.

■ The courses avail themselves of websites where students download the test questions they remember immediately after the exam. Because the tests do recycle some questions to ensure score consistency over time, the courses can prep students for actual exam questions.

■ They provide tricks (e.g., females in the test passages are always smarter than males) that help students choose correct answers just by looking at the choices, without understanding the passages.

■ Since many of the students are good at math, they recommend that five minutes into the math section, their students should flip back to the reading section and finish it. Flipping is prohibited, but this timing helps students escape the attention of the proctors, who look for it at the beginning and end of each test section.

■ They help students prepare essays and speeches on topics—such as biographies of famous Americans—that can be memorized and adapted to many situations, thus avoiding extemporaneous performances.

The upside of these efforts is that many of the students do fulfill dreams of getting into American schools. The downside is that many of these same students have such poor English skills that they cannot understand the lectures or participate in class discussions. Nor can they write class papers without help. Unfortunately, they score so well that they even sometimes test out of the transitional programs many schools have to help students with shaky English skills.[96]

Is New Oriental an ethical business?

What would Warren Buffett say (see page 88)?

What would Tony Hsieh say (see page 91)?

How does New Oriental fare using Michael Davis's tests (see page 91)?

What are New Oriental's effects on its students?

Why do American schools accept these students?

What could be done to make the situation more ethical?

4.7   Analyzing Communication Ethics

Reread the "Egg-semplary Ethics" sidebar, page 89. In small groups, discuss what you would have done in that situation.

■ What aspects of the situation would have made you break the confidentiality agreement?
■ What aspects of the case would make you keep quiet?

- Apply the tests in Michael Davis's ethical decision-making system (page 91). Which tests most help you to decide what you would do in this situation?

- Did everyone in your group reach the same conclusion? What reasons were most commonly given?

4.8 Analyzing Corporate Culture: I

Some businesses are deciding not to hire people with visible body art. Do you think such policies are allowable expressions of corporate culture, or are they a form of discrimination? Discuss your answers in small groups.

4.9 Analyzing Corporate Culture: II

Go to *Fortune*'s "100 Best Companies to Work For" website: http://money.cnn.com/magazines/fortune/best-companies/.

Look up six companies you find interesting. What are unique features of their corporate culture? What features seem to be common with many companies? Which features did you find particularly appealing? Write an e-mail for your instructor containing your findings.

4.10 Analyzing Customer Service

Go to a business on campus or in your community where you can observe customer service for a half hour. Make sure you observe at least three different kinds of service.

- Where did you go? Why?
- What categories of service did you observe?
- What examples of good service did you see?

- What examples of service that could be improved did you see? How would you improve it?
- If you were the manager of the business, what changes would you make to impact customer service?

Write an e-mail to your instructor containing your findings.

4.11 Analyzing Nonverbal Communication

Choose one of your courses and make notes on nonverbal communications you see in the classroom.

- What are some dominant traits you see among the students?
- What are some interesting behaviors you see in individual students?
- Does the nonverbal communication differ from the beginning and end of the class?

- What are nonverbal communications from the instructor?
- Overall, what does the nonverbal communication in the classroom tell you about student learning in that class?

Write an e-mail to your instructor containing your findings.

4.12 Analyzing Body Language: I

Go to www.ted.com and search for "Body Language." Watch the Ted Talk by social psychologist Amy Cuddy, "Your Body Language Shapes Who You Are." After watching the video, break into small groups and discuss the following questions.

- When have you made a judgment about someone based upon that person's nonverbal communication? Describe the situation: What were they doing? What did you think of them?
- Think back to the last stressful evaluative experience you had (such as an interview or class presentation). How did you feel during that time? Do you remember how you were standing or sitting?

- Practice some power poses. Each person in your group should practice a power pose for two minutes. After those two minutes, have each person present his or her career goals in a one-minute presentation to the rest of the group. Observe each other carefully. How does each person look? Discuss body language and presence.
- Outside-of-class activity: Tell your friends about the Ted Talk by Amy Cuddy, and encourage them to try their own power poses. Take pictures of them in their power poses and bring to class for discussion.

4.13   Analyzing Body Language: II

Go to a location such as your campus or city library where you can watch people at work and rest. Spend a half hour observing examples of body language around you. Make sure your half hour includes examples of at least one group at work, individuals at work, and individuals relaxing.

- What interesting examples of body language did you note?
- What were some common features of body language?

- Did you see any unique body language?
- Could you make assumptions about group relations based on the body language you saw exhibited by members of the group?
- How did the body language of individuals who were relaxing differ from that of the group members?

Write an e-mail for your instructor containing your findings.

4.14   Analyzing Your Time Management

For two days, write down exactly how you spend your time. Be specific. Don't just say "two hours studying." Instead, write how long you spent on each item of study (e.g., 15 min. reviewing underlinings in sociology chapter, 20 min. reviewing class notes, an hour and 20 min. reading accounting chapter). Include time spent on items such as grooming, eating, talking with friends (both in person and on phone), texting, watching television, and sleeping.

Now analyze your time record. Does anything surprise you? How much time did you spend studying? Is it enough? Did you spend more time studying your

most important subjects? Your hardest subjects? Did you spend time on projects that are due later in the term? Did you spend time on health-related items? Do you see items on which you spent too much time? Too little time? Did you spend any time on items that would fit in Stephen Covey's quadrant II (see page 101)?

As your instructor directs,

a.   Share your findings in small groups.

b.   Write an e-mail for your instructor containing your findings.

4.15   Analyzing the Business Environment Where You Work

In an e-mail to your instructor, describe and analyze the business environment at an organization where you have worked. Use this chapter as a guide for content. What

aspects of the environment did you like? Dislike? What aspects helped your job performance? What aspects hindered your job performance?

4.16   Participating in a Networking Event

In this exercise, you are going to participate in a networking event, an abbreviated "talk and walk."

To prepare for the event,

- Create business cards for yourself, using a computer application of your choice.
- List people in your class whom you would like to meet (give a visual description if you do not know their names).
- Make a list of questions you would like to have answered.
- Collect materials to use for taking notes during the event.

During the event, you will have six three-minute sessions to talk with a fellow student and exchange business cards. Your instructor will time the sessions and tell you when to change people. Remember that the other person also has questions she or he wants answered.

After the event, analyze what you have learned. Here are some questions to get you started:

- Who was the most interesting? Why?
- Who did you like the most? Why?
- Who would you most like to have on a team in this class? Why?
- Did you meet anyone who might become a professional contact? Explain.
- What lessons did you learn about networking?

As your instructor directs,

a.   Share your analyses in small groups; then prepare an informal oral report for the class.

b.   Write your analysis in an e-mail to your teacher.

c.   Write your analysis in an e-mail to post on your class website.

Notes

1. James O'Toole, "New York Sues Credit Suisse in Latest Mortgage Lawsuit," *CNNMoney,* November 20, 2012, http://money.cnn.com/2012/11/20/investing/credit-suisse-new-york/index.html?eref=mrss_igoogle_business.

2. Charles Riley and Emily Jane Fox, "GlaxoSmithKline in $3 Billion Fraud Settlement," *CNNMoney,* July 2, 2012, http://money.cnn.com/2012/07/02/news/companies/GlaxoSmithKline-settlement/index.htm; and Peter Loftus and Jon Kamp, "Glaxo To Pay $750 Million in Pact; Whistleblower Due Big Payment," *Wall Street Journal,* November 27, 2010, B3.

3. James O'Toole, "Visa, MasterCard Settle Antitrust Case," *CNNMoney,* July 13, 2012, http://money.cnn.com/2012/07/13/news/companies/visa-mastercard-settlement/index.htm.

4. Howard Mustoe and Gavin Finch, "HSBC Apologizes to Investors for Compliance Failures," *Businessweek.com,* July 30, 2012, http://www.businessweek.com/news/2012-07-30/hsbc-profit-beats-estimates-on-income-from-asset-sales.

5. Joe Palazzolo, "FCPA Inc.: The Business of Bribery," *Wall Street Journal,* October 2, 2012, B1.

6. Mary Williams Walsh and Ron Nixon, "S.&P. E-Mails on Mortgage Crisis Show Alarm and Gallows Humor," *DealBook,* February 5, 2013, http://dealbook.nytimes.com/2013/02/05/case-details-internal-tension-at-s-p-amid-subprime-problems/.

7. Michael Rothfeld, Susan Pulliam, and Chad Bray, "Fund Titan Found Guilty," *Wall Street Journal,* May 12, 2011, A1.

8. Ethics Resource Center, *2011 National Business Ethics Survey,* 12, 39, accessed April 11, 2013, http://www.ethics.org/nbes/files/FinalNBES-web.pdf.

9. Mary C. Gentile, "Keeping Your Colleagues Honest," *Harvard Business Review* 88, no. 2 (February 2010): 114–15.

10. "United Nations Global Compact Participants," *United Nations Global Compact,* October 23, 2012, http://www.unglobalcompact.org/ParticipantsAndStakeholders/index.html.

11. "About Us," *Clinton Global Initiative,* accessed April 12, 2013, http://www.clintonglobalinitiative.org/aboutus/default.asp.

12. Google, "About," accessed April 12, 2013, http://www.google.org/about.html.

13. "Robin Hood," accessed May 8, 2013, http://www.robinhood.org; and Andy Serwer, "The Legend of Robin Hood," *Fortune,* September 18, 2006, 103–14.

14. Merck, "The Merck MECTIZAN Donation Program—River Blindness," accessed April 23, 2013, http://www.merck.com/cr/docs/River%20Blindness%20Fact%20Sheet.pdf.

15. Marc Benioff and Karen Southwick, *Compassionate Capitalism: How Corporations Can Make Doing Good an Integral Part of Doing Well* (Franklin Lakes, NJ: Career Press, 2004), 101–04.

16. Quoted from Tony Hsieh, *Delivering Happiness: A Path to Profits, Passion, and Purpose* (New York: Business Plus, 2010), 243.

17. Michael Davis, *Ethics and the University* (New York: Routledge, 1999), 166–67.

18. M. Rose, "Three-Ring Ad Circus: Ogilvy & Mather's Surreal Canton Fun House," *Bloomberg Businessweek,* October 8, 2012, 88–89.

19. Leigh Buchanan, "Learning from the Best: Smart Strategies from the Top Small Company Workplaces," *Inc.,* June 2010, 92.

20. Ellen Byron, "Merger Challenge: Unite Toothbrush, Toothpaste: P&G and Gillette Find Creating Synergy Can Be Harder than It Looks," *Wall Street Journal,* April 24, 2007, A1.

21. Phred Dvorak, "Hotelier Finds Happiness Keeps Staff Checked In," *Wall Street Journal,* December 17, 2007, B3.

22. Hsieh, *Delivering Happiness,* 150–65.

23. Ibid., 148.

24. Daniel Goleman, *Emotional Intelligence: The Tenth Anniversary Edition* (New York: Bantam, 2005), xiv–xv.

25. Thomas Gordon and Judith Gordon Sands, *P.E.T. in Action* (New York: P. H. Wyden, 1976), 117–18.

26. Deborah Tannen, *That's Not What I Meant!: How Conversational Style Makes or Breaks Relationships,* Rei Rep ed. (New York: Harper Perennial, 2011).

27. Daniel N. Maltz and Ruth A. Borker, "A Cultural Approach to Male–Female Miscommunication," in *Language and Social Identity,* ed. John J. Gumperz (Cambridge: Cambridge University Press, 1982), 202.

28. Marie Helweg-Larson et al., "To Nod or Not to Nod: An Observational Study of Nonverbal Communication and Status in Female and Male College Students," *Psychology of Women Quarterly* 28, no. 4 (2004): 358–61.

29. Carol Kinsey Goman, "10 Common Body Language Traps for Women in the Workplace," *On Leadership* (blog), *Washington Post,* March 3, 2011, http://www.washingtonpost.com/blogs/on-leadership/post/10-common-body-language-traps-for-women-in-the-workplace/2011/03/03/AFl0GFbF_blog.html.

30. Alex Pentland, "We Can Measure the Power of Charisma," *Harvard Business Review* 88, no.1 (January 2010): 34.

31. Alex "Sandy" Pentland, "The Power of Nonverbal Communication," *Wall Street Journal,* October 20, 2008, R2.

32. Carol Kinsey Goman, "10 Simple and Powerful Body Language Tips for 2013," *Forbes,* January 7, 2013, http://www.forbes.com/sites/carolkinseygoman/2013/01/07/10-simple-and-powerful-body-language-tips-for-2013/2/; and "Leadership: Strike a Pose," *Inc.,* May 2012, 108–12.

33. Goleman, *Emotional Intelligence,* 161–62.

34. Ibid., 162.

35. "Social Studies," *Businessweek,* June 14, 2010, 72–3.

36. Jessica Hodgins, "'You Can't Make More Time': Randy Pausch's Heart-felt Views on Using Time to the Fullest," *BusinessWeek,* September 1, 2008, 71.

37. Stephen R. Covey, *The 7 Habits of Highly Effective People: Powerful Lessons in Personal Change* (New York: Free Press, 2004), 150–54.

38. Jared Sandberg, "Yes, Sell All My Stocks. No, the 3:15 from JFK. and Get Me Mr. Sister," *Wall Street Journal,* September 12, 2006, B1.

39. Toddi Gutner, "Beat the Clock: E-mails, Faxes, Phone Calls, Oh My. Here's How to Get It All Done," *BusinessWeek SmallBiz,* February/March 2008, 58.

40. Adam Gorlick, "Media Multitaskers Pay Mental Price, Stanford Study Shows," *Stanford Report,* August 24, 2009, http://news.stanford.edu/news/2009/august24/multitask-research-study-082409.html.

41. Rachel Emma Jackson, "Here's Why You Won't Finish This Article" *Wall Street Journal,* December 12, 2012, B1.

42. Sharon Begley, "Will the BlackBerry Sink the Presidency?" *Newsweek*, February 16, 2009, 37.

43. Nick Wingfield, Ian Sherr, and Ben Worthen, "Hacker Raids Sony Videogame Network," *Wall Street Journal*, April 27, 2011, A1; Parmy Olson, "FBI Agent's Laptop 'Hacked' to Grab 12 Million Apple IDs," *Forbes.com*, September 4, 2012, http://www.forbes.com/sites/parmyolson/2012/09/04/fbi-agents-laptop-hacked-to-grab-12-million-apple-ids-anonymous-claims/; David Goldman, "More Than 6 Million LinkedIn Passwords Stolen," *CNNMoney*, June 6, 2012, http://money.cnn.com/2012/06/06/technology/linkedin-password-hack/index.htm; and "Nation and World Watch," *Des Moines Register*, October 30, 2012, 2A.

44. Michael Chertoff, "How Safe Is Your Data?" *Wall Street Journal*, January 22, 2013, B16.

45. Stephanie Armour, "Employers Look Closely at What Workers Do on Job: Companies Get More Vigilant as Technology Increases their Risks," *USA Today*, November 8, 2006, 2B; and M. P. McQueen, "Laptop Lockdown: Companies Start Holding Employees Responsible for Security of Portable Devices They Use for Work," *Wall Street Journal*, June 28, 2006, D1.

46. American Management Association, "The Latest on Workplace Monitoring and Surveillance," March 13, 2008, http://www.amanet.org/training/articles/The-Latest-on-Workplace-Monitoring-and-Surveillance.aspx.

47. Chris Newmarker, "On the Off-Ramp to Adultery, There's No Fooling E-ZPass," *Des Moines Register*, August 12, 2007, 8A.

48. Armour, "Employers Look Closely at What Workers Do on Job"; M. P. McQueen, "Workers' Terminations for Computer Misuse Rise," *Wall Street Journal*, July 15, 2006, B4; and "Burger King Fires Workers over Blogs," *Wall Street Journal*, May 14, 2008, A18.

49. Dalia Fahmy, "Can You Be Fired for Sending Personal E-Mails at Work?" *ABC News*, December 17, 2009, http://abcnews.go.com/Business/GadgetGuide/supreme-court-employee-rights-privacy-workplace-emails/story?id59345057.

50. John Markoff, "Armies of Expensive Lawyers, Replaced by Cheaper Software," *New York Times*, March 4, 2011, http://www.nytimes.com/2011/03/05/science/05legal.html.

51. Karen Weise, "Who Does Google Think You Are?" *Bloomberg Businessweek*, February 6, 2012, 39–40.

52. Alexandra Alter, "Your E-Book is Reading You," *Wall Street Journal*, June 29, 2012, D1.

53. "Twitter Tirades Test Free-Speech Limits," *Des Moines Register*, November 25, 2010, 4A.

54. Lauren A.E. Schuker, "Secret Texting…Pass It On," *Wall Street Journal*, February 4, 2011, B11.

55. Nick Wingfield and Julia Angwin, "Microsoft Adds Privacy Tool," *Wall Street Journal*, March 15, 2011, B1.

56. Emily Steel and Jessica E. Vascellaro, "FTC Backs Web-Ad Self-Regulation: Agency Lays Out Principles for Protecting the Privacy of 'Targeted' Users," *Wall Street Journal*, February 13, 2009, B7.

57. Evelyn M. Rusli, "Facebook Simplifies Privacy Settings," *Wall Street Journal*, December 13, 2012, B4.

58. Julia Angwin and Tom McGinty, "Sites Feed Personal Details to New Tracking Industry," *Wall Street Journal*, July 31, 2010, A1; Scott Thurm and Yukari Iwatani Kane, "Your Apps Are Watching You," *Wall Street Journal*, December 18, 2010, C1.

59. Christopher W. Hart, "Beating the Market with Customer Satisfaction," *Harvard Business Review* 85, no. 3 (March 2007): 30–32.

60. "Frequently Asked Questions: What Can ACSI Tell Us," *American Customer Satisfaction Index*, accessed May 9, 2013, http://www.theacsi.org/index.php?option5com_content&view5article&id546&Itemid5124#what_can.

61. Dana Mattioli, "Customer Service as a Growth Engine," *Wall Street Journal*, June 7, 2010, B6.

62. "2012 Working Mother 100 Best Companies," *Working Mother*, accessed April 14, 2013, http://www.working-mother.com/best-company-list/129110/7271.

63. Elise Hu, "Working from Home: The End of Productivity or the Future of Work?" *NPR*, February 25, 2013, http://www.npr.org/blogs/alltechconsidered/2013/02/23/172792467/working-from-home-the-end-of-productivity-or-the-future-of-work.

64. "Daily Report: Yahoo's In-Office Policy Aims to Bolster Morale," *Bits*, blog entry, March 6, 2013, http://bits.blogs.nytimes.com/2013/03/06/daily-report-yahoos-in-office-policy-aims-to-bolster-morale/; and "Why Both Sides Are Wrong in the Debate Over Telecommuting," *Bloomberg.com*, March 4, 2013, http://www.bloomberg.com/news/2013-03-04/why-both-sides-are-wrong-in-the-debate-over-telecommuting-view.html.

65. Rachel Emma Silverman and Quentin Fottrell, "The Home Office in the Spotlight," *Wall Street Journal*, February 27, 2013, B6.

66. "Why Both Sides Are Wrong."

67. Betsy McKay and Suzanne Vranica, "Firms Use Earth Day to Show Their Green Side," *Wall Street Journal*, April 22, 2008, B7.

68. Gwendolyn Bounds, "Misleading Claims on 'Green' Labeling," *Wall Street Journal*, October 26, 2010, D4.

69. Marianne Mason and Robert D. Mason, "Communicating a Green Corporate Perspective: Ideological Persuasion in the Corporate Environmental Report," *Journal of Business and Technical Communication* 26, no. 4 (2012): 481, doi:10.1177/1050651912448872.

70. Susan Berfield, "Levi's Has a New Color for Blue Jeans: Green," *Bloomberg Businessweek*, October 22, 2012, 26–28; Ramit Plushnick-Masti, "Beverage Companies Investing Millions for Water Conservation," *Des Moines Register*, August 11, 2012, 7B; and PepsiCo, "PepsiCo Achieves Safe Water Access Goal," press release, March 28, 2013, http://www.pepsico.com/PressRelease/PepsiCo-Achieves-Safe-Water-Access-Goal03282013.html.

71. McDonald's Corporation, "McDonald's Canada: FAQs," accessed April 14, 2013, http://www.mcdonalds.ca/ca/en/contact_us/faq.html.

72. UPS, "Worldwide Facts," accessed April 14, 2013, http://www.ups.com/content/us/en/about/facts/worldwide.html.

73. Coca-Cola, "Our Company," accessed April 14, 2013, http://www.coca-colacompany.com/our-company/.

74. Walmart, "Our Locations," accessed April 14, 2013, http://corporate.walmart.com/our-story/locations.

75. Thomas L. Friedman, *The World Is Flat: A Brief History of the Twenty-First Century*, updated and expanded ed. (New York: Farrar, Straus, and Giroux, 2006), 14.

76. Ibid., 86.

77. Christine Uber Grosse, "Managing Communication within Virtual Intercultural Teams," *Business Communication Quarterly* (2002): 22; and Linda H. Heuring, "Patients First," *HRMagazine*, July 2003, 67–68.

78. Sue Shellenbarger, "Some Companies Rethink the Telecommuting Trend," *Wall Street Journal,* February 28, 2008, D1.

79. Heuring, "Patients First."

80. Jörgen Sandberg, "Understanding Competence at Work," *Harvard Business Review* 79, no. 3 (2001): 24–28.

81. "Xerox CEO: 'If You Don't Transform, You're Stuck,'" *NPR,* May23,2012,http://www.npr.org/2012/05/23/153302563/xerox-ceo-if-you-don-t-transform-you-re-stuck.

82. Tom Kelley and David Kelley, "Reclaim Your Creative Confidence," *Harvard Business Review* 90, no. 12 (December 2012): 115–18.

83. Ibid.

84. InnoCentive, "About Us: Facts & Stats," March 1, 2013, http://www.innocentive.com/about-innocentive/facts-stats.

85. Kelley and Kelley, "Reclaim Your Creative Confidence."

86. Linda Tischler, "A Designer Takes on His Biggest Challenge Ever," *Fast Company,* February 2009, 78–83, 101.

87. L. D. DeSimone et al., "How Can Big Companies Keep the Entrepreneurial Spirit Alive?" *Harvard Business Review* 73, no. 6 (1995): 183–92.

88. "How Google Fuels Its Idea Factory," *BusinessWeek,* May 12, 2008, 54–55.

89. U.S. Census Bureau, "Census Bureau Reports Nation Has Nearly 350,000 Fewer Nonemployer Business Locations," press release, June 24, 2010, http://www.census.gov/newsroom/releases/archives/business_ownership/cb10-93.html.

90. Andrew McAfee and Erik Brynjolfsson, "Big Data: The Management Revolution," *Harvard Business Review* 90, no. 10 (October 2012): 62.

91. "Bigger and Bigger," *Wall Street Journal,* January 22, 2013, B14.

92. L. Gordon Crovitz, "Why 'Big Data' Is a Big Deal," *Wall Street Journal,* March 25, 2013, A15.

93. Steven Rosenbush and Michael Totty, "How Big Data Is Changing the Whole Equation for Business," *Wall Street Journal,* March 11, 2013, R2.

94. McAfee and Brynjolfsson, "Big Data: The Management Revolution."

95. Max Messmer, "Soft Skills Are Key to Advancing Your Career," *Business Credit* 109, no. 4 (2007): 34.

96. Daniel Golden, "U.S. College Test Prep in China Is: [sic]" *Bloomberg Businessweek,* May 9, 2011, 58–63.

5 Planning, Composing, and Revising

Chapter Outline

NEWSWORTHY COMMUNICATION

"Pink Slime": Billion Dollar Words

In September 2012, Beef Products Inc. (BPI) sued ABC News for $1.2 billion over two words: *Pink Slime*.

For more than 30 years, BPI has produced "lean, finely textured beef," a product made from beef trimmings treated with ammonia and added as filler in some ground beef. Although cleared by the U.S. Department of Agriculture (USDA), its safety came into question from some 2011 news reports.

ABC News reports described BPI's product as *pink slime*, a term coined by a USDA microbiologist in 2002. The term caught on and quickly spread through social media.

The effect of *pink slime* was swift. Restaurant chains, grocery stores, and school cafeterias eliminated products that contained it. In 28 days, BPI's business dropped by 80%, and the company was forced to shut three of its plants and lay off more than 700 employees.

BPI's attorney blamed the losses on ABC News: "To call a food product slime is the most pejorative term that could be imagined. ABC's constant repetition of it . . . had a huge impact on the consuming public." ABC's lawyers disagreed, calling *pink slime* "the sort of 'loose, figurative, or hyperbolic language' that courts recognize demands protection under the First Amendment."

Two small but powerful words nearly destroyed BPI's business and could cost ABC more than a billion dollars. In preparing documents, professionals should always be careful of the wording they use and the impression it conveys to an audience.

Sources: Bill Tomson, "ABC Sued for 'Pink Slime' Defamation," *Wall Street Journal,* September 14, 2012, B3; Daniel P. Finney, "'Pink Slime': Two Small Words Trigger Big Lawsuit," *Des Moines Register,* September 14, 2012, 1A; Jonathan Stempel, "ABC News Sued for Defamation Over 'Pink Slime' Reports," *Reuters,* September 13, 2012, http://www.reuters.com/article/2012/09/13/us-usa-beef-pinkslime-lawsuit-idUSBRE88C0R720120913; and Martha Graybow, "ABC News Seeks Dismissal of Beef Products' Defamation Lawsuit," *Reuters,* October 31, 2012, http://www.reuters.com/article/2012/11/01/us-usa-beef-pinkslime-abclawsuit-idUSBRE8A002F20121101.

After studying this chapter, you will know

LO 5-1 Activities involved in the composing process, and how to use these activities to your advantage.

LO 5-2 Guidelines for effective word choice, sentence construction, and paragraph organization.

LO 5-3 Techniques to revise, edit, and proofread your communications.

Ethics and the Writing Process

As you plan a message,

- Identify all audiences of the message.
- In difficult situations, seek allies in your organization and discuss your options with them.

As you compose,

- Provide accurate and complete information.
- Use reliable sources of material. Document when necessary.
- Warn your readers of limits or dangers in your information.
- Promise only what you can deliver.

As you revise,

- Check to see that your language is clear to the audience and bias-free.
- Use feedback to revise text and visuals that your audience may misunderstand.
- Check your sources.
- Assume that no document is confidential. E-mail documents, texts, and IMs (instant messages) can be forwarded and printed without your knowledge; both electronic and paper documents, including drafts, can be subpoenaed for court cases.

Skilled performances look easy and effortless. In reality, as every dancer, musician, and athlete knows, they're the products of hard work, hours of practice, attention to detail, and intense concentration. Like skilled performances in other arts, writing rests on a base of work.

The Ways Good Writers Write

No single writing process works for all writers all of the time. However, good writers and poor writers seem to use different processes.[1] Good writers are more likely to

- Realize that the first draft can be revised.
- Write regularly.
- Break big jobs into small chunks.
- Have clear goals focusing on purpose and audience.
- Have several different strategies to choose from.
- Use rules flexibly.
- Wait to edit until after the draft is complete.

The research also shows that good writers differ from poor writers in identifying and analyzing the initial problem more effectively, understanding the task more broadly and deeply, drawing from a wider repertoire of strategies, and seeing patterns more clearly. Good writers also are better at evaluating their own work.

Thinking about the writing process and consciously adopting the processes of good writers will help you become a better writer.

Activities in the Composing Process **LO 5-1**

Composing can include many activities: planning, brainstorming, gathering, organizing, writing, evaluating, getting feedback, revising, editing, and proofreading. The activities do not have to come in this order. Not every task demands all activities.

Planning

- Analyzing the problem, defining your purposes, and analyzing the audience.

- Brainstorming information to include in the document.

- Gathering the information you need—from the message you're answering, a person, printed sources, or the web.

- Selecting the points you want to make and the examples, data, and arguments to support them.

- Choosing a pattern of organization, making an outline, creating a list.

Writing

- Putting words on paper or a screen. Writing can be lists, possible headings, fragmentary notes, stream-of-consciousness writing, and partial drafts.

- Creating rough drafts.

- Composing a formal draft.

Revising

- Evaluating your work and measuring it against your goals and the requirements of the situation and audience. The best evaluation results from *re-seeing* your draft as if someone else had written it. Will your audience understand it? Is it complete? Convincing? Friendly?

- Getting feedback from someone else. Is all the necessary information there? Is there too much information? Is your pattern of organization appropriate? Does a revision solve an earlier problem? Are there obvious mistakes?

- Adding, deleting, substituting, or rearranging. Revision can be changes in single words or in large sections of a document.

Editing

- Checking the draft to see that it satisfies the requirements of standard English. Here you'd correct spelling and mechanical errors and check word choice and format. Unlike revision, which can produce major changes in meaning, editing focuses on the surface of writing.

- Proofreading the final copy to see that it's free from typographical errors.

Note the following points about these activities:

- **The activities do not have to come in this order.** Some people may gather data *after* writing a draft when they see that they need more specifics to achieve their purposes.

A Writer on Writing

Donald Murray, a Pulitzer-winning journalist, former editor of *Time*, and author of a major text on revision, says this about writing:

"*The myth:* The writer sits down, turns on the faucet, and writing pours out—clean, graceful, correct, ready for the printer.

"*The reality:* The writer gets something—anything—down on paper, reads it, tries it again, rereads, rewrites, again and again."

He says his writing was held back by these three false beliefs:

- "Good writing was spontaneous writing.

- Rewriting was punishment for failure. . . .

- Revision was a matter of superficial correction that forced my natural style to conform to an old-fashioned, inferior style."

Adapted and quoted from Donald M. Murray, *The Craft of Revision* (Chicago: Holt, Rinehart, and Winston, 1991), 1.

- ■ **You do not have to finish one activity to start another.** Some writers plan a short section and write it, plan the next short section and write it, and so on through the document. Evaluating what is already written may cause a writer to do more planning or to change the original plan.

- ■ **Most writers do not use all activities for all the documents they write.** You'll use more activities when you write more complex or difficult documents about new subjects or to audiences that are new to you.

For many workplace writers, pre-writing is not a warm-up activity to get ready to write the "real" document. It's really a series of activities designed to gather and organize information, take notes, brainstorm with colleagues, and plan a document before writing a complete draft. And for many people, these activities do not include outlining. Traditional outlining may lull writers into a false sense of confidence about their material and organization, making it difficult for them to revise their content and structure if they deviate from the outline developed early in the process.

Using Your Time Effectively

To get the best results from the time you have, spend only one-third of your time actually "writing." Spend at least another one-third of your time analyzing the situation and your audience, gathering information, and organizing what you have to say. Spend the final third evaluating what you've said, revising the draft(s) to meet your purposes and the needs of the audience and the organization, editing a late draft to remove any errors in grammar and mechanics, and proofreading the final copy.

Do realize, however, that different writers, documents, and situations may need different time divisions to produce quality communications, especially if documents are produced by teams. Geographic distance will add even more time to the process.

Not all writing has to be completed in office settings. Some people work better outside, in coffee shops, or from home.

Brainstorming, Planning, and Organizing Business Documents

Spend significant time planning and organizing before you begin to write. The better your ideas are when you start, the fewer drafts you'll need to produce a good document. Start by using the analysis questions from Chapter 1 to identify purpose and audience. Use the strategies described in Chapter 2 to analyze audience and identify benefits. Gather information you can use for your document. Select the points you want to make—and the examples and data to support them.

Sometimes your content will be determined by the situation. Sometimes, even when it's up to you to think of information to include in a report, you'll find it easy to think of ideas. If ideas won't come, try the following techniques:

- **Brainstorming.** Think of all the ideas you can, without judging them. Consciously try to get at least a dozen different ideas before you stop. Good brainstorming depends on generating many ideas.

- **Freewriting.**[2] Make yourself write, without stopping, for 10 minutes or so, even if you must write "I will think of something soon." At the end of 10 minutes, read what you've written, identify the best point in the draft, then set it aside, and write for another 10 uninterrupted minutes. Read this draft, marking anything that's good and should be kept, and then write again for another 10 minutes. By the third session, you will probably produce several sections that are worth keeping—maybe even a complete draft that's ready to be revised.

- **Clustering.**[3] Write your topic in the middle of the page and circle it. Write down the ideas the topic suggests, circling them, too. (The circles are designed to tap into the nonlinear half of your brain.) When you've filled the page, look for patterns or repeated ideas. Use different colored pens to group related ideas. Then use these ideas to develop your content.

- **Talking to your audiences.** As research shows, talking to internal and external audiences helps writers to involve readers in the planning process and to understand the social and political relationships among readers. This preliminary work helps reduce the number of revisions needed before documents are approved.[4]

Thinking about the content, layout, or structure of your document can also give you ideas. For long documents, write out the headings you'll use. For short documents, jot down key points—information to include, objections to answer, benefits to develop. For an oral presentation, a meeting, or a document with lots of visuals, try creating a **storyboard,** with a rectangle representing each page or unit. Draw a box with a visual for each main point. Below the box, write a short caption or label.

Writing Good Business and Administrative Documents

After you have a collection of ideas, it is time to put them in a draft of your document. In *Bird by Bird: Some Instructions on Writing and Life,* writer Anne Lamott call this first draft the "down draft": you just get your ideas down—without worrying about writing skills such as supporting detail, organization, or mechanics.[5] Don't even worry about completeness at this point.

Overcoming Writer's Block

These actions help overcome writer's block:

1. **Prepare for writing.** Collect and arrange material. Talk to people; interact with some of your audiences. The more you learn about the company, its culture, and its context, the easier it will be to write—and the better your writing will be.

2. **Practice writing regularly and in moderation.** Try to write almost daily. Keep sessions to a moderate length; an hour to an hour and a half is ideal for many people.

3. **Talk positively to yourself:** "I can do this." "If I keep working, ideas will come." "It doesn't have to be perfect; I can make it better later."

4. **Talk to other people about writing.** Value the feedback you get from them. Talking to other people expands your repertoire of strategies and helps you understand your writing community.

If even a very rough draft seems daunting, try finding one small piece to write. Perhaps you can write up the information in a table or create some audience benefits. Just getting something on paper will help. Lamott tells the story of her 10-year-old brother trying to write his report on birds. He had had three months to write it, it was due the next day, and he had not started:

> He was at the kitchen table close to tears, surrounded by binder paper and pencils and unopened books on birds, immobilized by the hugeness of the task ahead. Then my father sat down beside him, put his arm around my brother's shoulder, and said, "Bird by bird, buddy. Just take it bird by bird.[6]

Lamott calls the second draft the "up draft": you start fixing up the first draft.[7] It is at this stage that you start turning your writing into professional writing.

Good business and administrative writing is closer to conversation and less formal than the style of writing that has traditionally earned high marks in college essays and term papers (see Figure 5.1).

Business Styles

Most people have several styles of talking, which they vary instinctively depending on the audience. Good writers have several styles, too. An e-mail to your boss about the delays from a supplier will be informal, perhaps even chatty; a letter to the supplier demanding better service will be more formal.

Figure 5.1	Different Levels of Style		
Feature	**Conversational style**	**Good business style**	**Traditional term paper style**
Formality	Highly informal	Conversational; sounds like a real person talking	More formal than conversation would be, but retains a human voice
Use of contractions	Many contractions	OK to use occasional contractions	Few contractions, if any
Pronouns	Uses first- and second-person pronouns	Uses first- and second-person pronouns	First- and second-person pronouns kept to a minimum
Level of friendliness	Friendly	Friendly	No effort to make style friendly
How personal	Personal; refers to specific circumstances of conversation	Personal; may refer to reader by name; refers to specific circumstances of audiences	Impersonal; may generally refer to readers but does not name them or refer to their circumstances
Word choice	Short, simple words; slang	Short, simple words but avoids slang	Many abstract words; scholarly, technical terms
Sentence and paragraph length	Incomplete sentences; no paragraphs	Short sentences and paragraphs	Longer sentences and paragraphs
Grammar	Can be ungrammatical	Uses standard English	Uses more formal standard English
Visual impact	Not applicable	Attention to visual impact of document	No particular attention to visual impact

Reports tend to be more formal than letters, memos, and e-mails because they may be read many years in the future by audiences the writer can barely imagine. Reports tend to avoid contractions, personal pronouns, and second person (since so many people read reports, *you* doesn't have much meaning). See Chapter 18 for more about report style.

Keep the following points in mind as you choose a level of formality for a specific document:

- Use a friendly, informal style to someone you've talked with.

- Avoid contractions, slang, and even minor grammatical lapses in paper documents to people you don't know. Abbreviations are OK in e-mail messages if they're part of the group's culture.

- Pay particular attention to your style when you write to people you fear or when you must give bad news. Research shows our style changes in stressful contexts. We tend to rely on nouns rather than on verbs and deaden our style when we are under stress or feel insecure.[8] Confident people are more direct. Edit your writing so that you sound confident, whether you feel that way or not.

The Plain Language Movement

More and more organizations are trying to simplify their communications. In the financial world, the U.S. Securities and Exchange Commission's *A Plain English Handbook: How to Create Clear SEC Disclosure Documents* asks for short sentences, everyday words, active voice, bullet lists, and descriptive headings. It cautions against legal and highly technical terms. Warren Buffett wrote the preface, saying the handbook was good news for him, because too often he had been unable to decipher the documents filed by public companies. He offers his own writing tip: write to a specific person. He says he pretends he is writing to his sisters when he writes his Berkshire Hathaway annual reports. The SEC has more recently applied the handbook standards to the brochures investment advisers give to clients and has urged them on hedge funds.[9]

In 2010, the Plain Writing Act became law. It requires all federal agencies to use clear prose that the public can readily understand. The website www.plainlanguage.gov explains the law, provides a 112-page manual to help agencies use plain language, and offers examples of good federal communication.

Of course, the news is full of examples where these efforts have failed. The same negative examples, however, also show the great need for clear, simple style. A major factor in the subprime mortgage disaster that precipitated the global recession of 2008 was material written in prose so complex that even experts couldn't understand the content. Many homeowners who signed adjustable-rate mortgages and subsequently lost their homes claim they did not understand all the consequences of what they were signing. Experts outside the mortgage business agree with the homeowners that the language was too complex for most people to understand.[10]

Communication consultants such as Gerard Braud urge clients to simplify their prose. He warns, "All communication affects [the] bottom line. . . . When a reader, listener, viewer or member of a live audience has to take even a nanosecond to decipher what you are saying because you are making it more complicated than it needs to be, you may lose that person."[11]

To Clarify or Not to Clarify

Former Federal Reserve Chair Alan Greenspan was known for his lack of clarity.

After one speech, a headline in the *Washington Post* read, "Greenspan Hints Fed May Cut Interest Rates," while the corresponding headline in the *New York Times* read, "Doubt Voiced by Greenspan on a Rate Cut."

Even his wife joked that he had to propose twice before she understood what he was saying.

Greenspan explained his prose style this way: "On questions that were too market-sensitive to answer, 'no comment' was indeed an answer. And so you construct . . . the sentence in some obscure way which made it incomprehensible. But nobody was quite sure I wasn't saying something profound."

Adapted from Greg Ip, "'Transparent' Vision: New Fed Chairman Hopes to Downplay Impact of His Words," *Wall Street Journal*, September 6, 2006, A1; Daniel Kadlec, "5 Ways the New Fed Chairman Will Be Different," *Time*, November 7, 2005, 49–50; and quote from Devin Leonard and Peter Coy, "An Interview with Alan Greenspan, *Economist*," *Bloomberg Businessweek*, August 13, 2012, 65.

| Figure 5.2 | Excerpts from Warren Buffett's 2012 Letter to Shareholders |

BERKSHIRE HATHAWAY INC.

To the Shareholders of Berkshire Hathaway Inc.:

Buffett's letter starts with a short financial summary of the past year.

In 2012, Berkshire achieved a total gain for its shareholders of $24.1 billion. We used $1.3 billion of that to repurchase our stock, which left us with an increase in net worth of $22.8 billion for the year. The per-share book value of both our Class A and Class B stock increased by 14.4%. Over the last 48 years (that is, since present management took over), book value has grown from $19 to $114,214, a rate of 19.7% compounded annually.*

A number of good things happened at Berkshire last year, but let's first get the bad news out of the way.

If this is the bad news, think how great the good news will be.

When the partnership I ran took control of Berkshire in 1965, I could never have dreamed that a year in which we had a gain of $24.1 billion would be subpar, in terms of the comparison we present on the facing page.

Contextualizes good news to make it even more impressive.

. . .

Despite tepid U.S. growth and weakening economies throughout much of the world, our "powerhouse five" had aggregate earnings of $10.1 billion, about $600 million more than in 2011.

. . .

Todd Combs and Ted Weschler, our new investment managers, have proved to be smart, models of integrity, helpful to Berkshire in many ways beyond portfolio management, and a perfect cultural fit. We hit the jackpot with these two. In 2012 each outperformed the S&P 500 by double-digit margins. They left me in the dust as well.

Uses humor (plus tiny type) and humility to underscore his point.

. . .

Supports green initiatives

MidAmerican's electric utilities serve regulated retail customers in ten states. Only one utility holding company serves more states. In addition, we are the leader in renewables: first, from a standing start nine years ago, we now account for 6% of the country's wind generation capacity. Second, when we complete three projects now under construction, we will own about 14% of U.S. solar-generation capacity.

---

* All per-share figures used in this report apply to Berkshire's A shares. Figures for the B shares are 1/1500th of those shown for A.

Source: Warren Buffett, "Letters 2012," Berkshire Hathaway Inc., accessed March 4, 2013 , http://www.berkshirehathaway.com/letters/2012ltr.pdf.

Individualized Styles

Good business style allows for individual variation. Warren Buffett is widely known for the style of his shareholder letters in the Berkshire Hathaway annual reports. He began the letters in 1966, and they have gotten better—and longer—ever since. In addition to intelligence, they are known for humor, colorful language, and originality. Carol Loomis, a senior editor at *Fortune* who has been the editor of Buffett's letters since 1977, notes she makes few changes to the letters.[12] Figure 5.2 shows excerpts from his 2012 letter. Buffett's direct style suggests integrity and openness. Later in the letter, Buffett adds some of the colorful prose for which he is famous:

- "Charlie and I have again donned our safari outfits and resumed our search for elephants."

- "Berkshire's year-end employment totaled a record 288,462 (see page 106 for details), up 17,604 from last year. Our headquarters crew, however, remained unchanged at 24. No sense going crazy."

- "Berkshire's ownership interest in all four companies is likely to increase in the future. Mae West had it right: 'Too much of a good thing can be wonderful.'"

- "If you are a CEO who has some large, profitable project you are shelving because of short-term worries, call Berkshire. Let us unburden you."

- "But wishing makes dreams come true only in Disney movies; it's poison in business."[13]

Half-Truths about Business Writing

Many generalizations about business writing are half-truths and must be applied selectively, if at all.

Half-Truth 1: "Write as You Talk."

Most of us use a colloquial, conversational style in speech that is too informal for writing. We use slang, incomplete sentences, and even grammatical errors.

Unless our speech is exceptionally fluent, "writing as we talk" can create awkward, repetitive, and badly organized prose. It's OK to write as you talk to produce your first draft, but edit to create a good written style.

Half-Truth 2: "Never Use *I*."

Using *I* too often can make your writing sound self-centered; using it unnecessarily will make your ideas seem tentative. However, when you write about things you've done or said or seen, using *I* is both appropriate and smoother than resorting to awkward passives or phrases like *this writer*.

Half-Truth 3: "Never Use *You*."

Certainly writers should not use *you* in formal reports, as well as other situations where the audience is not known or *you* may sound too informal. But *you* is widely used in situations such as writing to familiar audiences like our office mates, describing audience benefits, and writing sales text.

Half-Truth 4: "Never Begin a Sentence with *And* or *But*."

Beginning a sentence with *and* or *also* makes the idea that follows seem like an afterthought. That's OK when you want the effect of spontaneous speech in a written document, as you may in a sales letter. If you want to sound as though you have thought about what you are saying, put the *also* in the middle of the sentence or use another transition such as *moreover* or *furthermore*.

But tells the reader that you are shifting gears and that the following point not only contrasts with but also is more important than the preceding ideas. Presenting such verbal signposts to your reader is important. Beginning a sentence with *but* is fine if doing so makes your paragraph read smoothly.

Evaluating "Rules" about Writing

Some "rules" are grammatical conventions. For example, standard edited English requires that each sentence have a subject and verb, and that the subject and verb agree. Business writing normally demands standard grammar, but exceptions exist. Promotional materials such as brochures, advertisements, and sales letters may use sentence fragments to mimic the effect of speech.

Other "rules" may be conventions adopted by an organization so that its documents will be consistent. For example, a company might decide to capitalize job titles (e.g., *Production Manager*) even though grammar doesn't require the capitals.

Still other "rules" are attempts to codify "what sounds good." "Never use *I*" and "use big words" are examples of this kind of "rule." To evaluate these "rules," you must consider your audience, purposes, and situation. If you want the effect produced by an impersonal style and polysyllabic words, use them. But use them only when you want the distancing they produce.

Half-Truth 5: "Never End a Sentence with a Preposition."

Prepositions are those useful little words that indicate relationships: *with, in, under, to, at.* In job application letters, business reports, and important presentations, avoid ending sentences with prepositions. Most other messages are less formal; it's OK to end an occasional sentence with a preposition. Noting exceptions to the rule, Sir Winston Churchill famously scolded an editor who had presumptuously corrected a sentence ending with a preposition, "This is the kind of impertinence up with which I will not put."[14] Analyze your audience and the situation, and use the language that you think will get the best results.

Half-Truth 6: "Never Have a Sentence with More than 20 Words, or a Paragraph with More than 8 Lines."

While it is true that long sentences and paragraphs may sometimes be hard to read, such is not always the case. Long sentences with parallel clauses (see pages 137–38) may be quite clear, and a longer paragraph with a bulleted list may be quite readable. Your audience, purpose, and context should guide length decisions. Instructions for complicated new software may need shorter sentences and paragraphs, but an instruction paragraph on the six criteria for legitimate travel expenses may be longer than eight lines and still quite clear.

If your audience, however, believes in rigid guidelines, then you should follow them also.

Half-Truth 7: "Big Words Impress People."

Learning an academic discipline requires that you master its vocabulary. After you get out of school, however, no one will ask you to write just to prove that you understand something. Instead, you'll be asked to write or speak to people who need the information you have.

Sometimes you may want the sense of formality or technical expertise that big words create. But much of the time, big words just distance you from your audience and increase the risk of miscommunication. If you feel you need to use big words, make sure you use them correctly. When people misuse big words, they look foolish.

Half-Truth 8: "Business Writing Does Not Document Sources."

It is true that much business writing does not use sources, and that many businesses frequently use their own boilerplate (see page 147). However, if you borrow the words or ideas of someone outside your business, you must acknowledge your source or you will be plagiarizing. Even inside a business, if the source is not widely known or the material was particularly good or controversial, it is common to acknowledge the source. See Chapter 18 for help on documentation.

Ten Ways to Make Your Writing Easier to Read   LO 5-2

Direct, simple writing is easier to read. One study tested two versions of a memo report. The "high-impact" version was written with the "bottom line" (the purpose of the report) in the first paragraph, simple sentences in normal word order, active verbs, concrete language, short paragraphs, headings and lists, and first- and second-person pronouns. The high-impact version took 22% less time to read. Readers said they understood the report better, and tests showed that they really did.[15] Another study showed that high-impact instructions were more likely to be followed.[16]

Building a good style takes energy and effort, but it's well worth the work. Good style can make every document more effective; good style can help make you the good writer so valuable to every organization.

As You Choose Words

The best word depends on context: the situation, your purposes, your audience, the words you have already used.

1. Use words that are accurate, appropriate, and familiar.   Accurate words mean what you want to say. Appropriate words convey the attitudes you want and fit well with the other words in your document. Familiar words are easy to read and understand.

Sometimes choosing the accurate word is hard. Most of us have word pairs that confuse us. Grammarian Richard Lederer tells Toastmasters that these 10 pairs are the ones you are most likely to see or hear confused.[17]

Affect/Effect	Disinterested/Uninterested
Among/Between	Farther/Further
Amount/Number	Fewer/Less
Compose/Comprise	Imply/Infer
Different from/Different than	Lay/Lie

For help using the pairs correctly, see Appendix B.

Some meanings are negotiated as we interact with another person, attempting to communicate. Individuals are likely to have different ideas about value-laden words such as *fair* or *rich*.

Some word choices have profound implications.

- Because Super Storm Sandy was not labeled a hurricane by the National Weather Service or the National Hurricane Center (technically, it made landfall as a post-tropical depression), some officials and residents did not take it seriously enough, leading to damaging inaction. But once it hit, officials such as New Jersey's governor hastened to keep it labeled as a post-tropical depression so their residents could get more insurance money (many insurance policies limit hurricane payments).[18]

- Many hospitals are labeled as charities, a status that enables them to avoid millions of dollars in taxes. A survey of charity hospitals in one state found that in one-third of them less than 1% of expenditures went to charity care.[19]

- In 2012, the American Psychiatric Association approved the fifth edition of its diagnostic manual for mental disorders, dropping and adding some categories, changes that will impact the billions of dollars spent on mental health insurance payments and subsidized treatments.[20]

Can We Predict Earthquakes?

Seismologists define an earthquake *prediction* as a statement specifying exactly when and where an earthquake will occur: an earthquake will hit San Francisco July 30.

They define a *forecast* as a probability statement, usually over a lengthy time period: over the next 30 years, the probability of a major earthquake in the San Francisco area is 67%.

The U.S. Geological Survey states on its website that no scientist has ever predicted a major earthquake, nor does the Survey expect that fact to change in the foreseeable future. However, scientists can *forecast* earthquakes.

Adapted from Nate Silver, *The Signal and the Noise: Why So Many Predictions Fail—But Some Don't* (New York: Penguin, 2012), 148–49.

As the last example indicates, some word choices have major health repercussions. Smokers have sued tobacco companies for duping them into believing that "light" cigarettes were less harmful. *Recall,* when used in warnings about defective pacemakers and defibrillators, causes patients to ask for replacements, even though the replacement surgery is riskier than the defective device. For this reason, some physician groups prefer *safety advisory* or *safety alert.*[21]

Accurate Denotations

To be accurate, a word's denotation must match the meaning the writer wishes to convey. Denotation is a word's literal or dictionary meaning. Most common words in English have more than one denotation. The word *pound,* for example, means, or denotes, a unit of weight, a place where stray animals are kept, a unit of money in the British system, and the verb *to hit.* Coca-Cola spends millions each year to protect its brand names so that *Coke* will denote only that brand and not just any cola drink.

When two people use the same word or phrase to mean, or denote, different things, **bypassing** occurs. For example, a large mail-order drug company notifies clients by e-mail when their prescription renewals get stopped because the doctor has not verified the prescription. Patients are advised to call their doctors and remind them to verify. However, the company's website posts a sentence telling clients that the prescription is *being processed.* The drug company means the renewal is in the system, waiting for the doctor's verification. The patients believe the doctor has checked in and the renewal is moving forward. The confusion results in extra phone calls to the company's customer service number, delayed prescriptions, and general customer dissatisfaction.

Problems also arise when writers misuse words.

> Three major divisions of Stiners Corporation are poised to strike out in opposite directions.

(Three different directions can't be opposite each other.)

> Stiners has grown dramatically over the past five years, largely by purchasing many smaller, desperate companies.

This latter statement probably did not intend to be so frank. More likely, the writer relied on a computer's spell checker, which accepted *desperate* for *disparate,* meaning "fundamentally different from one another."

Appropriate Connotations

Words are appropriate when their **connotations,** that is, their emotional associations or colorings, convey the attitude you want. A great many words carry connotations of approval or disapproval, disgust or delight. Consider *firm* or *obstinate, flexible* or *wishy-washy.* Some businesses offer a cash discount; you rarely hear of a credit surcharge. Some companies offer an insurance discount if their employees follow specified good-health practices; the employees who do not follow those practices are paying a penalty, although it is not publicized that way.

A supervisor can "tell the truth" about a subordinate's performance and yet write either a positive or a negative performance appraisal, based on the connotations of the words in the appraisal. Consider an employee who pays close attention to details. A positive appraisal might read, "Terry is a meticulous team member who takes care of details that others sometimes ignore." But the same behavior might be described negatively: "Terry is hung up on trivial details."

Advertisers carefully choose words with positive connotations.

- In this youth-conscious society, hearing aids become personal communication assistants.[22]

- Expensive cars are never *used;* instead, they're *pre-owned, experienced,* or even *previously adored.*[23]

- Insurers emphasize what you want to *protect* (your home, your car, your life), rather than the losses you are insuring against (fire damage, auto accident, death).

Words may also connote categories. Some show status. Both *salesperson* and *sales representative* are nonsexist job titles. But the first sounds like a clerk in a store; the second suggests someone selling important items to corporate customers. Some words connote age: *adorable* generally connotes young children, not adults. Other words, such as *handsome* or *pretty,* connote gender.

Connotations change over time. The word *charity* had acquired such negative connotations by the 19th century that people began to use the term *welfare* instead. Now, *welfare* has acquired negative associations. Most states have *public assistance programs* instead.

Ethical Implications of Word Choice How positively can we present something and still be ethical? We have the right to package our ideas attractively, but we have the responsibility to give the public or our superiors all the information they need to make decisions.

Word choices have ethical implications in technical contexts as well. When scientists refer to 100-year floods, they mean a flood so big that it has a 1% chance of happening in any given year. However, a "1% annual chance flood" is awkward and has not become standard usage. On the other hand, many nonscientists believe a 100-year flood will happen only once every hundred years. After a 100-year flood swamped the Midwest in 1993, many people moved back into flood-prone homes; some even dropped their flood insurance. Unfortunately, both actions left them devastated by a second 100-year flood in 2008.[24]

Perhaps one of the best-known examples of ethical implications deals with the interrogation technique of waterboarding. President George W. Bush's attorney general said waterboarding was not torture; President Obama's attorney general said it was.[25]

Familiar Words Use familiar words, words that are in almost everyone's vocabulary. Use the word that most exactly conveys your meaning, but whenever you can choose between two words that mean the same thing, use the shorter, more common one. Some writers mistakenly believe that using long, learned words makes them seem smart. However, experimental evidence shows the opposite is usually true: needlessly pretentious diction is generally taken as a sign of lower intelligence—and causes low credibility.[26] Try to use specific, concrete words. They're easier to understand and remember.[27]

The following list gives a few examples of short, simple alternatives:

Formal and stuffy	Short and simple
ameliorate	improve
commence	begin

How Local Is "Local"?

Some consumers prefer to purchase food produced locally on the assumption that the food will be fresher and contain fewer chemicals. But what does *local* mean? One woman in Washington, D.C., found "local" strawberries whose packaging indicated they were actually grown in California.

Some states and retailers have established definitions for what qualifies as locally grown: Vermont says within state or 30 miles of sales place; Walmart says *local* means produce came from the state where it is being sold. However, definitions vary widely, and, given the diversity of crops and their growing regions, a nationwide standard is unlikely.

So, despite the economic boon to retailers of labeling a product as locally produced, the advantage to consumers is not always clear.

Adapted from "Locally Grown Produce? It All Depends on How You Define It," *Des Moines Register,* April 2, 2011, 8A.

Formal and stuffy	Short and simple
enumerate	list
finalize	finish, complete
prioritize	rank
utilize	use
viable option	choice

There are some exceptions to the general rule that "shorter is better."

- Use a long word if it is the only word that expresses your meaning exactly.

- Use a long word—or phrase—if it is more familiar than a short word: *a word in another language for a geographic place or area* is better than *exonym*.

- Use a long word if its connotations are more appropriate. *Exfoliate* is better than *scrape off dead skin cells*.

- Use a long word if your audience prefers it.

2. Use technical jargon sparingly; eliminate business jargon. There are two kinds of **jargon.** The first is the specialized terminology of a technical field. Many public figures enjoy mocking this kind of jargon. Even the *Wall Street Journal* does its share, mocking quotes like this one from a computer industry press release announcing a new "market offering":

> [The] offerings are leading-edge service configuration assurance capabilities that will help us to rapidly deploy high-demand IP services, such as level 3 virtual private networks, multi-cast and quality of service over our IP/MPLS network.[28]

A job application letter is one of the few occasions when it's desirable to use technical jargon: using the technical terminology of the reader's field helps suggest that you're a peer who also is competent in that field. In other kinds of messages, use technical jargon only when the term is essential and known to the reader. If a technical term has a "plain English" equivalent, use the simpler term.

The second kind of jargon is the **businessese** that some writers still use: *as per your request, enclosed please find, please do not hesitate*. None of the words in this second category of jargon are necessary. Indeed, some writers call these terms *deadwood*, since they are no longer living words. If any of the terms in the first column of Figure 5.3 appear in your writing, replace them with more modern language.

As You Write and Revise Sentences

At the sentence level, you can do many things to make your writing easy to read.

3. Use active voice most of the time. "Who does what" sentences with active voice make your writing more forceful.

A verb is in **active voice** if the grammatical subject of the sentence does the action the verb describes. A verb is in **passive voice** if the subject is acted upon. Passive voice is usually made up of a form of the verb *to be* plus a past participle. *Passive* has nothing to do with *past*. Passive voice can be past, present, or future:

Figure 5.3	Getting Rid of Business Jargon	
Instead of	**Use**	**Because**
At your earliest convenience	The date you need a response	If you need it by a deadline, say so. It may never be convenient to respond.
As per your request; 65 miles per hour	As you requested; 65 miles an hour	*Per* is a Latin word for *by* or *for* each. Use *per* only when the meaning is correct; avoid mixing English and Latin.
Enclosed please find	Enclosed is; Here is	An enclosure isn't a treasure hunt. If you put something in the envelope, the reader will find it.
Hereto, herewith	Omit	Omit legal jargon.
Please be advised; Please be informed	Omit—simply start your response	You don't need a preface. Go ahead and start.
Please do not hesitate	Omit	Omit negative words.
Pursuant to	According to; or omit	*Pursuant* does not mean *after.* Omit legal jargon in any case.
This will acknowledge receipt of your letter.	Omit—start your response	If you answer a letter, the reader knows you got it.
Trusting this is satisfactory, we remain	Omit	Eliminate-*ing* endings. When you are through, stop.

were received   (in the past)

is recommended   (in the present)

will be implemented   (in the future)

To spot a passive voice, find the verb. If the verb describes something that the grammatical subject is doing, the verb is in active voice. If the verb describes something that is being done to the grammatical subject, the verb is in passive voice.

Active Voice	**Passive Voice**
The customer received 500 widgets.	Five hundred widgets were received by the customer.
I recommend this method.	This method is recommended by me.
The state agencies will implement the program.	The program will be implemented by the state agencies.

To change from passive voice to active voice, you must make the agent the new subject. If no agent is specified in the sentence, you must supply one to make the sentence active.

Passive Voice	**Active Voice**
The request was approved by the plant manager.	The plant manager approved the request.
A decision will be made next month. No agent in sentence.	The committee will decide next month.
A letter will be sent informing the customer of the change. No agent in sentence.	[You] Send the customer a letter informing her about the change.

Passive voice has at least three disadvantages:

- If all the information in the original sentence is retained, passive voice makes the sentence longer and thus more time consuming to understand.[29]

- If the agent is omitted, it's not clear who is responsible for doing the action.

- Using much passive voice, especially in material that has a lot of big words, can make the writing boring and pompous.

Passive voice is desirable in these situations:

a. Use passive voice to emphasize the object receiving the action, not the agent.

> Your order was shipped November 15.

The customer's order, not the shipping clerk, is important.

b. Use passive voice to provide coherence within a paragraph. A sentence is easier to read if "old" information comes at the beginning of a sentence. When you have been discussing a topic, use the word again as your subject even if that requires passive voice.

> The bank made several risky loans in the late 1990s. These loans were written off as "uncollectible" in 2001.

Using *loans* as the subject of the second sentence provides a link between the two sentences, making the paragraph as a whole easier to read.

c. Use passive voice to avoid assigning blame.

> The order was damaged during shipment.

Active voice would require the writer to specify *who* damaged the order. The passive voice is more tactful here.

According to PlainLanguage.gov, changing writing to active voice is the most powerful change that can be made to government documents.[30] But even the self-proclaimed prescriptivist style editor Bill Walsh, a copy chief at the *Washington Post,* admits that sometimes passive voice is necessary—although not as often as many writers think.[31]

4. Use verbs—not nouns—to carry the weight of your sentence.   Put the weight of your sentence in the verb to make your sentences more forceful and up to 25% easier to read.[32] When the verb is a form of the verb *to be,* revise the sentence to use a more forceful verb.

Weak: The financial advantage of owning this equipment instead of leasing it is 10% after taxes.

Better: Owning this equipment rather than leasing it will save us 10% after taxes.

Nouns ending in *-ment, -ion,* and *-al* often hide verbs.

Weak	Better
make an adjustment	adjust
make a payment	pay
make a decision	decide
reach a conclusion	conclude
take into consideration	consider

make a referral	refer
provide assistance	assist

Use verbs to present the information more forcefully.

Weak: We will perform an investigation of the problem.

Better: We will investigate the problem.

Weak: Selection of a program should be based on the client's needs.

Better: Select the program that best fits the client's needs.

5. Eliminate wordiness.

Writing is **wordy** if the same idea can be expressed in fewer words. Unnecessary words increase writing time, bore your reader, and make your meaning more difficult to follow, since the reader must hold all the extra words in mind while trying to understand your meaning.

Good writing is concise, but it may still be lengthy. Concise writing may be long because it is packed with ideas. In Chapter 3, we saw that revisions to create you-attitude and positive emphasis and to develop benefits were frequently *longer* than the originals because the revision added information not given in the original.

Sometimes you may be able to look at a draft and see immediately how to condense it. When the solution isn't obvious, try the following strategies to condense your writing:

a. Eliminate words that add nothing.

b. Combine sentences to eliminate unnecessary words.

c. Put the meaning of your sentence into the subject and verb to cut the number of words.

You eliminate unnecessary words to save the reader's time, not simply to see how few words you can use. You aren't writing a telegram, so keep the little words that make sentences complete. (Incomplete sentences are fine in lists where all the items are incomplete.)

The following examples show how to use these methods.

a. **Eliminate words that add nothing.** Cut words if the idea is already clear from other words in the sentence. Substitute single words for wordy phrases.

Wordy: Keep this information on file for future reference.

Better: Keep this information for reference.

or: File this information.

Wordy: The reason we want to see changing our hardware manager to Hanson's is because Hanson's is able to collect hardware from a larger number of vendors than our current supplier.

Better: We recommend changing our hardware manager to Hanson's for their larger number of vendors.

Phrases beginning with *of, which,* and *that* can often be shortened.

Wordy: the question of most importance

Better: the most important question

Wordy: the estimate which is enclosed

Better: the enclosed estimate

Wordy: We need to act on the suggestions that our customers offer us.

Better: We need to act on customer suggestions.

Internet Influence on Conciseness

The Internet has changed the way we read. Author Christopher Johnson says the "sad irony is that we often waste our time clicking around because we don't want to waste our attention. We don't always give it willingly, but it can be captured."

That capturing is done through "microstyle," concise messages that are short, to the point, and attention-grabbing.

Johnson reminds us that in these micro-messages word choice is incredibly important, in anything from slogans, like Target's "Expect more, pay less," to new compound words like *YouTube.* Johnson advises writers that to make a small message a success, it should display careful word choice or humor.

Adapted from Daniel Akst, "The Soul of Brevity," *Wall Street Journal,* August 6–7, 2011, C10.

Meaningless Sentences

Editor Bill Walsh of the *Washington Post* gives these examples of meaningless sentences.

- *A donation of your car, truck or boat is tax-deductible to the maximum extent of the law.*

In other words, you're allowed to deduct it as much as you're allowed to deduct it. Good news: Your toenail clippings are also deductible to the maximum extent of the law.

- *You can use this scholarship at any participating school in the world.*

I have no doubt that this is true. But it raises one major question. . . .

- *Area schools will be back in session Monday, disappointing thousands of children who would rather stay home and watch John Wayne movies.*

No, they wouldn't. (How old are you, anyway?)

Quoted from Bill Walsh, *The Elephants of Style: A Trunkload of Tips on the Big Issues and Gray Areas of Contemporary American English* (New York: McGraw-Hill, 2004), 140, 149.

Sentences beginning with *There are* or *It is* can often be tighter.

Wordy: There are three reasons for the success of the project.

Tighter: Three reasons explain the project's success.

Wordy: It is the case that college graduates earn more money.

Tighter: College graduates earn more money.

Check your draft. If you find these phrases, or any of the unnecessary words shown in Figure 5.4, eliminate them.

b. **Combine sentences to eliminate unnecessary words.** In addition to saving words, combining sentences focuses the reader's attention on key points, makes your writing sound more sophisticated, and sharpens the relationship between ideas, thus making your writing more coherent.

Wordy: I conducted this survey by telephone on Sunday, April 21. I questioned two groups of upperclass students—male and female—who, according to the Student Directory, were still living in the dorms. The purpose of this survey was to find out why some upperclass students continue to live in the dorms even though they are no longer required by the University to do so. I also wanted to find out if there were any differences between male and female upperclass students in their reasons for choosing to remain in the dorms.

Tighter: On Sunday, April 21, I phoned upperclass men and women living in the dorms to find out (1) why they continue to live in the dorms even though they are no longer required to do so, and (2) whether men and women gave the same reasons.

c. **Put the meaning of your sentence into the subject and verb to cut the number of words.** Put the core of your meaning into the subject and verb of your main clause.

Wordy: The reason we are recommending the computerization of this process is because it will reduce the time required to obtain data and will give us more accurate data.

Better: Computerizing the process will give us more accurate data more quickly.

Wordy: The purpose of this letter is to indicate that if we are unable to mutually benefit from our seller/buyer relationship, with satisfactory material and satisfactory payment, then we have no alternative other than to sever the relationship. In other words, unless the account is handled in 45 days, we will have to change our terms to a permanent COD basis.

Figure 5.4	Words to Cut		
Cut the following words	**Cut redundant words**	**Substitute a single word for a wordy phrase**	
quite	a period of three months	at the present time	now
really	during the course of the negotiations	due to the fact that	because
very	during the year of 2013	in order to	to
	maximum possible	in the event that	if
	past experience	in the near future	soon (or give the date)
	plan in advance	on a regular basis	regularly
	refer back	prior to the start of	before
	the color blue	until such time as	until
	the month of November		
	true facts		

Better: A good buyer/seller relationship depends upon satisfactory material and payment. You can continue to charge your purchases from us only if you clear your present balance in 45 days.

6. Vary sentence length and sentence structure.

Readable prose mixes sentence lengths and varies sentence structure. A short sentence (under 10 words) can add punch to your prose. Long sentences (over 30 words) can be danger signs. The first-place Golden Gobbledygook Award goes to a 1,000-word sentence in a legal document filed in Oklahoma.[33]

You can vary sentence patterns in several ways. First, you can mix simple, compound, and complex sentences. (See Appendix B for more information on sentence structure.) **Simple sentences** have one main clause:

We will open a new store this month.

Compound sentences have two main clauses joined with *and, but, or,* or another conjunction. Compound sentences work best when the ideas in the two clauses are closely related.

We have hired staff, and they will complete their training next week.

We wanted to have a local radio station broadcast from the store during its grand opening, but the DJs were already booked.

Complex sentences have one main and one subordinate clause; they are good for showing logical relationships.

When the stores open, we will have specials in every department.

Because we already have a strong customer base in the northwest, we expect the new store to be just as successful as the store in the City Center Mall.

You can also vary sentences by changing the order of elements. Normally the subject comes first.

We will survey customers later in the year to see whether demand warrants a third store on campus.

To create variety, occasionally begin the sentence with some other part of the sentence.

Later in the year, we will survey customers to see whether demand warrants a third store on campus.

Use these guidelines for sentence length and structure:

- Always edit sentences for conciseness. Even a short sentence can be wordy.
- When your subject matter is complicated or full of numbers, make a special effort to keep sentences short.

Names Influence Eating Behaviors

Can renaming a food make it more appealing? Can the name make you eat more? Well, yes, especially if you're dieting.

Researchers called Jelly Belly candies "fruit chews" or "candy chews." Dieters rated "candy chews" as being less tasty than "fruit chews." In addition, dieters consumed 70% more when the candies were called "fruit chews" than they did when the candies were called "candy chews."

Adapted from Christopher Shea, "Salad Is a Magic Word," *Wall Street Journal*, April 23–24, 2011, C4.

- Use longer sentences to show how ideas are linked to each other; to avoid a series of short, choppy sentences; and to reduce repetition.

- Group the words in long and medium-length sentences into chunks that the reader can process quickly.

- When you use a long sentence, keep the subject and verb close together.

Let's see how to apply the last three principles.

Use long sentences to show how ideas are linked to each other; to avoid a series of short, choppy sentences; and to reduce repetition. The following sentence is hard to read not simply because it is long but because it is shapeless. Just cutting it into a series of short, choppy sentences doesn't help. The best revision uses medium-length sentences to show the relationship between ideas.

Too long:	It should also be noted in the historical patterns presented in the summary, that though there were delays in January and February which we realized were occurring, we are now back where we were about a year ago, and that we are not off line in our collect receivables as compared to last year at this time, but we do show a considerable over-budget figure because of an ultra-conservative goal on the receivable investment.
Choppy:	There were delays in January and February. We knew about them at the time. We are now back where we were about a year ago. The summary shows this. Our present collect receivables are in line with last year's. However, they exceed the budget. The reason they exceed the budget is that our goal for receivable investment was very conservative.
Better:	As the summary shows, although there were delays in January and February (of which we were aware), we have now regained our position of a year ago. Our present collect receivables are in line with last year's, but they exceed the budget because our goal for receivable investment was very conservative.

Group the words in long and medium-length sentences into chunks. The "better" revision above has seven chunks. At 27 and 24 words, respectively, these sentences aren't short, but they're readable because no chunk is longer than 10 words. Any sentence pattern will get boring if it is repeated sentence after sentence. Use different sentence patterns—different kinds and lengths of chunks—to keep your prose interesting.

Keep the subject and verb close together. Often you can move the subject and verb closer together if you put the modifying material in a list at the end of the sentence. For maximum readability, present the list vertically.

Hard to read:	Movements resulting from termination, layoffs and leaves, recalls and reinstates, transfers in, transfers out, promotions in, promotions out, and promotions within are presently documented through the Payroll Authorization Form.
Better:	The Payroll Authorization Form documents the following movements:

- Termination
- Layoffs and leaves
- Recalls and reinstates
- Transfers in and out
- Promotions in, out, and within

7. Use parallel structure.   **Parallel structure** puts words, phrases, or clauses in the same grammatical and logical form. In the following faulty example, *by reviewing* is a gerund, while *note* is an imperative verb. Make the sentence parallel by using both gerunds or both imperatives.

Faulty:	Errors can be checked by reviewing the daily exception report or note the number of errors you uncover when you match the lading copy with the file copy of the invoice.
Parallel:	Errors can be checked by reviewing the daily exception report or by noting the number of errors you uncover when you match the lading copy with the file copy of the invoice.
Also parallel:	To check errors, note

1. The number of items on the daily exception report.
2. The number of errors discovered when the lading copy and the file copy are matched.

Note that a list in parallel structure must fit grammatically into the umbrella sentence that introduces the list.

Faulty:	The following suggestions can help employers avoid bias in job interviews:

1. Base questions on the job description.
2. Questioning techniques.
3. Selection and training of interviewers.

Parallel:	The following suggestions can help employers avoid bias in job interviews:

1. Base questions on the job description.
2. Ask the same questions of all applicants.
3. Select and train interviewers carefully.

Also parallel:	Employers can avoid bias in job interviews by

1. Basing questions on the job description.
2. Asking the same questions of all applicants.
3. Selecting and training interviewers carefully.

Words must also be logically parallel. In the following faulty example, *juniors, seniors,* and *athletes* are not three separate groups. The revision groups words into non-overlapping categories.

Faulty:	I interviewed juniors and seniors and athletes.
Parallel:	I interviewed juniors and seniors. In each rank, I interviewed athletes and non-athletes.

Parallel structure is a powerful device for making your writing tighter, smoother, and more forceful.

Faulty:	Our customers receive these benefits:

- Use tracking information.
- Our products let them scale the software to their needs.
- The customer can always rely on us.

Parallel:	Our customers receive these benefits:

- Tracking information
- Scalability
- Reliability

8. Put your readers in your sentences. Use second-person pronouns (*you*) rather than third-person (*he, she, one*) to give your writing more impact. *You* is both singular and plural; it can refer to a single person or to every member of your organization.

Third-person:	Funds in a participating employee's account at the end of each six months will automatically be used to buy more stock unless a "Notice of Election Not to Exercise Purchase Rights" form is received from the employee.

| Second-person: | Once you begin to participate, funds in your account at the end of each six months will automatically be used to buy more stock unless you turn in a "Notice of Election Not to Exercise Purchase Rights" form. |

Be careful to use *you* only when it refers to your reader.

| Incorrect: | My visit with the outside sales rep showed me that your schedule can change quickly. |
| Correct: | My visit with the outside sales rep showed me that schedules can change quickly. |

As You Write and Revise Paragraphs

Paragraphs are visual and logical units. Use them to chunk your sentences.

9. Begin most paragraphs with topic sentences.

A good paragraph has **unity;** that is, it discusses only one idea, or topic. The **topic sentence** states the main idea and provides a scaffold to structure your document. Your writing will be easier to read if you make the topic sentence explicit and put it at the beginning of the paragraph.[34]

| Hard to read (no topic sentence): | In fiscal 2014, the company filed claims for refund of federal income taxes of $3,199,000 and interest of $969,000 paid as a result of an examination of the company's federal income tax returns by the Internal Revenue Service (IRS) for the years 2010 through 2012. It is uncertain what amount, if any, may ultimately be recovered. |
| Better (paragraph starts with topic sentence): | The company and the IRS disagree about whether the company is responsible for back taxes. In fiscal 2014, the company filed claims for a refund of federal income taxes of $3,199,000 and interest of $969,000 paid as a result of an examination of the company's federal income tax returns by the Internal Revenue Service (IRS) for the years 2010 through 2012. It is uncertain what amount, if any, may ultimately be recovered. |

A good topic sentence forecasts the structure and content of the paragraph.

> Plan B also has economic advantages.

(Prepares the reader for a discussion of B's economic advantages.)

> We had several personnel changes in June.

(Prepares the reader for a list of the month's terminations and hires.)

> Employees have complained about one part of our new policy on parental leaves.

(Prepares the reader for a discussion of the problem.)

When the first sentence of a paragraph is not the topic sentence, readers who skim may miss the main point. If the paragraph does not have a topic sentence, you will need to write one. If you can't think of a single sentence that serves as an "umbrella" to cover every sentence, the paragraph probably lacks unity. To solve the problem, either split the paragraph or eliminate the sentences that digress from the main point.

10. Use transitions to link ideas.

Transition words and sentences signal the connections between ideas to the reader. Transitions tell whether the next sentence continues the previous thought or starts a new idea; they can tell whether

Figure 5.5	Transition Words and Phrases		
To show addition or continuation of the same idea and also first, second, third in addition likewise similarly **To introduce another important item** furthermore moreover	**To introduce an example** for example (e.g.) for instance indeed to illustrate namely specifically **To contrast** in contrast on the other hand or	**To show that the contrast is more important than the previous idea** but however nevertheless on the contrary **To show cause and effect** as a result because consequently for this reason therefore	**To show time** after as before in the future next then until when while **To summarize or end** finally in conclusion

the idea that comes next is more or less important than the previous thought. Figure 5.5 lists some of the most common transition words and phrases.

These sentences use transition words and phrases:

Kelly wants us to switch the contract to Ames Cleaning, and I agree with her. (continuing the same idea)

Kelly wants us to switch the contract to Ames Cleaning, but I prefer Ross Commercial. (contrasting opinions)

As a result of our differing views, we will be visiting both firms. (showing cause and effect)

These are transitional sentences:

Now that we have examined the advantages of using Ames Cleaning, let's look at potential disadvantages. (shows movement between two sections of evaluation)

These pros and cons show us three reasons we should switch to Ross Commercial. (shows movement away from evaluation sections; forecasts the three reasons)

Organizational Preferences for Style

Different organizations and bosses may legitimately have different ideas about what constitutes good writing. If the style doesn't seem reasonable, ask. Often the documents that end up in files aren't especially good; later, other workers may find these and copy them, thinking they represent a corporate standard. Bosses may in fact prefer better writing.

Recognize that a style may serve other purposes than communication. An abstract, hard-to-read style may help a group forge its own identity. Researchers James Suchan and Ronald Dulek have shown that Navy officers preferred a passive, impersonal style because they saw themselves as followers. An aircraft company's engineers saw wordiness as the verbal equivalent of backup systems. A backup is redundant but essential to safety, because parts and systems do fail.[35]

Revising, Editing, and Proofreading LO 5-3

Once you have your document written, you need to polish it.

A popular myth about revising is that Abraham Lincoln wrote the Gettysburg address, perhaps the most famous of all American presidential speeches, on the back of an envelope as he traveled by train to the battlefield's dedication. The reality is that Lincoln wrote at least a partial draft of the speech before leaving for the trip and continued to revise it up to the morning of its delivery. Furthermore, the speech was on a topic he passionately believed in, one he had been pondering for years.[36]

Like Lincoln, good writers work on their drafts; they make their documents better by judicious revising, editing, and proofreading.

- **Revising** means making changes in content, organization, and tone that will better satisfy your purposes and your audience.

- **Editing** means making surface-level changes that make the document grammatically correct.

- **Proofreading** means checking to be sure the document is free from typographical errors.

What to Look for When You Revise

When you're writing to a new audience or have to solve a particularly difficult problem, plan to revise the draft at least three times. The first time, look for content and clarity: Have I said enough and have I said it clearly? The second time, check the organization and layout: Have I presented my content so it can be easily absorbed? Finally, check style and tone: Have I used you-attitude? The Thorough Revision Checklist summarizes the questions you should ask.

Often you'll get the best revision by setting aside your draft, getting a blank page or screen, and redrafting. This strategy takes advantage of the thinking you did on your first draft without locking you into the sentences in it.

As you revise, be sure to read the document through from start to finish. This is particularly important if you've composed in several sittings or if you've used text from other documents. Such drafts tend to be choppy, repetitious, or inconsistent. You may need to add transitions, cut repetitive parts, or change words to create a uniform level of formality throughout the document.

Sometimes revising and proofreading is more pleasant if done in an informal setting.

If you're really in a time bind, do a light revision, as outlined in the Light Revision Checklist. The quality of the final document may not be as high as with a thorough revision, but even a light revision is better than skipping revision altogether.

Checklist

Thorough Revision Checklist

Content and clarity

☐ Does your document meet the needs of the organization and of the reader—and make you look good?

☐ Have you given readers all the information they need to understand and act on your message?

☐ Is all the information accurate and clear?

☐ Is the message easy to read?

☐ Is each sentence clear? Is the message free from apparently contradictory statements?

☐ Is the logic clear and convincing? Are generalizations and benefits backed up with adequate supporting detail?

Organization and layout

☐ Is the pattern of organization clear? Is it appropriate for your purposes, audience, and context?

☐ Are transitions between ideas smooth? Do ideas within paragraphs flow smoothly?

☐ Does the design of the document make it easy for readers to find the information they need? Is the document visually inviting?

☐ Are the points emphasized by layout ones that deserve emphasis?

☐ Are the first and last paragraphs effective?

Style and tone

☐ Does the message use you-attitude and positive emphasis?

☐ Is the message friendly and free from sexist language?

☐ Does the message build goodwill?

Revisioning a Novel

Michael Chabon is a Pulitzer Prize author. His novel, *The Yiddish Policemen's Union,* had a blurb in his publisher's sales catalog plus an on-sale date when his editor made him revise it.

He spent eight months reworking the entire book, adding a flashback structure and paring down the language.

Altogether, he spent five years and four drafts working on the novel. In the process, he moved to a different plot and changed from a first-person to a third-person narrator. His editor sent him detailed notes in the margins of the drafts. On the final draft, she went over the manuscript page by page with him.

The novel won both Hugo and Nebula awards, science fiction's highest awards.

Adapted from Sam Schechner, "Chabon's Amazing Rewrite Adventures," *Wall Street Journal,* April 27, 2007, W3.

> ### Checklist
>
> ## Light Revision Checklist
>
> ☐ Have you given readers all the information they need to understand and act on your message?
>
> ☐ Is the pattern of organization clear and helpful?
>
> ☐ Is the logic clear and convincing? Are generalizations and benefits backed up with adequate supporting detail?
>
> ☐ Does the design of the document make it easy for readers to find the information they need?
>
> ☐ Are the first and last paragraphs effective?

What to Look for When You Edit

Even good writers need to edit, because no one can pay attention to surface correctness while thinking of ideas. As a matter of fact, even history-shaping documents like the Declaration of Independence became better with editing.

Editing should always *follow* revision. There's no point in taking time to fix a grammatical error in a sentence that may be cut when you clarify your meaning or tighten your style. Some writers edit more accurately when they print out a copy of a document and edit the hard copy.

Check your material to make sure you have acknowledged all information and opinions borrowed from outside the organization (see Chapter 18 for help on documentation). Using material from outside the organization without acknowledging the source is **plagiarism.** Check also that you have acknowledged company information that is controversial or not widely known.

Check your communication to make sure your sentences say what you intend.

Not:	Take a moment not to sign your policy.
But:	Take a moment now to sign your policy.
Not:	I wish to apply for the job as assistant manger.
But:	I wish to apply for the job as assistant manager.

One of the most famous editing errors in history was the so-called Wicked Bible, which left out a crucial *not*, thus changing one of the Ten Commandments into "Thou shalt commit adultery."

An extra *not* caused Arkansas to accidentally pass a law allowing its citizens of any age, even children, to marry if their parents agreed. The unintended law said this:

> In order for a person who is younger than eighteen (18) years of age and who is not pregnant to obtain a marriage license, the person must provide the county clerk with evidence of parental consent to the marriage.[37]

When you edit, you also need to check that the following are accurate:

- Sentence structure.
- Subject–verb and noun–pronoun agreement.
- Punctuation.
- Word usage.
- Spelling—including spelling of names.
- Numbers.

You need to know the rules of grammar and punctuation to edit. Errors such as sentence fragments and run-on sentences disturb most educated readers and make them wonder what other mistakes you might be making. Errors in punctuation can change the meaning of a sentence. Lynne Truss, author of the *New York Times* best seller on punctuation, *Eats, Shoots & Leaves*, offers "a popular 'Dear Jack' letter" to show the need for care:[38]

> Dear Jack,
> I want a man who knows what love is all about. You are generous, kind, thoughtful. People who are not like you admit to being useless and inferior. You have ruined me for other men. I yearn for you. I have no feelings whatsoever when we're apart. I can be forever happy—will you let me be yours?
>
> Jill

> Dear Jack,
> I want a man who knows what love is. All about you are generous, kind, thoughtful people, who are not like you. Admit to being useless and inferior. You have ruined me. For other men I yearn! For you I have no feelings whatsoever. When we're apart I can be forever happy. Will you let me be? Yours,
>
> Jill

Writers with a good command of grammar and mechanics can do a better job than the computer **grammar checkers** currently available. But even good writers sometimes use a good grammar handbook for reference. On the other hand, even good editors—such as Bill Walsh, copy desk chief for the business desk of the *Washington Post*—warn writers that handbooks should be used with a clear goal of clarifying text, not blindly following rules.[39]

Appendix B reviews grammar, punctuation, numbers, and words that are often confused.

Most writers make a small number of errors over and over. If you know that you have trouble with dangling modifiers or subject–verb agreement, for example, specifically look for them in your draft. Also look for any errors that especially bother your boss and correct them.

How to Catch Typos

To catch typos use a spell-checker. But you still need to proofread by eye. Spell-checkers work by matching words; they will signal any group of letters

What? Prof Reed? Why?

Amazing proofreading errors circulate on social media; don't let it happen to you.

A typo missed by the Mitt Romney campaign gained notoriety when it suggested that voters should stick by him for "A Better Amercia."

A humorous graduation announcement typo was from the "Lyndon B. Johnson School of Pubic Affairs."

The menu from a Phoenix restaurant listed the ingredients for its Candy Apple Martini as containing, "Apple Pucker, Butterscotch liqueur . . . ."

Too often we rely on spell checkers, "witch wont ketch wards spelled rite, butt know yews wright."

Adapted from Merrill Perlman, "Why 'Amercia' Needs Copy Editors," *CNN*, June 1, 2012, http://cnn.com/2012/06/01/opinion/perlman-romney-needs-editor/index.html?=eref=mrss_igoogle_cnn.

not listed in their dictionaries. However, they cannot tell you when you've used the wrong word but spelled it correctly.

Don't underestimate the harm that spelling errors can create. A large, Midwestern university lost its yearbook after an uncaught typo referred to the Greek community as the "geeks on campus." Greeks boycotted the yearbook, which went deeply into debt and out of business. The impact of typos on job documents is well known (see "The Cost of a Typo" sidebar for example). Proofread every document both with a spell-checker and by eye, to catch the errors a spell-checker can't find.

Proofreading is hard because writers tend to see what they know should be there rather than what really is there. It's easier to proof something you haven't written, so you may want to swap papers with a proofing buddy. (Be sure the person looks for typos, not content.)

To proofread,

- Read once quickly for meaning, to see that nothing has been left out.

- Read a second time, slowly. When you find an error, correct it and then *reread that line.* Readers tend to become less attentive after they find one error and may miss other errors close to the one they've spotted.

- To proofread a document you know well, read the lines backward or the pages out of order.

Always triple-check numbers, headings, the first and last paragraphs, and the reader's name.

Getting and Using Feedback

Getting feedback almost always improves a document. In many organizations, it's required. All external documents must be read and approved before they go out. The process of drafting, getting feedback, revising, and getting more feedback is called **cycling.** One researcher reported that documents in her clients' firms cycled an average of 4.2 times before reaching the intended audience.[40] Another researcher studied a major 10-page document whose 20 drafts made a total of 31 stops on the desks of nine reviewers on four different levels.[41] Being asked to revise a document is a fact of life in business.

You can improve the quality of the feedback you get by telling people which aspects you'd especially like comments about. For example, when you give a reader the outline or planning draft, you probably want to know whether the general approach and content are appropriate, and if you have included all major points. After your second draft, you might want to know whether the reasoning is convincing. When you reach the polishing draft, you'll be ready for feedback on style and grammar. The Questions to Ask Readers Checklist (page 148) offers suggestions.

Technology helps with both giving and receiving feedback. Word documents can be edited using review features such as Track Changes, a word-processing feature that records alterations made to a document. It is particularly useful when you are collaborating with a colleague to create, edit, or revise documents. Track Changes will highlight any text that has been added or deleted to your document, and it also allows you to decide whether to accept each change or reject it and return to your original text. In addition to Track Changes, many word processors include a comment feature that allows you to ask questions or make suggestions without altering the text itself. Documents can also be posted in the cloud using Google Docs, and can then be edited by multiple people.

It's easy to feel defensive when someone criticizes your work. If the feedback stings, put it aside until you can read it without feeling defensive. Even if you think that the reader hasn't understood what you were trying to say, the fact that the reader complained usually means the section could be improved. If the reader says "This isn't true," and you know the statement is true, several kinds of revision might make the truth clear to the reader: rephrasing the statement, giving more information or examples, or documenting the source.

Reading feedback carefully is a good way to understand the culture of your organization. Are you told to give more details or to shorten messages? Does your boss add headings and bullet points? Look for patterns in the comments, and apply what you learn in your next document.

Using Boilerplate

Boilerplate is language—sentences, paragraphs, even pages—from a previous document that a writer legitimately includes in a new document. In academic papers, material written by others must be quoted and documented—to neglect to do so would be plagiarism. However, because businesses own the documents their employees write, old text may be included without attribution.

Many legal documents, including apartment leases and sales contracts, are almost completely boilerplate. Writers may also use boilerplate they wrote for earlier documents. For example, a section from a proposal describing the background of the problem could also be used in the final report. A section from a progress report describing what the writer had done could be used with only a few changes in the methods section of the final report.

Writers use boilerplate both to save time and energy and to use language that has already been approved by the organization's legal staff. However, research has shown that using boilerplate creates two problems.[42] First, using unrevised boilerplate can create a document with incompatible styles and tones. Second, boilerplate can allow writers to ignore subtle differences in situations and audiences.

Readability Formulas

Readability formulas attempt to measure objectively how easy something is to read. However, since they don't take many factors into account, the formulas are at best a very limited guide to good style.

Computer packages that analyze style may give you a readability score. Some states' "plain English" laws require consumer contracts to meet a certain readability score. Some companies require that warranties and other consumer documents meet certain scores.

Readability formulas depend heavily on word length and sentence length. See the *Business and Administrative Communication* website to calculate readability using the two best-known readability formulas: the Gunning Fog Index and the Flesch Reading Ease Scale. Research has shown,[43] however, that using shorter words and sentences will not necessarily make a passage easy to read. Short words are not always easy to understand, especially if they have technical meanings (e.g., *waive, bear market, liquid*). Short, choppy sentences and sentence fragments are actually harder to understand than well-written, medium-length sentences.

No reading formula yet devised takes into account three factors that influence how easy a text is to read: the complexity of the ideas, the organization of the ideas, and the layout and design of the document.

MBAs Can't Write

The writing and presentation skills of MBAs have long been a complaint of employers. Too many words, employers say, and too many big words. Graduates are particularly inept at preparing short persuasive communications or writing for multiple audiences.

Now MBA programs are acting on the complaints. The Wharton School of Business now requires 12 communication classes, twice what it required before. Other business schools are adding writing coaches and having the writing coaches assign writing grades to papers for other courses.

Adapted from Diana Middleton, "Students Struggle for Words," *Wall Street Journal*, March 3, 2011, B8.

Instead of using readability formulas, test your draft with the people for whom it is designed. How long does it take them to find the information they need? Do they make mistakes when they try to use the document? Do they think the writing is easy to understand? Answers to these questions can give much more accurate information than any readability score.

Checklist
Questions to Ask Readers

Outline or planning draft

☐ Does the plan seem on the right track?

☐ What topics should be added? Should any be cut?

☐ Do you have any other general suggestions?

Revising draft

☐ Does the message satisfy all its purposes?

☐ Is the message adapted to the audience(s)?

☐ Is the organization effective?

☐ What parts aren't clear?

☐ What ideas need further development and support?

☐ Do you have any other suggestions?

Polishing draft

☐ Are there any problems with word choice or sentence structure?

☐ Did you find any inconsistencies?

☐ Did you find any typos?

☐ Is the document's design effective?

Summary by Learning Objectives

LO 5-1 **Activities involved in the composing process, and how to use these activities to your advantage.**

Processes that help writers write well include not expecting the first draft to be perfect, writing regularly, modifying the initial task if it's too hard or too easy, having clear goals, knowing many different strategies, using rules as guidelines rather than as absolutes, and waiting to edit until after the draft is complete.

Writing processes can include many activities: planning, gathering, brainstorming, organizing, writing, evaluating, getting feedback, revising, editing, and proofreading. *Revising* means changing the document to make it better satisfy the writer's purposes and the audience. *Editing* means making surface-level changes that make the document grammatically correct. *Proofreading* means checking to be sure the document is free from typographical errors. The activities do not have to come in any set order. It is not necessary to finish one activity to start another. Most writers use all activities only when they write a document whose genre, subject matter, or audience is new to them.

To think of ideas, try brainstorming, freewriting (writing without stopping for 10 minutes or so), and clustering (brainstorming with circled words on a page).

LO 5-2 **Guidelines for effective word choice, sentence construction, and paragraph organization.**

Good style in business and administrative writing is less formal, more friendly, and more personal than the style usually used for term papers.

Use the following techniques to make your writing easier to read.

As you choose words,

1. Use words that are accurate, appropriate, and familiar. Denotation is a word's literal meaning; connotation is the emotional coloring that a word conveys.

2. Use technical jargon sparingly; eliminate business jargon.

As you write and revise sentences,

3. Use active voice most of the time. Active voice is better because it is shorter, clearer, and more interesting.

4. Use verbs—not nouns—to carry the weight of your sentence.

5. Eliminate wordiness. Writing is wordy if the same idea can be expressed in fewer words.
   a. Eliminate words that add nothing.
   b. Combine sentences to eliminate unnecessary words.
   c. Put the meaning of your sentence into the subject and verb to cut the number of words.

6. Vary sentence length and sentence structure.

7. Use parallel structure. Use the same grammatical form for ideas that have the same logical function.

8. Put your readers in your sentences.

As you write and revise paragraphs,

9. Begin most paragraphs with topic sentences so that readers know what to expect in the paragraph.

10. Use transitions to link ideas.

LO 5-3 **Techniques to revise, edit, and proofread your communications.**

If the writing situation is new or difficult, plan to revise the draft at least three times. The first time, look for content and completeness. The second time, check the organization, layout, and reasoning. Finally, check style and tone.

Edit for surface-level changes to make your document grammatically correct.

Finally, proofread to catch typos. Use available technologies to help you.

Continuing Case

The All-Weather Case, set in an HR department in a manufacturing company, extends through all 19 chapters and is available at www.mhhe.com/locker11e. The portion for this chapter asks students to revise, edit, and proofread a document.

Exercises and Cases

*Go to www.mhhe.com/locker11e for additional Exercises and Cases.

5.1   Reviewing the Chapter

1. What are some techniques of good writers? Which ones do you use regularly? (LO 5-1–3)

2. What are ways to get ideas for a specific communication? (LO 5-1)

3. What activities are part of the composing process? Which one should you be doing more often or more carefully in your writing? (LO 5-1)

4. What are some half-truths about style? (LO 5-2)

5. What are some ways you can make your sentences more effective? (LO 5-2)

6. What are some ways you can make your paragraphs more effective? (LO 5-2)

7. How can you adapt good style to organization preferences? (LO 5-2)

8. How do revising, editing, and proofreading differ? Which one do you personally need to do more carefully? (LO 5-3)

9. How can you get better feedback on your writing? (LO 5-3)

5.2   Interviewing Writers about Their Composing Processes

Interview someone about the composing process(es) he or she uses for on-the-job writing. Questions you could ask include the following:

- What kind of planning do you do before you write? Do you make lists? formal or informal outlines?

- When you need more information, where do you get it?

- How do you compose your drafts? Do you dictate? Draft with pen and paper? Compose on screen? How do you find uninterrupted time to compose?

- When you want advice about style, grammar, and spelling, what source(s) do you consult?

- Does your superior ever read your drafts and make suggestions?

- Do you ever work with other writers to produce a single document? Describe the process you use.

- Describe the process of creating a document where you felt the final document reflected your best work. Describe the process of creating a document you found difficult or frustrating. What sorts of things make writing easier or harder for you?

As your instructor directs,

a. Share your results orally with a small group of students.

b. Present your results in an oral presentation to the class.

c. Present your results in an e-mail to your instructor.

d. Share your results with a small group of students and write a joint e-mail reporting the similarities and differences you found.

5.3   Analyzing Your Own Writing Processes

Save your notes and drafts from several assignments so that you can answer the following questions:

- Which practices of good writers do you follow?

- Which of the activities discussed in Chapter 5 do you use?

- How much time do you spend on each of the activities?

- What kinds of revisions do you make most often?

- Do you use different processes for different documents, or do you have one process that you use most of the time?

- What parts of your process seem most successful? Are there any places in the process that could be improved? How?

- What relation do you see between the process(es) you use and the quality of the final document?

As your instructor directs,

a. Discuss your process with a small group of other students.

b. Write an e-mail to your instructor analyzing in detail your process for composing one of the papers for this class.

c. Write an e-mail to your instructor analyzing your process during the term. What parts of your process(es) have stayed the same throughout the term? What parts have changed?

5.4 Evaluating the Ethical Implication of Connotations

In each of the following pairs, identify the more favorable term. When is its use justifiable?

1. wasted/sacrificed
2. illegal alien/immigrant
3. friendly fire/enemy attack
4. terminate/fire
5. inaccuracy/lying
6. budget/spending plan
7. feedback/criticism

5.5 Correcting Errors in Denotation and Connotation

Identify and correct the errors in denotation or connotation in the following sentences:

1. In our group, we weeded out the best idea each person had thought of.
2. She is a prudent speculator.
3. The three proposals are diametrically opposed to each other.
4. While he researched companies, he was literally glued to the web.
5. Our backpacks are hand sewn by one of roughly 16 individuals.
6. Raj flaunted the law against insider trading.

5.6 Eliminating Jargon and Simplifying Language

Revise these sentences to eliminate jargon and to use short, familiar words.

1. When the automobile company announced its strategic downsizing initiative, it offered employees a career alternative enhancement program.
2. Any alterations must be approved during the 30-day period commencing 60 days prior to the expiration date of the agreement.
3. As per your request, the undersigned has obtained estimates of upgrading our computer system. A copy of the estimated cost is attached hereto.
4. Please be advised that this writer is in considerable need of a new computer.
5. Enclosed please find the proposed draft for the employee negative retention plan. In the event that you have alterations which you would like to suggest, forward same to my office at your earliest convenience.

5.7 Changing Verbs from Passive to Active Voice

Identify passive voice in the following sentences and convert it to active voice. In some cases, you may need to add information to do so. You may use different words as long as you retain the basic meaning of the sentence. Remember that imperative verbs are active voice, too.

1. It has been suggested by the corporate office that all faxes are to be printed on recycled paper.
2. The office carpets will be cleaned professionally on Friday evening. It is requested that all staff members put belongings up on their desks.
3. The office microwave is to be cleaned by those who use it.
4. When the vacation schedule is finalized it is recommended that it be routed to all supervisors for final approval.
5. Material must not be left on trucks outside the warehouse. Either the trucks must be parked inside the warehouse or the material must be unloaded at the time of receiving the truck.

5.8 Using Strong Verbs

Revise each of the following sentences to replace hidden verbs with action verbs.

1. An understanding of stocks and bonds is important if one wants to invest wisely.
2. We must undertake a calculation of expected revenues and expenses for the next two years.
3. The production of clear and concise documents is the mark of a successful communicator.

4. We hope to make use of the company's website to promote the new product line.

5. If you wish to be eligible for the Miller scholarship, you must complete an application by January 31.

6. When you make an evaluation of media buys, take into consideration the demographics of the group seeing the ad.

7. We provide assistance to clients in the process of reaching a decision about the purchase of hardware and software.

5.9   Reducing Wordiness

1. Eliminate words that say nothing. You may use different words.

   a. There are many businesses that are active in community and service work.

   b. The purchase of another computer for the claims department will allow us to produce form letters quickly. In addition, return on investment could be calculated for proposed repairs. Another use is that the computer could check databases to make sure that claims are paid only once.

   c. Our decision to enter the South American market has precedence in the past activities of the company.

2. Combine sentences to show how ideas are related and to eliminate unnecessary words.

   a. Some customers are profitable for companies. Other customers actually cost the company money.

   b. If you are unable to come to the session on HMOs, please call the human resources office. You will be able to schedule another time to ask questions you may have about the various options.

   c. Major Japanese firms often have employees who know English well. U.S. companies negotiating with Japanese companies should bring their own interpreters.

   d. New procedure for customer service employees: Please be aware effective immediately, if a customer is requesting a refund of funds applied to their account a front and back copy of the check must be submitted if the transaction is over $500.00. For example, if the customer is requesting $250.00 back, and the total amount of the transaction is $750.00, a front and back copy of the check will be needed to obtain the refund.

5.10   Improving Parallel Structure

Revise each of the following sentences to create parallelism.

1. The orientation session will cover the following information:

   ■ Company culture will be discussed.

   ■ How to use the equipment.

   ■ You will get an overview of key customers' needs.

2. Five criteria for a good web page are content that serves the various audiences, attention to details, and originality. It is also important to have effective organization and navigation devices. Finally, provide attention to details such as revision date and the webmaster's address.

3. When you leave a voice mail message,

   ■ Summarize your main point in a sentence or two.

   ■ The name and phone number should be given slowly and distinctly.

   ■ The speaker should give enough information so that the recipient can act on the message.

   ■ Tell when you'll be available to receive the recipient's return call.

5.11   Revising Paragraphs

1. Make each of the following paragraphs more readable by opening each paragraph with a topic sentence. You may be able to find a topic sentence in the paragraph and move it to the beginning. In other cases, you'll need to write a new sentence.

   a. At Disney World, a lunch put on an expense account is "on the mouse." McDonald's employees "have ketchup in their veins." Business slang flourishes at companies with rich corporate cultures. Memos at Procter & Gamble are called "reco's" because the model P&G memo begins with a recommendation.

   b. The first item on the agenda is the hiring for the coming year. George has also asked that we review the agency goals for the next fiscal year. We should cover this early in the meeting since it may affect our hiring preferences. Finally, we need to announce the deadlines for grant proposals, decide which grants to apply for, and set up a committee to draft each proposal.

c. Separate materials that can be recycled from your regular trash. Pass along old clothing, toys, or appliances to someone else who can use them. When you purchase products, choose those with minimal packaging. If you have a yard, put your yard waste and kitchen scraps (excluding meat and fat) in a compost pile. You can reduce the amount of solid waste your household produces in four ways.

2. Revise each paragraph to make it easier to read. Change, rearrange, or delete words and sentences; add any material necessary.

a. Once a new employee is hired, each one has to be trained for a week by one of our supervisors at a cost of $1,000 each which includes the supervisor's time. This amount also includes half of the new employee's salary, since new hires produce only half the normal production per worker for the week. This summer $24,000 was spent in training 24 new employees. Absenteeism increased in the department on the hottest summer days. For every day each worker is absent we lose $200 in lost production. This past summer there was a total of 56 absentee days taken for a total loss of $11,200 in lost production. Turnover and absenteeism were the causes of an unnecessary expenditure of over $35,000 this summer.

b. One service is investments. General financial news and alerts about companies in the customer's portfolio are available. Quicken also provides assistance in finding the best mortgage rate and in providing assistance in making the decision whether to refinance a mortgage. Another service from Quicken is advice for the start and management of a small business. Banking services, such as paying bills and applying for loans, have long been available to Quicken subscribers. The taxpayer can be walked through the tax preparation process by Quicken. Someone considering retirement can use Quicken to ascertain whether the amount being set aside for this purpose is sufficient. Quicken's website provides seven services.

5.12 Revising, Editing, and Proofreading an E-mail

Dana Shomacher, an enthusiastic new hire of six months at Bear Foods, wants Stan Smith, regional head of HR at the grocery chain, to allow her to organize and publicize a food drive for Coastal Food Pantry. Revise, edit, and proof her e-mail.

> Hey Stan,
>
> I have this great idea for great publicity for Bear Foods that won't cost anything and will get us some really great publicity. Its something great we can do for our community. I wont Bear to conduct a food drive for Coastal Food Pantry. Their was an article in the Tribune about how they were having trouble keeping up with food requests and I thought what a great fit it would be for Bear.
>
> All our employees should donate food and we should also get our customer to donate also. We could set out some shopping carts for the donations. I could write an announcement for the Tribune and get some postures made for our front windows.
>
> I am willing to take care of all details so you won't have to do anything except say yes to this e-mail.
>
> Dana

After you have fixed Dana's e-mail, answer these questions in an e-mail to your instructor.

■ What revisions did you make? Why?

■ Many grocery stores already contribute to local food pantries. In addition to some staples, they provide items such as bakery goods that are past their sale date but still quite tasty, sacks for bagging groceries at the pantry, and even shopping carts to transport groceries to the cars of pantry clients. If Bear already contributes to Coastal, how should that fact change the content of Dana's e-mail?

■ What edits did you make? Why?

■ What impression do you think this e-mail made on the head of human resources? Explain. Do you think he granted Dana's request? Why or why not?

Submit both your version of Dana's e-mail and your analysis e-mail.

■ Make visual design choices that enhance and expand on your text without being simply decorative.

As your instructor directs,

a. Write an e-mail to your instructor explaining your choices for content and design.

b. In an oral presentation to the class, display your brochure and explain your content and design choices.

6.11   Creating an Infographic

Create an infographic for a campus, nonprofit, government, or business organization. As you work,

■ Analyze your intended audience. What are their needs? What factors are most likely to persuade them to view your infographic?

■ Choose a story. What's the important information? What idea or information do you want your audience to take away?

■ Make design choices that create a usable document and generate a positive response from your audience.

■ Make visual design choices that enhance and expand on your text without being simply decorative.

As your instructor directs,

a. Write an e-mail to your instructor explaining your choices for the content and design of your infographic.

b. In an oral presentation to the class, display your infographic and explain your content and design choices.

6.12   Creating a Web Page

Create a web page for a campus, nonprofit, government, or business organization that does not yet have one. As you work,

■ Analyze your intended audience. What are their needs? What factors are most likely to persuade them to use this site?

■ Choose a story. What's the important information? What action do you want them to take while they're browsing this site?

■ Make page design choices that create a usable site and generate a positive response from your audience.

■ Make visual design choices that enhance and expand on your text without being distracting.

As your instructor directs,

a. Write an e-mail to your instructor explaining your choices for content and design.

b. In an oral presentation to the class, display your site and explain your page and visual design choices. Provide the URL, or display images of the site as presentation visuals, so that classmates can evaluate your design as you present it.

6.13   Testing a Document

Ask someone to follow a set of instructions or to fill out a form. (Consider consumer instructions, forms for financial aid, and so forth.) As an alternative, you also might test a document you've created for a course.

■ Time the person. How long does it take? Is the person able to complete the task?

■ Observe the person. Where does he or she pause, reread, seem confused?

■ Interview the person. What parts of the document were confusing?

As your instructor directs,

a. Discuss the changes needed with a small group of classmates.

b. Write an e-mail to your instructor evaluating the document and explaining the changes that are needed. Include the document as an attachment to your e-mail.

c. Write to the organization that produced the document recommending necessary improvements.

d. In an oral presentation to the class, evaluate the document and explain what changes are needed.

6.14   Improving a Financial Aid Form

You've just joined the financial aid office at your school. The director gives you the form shown below and asks you to redesign it. The director says:

> We need this form to see whether parents have other students in college besides the one requesting aid. Parents are supposed to list all family members that the parents support—themselves, the person here, any other kids in college, and any younger dependent kids.
>
> Half of these forms are filled out incorrectly. Most people just list the student going here; they leave out everyone else.
>
> If something is missing, the computer sends out a letter and a second copy of this form. The whole process starts over. Sometimes we send this form back two or three times before it's right. In the meantime, students' financial aid is delayed—maybe for months. Sometimes things are so late that they can't register for classes, or they have to pay tuition themselves and get reimbursed later.
>
> If so many people are filling out the form wrong, the form itself must be the problem. See what you can do with it. But keep it to a page.

As your instructor directs,

a. Analyze the current form and identify its problems.

b. Revise the form. Add necessary information; reorder information; change the chart to make it easier to fill out.

c. Write an e-mail to the director of financial aid pointing out the changes you made and why you made them.

Hints:

- Where are people supposed to send the form? What is the phone number of the financial aid office? Should they need to call the office if the form is clear?

- Does the definition of *half-time* apply to all students or just those taking courses beyond high school?

- Should capital or lowercase letters be used?

- Are the lines big enough to write in?

- What headings or subdivisions within the form would remind people to list all family members whom they support?

- How can you encourage people to return the form promptly?

Please complete the chart below by listing all family members for whom you (the parents) will provide more than half support during the academic year (July 1 through June 30). Include yourselves (the parents), the student, and your dependent children, even if they are not attending college.

EDUCATIONAL INFORMATION, 201_ – 201_						
FULL NAME OF FAMILY MEMBER	AGE	RELATIONSHIP OF FAMILY MEMBER TO STUDENT	NAME OF SCHOOL OR COLLEGE THIS SCHOOL YEAR	FULL-TIME	HALF-TIME* OR MORE	LESS THAN HALF-TIME
STUDENT APPLICANT						

*Half-time is defined as 6 credit hours or 12 clock hours a term.

When the information requested is received by our office, processing of your financial aid application will resume.

Please sign and mail this form to the above address as soon as possible. Your signature certifies that this information, and the information on the FAF, is true and complete to the best of your knowledge. If you have any questions, please contact a member of the need analysis staff.

_____   _____
Signature of Parent(s)   Date

Notes

1. Edward Tufte, *Beautiful Evidence* (Cheshire, CT: Graphics Press, 2006), 153–55.
2. *Des Moines Register,* Front Page, October 14, 2011.
3. Charles Kostelnick and Michael Hassett, *Shaping Information: The Rhetoric of Visual Conventions* (Carbondale, IL: Southern Illinois University Press, 2003), 92, 94.
4. Ibid., 206–07.
5. Charles Kostelnick and David Roberts, *Designing Visual Language,* 2nd ed. (Boston: Allyn & Bacon, 2011), 81–83.
6. Rebecca Hagen and Kim Golombisky, *White Space is Not Your Enemy: A Beginners Guide to Communicating Visually Through Graphic, Web, and Multimedia Design,* 2nd ed. (New York: Focal Press, 2013), 7.
7. George A. Miller, "The Magical Number Seven, Plus or Minus Two: Some Limits on Our Capacity for Processing Information," *Psychological Review* 63, no. 2 (1956): 81–97.
8. Marlee M. Spafford, Catherine F. Schryer, Lorelei Lingard, and Marcellina Mian, "Accessibility and Order: Crossing Borders in Child Abuse Forensic Reports," *Technical Communication Quarterly* 19, no. 2 (2010): 118–43.
9. Jerry E. Bishop, "Word Processing: Research on Stroke Victims Yields Clues to the Brain's Capacity to Create Language," *Wall Street Journal,* October 12, 1993, A6; Anne Meyer and David H. Rose, "Learning to Read in the Computer Age," in *Reading Research to Practice,* ed. Jeanne S. Chall (Cambridge, MA: Brookline Books, 1998), 4–6.
10. Karen A. Schriver, *Dynamics in Document Design* (New York: Wiley, 1997), 274.
11. Jo Mackiewicz, "What Technical Writing Students Should Know about Typeface Personality," *Journal of Technical Writing and Communication* 34, no. 1–2 (2004): 113–31.
12. Miles A. Kimball and Ann R. Hawkins, *Document Design: A Guide for Technical Communicators* (Boston: Bedford/St. Martin's, 2008), 49, 125.
13. Mark Smiciklas, *The Power of Infographics* (Indianapolis: Que, 2012), 60–64.
14. Donna Kienzler, "Visual Ethics," *Journal of Business Communication* 34, no. 2 (1997): 171–72.
15. Harald Weinreich et al., "Not Quite the Average: An Empirical Study of Web Use," *ACM Transactions on the Web* 2, no. 1 (2008): 18.
16. "Lessons, Part 2," *Fast Company,* December 2012/January 2013, 98.
17. Jakob Nielsen, "F-Shaped Pattern for Reading Web Content," *Nielsen Norman Group: Jakob Nielsen's Alertbox,* April 17, 2006, http://www.nngroup.com/articles/f-shaped-pattern-reading-web-content/.
18. Jakob Nielsen, "Website Response Time," *Nielsen Norman Group: Jakob Nielsen's Alertbox,* June 21, 2010, http://www.nngroup.com/articles/website-response-times/.
19. Jakob Nielsen, "Top Ten Mistakes in Web Design," *Nielsen Norman Group: Jakob Nielsen's Alertbox,* January 1, 2011, http://www.nngroup.com/articles/top-10-mistakes-web-design/; and Emily Steel, "Neglected Banner Ads Get a Second Life," *Wall Street Journal,* June 20, 2007, B4.
20. "Corporate News: Target Settles with Blind Group on Web Access," *Wall Street Journal,* August 28, 2008, B4; and Lauren Pollock, "iTunes Eases Access for Blind," *Wall Street Journal,* September 29, 2008, B5.
21. Sarah Nassauer, "Marketing Decoder: Airline Boarding Passes," *Wall Street Journal,* May 3, 2012, D2.
22. Jakob Nielsen, "Why You Only Need to Test with 5 Users," *Nielsen Norman Group: Jakob Nielsen's Alertbox,* March 19, 2000, http://www.nngroup.com/articles/why-you-only-need-to-test-with-5-users/.
23. Jakob Nielsen, "Usability 101: Introduction to Usability," *Nielsen Norman Group: Jakob Nielsen's Alertbox,* January 4, 2012, http://www.nngroup.com/articles/usability-101-introduction-to-usability/.
24. Christopher Toth, "Revisiting a Genre: Teaching Infographics in Business and Professional Communication Courses," *Business and Professional Communication Quarterly* (March 2014). Page numbers not available at press time.

7 Communicating across Cultures

Chapter Outline

NEWSWORTHY COMMUNICATION

"Re-Treat" in China

To succeed in international markets, companies often need to adapt to local culture and tastes. American ice cream brands Baskin-Robbins and Dairy Queen have both had a presence in China since the early 1990s, but have had vastly different levels of success.

Dairy Queen, which entered China two years earlier than Baskin-Robbins, has opened more than 500 stores and plans to open another 500 by 2016.

Its success depends on how the company caters to local tastes: strong flavors and fruit-based desserts are popular in northern China, while green-tea-based flavors are favored in southern China. Dairy Queen relies on local owners to help the company balance between specialized local menus and costs of producing those products.

Competitor Baskin-Robbins, on the other hand, had opened only 90 stores in nearly 20 years. Part of the problem was with the branding

and slogans of the company: in China, Baskin-Robbins was known as "31 American Flavors." The company is now reviewing its strategy for China, including clarifying its brand, adapting its menu to local markets, and finding local master franchisees who can guide growth in different regions.

International business success depends on finding ways to appeal to local markets while being sensitive to cultures, values, and beliefs.

Source: Diana Bates, "Baskin-Robbins vs. Dairy Queen: A Delicious Cold War in China," *CNNMoney*, April 4, 2013, http://management.fortune.cnn.com/2013/04/04/baskin-robbins-dairy-queen-china/.

Learning Objectives

After studying this chapter, you will know

LO 7-1	**Why global business is important.**
LO 7-2	**Why diversity is becoming more important.**
LO 7-3	**How our values and beliefs affect our responses to other people.**
LO 7-4	**How nonverbal communication impacts cross-cultural communications.**
LO 7-5	**How to adapt oral communication for cross-cultural communications.**
LO 7-6	**How to adapt written communications for global audiences.**
LO 7-7	**Why it is important to check cultural generalizations.**

Marketing to Hispanic Audiences

Procter & Gamble (P&G) is changing marketing strategies to target more Hispanic shoppers. P&G is modifying some products and adding more Hispanic celebrities such as Jennifer Lopez and Eva Mendes to promote their products.

Hispanic families are typically younger and larger than the average American family and are a perfect market for items such as diapers and laundry detergents. P&G's researchers found that Hispanic shoppers are often willing to buy the slightly more expensive brands that P&G offers and that they are generally fans of fragrance in products.

Some specific items focused to Hispanic shoppers are Febreze air fresheners such as Brazilian Carnival and Hawaiian Aloha, and Downy fabric softener scented with lavender.

Adapted from Ellen Byron, "Hola: P&G Seeks Latino Shoppers," *Wall Street Journal,* September 15, 2011, B1.

Our values, priorities, and practices are shaped by the culture in which we grow up. Understanding other cultures is crucial if you want to work in an organization with a diverse group of employees, benefit from a global supply chain, sell your products to other cultures in your country, sell to other countries, manage an international plant or office, or work in this country for a multinational company headquartered in another country.

The successful intercultural communicator is

- Aware of the values, beliefs, and practices in other cultures.
- Sensitive to differences among individuals within a culture.
- Aware that his or her preferred values and behaviors are influenced by culture and are not necessarily "right."
- Sensitive to verbal and nonverbal behavior.
- Willing to ask questions about preferences and behaviors.
- Flexible and open to change.

The first step in understanding another culture is to realize that it may do things very differently, and that the difference is not bad or inferior. The second step is understanding that people within a single culture differ.

 WARNING: When pushed too far, the kinds of differences summarized in this chapter can turn into stereotypes, which can be just as damaging as ignorance.

Psychologists have shown that stereotypes have serious consequences and that they come into play even when we don't want them to. Asking African American students to identify their race before answering questions taken from the Graduate Record Examination, the standardized test used for admission to graduate schools, cut in half the number of items they got right.

Similarly, asking students to identify their sex at the beginning of Advanced Placement (AP) calculus tests, used to give high school students college credits, lowered the scores of women. If the sex question were moved to the end of the test, about 5% more women would receive AP credit.[1]

Don't try to memorize the material in this chapter as a rigid set of rules. Instead, use the examples to get a sense for the kinds of things that differ from one culture to another. Test these generalizations against your experience. When in doubt, ask.

Global Business LO 7-1

As we saw in Chapter 4, exports and imports are essential both to the success of individual businesses and to a country's economy as a whole. Even many small businesses have global supply chains. Most major businesses operate globally, and an increasing share of profits comes from outside the headquarters country:

- McDonald's earns 43% of its operating income internationally.

- 3M operates in more than 70 countries and has 65% of its sales internationally.

- Unilever sells products in over 190 countries; more than 55 % of its business is in emerging markets.

- Walmart's international sales earn "only" 28% of the company's sales, but that percentage is a huge $125 billion.[2]

Other businesses are following suit. Movie studios, for instance, are turning down scripts that would play well in the United States because they would not play well abroad. Such decisions are seen as sound, since foreign ticket sales are now two-thirds of the global film market. Studios are hiring more foreign actors for blockbusters, rewriting scripts for international audiences, and cutting back on comedies (American humor is frequently not funny abroad).[3] Other companies depend on international vendors or operations for services such as call centers, data centers, and accounting centers.

Local Culture Adaptations

As they expand globally, U.S. retailers are catering to local tastes and customs. When expanding to China, Walmart enraged consumers when its stores sold dead fish, and packaged meat, which shoppers saw as old merchandise. Walmart quickly learned to compensate by leaving meat uncovered and installing fish tanks to sell live fish. Walmart also sells live tortoises and snakes; Johnson's Baby Oil is stocked next to moisturizers containing sheep placenta, a native wrinkle "cure." Stores lure customers on foot or bikes with free shuttle buses and home deliveries for large items. Perhaps the biggest change is Walmart's acceptance of organized labor in China; in July 2006 it accepted its first union ever into its stores.

Other companies are also adapting their products to local preferences. Yum Brands, one of the most successful companies operating in China, serves fried shrimp and egg tarts along with Kentucky fried chicken, and Thai fried rice and seafood pizza at Pizza Huts. In the same market, Kraft Foods is offering green tea, mango, and mandarin orange cookies; beef stew; spicy chicken Ritz crackers; lobster cheese; and lemon-tea potato chips. In India, Dunkin' Donuts is offering mango doughnuts and smoothies.[4] Burger King sells a burger with

Marketing Disney to China

Six months after Hong Kong Disneyland opened, Disney officials were scrambling to understand why attendance was so low at the new park. They turned for answers to Chinese travel agents who book tours. Some of these agents believed Disney officials had not tried to understand the local market and Chinese culture.

After the disappointing start, Disney officials were eager to learn and ready to make changes. Using the travel industry feedback and other market research, Disney developed a new advertising campaign. Original ads had featured an aerial view of the park; new TV spots focused on people and showed guests riding attractions. A new print ad featuring a grandmother, mother, and daughter showed Disneyland as a place where families could have fun together.

Disney also worked to make visitors more comfortable inside the park. At an attraction offered in three different languages, guests gravitated toward the shortest line—usually the line for English-speaking guests. Now, three separate signs clearly mark which language will be used to communicate with guests in that line. Greater use of Mandarin-speaking guides and materials helped guests better enjoy shows and attractions. Also, additional seating was added in dining areas because Chinese diners linger longer than do Americans.

After incorporating these changes as well as others, Hong Kong Disneyland announced its first year in the black in February 2013.

Source: Merissa Marr and Geoffrey A. Fowler, "Chinese Lessons for Disney," *Wall Street Journal*, June 12, 2006, B1, B5; and Bruce Einhorn, "Disney's Hong Kong Theme Park Finally Turns a Profit," *Bloomberg Businessweek*, February 19, 2013, http://www.businessweek.com/articles/2013-02-19/disneys-hong-kong-theme-park-finally-turns-a-profit.

squid-ink-flavored catsup in Japan, where McDonald's sells a pie filled with mashed potatoes and bacon.[5]

KFC (formerly Kentucky Fried Chicken) achieved a marketing coup in Japan by suggesting that traditional American Christmas dinners centered on fried chicken. The campaign was so successful that Christmas takeout meals from KFC now must be reserved well in

What cultural barriers did Disney need to overcome to help Hong Kong Disneyland succeed? See "Marketing Disney to China" sidebar.

advance of the holiday. Signs in storefronts tell customers how many reservations are still available. Statues of Colonel Sanders are often dressed in kimonos or costumes for photo opportunities outside KFC stores.[6]

The costs for failing to adapt to local cultures can be high. AlertDriving, a Toronto company that provides training for companies' drivers, opened its services in more than 20 countries before it became aware of problems. The driving lessons had been poorly translated, and the instructions did not fit with local laws and customs. To make matters worse, the company did not learn about some of the problems for years because some clients considered criticism disrespectful. Eventually AlertDriving had to spend a million dollars to retranslate and rework all of its materials for local cultures, a costly lesson in cultural awareness.[7]

Outsourcing

Another major aspect of global business is **outsourcing**, sending corporate work to other companies. In the past this work was lower level: garment factories might be in Bangladesh; call or help centers might be in India. Now more companies are also outsourcing higher-level work such as research and accounting. And even outsourcing leaders, such as Tata Consultancy Services of India, are outsourcing; that company now has 8,500 employees in South America.[8]

Outsourcing has also moved from Near East countries to Eastern Europe and South America. IBM, Microsoft, Hewlett-Packard, and Ernst & Young have all opened offices in Poland, where they appreciate the highly educated and multilingual young workforce.[9]

International Career Experience

When plants, stores, and offices move overseas, people follow—from top executives to migrant workers. In fact, managers often find they need international experience if they want top-level jobs. Expatriate experience has also been shown to make them more creative and better problem solvers.[10] This effect, combined with booming overseas growth, means that executive headhunters are looking for people with deep bicultural fluency or experience in several countries, with China, India, and Brazil at the top of the list.[11] Responding to the need for global experience, business schools are stepping up their international offerings with classes, international case studies, overseas campuses, and student/faculty exchanges. For both young and experienced hires, second-language proficiency and multicultural awareness are sought.[12]

U.S. workers join a host of migrant workers already abroad. Nepalis work in Korean factories; Mongolians perform menial labor in Prague. Close to half of all migrants are women, many of whom leave children behind. They stay in touch through cell phones and the Internet.[13]

Migrant workers benefit the economies of both host and home countries. The money sent home by migrants, over $317 billion a year, is three times the world's total foreign aid. For seven countries, that income is over a quarter of their gross domestic product.[14] Thus, the money sent home is one of the major drivers of international development.

Thomas Friedman, Pulitzer Prize author and *New York Times* columnist, uses the metaphor of a flat world to describe the increasing globalization. In *The World Is Flat: A Brief History of the Twenty-First Century,* he says,

> What the flattening of the world means is that we are now connecting all the knowledge centers on the planet together into a single global network, which— if politics and terrorism do not get in the way—could usher in an amazing era of prosperity, innovation, and collaboration, by companies, communities, and individuals.[15]

Diversity in North America LO 7-2

Even if you stay in the United States and Canada, you'll work with people whose backgrounds differ from yours. Residents of small towns and rural areas may have different notions of friendliness than do people from big cities. Californians may talk and dress differently than people in the Midwest. The cultural icons that resonate for baby boomers may mean little to millennials. For many workers, local diversity has become as important as international diversity.

The past two decades have seen a growing emphasis on diversity. This diversity comes from many sources:

- Gender
- Race and ethnicity
- Regional and national origin
- Social class
- Religion
- Age
- Sexual orientation
- Physical ability

Many young Americans are already multicultural. According to 2010 U.S. census figures, only 59% of Americans aged 18 to 24 are non-Hispanic whites.[16] Some of them are immigrants or descendants of immigrants. In 2010, the largest numbers of immigrants to the United States have come from Mexico, China, India, the Philippines, Dominican Republic, Cuba, and Vietnam.[17] In 2002 Latinos became the largest minority group in the United States. The U.S. Census Bureau predicts that by 2042, the non-Hispanic white population will be less than 50% of the country's total population.[18] A comparable estimate from the Pew Research Center predicts the change will occur by 2050.[19] Already California, the District of Columbia, Hawaii, New Mexico, and Texas have a population that is more than 50% minorities; the Census Bureau labels these states as having a "majority-minority" population.[20]

Beyond Stereotypes

Learning about different cultures is important for understanding the different kinds of people we work with. However, leadership coaches Keith Caver and Ancella Livers caution that people are individuals, not just representatives of a cultural group. Based on their work with African American executives and middle managers, Caver and Livers have found that co-workers sometimes treat these individuals first as representatives of black culture, and only second as talented and experienced managers.

As an example, Caver and Livers cite the all-too-common situation of a newly hired black manager who participates in a management development activity. The new manager is prepared to answer questions about her area of business expertise, but the only questions directed toward her are about diversity. African American clients of Caver and Livers have complained that they are often called upon to interpret the behavior of famous black Americans such as Clarence Thomas or Jesse Jackson, and they wonder whether their white colleagues would feel their race qualifies them to interpret the deeds of famous white Americans.

In this example, stereotypes make well-intentioned efforts at communication offensive. To avoid such offense, consider not only culture, but also people's individual qualities and their roles and experiences. A person who communicates one way in the role of son or daughter may communicate very differently as an engineer or client.

Adapted from Keith A. Caver and Ancella B. Livers, "Dear White Boss," *Harvard Business Review* 80, no. 11 (November 2002), 76–81.

Bilingual Canada has long compared the diversity of its people to a mosaic. But now immigrants from Italy, China, and the Middle East add their voices to the medley of French, English, and Inuit. CHIN Radio in Toronto offers information in more than 30 languages.[21]

According to 2010 U.S. census figures, about 9 million people identified themselves as belonging to two or more races.[22] U.S. census figures also show that 20.0% of the population nationally and 43.1% in California speak a language other than English at home.[23] In cities such as Los Angeles and San Jose, over half the population speaks a language other than English at home (60.5% and 55.0%, respectively).[24]

Faced with these figures, organizations are making special efforts to diversify their workforces. Microsoft, for instance, has 40 employee networks; in addition to various national heritage groups such as Arabs, Brazilians, and ex-Yugoslavians, they cover various family roles (working parents), disabilities (visually impaired persons), age groups (boomers), and backgrounds (U.S. military veterans). The groups help provide a sense of community and also provide resources for recruiting and training.[25]

Diversified companies are smart; new evidence shows that diversity can improve business. Research analyzing the relationship between diversity levels and business performance of 250 U.S. businesses found a correlation between diversity and business success; companies with high levels of racial and ethnic minorities have the highest profits, market shares, and number of customers. On the other hand, organizations with low levels of diversity have the lowest profits, market shares, and number of customers.[26] When the Supreme Court heard arguments on considering race as a factor in admissions at the University of Texas, 57 companies, including Aetna, Dow Chemical, General Electric, Microsoft, Procter & Gamble, and Walmart, filed a brief arguing that a diverse workforce helps profits.[27]

Ways to Look at Culture

Each of us grows up in a culture that provides patterns of acceptable behavior and belief. We may not be aware of the most basic features of our own culture until we come into contact with people who do things differently. In India, children might be expected to touch the bare feet of elders to show respect, but in the United States such touching would be inappropriate.[28]

Anthropologist Edward Hall first categorized cultures as high-context or low-context, categories that are popular in the business milieu, although no longer in vogue in anthropology. In **high-context cultures**, most of the information is inferred from the social relationships of the people and the context of a message; little is explicitly conveyed. Chinese, Japanese, Arabic, and Latin American cultures are high-context. In **low-context cultures**, context is less important; most information is explicitly spelled out. German, Scandinavian, and North American cultures are low-context.

High- and low-context cultures value different kinds of communication and have different attitudes toward oral and written communication. As Figure 7.1 shows, low-context cultures like those of the United States favor direct approaches and may see indirectness as dishonest or manipulative. The written word is seen as more important than oral statements, so contracts are binding but promises may be broken. Details matter. Business communication practices in the United States reflect these low-context preferences.

Figure 7.1	Views of Communication in High- and Low-Context Cultures	
	High-context (Examples: Japan, Saudi Arabia)	**Low-context (Examples: Germany, North America)**
Preferred communication strategy	Indirectness, politeness, ambiguity	Directness, confrontation, clarity
Reliance on words to communicate	Low	High
Reliance on nonverbal signs to communicate	High	Low
Importance of relationships	High	Low
Importance of written word	Low	High
Agreements made in writing	Not binding	Binding
Agreements made orally	Binding	Not binding
Attention to detail	Low	High

Another way of looking at cultures is by using Geert Hofstede's cultural dimensions. Based on data collected by IBM, Hofstede's five dimensions are power/inequality, individualism/collectivism, masculinity/femininity, uncertainty avoidance, and long-term/short-term orientation. They are now applied to 74 countries and regions. To illustrate, Hofstede analyzes the United States as extremely high in individualism, but also high in masculinity, with men dominating a significant portion of the power structure. It has a lower power-distance index, indicating more equality at all social levels. It also has a lower uncertainty avoidance index, meaning it has fewer rules and greater tolerance for a variety of ideas and beliefs than do many countries.[29]

The discussion that follows focuses on national and regional cultures. But business communication is also influenced by the organizational culture and by personal culture, such as gender, race and ethnicity, social class, and so forth. As Figure 7.2 suggests, all of these intersect to determine what kind of communication is needed in a given situation. Sometimes one kind of culture may be more important than another. For example, in a study of aerospace engineers in Europe, Asia, and the United States, researchers found that the similarities of the professional discourse community outweighed differences in national cultures.[30]

Figure 7.2	National Culture, Organizational Culture, and Personal Culture Overlap

A $28 Billion Cross-Cultural Mistake

When Daimler-Benz and Chrysler proposed a $36 billion merger in 1998, both parties thought it was a good plan.

The merger was supposed to strengthen each other's place in the automotive market. But in 2007, a third party, Cerberus Capital Management, bought Daimler-Chrysler for just $7.4 billion. What went wrong?

The cultural differences reflected in the practices of the two companies were a significant factor. For example, the German workers of Daimler-Benz were used to daily, company-sanctioned beer breaks while the American workers worried that alcohol consumption during work would lead to accidents and legal suits.

In addition, the German professionals were used to a formal, hierarchical structure in the organization and formal business attire.

Differences in the corporate lifestyle later led to questions as to who got the better end of the deal. U.S. assembly line workers earned more wages per hour than their German counterparts. However, the German workers, who received a six-week annual vacation, fully paid health care and education, and a triennial soul-soothing spa break, undoubtedly had a better benefits package.

In addition, while the Daimler plant produced 850,000 vehicles a year with 120,000 employees, Chrysler manufactured 3 million with approximately the same number of employees. These cultural differences eventually overshadowed the positives of this merger.

Adapted from Associated Press, "A Chronology in the Takeover Saga of Global Automaker DaimlerChrysler AG," *Associated Press Archive*, May 14, 2007; Roberto A. Weber and Colin F. Camerer, "Cultural Conflict and Merger Failure: An Experimental Approach," *Management Science* 49, no. 4 (2003).

Values, Beliefs, and Practices   LO 7-3

Values and beliefs, often unconscious, affect our response to people and situations. Most North Americans, for example, value "fairness." "You're not playing fair" is a sharp criticism calling for changed behavior. In some countries, however, people expect certain groups to receive preferential treatment. Many people in the United States value individualism. Other countries may value the group. Japan's traditional culture emphasized the group, although there is evidence that this cultural value is changing.

Social relationships, which vary widely by country, also affect business communications. In countries such as Brazil and Saudi Arabia, where obligations to family and friends are extremely important, phone calls or even visits from family and friends may interrupt business meetings. In Saudi Arabia, segregation of women is so complete that a man and a woman should not be seen together in public unless married or family. In 2008, even France's president was asked not to bring his fiancée with him on a visit. Some buildings have elevators segregated by gender.[31]

Religion also affects business communication and business life. Practicing Muslims, Jews, and Christians observe days of rest and prayer on Friday, Saturday, and Sunday, respectively. During the holy month of Ramadan, Muslims fast from sunup to sundown; scheduling a business luncheon with a Muslim colleague during Ramadan would be inappropriate.

Even everyday practices differ from culture to culture. North Americans and Europeans put the family name last; Asians put it first. North American and European printing moves from left to right; Arabic reads from right to left. In the United States, a meeting on the fourth floor is actually on the fourth floor; in England, it is actually on the fifth floor of the building, because the British distinguish between ground and first floors. In China, the building may not have a fourth floor, because the word for *four* sounds like the word for *death,* so the number is considered unlucky.[32]

Food practices can lead to interesting business meals, with different ways of eating. Food delicacies also vary widely by country. In China you might eat scorpions, kidney pie in England, snails in France, durian in Indonesia, grasshoppers in Mexico, sheep's head in Saudi Arabia, and haggis in Scotland. Remember that our consumption of pork would horrify many Muslims, while our consumption of beef would disgust many Indians.[33]

Common business practices also differ among cultures (see Figure 7.3). In Middle Eastern—or predominantly Muslim—countries, business cards are exchanged only with the right hand, never with the "unclean" left hand. Cards should not be kept or put in a pigskin case; in India, avoid leather cases, also. In China, business cards are exchanged with both hands; they are complimented and put in a card case. In Russia, where hierarchy is important, cards should show your status by including items such as your title and the founding date of your company. In India, where education is specially valued, your card might show your graduate degrees.[34]

In today's electronically connected world, cultural practices can change swiftly. For instance, in China, where age has traditionally been revered, few political or business leaders now turn gray, even those who are in their fifties or sixties. Workers are also becoming less group oriented and more individualistic.[35] In such fluid contexts, communication becomes even more important. If you don't know, ask.

Nonverbal Communication   LO 7-4

Chapter 4 discussed the significance of nonverbal communication in interpersonal communication. **Nonverbal communication** is also important in intercultural settings. Be aware of usage differences in such areas as body language, touch, space, and time.

Figure 7.3	Customs for Business Meetings					
Country	**Icebreakers**	**Openers**	**Punctuality**	**Standing space bubble**	**Greeting**	**Faux pas**
Brazil	Soccer	Some small talk	You should be punctual; your contact may be 15–60 minutes late.	Less than one foot	Extended handshake; after acquaintance, embraces and air kisses	Refusing invitation to eat
China	Chinese discoveries and innovations	Research your contacts; they will have researched you. Show your awareness of a mutual interest.	Very important	2.5–3 feet	Slight bow; sometimes just a nod. With foreigners, handshake may follow bow.	Omitting official titles
Germany	Sports, international affairs, German literature	Maybe small talk, maybe straight to business. If small talk, discuss local culture, sites, food, beverages.	Of major importance. Arrive a few minutes early.	About 6 inches beyond handshake distance	Firm, brief handshake with direct eye contact but not a big smile	Using humor in business affairs; referring to Third Reich
India	Trade event, the specific city, Indian culture	Trading of information about hobbies, travels, maybe some about your family	You should be punctual. Allow time for traffic jams.	2–2.5 feet. May move closer after initial greeting	Some businessmen will shake hands. A more common greeting among Indians is the *namaste.**	Referring to caste system, Pakistan, or infrastructure
Japan	Many personal questions to ascertain your place in hierarchy	Try to establish pleasant mood rather than conveying lots of facts	Arrive 5–10 minutes early	Start 2.5–3 feet apart to leave room for the bow.	Enthusiastic verbal greeting. Many degrees of bowing (from the waist). Handshakes are gentle and last 5 seconds or more.	Not having a significant gift to exchange; prolonged eye contact
Russia	Russian cultural and scientific achievements	Explain your position with great clarity, evidence, and firmness.	Be punctual; your host may be 15 minutes late.	About 1.5 feet	Handshake with extended direct eye contact	Whistling, standing with hands in pockets
Saudi Arabia	Soccer or racing	Extensive inquiries into your journey, family; inquiring how host started in industry and became successful	Be punctual, but punctuality is not a virtue for natives.	About one foot; do not back away to increase space	Several styles of greeting currently in use; let your counterpart initiate	Misusing images of their flag; inquiries about women in general, host's female family members in particular

Namaste: palms together in front of chest, fingertips just below chin. Head may nod slightly.
Source: Terri Morrison and Wayne A. Conaway, *Kiss, Bow, or Shake Hands: Sales and Marketing: The Essential Cultural Guide—from Presentations and Promotions to Communicating and Closing* (New York: McGraw-Hill, 2012).

Communicating with Subsistence Consumers

Subsistence consumers may earn little money, but they still need to buy necessities. Corporations are learning how best to communicate with them.

Many of them lack basic reading skills, so visual cues are important. Cues such as store layout, package design, and brand logos need to remain consistent for them. Many buy products that look attractive because of packaging colors or pictures. They also tend to buy only brands they recognize by appearance, so changes in colors or visual design have negative impacts.

To better serve these customers, stores need to

- Display pictures of product categories, so shoppers can find the goods they need.

- Sell products in small quantities, including single-use or daily quantities.

- Provide easy-to-use packaging that keeps products safe in local conditions such as high humidity and lack of refrigeration.

- Price products in whole or half numbers, and display these prices graphically— such as a picture of the money needed to buy the product.

- Train store personnel to form relationships with consumers and offer friendly, individualized assistance.

- Capitalize on local social networks and word-of-mouth communications.

Adapted from Jose Antonio Rosa, Madhubalan Viswanathan, and Julie A. Ruth, "Emerging Lessons: For Multinational Companies, Understanding the Needs of Poorer Consumers Can Be Profitable and Socially Responsible," *Wall Street Journal*, October 20, 2008, R12; and Kelly L. Weidner, Jose Antonio Rosa, and Madhu Viswanathan, "Marketing to Subsistence Consumers: Lessons from Practice," *Journal of Business Research*, 63, no. 6 (2010): 559–69.

Body Language

Just as verbal languages differ, so body languages differ from culture to culture. The Japanese value the ability to sit quietly. They may see the U.S. tendency to fidget and shift as an indication of lack of mental or spiritual balance. Even in North America, interviewers and audiences usually respond negatively to nervous gestures such as fidgeting with a tie or hair or jewelry, tapping a pencil, or swinging a foot.

People use body language to signal such traits as interest, respect, emotional involvement, confidence, and agreement. Among Arab men, for instance, holding hands is an expression of affection and solidarity. Americans working in the Middle East are cautioned to avoid pointing their finger at people or showing the soles of their feet when seated.[36] Bill Gates made international news when he greeted the president of South Korea by shaking her hand with one hand and keeping his other hand in his pocket (a sign of disrespect in South Korea).

Eye Contact   North American whites see eye contact as a sign of attention; in fact, lack of eye contact is slightly suspect. But in many cultures, dropped eyes are a sign of appropriate deference to a superior. Japanese show respect by lowering their eyes when speaking to superiors. In some Latin American and African cultures, such as Nigeria, it is disrespectful for lower-status people to prolong eye contact with their superiors. Similarly, in the United States, staring is considered rude. For the English, however, polite people pay strict attention to speakers and blink their eyes to show understanding. In China, a widening of the eyes shows anger, in the United States—surprise. Among Arab men, eye contact is important; it is considered impolite not to face someone directly.[37] In Muslim countries, women and men are not supposed to have eye contact.

These differences can lead to miscommunication in the multicultural workplace. Superiors may feel that subordinates are being disrespectful when the subordinates are being fully respectful—according to the norms of their culture.

Facial Expression   The frequency of smiling and the way people interpret smiles may depend on the purpose smiles serve in a particular culture. In the United States, smiling varies from region to region. In Germany, Sweden, and the "less-smiley" U.S. cultures, smiling is more likely to be reserved for close relationships and genuine joy. Frequent smiles in other situations would therefore seem insincere. For other people, including those in Thailand, smiling can be a way to create harmony and make situations pleasant.

Research has shown that when they are interpreting emotions, Americans focus on the mouth, so smiles are important. Japanese often focus on the eyes. This distinction is apparent even in their emoticons. Americans use :) for a happy face and :(for a sad one; Japanese use ^-^ for a happy face and ;_; for a sad one.[38]

Gestures   U.S. citizens sometimes assume that they can depend on gestures to communicate if language fails. But the meanings of gestures vary widely in different cultures. Kissing is usually an affection gesture in the United States but is a greeting gesture in other countries. In Greece, people may nod their heads to signify *no* and shake their heads to signify *yes*.[39]

Gestures that mean approval in the United States may have very different meanings in other countries. The "thumbs up" sign, which means "good work" or "go ahead" in the United States and most of Western Europe, is a vulgar insult in Iraq, Iran, and Bangladesh. The circle formed with the thumb and first finger that means *OK* in the United States is obscene in Brazil and Germany. In India, the raised middle finger means you need to urinate.[40]

The V-sign is another gesture with multiple meanings. Made with the palm facing out, it was famously used by Churchill during WWII and by the hippies in the '60s and '70s. Made with the palm facing in, it is the equivalent of giving someone the finger in countries such as the United Kingdom, Ireland, and Australia. An American president made interesting headlines when he inadvertently used the V-sign on a visit to Australia.

Movements from other body parts besides the hands can also be significant. In Saudi Arabia, where feet are unclean, it would be highly improper to nudge anyone with your foot, or to sit with your legs crossed in a way that shows the sole of your shoe.[41]

Touch

Repeated studies have shown that babies need to be touched to grow and thrive and that older people are healthier both mentally and physically if they are touched. But some people are more comfortable with touch than others. Each kind of person may misinterpret the other. A person who dislikes touch may seem unfriendly to someone who's used to touching. A toucher may seem overly familiar to someone who dislikes touch.

Many parts of North America allow opposite-sex couples to hold hands or walk arm-in-arm in public but frown on the same behavior in same-sex couples. People in some other countries have the opposite expectation: male friends or female friends can hold hands or walk arm-in-arm, but an opposite-sex couple should not touch in public.

In U.S. business settings, people generally shake hands when they meet, but little other touching is considered appropriate. In Mexico, greetings may involve greater physical contact. Men may embrace one another, and women may kiss one another. In many European settings, business colleagues may shake hands when they encounter one another throughout the day. In countries along the Mediterranean, hugs and shoulder pats are common as well. In some European countries, greetings include light kisses. The typical pattern is to kiss the person's right cheek and then the left (or to kiss the air near the cheek). In Italy this pattern stops with two kisses; Belgians continue for three, and the French for four.[42]

Space

Personal space is the distance people want between themselves and other people in ordinary, nonintimate interchanges. Some research shows that many North Americans, North Europeans, and Asians want a bigger personal space than do many Latin Americans, French, Italians, and Arabs. Even people who prefer lots of personal space are often forced to accept close contact on a crowded elevator or subway, or in a small conference room.

Even within a culture, some people like more personal space than do others. In many cultures, people who are of the same age and sex take less personal space than do mixed-age or mixed-sex groups.

Time

Differences in time zones complicate international phone calls and videoconferences. But even more important are different views of time and attitudes toward time. Offices in the United States keep time by the calendar and

Nonverbal Communication Tips for China

- If you are going to shake hands with your boss, you must initiate the handshake; use a gentle, almost limp, hand to show respect. Some Chinese do not like to shake hands; in that case, use a small bow.

- Make sure you have a professional business card, and show you are impressed by others' business cards. Treat their cards with admiration and respect.

- Small gifts are expected. Give something like a watch (not too fancy, but a known Western brand), but never a clock (associated with death).

- Numbers have meaning. Four is unlucky, because it sounds like *death*, so you would never give anyone a set of four objects. Eight is lucky because it sounds like *wealth*.

- Do not point at someone to get their attention; that is considered a rude gesture. Instead, gracefully wave them over with your whole hand.

- Be aware that drinking and smoking are considered a normal part of business.

- Be prepared to eat foods that you are not familiar with, like offal (entrails and inner organs of animals). Fish heads, however, should be reserved for the most important person at the table.

Adapted from Eric Spitznagel, "Impress Your Chinese Boss," *Bloomberg Businessweek*, January 9, 2012, 80–81.

Chinese Brand Names

Companies may struggle with brand name interpretations when introducing new products to another country. This can be especially difficult when bringing a new product to China, where the language has thousands of characters.

Ideally, the Chinese name that is chosen will sound like the original and mean the same thing, but that ideal can be difficult to achieve. Companies naming products for the Chinese market have four approaches:

- No resemblance in sound or meaning: Pizza Hut's Chinese name means "Guarantee Wins Guests."

- Only sounds similar: Sony's Chinese name sounds similar, but means "Exploring Nun or Priest."

- Means the same but sounds different: General Motors chose this option.

- Sounds and means the same: Nike's Chinese name sounds like "Nike" and means, "Endurance Conquer."

Adapted from Marc Fetscherin, Ilan Alon, Romie Littrell, and Allan Chan, "In China? Pick Your Brand Name Carefully," *Harvard Business Review* 90, no. 9 (September 2012): 26.

https://www.cia.gov/library/publications/the-world-factbook/.

World Factbook published by the Central Intelligence Agency is a good starting point for learning about the people of another country. Extensive country-by-country information includes history, government, and economics.

the clock. Being "on time" is seen as a sign of dependability. Other cultures may keep time by the seasons, the moon, the sun, internal "body clocks," or a personal feeling that "the time is right."

North Americans who believe that "time is money" are often frustrated in negotiations with people who take a much more leisurely approach. Part of the problem is that people in many other cultures want to establish a personal relationship before they decide whether to do business with each other.

The problem is made worse because various cultures mentally measure time differently. Many North Americans measure time in five-minute blocks. Someone who's five minutes late to an appointment or a job interview feels compelled to apologize. If the executive or interviewer is running half an hour late, the caller expects to be told about the likely delay upon arriving. Some people won't be able to wait that long and will need to reschedule their appointments. But in other cultures, half an hour may be the smallest block of time. To someone who mentally measures time in 30-minute blocks, being 45 minutes late is no worse than being 10 minutes late is to someone who is conscious of smaller units.

Different cultures have different lead times for scheduling events. In some countries, you need to schedule important meetings at least two weeks in advance. In other countries, not only are people not booked up so far in advance, but a date two weeks into the future may be forgotten.

Anthropologist Edward Hall distinguishes between **monochronic cultures**, which focus on clock time, and **polychronic cultures**, which focus on relationships. People in monochronic cultures tend to schedule their time and do one task at a time; people in polychronic cultures tend to want their time unstructured and do multiple tasks at the same time. When U.S. managers feel offended because a Latin American manager also sees other people during "their" appointments, the two kinds of time are in conflict.[43]

Eating pizza with chopsticks illustrates how new cultural values interact with native culture to constantly create hybrid cultures.

Other Nonverbal Symbols

Many other symbols can carry nonverbal meanings: clothing, colors, age, and height, to name a few.

Clothing   In North America, certain styles and colors of clothing are considered more professional and credible. Some clothing denotes not only status but also occupational group. Cowboy boots, firefighter hats, and judicial robes all may, or may not, signal specific occupations. Tool belts, coveralls, hard hats, and stethoscopes may signal broader occupational groupings.

Colors   Colors can also carry meanings in a culture. Chinese tradition associates red with good fortune. Korean Buddhists use red to announce death. Black is the color of joy in Japan, the color of death in the United States.[44] White is the color of funerals in Eastern countries; in the United States it is the color of brides. UPS found its company color working against it when it entered the Spanish market. The brown trucks that distinguish the delivery company's brand in the United States are not a good image in Spain, where hearses are traditionally brown. When UPS realized its mistake, it altered its uniforms and truck colors in Spain, emphasizing the company logo rather than the color brown.[45]

Age In the United States, youth is valued. People color their hair and even have face-lifts to look as youthful as possible. In Japan, younger people generally defer to older people. Americans attempting to negotiate in Japan are usually taken more seriously if at least one member of the team is noticeably gray-haired.

Height Height connotes status in many parts of the world. Executive offices are usually on the top floors; the underlings work below. Even being tall can help a person succeed. A recent study found that white, non-Hispanic males of below-average height earned 10% less than males of above-average height. Each additional inch of height was linked to 2.5% greater income. Perhaps surprisingly, the measurement that produced this effect was the man's height when he was a teenager. Those who grew later in life did not enjoy the income benefits of greater height. For white women in the study, actual adult height was associated with greater income. The researchers lacked sufficient data on other ethnic groups except to say that there seems to be a height–income effect for black males that resembles the effect for white males.[46]

Oral Communication LO 7-5

Effective oral communication requires cultural understanding. In Japan, for instance, much information is transmitted nonverbally and indirectly. Subtlety and restraint are important; what is not said is just as important as what is said. Japanese are comfortable with silence, and pauses of 10 to 15 seconds are not uncommon.[47]

As Figure 7.3 suggests, even an act as specific as a business introduction may differ across cultures. These are general patterns, not absolutes, but they help communicators stay alert for audience preferences.

During business meetings, even words as distinct as *yes* and *no* may cause confusion. In some cultures where saying *no* is considered rude, a *yes* may mean merely "I heard you."

Learning at least a little of the language of the country where you hope to do business will help you in several ways. First, learning the language will give you at least a glimpse into the culture. Second, learning some of the language will help you manage the daily necessities of finding food and getting where you need to go while you're there. Finally, in business negotiations, knowing a little of the language gives you more time to think. You'll catch part of the meaning when you hear your counterpart speak; you can begin thinking even before the translation begins.

Frequently you will need good translators when you travel abroad on business. Brief them with the technical terms you'll be using; explain as much of the context of your negotiations as possible. A good translator can also help you interpret nonverbal behavior and negotiating strategies. Some translators can help their clients establish trust and credibility with international businesses.

**Safety Problem:
Multiple
Languages**

All mining is dangerous, but
platinum mining is particular so.
The mineral is frequently a mile
below the surface and in very
hard rock.

Safety at Anglo American Platinum's mines was further complicated by lack of a common
language. Workers, who come
from various countries and
tribes, speak a dozen languages
and are frequently not able to
warn each other of dangers.

For more than a hundred
years, Anglo has taught its miners Fanagolo, a 200-word pid-
gin language created for mining
tasks. But today's workers find
the language racially offensive.

Now Anglo is offering English
and Afrikaans classes, and
encouraging all its miners to
learn one of the two languages.

Adapted from Robert Guy
Matthews, "A Mile Down,
Saving Miners' Lives," *Wall
Street Journal*, July 19,
2010, B1.

Understatement and Exaggeration

To understand someone from another culture, you must understand the speaker's conversational style. The British have a reputation for understatement. Someone good enough to play at Wimbledon may say he or she "plays a little tennis." In many contexts, Americans accept exaggeration as a way to express positive thinking. Particularly in advertising, Americans expect some hype. Germans, in contrast, generally see exaggeration as a barrier to clear communication.[48]

Compliments

The kinds of statements that people interpret as compliments and the socially correct ways to respond to compliments also vary among cultures. Statements that seem complimentary in one context may be inappropriate in another. For example, women in business may be uncomfortable if male colleagues or superiors compliment them on their appearance: the comments may suggest that the women are being treated as visual decoration rather than as contributing workers.

Approaches to Negatives

Cultures also vary in the way they deal with unpleasant details. In Brazil and India, unpleasantness is suppressed, so a negative response would probably be indirect. It may be a statement that the issue or action is complicated, or an off-topic remark, such as one about a restaurant. To save face in Japan, bad news is never delivered in front of a group. In Saudi Arabia, face saving is also important, so again blunt *no*'s are rare. A polite *yes* may frequently be a *no*. A true yes will be followed by action such as a request for information or an appointment with a lawyer. Negative information is delivered through intermediaries.[49]

Writing to International Audiences   LO 7-6

Cultural preferences are also important in written documents. Germans, for instance, have a reputation for appreciating technical data and scientific detail. They are likely to be intolerant of claims that seem logically unsupportable. An American writing for a German audience should ensure that any claims are literally true.[50] The Muslim calendar, the Hijri, is a lunar one of 354 days. Paperwork for Saudi businesses might carry two sets of dates: Western dates, designated C.E. (Common Era), and Muslim dates, designated H. (Hijri).[51]

Most cultures are more formal in their writing than the United States. When you write to international audiences, you may need to use titles, not first names. Avoid contractions, slang, idioms, and sports metaphors.

Not: Let's knock these sales figures out of the ballpark.

But: Our goal is to increase sales 7%.

Do write in English unless you're extremely fluent in your reader's language. Be clear, but be adult. Don't write in second-grade English.

Not: We will meet Tuesday. Our meeting room will be Hanscher North. We will start at 9:30 AM.

But: We will meet Tuesday at 9:30 AM in Hanscher North.

Disaster communications that cross cultures have many complexities, but Apple CEO Steve Jobs wrote a message that moved audiences in multiple cultures. See "Communicating Compassion" sidebar on this page.

The patterns of organization that work for U.S. audiences may need to be modified in international correspondence. For instance, most North Americans develop an argument linearly; points in a contract such as price, quantity, and delivery date are presented in order, one at a time. However, businesspeople from other cultures may think holistically rather than sequentially, and the business relationship may be far more important than the actual contract, which may not even be considered binding.

In other documents, negative messages may need more buffering and requests may need to be indirect. A U.S. manager asking a direct question in an e-mail ("Were the contract numbers checked against Accounting's figures?") could cause hurt feelings among some international recipients, who might take the question as an accusation.

As Figures 7.4 and 7.5 suggest, the style, structure, and strategies that would motivate a U.S. audience may need to be changed for international readers. Relationships become more important, as do politeness strategies. The information in the figures suggests general patterns, not definitive delineations, but such suggestions help communicators look for ways to be more effective.

Communicating Compassion

When the 2011 earthquake and tsunami struck Japan, Apple was preparing to release its latest version of the popular iPad there. It was a critical time for the company's continued success. Hours after the earthquake, however, Apple suspended the iPad's launch, and all its employees in Japan received this message from CEO Steve Jobs:

"To Our Team in Japan,

We have all been following the unfolding disaster in Japan. Our hearts go out to you and your families, as well as all of your countrymen who have been touched by this tragedy.

If you need time or resources to visit or care for your families, please see HR and we will help you. If you are aware of any supplies that are needed, please also tell HR and we will do what we can to arrange delivery.

Again, our hearts go out to you during this unimaginable crisis.

Please stay safe."

The message itself was important—a statement of compassion from the CEO. But the way Apple continued to respond made the difference for thousands of employees and even more nonemployees. In cities with no power or Internet, Apple's self-contained stores stayed open, providing free wireless access, computer access, phone calls, charging stations, food, and places to sleep for stranded employees. Hundreds crowded into the stores to contact family and friends.

In high-context cultures like Japan's, which place great importance on actions and personal relationships, Apple's response to the disaster was admirable. The message from Jobs and the actions of local employees who helped thousands of people were compassionate gestures from a truly international company.

Adapted from "Steve Jobs Responds to Japan Quake," *International Business Times,* March 17, 2011, http://www.ibtimes.com/steve-jobs-responds-japan-quake-276013#; and Josh Ong, "Japan Apple Stores Serve as Rallying Point after Massive Quake," *Apple Insider,* March 14, 2011, http://appleinsider.com/articles/11/03/14/japan_apple_stores_serve_as_rallying_point_after_massive_quake.

Figure 7.4	Cultural Contrasts in Oral Communication		
	United States	**Europe**	**Asia**
Opening a conversation	Take the initiative	England: take the initiative	Japan: wait for an invitation to speak
Interrupting	Wait until speaker finishes	Italy: interruptions common; more than one person may speak at once	Japan: do not interrupt; silent periods common
Vocal characteristics	Modulated pace and volume	Spaniards may speak louder than the French	Indians speak English much faster than Americans
Disagreements	Stated calmly and directly	Spain: often accompanied by emotional outbursts	Japan: often communicated by silence
Praise	Key motivational factor	Russia: saved for extraordinary behavior, otherwise seen as false	Indonesia: may be offensive (suggests supervisor surprised by good job)

Source: Adapted from Richard M. Steers, Carlos J. Sanchez-Runde, and Luciara Nardon, *Management across Cultures: Challenges and Strategies* (New York: Cambridge University Press, 2010), 222–23.

Figure 7.5	Cultural Contrasts in Written Persuasive Documents		
	United States	**Japan**	**Arab countries**
Opening	Request action or get reader's attention	Offer thanks; apologize	Offer personal greetings
Way to persuade	Immediate gain or loss of opportunity	Waiting	Personal connections; future opportunity
Style	Short sentences	Modesty; minimize own standing	Elaborate expressions; many signatures
Closing	Specific request	Desire to maintain harmony	Future relationship, personal greeting
Values	Efficiency, directness, action	Politeness, indirectness, relationship	Status, continuation

Source: Adapted from Farid Elashmawi and Philip R. Harris, *Multicultural Management 2000: Essential Cultural Insights for Global Business Success* (Houston: Gulf, 1998), 139.

IBM in Africa

IBM would like to use its products and consulting experience to help Africa increase crop yields, power grid performance, and government efficiency.

Many parts of Africa desperately need this help. In various cities and town, thousands of people live in shacks made out of plastic tarps and old iron, living on very small amounts of water. In the city of Tshwane in South Africa, a quarter of the city's water supply is wasted due to leaking water tanks. IBM sent a team to do a free analysis of Tshwane's water system in order to build a business relationship with the local government.

IBM's revenue from Africa was $400 million in 2012 and is expected to more than double in a few years. If so, this growth will be even faster than sales growth in India was.

Working in Africa can be a risky venture for businesses, however. Because so many African governments are new and subject to failure, establishing a business relationship with them can be difficult.

Adapted from Sarah Frier, "Things Fall Apart. IBM Is Here to Help," *Bloomberg Businessweek,* February 25–March 3, 2013, 28–29.

Most writers will benefit from researching a culture before composing messages for people in it.

Response time expectations may also need to be modified. U.S. employees tend to expect fast answers to e-mails. However, other cultures with hierarchical organization structures may need extra response time to allow for approval by superiors. Pressing for a quick response may alienate the people whose help is needed and may result in false promises.[52]

In international business correspondence, list the day before the month:

Not: April 8, 2008

But: 8 April 2008

Spell out the month to avoid confusion.

Businesspeople from Europe and Japan who correspond frequently with North America are beginning to adopt U.S. directness and patterns of organization. Still, it may be safer to modify your message somewhat; it certainly is more courteous.

Learning More about International Business Communication   LO 7-7

Learning to communicate with people from different backgrounds shouldn't be a matter of learning rules. Instead, use the examples in this chapter to get a sense for the kinds of factors that differ from one culture to another. Test these generalizations against your experience. Remember that people everywhere have their own personal characteristics. And when in doubt, ask.

You can also learn by seeking out people from other backgrounds and talking with them. Many campuses have centers for international students. Some communities have groups of international businesspeople who meet regularly to discuss their countries. By asking all these people what aspects of the dominant U.S. culture seem strange to them, you'll learn much about what is "right" in their cultures.

Summary by Learning Objectives

LO 7-1   **Why global business is important.**

Exports are essential both to the success of individual businesses and to a country's economy as a whole. Even many small businesses have global supply chains.

LO 7-2   **Why diversity is becoming more important.**

Research has found a correlation between diversity and business success; companies with high levels of racial and ethnic minorities have the highest profits, the highest market shares, and highest number of customers.

LO 7-3   **How our values and beliefs affect our responses to other people.**

Although often unconscious, our values and beliefs impact our cross-cultural communications. Religious beliefs, social values, even everyday practices, all impact communication.

LO 7-4   **How nonverbal communication impacts cross-cultural communications.**

Nonverbal communication is communication that doesn't use words. Nonverbal communication can include body language, space, time, and other miscellaneous matters such as clothing, colors, age, and height.

Nonverbal signals can be misinterpreted just as easily as can verbal symbols (words). For instance, no gesture has a universal meaning across all cultures. Gestures that signify approval in North America may be insults in other countries, and vice versa.

LO 7-5   **How to adapt oral communication for cross-cultural communications.**

Learning a little of the language of the country helps, as does a good translator. Be particularly careful of compliments and approaches to negatives.

LO 7-6   **How to adapt written communications for global audiences.**

Cultural preferences are also important in written documents. Most cultures are more formal in their writing than the United States. Also, the patterns of organization that work for North American audiences may need to be modified in international correspondence.

LO 7-7   **Why it is important to check cultural generalizations.**

The successful intercultural communicator is

- Aware of the values, beliefs, and practices in other cultures.
- Sensitive to differences among individuals within a culture.
- Aware that his or her preferred values and behaviors are influenced by culture and are not necessarily "right."
- Sensitive to verbal and nonverbal behavior.
- Willing to ask about preferences and behaviors.
- Flexible and open to change.

Continuing Case

The All-Weather Case, set in an HR department in a manufacturing company, extends through all 19 chapters and is available at www.mhhe.com/locker11e. The portion for this chapter asks students to research and then write on Japanese customs.

Exercises and Cases

*Go to www.mhhe.com/locker11e for additional Exercises and Cases.

7.1   Reviewing the Chapter

1. Why is global business important? (LO 7-1)
2. What are the advantages of receiving an overseas assignment? (LO 7-1)
3. Why is diversity becoming more important than ever before? (LO 7-2)
4. What are low-context and high-context cultures? (LO 7-3)
5. How do our values and beliefs affect our responses to other people? (LO 7-3)

6. What are some forms of nonverbal communication? What variations would you expect to see in them among people of different cultures? (LO 7-4)

7. Why do people from monochronic cultures sometimes have trouble with people from polychronic cultures? (LO 7-4)

8. What are some characteristics of oral communications you should consider when communicating cross-culturally? (LO 7-5)

9. What are some cautions to consider when writing for international audiences? (LO 7-6)

10. Why is it important to check cultural generalizations? (LO 7-7)

7.2   Identifying Sources of Miscommunication

In each of the following situations, identify one or more ways that cultural differences may be leading to miscommunication.

1. Alan is a U.S. sales representative in South America. He makes appointments and is careful to be on time. But the person he's calling on is frequently late. To save time, Alan tries to get right to business. But his hosts want to talk about sightseeing and his family. Even worse, his appointments are interrupted constantly, not only by business phone calls but also by long conversations with other people and even the customers' children who come into the office. Alan's first progress report is very negative. He hasn't yet made a sale. Perhaps South America just isn't the right place to sell his company's products.

2. To help her company establish a presence in Asia, Susan wants to hire a local interpreter who can advise her on business customs. Kana Tomari has superb qualifications on paper. But when Susan tries to probe about her experience, Kana just says, "I will do my best. I will try very hard." She never gives details about any of the previous positions she's held. Susan begins to wonder if the résumé is inflated.

3. Stan wants to negotiate a joint venture with an Asian company. He asks Tung-Sen Lee if the people have enough discretionary income to afford his product. Mr. Lee is silent for a time, and then says, "Your product is good. People in the West must like it." Stan smiles, pleased that Mr. Lee recognizes the quality of his product, and he gives Mr. Lee a contract to sign. Weeks later, Stan still hasn't heard anything. If Asians are going to be so nonresponsive, he wonders if he really should try to do business with them.

4. Elspeth is very proud of her participatory management style. On assignment in India, she is careful not to give orders but to ask for suggestions. But people rarely suggest anything. Even a formal suggestion system doesn't work. And to make matters worse, she doesn't sense the respect and camaraderie of the plant she managed in the United States. Perhaps, she decides gloomily, people in India just aren't ready for a woman boss.

7.3   Interviewing for Cultural Information

Interview a person from an international community about cross-cultural communication. You might want to discuss issues such as these:

- Verbal and nonverbal communication, including body language.
- Tone and organization of professional communications.

- Attitude toward materialism.
- Time awareness differences.
- Concepts of personal space.

Compare the person's responses with your own values and write an e-mail to your instructor reflecting on the similarities and differences.

7.4   Analyzing Ads

Go to http://advertising.chinasmack.com/2011/weird -wonderful-chinese-advertising-of-2011.html, which is a website that portrays advertisements from China. In small groups, choose one advertisement to analyze. Compare it to a similar ad created in the Unites States.

- What are some differences you see in the advertisement?
- What does the advertisement say about cultural values in the country it is from?

- What message is the advertisement sending about a particular product or company?
- Does the advertisement require an explanation for our understanding?
- Would this particular advertisement be effective if shown in the United States?

Discuss your findings in small groups. As a group, prepare a short presentation for your classmates.

7.5 Comparing Company Web Pages for Various Countries

Many multinationals have separate web pages for their operations in various countries. For example, Coca-Cola's pages include pages for Belgium, France, and Japan. Analyze three of the country pages of a company of your choice.

- Is a single template used for pages in different countries, or do the basic designs differ?
- Are different images used in different countries? What do the images suggest?
- If you can read the language, analyze the links. What information is emphasized?
- To what extent are the pages similar? To what extent do they reveal national and cultural differences?

As your instructor directs,

a. Write an e-mail analyzing the similarities and differences you find. Attach printouts of the pages to your e-mail.

b. Make an oral presentation to the class. Paste the web pages into PowerPoint slides.

c. Join with a small group of students to create a group report comparing several companies' web pages in three specific countries. Attach printouts of the pages.

d. Make a group oral presentation to the class.

7.6 Researching Other Countries

Choose two countries in two different continents other than North America. Look them up in both http://www.cyborlink.com and http://www.kwintessential.co.uk. Note information a new manager in those countries would need to know. Working in small groups (make sure your group covers multiple continents and does not duplicate countries), share your information.

a. Which country would be the easiest one for a young U.S. manager to gain international experience? Why?

b. Which country would be the hardest? Why?

c. Which country would you like to be sent to by a company? Why?

7.7 Creating a Web Page

Create a web page of international information for managers who are planning assignments in another country or who work in this country for a multinational company headquartered in another country.

Assume that this page can be accessed from another of the organization's pages. Offer at least seven links. (More is better.) You may offer information as well as links to other pages with information. At the top of the page, offer an overview of what the page covers. At the bottom of the page, put the creation/update date and your name and e-mail address.

As your instructor directs,

a. Turn in a copy of your page(s). On another page, give the URLs for each link.

b. Write an e-mail to your instructor (1) identifying the audience for which the page is designed and explaining (2) the search strategies you used to find

material on this topic, (3) why you chose the pages and information you've included, and (4) why you chose the layout and graphics you've used.

c. Present your page orally to the class.

Hints:

- Limit your page to just one country or one part of the world.
- You can include some general information about working abroad and culture, but most of your links should be specific to the country or part of the world you focus on.
- Consider some of these topics: history, politics, geography, culture, money, living accommodations, transportation, weather, business practices, and so forth.
- Chunk your links into small groups under headings.

7.8 Comparing International Information

In small groups, find at least four websites providing information about a specific international community. Also, if possible, meet with a member of that community and discuss your findings. Do you find any clashing sources of evidence? What do the contradictions tell you

about your sources? What do they tell you about that international community in general?

Discuss your findings in small groups. As a group, prepare a short presentation for your classmates.

7.9   Planning an International Trip

Assume that you're going to the capital city of another country on business two months from now. (You pick the country.) Use a search engine to find out

- What holidays will be celebrated in that month.
- What the climate will be.
- What current events are in the news there.
- What key features of business etiquette you might consider.
- What kinds of gifts you should bring to your hosts.
- What sight-seeing you might include.

As your instructor directs,

a.   Write an e-mail to your instructor reporting the information you found.

b.   Post a message to the class analyzing the pages. Include the URLs as hot links.

c.   Make an oral presentation to the class.

d.   Join with a small group of students to create a group report on several countries in a region.

e.   Make a group oral presentation to the class.

7.10   Recommending a Candidate for an Overseas Position

Your company sells customized computer systems to businesses large and small around the world. The Executive Committee needs to recommend someone to begin a three-year term as manager of Eastern European marketing.

As your instructor directs,

a.   Write an e-mail to each of the candidates, specifying the questions you would like each to answer in a final interview.

b.   Assume that it is not possible to interview the candidates. Use the information here to write an e-mail to the CEO recommending a candidate.

c.   Write an e-mail to the CEO recommending the best way to prepare the person chosen for his or her assignment.

d.   Write an e-mail to the CEO recommending a better way to choose candidates for international assignments.

e.   Write an e-mail to your instructor explaining the assumptions you made about the company and the candidates that influenced your recommendation(s).

Information about the candidates:

All the candidates have applied for the position and say they are highly interested in it.

1.   **Deborah Gere,** 39, white, single. Employed by the company for eight years in the Indianapolis and New York offices. Currently in the New York office as assistant marketing manager, Eastern United States; successful. University of Indiana MBA. Speaks Russian fluently; has translated for business negotiations that led to the setting up of the Moscow office. Good technical knowledge, acceptable managerial skills, excellent communication skills, good interpersonal skills. Excellent health; excellent emotional stability. Swims. One child, age 12. Lived in the then–Soviet Union for one year as an exchange student in college; business and personal travel in Europe.

2.   **Claude Chabot,** 36, French, single. Employed by the company for 11 years in the Paris and London offices. Currently in the Paris office as assistant sales manager for the European Community; successful. No MBA, but degrees from MIT in the United States and l'Ecole Supérieure de Commerce de Paris. Speaks native French; speaks English and Italian fluently; speaks some German. Good technical knowledge, excellent managerial skills, acceptable communication skills, excellent interpersonal skills. Excellent health, good emotional stability. Plays tennis. No children. French citizen; lived in the United States for two years, in London for five years (one year in college, four years in the London office). Extensive business and personal travel in Europe.

3.   **Linda Moss,** 35, African American, married. Employed by the company for 10 years in the Atlanta and Toronto offices. Currently assistant manager of Canadian marketing; very successful. Howard University MBA. Speaks some French. Good technical knowledge, excellent managerial skills, excellent communication skills, excellent interpersonal skills. Excellent health; excellent emotional stability. Does Jazzercise classes. Husband is an executive at a U.S. company in Detroit; he plans to stay in the States with their children, ages 11 and 9. The couple plans to commute every two to six weeks. Has lived in Toronto for five years; business travel in North America; personal travel in Europe and Latin America.

4.   **Steven Hsu,** 42, of Asian American descent, married. Employed by the company for 18 years in the Los Angeles office. Currently marketing manager, Western United States; very successful. UCLA MBA. Speaks some Korean. Excellent technical knowledge, excellent managerial skills, good communication skills, excellent interpersonal skills. Good health, excellent emotional stability. Plays golf. Wife is an engineer who plans to do consulting work in Eastern Europe. Children ages 8, 5, and 2. Has not lived outside the United States; personal travel in Europe and Asia.

Your committee has received this e-mail from the CEO.

To: Executive Committee

From: Ed Conzachi

Subject: Choosing a Manager for the New Eastern European Office

Please write me an e-mail recommending the best candidate for manager of East European marketing. In your e-mail, tell me whom you're choosing and why; also explain why you have rejected the unsuccessful candidates.

This person will be assuming a three-year appointment, with the possibility of reappointment. The company will pay moving and relocation expenses for the manager and his or her family.

The Eastern European division currently is the smallest of the company's international divisions. However, this area is poised for growth. The new manager will supervise the Moscow office and establish branch offices as needed.

The committee has invited comments from everyone in the company. You've received these e-mails.

To: Executive Committee

From: Robert Osborne, U.S. Marketing Manager

Subject: Recommendation for Steve Hsu

Steve Hsu would be a great choice to head up the new Moscow office. In the past seven years, Steve has increased sales in the Western Region by 15%—in spite of recessions, earthquakes, and fires. He has a low-key, participative style that brings out the best in subordinates. Moreover, Steve is a brilliant computer programmer. He probably understands our products better than any other marketing or salesperson in the company.

Steve is clearly destined for success in headquarters. This assignment will give him the international experience he needs to move up to the next level of executive success.

To: Executive Committee

From: Becky Exter, Affirmative Action Officer

Subject: Hiring the New Manager for East European Marketing

Please be sensitive to affirmative action concerns. The company has a very good record of appointing women and minorities to key positions in the United States and Canada; so far our record in our overseas divisions has been less effective.

In part, perhaps, that may stem from a perception that women and minorities will not be accepted in countries less open than our own. But the experience of several multinational firms has been that even exclusionary countries will accept people who have the full backing of their companies. Another concern may be that it will be harder for women to establish a social support system abroad. However, different individuals have different ways of establishing support. To assume that the best candidate for an international assignment is a male with a stay-at-home wife is discriminatory and may deprive our company of the skills of some of its best people.

We have several qualified women and minority candidates. I urge you to consider their credentials carefully.

To: Executive Committee

From: William E. Dortch, Marketing Manager, European Economic Community

Subject: Recommendation for Debbie Gere

Debbie Gere would be my choice to head the new Moscow office. As you know, I recommended that Europe be divided and that we establish an Eastern European division. Of all the people from the States who have worked on the creation of the new division, Debbie is the best. The negotiations were often complex. Debbie's knowledge of the language and culture was invaluable. She's done a good job in the New York office and is ready for wider responsibilities. Eastern Europe is a challenging place, but Debbie can handle the pressure and help us gain the foothold we need.

To: Ed Conzachi, President

From: Pierre Garamond, Sales Representative, European Economic Community

Subject: Recommendation for Claude Chabot

Claude Chabot would be the best choice for manager of Eastern European marketing. He is a superb supervisor, motivating us to the highest level of achievement. He understands the complex legal and cultural nuances of selling our products in Europe as only a native can. He also has the budgeting and managerial skills to oversee the entire marketing effort.

You are aware that the company's record of sending U.S. citizens to head international divisions is not particularly good. European Marketing is an exception, but our records in the Middle East and Japan have been poor. The company would gain stability by appointing Europeans to head European offices, Asians to head Asian offices, and so forth. Such people would do a better job of managing and motivating staffs which will be comprised primarily of nationals in the country where the office is located. Ending the practice of reserving the top jobs for U.S. citizens would also send a message to international employees that we are valued and that we have a future with this company.

To: Executive Committee

From: Elaine Crispell, Manager, Canadian Marketing

Subject: Recommendation for Linda Moss

Linda Moss has done well as Assistant Manager for the last two and a half years. She is a creative, flexible problem solver. Her productivity is the highest in the office. Though she could be called a "workaholic," she is a warm, caring human being.

As you know, the Canadian division includes French-Speaking Montreal and a large Native Canadian population; furthermore, Toronto is an international and intercultural city. Linda has gained intercultural competence both on a personal and professional level.

Linda has the potential to be our first woman CEO 15 years down the road. She needs more international experience to be competitive at that level. This would be a good opportunity for her, and she would do well for the company.

7.11 Researching Diversity at Your School

Research your university's policies and practices regarding diversity. Conduct the following research:

- Locate your university's position statement on diversity for both employment and educational opportunities.
- Find diversity data for your university's student body.
- Gather pictures of the student body you can find from the Internet, brochures, and posters throughout your university.
- Analyze your findings. Do the pictures you find resemble the statistics you find?

As your instructor directs,

a. Write an e-mail to your instructor explaining your findings, opinions, and conclusions.

b. Share your results with a small group of students.

c. Write an e-mail message to the president of the university outlining your opinion on how your university is achieving diversity and what, if anything, needs to be done to improve its efforts.

d. Make a short oral presentation to the class discussing your findings and conclusions.

7.12 Analyzing Cross-Cultural Advertising Ethics

In China, Reckitt Benckiser Group recently adapted a marketing plan for its Veet hair-removal cream, encouraging Chinese women to be more conscious of body hair. Chinese women physically do not have much body hair and traditionally have not been concerned about it, so they are a new target audience. The company gave away free samples at universities, with careful use instructions. Reckitt Benckiser Group then promoted the product as an absolute necessity to avoid embarrassment and to be professional. Veet even hired a Chinese actress, Yang Mi, to endorse Veet.

Discuss these questions as a group:

- Is it ethical to convince a specific audience that a natural feature of their body is a negative?

- How might this new product affect Chinese culture?
- If you were working on the marketing team for Veet, what would you do if someone on the team introduced the new marketing strategy?

As your instructor directs,

a. Write an e-mail to your instructor explaining your findings, opinions, and conclusions.

b. Share your results with a small group of students.

c. Make a short oral presentation to the class discussing your findings and conclusions.

Notes

1. Sharon Begley, "Studies Take Measure of How Stereotyping Alters Performance," *Wall Street Journal*, February 23, 2007, B1; and Claude Steele and Joshua Aronson, "Stereotype Threat and Intellectual Test Performance of African Americans," *Journal of Personality and Social Psychology* 69, no. 5 (1995): 797–811.

2. McDonald's, *McDonald's 2012 Annual Report*, March 13, 2013, http://www.aboutmcdonalds.com/content/dam/AboutMcDonalds/Investors/Investor%202013/2012%20Annual%20Report%20Final.pdf; 3M, "3M Facts Year-end 2012," accessed May 15, 2013, http://multimedia.3m.com/mws/mediawebserver?mwsId=SSSSSuH8gc7nZxtUNY_BPY_BevUqe17zHvTSevTSeSSSSSS--; Unilever, "Unilever Annual Report 2012," accessed May 15, 2013, http://unilever.com/images/ir_Unilever_AR12_tcm13-348376.pdf; Walmart, *Walmart 2012 Annual Report*, http://www.walmartstores.com/sites/annual-report/2012/WalMart_AR.pdf.

3. Lauren A. E. Schuker, "Plot Change: Foreign Forces Transform Hollywood Films," *Wall Street Journal*, July 31, 2010, A1.

4. Laurie Burkitt, "China Loses Its Taste for Yum," *Wall Street Journal*, December 3, 2012, B9; Laurie Burkitt, "Kraft Craves More of China's Snacks Market," *Wall Street Journal*, May 30, 2012, B6; and Margherita Stancati, "Dunkin' Donuts Goes to India," *Wall Street Journal*, May 9, 2012, B3.

5. Dan Myers, "The 5 Craziest McDonald's Pies," *USAToday.com*, January 29, 2013, http://www.usatoday.com/story/travel/destinations/2013/01/29/the-5-craziest-mcdonalds-pies/1873913/.

6. Terri Morrison and Wayne A. Conaway, *Kiss, Bow, or Shake Hands: Sales and Marketing: The Essential Cultural Guide—from Presentations and Promotions to Communicating and Closing* (New York: McGraw-Hill, 2012), 140.

7. Emily Maltby, "Expanding Abroad? Avoid Cultural Gaffes," *Wall Street Journal*, January 19, 2010, B5.

8. John Helyar, "Outsourcing: A Passage Out of India," *Bloomberg Businessweek*, March 19, 2012, 36.

9. Ibid.

10. William W. Maddux, Adam D. Galinshky, and Carmit T. Tadmor, "Be a Better Manager: Live Abroad," *Harvard Business Review* 88, no. 9 (2010): 24.

11. Joann S. Lublin, "Hunt Is On for Fresh Executive Talent: Recruiters List Hot Prospects, Cultural Flexibility in Demand," *Wall Street Journal*, April 11, 2011, B1.

12. Diana Middleton, "Schools Set Global Track, for Students and Programs," *Wall Street Journal*, April 7, 2011, B7.

13. Eunkyung Seo, "South Korea's Hottest Import: Workers," *Bloomberg Businessweek*, February 25, 2013, 12; and Jason DeParle, "Global Migration: A World Ever More on the Move," *New York Times*, June 26, 2010, http://www .nytimes.com/2010/06/27/weekinreview/27deparle .html?pagewanted=all&_r=0.

14. DeParle, "Global Migration."

15. Thomas L. Friedman, *The World Is Flat: A Brief History of the Twenty-first Century,* updated and expanded ed. (New York: Farrar, Straus and Giroux, 2006), 8.

16. U.S. Census Bureau, "Statistical Abstract of the United States, Table 12: Resident Population Projections by Race, Hispanic Origin, and Age: 2010 and 2015," accessed May 16, 2013, http://www.census.gov/compendia/ statab/2012/tables/12s0012.pdf.

17. U.S. Census Bureau, "Statistical Abstract of the United States, Table 50: Persons Obtaining Legal Permanent Resident Status by Country of Birth: 1981 to 2010," accessed May 16, 2013, http://www.census.gov/compendia/ statab/2012/tables/12s0050.pdf.

18. Conor Dougherty, "Whites to Lose Majority Status in U.S. by 2042," *Wall Street Journal*, August 14, 2008, A3.

19. Jeffery Passel, Gretchen Livingston, and D'Vera Cohn, "Explaining Why Minority Births Now Outnumber White Births," *Pew Research Social & Demographic Trends*, May 17, 2012, http://www.pewsocialtrends.org/2012/05/17/ explaining-why-minority-births-now-outnumber-white-births/.

20. U.S. Census Bureau, "2010 Census Shows America's Diversity," news release, March 24, 2011, http://www .census.gov/newsroom/releases/archives/2010_census/ cb11-cn125.html.

21. CHIN Radio, "CHIN Radio," accessed May 16, 2013, http://chinradio.com/chin-radio/.

22. U.S. Census Bureau, "2010 Census Shows America's Diversity."

23. U.S. Census Bureau, "Statistical Abstract of the United States, Table 54: Language Spoken at Home by State: 2009," accessed May 16, 2013, http://www.census.gov/ compendia/statab/2012/tables/12s0054.pdf.

24. Ibid.

25. Microsoft Corporation, "Employee Resource Groups and Networks at Microsoft," accessed May 14, 2013, http:// www.microsoft.com/en-us/diversity/programs/ergen/ default.aspx.

26. Cedric Herring, "Does Diversity Pay?: Race, Gender, and the Business Case for Diversity," *American Sociological Review* 74 (April 2009): 208–24.

27. Paul M. Barrett, "Selling the Supremes on Diversity," *Bloomberg Businessweek*, October 22, 2012, 38.

28. Abhijit Rao, e-mail message to author, August 15, 2013.

29. Hofstede Centre, "What about the USA?" accessed May 14, 2013, http://www.geert-hofstede.com/hofstede_ united_states.shtml.

30. John Webb and Michael Keene, "The Impact of Discourse Communities on International Professional Communication," in *Exploring the Rhetoric of International Professional Communication: An Agenda for Teachers and Researchers,* ed. Carl R. Lovitt and Dixie Goswami (Amityville, NY: Baywood, 1999), 81–109.

31. Morrison and Conaway, *Kiss, Bow, or Shake Hands,* 29, 174–83.

32. Richard M. Steers, Carlos J. Sanchez-Runde, and Luciara Nardon, *Management across Cultures: Challenges and Strategies* (New York: Cambridge University Press, 2010), 205–6.

33. Morrison and Conaway, *Kiss, Bow, or Shake Hands,* 272

34. Morrison and Conaway, *Kiss, Bow, or Shake Hands,* 94, 178; "Business Cards," *BusinessWeek SmallBiz,* June/July 2008, 28; and Roy A. Cook and Gwen O. Cook, *Guide to Business Etiquette* (New York: Prentice Hall, 2011), 113.

35. Kathryn King-Metters and Ricard Metters, "Misunderstanding the Chinese Worker: Western Impressions Are Dated—And Probably Wrong," *Wall Street Journal,* July 7, 2008, R11; Jason Leow, "Chinese Bigwigs Are Quick to Reach for the Hair Color: Politicians and Executives Look for Youth in a Bottle of Black Dye on the Sly," *Wall Street Journal,* December 11, 2007, A1, A24.

36. Robert T. Moran, Philip R. Harris, and Sarah V. Moran, *Managing Cultural Differences: Global Leadership Strategies for the 21st Century,* 7th ed. (Boston: Elsevier, 2007), 341–42.

37. Ibid., 64.

38. Steers, Sanchez-Runde, and Nardon, *Management across Cultures,* 219.

39. Moran, Harris, and Moran, *Managing Cultural Differences,* 579.

40. Mike Kilen, "Watch Your Language: Rude or Polite? Gestures Vary with Cultures," *Des Moines Register,* May 30, 2006, E1–2.

41. Morrison and Conaway, *Kiss, Bow, or Shake Hands,* 180.

42. Martin J. Gannon, *Understanding Global Cultures: Metaphorical Journeys through 23 Nations,* 2nd ed. (Thousand Oaks, CA: Sage, 2001), 13.

43. Edward Twitchell Hall, *Hidden Differences: Doing Business with the Japanese* (Garden City, NY: Anchor-Doubleday, 1987), 25.

44. Moran, Harris, and Moran, *Managing Cultural Differences,* 445, 78.

45. Malcolm Fleschner, "Worldwide Winner," *Selling Power,* November–December 2001, 54–61.

46. Ira Carnahan, "Presidential Timber Tends to Be Tall," *Forbes,* May 19, 2004, http://www.forbes.com/2004/05/19/cz_ ic_0519beltway.html.

47. Morrison and Conaway, *Kiss, Bow, or Shake Hands,* 138–39.

48. Craig Storti, *Old World, New World: Bridging Cultural Differences: Britain, France, Germany, and the U.S.* (Yarmouth, ME: Intercultural Press, 2001), 209.

49. Morrison and Conaway, *Kiss, Bow, or Shake Hands,* 30, 96, 133, 182.

50. Storti, *Old World, New World;* and Morrison and Conaway, *Kiss, Bow, or Shake Hands,* 76.

51. Morrison and Conaway, *Kiss, Bow, or Shake Hands,* 181, 185.

52. Nick Easen, "Don't Send the Wrong Message," *Business 2.0,* August 2005, 102.

8 Working and Writing in Teams

Chapter Outline

NEWSWORTHY COMMUNICATION

Animating Teamwork

In the business of making animated movies, working together as a team is incredibly important. To produce the dazzling effects we see in films such as Disney/Pixar's *Brave* requires collaboration between hundreds of people organized into focused teams. For example, one team of 14 animators at Pixar worked solely on Princess Merida's hair and the complex muscles on her horse.

Because of the importance of teamwork in animation, recruiters from major animation studios including Pixar, DreamWorks, and Sony turn to an unexpected source: Brigham Young University in Provo, Utah. The 13-year-old animation program at BYU has turned out dozens of animators who are now contributing in major ways to blockbuster animated features.

What makes the difference at BYU? It's not necessarily talent. In fact, recruiters note that the students at BYU may not be as talented artistically as the students who come out of more traditional art schools. But, as one recruiter says, the BYU students have "a different mind-set." The BYU program is focused on collaboration, not individual artistic expression. All of the students work together on a single short film rather than individual projects. One result is that the students learn the best ways to contribute individually to a team effort.

The teamwork at BYU is being noticed in the movie industry. The program has won several awards for its films, including Student Oscars, and its graduates are hired quickly by leading studios. The focus on collaborative teamwork prepares BYU students for the realities of modern animated filmmaking.

Source: Jon Mooallem, "When Hollywood Wants Good, Clean Fun, It Goes to Mormon Country," *New York Times,* May 23, 2013, http://www.nytimes.com/2013/05/26/magazine/when-hollywood-wants-good-clean-fun-it-goes-to-mormon-country.html.

Learning Objectives

After studying this chapter, you will know

LO 8-1 Different kinds of productive and nonproductive roles in teams.

LO 8-2 Group decision-making strategies.

LO 8-3 Characteristics of successful teams.

LO 8-4 Techniques for resolving conflict.

LO 8-5 Techniques for making meetings effective.

LO 8-6 Technologies to use in teamwork.

LO 8-7 Techniques for collaborative writing.

http://www
.teamtechnology
.co.uk/

Log on to this website to find a wide range of articles and resources about interacting effectively in team settings. More specifically, click on "Team Roles" to find interactive links to aid in assessing yourself as a team member as well as determining roles of your fellow group members.

http://www
.effectivemeetings
.com/

Log on to EffectiveMeetings .com for articles offering advice about making meetings effective. What advice offered in these articles do you think would be helpful for conducting meetings with your fellow group members?

Teamwork is crucial to success in an organization. The ability to work in a team is in the top 10 skills employers seek in job candidates.[1] Some teams produce products, provide services, or recommend solutions to problems. Other teams—perhaps in addition to providing a service or recommending a solution—also produce documents. Today teamwork is facilitated by a wide range of technology tools such as wikis, chats, Skype, and teleconferencing, as well as collaborative features in Google Docs, Microsoft Office, and Prezi. (For more on the use of technology, see Chapter 9).

Teamwork comes into play when a job is too big or the time is too short for one person to do the work, and also when no one person has the needed knowledge and skills. High stakes call for teamwork, both because the efforts of multiple talented people are needed and because no one person wants the sole responsibility for a possible failure. Many companies see teamwork as a way to foster creativity and to produce better results.

Interpersonal communication, communication between people, is crucial for good teamwork. It relies heavily on interpersonal skills such as listening and networking. Chapter 4 discusses interpersonal skills vital for good teamwork. Skills in conflict resolution, meeting organization, and collaborative writing also help teamwork. These skills will make you more successful in your job, social groups, community service, and volunteer work. On writing teams, giving careful attention to both teamwork and the writing process (see Chapter 5) improves both the final product and members' satisfaction with the team.

Team Interactions **LO 8-1**

Teams can focus on different dimensions:

- **Informational dimensions** focus on content: the problem, data, and possible solutions.

- **Procedural dimensions** focus on method and process. How will the team make decisions? Who will do what? When will assignments be due?

- **Interpersonal dimensions** focus on people, promoting friendliness, cooperation, and team loyalty.

Different kinds of communication dominate during these stages of a task team's life: formation, coordination, and formalization.

During **formation,** when members meet and begin to define their task, teams need to develop social cohesiveness and procedures for meeting and acting. Interpersonal and procedural comments reduce the tension that always exists in a new team. Diving immediately into project work or insisting on information in this first stage can hurt the team's long-term productivity.

Teams are often most effective when they explicitly adopt ground rules. Figure 8.1 lists some common ground rules used by workplace teams.

During formation, conflicts frequently arise when the team defines tasks and procedures. Successful teams anticipate and resolve conflicts by clarifying what each member is supposed to do. They also set procedures: When and how often will they meet? Will decisions be made by a leader, as is the case with many advisory groups? By consensus or vote? Will the team evaluate individual performances? Will someone keep minutes? Successful teams analyze their tasks thoroughly and resolve conflicts through interpersonal communication before they begin to search for solutions.

Coordination is the longest phase and the phase during which most of the team's work is done. While procedural and interpersonal comments help maintain direction and friendliness, most of the comments should deal with information. Good information is essential to good decisions. Successful teams deliberately seek numerous possible solutions and carefully consider each before choosing the best one. They particularly avoid the temptation of going with the first solution that arises. Conflict may occur as the team debates these solutions.

In **formalization,** the group finalizes its work. The success of this phase determines how well the group's decision will be implemented. In this stage, the group seeks to forget earlier conflicts.

Roles in Teams

Individual members can play multiple roles within teams, and these roles can change during the team's work. Roles on teams can be positive or negative, as Figure 8.2 explains.

Forming Team Expectations

The initial meeting between team members can set the tone for successful teamwork. A contribution scorecard can help teams in the formation stage to establish expectations and goals. Team members fill out the scorecard in four areas:

1. Your development goals.
2. Steps you need to take to move toward your goals.
3. The knowledge and experience you can bring to bear on this project.
4. Ways to leverage the range of your knowledge and experience.

After the initial meeting, team members use the scorecards to monitor and evaluate their progress. The team as a whole revisits the scorecards during the project to manage expectations and make progress toward goals.

Adapted from Heidi K. Gardner, "Coming Through When It Matters Most," *Harvard Business Review,* April 2012, 88.

Figure 8.1	Possible Team Ground Rules

- Start team meetings on time; end on time.
- Attend regularly.
- Come to the meeting prepared.
- Leave the meeting with a clear understanding of what each member is to do next.
- Focus comments on the issues.
- Avoid personal attacks.
- Listen to and respect members' opinions.
- Have everyone speak on key issues and procedures.
- Address problems as you become aware of them. If you have a problem with another person, tell that person, not everyone else.
- Do your share of the work.
- Communicate immediately if you think you may not be able to fulfill an agreement.
- Produce your work by the agreed-upon time.

Teamwork Myths

Myth:	Harmony is good.
Reality:	Well-managed conflict can generate more creative solutions and help a group's performance.
Myth:	Add new members for fresh ideas and energy.
Reality:	The longer group membership stays stable, the better groups perform.
Myth:	With today's technology, in-the-room team meetings are no longer necessary.
Reality:	Long-distance teams have a considerable disadvantage, so much so that many businesses pay the money to bring them together at key times.
Myth:	Larger teams are better, particularly when they include representatives of all constituencies.
Reality:	Large size is one of the worst impediments to team effectiveness. It allows individuals to shirk their share of the workload and requires more effort poured into coordinating activities.

Adapted from J. Richard Hackman, "Six Common Misperceptions about Teamwork," *Harvard Business Review* (blog), June 7, 2011, http://blogs.hbr.org/cs/2011/06/six_common_misperceptions_abou.html.

Figure 8.2	Positive and Negative Team Actions

Positive roles and actions that help the team achieve its task goals include the following:

- **Seeking information and opinions**—asking questions, identifying gaps in the team's knowledge.
- **Giving information and opinions**—answering questions, providing relevant information.
- **Summarizing**—restating major points, summarizing decisions.
- **Synthesizing**—pulling ideas together, connecting different elements of the team's efforts.
- **Evaluating**—comparing team processes and products to standards and goals.
- **Coordinating**—planning work, giving directions, and fitting together contributions of team members.

Positive roles and actions that help the team build loyalty, resolve conflicts, and function smoothly include the following behaviors:

- **Encouraging participation**—demonstrating openness and acceptance, recognizing the contributions of members, calling on quieter team members.
- **Relieving tensions**—joking and suggesting breaks and fun activities.
- **Checking feelings**—asking members how they feel about team activities and sharing one's own feelings with others.
- **Solving interpersonal problems**—opening discussion of interpersonal problems in the team and suggesting ways to solve them.
- **Listening actively**—showing team members that they have been heard and that their ideas are being taken seriously.

Negative roles and actions that hurt the team's product and process include the following:

- **Blocking**—disagreeing with everything that is proposed.
- **Dominating**—trying to run the team by ordering, shutting out others, and insisting on one's own way.
- **Clowning**—making unproductive jokes and diverting the team from the task.
- **Overspeaking**—taking every opportunity to be the first to speak; insisting on personally responding to everyone else's comments.
- **Withdrawing**—being silent in meetings, not contributing, not helping with the work, not attending meetings.

Some actions can be positive or negative depending on how they are used. Active participation by members helps teams move forward, but too much talking from one member blocks contributions from others. Criticizing ideas is necessary if the team is to produce the best solution, but criticizing every idea raised without ever suggesting possible solutions blocks a team. Jokes in moderation can defuse tension and make the team work more fun. Too many jokes or inappropriate jokes can make the team's work more difficult.

Leadership in Teams

You may have noted that "leader" was not one of the roles listed in Figure 8.2. Every team has one or more leaders, who also perform some of the actions listed in the figure. Frequently the leader is formally designated or chosen, but sometimes leaders emerge during the teamwork process. Being a leader does *not* mean doing all the work yourself. Indeed, someone who implies that he or she has the best ideas and can do the best work is likely hindering the work of the team.

Effective teams balance three kinds of leadership, which parallel the three team dimensions:

- Informational leaders generate and evaluate ideas and text.

- Interpersonal leaders monitor the team's process, check people's feelings, and resolve conflicts.

- Procedural leaders set the agenda, make sure that everyone knows what's due for the next meeting, communicate with absent team members, and check to ensure assignments are carried out.

While it's possible for one person to assume all these responsibilities, in many teams the three kinds of leadership are taken on by three (or more) different people. Some teams formally or informally rotate or share these responsibilities, so that everyone—and no one—is a leader.

Studies have shown that people who talk a lot, listen effectively, and respond nonverbally to other members of the team are considered to be leaders.[2] As team projects progress, team leadership evolves and shifts in response to the needs of the team. For example, in the early brainstorming stages, the informational leader may take charge of meetings. As the team moves into making assignments, however, the procedural leader may take over.

Effective team leaders must be more than simply the boss. Leaders employ interpersonal communication and persuasion to help create a good team environment and to encourage productivity. The best leaders work with other team members, talk *and* listen to followers, help all team members develop their skills, and communicate a clear strategy to achieve the team's goals.

Different projects require different types of leaders. Defining or appointing a leader for a project has been shown to increase productivity and reduce conflict in teams. If too many people attempt to lead, more conflicts arise and productivity goes down. If no one tries to lead, teams experience less conflict, but also much less productivity.[3] Choosing a good leader has a direct effect on productivity. In fact, one study showed that a good leader increases the output of the team as much as if the team had an extra member.[4]

Understanding effective leadership can help teams minimize conflict, generate more and better ideas, and ultimately have a better experience.

Decision-Making Strategies LO 8-2

Probably the least effective decision-making strategy is to let the person who talks first, last, loudest, or most determine the decision. Most teams instead aim to air different points of view with the objective of identifying the best choice, or at least a choice that seems good enough for the team's purposes. The team discussion considers the pros and cons of each idea. In many teams, someone willingly plays **devil's advocate** to look for possible flaws in an idea. To give ideas a fair hearing, someone should also develop an idea's positive aspects.

After the team has considered alternatives, it needs a method for picking one to implement. Typical selection methods include voting and consensus. **Voting** is quick but may leave people in the minority unhappy with and uncommitted to the majority's plan. Coming to **consensus** takes time but usually results in speedier implementation of ideas. Airing preferences early in the process, through polls before meetings and straw votes during meetings, can sometimes help teams establish consensus more quickly. Even in situations where consensus is not possible, good teams ensure everyone's ideas are considered. Most people will agree to support the team's decision, even if it was not their choice, as long as they feel they have been heard.

Businesspeople in different nations have varying preferences about these two methods. An international survey of 15,000 managers and employees found that four-fifths of the Japanese respondents preferred consensus, but a little more than one-third of the Americans did. Other nations in which consensus was preferred included Germany, the Netherlands, Belgium, and France.[5]

Two strategies that are often useful in organizational teams are the standard problem-solving process and dot planning.

The standard problem-solving process has multiple steps:

1. Identify the task or problem. What is the team trying to do?
2. Understand what the team has to deliver, in what form, by what due date. Identify available resources.
3. Gather information, share it with all team members, and examine it critically.
4. Establish criteria. What would the ideal solution include? Which elements of that solution would be part of a less-than-ideal but still acceptable solution? What legal, financial, moral, or other limitations might keep a solution from being implemented?
5. Brainstorm solutions (see Figure 8.3).
6. Measure the alternatives against the criteria.
7. Choose the best solution.

Dot planning offers a way for large teams to choose priorities quickly. First, the team brainstorms ideas, recording each on pages that are put on the wall. Then each individual gets two strips of three to five adhesive dots in different colors. One color represents high priority, the other lower priority. People then walk up to the pages and stick dots by the points they care most about. Some teams allow only one dot from one person on any one item; others allow someone who is really passionate about an idea to put all of his or her dots on it. The dots make it easy to see which items the team believes are most and least important.

Figure 8.3	Brainstorming Techniques

Here are some techniques that will help produce successful team brainstorming sessions:

- Identify a clear, concrete goal before you start. That allows you to establish some boundaries for ideas—about practicality or cost, for example—and helps you keep your brainstorming session focused.

- Ensure everyone involved in the meeting knows the goal ahead of time. This step gives everyone a chance to have ideas ready when they come to the meeting.

- Set limits on meeting duration and size. An hour is enough time for a focused discussion, and it's easier for everyone to participate and be heard in a small team.

- Let the ideas flow freely without judgment. Any idea, however impractical, might inspire the best solution, and spending time weeding out weak ideas can stifle creativity.

- Build on each other's ideas.

- Brainstorm with a diverse team. Good ideas come from teams of people with different perspectives.

What happens if your team can't agree, or can't reach consensus? Team-building expert Bob Frisch suggests some strategies for working through a deadlock. In addition to using standard group techniques (setting clear goals, brainstorming solutions, and weighing the pros and cons of each solution), you should

- Use the current sticking point as the start for a new round of brainstorming. If there are two solutions that your team can't choose between, break the deadlock by brainstorming new solutions that combine the old ones. That will get the team making progress again and get new ideas on the table.

- Instead of rushing to a decision, allow time for team members to consider the options. Sometimes people refuse to compromise to avoid making a bad snap decision. Giving your team time to consider the options will take the pressure off. For especially complex decisions, schedule multiple meetings with time in between to do research and to digest the pros and cons of each solution.

- Allow team members to make their decisions confidentially. People might refuse to state an opinion—or change an opinion—if they feel their opinions and reasoning will be judged negatively by the group. A secret ballot or other confidential form of "discussion" can help break a deadlock by giving team members an opportunity to voice their opinions without being judged or embarrassed.[6]

Feedback Strategies

As soon as the team begins to put its decisions into play, it needs to begin generating and heeding feedback. Sometimes this feedback will be external; it will come from supervisors, suppliers, clients, and customers. It should also, however, come from within the team. Teams frequently evaluate individual team members' performances, team performance, task progress, and team procedures.

Feedback should be frequent and regular. Many teams have weekly feedback as well as feedback connected to specific stages of their task. Regular feedback is a good way to keep team members contributing their share of the work in a timely fashion. While feedback needs to be honest and incorporate criticism, such critiques can be phrased as positively as possible ("please get your figures in for the Wednesday update" rather than "do you think you can make the Wednesday deadline this time?"). And don't forget to praise. Research shows that teams with a higher ratio of positive-to-negative interactions do better work.[7]

Characteristics of Successful Student Teams LO 8-3

Studies of student teams completing class projects have found that students in successful teams were not necessarily more skilled or more experienced than students in less successful teams. Studies by a professor at MIT found patterns of communication to be "the most important predictor of a team's success."[8] Successful and less successful teams communicate differently.

- Successful teams assign specific tasks, set clear deadlines, and schedule frequent meetings. They also regularly communicate as a team about each member's progress. In less successful teams, members are not sure what they are supposed to be doing or when it is needed. Less successful teams meet less often.

- Successful teams meet and talk through plans and conflicts face-to-face. They use nonverbal cues as well as listening skills to build trust and communicate ideas. Less successful teams rely more on e-mail, social networking, and other electronic communication tools.

- Successful teams recognize that they have to build trust with each other through goodwill, active listening, and consistent participation. Teams who trust each other tend to work together to solve problems that impact the whole team. Less successful teams expect members to complete their own parts, and fail to bring those parts together into a coherent whole, behaviors that also appear in unsuccessful workplace teams.[9]

- Successful teams recognize the contribution of every team member to the team's success, and take time to acknowledge each member during team meetings. When team members know that their efforts are noticed and appreciated by their peers, they're much more willing to contribute to the team. Less successful teams take individual contributions for granted.

- Successful teams listen carefully to each other and respond to emotions as well as words. Less successful teams pay less attention to what is said and how it is said.

- In successful teams, members work more evenly and actively on the project.[10] They find ways to cater to each other's schedules and work preferences. Successful teams even find ways to use members who don't like working in teams. For example, a student who doesn't want to be a "team player" can be a freelancer for her team, completing assignments by herself and e-mailing them to the team. Less successful teams have a smaller percentage of active members and frequently have some members who do very little on the final project.

- Successful teams make important decisions together. In less successful teams, a subgroup or an individual makes decisions.

- Successful teams listen to criticism and try to improve their performance on the basis of it. In less successful teams, criticism is rationalized.

- Successful teams deal directly with conflicts that emerge; unsuccessful teams try to ignore conflicts.

As you no doubt realize, these characteristics of good teams actually apply to most teams, not just student teams. A survey of engineering project teams found that 95% of the team members thought that good communication was the reason for team success, and poor communication the reason for team failures.[11]

Peer Pressure and Groupthink

Teams that never express conflict may be experiencing groupthink. Groupthink is the tendency for teams to put such a high premium on agreement that they directly or indirectly punish dissent.

Research has shown that teams produce better documents when they disagree over substantive issues of content and document design. The disagreement does not need to be angry: someone can simply say, "Yes, and here's another way we could do it." Deciding among two (or more) alternatives forces the proposer to explain the rationale for an idea. Even when the team adopts the original idea, considering alternatives rather than quickly accepting the first idea produces better writing.[12]

Many people feel so much reluctance to express open disagreement that they will say they agree even when objective circumstances would suggest the first speaker cannot be right. In a series of classic experiments in the 1950s, Solomon Asch showed the influence of peer pressure. People sitting around a table were shown a large card with a line and asked to match it to the line of the same length on another card. It's a simple test: people normally match the lines correctly almost 100% of the time. However, in the experiment, all but one of the people in the group had been instructed to give false answers for several of the trials. When the group gave an incorrect answer, the focal person accepted the group's judgment 36.8% of the time. When someone else also gave a different answer—even if it was another wrong answer—the focal person accepted the group's judgment only 9% of the time.[13]

The experimenters varied the differences in line lengths, hoping to create a situation in which even the most conforming subjects would trust their own senses. But some people continued to accept the group's judgment, even when one line was seven inches longer than the other.

A classic example of groupthink, and one illustrating the sometimes constraining influence of a powerful team leader, occurred during President Kennedy's administration. The deliberations of Kennedy and his advisers illustrated classic characteristics of groupthink such as premature agreement and suppression of doubts. Kennedy guided the discussions in a way that minimized disagreements. The result was the disastrous decision to launch the Bay of Pigs invasion, whose failure led to the Cuban Missile Crisis. However, Kennedy subsequently analyzed what had gone wrong with the decision process, and he had his advisers do likewise. He used these analyses to change the process for the Cuban Missile Crisis. Although the team again included Kennedy and many of the same advisers, it avoided groupthink. Kennedy ordered the team to question, allowed free-ranging discussions, used separate subteam meetings, and sometimes left the room himself to avoid undue influence of the discussions.[14]

Teams that "go along with the crowd" and suppress conflict ignore the full range of alternatives, seek only information that supports the positions they already favor, and fail to prepare contingency plans to cope with foreseeable setbacks. A business suffering from groupthink may launch a new product that senior executives support but for which there is no demand. Student teams suffering from groupthink turn in inferior documents.

The best correctives to groupthink are to consciously search for additional alternatives, to test one's assumptions against those of a range of other people, and to protect the right of people on a team to disagree. When power roles are a factor, input may need to be anonymous.

Working on Diverse Teams

In any organization, you will work with people whose backgrounds and working styles differ from yours. Residents of small towns and rural areas have different notions of friendliness than do people from big cities. The values and attitudes of marketing people tend to differ from those of researchers or engineers. In addition, differences arise from gender, class, race and ethnicity, religion, age, sexual orientation, and physical ability. Even people who share some of these characteristics are likely to differ in personality type.

These differences affect how people behave on teams and what they expect from teams. For example, in a business negotiation, people from Asia are more likely to see the goal of negotiation as development of a relationship between the parties. In contrast, American negotiators (especially the lawyers on the team) are more likely to see the purpose of a negotiation as producing a signed contract.[15] Such differences are likely to affect what people talk about and how they talk. Some Western cultures use direct approaches; other cultures,

There's No Boss

At Valve Corp., a video game maker, there are no bosses, supervisors, or even assigned projects. In fact, since its founding in 1996, Valve has never had a boss. All of the employees are equal, and they make decisions on projects, hiring, firing, and even salaries by team consensus.

How does it work? Employees develop their own projects and recruit peers in the company to help them. As the teams work, a leader emerges for the project and acts as the manager and coordinator until the project ends. Team members can move in and out of teams at will, which allows them to work on projects they care about.

Working without bosses can be a challenge, and it takes many employees months to adjust to working at Valve. But it seems to be working. Employees feel an ownership of the company and its products. They are more satisfied with their experience at work and with their final products.

Would you like to work at Valve?

Adapted from Rachel Emma Silverman, "Who's the Boss? There Isn't One," *Wall Street Journal*, June 20, 2012, B1.

International Teams

IBM programmer Rob Nicholson has 50 colleagues from three countries—England, India, and Canada—on his software team.

Global teams such as his have to work to overcome language and cultural barriers. Workers worried about having their jobs outsourced have to learn to share information. Workers from more polite or reserved cultures have to conquer their reluctance to interrupt people and instead contact colleagues immediately with questions.

The team collaborates through sophisticated electronic communications. Team wikis allow members to post reports on their own progress and comment on the work of other team members. Team members get automatic alerts when major components of their project change. Completed program segments are put into a shared database. Work stations display photos and personal details of team members so new programmers can learn about their teammates and where to go for help. Instant messaging keeps team members in touch.

A vital task for this team is dividing the work into small pieces. Most projects are divided into two-week chunks; those chunks are further divided into pieces that one programmer can complete in one or two days. The task list is kept on the team wiki. As programmers complete their tasks, they take the top task from the wiki list.

When the software fails a test, the entire team stops programming and focuses on finding the problem. In fact, the British office has rigged a red emergency light on its testing machine.

Clear and frequent communications among team members are a vital key for the success of the project.

Adapted from Phred Dvorak, "How Teams Can Work Well Together from Far Apart," *Wall Street Journal,* September 17, 2007, B4.

Diverse teams can extend the range of group efforts and ideas.

especially Eastern cultures, consider such approaches rude and respond by withholding information.

Other pitfalls of team differences exist. Sometimes people who sense a difference may attribute problems in the team to prejudice, when other factors may be responsible. Also, a significant body of research shows that accurate interpretation of emotions in diverse teams is influenced by factors such as gender, nationality, race, and status.[16]

On the other hand, another body of research shows that ethnically diverse teams produce more and higher-quality ideas.[17] One study showed that simply including more women actually increases the team's ability to perform better.[18] Research has also found that over time, as team members focus on their task, mission, or profession, cultural differences become less significant than the role of being a team member.[19]

Sometimes the culture to which the team belongs is a distinct asset, uniting strangers in positive ways and giving them strengths to use in high-stakes situations. With their team skills enhanced by the organizational culture, airline crews and emergency teams may perform heroically in a crisis.

Savvy team members play to each other's strengths and devise strategies for dealing with differences. These efforts can benefit the whole team. A study of multicultural teams published in the *Harvard Business Review* found acknowledging cultural gaps openly and cooperatively working through them an ideal strategy for surmounting cultural differences. For example, a U.S. and U.K. team used their differing approaches to decision making to create a higher-quality decision. The U.K. members used their slower approach to analyze possible pitfalls, and the U.S. members used their "forge ahead" approach to move the project along. Both sides appreciated the contributions of the other members.[20]

Conflict Resolution   LO 8-4

Conflicts are going to arise in any group of intelligent people who care about their task. Yet many of us feel so uncomfortable with conflict that we pretend it doesn't exist. Conflict does not mean the team has failed. In fact, conflicts are often the result of working through different perspectives to create opportunities. Although conflicts can be healthy for a project, they must be resolved to maintain effective teamwork. Unacknowledged or unresolved conflicts rarely go away: they fester, making the next interchange more difficult.

To reduce the number of conflicts in a team,

- ■ Make responsibilities and ground rules clear at the beginning.

- ■ Discuss problems as they arise, rather than letting them fester till people explode.

- ■ Realize that team members are not responsible for each others' happiness.

Despite these efforts, most teams experience some conflict, and that conflict needs to be resolved. When a conflict is emotionally charged, people will need a chance to calm themselves before they can arrive at a well-reasoned solution. Meeting expert John Tropman recommends the "two-meeting rule" for controversial matters. The first meeting is a chance for everyone to air a point of view about the issue. The second meeting is the one at which the team reaches a decision. The time between the two meetings becomes a cooling-off period.[21]

Figure 8.4 suggests several possible solutions to conflicts that student teams experience. Often the symptom arises from a feeling of not being respected or appreciated by the team. Therefore, many problems can be averted if people advocate for their ideas in a positive way. One way to do this is to devote as much effort to positive observations as possible. Another technique is to state analysis rather than mere opinions. Instead of "I wouldn't read an eight-page brochure," the member of a team could say, "Tests we did a couple of years ago found a better response for two-page brochures. Could we move some of that information to our website?" As in this example, an opinion can vary from person to person; stating an opinion does not provide a basis for the team to make a decision. In contrast, analysis provides objective information for the team to consider.

Steps in Conflict Resolution

Dealing successfully with conflict requires attention both to the issues and to people's feelings. The following techniques will help you resolve conflicts constructively.

1. Make Sure the People Involved Really Disagree.   Sometimes different conversational styles, differing interpretations of data, or faulty inferences create apparent conflicts when no real disagreement exists.

Someone who asks "Are those data accurate?" may just be asking for source information, not questioning the conclusions the team drew from the data.

Sometimes someone who's under a lot of pressure may explode. But the speaker may just be venting anger and frustration; he or she may not in fact be angry at the person who receives the explosion. One way to find out if a person is just venting is to ask, "Is there something you'd like me to do?"

2. Check that Everyone's Information Is Correct.   Sometimes people are operating on outdated or incomplete information. People may also act on personal biases or opinions rather than data.

A Team Disaster

Successful teams must be built on excellent cooperation and communication. The Deepwater Horizon disaster in the Gulf of Mexico exposed the failures of the teams involved with the operation.

The corporations involved did not work together as a team. The team on the oil rig did not understand who had authority during an emergency. Written safety guidelines on the rig required multiple people to make decisions about responding to emergencies, but crew members wasted critical minutes when the rig caught fire attempting to decide whether they could shut off the well. As the captain of the rig and 10 other managers and crew members discussed the situation, Andrea Fleytas, a 23-year-old rig worker, took charge and radioed a distress signal to the Coast Guard. She was promptly reprimanded for doing so without the captain's permission.

Successful teams, whether composed of individuals or corporations working together, must be built on excellent cooperation and communication. People on the teams must be aware of correct procedures and their own roles and responsibilities. In the case of the Deepwater Horizon disaster, failures in teamwork at all levels ended up in a human and environmental tragedy.

Sources: Stephen Power and Ben Casselman, "White House Probe Blames BP, Industry in Gulf Blast," *Wall Street Journal,* January 6, 2011, A2; and Douglas A. Blackmon, Vanessa O'Connell, Alexandra Berzon, and Ana Campoy, "There Was 'Nobody in Charge,'" *Wall Street Journal,* May 28, 2010, A6–A7.

Figure 8.4	Troubleshooting Team Problems
Symptom	**Possible solutions**
We can't find a time to meet that works for all of us.	a. Find out why people can't meet at certain times. Some reasons suggest their own solutions. For example, if someone has to stay home with small children, perhaps the team could meet at that person's home. b. Assign out-of-class work to "committees" to work on parts of the project. c. Use technology (e.g., Skype, Google Docs, wikis, e-mail) to share, discuss, and revise drafts.
One person isn't doing his or her fair share.	a. Find out what is going on. Is the person overcommitted? Does he or she feel unappreciated? Is he or she unprepared? Those are different problems you'd solve in different ways. b. Early on, do things to build team loyalty. Get to know each other as writers and as people. Sometimes do something fun together. c. Encourage the person to contribute. "Mary, what do you think?" "Jim, which part of this would you like to draft?" Then find something to praise in the work. "Thanks for getting us started." d. If someone misses a meeting, assign someone else to bring the person up to speed. People who miss meetings for legitimate reasons (job interviews, illness) but don't find out what happened may become less committed to the team. e. Consider whether strict equality is the most important criterion. On a given project, some people may have more knowledge or time than others. Sometimes the best team product results from letting people do different amounts of work. f. Even if you divide up the work, make all decisions as a team: what to write about, which evidence to include, what graphs to use, what revisions to make. People excluded from decisions become less committed to the team.
I seem to be the only one on the team who cares about quality.	a. Find out why other members "don't care." If they received low grades on early assignments, stress that good ideas and attention to detail can raise grades. Perhaps the team should meet with the instructor to discuss what kinds of work will pay the highest dividends. b. Volunteer to do extra work. Sometimes people settle for something that's just OK because they don't have the time or resources to do excellent work. They might be happy for the work to be done—if they don't have to do it. c. Be sure that you're respecting what each person can contribute. Team members sometimes withdraw when one person dominates and suggests that he or she is "better" than other members. d. Fit specific tasks to individual abilities. People generally do better work in areas they see as their strengths. A visual learner who doesn't care about the written report may do an excellent job on the accompanying visuals.
People in the team don't seem willing to disagree. We end up going with the first idea suggested.	a. Brainstorm so you have multiple possibilities to consider. b. After an idea is suggested, have each person on the team suggest a way it could be improved. c. Appoint someone to be a devil's advocate. d. Have each person on the team write a draft. It's likely the drafts will be different, and you'll have several options to mix and match. e. Talk about good ways to offer criticism. Sometimes people don't disagree because they're afraid that other team members won't tolerate disagreement.
One person just criticizes everything.	a. Ask the person to follow up the criticism with a suggestion for improvement. b. Talk about ways to express criticism tactfully. "I think we need to think about x" is more tactful than "You're wrong." c. If the criticism is about ideas and writing (not about people), value it. Ideas and documents need criticism if we are to improve them.

3. Discover the Needs Each Person Is Trying to Meet. Sometimes determining the real needs makes it possible to see a new solution. The **presenting problem** that surfaces as the subject of dissension may or may not be the real problem. For example, a worker who complains about the hours he's putting in may in fact be complaining not about the hours themselves but about not feeling appreciated. A supervisor who complains that the other supervisors don't invite her to meetings may really feel that the other managers don't accept her as a peer. Sometimes people have trouble seeing beyond the presenting problem because they've been taught to suppress their anger, especially toward powerful people. One way to tell whether the presenting problem is the real problem is to ask, "If this were solved, would I be satisfied?" If the answer is *no*, then the problem that presents itself is not the real problem. Solving the presenting problem won't solve the conflict. Keep probing until you get to the real conflict.

4. Search for Alternatives. Sometimes people are locked into conflict because they see too few alternatives. People tend to handle complexity by looking for ways to simplify. In a team, someone makes a suggestion, so the team members discuss it as if it is the only alternative. The team generates more alternatives only if the first one is unacceptable. As a result, the team's choice depends on the order in which team members think of ideas. When a decision is significant, the team needs a formal process to identify alternatives before moving on to a decision. Many teams use brainstorming when they search for alternatives.

5. Repair Negative Feelings. Conflict can emerge without anger and without escalating the disagreement, as the next section shows. But if people's feelings have been hurt, the team needs to deal with those feelings to resolve the conflict constructively. Only when people feel respected and taken seriously can they take the next step of trusting others on the team.

Criticism Responses

Conflict is particularly difficult to resolve when someone else criticizes or attacks us directly. When we are criticized, our natural reaction is to defend ourselves—perhaps by counterattacking. The counterattack prompts the critic to defend him- or herself. The conflict escalates; feelings are hurt; issues become muddied and more difficult to resolve.

Just as resolving conflict depends on identifying the needs each person is trying to meet, so dealing with criticism depends on understanding the real concern of the critic. Constructive ways to respond to criticism and get closer to the real concern include paraphrasing, checking for feelings, checking inferences, and buying time with limited agreement.

Paraphrasing To **paraphrase,** repeat in your own words the verbal content of the critic's message. The purposes of paraphrasing are (1) to be sure that you have heard the critic accurately, (2) to let the critic know what his or her statement means to you, and (3) to communicate that you are taking the critic and his or her feelings seriously.

Criticism:	You guys are stonewalling my requests for information.
Paraphrase:	You think that we don't give you the information you need.

A Team of Rivals

A major focus of Doris Kearns Goodwin's book *Team of Rivals* is Abraham Lincoln's leadership style, particularly the way he built his leadership team. President Obama said if he could take only one book, apart from the Bible, with him to the White House it would be this book.

The following are some of Goodwin's key points:

- Lincoln chose his cabinet from his most able rivals, men who were guaranteed to hold different views. His ability to weave these men into an effective team showed great emotional intelligence.

- These men were confident enough that they were not afraid to question Lincoln or argue with him. The resulting exchange of ideas strengthened Lincoln's decision making.

- These men also had temperaments different from Lincoln's, helping Lincoln find a balanced approach to leading the war.

- Lincoln shared both credit for successes and responsibility for failures, including failures of others. Goodwin calls this tactic creating "a reservoir of good feeling." Through this approach Lincoln earned the intense loyalty of his team.

Adapted from Doris Kearns Goodwin, "Leadership Lessons from Abraham Lincoln," *Harvard Business Review* 87, no.4 (2009): 43–47.

Scientific Teams

For centuries Western innovation has been led by individuals, such as Da Vinci, Darwin, and Einstein. But in recent years, teamwork has become the model that drives innovation, especially in the sciences.

Benjamin Jones, a professor at Northwestern University's Kellogg School of Management, analyzed 19.9 million papers and 2.1 million patents, and found that 99% of scientific subfields have seen not only increased levels of teamwork but also increases in the sizes of teams.

According to Jones, the best research now comes from teams. Among the most cited studies, papers authored by teams are cited more than twice as often as papers by individual authors. Papers cited more than 1,000 times—"home run papers"—are more than six times as likely to be the result of team research.

What is behind this shift toward teamwork? In part, Jones claims, researchers develop narrow expertise during years of graduate study, requiring them to rely on colleagues in other fields to provide connections between areas of study. Additionally, the complex nature of twenty-first-century problems demands collaborative efforts in order to truly transform our understanding of those problems.

Adapted from Jonah Lehrer, "Sunset of the Solo Scientist," *Wall Street Journal*, February 5, 2011, C12.

Checking for Feelings

When you check the critic's feelings, you identify the emotions that the critic seems to be expressing verbally or nonverbally. The purposes of checking feelings are to try to understand (1) the critic's emotions, (2) the importance of the criticism for the critic, and (3) the unspoken ideas and feelings that may actually be more important than the voiced criticism.

| Criticism: | You guys are stonewalling my requests for information. |
| Feelings check: | You sound pretty angry, yes? |

Always *ask* the other person if you are right in your perception. Even the best reader of nonverbal cues is sometimes wrong.

Checking for Inferences

When you check the inferences you draw from criticism, you identify the implied meaning of the verbal and nonverbal content of the criticism, taking the statement a step further than the words of the critic to try to understand *why* the critic is bothered by the action or attitude under discussion. The purposes of checking inferences are (1) to identify the real (as opposed to the presenting) problem and (2) to communicate the feeling that you care about resolving the conflict.

| Criticism: | You guys are stonewalling my requests for information. |
| Inference: | Are you saying that you need more information from our team? |

Inferences can be faulty. In the above interchange, the critic might respond, "I don't need more information. I just think you should give it to me without my having to file three forms in triplicate every time I want some data."

Buying Time with Limited Agreement

Buying time is a useful strategy for dealing with criticisms that really sting. When you buy time with limited agreement, you avoid escalating the conflict (as an angry statement might do) but also avoid yielding to the critic's point of view. To buy time, restate the part of the criticism you agree to be true. (This is often a fact, rather than the interpretation or evaluation the critic has made of that fact.) *Then let the critic respond, before you say anything else.* The purposes of buying time are (1) to allow you time to think when a criticism really hits home and threatens you, so that you can respond to the criticism rather than simply reacting defensively, and (2) to suggest to the critic that you are trying to hear what he or she is saying.

| Criticism: | You guys are stonewalling my requests for information. |
| Limited agreement: | It's true that the cost projections you asked for last week still aren't ready. |

DO NOT go on to justify or explain. A "Yes, but . . . " statement is not a time-buyer.

You-Attitude in Conflict Resolution

You-attitude means looking at things from the audience's point of view, respecting the audience, and protecting the audience's ego (see Chapter 3 for more on you-attitude). Resolving conflicts or persuading others involves three kinds of awareness: situational awareness (showing that you understand the situation), personal awareness (showing that you understand the other person), and solution awareness (showing that you understand or are seeking a path to resolution).[22] The way you communicate your awareness comes through in how you employ you-attitude.

The *you* statements that many people use when they're angry attack the audience; they do not illustrate you-attitude. Instead, substitute statements about your own feelings. In conflict, *I* statements show good you-attitude!

Lacks you-attitude:	You never do your share of the work
You-attitude:	I feel that I'm doing more than my share of the work on this project.
Lacks you-attitude:	Even you should be able to run the report through a spelling checker.
You-attitude:	I'm not willing to have my name on a report with so many spelling errors. I did lots of the writing, and I don't think I should have to do the proofreading and spell checking, too.

Effective Meetings LO 8-5

Meetings have always taken a large part of the average manager's week. Although technology has eliminated some meetings, the increased number of teams means that meetings are even more frequent. Despite their advantages for communication, meetings are not always good. Many productive workers see them as too often a waste of time, interrupting valuable work, while less productive workers see them as a pleasant break. However, meetings can easily be made more effective.

Meetings can have multiple purposes:

- To share information.
- To brainstorm ideas.
- To evaluate ideas.
- To develop plans.
- To make decisions.
- To create a document.
- To motivate members.

When meetings combine two or more purposes, it's useful to make the purposes explicit. For example, in the meeting of a company's board of directors, some items are presented for information. Discussion is possible, but the group will not be asked to make a decision. Other items are presented for action; the group will be asked to vote. A business meeting might specify that the first half hour will be time for brainstorming, with the second half hour devoted to evaluation.

Formal meetings are run under strict rules, like the rules of parliamentary procedure summarized in *Robert's Rules of Order*. Motions must be made formally before a topic can be debated. Each point is settled by a vote. **Minutes** record each motion and the vote on it. Formal rules help the meeting run smoothly if the group is very large or if the agenda is very long. **Informal meetings,** which are much more common in the workplace, are run more loosely. Votes may not be taken if most people seem to agree. Minutes may not be kept. Informal meetings are better for team-building and problem solving.

Fun at Berkshire Hathaway's Annual Meeting

[In his 2012 letter to the shareholders of Berkshire Hathaway, Chairman and CEO Warren Buffett gives a three-page preview of what to anticipate at the annual meeting. Here are some colorful excerpts.]

- The doors will open at 7 a.m., and at 7:30 we will have our second International Newspaper Tossing Challenge. The target will be the porch of a Clayton Home, precisely 35 feet from the throwing line. Last year I successfully fought off all challengers. But now Berkshire has acquired a large number of newspapers and with them came much tossing talent (or so the throwers claim).

- If you decide to leave during the day's question periods, please do so while *Charlie* is talking.

- The best reason to exit, of course, is to *shop*. . . . Remember: Anyone who says money can't buy happiness simply hasn't shopped at our meeting.

- Around 1 p.m. on Sunday, I will begin clerking at Borsheims. Last year my sales totaled $1.5 million. This year I won't quit until I hit $2 million. Because I need to leave well before sundown, I will be desperate to do business. Come take advantage of me. Ask for my "Crazy Warren" price.

Bullets quoted from Warren Buffett, "Letters 2012," Berkshire Hathaway Inc., accessed April 24, 2013, http://www.berkshirehathaway.com/letters/2012ltr.pdf.

Planning the **agenda** is the foundation of a good meeting. A good agenda indicates

- A list of items for consideration.
- Whether each item is presented for information, for discussion, or for a decision.
- Who is sponsoring or introducing each item.
- How much time is allotted for each item.

Although a time schedule on an agenda is frequently not followed exactly, it does inform participants about the relative importance of the agenda items. In general, the information on an agenda should be specific enough that participants can come to the meeting prepared with ideas, background information, and any other resources they need for completing each agenda item.

Many groups start their agendas with routine items on which agreement will be easy. Doing so gets the meeting off to a positive start. However, it may also waste the time when people are most attentive. Another approach is to put routine items at the end. If there's a long list of routine items, sometimes you can dispense with them in an omnibus motion. An **omnibus motion** allows a group to approve many items together rather than voting on each separately. A single omnibus motion might cover multiple changes to operational guidelines, or a whole slate of candidates for various offices, or various budget recommendations. It's important to schedule controversial items early in the meeting, when energy levels are high, and to allow enough time for full discussion. Giving a controversial item only half an hour at the end of the day or evening makes people suspect that the leaders are trying to manipulate them.

Pay attention to people and process as well as to the task at hand. At informal meetings, a good leader observes nonverbal feedback and invites everyone to participate. If conflict seems to be getting out of hand, a leader may want to focus attention on the group process and ways that it could deal with conflict, before getting back to the substantive issues. Highly sensitive topics may require two or more meetings, the first to air the subject and people's feelings and the second to vote. The time between the two gives participants an opportunity to cool off and informally discuss the issues involved.

If the group doesn't formally vote, the leader should summarize the group's consensus after each point. At the end of the meeting, the leader should summarize all decisions and remind the group who is responsible for implementing or following up on each item. If no other notes are taken, someone should record the decisions and assignments. Long minutes will be most helpful if assignments are set off visually from the narrative.

Technology in Teams LO 8-6

Now that companies are more spread out geographically than ever before, team members may be scattered across different offices, states, and even countries. Yet the teams are still expected to work together effectively and produce results. New technologies provide ways for distributed teams to meet, create schedules and assignments, and collaborate on projects.

Technologies for Meetings

There are many options for virtual meetings with teams. For one-on-one meetings or small teams, video chatting through applications such as Skype, FaceTime, or Google+ allows for quick, free meetings. Skype and FaceTime are specifically designed for one-on-one conversations, but allow additional people to join. Google+, on the other hand, is designed for multiple people to connect at the same time. It actively manages the video streams to show the person who is currently talking.

For larger meetings that include formal presentations or require more stability, many companies use GoToMeeting.com, which provides videoconferencing services for a monthly fee. Participants in the meetings can simply log on to the website and be connected to the video and audio of the meeting and gain access to presentation slides and other materials. Other companies use streaming web video combined with social networking, e-mail, or online comment forms to create a collaborative setting for a meeting.

Technologies for Scheduling and Assignments

Productive meetings include creating schedules and making assignments for team members. Keeping track of these schedules and assignments can be complicated, particularly if the members of the team are in different locations or in different time zones. Simple online calendars, such as Google's calendar, can manage deadlines and simple tasks. More complex assignments may require something such as Microsoft Outlook, which can organize calendars, assignments, communications, and documents. Other applications also provide specialized project management tools. Producteev, for example, uses a web interface to create to-do lists, manage assignments and deadlines, coordinate tasks within assignments, and organize documents. Many additional applications and services can perform the same services.

Technologies for Collaboration

Team members also need to collaborate on documents, presentations, and products. Google Docs uses a simple interface that allows team members to write, edit, and comment on the same document in real time. Newer versions of Microsoft Office offer similar tools for collaboration; team members can write, edit, and comment on shared Word, Excel, and PowerPoint documents. For presentation slides, Prezi and SlideRocket offer online tools to facilitate collaboration. DropBox, Microsoft SkyDrive, and Google Docs all offer online storage for teams to share documents and project files. Wikis also allow teams to share ideas and write collaboratively.

Collaborative Writing LO 8-7

Whatever your career, it is likely that some of the documents you produce will be written with a team. Collaborative writing is often prompted by one of the following situations:

- The task is too big or the time is too short for one person to do all the writing.

- No one person has all the knowledge required to do the writing.

- The stakes for the task are so high that the organization wants the best efforts of as many people as possible; no one person wants the sole responsibility for the success or failure of the document.

Collaborative writing can be done by two people or by a much larger group. The team can be democratic or run by a leader who makes decisions alone. The team may share or divide responsibility for each stage in the writing process.

Teams commonly divide the work in several ways. One person might do the main writing, with others providing feedback. Another approach is to divide the whole project into smaller tasks and to assign each task to a different team member. This approach shares the workload more evenly but is harder to coordinate, although technology, such as wikis or Google Docs, helps. Sometimes team members write together simultaneously, discussing and responding to each other's ideas. This approach helps consensus but is time-consuming.

Research in collaborative writing suggests strategies that produce the best writing. As noted earlier, research has found that student teams that voiced disagreements as they analyzed, planned, and wrote a document produced significantly better documents than those that suppressed disagreement, going along with whatever was first proposed.[23] A case study of two collaborative writing teams in a state agency found that the successful team distributed power in an egalitarian way, worked to soothe hurt feelings, and was careful to involve all team members. In terms of writing process, the successful team understood the task as a response to a rhetorical situation (with a specific audience, purpose, and situation), planned revisions as a team, saw supervisors' comments as legitimate, and had a positive attitude toward revision.[24]

Planning the Work and the Document

Collaborative writing is most successful when the team articulates its understanding of the document's purposes, audiences, and contexts, and explicitly discusses the best way to achieve rhetorical goals. Businesses schedule formal planning sessions for large projects to set up a time line specifying intermediate and final due dates, meeting dates, who will attend each meeting, and who will do what. Putting the plan in writing reduces misunderstandings during the project.

When you plan a collaborative writing project,

- Make your analysis of the problem, audience, context, and purposes explicit so you know where you agree and where you disagree. It usually helps to put these in writing.

- Plan the organization, format, and style of the document before anyone begins to write to make it easier to blend sections written by different authors. Decide who is going to do what and when each piece of the project will be due.

- Consider your work styles and other commitments when making a time line. A writer working alone can stay up all night to finish a single-authored document. But members of a team need to work together to accommodate each other's styles and to enable members to meet other commitments.

- Decide how you will give constructive feedback on each person's work.

- Build some leeway into your deadlines. It's harder for a team to finish a document when one person's part is missing than it is for a single writer to finish the last section of a document on which he or she has done all the work.

All team members need to give input on important planning issues, especially to analysis and organization.

Composing the Drafts

When you draft a collaborative writing project,

- Decide who will write what. Will one person write an entire draft? Will each team member be assigned a portion of the draft? Will the whole team write the draft together? Most writers find that composing alone is faster than composing in a group. However, composing together may reduce revision time later, since the group examines every choice as it is made. Even so, it is still generally faster to have individuals compose drafts.

- Decide how you will share drafts. Which technologies will you use so everyone can work on a draft? International teams particularly need to use electronic media to compose drafts.

- Carefully label and date drafts so everyone is working on the most current version. Make sure everyone knows the date of the latest draft.

- If the quality of writing is crucial, have the best writer(s) draft the document after everyone has gathered the necessary information.

Revising the Document

Revising a collaborative document requires attention to content, organization, and style. The following guidelines can make the revision process more effective:

- Evaluate the content and discuss possible revisions as a team. Brainstorm ways to improve each section so the person doing the revisions has some guidance.

- Evaluate the organization and discuss possible revisions as a team. Would a different organization make the message clearer?

- Recognize that different people favor different writing styles. If the style satisfies the demands of standard English and the conventions of business writing, accept it even if you wouldn't say it that way.

- When the team is satisfied with the content of the document, one person—probably the best writer—should make any changes necessary to make the writing style consistent throughout.

Editing and Proofreading the Document

Since writers' mastery of standard English varies, a team report needs careful editing and proofreading.

- Have at least one person check the whole document for correctness in grammar, mechanics, and spelling and for consistency in the way that format elements (particularly headings), names, and numbers are handled.

- Run the document through a spell checker.

- Even if you use a computerized spell checker, at least one human being should proofread the document too.

Blue Man Group Work

The Blue Man Group started in 1988 as a trio of performance artists doing street theater in New York City. Today, Blue Man Group is an entertainment franchise with about 70 Blue Men employed in nine theater shows plus touring concerts. They fill stadiums, they've founded their own creativity-based early childhood program, and they've been nominated for a Grammy. How did they do it? Teamwork.

As Matt Goldman, one of the founding Blue Men, notes, "Three is the smallest unit where you can have an outsider." The Blue Man Group uses consensus to create music, original instruments, and shows—and to run the business. They discuss decisions until they reach a point where all three members can agree. That lets each member bring his or her own unique contributions to the process, while ensuring that the whole team is satisfied with the result. "It takes longer, but we find if you keep talking things through, you reach a better choice."

Working as part of a team is one of the most challenging communication tasks you can face in a professional setting. But it can be rewarding. Chris Wink, another of the founding Blue Men, says, "If you can be a good collaborator, it's like a superpower because you can connect your gifts with that of someone else."

As a team member, you'll use your audience analysis skills to build goodwill with people inside *and* outside of your team, and your organizational skills to keep both your communication and your work moving smoothly.

Sources: Liz Welch, "How We Did It: The Blue Man Group, from Downtown Performance Art to Global Entertainment Empire," *Inc.,* August 2008, 110–12; and Dinah Eng, "The Color Blue Just Felt Right," *Fortune,* October 8, 2012, 41.

Like any member of the writing team, those handling the editing tasks need to consider how they express their ideas. In many situations, the editor plays the role of diplomat, careful to suggest changes in ways that do not seem to call the writer's abilities into question. Describing the reason for a change is typically more helpful than stating an opinion. Writers are more likely to allow editing of their prose if they know a sentence has a dangling modifier, or a paragraph needs work on parallel structure. Using words like *could* and *should* to modify a direction can add a tone of politeness.

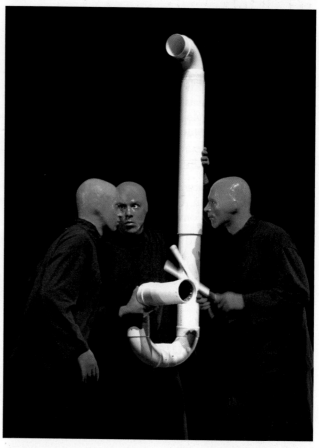

The Blue Man Group uses consensus to create shows and run the business. See "Blue Man Group Work" sidebar on this page.

Making the Team Process Work

The information in this chapter can help your team interact effectively, run meetings efficiently, and deal with conflict constructively. The following suggestions apply specifically to writing teams:

- Give yourselves plenty of time to discuss problems and find solutions. Writing a team report may require hours of discussion time in addition to the time individuals spend doing research and writing drafts.

- Take the time to get to know team members and to build team loyalty. Team members will work harder and the final document will be better if the team is important to members.

- Be a responsible team member. Produce your drafts on time.

- Be aware that people have different ways of expressing themselves in writing.

- Because talking is "looser" than writing, people on a team can think they agree when they don't. Don't assume that because the discussion went smoothly, a draft written by one person will necessarily be acceptable.

- Use collaborative technologies wisely to help the writing process rather than hinder it.

- Allow more time at all stages of the writing process than you would if you were writing the document by yourself.

Summary by Learning Objectives

LO 8-1 **Different kinds of productive and nonproductive roles in teams.**

Effective teams balance informational, interpersonal, and procedural team roles.

LO 8-2 **Group decision-making strategies.**

Groupthink is the tendency for groups to put such a high premium on agreement that they directly or indirectly punish dissent. The best correctives to groupthink are to consciously search for additional alternatives, to test one's assumptions against those of a range of other people, and to protect the right of each person in the group to disagree.

LO 8-3 **Characteristics of successful teams.**

Successful teams set clear deadlines, schedule frequent meetings, deal directly with conflict, have an inclusive decision-making style, and have a higher proportion of members who worked actively on the project.

LO 8-4 **Techniques for resolving conflict.**

- To resolve conflicts, first make sure the people involved really disagree. Next, check to see that everyone's information is correct. Discover the needs each person is trying to meet. The presenting problem that surfaces as the subject of dissension may or may not be the real problem. Search for alternatives. Repair negative feelings.

- Constructive ways to respond to criticism include paraphrasing, checking for feelings, checking inferences, and buying time with limited agreement.

- Use statements about your own feelings to own the problem and avoid attacking the audience. In conflict, *I* statements are good you-attitude!

LO 8-5 **Techniques for making meetings effective.**

To make meetings more effective,

- State the purpose of the meeting at the beginning.

- Distribute an agenda that indicates whether each item is for information, discussion, or action, and how long each is expected to take.

- Allow enough time to discuss controversial issues.

- Pay attention to people and process as well as to the task at hand.

- If you don't take formal votes, summarize the group's consensus after each point. At the end of the meeting, summarize all decisions and remind the group who is responsible for implementing or following up on each item.

LO 8-6 **Technologies to use in teamwork.**

Modern technologies allow for team collaboration through meetings, scheduling, and creating documents and presentations.

LO 8-7 **Techniques for collaborative writing.**

Collaborative writing means working with other writers to produce a single document. Writers producing a joint document need to pay attention not only to the basic steps in the writing process but also to the processes of team formation and conflict resolution. They also need to allow more time than they would for single-authored documents.

Continuing Case

The All-Weather Case, set in an HR department in a manufacturing company, extends through all 19 chapters and is available at www.mhhe.com/locker11e. The portion for this chapter asks students to suggest how two team leaders could be more effective.

Exercises and Cases

8.1   Reviewing the Chapter

1. What are 10 kinds of productive roles in teams? Which roles do you prefer to play? (LO 8-1)

2. What are five kinds of nonproductive roles in teams? (LO 8-1)

3. What are some team decision-making strategies? (LO 8-2)

4. Name five characteristics of successful teams. (LO 8-3)

5. What is groupthink? Have you ever experienced it? (LO 8-3)

6. What are some techniques for resolving conflict? (LO 8-4)

7. What are some techniques for responding to criticism? (LO 8-4)

8. What are some techniques for making meetings effective? (LO 8-5)

9. What are some technology tools for collaboration? (LO 8-6)

10. What are some techniques for collaborative writing? (LO 8-7)

11. Have you ever been part of a team that wrote a document as a whole group rather than assigning out pieces? If so, how did the process work for your team? (LO 8-7)

8.2   Brainstorming Ways to Resolve Conflicts

Suggest one or more ways that each of the following teams could deal with the conflict(s) it faces.

1. Mike and Takashi both find writing hard. Elise has been getting better grades than either of them, so they offer to do all the research if she'll organize the document and write, revise, edit, and proofread it. Elise thinks that this method would leave her doing a disproportionate share of the work. Moreover, scheduling the work would be difficult, since she wouldn't know how good their research was until the last minute.

2. Because of their class and work schedules, Lars and Andrea want to hold team meetings from 8 to 10 p.m., working later if need be. But Juan's wife works the evening shift, and he needs to be home with his children, two of whom have to be in bed before 8. He wants to meet from 8 to 10 a.m., but the others don't want to meet that early.

3. Lynn wants to divide the work equally, with firm due dates. Marcia is trying to get into medical school. She says she'd rather do the lion's share of the work so that she knows it's good.

4. Jessie's father is terminally ill. This team isn't very important in terms of what's going on in her life, and she knows she may have to miss some team meetings.

5. Sherry is aware that she is the person on her team who always points out the logical flaws in arguments: she's the one who reminds the team members that they haven't done all the parts of the assignment. She doesn't want her team to turn in a flawed product, but she wonders whether the other team members see her as too critical.

6. Jim's team missed several questions on the team quiz. Talking to Tae-Suk after class, Jim learns that Tae-Suk knew all the answers. "Why didn't you say anything?" Jim asks angrily. Tae-Suk responds quietly, "Todd said that he knew the answers. I did not want to argue with him. We have to work together, and I do not want anyone to lose face."

8.3   Comparing Meeting Minutes

Have two or more people record the minutes of each class or team meeting for a week. Compare the accounts of the same meeting.

- To what extent do they agree on what happened?
- Does one contain information missing in other accounts?
- Do any accounts disagree on a specific fact?
- How do you account for the differences you find?

As your instructor directs,

a. Discuss your findings with your team.

b. Share your team findings orally with the class.

c. Describe and analyze your findings in an e-mail to your instructor.

8.4 Preparing a Contribution Scorecard

"Forming Team Expectations," the sidebar on page 215, discussed using a contribution scorecard to help set and measure expectations for team work. With a small group, prepare a sample contribution scorecard using the following steps:

- List your development goals.
- Outline steps you need to take to move toward your goals.
- Detail the knowledge and experience you can bring to bear on your project.

- List ways to leverage the range of your knowledge and experience.

With your group, discuss the following questions:

- How does a contribution scorecard set expectations for your team?
- Do you think it will help your team in your day-to-day tasks? How?
- How could a contribution scorecard help you measure your performance as a team?

8.5 Recommending a Policy on Student Entrepreneurs

Assume that your small team comprises the officers in student government on your campus. You receive this e-mail from the Dean of Students:

As you know, campus policy says that no student may use campus resources to conduct business-related activities. Students can't conduct business out of dorm rooms or use university e-mail addresses for business. They can't post business web pages on the university server.

On the other hand, a survey conducted by the Kauffman Center for Entrepreneurial Leadership showed that 7 out of 10 teens want to become entrepreneurs.

Should campus policy be changed to allow students to use dorm rooms and university e-mail addresses for business? (And then what happens when roommates complain and our network can't carry the increased e-mail traffic?) Please recommend what support (if any) should be given to student entrepreneurs.

Your team will be writing a report recommending what (if anything) your campus should do for student entrepreneurs and supporting your recommendation.

Hints:

- Does your campus offer other support for entrepreneurs (courses, a business plan competition, a start-up incubator)? What should be added or expanded?
- Is it realistic to ask alumni for money to fund student start-ups?
- Are campus dorms, e-mail, phone, and delivery services funded by tax dollars? If your school is a public institution, do state or local laws limit business use?

You need to

- Send e-mail messages to team members describing your initial point of view on the issue and discussing the various options.
- Help your team write the report.
- Write an e-mail to your instructor telling how satisfied you are with
  - The decision your team reached.
  - The process you used to reach it.
  - The document your team produced.

8.6   Recommending a Fair Way to Assign Work around the Holidays

Assume your team comprises a hospital's Labor-Management Committee. This e-mail arrives from the hospital administrator:

> Subject: Allocating Holiday Hours
>
> It's that time of year again, and we're starting to get requests for time off from every department. We have shifts where every physician and half the nurses want time off. Don't these people realize that we can't close down over a holiday? And what's worse is that some of the shift leads are giving preferential treatment to their friends. The head of the nurses' union has already started complaining to me.
>
> We need a comprehensive, hospital-wide procedure for assigning holiday vacation time that doesn't make us shut down wards. It needs to be flexible, because people like to take a week off around Christmas. But we have to set limits: no more than one-quarter of the staff can take time off at any one time. And those nurses like to swap shifts with each other to arrange their days off into larger blocks, so we need to cover that too.
>
> Write up a policy to keep these people in line. Be sure to throw in the safety concerns and regulatory stuff.

Your team will be performing these tasks:

a. Write a team response recommending a new policy and supporting your recommendations. Include two transmittal e-mails: one to the hospital administrator, and one to the hospital's medical and nursing staff. Take care to address the two audiences' different needs and expectations with good you-attitude and positive emphasis.

b. Create a one-page notice describing your new policy. This notice should be suitable for posting at the duty desk for each ward—in full view of both your employees and your customers (the patients). Create an effective visual design that emphasizes and organizes the text.

You personally need to

- Send e-mail messages to team members describing your initial point of view on the issue and discussing the various options.
- Help your team write the documents.
- Write an e-mail to your instructor telling how satisfied you are with
  - The decisions your team reached.
  - The process you used to reach them.
  - The documents your team produced.

8.7   Recommending a Dress Policy

Assume your small team comprises your organization's Labor-Management Committee.
    This e-mail arrives from the CEO:

> In the last 10 years, we became increasingly casual. But changed circumstances seem to call for more formality. Is it time to reinstate a dress policy? If so, what should it be?

Your team will be writing a response recommending the appropriate dress for employees and supporting your recommendation.

Hint:

Agree on an office, factory, store, or other workplace to use for this problem.

You personally need to

- Send e-mail messages to team members describing your initial point of view on the issue and discussing the various options.
- Help your team write the response.

- Write an e-mail to your instructor telling how satisfied you are with
  - The decision your team reached.
  - The process you used to reach it.
  - The document your team produced.

8.8   Responding to Customer Complaints

Assume your small team comprises the Social Networking Committee at the headquarters of a chain of restaurants. After the managers of one of the restaurants appear on a reality television show, your team begins to receive negative online reviews on sites such as Yelp and Facebook. The negative reviews focus on the character and behavior of the restaurant managers. The CEO of the company asks your team to write a response to the criticisms to post online. He wants you to focus on the company's values and service.

Your team will be writing a group response to online criticisms. You will need to agree on how best to present your company, how to write about the managers who appeared on the TV show, and how to respond to the negative reviews.

You personally need to

- Send e-mail messages to team members describing your initial point of view on the issue and discussing the various options.
- Help your team write the response.
- Write an e-mail to your instructor telling how satisfied you are with
  - The decision your team reached.
  - The process you used to reach it.
  - The document your team produced.

8.9   Answering an Ethics Question

Assume your team comprises your organization's Ethics Committee. You receive the following anonymous note:

> People are routinely using the company letterhead to write letters to members of Congress, senators, and even the president stating their positions on various issues. Making their opinions known is of course their right, but doing so on letterhead stationery implies that they are speaking for the company, which they are not.
>
> I think that the use of letterhead for anything other than official company business should be prohibited.

Your team will be determining the best solution to the problem and then communicating it in a message to all employees.

You personally need to

- Send e-mail messages to team members describing your initial point of view on the issue and discussing the various options.
- Help your team write the message.

- Write an e-mail to your instructor telling how satisfied you are with
  - The decision your team reached.
  - The process you used to reach it.
  - The document your team produced.

8.10   Interviewing Workers about Collaborating

Interview someone who works in an organization about his or her on-the-job collaboration activities. Possible questions to ask include the following:

- How often do you work on collaborative projects?
- Do your collaborative projects always include people who are in your immediate office? How often do you collaborate with people via technology?
- How do you begin collaborative projects? What are the first steps you take when working with others?

- How do you handle disagreements?
- What do you do when someone isn't doing his/her share of the work on a collaborative project?
- What do you do to see every person meets team deadlines?
- How do you handle unexpected problems? Illness? Injury? Broken equipment?
- What advice can you give about effectively collaborating on projects?

As your instructor directs,

a. Share your information with a small team of students in your class.

b. Present your findings orally to the class.

c. Present your findings in an e-mail to your instructor.

d. Join with other students to present your findings in a team report.

8.11   Networking for Team Formation

In this exercise, you are going to participate in a networking event, an abbreviated "talk and walk."

To prepare for the event,

- Prepare business cards for yourself, using a computer application of your choice.
- Prepare a list of people in your class whom you would like to meet (give visual descriptions if you do not know their names).
- Prepare a list of questions you would like to have answered.
- Collect materials to use for taking notes during the event.

During the event, you will have six three-minute sessions to talk with a fellow student and exchange business cards. Remember, the other person also has questions he or she wants answered. Your instructor will time the sessions and tell you when to change people.

After the event, analyze what you have learned. Here are some questions to get you started:

- Who was the most interesting? Why?
- Whom did you like the most? Why?
- Whom would you most like to have on a team in this class? Why?
- Did you meet anyone you didn't want to work with? Explain.
- What lessons did you learn about networking?

Write an e-mail to your teacher containing your analysis.

8.12   Writing a Team Action Plan

Before you begin working on a team project, develop a team action plan to establish a framework that will hold your team members accountable for their work.

After reading the project assignment sheet and meeting your team, decide upon answers for the following questions:

- Will you have a team leader? If so, who? Why is that person qualified to be the team leader? What are that person's responsibilities? How will you proceed if the team leader is unable to meet those responsibilities?
- What will be each team member's role? What is each team member's qualification for that role?
- How are you dividing your work? Why did you choose to divide the work the way you did?
- What are the tasks your team needs to accomplish? For each task in the assignment, identify a concrete deliverable (What do you need to hand in?), a concrete measure for success (How will your team decide if you completed that task well?), and a work schedule (When does each task need to be done?)
- How will you resolve disagreements that may arise while working on the project? How will your team make decisions: By majority? By consensus?
- When and where will you hold meetings? Decide whether you can hold meetings if all team members are not present. How will you inform team members of what occurred at meetings if they were not present?
- Define what "absence" means for your team. Are all absences equal? How should a team member who's going to be absent let the team know? How far in advance does your team need to know about an absence? How many absences from one team member will be too many? What are the consequences of too many absences?
- Create a policy dealing with people who don't attend class during your preparation days or during your presentation; people who don't attend meetings outside class; people who miss deadlines, don't do their work at all or in a timely manner, or who consistently turn in incomplete or poor-quality work. What penalties will you apply? (Some ideas: you might consider loss of points, grade reductions, failure, a team firing, or a team intervention.)
- Will you report problem members to your instructor? If so, at what point? What role do you want your instructor to have in dealing with problem members?

After your team determines and agrees on an action plan, the team's secretary should send your answers in an e-mail to your instructor, who will keep the document on file in case a problem arises.

8.13 Writing Team Meeting Minutes

As you work in a collaborative team setting, designate a different member to take minutes for each meeting.

As your instructor directs, your minutes should include:

- Name of the team holding the meeting.
- Members who were present.
- Members who were absent.
- Place, time, and date of meeting.
- Work accomplished, and who did it, during the meeting.

- Actions that need to be completed, the person responsible, and the due date.
- Decisions made during the meeting.
- New issues raised at the meeting but not resolved should be recorded for future meetings.
- Signature of acting secretary.

Remember to keep your minutes brief and to the point. When the minutes are complete, e-mail them to your fellow team members and cc: them to your instructor.

8.14 Keeping a Journal about a Team

As you work on a team, keep a journal after each team meeting.

- Who did what?
- What roles did you play in the meeting?
- What decisions were made? How were they made?
- What conflicts arose? How were they handled?
- What strategies could you use to make the next meeting go smoothly?
- Record one observation about each team member.

At the end of the project, analyze your journals. In an e-mail to your instructor, discuss

- Patterns you see.
- Roles of each team member, including yourself.

- Decision making in your team.
- Conflict resolution in your team.
- Strengths of your team.
- Areas where your team could improve.
- Strengths of the deliverables.
- Areas where the deliverables could be improved.
- Changes you would make in the team and deliverables if you had the project to do over.

8.15 Analyzing the Dynamics of a Team

Analyze the dynamics of a task team of which you were a member. Answer the following questions:

1. Who was the team's leader? How did the leader emerge? Were there any changes in or challenges to the original leader?
2. Describe the contribution each member made to the team and the roles each person played.
3. Did any members of the team officially or unofficially drop out? Did anyone join after the team had begun working? How did you deal with the loss or addition of a team member, both in terms of getting the work done and in terms of helping people work together?
4. What planning did your team do at the start of the project? Did you stick to the plan or revise it? How did the team decide that revision was necessary?
5. How did your team make decisions? Did you vote? Reach decisions by consensus?
6. What problems or conflicts arose? Did the team deal with them openly? To what extent did they interfere with the team's task?
7. Evaluate your team both in terms of its task and in terms of the satisfaction members felt. How did this team compare with other task teams you've been part of? What made it better or worse?

8. What were the strengths of the team? Weaknesses?
9. How did the team's strengths and weaknesses impact the quality of the work produced?
10. If you had the project to do over again, what would you do differently?

As you answer the questions,

- Be honest. You won't lose points for reporting that your team had problems or did something "wrong."
- Show your knowledge of good team dynamics. That is, if your team did something wrong, show that you know what *should* have been done. Similarly, if your team worked well, show that you know *why* it worked well.
- Be specific. Give examples or anecdotes to support your claims.

As your instructor directs,

a. Discuss your answers with the other team members.
b. Present your findings in an individual e-mail to your instructor.
c. Join with the other team members to write a collaborative e-mail to your instructor.

8.16 Dealing with a "Saboteur"

It's often said that "there's no *I* in *team*" because on the best teams, everyone works together for the good of the group. What happens when you encounter a team member who believes that "there's a *me* in *team*" and ignores or undermines the team's success in order to achieve personal goals?

Consider this scenario. You're on a team of four students, and you've all been working for the past month to complete a major class project. When you were planning your project, one team member—let's say Lee—argued with your team's decisions, but agreed to go along with the majority. Lee contributed the bare minimum to your team's work, sat silently during meetings, and when you asked for help overcoming a problem with the project, Lee responded with a shrug, "I told you at the start that I thought this was a bad idea. I guess we're all going to get a failing grade."

Now you're at your last team meeting before the assignment is due. Lee reveals a decision to quit the team and turn in a separate project. Lee doesn't want a grade that "will suffer from all your 'second-rate' efforts," and tells you that s/he already complained to your instructor about the rest of you.

As your instructor directs,

a. Write an e-mail to your instructor in which you explain your individual response to this scenario. What would you do? How should your team proceed?

b. Work as a group to establish a working policy that might address this scenario before it happens.

   - What policies would you need to protect the group from individual members who are out for themselves?
   - What policies would you need to protect team members from having the team take advantage of them?
   - What is your instructor's role in your team's policy?
   - How would your team evaluate each member's contributions fairly?

Notes

1. "Top 10 Skills for Job Candidates," *NACE*, April 3, 2013, http://www.naceweb.org/Publications/Spotlight_Online/2013/0403/Top_10_Skills_for_Job_Candidates.aspx.
2. Kevin S. Groves, "Leader Emotional Expressivity, Visionary Leadership, and Organizational Change," *Leadership Organizational Development Journal* 27, no. 7 (2006): 566–83; and Ajay Mehra et al., "Distributed Leadership in Teams: The Network of Leadership Perceptions and Team Performance," *The Leadership Quarterly* 17, no. 3 (2006): 232–45.
3. "Why Hierarchies Are Good for Productivity (And Too Much Testosterone Is Not)," *Inc.*, September 2012, 26.
4. Edward P. Lazear, Kathryn L. Shaw, and Christopher T. Stanton, "The Value of Bosses," National Bureau of Economic Research Working Paper No. 18317, August 2012.
5. Jeswald W. Salacuse, *The Global Negotiator: Making, Managing, and Mending Deals around the World in the Twenty-First Century* (New York: Palgrave Macmillan, 2003), 92.
6. Bob Frisch, "When Teams Can't Decide," *Harvard Business Review* 86, no. 11 (2008): 121–26.
7. Sue Shellenbarger, "Work & Family Mailbox," *Wall Street Journal*, February 9, 2011, D3.
8. Alex "Sandy" Pentland, "The New Science of Building Great Teams," *Harvard Business Review* 90, no. 4 (2012): 60.
9. Kimberly Merriman, "Low-Trust Teams Prefer Individualized Pay," *Harvard Business Review* 86, no. 11 (2008): 32.
10. Sari Lindblom-Ylanne, Heikki Pihlajamaki, and Toomas Kotkas, "What Makes a Student Group Successful? Student–Student and Student–Teacher Interaction in a Problem-Based Learning Environment," *Learning Environments Research* 6, no. 1 (2003): 59–76.
11. Sue Dyer, "The Root Causes of Poor Communication," *Cost Engineering* 48, no. 6 (2006): 8–10.
12. Rebecca E. Burnett, "Conflict in Collaborative Decision-Making," in *Professional Communication: The Social Perspective*, ed. Nancy Roundy Blyler and Charlotte Thralls (Newbury Park, CA: Sage, 1993), 144–62; and Rebecca E. Burnett, "Productive and Unproductive Conflict in Collaboration," in *Making Thinking Visible: Writing, Collaborative Planning, and Classroom Inquiry*, ed. Linda Flower et al. (Urbana, IL: NCTE, 1994), 239–44.
13. Solomon F. Asch, "Opinions and Social Pressure," *Scientific American* 193, no. 5 (1955): 31–35. For a review of literature on groupthink, see Marc D. Street, "Groupthink: An Examination of Theoretical Issues, Implications, and Future Research Suggestions," *Small Group Research* 28, no. 1 (1997): 72–93.
14. Jared Diamond, *Collapse: How Societies Choose to Fail or Succeed* (New York: Penguin Books, 2005), 439.
15. Francesca Bariela-Chiappini et al., "Five Perspectives on Intercultural Business Communication," *Business Communication Quarterly* 66, no. 3 (2003): 73–96.
16. Ursula Hess and Pierre Philippot, *Group Dynamics and Emotional Expression* (New York: Cambridge University Press, 2007).
17. Kristina B. Dahlin, Laurie R. Weingart, and Pamela J. Hinds, "Team Diversity and Information Use," *Academy of Management Journal* 68, no. 6 (2005): 1107–23; Susannah B. F. Paletz et al., "Ethnic Composition and Its Differential Impact on Group Processes in Diverse Teams," *Small Group Research* 35, no. 2 (2004): 128–57; and Leisa D. Sargent and Christina Sue-Chan, "Does Diversity Affect Efficacy? The Intervening Role of Cohesion and Task Interdependence," *Small Group Research* 32, no. 4 (2001): 426–50.
18. Anita Woolley and Thomas Malone, "What Makes a Team Smarter? More Women," *Harvard Business Review* 89, no. 6 (2011): 32.

19.   Salacuse, *The Global Negotiator,* 96–97.

20.   Jeanne Brett, Kristin Behfar, and Mary C. Kern, "Managing Multicultural Teams," *Harvard Business Review* 84, no. 11 (2006): 84–91.

21.   John E. Tropman, *Making Meetings Work,* 2nd ed. (Thousand Oaks, CA: Sage, 2003), 28.

22.   Mark Goulston and John Ullmen, "How to Really Understand Someone Else's Point of View," *HBR Blog Network,* April 22, 2013, http://blogs.hbr.org/cs/2013/04/how_to_really_understand_someo.html.

23.   Burnett, "Productive and Unproductive Conflict in Collaboration."

24.   Kitty O. Locker, "What Makes a Collaborative Writing Team Successful? A Case Study of Lawyers and Social Service Workers in a State Agency," in *New Visions in Collaborative Writing,* ed. Janis Forman (Portsmouth, NJ: Boynton, 1991), 37–52.

9

Sharing Informative and Positive Messages with Appropriate Technology

Chapter Outline

NEWSWORTHY COMMUNICATION

Providing Bedside Information

Delos Cosgrove, CEO of the Cleveland Clinic, realized he had a problem. Although the clinic was recognized by *U.S. News & World Report* for being one of the top five hospitals in the country, its patients weren't satisfied. In particular, patients wanted better communication from doctors, nurses, and staff throughout their hospital stays.

To address this issue, the Cleveland Clinic changed how it provided patients with information. Now, before coming in for a procedure, patients receive a packet telling them what to expect throughout their stay. While in the hospital, patients receive from doctors, nurses, and staff consistent information about efforts at care. And after the procedure, the Cleveland Clinic has improved how patients receive information about after care and billing.

The results of this better communication have been striking. In overall patient satisfaction, the Cleveland Clinic has jumped from the 55th percentile to the 92nd percentile in just five years. In other areas, such as ratings of communication from doctors, nurses, and staff, the clinic has improved by more than 50 percentile points. The excellence in patient care at the Cleveland Clinic has remained constant. Improved communication of informative and positive messages has made all the difference.

Source: James I. Merlino and Ananth Raman, "Health Care's Service Fanatics," *Harvard Business Review* 91, no. 5 (2013): 108–16.

Learning Objectives

After studying this chapter, you will know

LO 9-1 What the purposes of informative and positive messages are.

LO 9-2 What kinds of newer communication hardware are entering offices.

LO 9-3 When and how to use common business media effectively.

LO 9-4 How to organize informative and positive messages.

LO 9-5 How to compose some of the common varieties of informative and positive messages.

Information about Your Medicine

Informing people about their medicines is not so simple. Hospitals annually treat 1.9 million people for medication problems; emergency rooms treat an additional 838,000. These figures are up 52% from 2004.

Part of the problem results from the growing complexity of medication regimes, particularly for the elderly and those with multiple, chronic conditions. These regimes are becoming so complex that even well-educated patients make mistakes.

Another group with special problems consists of patients with low literacy. In one study, only 34% of such patients could accurately demonstrate the precise number of pills they were to take, even after correctly repeating "take two twice a day."

These patients are not alone. Another study showed that more than half of adults misunderstood at least one of the common prescription warnings.

Experts are recommending language changes on medicine labels: "use only on your skin" to replace "for external use only," or "limit your time in the sun" to replace "avoid prolonged or excessive exposure to direct sunlight." They are also recommending new drug information sheets.

Adapted from Laura Landro, "'Use Only as Directed' Isn't Easy," *Wall Street Journal*, April 26, 2011, D1.

Business messages must meet the needs of the sender (and the sender's organization), be sensitive to the audience, and accurately reflect the topic being discussed. Informative and positive messages are the bread-and-butter messages in organizations.

When we need to convey information to which the receiver's basic reaction will be neutral, the message is **informative.** If we convey information to which the receiver's reaction will be positive, the message is a **positive or good news message.** Neither message immediately asks the receiver to do anything. You usually do want to build positive attitudes toward the information you are presenting, so in that sense, even an informative message has a persuasive element. Chapter 10 will discuss messages where the receiver will respond negatively; Chapter 11 will discuss messages where you want the receiver to change beliefs or behavior.

Informative and positive messages include acceptances; positive answers to requests; information about meetings, procedures, products, services, or options; announcements of policy changes that are neutral or positive; and changes that are to the receiver's advantage.

Purposes of Informative and Positive Messages **LO 9-1**

Even a simple informative or good-news message usually has several purposes:

Primary purposes
To give information or good news to the receiver or to reassure the receiver.
To have the receiver view the information positively.

Secondary purposes
To build a good image of the sender.
To build a good image of the sender's organization.
To cement a good relationship between the sender and the receiver.
To de-emphasize any negative elements.
To reduce or eliminate future messages on the same subject.

Informative and positive messages are not necessarily short. Instead, the length of a message depends on your purposes, the audience's needs, and the complexity of the situation.

In addition to these concerns, you also have to ensure you are communicating with appropriate tools and media.

Communication Hardware LO 9-2

Businesses are quick to adopt new forms of technology that can enhance the experience of workers and improve the bottom line. New software programs and devices continually enter the market to help businesses. However, acquiring new technology and helping workers master it entail an enormous capital investment. Learning to use new-generation software and improved hardware takes time and may be especially frustrating for people who were perfectly happy with old technology.

Some of the most popular workplace tools that improve productivity are smartphones, portable media players, tablets, and videoconferences.

Smartphones

Smartphones, such as Apple's iPhone, Windows Phone, or any in the Android lineup, allow users to send and receive e-mail, access websites, conduct word processing, learn their next tasks, update a job's status, check order or inventory statuses, complete a time sheet, and make phone calls. Many of these devices have touch screens with full QWERTY keyboards. These devices can also receive streaming video and audio. Some smartphones even have add-on devices that allow businesses to perform credit card transactions directly from the phones.

Every day more applications become available for these smartphones, which can enhance productivity. With the full functionality of these devices, employees can be connected to their work 24/7. However, this does not mean they should be. Be considerate and try to limit business calls, e-mails, and text messages to business hours. Some restaurants are even offering discounts to customers if they check their phones with receptionists and dine without electronic disruptions.[1]

Technology plays a large role in the changing face of business communication. Conference rooms are frequently equipped with laptops, projectors, and videoconferencing equipment, making it possible for people to have meetings across continents and time zones.

Portable Media Players

Portable media players (such as iPods and MP3 players) feature the ability to receive streaming video and audio. Some organizations give employees these devices pre-loaded with recordings of meetings, new product information, or general announcements. These devices help keep employees connected, even when they're not in the office.

Tablets

Tablets (such as Apple's iPad, Motorola's Xoom, or Samsung's Galaxy Tab) offer many of the smartphone features mentioned above, without the ability to place calls. Their advantage is the size, usually ranging from 7 to 10 inches, which makes viewing websites, watching instructional videos, or typing e-mails much easier on the eye than small phone screens do. As with portable media players, some organizations give employees these devices loaded with workplace information or applications to improve productivity. While some tablets need WiFi to keep employees online, many versions offer connections through cellular networks.

Videoconferences

With rising travel costs, many businesses are seeking alternatives to traditional face-to-face meetings. One solution is videoconferences, which allow two or more parties to communicate and hold meetings with full audio and visual capabilities. They can occur across different time zones or between different nations instantaneously. As an added benefit, meetings never have to be delayed or postponed because of late flights or weather problems.

One type of videoconferencing is telepresence, which uses high-end 50-inch plasma screens and broadcast-quality cameras to create virtual meetings that are almost lifelike. PepsiCo, Bank of America, and Procter & Gamble are just some of the companies that have adopted this technology. Banks are using telepresence to help their top advisers counsel clients face-to-face in multiple locations. These state-of-the-art telepresence rooms can be pricey, costing up to $300,000. Some of the cost is associated with the equipment necessary to create a room, but most of the cost comes from the large amounts of bandwidth required for the conferencing. Projected revenue for telepresence services will reach $2.3 billion by 2015.[2]

Lower-cost alternatives for videoconferencing exist as well. Services such as Skype, Apple's FaceTime, or GoToMeeting allow employees to connect and collaborate remotely with web cameras that are standard on many newer laptops or tablets. Cisco and Logitech have also introduced systems that require high-definition TVs and a broadband connection for videoconferencing in the comfort of your home.

Information Overload

One of the realities of communication today is information overload—having more information than one can process, understand, or act upon. Technology enables other people to bombard us with junk mail, sales calls, advertisements, and spam. Spam clutters computer mailboxes—or leads to filters that stop some needed e-mail. Spam also means that many people do not open e-mail if they do not recognize the sender or the topic.

Individual messages are also getting more complex. Credit card contracts were typically about 400 words in 1980; now many are 20,000 words.

Information hidden in fine print costs landline phone customers $2 billion annually, according to the Federal Communications Commission.[3]

Basex, a knowledge economy research and advisory company, surveyed knowledge workers and found that more than 50% of them felt that the amount of information coming to them daily was detrimental to accomplishing their work. In fact, 94% of them reported that at some point they were overwhelmed by information to the point of incapacity.[4] A similar survey by Xerox of government and education workers found that 58% spent almost half their work time sorting, filing, or deleting information, and that this effort amounts to over $31 billion spent annually on managing information.[5]

On another level, even more routine communications are becoming overwhelming. With fast and cheap e-mails, text messages, instant messages, and tweets, plus the genuine belief in more transparent business procedures, businesses send more announcements of events, procedures, policies, services, and employee news. Departments send newsletters. Employees send announcements of and best wishes for births, birthdays, weddings, and promotions. Customers send comments about products, service, policies, and advertisements.

Yet another factor in overload is inappropriate e-mails. This group includes jokes, personal information, and non-job-related e-mails, as well as e-mails that are unnecessarily long, trivial, and irrelevant. Too many people forward too many messages to uncaring receivers, and the "Reply to All" button has a notorious reputation.

According to the Radicati Group, a technology market research firm, the average corporate e-mail user sends and receives 110 e-mails per day.[6] Pingdom, an Internet usage monitoring company, calculates that 144 billion e-mail messages were sent *daily* in 2012, of which 68.8% were spam.[7]

With this flood of information, you need to protect your communication reputation.

WARNING: You do not want to be the person whose e-mails or voice mail messages are opened last because they take so long to get to the point, or even worse, the person whose messages are rarely opened at all because you send so many that aren't important or necessary.

One research study on e-mail overload found that length was not the problem: most e-mails in the study were four lines or less. Rather, the study found three factors that contributed to the perception of e-mail overload. The first, unstable requests, included requests that got refined in the process of e-mail correspondence and frequently morphed into requests for more work. The second, pressure to respond, included requests for information within hours. People in the study noted that they were never away from their e-mail, and that these requests could come any time. The third factor, delegation of tasks and shifting interactants, included tasks that were indirectly delegated (Could anyone get me the figures on X for the noon meeting?) or that recipients of the group e-mail then gave to their own subordinates.[8]

Some organizations and software applications are taking a stand to help employees deal with information overload. For instance, software add-ons for e-mail systems can now prioritize messages after analyzing which senders have the most importance. Some companies are declaring e-mail-free days, where employees are encouraged to meet face-to-face. Other companies are developing choice engines to help consumers more easily make difficult decisions. Two well-known travel choice engines are Expedia and Travelocity. Two newer choice engines are BrightScope, which analyzes and ranks 401(k) plans, and FirstFuel, which analyzes energy consumption data.[9]

Using Common Media   LO 9-3

In the office, most informative and positive communications are made through six channels: face-to-face contacts, phone calls, instant messages and text messaging, e-mails, letters, and memos. Many people have personal preferences that need to be recognized. They may keep up with their e-mail but avoid listening to voice mail messages; they may enjoy drop-in visitors but think instant messages are silly. Similarly, some channels seem better fitted for some situations than others.

Face-to-Face Contacts

Some businesses are encouraging their employees to write fewer e-mails and visit each other's desks more often. They believe such visits contribute to a friendlier, more collaborative work environment. Research with tracking sensors shows they are right; the most productive workers have the most face-to-face contacts.[10]

Visits are a good choice when

- You know a colleague welcomes your visits.
- You are building a business relationship with a person.
- A real-time connection saves messages (e.g., setting a meeting agenda).
- Your business requires dialogue or negotiation.
- You need something immediately (like a signature).
- Discretion is vital and you do not want to leave a paper trail.
- The situation is complex enough that you want as many visual and aural cues as possible.

Use these tips for effective face-to-face contact:

- Ensure the timing is convenient for the recipient.
- If you are discussing something complex, have appropriate documents in hand.
- Don't usurp recipients' space. Don't put your papers on top of their desk or table without permission.
- Look for "time to go" signs. Some people have a limited tolerance for small talk, especially when they are hard at work on a task.

Tony Hsieh, CEO of Zappos, is a big fan of face-to-face contacts. He says, "The best things happen when people are running into each other." To insure this happens, only one entrance is used at the Zappos office building.[11] Other companies are scheduling group breaks to increase face-to-face contacts.

Phone Calls

Phone calls provide fewer contextual cues than face-to-face visits, but more cues than electronic or paper messages. Phone calls are a good choice when

- Tone of voice is important.
- A real-time connection saves multiple phone calls or e-mails (e.g., setting a meeting time).

- You need something immediately (like an OK).

- You do not want to leave a paper trail (but remember that phone records are easily obtained).

Use these tips for effective phone calls (also see Figure 9.1):

- Ensure the timing is convenient for the recipient; try to limit cell phone calls to business hours.

- Promptly return calls to your voice mail.

- Speak clearly, especially when giving your name and phone number (even more important when leaving your name and phone number on voice mail). Do not assume the recipient has a phone that records your number.

- Use an information hook: I am calling about. . . .

- Keep the call short and cordial. If you need to leave a message, keep it brief: one or two sentences. Most people resent long voice mail messages.

- Repeat your phone number at the end of the call. Too often, people don't write the number down at the beginning of the call.

- Focus on the call; do not do other work. Most people can tell if you are reading e-mail or web pages while talking to them, and they get the message that their concern is not important to you.

Remember that unplanned phone calls are an interruption in a busy worker's day. If that person works in an open office, as many do, the call will also interrupt other employees to some extent. For this reason, and also because of the increase in texting, voice mail messages are declining. Voice mail retrieval is declining even more rapidly, so even if you leave a message, you cannot be sure it will be heard.[12]

Instant Messaging and Text Messaging

Formerly limited primarily to students, instant and text messaging are gaining acceptance in the business world, especially among people who work closely together. Instant messaging services, such as AOL Instant Messenger, Google Chat, and Yahoo Messenger, have quickly found their way into office settings.

Because they are less intrusive than phone calls or visits, these messages are good for short messages on noncritical topics, such as running commentary,

Figure 9.1	Voice Mail Pet Peeves

- Callback numbers that are mumbled or given too quickly.
- Messages longer than 30 seconds.
- Messages that require serious note taking (when an e-mail would have been better).
- Too much or too little information.
- Demands to return the call without saying why.
- Messages expecting an immediate response.
- Angry messages.

questions, or clarifications on tasks you and your colleagues are working on simultaneously. And because they are generally answered immediately, they can decrease the time needed to solve an issue. Some organizations also believe that IMing fosters better collaborations among employees, particularly those who work from home. Researchers have found that people do not like to use IMs for larger tasks, more complex questions or instructions, or messages connected in any way with conflict.[13]

Audience preferences will be important, especially with abbreviations. Although even the *Oxford English Dictionary* lists LOL, BFF, IMHO, and OMG, some people will not recognize other abbreviations. And abbreviations such as OMG disturb some readers.

In many organizations, text messages to all but close friends are expected to look professional.

Not this: that time should work. bring the donuts and coffee!!! i'm hungry! CU L8r

But this: 3 works for me, too. I'll bring copies of the Wolford schedule. See you there.

Remember that, like e-mails, these messages can be saved, forwarded, and printed. They too leave a paper trail, and many businesses monitor them. Do not use them to send sensitive information, such as files or passwords, and always keep them professional in both mechanics and content. Florida Congressman Mark Foley lost his position for holding sexual and otherwise inappropriate IM conversations with underage pages.

Wikis

With the popularity of websites such as Wikipedia, the business world has been quick to follow suit. Many organizations are using wikis, an online form of content knowledge management, in which users can post information or collaborate on projects. The access to these wikis is limited to employees of the particular organization using them, much like intranets. Employees can use wikis to

- Bookmark and summarize web pages.
- Upload drafts of working documents.
- Create new entries about workplace practices.

Other employees can then quickly search for information using key words or modify existing uploaded documents.

Wikis are a great way for corporations to create knowledge databases of workplace practices for their particular organization. In addition, wikis reduce the e-mailing of drafts between employees who are collaborating on a project. As an added bonus, every change made to documents on a wiki can be tracked. Moreover, when employees leave an organization, their job knowledge is still stored on the wiki and can be a valuable resource for new employees.

Social Media

Many organizations are adapting social media tools at an ever-increasing rate. And they have good reason to do so. In addition to reaching thousands of clients in a single message, social media offer a relatively inexpensive way to connect. Employees can post profiles, updates, tweets, blogs, or useful links, all for free. They can also do all of these activities from the smartphones, portable media players, or tablets that many organizations give their employees.

For businesses, the challenge of social media is figuring out how to harness the positives to increase productivity, particularly when dealing with customers. Dell Inc. has created a social media university for employees who are interested in learning the basics of social media by taking four courses. Over 9,000 employees started the program to better integrate social media into their positions.[14]

Like Dell, many organizations use social networking sites to establish an identity and harness a relationship with clients. The U.S. Army has a social media division in charge of recruiting. Even the Pope has encouraged priests to tap into digital media options.

Some businesses seem to adapt easily to social media. Blendtec, a manufacturer of blenders, became a media star with a series of YouTube videos, *Will It Blend?*, which put various objects (computer games, iPod, iPad) in its blenders. The video with the iPhone has been viewed almost 12 million times, and Blendtec sales have increased sevenfold. Other businesses have to be more cautious. Mutual funds were slow to embrace social media, partly because of industry regulations. In 2013 however, the Securities and Exchange Commission ruled that informational postings on social media were allowed as long as companies had told investors which sites were going to be used.[15]

Four of the most common ways to connect with customers are Facebook, Twitter, LinkedIn, and blogs.

Facebook   Facebook is a social networking tool where users create a profile and then can chat and share interests with other users. The site has over a billion users worldwide and has become one of the most popular sites in the United States.

Beyond buying advertising space, organizations use Facebook as a communication channel with customers by providing updates about business activities, introducing new products or services, providing tips on old ones, informing about upcoming events, encouraging participation in philanthropic causes, or offering discounts or incentives. Organizations can also create focus groups where they can receive or share feedback from clients about products and services.

Organizations get data from Likes, links clicked, and customer comments. Dr Pepper measures the social conversation about its brand from the 8.5 million fan base and adjusts marketing messages accordingly. As a result, Dr Pepper gets free marketing when users pass messages on to other Facebook friends.[16]

As an added bonus to businesses, Facebook connections can increase awareness about their brand by boosting their presence in search engines. Best of all, Facebook easily integrates with other social media platforms, such as Twitter, which offer organizations a complete media link to consumers.

Employees within the same organization can build stronger relationships by friending each other. In some organizations, teams have even established Facebook groups to promote camaraderie and create a place to discuss project documents and other concerns.

Because of its interactivity, Facebook, like Twitter, is time-consuming for corporate writers. Customers posting to a corporate site expect prompt responses. They also can post misinformation and vulgarities, so it is important that organizations have policies to help guide their social media writers.

Employees on Facebook need to remember the public nature of the site. In fact, poor judgment has cost some workers their jobs as a result of posting controversial updates about their employers or uploading inappropriate photos.

Social Media at Work

Many younger employees are joining the job market with their own social media participation or brand. Often, this is referred to as "co-branding," using social media to build a personal public identity. Such employees can bring with them both positives and negatives for the employer.

Positives for the company include prestige, business leads, and free media attention, as well as the recruitment of other media-savvy employees.

Such employees can also bring negatives:

- Online popularity can swell egos—and salary expectations.

- Employees may find themselves spending an excessive amount of time on their social media, and neglecting other work.

- Inside information can easily be shared online.

- A focus or tone in conflict with the corporate image can do much damage, as can a single ill-conceived tweet.

- Team collaboration can be damaged by jealousy.

Adapted from Alexandra Samuel, "Your Employee Is an Online Celebrity. Now What Do You Do?" *Wall Street Journal*, October 29, 2012, B7.

For example, an Atlanta police officer was terminated after posting sensitive job information; Virgin Atlantic fired 13 crew members after they posted mean comments about passengers and spiteful opinions about the airline's safety standards.[17]

Twitter   Twitter is a microblog that allows users to let their followers know what they're doing by posting tweets, short messages of 140 characters or less.

Twitter offers another way for organizations to create a following, share information, brand themselves, and even eavesdrop on what people say about their competitors. Organizations can follow what other people tweet about them and use the service to provide an additional form of customer service. For example, when a patron in a Fort Worth branch of Chipotle tweeted about the restaurant lacking corn tortillas, the corporate office called the manager before the customer even left.[18]

Similar to many restaurants and other organizations, Chipotle has service representatives dedicated to social media relations. With over 400 million tweets sent per day worldwide in March 2013 when Twitter turned seven,[19] it can be overwhelming for organizations to manage their image and plan appropriate 140-word responses.

As an employee, you should consider your audience and context before tweeting, just as you should with all other forms of business communication. Avoid sending tweets like the following:

@bossman_GGSA I'm totes going to be late for work today. whacky traffic and coffee shop line is ridic UGH! #suckydaysofar #fail #IhateMondays

This person has probably selected the wrong medium to communicate with the boss, and the slang, uncommon acronym, and multiple hashtags are not appropriate for workplace communication. Instead, be upbeat and positive with workplace tweets:

Had a great presentation today with bossman. Lots of great feedback and excited to move onto the next phase!

Although Twitter messages as business communications are still relatively new compared to letters and e-mails, they have already developed some commonly accepted guidelines:

- Clarity is important. Although tweets are limited to 140 characters, they still need to use enough words so they are not cryptic.

- Don't waste people's time with tweets. If audience responses could be "Who cares?" don't send it. This guideline particularly applies to most tweets describing what you are doing at the moment.

- Be sparing with hashtags and acronyms.

- Slang is generally inappropriate for workplace tweets.

Remember that if your Twitter account is connected to your workplace followers, your tweets not only represent your views but should also reflect positively on your organization. As is true with all social media, you must be careful what you say. Tweets can be searched on Google and can be recalled in defamation lawsuits. Comedian Gilbert Gottfried, the voice of the Aflac duck, got fired over insensitive tweets about the Japanese earthquake and tsunami. New York Congressman Anthony Weiner had to step down after sexual tweets were reported in the media. As a final note to make us all even more cautious, the Library of Congress archives all tweets. As of late 2012, they were collecting almost half a billion tweets daily.[20]

LinkedIn LinkedIn allows professionals to connect with colleagues and other industry members. More than 100 million people use the site. Unlike Facebook or Twitter, which can easily blur the professional and personal line, LinkedIn profiles tend to remain strictly work oriented.

Professionals can use the site to network and earn recommendations from past and current clients. Another section allows your connections to endorse skills and expertise you may have. These referrals, in turn, could create more business opportunities. Employees can also join industry associations or alumni groups to expand their network of connections. LinkedIn Answers provides a forum for industry professionals to ask questions and share their expertise, which may also spark new clients. For job searches, LinkedIn allows users to search for new job opportunities, post a résumé, or recruit new employees.

Blogs Blogs allow businesses to connect with customers and clients in a more social way than they can on traditional websites. Internal corporate blogs allow managers and employees to share ideas and information.

Many public corporate blogs offer information relevant to their business: a catering service may offer food safety tips and recipes; a travel agency may offer travel tips and descriptions of exotic destinations. Other popular content includes employee stories, glimpses inside the business, insider business tips, and question-and-answer features.

Good blogs present their content in ways that inspire conversations and encourage readers to comment and then to share the information. The best blogs offer a unique perspective that enables them to stand out from the millions of other blogs on the Internet. While all blogs should be visually attractive, bloggers need to remember that many of their readers will have opted to turn off the visuals. Too many visuals will create an empty-looking blog.

Other Social Media Other social media sites are on the rise, and it seems as if new ones are added daily. Figure 9.2 lists a few that professionals have been quick to adapt to their business needs.

The realm of social media is expanding exponentially. Some systems are designed specifically for businesses. The social media team for Clorox started Clorox Connect, which is a website where suppliers and customers can brainstorm on new product ideas. They have adapted a game model where users

Small Businesses Prefer LinkedIn Over Twitter

In a recent survey by the *Wall Street Journal* of 835 small-business owners, only 3% believed that Twitter could promote their organization. On the other hand, LinkedIn earned a high 41% of respondents who believed the site was beneficial to their business. LinkedIn surpassed other popular social media sites such as Facebook, YouTube, and Google+.

The finding suggests that Twitter is not doing enough to educate small-business owners about the benefits of using their service in the same way that LinkedIn has.

Much of the focus from Twitter has been on larger businesses, which were the only ones allowed to buy ads through the service. But unlike large organizations, which may have entire teams dedicated to social media, small-business owners do not have the human power or time to figure out how Twitter can be used to heighten their business.

What do you think? Can you determine advantages that Twitter might offer small businesses? What benefits might they gleam from a Twitter presence that they cannot get from LinkedIn?

Adapted from Emily Maltby and Shira Ovide, "Small Firms Say LinkedIn Works, Twitter Doesn't," *Wall Street Journal*, January 31, 2013, http://online.wsj.com/article/SB1000 1424127887323926104578273683427129660.html.

Figure 9.2	Social Media Sites for Professionals

Xing—Similar features as LinkedIn, but more popular in Europe and India.
Google1—Google's version of Facebook containing many similar options.
Ning—A site for users to create their own social networking site adapted to their business.
NetParty—A site for young professionals to connect online to meet up for happy hour and other after-work activities.
Yammer—A Facebook–Twitter mashup tool exclusively for internal corporate communications.
Sermo—Site dedicated exclusively to the medical profession; helps doctors solicit opinions, share information, and improve patient care.

who contribute helpful ideas gain more visibility and are invited to take part in more difficult problem-solving exercises.[21]

Other systems have mixed uses. On the for-profit, health data-sharing site PatientsLikeMe, consenting participants provide detailed medical histories and discuss treatment problems. They can also connect with other patients. Information shared on the site is collated for multiple uses. It can be used by patients to manage their own conditions, but it also is available to selected researchers, drug companies, and equipment and service providers to help improve treatments and quality of life.[22]

Another way that businesses are trying to reach customers is through **widgets**, tiny software programs that can be dragged, dropped, and embedded into social media sites. Widgets change the way people use the Internet. In the past, people surfed from page to page, but now widgets can bring the power of all those pages into a central location, like a social networking site.

Of course, like all technological tools, social media sites have some drawbacks. If workers spend much of their day immersed in social media, how much of their regular work routine is not being completed? A survey of 1,400 large U.S. companies reported that more than half have some restrictions on social media use.[23] Other companies monitor what employees do on social media. However, it can be hard to differentiate between social media use for professional and personal purposes, especially when some employees have a single account.

A final thought about social media: once workers post information about themselves or their company, electronic copies of that information are stored indefinitely.

E-mails, Letters, and Memos

When people think of business communications, many think of e-mails, letters, and paper memos. Letters go to people outside your organization; memos go to people in your organization; e-mails can go anywhere. Today most memos are sent as e-mails rather than paper documents.

E-mails, letters, and memos use different formats. The most common formats are illustrated in Appendix A. The simplified letter format is very similar to memo format: it uses a subject line and omits the salutation and the complimentary close. Thus, it is a good choice when you don't know the reader's name.

The differences in audience and format are the only differences among these documents. All of these messages can be long or short, depending on how much you have to say and how complicated the situation is. All of these messages can be informal when you write to someone you know well, or more formal when you write to someone you don't know, to several audiences, or for the record. All of these messages can be simple responses that you can dash off in minutes; they can also take hours of analysis and revision when you're facing a new situation or when the stakes are high.

E-mail Usage E-mails are still the most common form of business communication. According to a widely cited research firm, employees send and receive about 110 e-mails daily. Some estimates say that many employees spend at least a third of their in-office time on e-mail.[24] It is commonly used for these purposes:

E-mails, instant and text messages, telephone calls, social media entries, and web searches can all be tracked by your employer and used in lawsuits. You should always observe professional practices while in the workplace.

- To accomplish routine, noncontroversial business activities (setting up meetings/appointments, reminders, notices, quick updates, information sharing).

- To save time: People can look through 60 to 100 e-mails an hour.

- To save money: one e-mail can go to many people, including global teams.

- To allow readers to deal with messages at their convenience, when timing is not crucial.

- To communicate accurately.

- To provide readers with details for reference (meetings).

- To create a paper trail.

E-mails do not work well for some purposes. Negative critiques and bad news generally have better outcomes when delivered in person. Sarcasm and irony are too frequently misinterpreted to be safely used. Similarly, avoid passing on gossip in your e-mails. The chances of having your gossip forwarded with your name attached are just too great.

E-mail Etiquette   E-mail usage has developed etiquette rules for behaviors to avoid (see also Figure 9.3). First on most lists is avoiding the "Reply to all" button unless you are sure everyone on the list needs the information. This button is so irritating that some companies install software to disable the button, and Microsoft has a free disabling add-on for Outlook.

Another important rule is greatly limiting use of high-priority markers or subject line words such as URGENT or READ NOW (e-mails containing subject lines with too many capital letters will be trashed by many spam filters). Yet another urgency misstep is calling, or e-mailing again, right away to see if the recipient has read your e-mail. If you need such a fast response, you probably need to phone.

Figure 9.3	E-mail Pet Peeves

- Missing or vague subject lines.
- Copying everyone ("Reply to all"), rather than just the people that might find the information useful/interesting.
- Too much information/too little information.
- Too many instant messaging acronyms.
- Lack of capitalization and punctuation.
- Long messages without headings or bullets.
- Delayed response e-mails that don't include the original message. Sometimes readers have no idea what the e-mails are responding about.
- Writers who send a general request to multiple people, creating confusion about who is responsible for handling the request.
- People who expect an immediate answer.
- People who never respond to queries.
- People who don't read their e-mail carefully enough to absorb a simple message.
- People who send too many unimportant e-mails.
- Superfluous images and attachments.
- Flaming (angry messages, frequently with extreme language).

These etiquette missteps are all irritating, but one behavior that can get you into serious trouble is answering someone else's e-mail without that person's permission. Even if it is a group e-mail, and even if you answer in an effort to save someone else the bother, if the answer belongs in the responsibilities of someone else, let that person answer it.

Salutations for e-mails are in a state of transition. *Dear* is saved mostly for formal e-mails; *Hey* is generally considered too informal for business use. Many writers are now starting their e-mails with *Hi* or *Hello* (e.g., "Hi Udi,"). And when e-mailing people with whom they are in constant contact, many writers use no salutation at all.

Common E-mail Miscommunication Causes   Many people read their e-mails quickly. They may read for only a few seconds or lines to decide if the e-mail is pertinent. Value your readers' time by designing your e-mail to help them:

- Put the most important information in the first sentence.

- If your e-mail is more than one screen long, use an overview, headings, and enumeration to help draw readers to successive screens.

- Limit your e-mail to one topic. Delete off-topic material.

The ubiquitous e-mail thread is a common cause of information sent to the wrong audience. Frequently it is safer to send a new e-mail, addressed just to the specific people who need to know.

A major factor in e-mail miscommunication is the lack of nonverbal cues. Many of the billions of e-mails sent daily contain intentional and unintentional emotions that can cause misinterpretation of information.

Remember that e-mails are public documents and may be widely forwarded. Use standard capitalization and spelling; save lowercase and instant message abbreviations for friends, if you use them at all. Features that express emotion, such as underlining, all caps, exclamation points, and emoticons, should be used with great caution. Even a quick confirmation to your boss should look professional.

Keep in mind the possibility that your e-mail may not be read. E-mails outside your company may be deflected by a misspelled address, an in-box filter, or an Internet malfunction. With the high volume of items in most in-boxes, it is easy for an e-mail to move off the screen and out of the receiver's awareness. If you do not receive a response within a reasonable time, follow up. Remember that many people do not consider a one- to two-hour turnaround time reasonable for e-mail. If the item is that urgent, you should choose another means of communication.

 WARNING: Never put anything in an e-mail that would embarrass you or harm your career if your employer, colleague, parent, or child saw it.

E-mail Misbehaviors   Examples abound of public and corporate officials forced to resign because of misbehaviors documented in e-mails they sent to others; reread the list in Chapter 1. But the senders don't have to be officials to cause the organization trouble.

- An employee e-mail arranging for a group to leave work early and go drinking at a topless bar was used as evidence of poor oversight in a product-contamination lawsuit against the company.[25]

- Employee e-mails were crucial in the federal suit filed against Standard & Poor's over credit ratings for bundled mortgage securities that the government claimed were fraudulently inflated.

- Leaked e-mails from the Climate Research Unit (located at East Anglia University in the United Kingdom) showing bias and exclusion not only created a furor for that research group, but also called into question all research on global warming.

A survey by the American Management Association found that over a quarter of bosses have fired employees for e-mail misuse.[26] And of course WikiLeaks has reminded everyone of the dangers hiding in even supposedly secure e-mails.

Organizing Informative and Positive Messages LO 9-4

The patterns of organization in this chapter and others follow standard conventions of business. The patterns will work for many of the writing situations most people in business, nonprofits, and government face. Using the appropriate pattern can help you compose more quickly, create a better final product, and demonstrate you know the conventions.

 WARNING: The patterns should never be used blindly. You must always consider whether your audience, purpose, and context would be better served with a different organization.

If you decide to use a pattern:

- Be sure you understand the rationale behind each pattern so that you can modify the pattern when necessary.

- Realize not every message that uses the basic pattern will have all the elements listed.

- Realize sometimes you can present several elements in one paragraph; sometimes you'll need several paragraphs for just one element.

Figure 9.4 shows how to organize informative and positive messages. Figures 9.5 and 9.6 illustrate two ways the basic pattern can be applied.

The letter in Figure 9.5 announces a change in a magazine's ownership. Rather than telling subscribers that their magazine has been acquired, which sounds negative, the first two paragraphs describe the change as a merger that will give subscribers greater benefits from the combined magazine. Paragraph 3 provides details about how the arrangement will work, along with a way to opt out. A possible negative is that readers who already have subscriptions to both magazines will now receive only one. The company addresses this situation positively by extending the subscription to the jointly published magazine. The goodwill ending has all the desired characteristics: it is positive ("we're confident"), personal ("your continued loyalty"), and forward-looking ("you will enjoy").

The e-mail in Figure 9.6 announces a new employee benefit. The first paragraph summarizes the new benefits. Paragraphs 2 and 3 give major details;

Use To/CC/BCC Lines to Your Advantage

To
Send your e-mail only to people who will want or need it. If you are sending to multiple people, decide in which order to place the names. Is organizational rank important? Should you alphabetize the list? Don't hit "reply to all" unless all will appreciate your doing so.

CC
CC stands for "carbon copy," from the days of typewriters when carbon paper was used to make multiple copies.

CC people who are not directly involved in the business of the e-mail but are interested in it. Marketing may not be helping you produce your new software, but the department may want to stay abreast of the changes to start generating marketing ideas. A committee might CC a secretary who does not attend committee meetings but does maintain the committee's paper records.

Sometimes the CC line is used politically. For example, an administrative assistant doing routine business may CC the boss to give added weight to the e-mail.

BCC
BCC stands for "blind carbon copy," a copy that the listed receivers do not know is being sent. Blind copies can create ill will when they become known, so be careful in their use.

| Figure 9.4 | How to Organize Informative and Positive Messages |

1. **Start with good news or the most important information.** Summarize the main points. If the audience has already raised the issue, make it clear that you're responding.

2. **Give details, clarification, background.** Answer all the questions your audience is likely to have; provide all the information necessary to achieve your purposes. If you are asking or answering multiple questions, number them. Enumeration increases your chances of giving or receiving all the necessary information. Present details in the order of importance to the reader or in some other logical order.

3. **Present any negative elements—as positively as possible.** A policy may have limits; information may be incomplete; the audience may have to satisfy requirements to get a discount or benefit. Make these negatives clear, but present them as positively as possible.

4. **Explain any benefits.** Most informative messages need benefits. Show that the policy or procedure helps your audience, not just the company. Give enough detail to make the benefits clear and convincing. In letters, you may want to give benefits of dealing with your company as well as benefits of the product or policy.

   In a good-news message, it's often possible to combine a short benefit with a goodwill ending.

5. **Use a goodwill ending: positive, personal, and forward-looking.** Shifting your emphasis away from the message to the specific audience suggests that serving the audience is your real concern.

further details are saved for the plan's brochure. Negative elements are stated as positively as possible. The last section of the e-mail gives benefits and a goodwill ending.

Subject Lines for Informative and Positive Messages

A **subject line** is the title of a document. It aids in filing and retrieving the document, tells readers why they need to read the document, and provides a framework in which to set what you're about to say. Subject lines are standard in memos and e-mails. Letters are not required to have subject lines (see Appendix A, "Formats for Letters, and E-mail Messages").

A good subject line meets three criteria: it is specific, concise, and appropriate to the kind of message (positive, negative, persuasive).

Making Subject Lines Specific

The subject line needs to be specific enough to differentiate its message from others on the same subject, but broad enough to cover everything in the message.

Too general: Training Sessions

Better: Dates for 2012 Training Sessions

Figure 9.5	A Positive Informational Letter

eBus**CompanyToday**

P.O. Box 12345
Tampa, FL   33660
813-555-5555

June 17, 2014

Dear Ms. Locker:

Main point presented as good news

We're excited to share some great news! *eBusCompanyToday* has merged with another business magazine, *High-Tech Business News*. This merged publication will be called *High-Tech Business News* and will continue to be edited and published by the *eBusCompanyToday* staff.

Details focus on benefits to the reader

The "new" *High-Tech Business News* is a great tool for navigating today's relentlessly changing marketplace, particularly as it's driven by the Internet and other technologies. It reports on the most innovative business practices and the people behind them; delivers surprising, useful insights; and explains how to put them to work. Please be assured that you will continue to receive the same great editorial coverage that you've come to expect from *eBusCompanyToday*.

You will receive the "new" *High-Tech Business News* in about 4 weeks, starting with the combined August/September issue. If you already subscribe to *High-Tech Business News*, your subscription will be extended accordingly. And if you'd rather not receive this publication, please call 1-800-555-5555 within the next 3 weeks.

Option to cancel is offered but not emphasized

Positive, personal, forward-looking ending

Thank you for your continued loyalty to *eBusCompanyToday*; we're confident that you will enjoy reading *High-Tech Business News* every month.

Sincerely,

Alan Schmidt

Alan Schmidt, Editor and President

High-Tech Business News is published monthly except for two issues combined periodically into one and occasional extra, expanded or premium issues.

Figure 9.6   A Positive E-mail, Sent to Chamber of Commerce Employees and Members

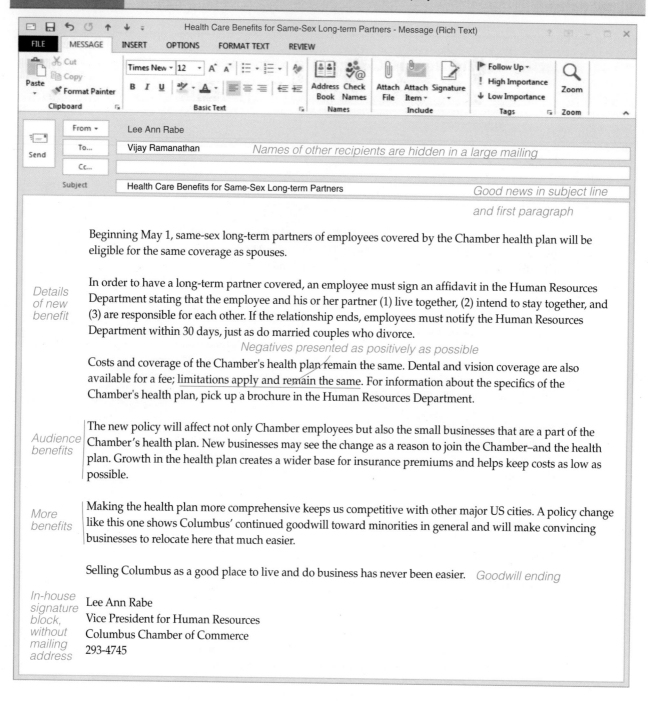

Good news in subject line and first paragraph

Beginning May 1, same-sex long-term partners of employees covered by the Chamber health plan will be eligible for the same coverage as spouses.

Details of new benefit

In order to have a long-term partner covered, an employee must sign an affidavit in the Human Resources Department stating that the employee and his or her partner (1) live together, (2) intend to stay together, and (3) are responsible for each other. If the relationship ends, employees must notify the Human Resources Department within 30 days, just as do married couples who divorce.

Negatives presented as positively as possible

Costs and coverage of the Chamber's health plan remain the same. Dental and vision coverage are also available for a fee; limitations apply and remain the same. For information about the specifics of the Chamber's health plan, pick up a brochure in the Human Resources Department.

Audience benefits

The new policy will affect not only Chamber employees but also the small businesses that are a part of the Chamber's health plan. New businesses may see the change as a reason to join the Chamber–and the health plan. Growth in the health plan creates a wider base for insurance premiums and helps keep costs as low as possible.

More benefits

Making the health plan more comprehensive keeps us competitive with other major US cities. A policy change like this one shows Columbus' continued goodwill toward minorities in general and will make convincing businesses to relocate here that much easier.

Selling Columbus as a good place to live and do business has never been easier.   *Goodwill ending*

In-house signature block, without mailing address

Lee Ann Rabe
Vice President for Human Resources
Columbus Chamber of Commerce
293-4745

Making Subject Lines Concise

Most subject lines are relatively short. MailerMailer, a web-based e-mail management service, found that e-mails whose subject lines were 4 to 15 characters were more likely to be opened by readers than subject lines with more than 35 characters.[27]

Wordy: Student Preferences in Regards to Various Pizza Factors

Better: Students' Pizza Preferences

If you can't make the subject both specific and short, be specific.

Making Subject Lines Appropriate for the Pattern of Organization

Since your subject line introduces your reader to your message, it must satisfy the psychological demands of the situation; it must be appropriate to your purposes and to the immediate response you expect from your reader.

In general, do the same thing in your subject line that you would do in the first paragraph. When you have good news for the reader, build goodwill by highlighting it in the subject line. When your information is neutral, summarize it concisely for the subject line.

> Subject: Discount on Rental Cars Effective January 2
>
> Starting January 2, as an employee of Amalgamated Industries you can get a 15% discount on cars you rent for business or personal use from Roadway Rent-a-Car.

> Subject: Update on Videoconference with France
>
> In the last month, we have chosen the participants and developed a tentative agenda for the March 21 videoconference with France.

Pointers for E-mail Subject Lines

Many people skim through large lists of e-mails daily, so subject lines in e-mails are even more important than those in letters and memos. Subject lines must be specific, concise, and catchy. In these days of spam, some e-mail users get so many messages that they don't bother reading messages if they don't recognize the sender or if the subject doesn't catch their interest. Create a subject line that will help your e-mail get read:

- Use important information in the subject line. Many people delete blanks and generic tags such as "hello," "your message," "thank you," and "next meeting," if they don't recognize the sender, especially now that so much spam has common business tags.

- Put good news in the subject line.

- Name drop to make a connection: Lee Pizer gave me your name.

- Make e-mail sound easy to deal with: Two Short Travel Questions.

- New topics need new subject lines; do not attach a new topic to an e-mail string on a different topic.

- Do not use indefinite dates such as Today, Tomorrow, Next Week, or even Wednesday, as subject lines. They are no longer clear if read at a later time.

- When you reply to a message, check to see that the automatic subject line "Re: [subject line of message to which you are responding]" is still appropriate. If it isn't, you may want to create a new subject line. And if a series of messages arises, you probably need a new subject line. "Re: Re: Re: Re: Question" is not an effective subject line.

The following subject lines would be acceptable for informative and good-news e-mail messages:

Travel Plans for Sales Meeting
Your Proposal Accepted
Reduced Prices during February
Your Funding Request Approved

Managing the Information in Your Messages

Information control is important. You want to give your audience the information they need, but you don't want to overwhelm them with information. Sometimes you will have good reasons for not providing all the information they want.

When you are the person in the know, it is easy to overestimate how much your audience knows. After Hurricane Sandy, scientists at the National Hurricane Center learned that law enforcement and hospital personnel, as well as local and state officials, did not understand the warnings issued about storm surge. To clear up confusion, scientists learned they should give surge figures in heights, rather than depths (the figures would be exactly the same, of course) and to provide clearer information on how far inland the surge would reach.[28]

But, of course, information management is not always that simple. Pharmaceutical companies struggle with how much information to provide about their drugs. In 2004, the Food and Drug Administration (FDA) publicized an analysis showing that young people on antidepressants had a 2% risk of suicidal thoughts. There were no actual suicides reported in the studies, just suicidal thoughts. Nevertheless, the FDA put a Black Box warning—the strongest possible warning—on antidepressants. Parents and physicians began backing away from the medications. Use of SSRI (selective serotonin reuptake inhibitors) medications in young people declined 14%, and suicides increased 18% among young people the first year of the warnings.[29]

Sometimes organizations get in trouble because their information management withholds information that others—shareholders, regulators, customers, etc.—believe should be revealed. Credit Suisse paid $120 million to settle with the Securities and Exchange Commission over allegations that it failed to disclose relevant mortgage practices. New federal regulations in 2012 require 401(k) plans to provide new, more detailed fee disclosures consolidated into one document.[30]

Other concerns about managing information are more prosaic.

Transocean mishandled a positive message. See the sidebar "Too Much Positive Spin" on the next page.

- If you send out regularly scheduled messages on the same topic, such as monthly updates of training seminars, develop a system that lets people know immediately what is new. Use color for new or changed entries. Put new material at the top.

- If you are answering multiple questions, use numbers.

- If your e-mail is long (more than one screen), use overviews, headings, and bullets so readers can find the information they need.

- If you are asking people to complete processes involving multiple steps or complicated knowledge, use checklists. Once maligned as too elementary, checklists are being recognized as a major tool to prevent errors. Atul Gawande has popularized the trend with his book, *The Checklist Manifesto: How to Get Things Right,* showing how checklists are used in fields as diverse as aviation, construction, and medicine to eliminate mistakes.

- If you send messages with an attachment, put the most vital information in the e-mail too. Don't make readers open an attachment merely to find out the time or location of a meeting.

Check your message for accuracy and completeness. Remember all the e-mails you receive about meetings that forget to include the time, place, or date, and don't let your e-mails fall in that incomplete category. Make a special effort to ensure that promised attachments really are attached. Be particularly careful with the last messages you send for the day or the week, when haste can cause errors.

Using Benefits in Informative and Positive Messages

Not all informative and positive messages need benefits. You don't need benefits when

- You are presenting factual information only.

- The audience's attitude toward the information doesn't matter.

- The benefits may make the audience seem selfish.

- The benefits are so obvious that to restate them insults the audience's intelligence.

You do need benefits when

- Presenting policies.

- Shaping your audience's attitudes toward the information or toward your organization.

- Stressing benefits presents the audience's motives positively.

- Presenting benefits that may not be obvious.

Benefits are hardest to develop when you are announcing policies. The organization probably decided to adopt the policy because it appeared to help the organization; the people who made the decision may not have thought at all about whether it would help or hurt employees. Yet benefits are most essential in this kind of message so employees see the reason for the change and support it.

When you present benefits, be sure to present advantages *to the audience.* Most new policies help the organization in some way, but few workers will

Too Much Positive Spin

In March 2011 Transocean issued its annual report, which stated, "We recorded the best year in safety performance in our Company's history."

Unfortunately, Transocean is the owner of Deepwater Horizon, the oil rig that exploded in the Gulf of Mexico, killing 11 workers, injuring another 17, and triggering the largest—and most publicized—oil spill in the history of the United States. Millions of barrels of oil gushed into the ocean over three months, causing an environmental disaster.

In its report, Transocean attempted to minimize the accident to place greater emphasis on its good news: "Notwithstanding the tragic loss of life in the Gulf of Mexico, we achieved an exemplary statistical safety record as measured by our total recordable incident rate and total potential severity rate."

The strategy backfired. News articles about the report focused on the phrase "the best year in safety performance" and the six-figure bonuses and salary increases for the executives, all only months after the disaster.

By failing to craft its positive annual report with sensitivity to the situation, Transocean saw a positive message turned into another negative strike against the company.

Sources: Transocean website, accessed June 7, 2011, http://www.deepwater.com; "Despite Gulf Oil Spill, Rig Owner Executives Get Big Bonuses," *CNN*, April 4, 2011, http://edition.cnn.com/2011/BUSINESS/04/03/gulf.spill.bonuses/index.html; and "Gulf Oil Rig Owner Apologizes for Calling 2010 'Best Year' Ever," *CNN*, April 4, 2011, http://www.cnn.com/2011/US/04/04/gulf.spill.bonuses/index.html?hpt=T2.

see their own interests as identical with those of the organization. Employees' benefits need to be spelled out, as do those of customers. To save money, an organization may change health care providers, but the notice to employees should spell out new benefits for employees and their families. Airlines announced new check-in kiosks to customers as a way to avoid lines and save travelers' time.

To develop benefits for informative and positive messages, use the steps suggested in Chapter 2. Be sure to think about benefits that come from the activity or policy itself, in addition to any financial benefits. Perhaps a policy improves customers' experience or the hours employees spend at work.

Ending Informative and Positive Messages

Ending a letter or e-mail gracefully can be a problem in short informative and positive messages. In an e-mail where you have omitted details and proof, you can tell readers where to get more information. In long messages, you can summarize your basic point. In a short message containing all the information readers need, either write a goodwill paragraph that refers directly to the reader or the reader's organization, or just stop. In many short e-mails, just stopping is the best choice.

Goodwill endings should focus on the business relationship you share with your reader rather than on the reader's hobbies, family, or personal life. Use a paragraph that shows you see your reader as an individual. Possibilities include complimenting the reader for a job well done, describing a benefit, or looking forward to something positive that relates to the subject of the message.

> Thank you so much for sending those two extra sales tables. They were just what I needed for Section IV of the report.

When you write to one person, a good last paragraph fits that person so specifically that it would not work if you sent the same basic message to someone else or even to a person with the same title in another organization. When you write to someone who represents an organization, the last paragraph can refer to your company's relationship to the reader's organization. When you write to a group (for example, to "All Employees"), your ending should apply to the whole group.

> Remember that the deadline for enrolling in this new benefit plan is January 31.

Some writers end every message with a standard invitation:

> If you have questions, please do not hesitate to ask.

That sentence implies both that your message did not answer all questions, and that readers will hesitate to contact you. Both implications are negative. But revising the line to say "feel free to call" is rarely a good idea. People in business aren't shrinking violets; they will call if they need help. Don't make more work for yourself by inviting calls to clarify simple messages. Simply omit this sentence.

Story in Informative Messages

Now that employees are used to easy and fast accessibility of information, employers are looking for ways to help information cohere and stick, both among factoids and within employees' minds. One way to achieve this goal that is gaining business attention is through the power of stories.

In the business world, stories are narratives but not fiction, and they are usually brief—a paragraph or two. Nevertheless, these stories enable us to put facts in a context, frequently with emotional underpinnings. The context and the emotion help us to understand and remember information.

- When a popular driver for a city bus company was nearly crushed to death between two parked buses, the company used the story of the driver's accident and agonizing recovery to help drivers remember the safety procedure designed to prevent such accidents in the future.

- Popular business books such as *Fish* and *Who Moved My Cheese?* are told as fables.

- A software company has its experienced technical support personnel help new employees, freshly out of their four-month technical training, by telling stories of a particular problem with a particular customer and how it was solved. The stories help new employees put their technical knowledge into a human context.

Humor in Informative Messages

Some communicators use humor to ensure their messages are read or heard. In fact, four decades of research show that skillfully used humor can help in some communication situations. The research also shows that the best executives use humor twice as often as do mediocre managers.[31]

Humor is a risky tool because of its tendency to rile some people. However, if you know your audience well, humor may help ensure that they absorb your message.

If you decide to use humor, these precautions will help keep it useful.

- Do not direct it against other people, even if you are sure they will never see your message. The Internet abounds with proof that such certainties are false. In particular, never aim humor against a specific group of people.

- Political, religious, and sexual humor should always be avoided; it is against discrimination policies in many businesses.

- Use restraint with your humor; a little levity goes a long way.

Used with care, humor in carefully chosen situations can help your communications. An information technology person sent the following e-mail in his nonprofit organization:[32]

My set of screw driver tips is missing. I may well have loaned them to someone, perhaps weeks ago. If you have them, please return them to me. I use them when someone reports that they have a screw loose.

He got his tips back promptly. Because he had a reputation for clever e-mails, people regularly read his messages.

The Importance of Storytelling

Many global corporations have noted that field reports often go unread. The World Bank Group's International Finance Corporation is working to change that. It has initiated a new program, SmartLessons, to help transfer information by embedding it in stories.

IFC suggests the following tips when using stories:

- Be honest; include setbacks.
- Convey the emotional impact of events.
- Give credit where it is due.
- Allow readers to rate their stories. SmartLessons even gives prizes to those who are top-rated.

SmartLessons can be searched by criteria such as geographic location and topic, and they are successful. Of the 159 IFC-tracked intranets, it is the most popular.

Adapted from Shad Morris and James B. Oldroyd, "To Boost Knowledge Transfer, Tell Me a Story," *Harvard Business Review*, May 2009, 23; and "SmartLessons," Internation Finance Corporation, 2013, http://smartlessons.ifc .org/smartlessons/page .html?page=834.

Varieties of Informative and Positive Messages LO 9-5

Many messages can be informative, negative, or persuasive depending on what you have to say. A transmittal, for example, can be positive when you're sending glowing sales figures or persuasive when you want the reader to act on the information. A performance appraisal is positive when you evaluate someone who's doing superbly, negative when you want to compile a record to justify firing someone, and persuasive when you want to motivate a satisfactory worker to continue to improve. Each of these messages is discussed in the chapter of the pattern it uses most frequently. However, in some cases you will need to use a pattern from a different chapter.

Transmittals

When you send someone something, you frequently need to attach a transmittal message explaining what you're sending. A transmittal can be as simple as a small yellow sticky note with "FYI" ("for your information") written on it, or it can be a separate typed document.

Organize a transmittal message in this order:

1. Tell the reader what you're sending.
2. Summarize the main point(s) of the document.
3. Indicate any special circumstances or information that would help the reader understand the document. Is it a draft? Is it a partial document that will be completed later?
4. Tell the reader what will happen next. Will you do something? Do you want a response? If you do want the reader to act, specify exactly what you want the reader to do and give a deadline.

Frequently transmittals have important secondary purposes. A transmittal from marketing to a store might have the primary purpose of giving the client a chance to affirm the marketing plan. If there's anything wrong, marketing wants to know *before* spending money developing the plan. But an important secondary purpose is to build goodwill: "I'm working on your plan; I'm earning my fee."

Summaries

You may be asked to summarize a conversation, a document, or an outside meeting for colleagues or superiors. (Minutes of an internal meeting are usually more detailed. See Chapter 8 for advice on writing minutes of meetings.)

In a summary of a conversation for internal use, identify the people who were present, the topic of discussion, decisions made, and who does what next.

To summarize a document, start with the main point. Then go on to summarize supporting evidence or details for that point. Add

Signs with information about nutritional content of food help consumers make healthier choices.

The CDC used zombie popularity to help spread information on disaster preparedness. See sidebar on this page.

Preparing for Zombies

How do you get people to read information they think is going to be boring?

The Centers for Disease Control started a zombie apocalypse campaign as a way to direct attention to disaster preparedness. The zombie-themed messages were a unique way to raise interest in the campaign and reached a wider audience with their important safety and natural disaster information. They were particularly effective with younger audiences, who were not familiar with how to prepare for disasters—a primary audience the CDC wanted to reach.

Many emergency departments, like those in the CDC, have a limited budget, so posting humorous blog posts to their websites is one way to bring in readers while still disseminating important safety information.

Ten minutes after posting the zombie information, the CDC blog site crashed as 30,000 tried to read it. Once restored, the site had more than 60,000 views per hour. Officials were understandably pleased. As one official noted, preparing for a zombie disaster is not much different than preparing for a natural disaster.

Adapted from Sydney Lupkin, "Government Zombie Promos are Spreading," abcnews.go.com, September 7, 2012, http://abcnews .go.com/blogs/health/2012/ 09/07/government-zombie- promos-are-spreading/.

the subsidiary points if your audience needs them. In some cases, your audience may also want you to evaluate the document. Should others in the company read this report? Should someone in the company write a letter to the editor responding to this newspaper article?

After you visit a client or go to a conference, you may be asked to share your findings and impressions with other people in your organization. Chronological accounts are the easiest to write but the least useful for the reader. Your company doesn't need a blow-by-blow account of what you did; it needs to know what *it* should do as a result of the meeting.

Summarize a visit with a client or customer in this way:

1. Put the main point from your organization's point of view—the action to be taken, the perceptions to be changed—in the first paragraph.

2. Provide an **umbrella paragraph** to cover and foreshadow the points you will make in the report.

3. Provide necessary detail to support your conclusions and cover each point. Use lists and headings to make the structure of the document clear.

In the following example, the revised first paragraph summarizes the sales representative's conclusions after a call on a prospective client.

Weak original:

> On October 10th, Rick Patel and I made a joint call on Consolidated Tool Works. The discussion was held in a conference room, with the following people present:
> 1. Kyle McCloskey (Vice President and General Manager)
> 2. Bill Petrakis (Manufacturing Engineer)
> 3. Garett Lee (Process Engineering Supervisor)
> 4. Courtney Mansor-Green (Project Engineer)

Improved revision:

> Consolidated Tool Works is an excellent prospect for purchasing a Matrix-Churchill grinding machine. To get the order, we should
> 1. Set up a visit for CTW personnel to see the Matrix-Churchill machine in Kansas City;
> 2. Guarantee 60-day delivery if the order is placed by the end of the quarter; and
> 3. Extend credit terms to CTW.

Thank-You and Positive Feedback Notes

We all like to feel appreciated. Praising or congratulating people can cement good feelings between you and them and enhance your own visibility.

> Congratulations, Sam, on winning the Miller sales award. I bet winning that huge Lawson contract didn't hurt any!

Make your praise sound sincere by offering specifics and avoiding language that might seem condescending or patronizing. For example, think how silly it would sound to praise an employee for completing basic job requirements or to gush that one's mentor has superior knowledge. In contrast, thanks for a kind deed and congratulations or praise on completing a difficult task are rewarding in almost any situation.

Sending a **thank-you note** will make people more willing to help you again in the future. Thank-you notes can be short but must be prompt. They need to be specific to sound sincere.

> Chris, thank you for the extra-short turnaround time. You were a major reason we made the deadline.

Most thank-you notes are e-mails now, so handwritten ones stand out.

If you make it a habit to watch for opportunities to offer thanks and congratulations, you may be pleasantly surprised at the number of people who are extending themselves. During his six-year term, Douglas Conant, chief executive of Campbell, sent over 16,000 handwritten thank-you notes to employees ranging from top executives to hourly workers.[33] As Kenneth Blanchard and Spencer Johnson, authors of the business best seller *The One Minute Manager,* note, "People who feel good about themselves produce good results."[34]

Positive Responses to Complaints

Complaining customers expect organizations to show that they are listening and want to resolve the problem. When you grant a customer's request for an adjusted price, discount, replacement, or other benefit to resolve a complaint, do so in the very first sentence.

Dear Professor Carlton,

Thank you for all your help this semester. My writing skills have improved greatly as have my organizational skills. The extra time you gave me really paid off. I've already had three job interviews due to the job packet I prepared for your course. I will miss your funny dog stories!!! Thanks again for everything!

Pat Robbins

Thank-you notes can be written on standard business stationery, using standard formats. But one student noticed that his professor really liked dogs and told funny dog stories in class. So the student found a dog card for a thank-you note.

Your Visa bill for a night's lodging has been adjusted to $163. Next month a credit of $37 will appear on your bill to reimburse you for the extra amount you were originally asked to pay.

Don't talk about your own process in making the decision. Don't say anything that sounds grudging. Give the reason for the original mistake only if it reflects credit on the company. (In most cases, it doesn't, so the reason should be omitted.)

Solving a Sample Problem

Workplace problems are richer and less well defined than textbook problems and cases. But even textbook problems require analysis before you begin to write. Before you tackle the assignments for this chapter, examine the following problem. See how the analysis questions from Chapter 1 probe the basic points required for a solution. Study the two sample solutions to see what makes one unacceptable and the other one good. Note the recommendations for revision that could make the good solution excellent. The checklist at the end of the chapter can help you evaluate a draft.

Problem

At Interstate Fidelity Insurance (IFI) there is often a time lag between receiving a payment from a customer and recording it on the computer. Sometimes, while the payment is in line to be processed, the computer sends out additional past-due notices or collection letters. Customers are frightened or angry and ask for an explanation. In most cases, if they just waited a little while, the situation would be straightened out. But policyholders are afraid that they'll be without insurance because the company thinks the bill has not been paid.

IFI doesn't have the time to check each individual situation to see if the check did arrive and has been processed. It wants you to write an e-mail that will persuade customers to wait. If something is wrong and the payment never reached IFI, IFI would send a legal notice to that effect saying the policy would be canceled by a certain date (which the notice would specify) at least 30 days after the date on the original premium bill. Continuing customers always get this legal notice as a third chance (after the original bill and the past-due notice).

Prepare a form e-mail that can go out to every policyholder who claims to have paid a premium for automobile insurance and resents getting a past-due notice. The e-mail should reassure readers and build goodwill for IFI.

Analysis of the Problem

1. Who is (are) your audience(s)?

    Automobile insurance customers who say they've paid but have still received a past-due notice. They're afraid they're no longer insured. Since it's a form response, different readers will have different situations. In some cases payments did arrive late, in some cases the company made a mistake, in some the customer never paid (check was lost in mail, unsigned, bounced, etc.).

2. What are your purposes in writing?

    To reassure readers that they're covered for 30 days. To inform them that they can assume everything is OK *unless* they receive a second notice. To avoid further correspondence on this subject. To build goodwill for IFI: (a) we don't want to suggest IFI is error-prone or too cheap to hire enough people to do the necessary work; (b) we don't want readers to switch companies; (c) we do want readers to buy from IFI when they're ready for more insurance.

3. What information must your message include?

    Readers are still insured. We cannot say whether their checks have now been processed (company doesn't want to check individual accounts). Their insurance will be canceled if they do not pay after receiving the second past-due notice (the legal notice).

4. How can you build support for your position? What reasons or benefits will your audience find convincing?

    We provide personal service to policyholders. We offer policies to meet all their needs. Both of these points would need specifics to be interesting and convincing.

5. What aspects of the total situation may affect audience response? The economy? The time of year? Morale in the organization? The relationship between the communicator and audience? Any special circumstances?

    The insurance business is highly competitive—other companies offer similar rates and policies. The customer could get a similar policy for about the same money from someone else. The economy is making money tight, so customers will want to keep insurance costs low. Yet the fact that prices are steady or rising means that the value of what they own is higher—they need insurance more than ever.

    Many insurance companies are refusing to renew policies (car, liability, home). These refusals to renew have gotten lots of publicity, and many people have heard horror stories about companies and individuals whose insurance has been canceled or not renewed after a small number of claims. Readers don't feel very kindly toward insurance companies.

    People need car insurance. If they have an accident and aren't covered, they not only have to bear the costs of that accident alone but also (depending on state law) may need to place as much as $50,000 in a state escrow account to cover future accidents. They have a legitimate worry.

We are slow in processing payments. We don't know if the checks have been processed. We will cancel policies if their checks don't arrive.

Discussion of the Sample Solutions

The solution in Figure 9.7 is unacceptable. The red marginal comments show problem spots. Since this is a form response, we cannot tell customers we have their checks; in some cases, we may not. The e-mail is far too negative. The explanation in paragraph 2 makes IFI look irresponsible and uncaring. Paragraph 3 is far too negative. Paragraph 4 is too vague; there are no benefits; the ending sounds selfish. A major weakness with the solution is that it lifts phrases straight out of the problem; the writer does not seem to have thought about the problem or about the words he or she is using. Measuring the draft against the answers to the questions for analysis suggests that this writer should start over.

The solution in Figure 9.8 is much better. The blue marginal comments show the e-mail's good points. The message opens strongly with the good news that is true for all audiences. Paragraph 2 explains IFI's policy in more positive terms. The negative information is buried in paragraph 3 and is presented positively: the notice is information, not a threat; the 30-day extension is a "grace period." Telling the reader now what to do if a second notice arrives eliminates the need for a second exchange of letters. Paragraph 4 offers

Figure 9.7	An Unacceptable Solution to the Sample Problem

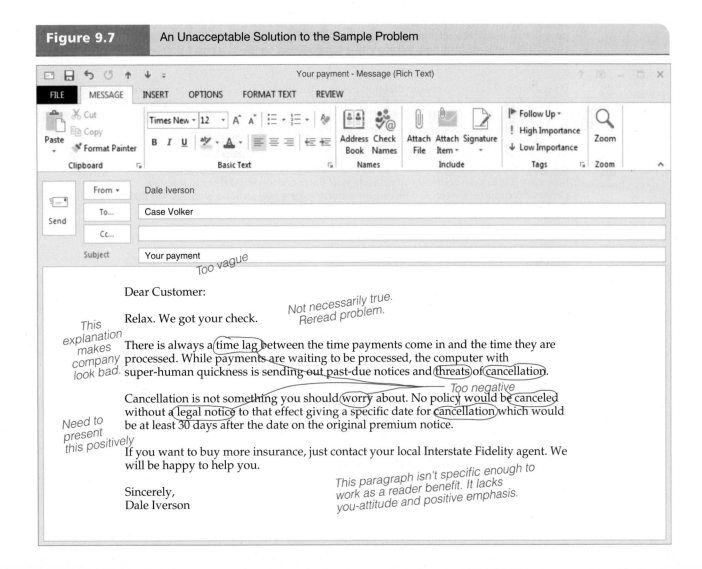

Figure 9.8	A Good Solution to the Sample Problem

Your auto insurance - Message (Rich Text)

FILE **MESSAGE** INSERT OPTIONS FORMAT TEXT REVIEW

Paste — Clipboard | Times New ▾ 12 ▾ A˄ A˅ B *I* U̲ ... | Address Book Check Names — Names | Attach File Attach Item ▾ Signature ▾ — Include | Follow Up ▾ ! High Importance ↓ Low Importance — Tags | Zoom — Zoom

From ▾   Dale Iverson

To...   Case Volker

Cc...

Subject   Your auto insurance

Dear Customer: *Better: use computer to personalize. Put in name and address of a specific reader*

Your auto insurance is still in effect.   *Good ¶ 1. True for all readers*

Good to treat notice as information, tell reader what to do if it arrives

Past-due notices are mailed out if the payment has not been processed within three days after the due date. This may happen if a check is delayed in the mail or arrives without a signature or account number. When your check arrives with all the necessary information, it is promptly credited to your account.   *Good you-attitude*

Even if a check is lost in the mail and never reaches us, you still have a 30-day grace period. If you do get a second notice, you'll know that we still have not received your check. To keep your insurance in force, just stop payment on the first check and send a second one.

Benefits of using IFI

IFI is always checking to ensure that you get any discounts you're eligible for: multicar, accident-free record, good student. If you have a claim, your agent finds quality repair shops quickly, whatever car you drive. You get a check quickly—usually within 3 *Too negative* working days—without having to visit dealer after dealer for time-consuming estimates.

Better to put in agent's name, phone number

Need to add benefits of insuring with IFI

Today, your home and possessions are worth more than ever. You can protect them with Interstate Fidelity's homeowners' and renters' policies. Let your local agent show you how easy it is to give yourself full protection. If you need a special rider to insure a personal computer, jewelry, a coin or gun collection, or a fine antique, you can get that from IFI, too.   *Good specifics*

Whatever your insurance needs—auto, home, life, or health—one call to IFI can do it all.

Sincerely,   *Acceptable ending*
Dale Iverson

---

benefits for being insured by IFI. Paragraph 5 promotes other policies the company sells and prepares for the last paragraph.

As the red comments indicate, this good solution could be improved by personalizing the salutation and by including the name and number of the local agent. Computers could make both of those insertions easily. This good response could be made excellent by revising paragraph 4 so that it doesn't end on a negative note and by using more benefits. For instance, can agents advise clients of the best policies for them? Does IFI offer good service—quick, friendly, unpressured—that could be stressed? Are agents well trained? All of these might yield ideas for additional benefits.

Checklist

Checklist for Informative and Positive Messages

☐ In positive messages, does the subject line give the good news? In either message, is the subject line specific enough to differentiate this message from others on the same subject?

☐ Does the first paragraph summarize the information or good news? If the information is too complex to fit into a single paragraph, does the paragraph list the basic parts of the policy or information in the order in which the message discusses them?

☐ Is all the information given in the message? What information is needed will vary depending on the message, but information about dates, places, times, and anything related to money usually needs to be included. When in doubt, ask!

☐ In messages announcing policies, is there at least one benefit for each segment of the audience? Are all benefits ones that seem likely to occur in this organization?

☐ Is each benefit developed, showing that the benefit will come from the policy and why the benefit matters to this audience? Do the benefits build on the specific circumstances of the audience?

☐ Does the message end with a positive paragraph—preferably one that is specific to the readers, not a general one that could fit any organization or policy?

And, for all messages, not just informative and positive ones,

☐ Does the message use you-attitude and positive emphasis?

☐ Is the tone friendly?

☐ Is the style easy to read?

☐ Is the visual design of the message inviting?

☐ Is the format correct?

☐ Does the message use standard grammar? Is it free from typos?

Originality in a positive or informative message may come from

☐ Creating good headings, lists, and visual impact.

☐ Developing benefits.

☐ Thinking about audiences; giving details that answer their questions and make it easier for them to understand and follow the policy.

Summary by Learning Objectives

LO 9-1   **What the purposes of informative and positive messages are.**

Informative and positive messages have a primary purpose of providing information and good news in a positive manner, as well as multiple secondary purposes such as creating a positive image of the sender and the sender's organization.

LO 9-2   **What kinds of newer communication hardware are entering offices.**

Smartphones, portable media players, tablets, and videoconferencing equipment are enhancing business communications.

LO 9-3   **When and how to use common business media effectively.**

Good communicators need to thoughtfully select one of the common modes of communications: face-to-face contact, phone calls, instant messages and text messaging, social media, letters, e-mails, and paper memos. Media choices depend on the audience, context, and purpose of the message.

LO 9-4   **How to organize informative and positive messages.**

Informative and positive messages normally use the following pattern of organization:

1.   Start with good news or the most important information; summarize the main points.
2.   Give details, clarification, background.
3.   Present any negative elements—as positively as possible.

4.   Explain any benefits.
5.   Use a goodwill ending: positive, personal, and forward-looking.

- A subject line is the title of a document. A good subject line meets three criteria: it's specific; it's concise; and it's adapted to the kind of message (positive, negative, persuasive). If you can't make the subject both specific and short, be specific.

- The subject line for an informative or positive message should highlight any good news and summarize the information concisely.

- Good messages provide the necessary information without overwhelming their audience.

- Use benefits in informative and positive messages when you want to shape your audience's attitudes toward the information or toward your organization.

- Goodwill endings should focus on the business relationship you share with your audience or the audience's organization. The last paragraph of a message to a group should apply to the whole group.

LO 9-5   **How to compose some of the common varieties of informative and positive messages.**

Some common informative and positive messages are transmittals, summaries, thank-you notes, positive feedback, and positive responses to complaints. All usually follow some variation of the pattern presented above.

Continuing Case

The All-Weather Case, set in an HR department in a manufacturing company, extends through all 19 chapters and is available at www.mhhe.com/locker11e. The portion for this chapter asks students to reorganize and rewrite an informational message.

Exercises and Cases

*Go to www.mhhe.com/locker11e for additional Exercises and Cases.

9.1   Reviewing the Chapter

1.   What are the purposes of informative and positive messages? (LO-9-1)
2.   What technological changes are occurring in business communication? (LO 9-2)
3.   What are the multiple purposes of informative and good-news messages? (LO 9-3)

4.   How does information overload impact your communications? (LO 9-3)
5.   When do you use face-to-face contacts? Phone calls? Instant messages? Text messaging? Social media? Letters? Memos and e-mails? (LO 9-3)

6. What are some tips for effectively using face-to-face contacts? Phone calls? Instant messages? Text messaging? Social media? Letters? Memos and e-mails? (LO 9-3)

7. How do you organize informative and positive messages? (LO 9-4)

8. What are some concerns to consider when choosing and ordering the information in your message? (LO 9-4)

9. What are tips for composing some of the common varieties of informative and positive messages? (LO 9-5)

9.2   Reviewing Grammar

Good letters and e-mails need correct grammar. Practice yours by doing the exercises from Appendix B on correcting sentence errors (B.8) and editing for grammar and usage (B.9).

9.3   Describing the Role of Technology Where You Work

Analyze the role of technology in an organization where you—or a friend or family member—have worked.

■ What kinds of communication technology do you use most?

■ What are some of the newest communication technologies introduced there?

■ What kinds of technology upgrades do you wish would be made?

■ Are certain kinds of technology used for certain situations? (For instance, are layoffs announced face-to-face or by e-mail?)

■ What kinds of data security measures are in force?

■ Has anyone there gotten in trouble for misuse of technology?

As your instructor directs,

a. Share your information in small groups.

b. Present your group findings to your classmates.

c. Post your information online for your classmates.

9.4   Saying Yes to a Subordinate—E-mails for Discussion

Today, you get this request from a subordinate.

Subject: Request for Leave

You know that I've been feeling burned out. I've decided that I want to take a three-month leave of absence this summer to travel abroad. I've got five weeks of vacation time saved up; I would take the rest as unpaid leave. Just guarantee that my job will be waiting when I come back!

You decide to grant the request. The following messages are possible responses. How well does each message meet the criteria in the checklist for informative and positive messages?

1.

Subject: Re: Request for Leave

I highly recommend Italy. Spend a full week in Florence, if you can. Be sure to visit the Brancacci Chapel—it's been restored, and the frescoes are breathtaking. And I can give you the names of some great restaurants. You may never want to come back!

2.

Subject: Your Request for Leave

As you know, we are in a very competitive position right now. Your job is important, and there is no one who can easily replace you. However, because you are a valued employee, I will permit you to take the leave you request, as long as you train a replacement before you leave.

3.

Subject: Your Request for Leave Granted

Yes, you may take a three-month leave of absence next summer using your five weeks of accumulated vacation time and taking the rest as unpaid leave. And yes, your job will be waiting for you when you return!

I'm appointing Garrick to take over your duties while you're gone. Talk with him to determine how much training time he'll need, and let me know when the training is scheduled.

Have a great summer! Let us know every now and then how you're doing!

9.5   Introducing a Suggestion System—E-mails for Discussion

Your organization has decided to institute a suggestion system. Employees on hourly pay scales will be asked to submit suggestions. (Managers and other employees on salary are not eligible for this program; they are supposed to be continually suggesting ways to improve things as part of their regular jobs.) If the evaluating committee thinks the suggestion will save money, the employee will receive 10% of the first year's estimated annual savings. If the suggestion won't save money but will improve work conditions, service, or morale, the employee will get a check for $100.

The following e-mails are possible approaches. How well does each message meet the criteria in the checklist for informative and positive messages?

1.

Subject: Suggestion System (SS)

I want to introduce you to the Suggestion System (SS). This program enables the production worker to offer ideas about improving his job description, working conditions, and general company procedures. The plan can operate as a finely tuned machine, with great ideas as its product.

Operation will begin October 1. Once a week, a designate of SS will collect the ideas and turn them over to the SS Committee. This committee will evaluate and judge the proposed changes.

Only employees listed as factory workers are eligible. This excludes foremen and the rest of supervisory personnel. Awards are as follows:

1. $100 awards will be given to those ideas judged operational. These are awarded monthly.
2. There will be grand prizes given for the best suggestions over the six-month span.

Ideas are judged on feasibility, originality, operational simplicity, and degree of benefit to the worker and company. Evaluation made by the SS Committee is final. Your questions should be channeled to my office.

2.

Subject: Establishment of Suggestion System

We announce the establishment of a Suggestion System. This new program is designed to provide a means for hourly employees to submit suggestions to company management concerning operations and safety. The program will also provide an award system to compensate nonmanagement employees for implemented suggestions.

Here is how the program will work: beginning October 1, suggestions can be submitted by hourly workers to the company on Form 292, which will be furnished to all plants and their departments by October 1st. On the form, the submitting employee should include the suggestion, his or her name, and the department number. The form can be deposited in a suggestion drop box, which will be located near the personnel office in each plant.

Any suggestion dealing with the improvement of operations, safety, working conditions, or morale is eligible for consideration. The award structure for the program will be as follows:

1. For an implemented suggestion which improves safety or efficiency with no associated monetary benefits or cost reduction: $100.00.

2. For an implemented suggestion which makes or saves the company money: 10% of the first year's estimated annual savings or additional revenue.

It is hoped that we will have a good initial and continuous response from all hourly employees. This year, we are out to try to cut production costs, and this program may be the vehicle through which we will realize new savings and increased revenues. New ideas which can truly increase operational efficiency or cut safety problems will make the company a nicer place for all employees. A safer work environment is a better work environment. If department operations can be made more efficient, this will eventually make everyone's job just a little easier, and give that department and its employees a sense of pride.

3.

Subject: New Employee Suggestion System

Beginning October 1, all of you who are hourly employees of Tyfor Manufacturing will be able to get cash awards when your suggestions for improving the company are implemented.

Ideas about any aspect of Tyfor Manufacturing are eligible: streamlining behind-the-counter operations, handling schedule problems, increasing the life of line machines.

■ If your idea cuts costs or increases income (e.g., increasing production, decreasing line accidents), you'll receive 10% of the first year's estimated annual savings.

■ If the idea doesn't save money but does improve service, work conditions, or morale, you'll receive a check for $100.

To submit a suggestion, just pick up a form from your manager. On the form, explain your suggestion, describe briefly how it could be implemented, and show how it will affect Tyfor Manufacturing. Return the completed form in the new suggestion box behind the back counter. Suggestions will be evaluated at the end of each month. Turn in as many ideas as you like!

Think about ways to solve the problems you face every day. Can we speed up the materials check-in process? Cut paperwork? Give customers faster service? Decrease the percentage of line flaws?

Your ideas will keep Tyfor Manufacturing competitive. Ten years ago, Tyfor Manufacturing was the only supplier in the Midwest. Now we have three regional competitors, in addition to numerous international ones. Efficiency, creativity, and quality can keep Tyfor Manufacturing ahead.

Employees whose ideas are implemented will be recognized in the regional Tyfor Manufacturing newsletter. The award will also be a nice accomplishment to add to any college application or résumé. By suggesting ways to improve Tyfor Manufacturing, you'll demonstrate your creativity and problem-solving abilities. And you'll be able to share the credit for keeping Tyfor Manufacturing a profitable manufacturing concern.

9.6   Critiquing a Letter—Economic Stimulus Payment Notice

The following letter was sent to more than 130 million households after the U.S. Congress passed a stimulus package in early 2008. Critique it in small groups. Here are some questions to get you started:

1.   What are the purposes of this letter?

2.   How well does this letter inform the audience of its purpose?

3.   Does the letter violate any of the guidelines for constructing informational messages you read about in this chapter? If so, which ones?

4. What kind of impression is given to readers by the document design choices?

As your instructor directs,

a. Write an e-mail to your instructor summarizing your group discussion.

b. As a group, record your answers to the questions, plus other observations you made. Trade summaries with another group. Where did they agree with you? Disagree? What observations did they make that your group did not? Write an e-mail to your instructor summarizing the differences between the two critiques. Submit the e-mail and the two critiques to your instructor.

IRS
Department of the Treasury
Internal Revenue Service
Notice 1377 (February 2008)
Catalog Number 51255B
www.irs.gov

Economic Stimulus Payment Notice

Dear Taxpayer:

We are pleased to inform you that the United States Congress passed and President George W. Bush signed into law the Economic Stimulus Act of 2008, which provides for economic stimulus payments to be made to over 130 million American households. Under this new law, you may be entitled to a payment of up to $600 ($1,200 if filing a joint return), plus additional amount for each qualifying child.

We are sending this notice to let you know that based on this new law the IRS will begin sending the one-time payments starting in May. To receive a payment in 2008, individuals who qualify will not have to do anything more than file a 2007 tax return. The IRS will determine eligibility, figure the amount, and send the payment. This payment should not be confused with any 2007 income tax refund that is owed to you by the federal government. Income tax refunds for 2007 will be made separately from this one-time payment.

For individuals who normally do not have to file a tax return, the new law provides for payments to individuals who have a total of $3,000 or more in earned income, Social Security benefits, and/or certain veterans' payments. Those individuals should file a tax return for 2007 to receive a payment in 2008.

Individuals who qualify may receive as much as $600 ($1,200 if married filing jointly). Even if you pay no income tax but have a total of $3,000 or more in earned income, Social Security benefits, and/or certain veterans' payments, you may receive a payment of $300 ($600 if married filing jointly).

In addition, individuals eligible for payments may also receive an additional amount of $300 for each child qualifying for the child tax credit.

For taxpayers with adjusted gross income (AGI) of more than $75,000 (or more than $150,000 if married filing jointly), the payment will be reduced or phased out completely.

To qualify for the payment, an individual, spouse, and any qualifying child must have a valid Social Security number. In addition, individuals cannot receive a payment if they can be claimed as a dependent of another taxpayer or they filled a 2007 Form 1040NR, 1040NR-EZ, 1040-PR, or 1040-SS.

All individuals receiving payments will receive a notice and additional information shortly before the payment is made. In the meantime, for additional information, please visit the IRS website at _www.irs.gov_.

Source: Internal Revenue Service, "Economic Stimulus Payment Notice," February 2008, http://www.irs.gov/pub/irs-utl/economic_stimulus_payment_notice.pdf.

9.7   Critiquing a Letter—Introducing Kindle

When Amazon brought Kindle to market in 2007, CEO Jeff Bezos sent shareholders a letter telling the story of the creation of the device. Read the letter at http://media .corporate-ir.net/media_files/irol/97/97664/2007letter .pdf. Critique the letter in small groups. Here are some questions to get you started:

1. What are the purposes of this letter?
2. How well are these purposes accomplished?
3. What information does Bezos provide about Kindle? Why do you think he chose this information?
4. How is the information organized?
5. Where do you see you-attitude and positive tone? Do they contribute to the letter's effectiveness? Why or why not?

As your instructor directs,

a. Write an e-mail to your instructor summarizing your group discussion.
b. As a group, record your answers to the questions, plus other observations you made. Trade summaries with another group. Where did they agree with you? Disagree? What observations did they make that your group did not? Write an e-mail to your instructor summarizing the differences between the two critiques. Submit the e-mail and the two critiques to your instructor.

9.8   Critiquing a Letter—Airline Merger

The following letter was sent by Northwest Airlines before its merger with Delta. Critique the letter in small groups. Here are some questions to get you started:

1. What are the purposes of this letter?
2. How well are these purposes accomplished?
3. What information does the letter provide that an ordinary traveler would find useful?
4. How is the information organized?
5. Where do you see you-attitude and positive tone? Do they contribute to the letter's effectiveness? Why or why not?

As your instructor directs,

a. Write an e-mail to your instructor summarizing your group discussion.
b. As a group, record your answers to the questions, plus other observations you made. Trade summaries with another group. Where did they agree with you? Disagree? What observations did they make that your group did not? Write an e-mail to your instructor summarizing the differences between the two critiques. Submit the e-mail and the two critiques to your instructor.

Dear Steven Schmidt,

As a valued Northwest Airlines customer and WorldPerks® member, I wanted you to be among the first to hear that we have announced a merger with Delta Air Lines. Subject to regulatory review, our two airlines are joining forces to create America's premier global airline which, upon closing of the merger, will be called Delta Air Lines.

By combining Northwest and Delta, we are building a stronger, more resilient airline that will be a leader in providing customer service and value. Our combined airline will offer unprecedented access to the world, enabling you to fly to more destinations, have more flight choices and more ways than ever to earn and redeem your WorldPerks miles.

You can be assured that your WorldPerks miles and Elite program status will be unaffected by this merger. In addition, you can continue to earn miles through use of partners like WorldPerks Visa®. And once the new Delta Air Lines emerges you can look forward to being a part of the world's largest frequent flyer program with expanded benefits.

The combined Delta Air Lines will serve more U.S. communities and connect to more worldwide destinations than any global airline. Our hubs—both Delta's and Northwest's—will be retained and enhanced. We will be the only U.S. airline to offer direct service from the United States to all of the world's major business centers in Asia, Latin America, Europe, Africa and around North America.

Both airlines bring tremendous strengths to this new partnership. Our complementary service networks form an end-to-end system that is truly greater than the sum of its parts. This is a merger by addition, not subtraction, which means all of our hubs—both Northwest's and Delta's—will be retained. In addition, building on both airlines' proud decades-long history of serving small communities, we plan to enhance global connections to small towns and cities across the U.S.

All of these positive benefits of our combination mean that we can:

- Offer a true global network where our customers will be able to fly to more destinations, have more schedule options and more opportunities to earn and redeem frequent flyer miles in what will become the world's best and most comprehensive frequent flyer program.

- Continue to serve our current roster of destinations and to maintain our hubs in Atlanta, Cincinnati, Detroit, Memphis, Minneapolis/St. Paul, New York, Salt Lake City, Amsterdam, and Tokyo.

- Improve our customers' travel experience, through new products and services including enhanced self-service tools, better bag-tracking technology, more onboard services, including more meal options, new seats and refurbished cabins.

While we work to secure approval of our merger, which may take up to 6 to 8 months, it will be business-as-usual at both airlines. We will continue to operate as independent airlines and the people of Northwest will remain focused on providing you with the very best in safe, reliable and convenient air travel. At the same time, both airlines will be planning for a seamless integration of our two airlines, one that delivers to you the enhanced benefits that will earn—and retain—your preference.

As we work through this process, we will keep you informed at every step along the way. Thank you for your business and we look forward to serving you on your next Northwest flight.

Sincerely,

Bob Soukup

Managing Director, WorldPerks

9.9   Discussing an Ethics Situation: Fired for an E-mail

This really happened! The details have been changed—to protect the innocent, of course.

Jonah Delaney, a 22-year-old employee of a large health maintenance organization, sent an e-mail throughout the company charging that the multibillion-dollar conversion to electronic medical records was a mess.

In his e-mail, he noted he wasn't concerned just about the money; he was more concerned about medical professionals having the tools they needed "to save lives."

Delaney believed he would be protected by the HMO's policy encouraging people to report ethical problems. He was not; in fact, he was fired. The CIO "coincidentally" resigned at the same time. Delaney's criticism got a government watchdog agency to monitor the HMO and a large newspaper to run the story.

Would you risk your job for an ethics issue this large? A smaller ethics issue? How could Mr. Delaney have handled differently the problem he saw?

9.10   Writing Common Informational E-mails

Some of the most common e-mails are meeting announcements, away notices, and maintenance notices. Create these three messages:

1. Write an e-mail announcing a staff meeting to hear a consultant's presentation on business etiquette.

2. Write a computer away-notice for your upcoming sales trip.

3. Write an e-mail announcing maintenance work (e.g., updating a server, paving a parking lot or sidewalk, repairing an entrance).

In small groups, compare messages. Were all messages equally clear? Did some messages accidentally omit necessary information? What kinds of information? Did all messages use you-attitude and positive tone? Were benefits included where appropriate? How long did it take each of you to write the three messages?

As your instructor directs,

a. Share your findings with the class.

b. Write an informational e-mail to your instructor summarizing your findings.

c. Write an informational e-mail to your instructor summarizing what you learned about your ability to write short, commonplace e-mails.

9.11 Managing Overdraft Information

Banks make billions of dollars from overdraft fees. They maintain that the overdraft service allows customers to make vital purchases even when their account is empty.

On the other side, many customers are furious at how the current system allows them to rack up hundreds of dollars in overdraft fees without knowing they are doing so. Many of them claim they did not know they had overdraft service until they saw the fees. They want to be alerted when a purchase will result in an overdraft. They also object to the bank practice of processing a large purchase before several small ones that occurred at almost the same time, so that each small purchase gets an overdraft fee that it would not have gotten if the large purchase had been processed last.

In small groups, discuss how much overdraft information should be shared. Here are some questions to get you started:

- For what groups are overdraft services a benefit?
- Which groups do such services hurt most?
- Should people be automatically enrolled in such services, as is now the case for most customers?
- Should banks notify customers that they are about to incur an overdraft fee? How would third-party processors affect such notifications?

Write an e-mail to your instructor summarizing your group's discussion.

9.12 Revising a Letter

You work for a local fitness center called Super Fit. The owners of Super Fit would like to expand their business and add a running track and a large pool. They have drafted the following letter to send out to their current members, informing them of the updates and new services.

Dear Sir or Ma'am,

We are excitedly writing to let you know about some thrilling new changes here at Super Fit! We have decided to expand our curent business to fit our clients needs. So, as of January 2014, we will have a brand new running track and a new lap pool. Both the running track and the pool will be very large, and will be able to accommodate many runners and swimmers. We will also offer a few other new services too.

We are proud to note that your membership fee will not increase at all. We appreciate your business and hope you will consider telling your friends about Super Fit and all that we offer! We would also like to offer you a 50% off of one month's fee if you refer a friend to us and they sign a membership contract.

Remeber, stay fit with Super Fit!

With love,

Bob and Joanie

1. Bob and Joanie have asked you to look over their letter and make improvements. Write the new letter and an e-mail to Bob and Joanie explaining your changes.

2. Discuss how you would reach out to new customers with this information. Draft a poster or a flyer, designed to grab potential new members' attentions. How will you change the scope of the information for this new audience?

9.13 Creating a Human Resources Web Page

As firms attempt to help employees balance work and family life (and as employers become aware that personal and family stresses affect performance at work), human resource departments sponsor an array of programs and provide information on myriad subjects. However, some people might be uncomfortable asking for help, either because the problem is embarrassing (needing help to deal with drug abuse, domestic violence, or addiction to gambling) or because focusing on nonwork issues (e.g., child care) might lead others to think they aren't serious about their jobs. The web allows organizations to post information that employees can access privately—even from home.

Create a web page that could be posted by human resources to help employees with one of the challenges they face. Possible topics include

- Appreciating an ethnic heritage.
- Buying a house.
- Caring for dependents: child care, helping a child learn to read, living with teenagers, elder care, and so forth.
- Staying healthy: exercise, yoga, massage, healthy diet, and so forth.
- Dealing with a health problem: alcoholism, cancer, diabetes, heart disease, obesity, and so forth.
- Dressing for success or dressing for casual days.
- Managing finances: basic budgeting, deciding how much to save, choosing investments, and so forth.
- Nourishing the spirit: meditation, religion.
- Getting out of debt.
- Planning for retirement.
- Planning vacations.

- Reducing stress.
- Resolving conflicts on the job or in families.

Assume this page can be accessed from another of the organization's pages. Offer at least seven links. (More is better.) You may offer information as well as links to other pages with information. At the top of the page, offer an overview of what the page covers. At the bottom of the page, put the creation/update date and your name and e-mail address.

As your instructor directs,

a. Turn in one printed copy of your web page(s). On another page, give the URLs for each link.
b. Electronically submit your web page files.
c. Write an e-mail to your instructor identifying the audience for which the page is designed and explaining (1) the search strategies you used to find material on this topic, (2) why you chose the pages and information you've included, and (3) why you chose the layout and graphics you've used.
d. Present your page orally to the class.

Hints:

- Pick a topic you know something about.
- Realize that audience members will have different needs. You could explain the basics of choosing day care or stocks, but don't recommend a specific day care center or a specific stock.
- If you have more than nine links, chunk them in small groups under headings.
- Create a good image of the organization.

9.14 Giving New Information

The Coffee Place, the local coffee shop/café where you work, has now developed a gluten-free menu at the request of customers.

In a group, list ways The Coffee Place can get this information to customers. What are the benefits of using those particular media?

As a group, design a document that delivers this new information. How can you extend the benefit of developing a gluten-free diet to your customers who don't care about gluten? Share your document with the class.

9.15 Investigating E-mail

Interview a professional you know about his/her use of e-mail. You might consider questions such as these:

- How many e-mails do you receive on an average day? Send?
- How much time do you spend handling e-mails on an average day?
- What are the most common kinds of e-mails you receive? Send?

- What are the most difficult kinds of e-mails for you to write? Why?
- What are your pet peeves about e-mails?

Write up your findings in an informational e-mail to your instructor.

9.16   Reminding Guests about the Time Change

Annually in the United States, cities switch to daylight saving time and then back again. The time change can be disruptive for hotel guests, who may lose track of the date, forget to change the clocks in their rooms, and miss appointments as a result.

Prepare a form letter to leave in each hotel room reminding guests of the impending time change. What should guests do?

Write the letter.

Hints:

- Use an attention-getting page layout so readers don't ignore the message.
- Pick a specific hotel or motel chain you know something about.
- Use the letter to build goodwill for your hotel or motel chain. Use specific references to services or features the hotel offers, focusing not on what the hotel does for the reader, but on what the reader can do at the hotel.

9.17   Announcing an Employee Fitness Center

Your company is ready to open an employee fitness center with on-site aerobics and yoga classes, stationary bikes, treadmills, and weight machines. The center will be open 6 a.m. to 10 p.m. daily; at least one qualified instructor will be on duty at all times. Employees get first preference; if there is extra room, clients, spouses, and children 14 and older may also use the facilities. Locker rooms and showers will also be available.

Your company hopes that the fitness center will help out-of-shape employees get the exercise they need to be more productive. Other companies have saved between $2.30 and $10.10 for every $1.00 spent on wellness programs. The savings come from lower claims on medical insurance, less absenteeism, and greater productivity.

Write the e-mail announcing the center.

Hints:

- Who pays the medical insurance for employees? If the employer pays, then savings from healthier employees will pay for the center. If another payment plan is in effect, you'll need a different explanation for the company's decision to open the fitness center.
- Stress benefits apart from the company's saving money. How can easier access to exercise help employees? What do they do? How can exercise reduce stress, improve strength, help employees manage chronic illnesses such as diabetes and high blood pressure, and increase productivity at work?
- What kind of record does the company have of helping employees be healthy? Is the fitness center a departure for the company, or does the company have a history of company sports teams, stop-smoking clinics, and the like?
- What is the company's competitive position? If the company is struggling, you'll need to convince readers that the fitness center is a good use of scarce funds. If the company is doing well, show how having fit employees can make people even more productive.
- Stress fun as a benefit. How can access to the center make employees' lives more enjoyable?

9.18   Providing Information to Job Applicants

Your company is in a prime vacation spot, and as personnel manager you get many letters from students asking about summer jobs. Company policy is to send everyone an application for employment, a list of the jobs you expect to have open that summer with the rate of pay for each, a description of benefits for seasonal employees, and an interview schedule. Candidates must come for an interview at their own expense and should call to schedule a time in advance. Competition is keen: only a small percentage of those interviewed will be hired.

Write a form letter to students who've written to you asking about summer jobs. Give them the basic information about the hiring procedure and tell them what to do next. Be realistic about their chances, but maintain their interest in working for you.

9.19   Announcing a Tuition Reimbursement Program

Your organization has decided to encourage employees to take courses by reimbursing each eligible employee a maximum of $3,500 in tuition and fees during any one calendar year. Anyone who wants to participate in the program must apply before the first class meeting; the application must be signed by the employee's immediate supervisor. The Office of Human Resources will evaluate applications. That office has application forms; it also has catalogs from nearby schools and colleges.

The only courses employees may choose are those either related to the employee's current position (or to a position in the company that the employee might hold someday) or part of a job-related degree program. Again, the degree must be one that would help the employee's current position or that would qualify him or her for a promotion or transfer in the organization.

Only tuition and fees are covered, not books or supplies. People whose applications are approved will be reimbursed when they have completed the course with a grade of C or better. An employee cannot be reimbursed until he or she submits a copy of the approved application, an official grade report, and a statement of the tuition paid. If someone is eligible for other financial aid (scholarship, veterans benefits), the company will pay tuition costs not covered by that aid as long as the employee does not receive more than $3,500 and as long as the total tuition reimbursement does not exceed the actual cost of tuition and fees.

Part-time employees are not eligible; full-time employees must work at the company a year before they can apply to participate in the program. Courses may be at any appropriate level (high school, college, or graduate). However, the Internal Revenue Service currently requires workers to pay tax on any reimbursement for graduate programs. Undergraduate and basic education reimbursements of $3,500 or less a year are not taxed.

As director of human resources, write an e-mail to all employees explaining this new benefit.

Hints:

- Pick an organization you know something about. What do its employees do? What courses or degrees might help them do their jobs better?

- How much education do employees already have? How do they feel about formal schooling?

- The information in the problem is presented in a confusing order. Put related items together.

- The problem stresses the limits of the policy. Without changing the provisions, present them positively.

- How will having a better educated workforce help the organization? Think about the challenges the organization faces, its competitive environment, and so forth.

9.20   Summarizing Information

Summarize one or more of the following:

1. An article from a recent edition of *Bloomberg Businessweek* or *Harvard Business Review.*

2. One of Jakob Nielsen's articles at http://www.nngroup.com/articles/author/jakob-nielsen.

3. An article about college, career development, or job searching from Quintessential Careers, http://www.quintcareers.com/articles.html.

4. Online information about options for recycling or donating used, outdated computers.

5. Options for consolidating student loans and other finances.

6. Online information about protecting your credit card or debit card.

7. An article or web page assigned by your instructor.

As your instructor directs,

a. Write a summary of no more than 100 words.

b. Write a 250- to 300-word summary.

c. Write a one-page summary.

d. In a small group compare your summaries. How did the content of the summaries vary? How do you account for any differences?

Notes

1. Erin Kim, "Restaurant Offers 5% Discount to Eat Without Your Phone," *CNNMoney,* August 16, 2012, http://money.cnn.com/2012/08/16/technology/restaurant-cell-phone-discount/index.html.

2. Drake Bennett, "I'll Have My Robots Talk to Your Robots," *Bloomberg Businessweek,* February 21, 2011, 51–61.

3. Alan Siegel and Irene Etzkorn, "When Simplicity Is the Solution," *Wall Street Journal,* March 30, 2013, C1.

4. Jonathan B. Spira, "The Knowledge Worker's Day: Our Findings," *Basex* (blog), November 4, 2010, http://www.basexblog.com/2010/11/04/our-findings/.

5. Xerox Newsroom, "For Government Workers: Easing Information Overload Will Save," news release, February 19, 2009, http://news.xerox.com/pr/xerox/NR_2009Feb19_Xerox_and_Harris_Interactive_Public_Sector_Survey.aspx.

6. Ellen Lee, "How to (Finally!) Manage Your Email" *USAToday.com,* November 22, 2012, http://www.usatoday.com/story/tech/2012/11/22/manage-email/1704111/.

7. "Internet 2012 in Numbers," *Royal Pingdom* (blog), January 16, 2013, http://royal.pingdom.com/2013/01/16/internet-2012-in-numbers/.

8. Gail Fann Thomas and Cynthia L. King, "Reconceptualizing E-Mail Overload," *Journal of Business and Technical Communication* 20, no. 3 (2006): 252–87.

9. Richard H. Thaler and Will Tucker, "Smarter Information, Smarter Consumers," *Harvard Business Review* 91, no. 1 (January–February 2013): 49.

10. Rachael Emma Silverman, "Tracking Sensors Invade the Workplace," *Wall Street Journal,* March 7, 2013, B1.

11. Tony Hsieh, "Embrace Accidents," *Inc.,* February 2013, 50.

12. Roger Yu, "Voice Mail in Decline with Rise of Text, Loss of Patience," *USAToday.com,* September 3, 2012, http://usatoday30.usatoday.com/tech/news/story/2012-09-03/voicemail-decline/57556358/1.

13. Pilar Pazos, Jennifer M. Chung, and Marina Micari, "Instant Messaging as a Task-Support Tool in Information Technology Organizations," *Journal of Business Communication* 50, no. 12 (2013): 68–86.

14. Geoffrey A. Fowler, "Are You Talking to Me?" *Wall Street Journal,* April 25, 2011, R5.

15. Soumitra Dutta, "Managing Yourself: What's Your Personal Social Media Strategy?" *Harvard Business Review* 88, no. 11 (November 2010): 127; Emily Glazer, "Fund Firms Cautiously Tweet Their Way into a New World," *Wall Street Journal,* February 7, 2011, R1; and Jessica Holzer and Greg Bensinger, "SEC Embraces Social Media: New Way to Make Disclosures Gets Go-Ahead if Investors Are Told Where to Look," *Wall Street Journal,* April 3, 2013, A1.

16. Fowler, "Are You Talking to Me?"

17. Christopher Steiner and Helen Coster, "11 Career Ending Facebook Faux Pas," *Forbes,* April 13, 2010, http://www.forbes.com/2010/04/13/how-facebook-ruined-my-career-entrepreneurs-human-resources-facebook_slide.html.

18. Serena Dai, "Tweeting Diners Get Quick Response," *Des Moines Register,* September 25, 2010, 3E.

19. Hayley Tsukayama, "Twitter Turns 7: Users Send Over 400 Million Tweets Per Day," *Washington Post,* March 21, 2013, http://articles.washingtonpost.com/2013-03-21/business/37889387_1_tweets-jack-dorsey-twitter.

20. Erin Allen, "Update on the Twitter Archive at the Library of Congress," *Library of Congress Blog,* January 4, 2013, http://blogs.loc.gov/loc/2013/01/update-on-the-twitter-archive-at-the-library-of-congress/.

21. H. James Wilson, PJ Guinan, Salvatore Parise, and Bruce D. Weinberg, "What's Your Social Media Strategy?" *Harvard Business Review* 89, no. 7/8 (2011): 23.

22. "About PatientsLikeMe," *PatientsLikeMe,* accessed May 17, 2013, http://www.patientslikeme.com/about.

23. "Social Networking Rules Vary among Businesses," *Des Moines Register,* October 19, 2009, 6E.

24. Lee, "How To (Finally!) Manage Your Email"; and Alina Tugend, "What To Think about before You Hit 'Send,'" *New York Times,* April 20, 2012, http://www.nytimes.com/2012/04/21/your-money/what-to-think-about-before-you-hit-send.html?pagewanted=all&_r=0.

25. Jane Larson, "Be Careful with Business E-Mail Content," *Des Moines Register,* January 21, 2008, 2D.

26. Tugend, "What To Think about before You Hit 'Send.'"

27. MailerMailer, *Email Marketing Metrics Report,* July 2012, http://www.mailermailer.com/resources/metrics/index.rwp.

28. Jennifer Kay, "Hurricane Center Tries to Raise Storm Surge Awareness," *Des Moines Register,* May 25, 2013, 12A.

29. Gilbert Ross, "Black Box Backfire," *Wall Street Journal,* April 21, 2007, A8.

30. Mark Jewell, "New 401(k) Fee Disclosures Are Coming; 4 Key Items to Look for in Documents," *Des Moines Register,* July 8, 2012, 1D.

31. Daniel H. Pink, *A Whole New Mind: Why Right-Brainers Will Rule the Future* (New York: Riverhead Books, 2006), 198.

32. Bob Mills, e-mail message to author.

33. "Lighting a Fire under Campbell," *BusinessWeek,* December 4, 2006, 96.

34. Kenneth Blanchard and Spencer Johnson, *The One Minute Manager* (New York: William Morrow, 1982), 19.

10 Delivering Negative Messages

Chapter Outline

NEWSWORTHY COMMUNICATION

"We Heard You"

Companies often need to take extra care in creating messages to regain lost trust and business of their customers. Often, this involves acknowledging mistakes and offering apologies, like J.C. Penney did in early 2013.

In November 2011, retailer J.C. Penney attempted to revitalize its image and appeal to younger shoppers. The company hired CEO Ron Johnson, the former head of Apple's retail stores, to lead the effort. Johnson made huge changes to the layout of J.C. Penney stores, the brands it carried, and the customer experience. The changes failed. After only 17 months, Johnson was fired because of drastic declines in revenue and increasingly unhappy customers.

Shortly after firing Johnson, J.C. Penney released a 30-second video through social media in May 2013. The video's simple message was an apology and a commitment to listen to its customers: "It's no secret, recently J.C. Penney changed. Some changes you liked and some you didn't. But what matters with mistakes is what we learn. We learned a very simple thing: to listen to you, to hear what you need, to make your life more beautiful. Come back to J.C. Penney. We heard you."

While it is too early to determine the long-term effect of J.C. Penney's apology, the early indications were good. Customers responded positively on social media and in the stores. Only two weeks after posting the apology, J.C. Penney replaced it with a video thanking customers for their renewed support.

Communicating negative messages effectively can help a company rebuild customer support, even after serious mistakes.

Sources: Claire O'Connor, "J.C. Penney Releases Apology Ad Begging Shoppers to Come Back," *Forbes.com,* May 1, 2013, http://www.forbes.com/sites/clareoconnor/2013/05/01/j-c-penney-releases-apology-ad-begging-shoppers-to-come-back/; and Matt Brownell, "J.C. Penney Is Done Apologizing," *Daily Finance,* May 14, 2013, http://www.dailyfinance.com/on/jcpenney-apology-ad-removed/.

After studying this chapter, you will know

LO 10-1 Different purposes of negative messages.

LO 10-2 Different ways to organize negative messages.

LO 10-3 Ways to construct the different parts of negative messages.

LO 10-4 How to improve the tone of negative messages.

LO 10-5 Ways to construct different kinds of negative messages.

LO 10-6 How, and how not, to use technology for negative messages.

Bad News Weather

The National Weather Service (NWS) has decided to add more detailed and frightening information to the tornado warnings that are issued so residents will pay more attention. They have found that many people do not take the warnings seriously; sometimes, when people finally do take shelter, it is too late. The NWS will be adding specific warnings for powerful storms, like this one used for a storm in Kansas:

IMPACT—This is a life-threatening situation. You could be killed if not underground or in a tornado shelter. Complete destruction of entire neighborhoods is likely. Many well-built homes and businesses will be completely swept from their foundations. Debris will block most roadways. Mass devastation is highly likely making the area unrecognizable to survivors. TORNADO DAMAGE THREAT – Catastrophic.

The NWS hopes that these more vivid descriptions, which will be used rarely, will save more lives in the event of especially destructive storms, like those that hit Joplin, Missouri, in 2001 and Moore, Oklahoma, in 2013.

Adapted from Dennis Magee, "Sudden Impact: Weather Service Hones Warnings So Residents Will Take Heed," *Ames Tribune*, March 24, 2013, A4; and Bill Draper, "'Unsurvivable!' New Tornado Warnings Aim to Scare People to Shelter," *Des Moines Register*, April 3, 2012, 1A.

In a negative message, the basic information we have to convey is negative; we expect the audience to be disappointed or angry. Some jobs entail conveying more negative messages than others. Customer service representatives, employee relations personnel, and insurance agents all have to say no on a regular basis.

Negative communications such as refusals, rejections, recalls, and apologies are hard to compose. Yet they are so important. Good ones restore corporate reputations as well as customer and employee goodwill. Bad ones can lead to lawsuits. Corporate officers can be promoted or fired on the basis of a negative communication.

Mishandled negative communication can be expensive, in terms of both money and reputation. Toyota suffered extensive bad press when it dithered over its response to acceleration problems in its cars; British Petroleum experienced the same bad publicity when it initially downplayed its oil well catastrophe in the Gulf of Mexico. Businesses don't have to be large to worry about negative messages; local businesses routinely lose customers when they mishandle complaints.

One Silicon Valley company calculated the costs of negative communications from a salesperson known for negative interpersonal skills and e-mails. The costs included managerial time, HR time, anger management training and counseling, among others, and came to $160,000 for just one year. The company deducted 60% of that cost from the employee's bonus. A British study estimated the costs of bullying in firms with 1,000 employees to be about $2 million a year per firm.[1]

Withholding negative news can be equally expensive. Johnson & Johnson failed to notify the public about problems with its hip implant and is facing potentially thousands of lawsuits. Pharmaceutical companies have been sued for failing to disclose significant drug risks. Banks are being sued for keeping information from investors about flaws in bundled mortgages. Some of these lawsuits are for billions of dollars.

Purposes of Negative Messages **LO 10-1**

Negative messages include rejections and refusals, announcements of policy changes that do not benefit the audience, requests the audience will see as insulting or intrusive, negative performance reviews, disciplinary notices, and product recalls or notices of defects.

A negative message always has several purposes:

Primary purposes

- To give the audience the bad news.
- To have the audience understand and accept the message.
- To maintain as much goodwill as possible.

Secondary purposes

- To maintain, as much as possible, a good image of the communicator and the communicator's organization.
- To reduce or eliminate future communication on the same subject so the message doesn't create more work for the sender.

In many negative situations, the communicator and audience will continue to deal with each other. Even when further interaction is unlikely (for example, when a company rejects a job applicant or refuses to renew a customer's insurance), the firm wants anything the audience may say about the company to be positive or neutral rather than negative.

Some messages that at first appear to be negative can be structured to create a positive feeling: a decision that may be negative in the short term may be shown to be a positive one in the long term; or the communication of a problem can be directly connected to an effective solution.

Even when it is not possible to make the audience happy with the news we must convey, we still want the audience members to feel that

- They have been taken seriously.
- Our decision is fair and reasonable.
- If they were in our shoes, they would make the same decision.

Organizing Negative Messages   LO 10-2

The best way to organize a negative message depends on your audience and on the severity of the negative information. This chapter presents several possible patterns and connects them with their most likely contexts.

 WARNING: The patterns should never be used blindly. You must always consider whether your audience, purpose, and context would be better served with a different organization.

Giving Bad News to Clients and Customers

When you must give bad news to clients and customers, you need to be clear, but you also need to maintain goodwill. People are increasingly skeptical and have a hard time trusting organizations. One study found that in order to accept a message as true, more than 70% of people need exposure to it more than three times.[2] Compromises or alternatives can help you achieve clarity and goodwill. See the first column in Figure 10.1 for a way to organize these messages.

Figure 10.2 illustrates another basic pattern for negative messages. This letter omits the reason for the policy change, probably because the change benefits the company, not the customer. Putting the bad news first (though pairing

Restoring Goodwill at Delta

After large numbers of customer complaints, Delta Air Lines sent all 11,000 flight agents back to training.

In daylong seminars, agents learned how to respond to customer complaints and worries with a positive attitude and a focus on improving the customer's experience. The seminars included these key points:

- *Be positive.* The agents were taught to smile and express appreciation for the customers' business, especially when the customers were unhappy or had problems.
- *Be honest.* If a passenger was going to miss her flight, the agents learned to tell her immediately and offer to help rebook, rather than encouraging her to rush through the airport.
- *Recognize the customer's feelings.* Empathizing with a frustrated customer can make the difference between a bad experience and a good experience.
- *Don't place blame.* Customers know when they've made poor decisions, such as arriving late or not allowing enough time to get through airport security. Agents should work to help the customers and solve problems as much as possible.

Adapted from Scott McCartney, "Delta Sends Its 11,000 Agents to Charm School," *Wall Street Journal*, February 3, 2011, D3.

Handwritten note at top: how to do it among multiple cultures

Figure 10.1   How to Organize Negative Messages

Negative messages to clients and customers	Negative messages to superiors	Negative messages to peers and subordinates
1. **When you have a reason that the audience will understand and accept, give the reason before the refusal.** A good reason prepares the audience to expect the refusal.	1. **Describe the problem.** Tell what's wrong, clearly and unemotionally.	1. **Describe the problem.** Tell what's wrong, clearly and unemotionally.
2. **Give the negative information or refusal just once, clearly.** Inconspicuous refusals can be missed, making it necessary to say _no_ a second time.	2. **Tell how it happened.** Provide the background. What underlying factors led to this specific problem?	2. **Present an alternative or compromise, if one is available.** An alternative not only gives the audience another way to get what they want but also suggests that you care about them and helping them meet their needs.
3. **Present an alternative or compromise, if one is available.** An alternative not only gives the audience another way to get what they want but also suggests that you care about them and helping them meet their needs.	3. **Describe the options for fixing it.** If one option is clearly best, you may need to discuss only one. But if your superiors will think of other options, or if different people will judge the options differently, describe all the options, giving their advantages and disadvantages.	3. **If possible, ask for input or action.** People in the audience may be able to suggest solutions. And workers who help make a decision are far more likely to accept the consequences.
4. **End with a positive, forward-looking statement.**	4. **Recommend a solution and ask for action.** Ask for approval so that you can make the necessary changes to fix the problem.	

it immediately with an alternative) makes it more likely that the recipient will read the letter. If this letter seemed to be just a routine renewal, or if it opened with the good news that the premium was lower, few recipients would read the letter carefully, and many would not read it at all. Then, if they had accidents and found that their coverage was reduced, they'd blame the company for not communicating clearly. Emphasizing the negative here is both good ethics and good business.

Giving Bad News to Superiors

Your superior expects you to solve minor problems by yourself. But sometimes, solving a problem requires more authority or resources than you have. When you give bad news to a superior, also recommend a way to deal with the problem. Turn the negative message into a persuasive one. See the middle column in Figure 10.1.

When you are the superior, be sure that you do not block the transmittal of negative news to you (see Figure 10.3). Employees reporting negative situations (whistle-blowing) are frequently penalized; one study found the percentage being penalized to be 82%. Despite the penalties, the study found that 19% of corporate fraud was uncovered by employees.[3]

If employees believe that relaying bad news to you will gain them group support for solving their problems, you are far more likely to hear of problems at an early stage, when they are easier to solve. Alan Mulally, president and CEO of Ford, relates that when he joined Ford, the first economic forecast was for a $17 billion loss, yet at his first staff meeting, all the charts were green, indicating financial health. At the second meeting, one brave executive dared to present a chart with red, and everyone present looked to Mulally to see his reaction. His response was to ask everyone present what they could do to help get that particular vehicle launch back on track. In the following weeks, charts were all different colors because his staff knew it was safe to be honest. He

Handwritten note at left: employees providing bad news

Figure 10.2   A Negative Letter

Vickers
Insurance Company

3373 Forbes Avenue
Rosemont, PA 19010
(215) 572-0100

Negative information highlighted so reader won't ignore message

Liability Coverage Is Being Discontinued— Here's How to Replace It!

Negative

Alternative

Dear Policyholder:

Negative

When your auto insurance is renewed, it will no longer include liability coverage unless you select the new Assurance Plan. Here's why.

Liability coverage is being discontinued. It, and the part of the premium which paid for it, will be dropped from all policies when they are renewed.

Positive information underlined for emphasis

This change could leave a gap in your protection. But you can replace the old Liability Coverage with Vickers' new Assurance Plan.

Alternative

No reason is given. The change probably benefits the company rather than the reader, so it is omitted.

With the new Assurance Plan, you receive benefits for litigation or awards arising from an accident—regardless of who's at fault. The cost for the Assurance Plan at any level is based on the ages of drivers, where you live, your driving record, and other factors. If these change before your policy is renewed, the cost of your Assurance Plan may also change. The actual cost will be listed in your renewal statement.

To sign up for the Assurance Plan, just check the level of coverage you want on the enclosed form and return it in the postage-paid envelope within 14 days. You'll be assured of the coverage you select.

Forward-looking ending emphasizes reader's choice

Sincerely,

C. J. Morgan

C. J. Morgan
President

Alternative

P.S. The Assurance Plan protects you against possible legal costs arising from an accident. Sign up for the plan today and receive full coverage from Vickers.

and his staff were then able to concentrate on creating ways to turn reds into greens and move the company forward to financial health.[4]

Giving Bad News to Peers and Subordinates

When passing along serious bad news to peers and subordinates, many people use the organization suggested in the last column in Figure 10.1.

Delivering Cancer News

Oncologists, doctors who specialize in treating cancer, have one of the toughest jobs when it comes to delivering negative news. These doctors often inform patients that they have a difficult battle to face or that there is almost no hope and death may be imminent.

Some medical schools now insist that students learn how to deliver bad news to patients, particularly those suffering from cancer. These medical programs have added classes where students learn to give the negative news through verbal and nonverbal forms of communication. Some of these schools also use role-playing with patient actors. The medical students have to inform the actors of an unwanted diagnosis and appropriately deal with the actor's response. Some studies suggest that the manner in which bad news is presented to a patient has significant effects on their overall health.

As an additional resource for doctors to be upfront with their patients, the American Society of Clinical Oncology has developed a booklet. It helps patients understand their options when they learn they have cancer. The goal is to help improve their quality of life, maximize their remaining time, and plan for end-of-life care. The society believes that currently less than 40% of patients have conversations with their doctors about their options.

Adapted from Dawn Sagario, "Doctors Learn to Convey Facts in Appropriate, Thoughtful Way," *Des Moines Register,* October 17, 2006, E1, E2; "Oncology Group Promotes Candor on End-of-Life-Care," *Des Moines Register,* February 8, 2011, 6A.

Figure 10.3	How to Deal with Criticism

1. **Listen carefully,** even if you don't value the person. Focus on the criticism, not your response.
2. **Ask questions.** They will help clarify the criticism, show that you are listening carefully, and probably help you judge the quality of the criticism.
3. **Determine accuracy.** Even a criticism that seems off base may have some elements of truth.
4. **Stay calm and objective.** Save anger and defensiveness for private moments.
5. **Fix the problem.** Sometimes clarifying a misunderstanding is sufficient. Other times you will need to make a change.

No serious negative (such as being downsized or laid off) should come as a complete surprise, nor should it be delivered by e-mail. Managers may be inclined to use electronic forms of communication to deliver bad news, but they should resist the temptation in most situations. Six factors should be considered when choosing a channel for delivering bad news:

- The severity of the message.
- The degree of surprise involved.
- The context of the problem.
- The type and complexity of the explanation.
- The corporate culture.
- The relationship between the superior and subordinates.

When Chrysler cut 25% of its dealers, it sent the bad news the same day it went public with the list of cut dealerships. Thus, many dealers first heard about their cuts on the news, not from Chrysler's letter, creating even more bad press for the automaker.

People sending bad news must always juggle the efficiency of delivering the message with its impact on receivers. Research shows that managers who deliver bad news in face-to-face settings are more appreciated and accepted by employees.[5]

Managers can prepare for possible negatives by giving full information as it becomes available. It is also possible to let the people who will be affected by a decision participate in setting the criteria. Someone who has bought into the criteria for retaining workers is more likely to accept decisions using such criteria. And in some cases, the synergism of groups may make possible ideas that management didn't think of or rejected as "unacceptable."

When the bad news is less serious, as in Figure 10.4, try using the pattern in the first column of Figure 10.1 unless your knowledge of the audience suggests that another pattern will be more effective.

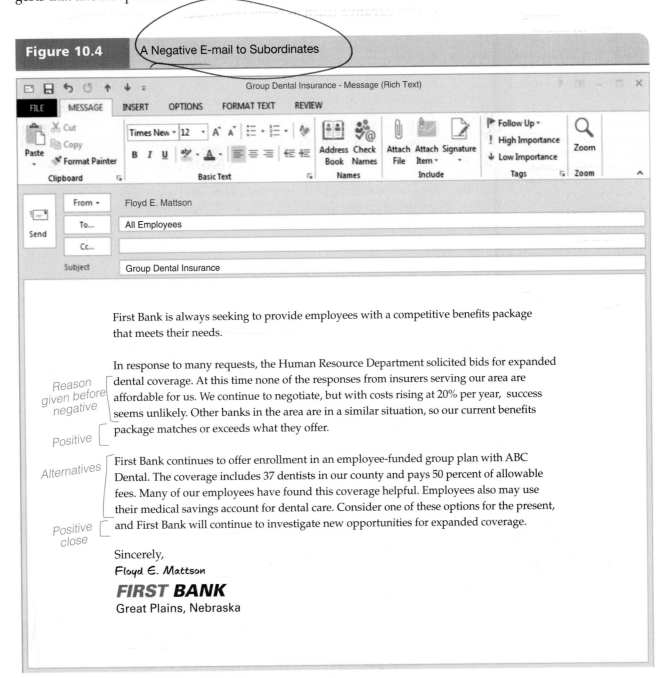

Figure 10.4   A Negative E-mail to Subordinates

First Bank is always seeking to provide employees with a competitive benefits package that meets their needs.

Reason given before negative — In response to many requests, the Human Resource Department solicited bids for expanded dental coverage. At this time none of the responses from insurers serving our area are affordable for us. We continue to negotiate, but with costs rising at 20% per year, success seems unlikely. Other banks in the area are in a similar situation, so our current benefits

Positive — package matches or exceeds what they offer.

Alternatives — First Bank continues to offer enrollment in an employee-funded group plan with ABC Dental. The coverage includes 37 dentists in our county and pays 50 percent of allowable fees. Many of our employees have found this coverage helpful. Employees also may use their medical savings account for dental care. Consider one of these options for the present,

Positive close — and First Bank will continue to investigate new opportunities for expanded coverage.

Sincerely,

Floyd E. Mattson

FIRST BANK
Great Plains, Nebraska

The Parts of a Negative Message LO 10-3

This section provides more information about wording each part of a negative message.

Subject Lines

Many negative messages put the topic, but not the specific negative, in the subject line.

> Subject: Status of Conversion Table Program

Other negative message subject lines focus on solving the problem.

> Subject: Improving Our Subscription Letter

Use a negative subject line in messages when you think readers may ignore what they believe is a routine message. Also use a negative subject line when the reader needs the information to make a decision or to act.

> Subject: Elevator to Be Out Friday, June 17

Many people do not read all their messages, and a neutral subject line may lead them to ignore the message.

Buffers

Traditionally, textbooks recommended that negative messages open with buffers. A buffer is a neutral or positive statement that allows you to delay the negative. Some research suggests that buffers do not make readers respond more positively,[6] and good buffers are hard to write. However, in special situations, you may want to use a buffer. The first sentence in the First Bank e-mail (Figure 10.4) is a buffer.

To be effective, a buffer must put the reader in a good frame of mind, not give the bad news but not imply a positive answer either, and provide a natural transition to the body of the letter. The kinds of statements most often used as buffers are good news, facts and chronologies of events, references to enclosures, thanks, and statements of principle.

1. **Start with any good news or positive elements the letter contains.**

> Starting Thursday, June 26, you'll have easier access to your money 24 hours a day at First National Bank.

Letter announcing that the drive-up windows will be closed for two days while new automatic teller machines are installed

2. **State a fact or provide a chronology of events.**

> In December the Delegate Assembly voted in a new graduated dues schedule.

Announcement of a new dues structure that will raise most members' dues

3. **Refer to enclosures in the letter.**

> A new sticker for your car is enclosed. You may pick up additional ones in the office if needed.

Letter announcing increase in parking rental rates

4. **Thank the reader for something he or she has done.**

> Thank you for scheduling appointments for me with so many senior people at First National Bank. My visit there March 14 was very informative.

Letter refusing a job offer

5. **State a general principle.**

> Good drivers should pay substantially less for their auto insurance. The Good Driver Plan was created to reward good drivers (those with five-year accident-free records) with our lowest available rates. A change in the plan, effective January 1, will help keep those rates low.

Letter announcing that the company will now count traffic tickets, not just accidents, in calculating insurance rates—a change that will raise many people's premiums

Some audiences will feel betrayed by messages whose positive openers delay the central negative point. Therefore, use a buffer only when the audience (individually or culturally) values harmony or when the buffer serves another purpose. For example, when you must thank the reader somewhere in the letter, putting the "thank you" in the first paragraph allows you to start on a positive note.

Buffers are hard to write. Even if you think the reader would prefer to be let down easily, use a buffer only when you can write a good one.

Reasons

Research shows that audiences who described themselves as "totally surprised" by negative news had many more negative feelings and described their feelings as being stronger than did those who expected the negative.[7] A clear and convincing reason prepares the audience for the negative, resulting in people who more easily accept it.

The following reason is inadequate.

Weak reason: The goal of the Knoxville CHARGE-ALL Center is to provide our customers faster, more personalized service. Since you now live outside the Knoxville CHARGE-ALL service area, we can no longer offer you the advantages of a local CHARGE-ALL Center.

If the reader says, "I don't care if my bills are slow and impersonal," will the company let the reader keep the card? No. The real reason for the negative is that the bank's franchise allows it to have cardholders only in a given geographic region.

Real reason: Each local CHARGE-ALL center is permitted to offer accounts to customers in a several-state area. The Knoxville CHARGE-ALL center serves customers east of the Mississippi. You can continue to use your current card until it expires. When that happens, you'll need to open an account with a CHARGE-ALL center that serves Texas.

Don't hide behind "company policy": your audience will assume the policy is designed to benefit you at their expense. If possible, show how your audience benefits from the policy. If they do not benefit, don't mention policy.

Weak reason:	I cannot write an insurance policy for you because company policy does not allow me to do so.
Better reason:	Gorham insures cars only when they are normally garaged at night. Standard insurance policies cover a wider variety of risks and charge higher fees. Limiting the policies we write gives Gorham customers the lowest possible rates for auto insurance.

Avoid saying that you *cannot* do something. Most negative messages exist because the communicator or company has chosen certain policies or cutoff points. In the example above, the company could choose to insure a wider variety of customers if it wanted to do so.

As a middle manager, you will often enforce policies that you did not design and announce decisions that you did not make. Don't pass the buck by saying, "This was a terrible decision." Carelessly criticizing your superiors is never a good idea.

If you have several reasons for saying *no*, use only those that are strong and watertight. If you give five reasons and the audience dismisses two of them, the audience may feel that they've won and should get the request.

Weak reason:	You cannot store large bulky items in the dormitory over the summer because moving them into and out of storage would tie up the stairs and the elevators just at the busiest times when people are moving in and out.

If students say they will move large items before or after the two days when most people are moving in or out, you are still not going to grant the request, because you do not have the storage room. If you do not have a good reason, omit the reason rather than use a weak one.

Even if you have a strong reason, omit it if it makes the company look bad.

Reason that hurts company:	Our company is not hiring at the present time because profits are down. In fact, the downturn has prompted top management to reduce the salaried staff by 5% just this month, with perhaps more reductions to come.
Better:	Our company does not have any openings now.

Refusals

Deemphasize the refusal by putting it in the same paragraph as the reason, rather than in a paragraph by itself.

Sometimes you may be able to imply the refusal rather than stating it directly.

Direct refusal:	You cannot get insurance for just one month.
Implied refusal:	The shortest term for an insurance policy is six months.

Be sure the implication is crystal clear. Any message can be misunderstood, but an optimistic or desperate audience is particularly unlikely to understand a negative message. One of your purposes in a negative message is to close the door on the subject. You do not want to have to send a second message saying that the real answer is *no*.

Alternatives

Giving your audience an alternative or a compromise, if one is available, is a good idea for several reasons:

- It offers the audience another way to get what they want.
- It suggests that you really care about your audience and about helping to meet their needs.
- It enables your audience to reestablish the psychological freedom you limited when you said *no*.
- It allows you to end on a positive note and to present yourself and your organization as positive, friendly, and helpful.

When you give an alternative, give your audience all the information they need to act on it, but don't take the necessary steps. Let your audience decide whether to try the alternative.

Negative messages limit your audience's freedom. People may respond to a limitation of freedom by asserting their freedom in some other arena. This phenomenon, called **psychological reactance**,[8] is at work when a customer who has been denied credit no longer buys even on a cash basis, a subordinate who has been passed over for a promotion gets back at the company by deliberately doing a poor job, or someone who has been laid off sabotages the company's computers. The news repeatedly has stories of workers disgruntled by negative news who return to the workplace and kill co-workers.

An alternative allows your audience to react in a way that doesn't hurt you. By letting your audience decide for themselves whether they want the alternative, you allow them to reestablish their sense of psychological freedom.

The specific alternative will vary depending on the circumstances. Some stores create goodwill by directing customers to other businesses for out-of-stock items. In Figure 10.2, the company offers the new Assurance Plan.

Endings

If you have a good alternative, refer to it in your ending. In Figure 10.2 the writer explains how to sign up for the Assurance Plan.

The best endings look positively to the future:

> Wherever you have your account, you'll continue to get all the service you've learned to expect from CHARGE-ALL, and the convenience of charging items at over a million stores, restaurants, and hotels in the United States and abroad—and in Knoxville, too, whenever you come back to visit!

Letter refusing to continue charge account for a customer who has moved

Avoid endings that seem insincere.

> We are happy to have been of service, and should we be able to assist you in the future, please contact us.

This ending lacks you-attitude and would not be good even in a positive message. In a situation where the company has just refused to help, it's likely to sound sarcastic.

4x a week. [handwritten]

Apologies

Apologizing is never an easy task, but it's something most of us do. New research suggests that people, on average, say they're sorry four times a week. And most people have an easier time saying they're sorry to friends and strangers than they do family members or partners.[9]

Organizations have to routinely offer apologies, too. The news frequently has stories of corporations providing apologies. Apple apologized to customers for its map app; American Airlines apologized for increases in delayed and canceled flights.[10] Descriptions of other apologies from Jawbone and Toyota can be found in sidebars in this chapter.

Not all negative messages, however, need to include apologies. In business documents, apologize only when you are at fault. If you need to apologize, do it early, briefly, and sincerely. Do so only once, early in the message. Do not dwell on the bad things that have happened. The reader already knows this negative information. Instead, focus on what you have done to correct the situation.

No explicit apology is necessary if the error is small and if you are correcting the mistake.

Negative:	We're sorry we got the nutrition facts wrong in the recipe.
Better:	You're right. We're glad you made us aware of this. The correct amounts are 2 grams of fat and 4 grams of protein.

Do not apologize when you are not at fault. The phrase "I'm sorry" is generally interpreted in the United States to mean the sorry person is accepting blame or responsibility. When you have done everything you can and when a delay or problem is due to circumstances beyond your control, you aren't at fault and don't need to apologize. It may, however, be appropriate to include an explanation so the reader knows you weren't negligent. In the previous example acknowledging an error, the writer might indicate the source of the error (such as a reference book or a government website). If the news is bad, put the explanation first. If you have good news for the reader, put it before your explanation.

Negative:	I'm sorry that I could not answer your question sooner. I had to wait until the sales figures for the second quarter were in.
Better (neutral or bad news):	We needed the sales figures for the second quarter to answer your question. Now that they're in, I can tell you that. . . .
Better (good news):	The new advertising campaign is a success. The sales figures for the second quarter are finally in, and they show that. . . .

If the error or problem is significant, offer a solution. Even if the customer has some responsibility, offer to fix the problem. The cost of doing so is almost always less than repairing a reputation smeared on social media.

Negative:	I'm sorry that the chairs will not be ready by August 25 as promised.
Better:	Because of a strike against the manufacturer, the desk chairs you ordered will not be ready until November. Do you want to keep that order, or would you like to look at the models available from other suppliers?

Sometimes you will be in a fortunate position where you can pair your apology with an appropriate benefit.

---

ral
ls
Hard

After decades of business exchanges, Americans and Japanese still have troubling apologizing appropriately to each other. Americans often see apologies as a way of taking the blame. Japanese often see it as a desire to repair a damaged relationship, without guilt being automatically involved.

These reactions to apologies are deeply tied to culture. Because Western cultures are more individualistic, Americans tend to assume that an apology is a person's way of taking responsibility for a mistake. However, in a more group-oriented culture such as Japan's, apologies are often regarded as a way of expressing regret that the event occurred.

International companies need to keep these cultural differences in mind when encountering apologies. Many Americans, for example, seemed unimpressed by profuse apologies from Toyota's CEO after the accelerator recalls. Similarly, the Japanese were upset when a U.S. submarine commander who accidentally sank a Japanese fishing boat didn't apologize immediately.

Adapted from William W. Maddux, Peter H. Kim, Tetsushi Okumura, and Jeanne M. Brett, "Why 'I'm Sorry' Doesn't Always Translate," *Harvard Business Review*, June 2012, 26.

I'm sorry in America [handwritten]

People say they are sorry an average of four times a week.

- When the Hallmark Flowers website stopped taking orders the week before Mother's Day, Hallmark sent an e-mail asking customers to try again and offering free shipping for a day.[11]

- When Apple sharply cut the price on the iPhone a few months after it came on the market, Steve Jobs offered an apology to earlier buyers and provided them with a $100 Apple store credit.

- Many airlines now have computer programs that generate apology letters for customers on flights with lengthy delays or other major problems; the letters frequently offer additional frequent-flyer miles or discount vouchers for future trips.[12]

Sincere apologies go hand in hand with efforts to rectify the problem. Toyota's apology letter to customers for the sticking accelerator problem noted the company was training dealers to make the repair and also stopping production of the involved models to concentrate on the repairs.

Some hospitals have found that disclosing medical errors, apologizing, and quickly offering a financial settlement to the victims actually reduces litigation. After a policy of full disclosure and apology was established at the University of Michigan Medical Center to help communicate with wronged patients, the number of lawsuits declined 65%.[13]

Tone in Negative Messages   LO 10-4

Tone—the implied attitude of the author toward the reader and the subject—is particularly important when you want readers to feel that you have taken their requests seriously. Check your draft carefully for positive emphasis and you-attitude (see Chapter 3), both at the level of individual words and at the level of ideas. In many situations, empathizing with your audience will help you create a more humane message.

Figure 10.5 lists some words and phrases to avoid in negative messages. Figure 3.3 in Chapter 3 suggests more negative words to avoid.

Even the physical appearance and timing of a message can convey tone. An obvious form rejection letter suggests that the writer has not given much consideration to the reader's application. An immediate negative suggests that the rejection didn't need any thought. A negative delivered just before a major holiday seems especially unfeeling.

It's easy to get angry in negative situations; avoid that temptation.

Tone is equally important in everyday oral communication of negatives (see Figure 10.6). In these situations, harsh negative tone is frequently labeled incivility or rudeness. A study of 14,000 people in 17 industries found that 98% of them said they had been treated rudely at work, and half said that rudeness occurred at least once a week. That rudeness was expensive. Among workers receiving it,

48% deliberately decreased work effort.

38% deliberately decreased work quality.

78% reported a loss of commitment to the organization.

25% took out frustration on customers.

12% left their job because of it.[14]

Rudeness to customers is, of course, equally damaging. And the rudeness does not have to be directed at them. Customers witnessing even a single rudeness directed at another employee are unlikely to deal with the company again.[15]

Alternative Strategies for Negative Situations

Whenever you face a negative situation, consider recasting it as a positive or persuasive message. Southwest Airlines, the low-cost airline, is famous for saying no to its customers. It says no to such common perks as reserved

Figure 10.5	Avoid These Phrases in Negative Messages
Phrase	**Because**
I am afraid that we cannot	You aren't fearful. Don't hide behind empty phrases.
I am sorry that we are unable	You probably are able to grant the request; you simply choose not to. If you are so sorry about saying no, why don't you change your policy and say *yes*?
I am sure you will agree that	Don't assume that you can read someone's mind.
Unfortunately	*Unfortunately* is negative in itself. It also signals that a refusal is coming.

Figure 10.6	Possible Responses for Some Common Negative Situations
Situation	**Possible response**
Your boss or client asks you to agree on a controversial topic.	I just don't like to get into this topic in the office.
Your co-worker is ranting about a controversial topic.	Yes, that is an important topic. (Then leave quickly.)
As a member of a minority group, you are asked how people in your group would respond: As an older worker, how do you think older workers feel about mandatory weight and blood pressure checks?	Turn the question: As a middle-aged worker, how do *you* think middle-aged people will respond? Sometimes careful humor will work: Yes, we older workers do think that. Also, we all got together across the nation and decided that smoothies should be eliminated.
You are using "should have" statements: You should have been checking with clients weekly.	Use "I want" statements and look to future improvement: In the future, I want you to check with your clients weekly.
You are angry about a problem.	Point out how the problem impacts other people or the company (not just yourself). Work together to find ways to prevent the problem from happening in the future.

seats, meals, and inter-airline baggage transfers. But it recasts all those negatives into its two biggest positives, low-cost fares and conveniently scheduled frequent flights.[16]

Recasting the Situation as a Positive Message

If the negative information will directly lead to a benefit that you know readers want, use the pattern of organization for informative and positive messages:

Situation:	Your airline has been mailing out quarterly statements of frequent-flier miles earned. To save money, you are going to stop mailing statements and ask customers to look up that information at your website.
Negative:	Important Notice: This is your last Preferred Passenger paper statement.
Positive emphasis:	New, convenient online statements will replace this quarterly mailing. Now you can get up-to-the-minute statements of your miles earned. Choose e-mail updates or round-the-clock access to your statement at our website, www.aaaair.com. It's faster, easier, and more convenient.

After Taco Bell had a law firm voluntarily withdraw a suit that questioned the amount of meat in the restaurant chain's ground beef, the company turned the negative situation into a positive. Taco Bell bought full pages in the *Wall Street Journal* and *New York Times* and ran advertisements with a headline, "Thank you for suing us." The company used the rest of the space to discuss the ingredients in its ground beef and to avoid a public relations scandal.[17]

Recasting the Situation as a Persuasive Message

Sometimes a negative situation can be recast as a persuasive message. Often magazines that are raising their rates send a persuasive letter to subscribers urging them to send in renewals early so they can beat the increases.

If your organization has a problem, ask the audience to help solve it. A solution that workers have created will be much easier to implement.

If you are criticizing someone, your real purpose may be to persuade the person to act differently. Chapter 11 offers patterns for such problem-solving persuasive messages.

Varieties of Negative Messages   LO 10-5

Some of the most common negative messages are claims and complaints. Three of the most difficult kinds of negative messages to write are rejections and refusals, disciplinary notices and negative performance reviews, and lay-offs and firings.

Claims and Complaints

Claims and complaint messages are needed when something has gone wrong: you didn't get the files you needed in time for the report; the supplier didn't send enough parts; the copy machine breaks down daily. Many claims and complaints are handled well with a quick phone call or office visit, but sometimes you will need a paper trail.

Technology has certainly influenced the way complaints are processed. United Airlines stopped its customer relations phone service. Complaint responses are now handled by United representatives through e-mail and letters. The company believes customers will get a better quality of feedback.[18] Delta Air Lines has a team of customer service agents who monitor social media applications such as Twitter for real-time complaints. When travelers complain about the company, the agents try to solve problems before they go viral by offering updated gate information or rebooking details. Sometimes they even bend the rules to null complaints in the Twittersphere.[19]

A lot of consumers are angry these days, and organizations should be responsive to their complaints. According to the Edelman Trust Barometer, people believe negative news about an organization with a low trust level after one or two encounters, while people believe positive news only after four or five.[20]

Organizations, like Delta, need fast response times in handling complaints before a situation tarnishes their brand. The speed of complaints is growing faster with websites exclusively dedicated to the issue. Sites such as Angie's List, Consumer Affairs, Planet Feedback, Ripoff Report, Tello, and Yelp offer forums for disgruntled customers. Many of these sites also have smartphone applications that allow consumers to report incidents almost instantaneously. To stay on top of the reviews, new electronic tools are emerging that help organizations scan for key words and monitor reviews related to their brand.

When writing a claim or complaint, you generally will use a direct organization: put a clear statement of the problem in the first sentence. An indirect approach, such as starting with a buffer, may be interpreted as a weak claim.

Give supporting facts—what went wrong, the extent of the damage. Give identifiers such as invoice numbers, warranty codes, and order dates. If this is a claim, specify what is necessary to set things right (be realistic!). Avoid anger and sarcasm; they will only lessen your chances of a favorable settlement. In particular, avoid saying you will never use the company, service, machine again. Such a statement may eliminate your audience's will to rectify the problem. See Figure 10.7 for suggestions for e-mail claims to airlines.

Rejections and Refusals

When you refuse requests from people outside your organization, try to give an alternative if one is available. For example, you may not be able to replace for free an automotive water pump that no longer is on warranty. But you may be able to offer your customer a rebuilt one that is much less expensive than a new pump.

Politeness and length help. In two studies, job applicants preferred rejection letters that said something specific about their good qualities, that phrased the refusal indirectly, that offered a clear explanation of the procedures for making a hiring decision, that offered an alternative (such as another position the applicant might be qualified for), and that were longer.[21] Furthermore, businesses that follow this pattern of organization for rejection letters will retain applicants who still view the organization favorably, who may recommend the organization to others interested in applying there, and who likely will not file lawsuits.[22]

Double-check the words in a refusal to be sure the reason can't backfire if it is applied to other contexts. The statement that a plant is too dangerous for a group tour could be used as evidence against the company in a worker's compensation claim.

Similarly, writing resignation letters for a variety of reasons—leaving a job, opting out of a fellowship—can be a delicate practice and can have serious future implications. Many audiences will see the letter as a statement that their organization is not good enough. The best letters try to neutralize these feelings. A negative and poorly worded resignation letter can impact your chances for receiving a positive recommendation or reference in the future.

Figure 10.7	Airline Complaint Tips

These tips can improve your chances of a favorable response from an airline:

- Use data: flight, reservation, frequent flyer numbers; date, time, exactly what happened, names of personnel.
- Ask for the compensation you want.
- Be realistic. You will not get compensation for a routine delay.
- Be direct and short.
- Stay polite; don't threaten. Particularly don't say you will never fly with them again, because that eliminates their will to compensate you.
- Use correct grammar, punctuation, spelling, and capitalization.
- Start by sending your e-mail through the airline's web page.

Source: Sascha Segan, "How to Complain to the Airlines," May 23, 2010, http://www.frommers.com/articles/6806.html.

When you refuse requests within your organization, use your knowledge of the organization's culture and of the specific individual to craft your message. Some organizations share more negative information than others. Some individuals prefer a direct no; others may find a direct negative insulting. The sample problem at the end of this chapter is a refusal to someone within the company.

Disciplinary Notices and Negative Performance Reviews

Performance reviews, discussed in more detail in Chapter 11, will be positive when they are designed to help a basically good employee improve. But when an employee violates company policy or fails to improve after repeated negative reviews, the company may discipline the employee or build a dossier to support firing him or her.

Present disciplinary notices and negative performance reviews directly, with no buffer. A buffer might encourage the recipient to minimize the message's importance—and might even become evidence in a court case that the employee had not been told to shape up "or else." Cite quantifiable observations of the employee's behavior, rather than generalizations or inferences based on it.

Weak:	Lee is apathetic about work.
Better:	Lee was absent 15 days and late by one hour 6 days in the quarter beginning January 1.
Weak:	Vasu is careless with her written documents.
Better:	Vasu had multiple spelling errors in her last three client letters; a fourth letter omitted the date of the mandatory federal training seminar.

Not all disciplinary notices are as formal as performance reviews. Blanchard and Johnson, of *One Minute Manager* fame, present what they call the One Minute Reprimand. Much of the effectiveness of these reprimands comes from the fact that supervisors tell their employees from the beginning, before any reprimands are needed, that there will be explicit communication about both positive and negative performances. The reprimand itself is to come immediately after negative behavior and specify exactly what is wrong. It distinguishes between positive feelings for the employee and negative feelings for his or her performance in the specific situation.[23]

Layoffs and Firings

If a company is in financial trouble, management needs to communicate the problem clearly. Sharing information and enlisting everyone's help in finding solutions may make it possible to save jobs. Sharing information also means that layoff notices, if they become necessary, will be a formality; they should not be new information to employees.

Give the employee an honest reason for the layoff or firing. Based on guidance from your organization's human resource experts, state the reasons in a way that is clear but does not expose the organization to legal liabilities. Research shows that workers given no explanation for being fired are 10 times more likely to sue than workers who receive a complete explanation.[24]

Show empathy for affected employees; think about how you would feel if you were losing your job. Show how the company will help them with severance pay and other aid, such as job search advice. Remember that many studies show that layoffs may temporarily help the bottom line, but they rarely provide long-term savings. They also hurt the productivity of remaining employees.[25]

Firings for unsatisfactory performance have always been a part of business. Now, however, as technology blurs the line between work and home, firings are also happening for personal reasons, even if the behavior is not tied to work and occurs off-site. The CEO of HBO was asked to resign after he was accused of assaulting his girlfriend in a parking lot. Kaiser Aluminum's CFO had to resign because of a personal relationship with another employee, as did Boeing's former President and CEO Harry Stonecipher.[26]

Information about layoffs and firings is normally delivered orally but accompanied by a written statement explaining severance pay or unemployment benefits that may be available. RadioShack made negative headlines when it fired 400 employees with a two-sentence e-mail.

Using Technology for Negative Messages

As this chapter has said, disastrous news, such as layoffs and firings, should be delivered in person. Sometimes, however, large corporations widely spread geographically have to use electronic media to deliver negative news so all employees hear the news at approximately the same time. Yahoo's CEO Marissa Mayer delivered by e-mail a ban on telecommuting (see Chapter 4 for more information). IBM's CEO Virginia Rometty delivered by a video posted on the company's internal blog an announcement of an earnings drop, the reason for it (employees moving too slowly with opportunities), and a plan to respond more quickly. Both CEOs made headlines and news blogs for weeks with their messages.[27]

A growing technology for negative messages is social media (see Chapter 9 for more on the use of social media). In fact, social media are playing such a large role that Google, Microsoft, and Yahoo offer free services to help companies track references on social media.

Many large corporations now have teams of employees handling negative tweets and Facebook postings. Doing so is a delicate operation. Customers posting to these sites expect prompt responses, an expectation that does not allow corporate writers much time to explore the situation or craft their message.

An ill-conceived response to a posting can easily go viral. When United baggage handlers broke a guitar and the company refused reparations, the musician wrote a song and posted it as a music video, "United Breaks Guitars," on YouTube. In 10 days the video had 3 million views and 14,000 comments. Within four days of the posting, United's stock dropped 10%, the equivalent of $180 million.[28]

Getting into a verbal brawl on a public forum does no good for a business. It is far better to work out a customer problem off-line. If that is not possible, try posting your phone number and asking the customer to call so you can help. Many problems need personal information, such as the customer's credit card number, to solve and cannot be solved on a public forum. After a problem is fixed, companies can respond to further references with a brief, nondefensive statement that they handled the situation (or even better, fixed the problem) and regret the mistake.

When these efforts fail, many companies try to fill the first page of corporate search results with positive material: the corporate website, press releases, flattering articles and blog posts, and other positive material. Most searches have only 10 results on the first page, and most searchers do not go beyond the first page.[29]

Many reputation management consultants note that social media are not effective channels to solve customer complaints. Solutions generally involve back and forth communication, thus expanding the negativity, and end up being resolved in more private communication. Such consultants point out that companies should see to it that better, more preferred channels, such as the phone and websites, are fast and effective at solving problems, so customers will turn to them first.[30]

Companies should also work on maintaining goodwill before problems arise by posting positive information on their web and Facebook pages and by answering user questions on the corporate sites. When McDonald's Canada invited its customers to ask anything they wanted to know, they got some harsh questions: Do Chicken McNuggets have pink sludge? Is your meat rinsed with ammonia? Why don't your burgers rot? In response, McDonald's produced and posted videos taking consumers behind the scenes for meat production.[31]

Solving a Sample Problem

Solving negative problems requires careful analysis. The checklist at the end of the chapter can help you evaluate your draft.

Problem

You're director of employee benefits for a Fortune 500 company. Today, you received the following e-mail:

> From: Michelle Jagtiani
> Subject: Getting My Retirement Benefits
>
> Next Friday will be my last day here. I am leaving [name of company] to take a position at another firm.
>
> Please process a check for my retirement benefits, including both the deductions from my salary and the company's contributions for the last six and a half years. I would like to receive the check by next Friday if possible.

You have bad news for Michelle. Although the company does contribute an amount to the retirement fund equal to the amount deducted for retirement from the employee's paycheck, employees who leave with less than seven years of employment get only their own contributions. Michelle will get back only the money that has been deducted from her own pay, plus 3½% interest compounded quarterly. Her payments and interest come to just over $17,200; the amount could be higher depending on the amount of her last paycheck, which will include compensation for any unused vacation days and sick leave. Furthermore, since the amounts deducted were not considered taxable income, she will have to pay income tax on the money she will receive.

You cannot process the check until after her resignation is effective, so you will mail it to her. You have her home address on file; if she's moving, she needs to let you know where to send the check. Processing the check may take two to three weeks.

Write an e-mail to Michelle.

Analysis of the Problem

Use the analysis questions in the first chapter to help you solve the problem.

1. Who is (are) your audience(s)?

    Michelle Jagtiani. Unless she's a personal friend, we probably wouldn't know why she's leaving and where she's going.

    There's a lot we don't know. She may or may not know much about taxes; she may or may not be able to take advantage of tax-reduction strategies. We can't assume the answers because we wouldn't have them in real life.

2. What are your purposes in communicating?

    To tell her that she will get only her own contributions, plus 3½% interest compounded quarterly; that the check will be mailed to her home address two to three weeks after her last day on the job; and that the money will be taxable as income.

    To build goodwill so that she feels that she has been treated fairly and consistently. To minimize negative feelings she may have.

    To close the door on this subject.

3. What information must your message include?

    When the check will come. The facts that her check will be based on her contributions, not the employer's, and that the money will be taxable income. How lump-sum retirement benefits are calculated. The fact that we have her current address on file but need a new address if she's moving.

4. How can you build support for your position? What reasons or benefits will your audience find convincing?

    Giving the amount currently in her account may make her feel that she is getting a significant sum of money. Suggesting someone who can give free tax advice (if the company offers this as a fringe benefit) reminds her of the benefits of working with the company. Wishing her luck with her new job is a nice touch.

5. What aspects of the total situation may be relevant?

    Since this is right after taxes are due, she may be particularly interested in the tax advice. With the weak economy, she may have been counting on the extra money. On the other hand, most people take another job to get more money, so maybe she is too. We don't know for sure. Since she and I don't know each other, I don't know about her special circumstances.

Discussion of the Sample Solutions

The solution in Figure 10.8 is not acceptable. The subject line gives a bald negative with no reason or alternative. The first sentence has a condescending

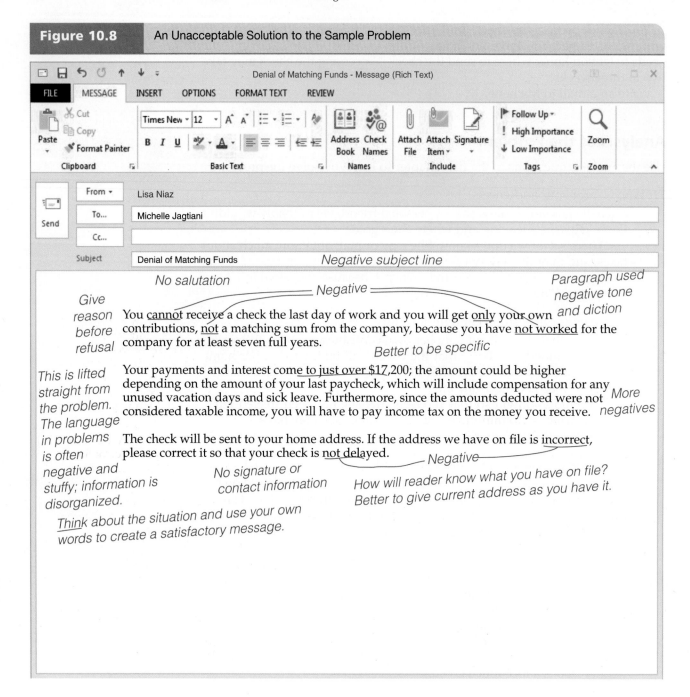

Figure 10.8   An Unacceptable Solution to the Sample Problem

tone that is particularly offensive in negative messages; it also focuses on what is being taken away rather than what remains. Paragraph 2 lacks you-attitude and is vague. The e-mail ends with a negative. There is nothing anywhere in the e-mail to build goodwill.

The solution in Figure 10.9, in contrast, is effective. The policy serves as a buffer and explanation. The negative is stated clearly but is buried in the paragraph to avoid overemphasizing it. Paragraph 2 emphasizes the positive by specifying the amount in the account and the fact that the sum might be even higher.

| Figure 10.9 | An Effective Solution to the Sample Problem |

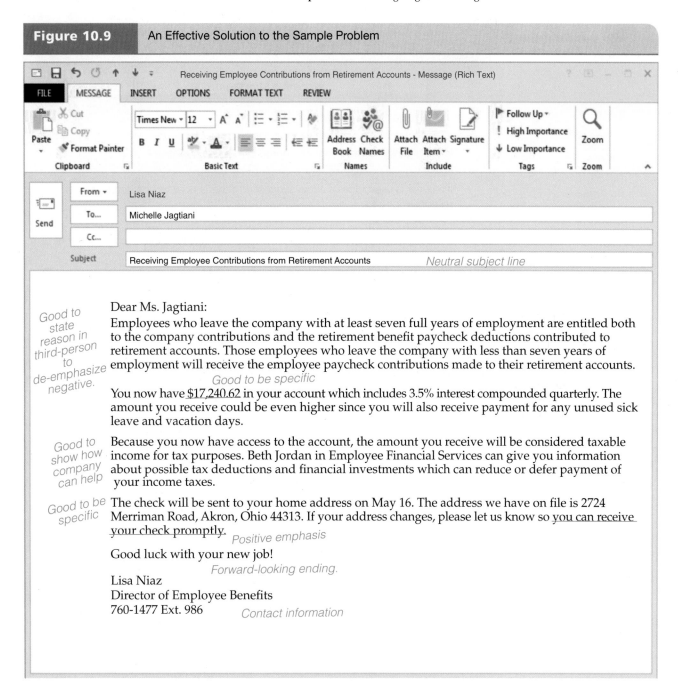

Receiving Employee Contributions from Retirement Accounts - Message (Rich Text)

FILE   MESSAGE   INSERT   OPTIONS   FORMAT TEXT   REVIEW

From ▾   Lisa Niaz

To...   Michelle Jagtiani

Cc...

Subject   Receiving Employee Contributions from Retirement Accounts   *Neutral subject line*

Dear Ms. Jagtiani:

Good to state reason in third-person to de-emphasize negative.
Employees who leave the company with at least seven full years of employment are entitled both to the company contributions and the retirement benefit paycheck deductions contributed to retirement accounts. Those employees who leave the company with less than seven years of employment will receive the employee paycheck contributions made to their retirement accounts.

Good to be specific
You now have $17,240.62 in your account which includes 3.5% interest compounded quarterly. The amount you receive could be even higher since you will also receive payment for any unused sick leave and vacation days.

Good to show how company can help
Because you now have access to the account, the amount you receive will be considered taxable income for tax purposes. Beth Jordan in Employee Financial Services can give you information about possible tax deductions and financial investments which can reduce or defer payment of your income taxes.

Good to be specific
The check will be sent to your home address on May 16. The address we have on file is 2724 Merriman Road, Akron, Ohio 44313. If your address changes, please let us know so you can receive your check promptly. *Positive emphasis*

Good luck with your new job!
Forward-looking ending.

Lisa Niaz
Director of Employee Benefits
760-1477 Ext. 986   *Contact information*

Paragraph 3 contains the additional negative information that the amount will be taxable but offers the alternative that it may be possible to reduce taxes. The writer builds goodwill by suggesting a specific person the reader could contact.

Paragraph 4 tells the reader what address is in the company files (Michelle may not know whether the files are up-to-date), asks that she update it if necessary, and ends with the reader's concern: getting her check promptly.

The final paragraph ends on a positive note. This generalized goodwill is appropriate when the writer does not know the reader well.

	Checklist
	Negative Messages

◻ Is the subject line appropriate?

◻ Is the organization and content appropriate for the audience?

◻ If a buffer is used, does it avoid suggesting either a positive or a negative response?

◻ Is the reason, if it is given, presented before the refusal? Is the reason watertight, with no loopholes?

◻ Is the negative information clear?

◻ Is an alternative given if a good one is available? Does the message provide all the information needed to act on the alternative but leave the choice up to the audience?

◻ Does the last paragraph avoid repeating the negative information?

◻ Is tone acceptable—not defensive, but not cold, preachy, or arrogant either?

Originality in a negative message may come from

◻ An effective buffer, if one is appropriate.

◻ A clear, complete statement of the reason for the refusal.

◻ A good alternative, clearly presented, which shows that you're thinking about what the audience really needs.

◻ Adding details that show you're thinking about a specific organization and the specific people in that organization.

Summary by Learning Objectives

LO 10-1   **Different purposes of negative messages.**

A good negative message conveys the negative information clearly while maintaining as much goodwill as possible. The goal is to make recipients feel that they have been taken seriously, that the decision is fair and reasonable, and that they would have made the same decision. A secondary purpose is to reduce or eliminate future communication on the same subject.

LO 10-2   **Different ways to organize negative messages.**

The best way to organize negative messages depends on the particular audiences and situations involved. Figure 10.1 suggests possible organizations.

LO 10-3 **Ways to construct the different parts of negative messages.**

- A buffer is a neutral or positive statement that allows you to delay the negative message. Buffers must put the audience in a good frame of mind, not give the bad news but not imply a positive answer either, and provide a natural transition to the body of the message. Use a buffer only when the audience values harmony or when the buffer serves a purpose in addition to simply delaying the negative.

- A good reason prepares the audience for the negative and must be watertight. Give several reasons only if all are watertight and are of comparable importance. Omit the reason for the refusal if it is weak or if it makes your organization look bad. Do not hide behind company policy.

- Make the refusal crystal clear.

- Giving the audience an alternative or a compromise
  - Offers the audience another way to get what they want.
  - Suggests that you really care about the audience and about helping to meet their needs.
  - Allows you to end on a positive note and to present yourself and your organization as positive, friendly, and helpful.

LO 10-4 **How to improve the tone of negative messages.**

Tone—the implied attitude of the author toward the reader and the subject—is particularly important when you have to convey negative news. Check your draft carefully for positive emphasis and you-attitude (see Chapter 3), both at the level of individual words and at the level of ideas.

LO 10-5 **Ways to construct different kinds of negative messages.**

Many negative situations can be redefined as informative, positive, or persuasive messages. Most of the others follow the suggested structures of Figure 10.1.

LO 10-6 **How, and how not, to use technology for negative messages.**

- Disastrous news, such as layoffs and firings, should be delivered in person. Sometimes, however, large corporations widely spread geographically have to use electronic media to deliver negative news so all employees hear the news at approximately the same time.

- Handling negative tweets and Facebook postings is a delicate operation; an ill-conceived response to a posting can easily go viral.

- Social media are not effective channels to solve customer complaints. Channels such as the phone and websites are fast and effective at solving problems.

Continuing Case

The All-Weather Case, set in an HR department in a manufacturing company, extends through all 19 chapters and is available at www.mhhe.com/locker11e. The portion for this chapter asks students to revise a negative message.

Exercises and Cases

*Go to www.mhhe.com/locker11e for additional Exercises and Cases.

10.1 Reviewing the Chapter

1. What are the purposes of negative messages? (LO 10-1)

2. What are the reasons behind the patterns of organization for negative messages in different situations (Figure 10.1)? (LO 10-2)

3. What are the parts of negative messages? How may those parts be changed for different contexts? (LO 10-3)

4. When should you not use a buffer? (LO 10-3)

5. When should you not apologize? (LO 10-3)

6. What are some ways you can maintain a caring tone in negative messages? (LO 10-4)

7. What are some different varieties of negative messages? What are some examples from the chapter text and sidebars? (LO 10-5)

8. What are some cautions for using technology to convey negative news? (LO 10-6)

10.2   Reviewing Grammar

Negative news is frequently placed in dependent clauses to help de-emphasize it. Unfortunately, some dependent clauses and phrases are dangling or misplaced modifiers. Do the exercise from Appendix B on improving modifiers (B.6) to help you learn to recognize this error.

10.3   Letters for Discussion—Credit Refusal

As director of customer service at C'est Bon, an upscale furniture store, you manage the store's credit. Today you are going to reject an application from Frank Steele. Although his income is fairly high, his last two payments on his college loans were late, and he has three bank credit cards, all charged to the upper limit, on which he's made just the minimum payment for the past three months.

The following letters are possible approaches to giving him the news. How well does each message meet the criteria in the checklist for negative messages?

1.

Dear Mr. Steele:

Your request to have a C'est Bon charge account shows that you are a discriminating shopper. C'est Bon sells the finest merchandise available.

Although your income is acceptable, records indicate that you carry the maximum allowable balances on three bank credit cards. Moreover, two recent payments on your student loans have not been made in a timely fashion. If you were given a C'est Bon charge account, and if you charged a large amount on it, you might have difficulty paying the bill, particularly if you had other unforeseen expenses (car repair, moving, medical emergency) or if your income dropped suddenly. If you were unable to repay, with your other debt you would be in serious difficulty. We would not want you to be in such a situation, nor would you yourself desire it.

Please reapply in six months.

Sincerely,

2.

Dear Frank:

No, you can't have a C'est Bon credit card—at least not right now. Get your financial house in order and try again.

Fortunately for you, there's an alternative. Put what you want on layaway. The furniture you want will be held for you, and paying a bit each week or month will be good self-discipline.

Enjoy your C'est Bon furniture!

Sincerely,

3.

Dear Mr. Steele:

Over the years, we've found that the best credit risks are people who pay their bills promptly. Since two of your student loan payments have been late, we won't extend store credit to you right now. Come back with a record of six months of on-time payments of all bills, and you'll get a different answer.

You might like to put the furniture you want on layaway. A $50 deposit holds any item you want. You have six months to pay, and you save interest charges.

You might also want to take advantage of one of our Saturday Seminars. On the first Saturday of each month at 11 AM, our associates explain one topic related to furniture and interior decorating. Upcoming topics are

How to Wallpaper a Room	February 5
Drapery Options	March 6
Persian Carpets	April 1

Sincerely,

10.4   E-mail Situations for Discussion—Sending a Negative News E-mail

Read the following situations and decide how you would handle them. You know that you will need to inform your boss, but how will you report what happened? Will you apologize? What channel will you use? Discuss as a class.

■ Your boss was looking for a new part-time assistant, just for the summer. You knew a friend of yours was looking for a summer job, so you referred him to your boss. Your boss hired your friend on your recommendation, but you've learned from your friend that this is not quite what he had in mind. Your friend is tired of getting up early to come to the office and doesn't feel like being an assistant anymore. He is thinking about simply not showing up for work next week. How do you let your boss know what is going on?

■ You were driving the company car to go pick up some coffee for everyone, when you received a text from the office secretary. She added a few more coffee orders to your list, and you texted her back: "OK, got it." However, you weren't paying attention and got into a minor fender bender. You know that texting while driving could be a large liability for your company. What should you do? What will you tell your boss?

■ You are supervising two interns for the summer, and one has come to you with a complaint about sexual harassment. She noted that the other intern makes her feel uncomfortable when he makes sexual jokes and comments toward her. You know that you need to report the incidents. What will you say to your boss and the HR representative?

10.5   E-mails for Discussion—Ending a Tradition

Your boss has asked you to draft a companywide e-mail that explains a change in policy. Previously, the company would buy a cake for each employee's birthday and there would be a small celebration in the office. However, due to budget cuts, the company will no longer be purchasing cakes for each employee. Your boss is worried that this bad news will hurt office morale, and wants you to break the news gently. Analyze the following e-mails. How well does each relate the news? How well does each message follow the negative messages checklist?

Subject: No more cake

Hello everyone,

We are sending this e-mail to let everyone know that due to budget cuts, we will no longer be purchasing cakes for employee birthday parties. Sorry! If you want to bring in your own cake, that would be fine.

Subject: Budget Cut Information

We regret to inform you that due to some changes to the current budget, we have decided that the company can no longer afford to purchase birthday cakes for each employee's birthday. We do, however, encourage everyone to bring in treats or cake on their own birthday so we can still continue with the office birthday tradition.

Thank you for your understanding!

Management.

Subject: Cake

This e-mail is to inform you that the company will no longer be buying cakes for employee's birthdays. It has simply become too expensive for the company to buy that many cakes every single year.

I would like to remind everyone, before you start sending out angry e-mail replies, that our country has been in an economic downturn and we are still recovering from that. Look at the bigger picture and try to appreciate the fact that you all still have jobs.

Thanks.

10.6   Revising a Negative Message

Rewrite the following negative message so it follows the guidelines for negative messages:

Dear Valued Employee:

I'm afraid the company will not be able to grant you your requested vacation time at this particular time. You recently took your allotted time of maternity leave, and the company has a policy that states employees may not take vacation time so soon after a long leave (even if it was for a baby).

The company also had to pay for your replacement to work here while you were on maternity leave, so we would appreciate it if you would clock some hours in the office.

I can recommend to you that you try submitting your vacation request again in approximately 10–12 weeks. Other than that, there is nothing that I can do for you.

We are so glad to have you as a valued employee here at VegCo.

Have a Veggie-riffic day!

Claire- HR

10.7   Practicing Negative Responses for the Office

Write a brief response for these office situations. Remember, you do not want to alienate your co-workers.

1. Turn down a request to volunteer. (What are some responses that almost guarantee getting recruited?)
2. Turn down a request to contribute to a fund-raiser.
3. Ask a colleague who loves to spread hurtful gossip to please stop sharing it with you.
4. Ask a colleague to wipe her sweat off the piece of equipment she has been using before you in the company gym.
5. Ask colleagues to refrain from using their electronic devices during your meeting.
6. Ask a colleague to take down an unflattering picture of you from his Facebook page.
7. Turn down a lunch request from a colleague who has already asked you several times before.

   In small groups, discuss your answers. Pick your best answer for each situation and share it with the class.

10.8   Notifying College Seniors That They May Not Graduate

State University asks students to file an application to graduate one term before they actually plan to graduate. The application lists the courses the student has already had and those he or she will take in the last term. Your office reviews the lists to see that the student will meet the requirements for total number of hours, hours in the major, and general education requirements. Some students have forgotten a requirement or not taken enough courses and cannot graduate unless they take more courses than those they have listed.

As your instructor directs,

Write form e-mail messages to the following audiences. Leave blanks for the proposed date of graduation and specific information that must be merged into the message:

a. Students who have not taken enough total hours.

b. Students who have not fulfilled all the requirements for their majors.

c. Students who are missing one or more general education courses.

d. Advisers of students who do not meet the requirements for graduation.

10.9 Correcting a Mistake

Today, as you reviewed some cost figures, you realized they didn't fit with the last monthly report you filed. You had pulled the numbers together from several sources, and you're not sure what happened. Maybe you miscopied, or didn't save the final version after you'd checked all the numbers. But whatever the cause, you've found errors in three categories. You gave your boss the following totals:

Personnel	$2,843,490
Office supplies	$43,500
Telephone	$186,240

E-mail your boss to correct the information.

As your instructor directs,

Write e-mail messages for the following situations:

a. The correct numbers are

Personnel	$2,845,490
Office supplies	$34,500
Telephone	$186,420

b. The correct numbers are

Personnel	$2,845,490
Office supplies	$84,500
Telephone	$468,240

Variations for each situation:

1. Your boss has been out of the office; you know she hasn't seen the data yet.

2. Your boss gave a report to the executive committee this morning using your data.

Hints:

- How serious is the mistake in each situation?
- In which situations, if any, should you apologize?
- Should you give the reason for the mistake? Why or why not?
- How do your options vary depending on whether your job title gives you responsibility for numbers and accounting?

10.10 Vetoing an Employee Benefit

Your newspaper ran an article on the front page of the business section featuring a local business that provides employees with unlimited vacation days. Now your Employees Council has come to you requesting the same perk. They say they are all responsible adults who would see that their work is covered, and note that it would be an excellent recruitment tool for top-notch people (and you are the owner of an expanding company). You promised to consider their request carefully, and you have. Now you owe them an answer. Write an e-mail to send to all your employees telling them you will not be offering that perk. When writing, consider these questions:

- Is your audience uniform? Do all your employees think unlimited vacation is a good idea?
- How should you organize your e-mail?
- Where can you use positive tone and you-attitude in your e-mail?
- What explanation will you give?
- How will the size of your company affect your explanation (20 employees might need different reasons than 100 employees)?
- Is there an alternative you can propose?

10.11 Discussing an Apology Letter

Reread the sidebar "A Successful Apology" on page 299; then read Rahman's apology at https:// jawbone.com/ up/guarantee. In small groups, discuss the following questions:

- Which pattern of organization (Figure 10.1) does the apology use?
- How well does the apology letter follow the negative messages checklist?

- How effective do you think this letter was? Why?
- If you were one of Jawbone's customers with a defective UP wristband, how would you react to this letter? Why?
- Is the full refund (alternative) enough to appease angry customers?
- What is the tone of the apology letter?
- If you could make any changes to this letter, what would they be?

10.12   Preparing a Class Civility Policy

Create a civility policy for your business communication classroom.

- What oral behaviors do you want to address?
- What nonverbal behaviors should you address?
- What negative consequences could your guidelines have?

Watch the tone of your policy to ensure it follows your own civility guidelines.

1. Write a draft of a policy yourself. Address at least six oral behaviors and four nonverbal behaviors.

2. In small groups, compare policies. Construct a policy as a group, including all the good ideas. Post your group's draft on your class website.

3. Read the policies of the other groups in your class. In your same small group, revise your group policy into a final draft and submit it to your instructor. Include an e-mail explaining your choices for inclusions and their wording. Also explain why you rejected some items.

10.13   Telling Employees to Remove Personal Websites

You're director of management and information systems in your organization. At your monthly briefing for management, a vice president complained that some employees have posted personal web pages on the company's web server.

"It looks really unprofessional to have stuff about cats and children and musical instruments. How can people do this?"

You took the question literally. "Well, some people have authorization to post material—price changes, job listings, marketing information. Someone who has authorization could put up anything."

Another manager said, "I don't think it's so terrible—after all, there aren't any links from our official pages to these personal pages."

A third person said, "But we're paying for what's posted—so we pay for server space and connect time. Maybe it's not much right now, but as more and more people become web-literate, the number of people putting up unauthorized pages could spread. We should put a stop to this now."

The vice president agreed. "The website is carefully designed to present an image of our organization.

Personal pages are dangerous. Can you imagine the flak we'd get if someone posted links to pornography?"

You said, "I don't think that's very likely. If it did happen, as system administrator, I could remove the page."

The third speaker said, "I think we should remove all the pages. Having any at all suggests that our people have so much extra time that they're playing on the web. That suggests that our prices are too high and may make some people worry about quality. In fact, I think that we need a new policy prohibiting personal pages on the company's web server. And any pages that are already up should be removed."

A majority of the managers agreed and told you to write a message to all employees. Create an e-mail message to tell employees that you will remove the personal pages already posted and that no more will be allowed.

Hints:

- Suggest other ways that people can post personal web pages.
- Give only reasons that are watertight and make the company look good.

10.14   Refusing to Waive a Fee

As the licensing program coordinator for your school, you evaluate proposals from vendors who want to make or sell merchandise with the school's name, logo, or mascot. If you find the product acceptable, the vendor pays a $250 licensing fee and then 6.5% of the wholesale cost of the merchandise manufactured (whether or not it is sold). The licensing fee helps to support the cost of your office; the 6.5% royalty goes into a student scholarship fund. At well-known universities or those with loyal students and alumni, the funds from such a program can add up to hundreds of thousands of dollars a year.

On your desk today is a proposal from a current student, Meg Winston.

I want to silk-screen and sell T-shirts printed with the name of the school, the mascot, and the words "We're Number One!" (A copy of the design I propose is enclosed.) I ask that you waive the $250 licensing fee you normally require and limit the 6.5% royalty only to those T-shirts actually sold, not to all those made.

I am putting myself through school by using student loans and working 30 hours a week. I just don't have $250. In my marketing class, we've done feasibility analyses, and I've determined that the shirts can be sold if the price is low enough. I hope to market these shirts in an independent study project with Professor Doulin, building on my marketing project earlier this term. However, my calculations show that I cannot price the shirts competitively if just one shirt must bear the 6.5% royalty for all the shirts produced in a batch. I will of course pay the 6.5% royalty on all shirts sold and not returned. I will produce the shirts in small batches (50–100 at a time). I am willing to donate any manufactured but unsold shirts to the athletic program so that you will know I'm not holding out on you.

By waiving this fee, you will show that this school really wants to help students get practical experience in business, as the catalog states. I will work hard to promote these shirts by getting the school president, the coaches, and campus leaders to endorse them, pointing out that the money goes to the scholarship fund. The shirts themselves will promote school loyalty, both now and later when we're alumni who can contribute to our alma mater.

I look forward to receiving the "go-ahead" to market these shirts.

The design and product are acceptable under your guidelines. However, you've always enforced the fee structure across the board, and you see no reason to make an exception now. Whether the person trying to sell merchandise is a student or not doesn't matter; your policy is designed to see that the school benefits whenever it is used to sell something. Students aren't the only ones whose cash flow is limited; many businesses would find it easier to get into the potentially lucrative business of selling clothing, school supplies, and other items with the school name or logo if they got the same deal Meg is asking for. (The policy also lets the school control the kinds of items on which its name appears.) Just last week, your office confiscated about 400 T-shirts and shorts made by a company that had used the school name on them without permission; the company has paid the school $7,500 in damages.

Write a letter to Meg rejecting her special requests. She can get a license to produce the T-shirts, but only if she pays the $250 licensing fee and the royalty on all shirts made.

10.15 Correcting Misinformation

You're the director of the city's Division of Water. Your mail today contains this letter:

When we bought our pool, the salesman told us that you would give us a discount on the water bill when we fill the pool. Please start the discount immediately. I tried to call you three times and got nothing but busy signals.

Sincerely,

Larry Shadburn-Butler

Larry Shadburn-Butler

The salesperson was wrong. You don't provide discounts for pools (or anything else). At current rates, filling a pool with a garden hose costs from $8.83 (for a 1,800-gallon pool) to $124.67 (for 26,000 gallons) in the city. Filling a pool from any other water source would cost more. Rates are 30% higher in the suburbs and 50% higher in unincorporated rural areas. And you don't have enough people to answer phones. You tried a voice mail system but eliminated it when you found people didn't have time to process all the messages that were left. But the city budget doesn't allow you to hire more people.

As your instructor directs,

a. Write a letter to Mr. Shadburn-Butler.

b. Write a letter to all the stores that sell swimming pools, urging them to stop giving customers misinformation.

c. Write a notice for the one-page newsletter that you include with quarterly water bills. Assume that you can have half a page for your information.

10.16   Analyzing Job Rejection Letters

Here are three rejections letters to an applicant who applied for an accounting position.

1. We realize that the application process for the accounting position at AlphaBank required a substantial amount of thought, time, and effort on your part. Therefore, we would like to express our sincere appreciation for your willingness to participate in the search process.

   The task of selecting a final candidate was difficult and challenging due to the quality of the applicant pool. We regret to inform you that we selected another candidate who we believe will best meet the needs of AlphaBank.

   We thank your for your interest in employment at AlphaBank and extend our best wishes as you pursue your professional goals.

2. Thank you for your interest in the accounting position at AlphaBank. I'm sorry to inform you that you were not one of the finalists. The position has now been filled.

   The search committee and I wish you the best in your future employment searches.

3. Thank you for your interest in the accounting position at AlphaBank.

   I'm sorry to inform you that the search committee has decided to offer the position to another candidate. This was an extremely difficult decision for us to make. We were all impressed with your résumé and credentials.

   Again, thank you for your interest in AlphaBank.

Analyze these three job rejection letters by answering the following questions:

- Do these letters use buffers? If so, how effective are they?
- What reasons do the letters give, if any?
- Does the letter attempt to build goodwill with the audience? If yes, how so?
- Do any of the letters offer an alternative?
- How do you think recipients will react to each of the letters? Which (if any) are more preferable?

As your instructor directs,

a. Discuss your findings in a small group.
b. Present your findings orally to the class.
c. Present your findings in an e-mail to your instructor.

10.17   Creating Equal Work Distribution

You noticed recently that Clare, the woman who works next to you at a call center, takes extended lunches and makes a lot of personal phone calls. As the result of her phone calls and breaks, you and your co-workers complete more work throughout the day. After discussing the situation with a close friend, you decide you are going to tell the boss about her behavior.

As your instructor directs,

a. Write an e-mail to your boss in which you discuss Clare's behavior and ask for a resolution.

b. Partner with a classmate and role-play the situation of telling the boss. One of you is the employee and one of you is the boss.
c. Partner with a classmate and role-play the situation of confronting Clare. One of you is the employee and one of you is Clare.

Hints:

- How can you deliver the negative news without sounding like a tattletale?
- How can you make the situation seem severe enough so that your boss takes action?

10.18 Turning Down a Faithful Client

You are Midas Investment Services' specialist in estate planning. You give talks to various groups during the year about estate planning. You ask nonprofit groups (churches, etc.) just to reimburse your expenses; you charge for-profit groups a fee plus expenses. These fees augment your income nicely, and the talks also are marvelous exposure for you and your company.

Every February for the past five years, Gardner Manufacturing Company has hired you to conduct an eight-hour workshop (two hours every Monday night for four weeks) on retirement and estate planning for its employees who are over 60 or who are thinking of taking early retirement. These workshops are popular and have generated clients for your company. The session last February went smoothly, as you have come to expect.

Today, out of the blue, you got a letter from Hope Goldberger, director of employee benefits at Gardner, asking you to conduct the workshops every Tuesday evening *next* month at your usual fee. She didn't say whether this is an extra series or whether this will replace next February's series.

You can't do it. Your spouse is giving an invited paper at an international conference in Paris next month, and the two of you are taking your children, ages 13 and 9, on a three-week trip to Europe. (You've made arrangements with school authorities to have the kids miss three weeks of classes.) You've been looking forward to and planning the trip for eight months.

Unfortunately, Midas Investment Services is a small group, and the only other person who knows anything about estate planning is a terrible speaker. You could suggest a friend at another financial management company, but you don't want Gardner to turn to someone else permanently; you enjoy doing the workshops and find them a good way to get leads.

Write the letter to Ms. Goldberger.

10.19 Getting Information from a Co-worker

Your boss has been pressuring you because you are weeks late turning in a termination report. However, you cannot begin your section of the report until your colleague, Matt Churetta, finishes his section. Right now, he is the problem. Here is a series of e-mail exchanges between you and Matt:

7/25/2014

Matt,

The boss wants the termination report now. Send over your section as soon as you finish.

Thanks,

Matt's reply:

7/31/2014

My apologies about the report.

On another note, I'm waiting to see my oncology surgeon to see what the course of treatment will be for the esophageal cancer. I will keep you posted on the process.

Please let me know if there is anything else coming up.

Thanks,

8/15/2014

Matt,

I had no idea that you are dealing with esophageal cancer. Definitely keep me posted on your condition. Best wishes as you work through your treatment.

I need your section of the termination report as soon as you finish it. The boss has been waiting patiently for the finished version.

Thanks,

Matt's reply:

> 8/26/2014
>
> Report is coming along. The last two weeks have been difficult dealing with all the tests, doctors' appointments, etc. I will beat this deal!!!
>
> Take Care,

It is now September, and over a month has passed from the termination report's original due date. While you are sympathetic to Matt's situation, the boss is demanding the finished report.

As your instructor directs,

a. Write an e-mail to Matt telling him you have to have his portion of the report as soon as possible.

You are concerned for your job security, as well as his, if this report is not finalized soon.

b. Write an e-mail to your boss explaining the situation.

c. Write an e-mail to your instructor that focuses on the ethical choices you had to make while constructing the two messages.

10.20 Sending Negative Messages to Real Audiences

As your instructor directs, write a negative letter that responds to one of the following scenarios:

■ Write a letter to the owner of a restaurant where you received poor service.

■ Write a letter to a company whose product unsatisfactorily met your expectations or needs.

■ Identify a current political topic on which you disagree with your congressional representative. Write a letter that outlines your views for him/her and calls for change.

■ Identify a television advertisement with which you disagree. Write a letter to the company explaining your position and request that the advertisement be altered or taken off the air.

Hints:

■ For all of these scenarios, your main goal should be to promote change.

■ Express your complaint as positively as possible.

■ Remember to consider your audience's needs; how can you build support for your position?

Notes

1. Robert I. Sutton, *The No Asshole Rule: Building a Civilized Workplace and Surviving One That Isn't* (New York: Warner Business Books, 2007), 45–48.
2. L. Gordon Crovitz, "The Business of Restoring Trust," *Wall Street Journal*, January 31, 2011, A13.
3. Ben Levisohn, "Getting More Workers to Whistle," *Business-Week*, January 28, 2008, 18.
4. Alan Mulally, "Get Honest Feedback," *Bloomberg Business-week*, April 12, 2012, 95.
5. Peter D. Timmerman and Wayne Harrison, "The Discretionary Use of Electronic Media: Four Considerations for Bad News Bearers," *Journal of Business Communication* 42, no. 4 (2005): 379–89.
6. Kitty O. Locker, "Factors in Reader Responses to Negative Letters: Experimental Evidence for Changing What We Teach," *Journal of Business and Technical Communication* 13, no. 1 (January 1999): 21.
7. Ibid., 25–26.
8. Sharon S. Brehm and Jack W. Brehm, *Psychological Reactance: A Theory of Freedom and Control* (New York: Academic Press, 1981), 3.
9. Elizabeth Bernstein, "I'm Very, Very, Very Sorry . . . Really?" *Wall Street Journal*, October 19, 2010, D1, D2.
10. "American Airlines Apologizes to Top Customers for Flight Woes," *USAToday.com*, September 24, 2012,

http://travel.usatoday.com/flights/story/2012/09/24/american-airlines-apologizes-to-top-customers-for-flight-woes/57824790/1.
11. hallmark@update.hallmark.com, e-mail message to author, May 8, 2007.
12. Scott McCartney, "What Airlines Do When You Complain," *Wall Street Journal*, March 20, 2007, D1; and Nick Wingfield, "Steve Jobs Offers Rare Apology Credit for iPhone," *Wall Street Journal*, September 7, 2007, B1.
13. Janet Paskin, "Don't Apologize," *Bloomberg Businessweek*, April 22, 2013, 88.
14. Christine Porath and Christine Pearson, "The Price of Incivility: Lack of Respect Hurts Morale—And the Bottom Line," *Harvard Business Review* 91, no. 1–2 (January–February 2013): 115–21.
15. Ibid., 116, 118.
16. William Ury, *The Power of a Positive No: How to Say No and Still Get to Yes* (New York: Bantam, 2007), 19.
17. Nathan Becker, "Taco Bell Plans Spin as Critic Drops Beef," *Wall Street Journal*, April 20, 2011, B7.
18. "United Airlines to Unplug Number of Complaints," *Wall Street Journal*, February 11, 2009, D6.
19. Scott McCartney, "The Airlines' Squeaky Wheels Turn to Twitter," *Wall Street Journal*, October 28, 2010, D1, D5.
20. Crovitz, "The Business of Restoring Trust."

21. Stephen W. Gilliland et al., "Improving Applicants' Reactions to Rejection Letters: An Application of Fairness Theory," *Personnel Psychology* 54, no. 3 (2001): 669–704; Robert E. Ployhart, Karen Holcombe Ehrhart, and Seth C. Hayes, "Using Attributions to Understand the Effects of Explanations on Applicant Reactions: Are Reactions Consistent with the Covariation Principle?" *Journal of Applied Social Psychology* 35, no. 2 (2005): 259–96.

22. John P. Hausknecht, David V. Day, and Scott C. Thomas, "Applicant Reactions to Selection Procedures: An Updated Model and Meta-Analysis," *Personnel Psychology* 57, no. 3 (2004): 639–84.

23. Kenneth Blanchard and Spencer Johnson, *The One Minute Manager* (New York: William Morrow, 1982), 59.

24. Dana Mattioli, Joann S. Lublin, and Rachel Emma Silverman, "Bad Call: How Not to Fire a Worker," *Wall Street Journal*, September 9, 2011, B2.

25. Carol Hymowitz, "Though Now Routine, Bosses Still Stumble During Layoff Process," *Wall Street Journal*, June 25, 2007, B1.

26. Carol Hymowitz, "Personal Boundaries Shrink as Companies Punish Bad Behavior," *Wall Street Journal*, June 18, 2007, B1.

27. Claire Suddath, "I'm Sorry to Have to Say This . . . : The Right Way for a CEO to Deliver Bad News," *Bloomberg Businessweek,* May 13, 2013, 80.

28. Jonah Berger, *Contagious: Why Things Catch On* (New York: Simon & Schuster, 2013), 111–12.

29. Anne Fisher, "Getting Slammed Online? How to Do Damage Control," *CNNMoney,* July 27, 2012, http://management.fortune.cnn.com/2012/07/27/getting-slammed-online-how-to-do-damage-control/.

30. Matt Dixon and Lara Ponomareff, "Should You Bother Using Social Media to Serve Customers?" *HBR Blog Network,* December 10, 2012, http://blogs.hbr.org/cs/2012/12/should_you_bother_using_social.html.

31. Danielle Sacks, "Can You Hear Me Now?" *Fast Company,* February 2013, 39.

11 Crafting Persuasive Messages

Chapter Outline

NEWSWORTHY COMMUNICATION

What's in a Name?

Using names and slang for Native Americans as mascots has been contentious for decades. Protests by Native American groups have helped convince most sports leagues and teams in the United States to change to less offensive mascots.

There are, however, some notable holdouts. In May 2013, Washington Redskins owner Dan Snyder declared that he would "never change the name" of his National Football League team, even in the face of a proposed law that would revoke trademarks based on racist language.

In response to Snyder's declaration, 10 members of the U.S. Congress wrote a letter, not to threaten Snyder, but to persuade him to make the choice to change the team's name. In the letter, they used several persuasive strategies:

■ They made a direct request for Snyder to change the name in the first sentence of the letter.

■ They anticipated his objections by acknowledging the "complexities involved in changing" the Redskins' name.

■ They explained the effects of the proposed law and cited widespread support for the law among Native American groups.

■ They attempted to build on common beliefs by quoting from the NFL's "Diversity Mission Statement."

■ They appealed to Snyder's emotions by describing the response to racist mascots among Native American youth.

■ They closed the letter with a request to work *with* Snyder "to find a solution to this important matter."

Well-written persuasive messages can be powerful, but even those messages sometimes take additional persuasion to bring change.

Source: "Read the Letter Congress Members Sent to D.C. NFL Team Owner Dan Snyder," *Indian Country Today Media Network,* May 29, 2013, http://indiancountrytodaymedianetwork.com/2013/05/29/read-letter-congress-members-sent-dc-nfl-team-owner-dan-snyder-149588.

After studying this chapter, you will know how to

LO 11-1   Identify the purposes of persuasive messages.

LO 11-2   Analyze a persuasive situation.

LO 11-3   Identify basic persuasive strategies.

LO 11-4   Write persuasive direct requests.

LO 11-5   Write persuasive problem-solving messages.

LO 11-6   Write sales and fund-raising messages.

LO 11-7   Use technology for persuasive messages.

Persuasion is almost universal in good business communications. If you are giving people information, you are persuading them to consider it good information, to remember it, or to use it. If you are giving people negative news, you are trying to persuade them to accept it. If you work for a company, you are a "sales representative" for it. Your job depends on its success.

In his book, *To Sell Is Human,* Daniel Pink reports the results of a large survey of full-time U.S. employees asking them what they did at work. These were the two major findings:

1. "People are now spending about 40 percent of their time at work engaged in non-sales selling—persuading, influencing, and convincing others in ways that don't involve anyone making a purchase. Across a range of professions, we are devoting roughly twenty-four minutes of every hour to moving others.

2. People consider this aspect of their work crucial to their professional success—even in excess of the considerable amount of time they devote to it."[1]

In our work, some communications seem more obviously persuasive to us than others. Employees try to persuade their supervisors to institute flex hours or casual Fridays; supervisors try to persuade workers to keep more accurate records, thus reducing time spent correcting errors; or to follow healthier lifestyles, thus reducing health benefit costs. You may find yourself persuading your colleagues to accept your ideas, your staff to work overtime on a rush project, and your boss to give you a raise.

Whether you're selling safety equipment or ideas, effective persuasion is based on accurate logic, effective emotional appeal, and credibility or trust. Reasons have to be ones the audience finds important; emotional appeal is based on values the audience cares about; credibility depends on your character and reputation.

Purposes of Persuasive Messages   **LO 11-1**

Persuasive messages include requests, proposals and recommendations, sales and fund-raising messages, job application letters, and efforts to change people's behavior, such as collection letters, criticisms or performance reviews where you want people to improve behavior, and public-service ads designed to reduce behaviors such as drunken driving or increase behaviors such as supporting charities. Reports are persuasive messages if they recommend action.

This chapter gives general guidelines for persuasive messages. Chapter 17 discusses proposals; reports are the subject of Chapter 18. Chapter 13 covers job application letters.

All persuasive messages have several purposes:

Primary purpose

- To have the audience act or change beliefs.

Secondary purposes

- To build a good image of the communicator.

- To build a good image of the communicator's organization.

- To cement a good relationship between the communicator and audience.

- To overcome any objections that might prevent or delay action.

- To reduce or eliminate future communication on the same subject so the message doesn't create more work for the communicator.

Analyzing Persuasive Situations LO 11-2

Choose a persuasive strategy based on your answers to the five questions in Figure 11.1. Use these questions to analyze persuasive situations:

UNICEF combines photos and text on its website to present persuasive arguments for supporting its efforts to aid the hungry, sick, and homeless. This screen features a nutrition treatment center.

Source: http://www.unicef.org/photography/photo_2013.php#UNI130560

Figure 11.1	Questions for Analyzing Persuasive Messages

1. What do you want people to do?
2. What objections, if any, will the audience have?
3. How strong is your case?
4. What kind of persuasion is best for the situation?
5. What kind of persuasion is best for the organization and the culture?

1. What Do You Want People to Do?

Identify the specific action you want and the person who has the power to do it. If your goal requires several steps, specify what you want your audience to do *now*. For instance, your immediate goal may be to have people come to a meeting or let you make a presentation, even though your long-term goal is a major sale or a change in policy.

2. What Objections, If Any, Will the Audience Have?

If you're asking for something that requires little time, money, or physical effort and for an action that's part of the person's regular duties, the audience is likely to have few objections.

However, that is often not the case, and you'll encounter some resistance. People may be busy and have what they feel are more important things to do. They may have other uses for their time and money. To be persuasive, you need to show your audience that your proposal meets their needs; you need to overcome any objections.

The easiest way to learn about objections your audience may have is to ask. Particularly when you want to persuade people in your own organization or your own town, talk to knowledgeable people. Phrase your questions non-defensively, in a way that doesn't lock people into taking a stand on an issue: "What concerns would you have about a proposal to do *x*?" "Who makes a decision about *y*?" "What do you like best about [the supplier or practice you want to change]?" Ask follow-up questions to be sure you understand: "Would you be likely to stay with your current supplier if you could get a lower price from someone else? Why?"

People are likely to be most aware of and willing to share objective concerns such as time and money. They will be less willing to tell you their real objection when it is emotional or makes them look bad. People have a **vested interest** in something if they benefit directly from keeping things as they are. People who are in power have a vested interest in retaining the system that gives them their power. Someone who designed a system has a vested interest in protecting that system from criticism. To admit that the system has faults is to admit that the designer made mistakes. In such cases, you'll need to probe to find out what the real reasons are.

Whether your audience is inside or outside your organization, they will find it easier to say *yes* when you ask for something that is consistent with their self-image.

3. How Strong Is Your Case?

The strength of your case is based on three aspects of persuasion: argument, credibility, and emotional appeal.

Argument refers to the reasons or logic you offer. Sometimes you may be able to prove conclusively that your solution is best. Sometimes your reasons may not be as strong, the benefits may not be as certain, and obstacles may be difficult or impossible to overcome. For example, suppose you wanted to persuade your organization to offer a tuition reimbursement plan for employees. You'd have a strong argument if you could show that tuition reimbursement would improve the performance of marginal workers or that reimbursement would be an attractive recruiting tool in a tight job market. However, if dozens of fully qualified workers apply for every opening you have, your argument would be weaker. The program might be nice for workers, but you'd have a hard job proving that it would help the company.

Some arguments are weakened by common errors known as logical **fallacies.** Figure 11.2 defines some common logical fallacies.

Credibility is the audience's response to you as the source of the message. Credibility in the workplace has three sources: expertise, image, and relationships.[2] Citing experts can make your argument more credible. In some organizations, workers build credibility by getting assigned to high-profile teams. You build credibility by your track record. The more reliable you've been in the past, the more likely people are to trust you now.

We are also more likely to trust people we know. That's one reason new CEOs make a point of visiting as many branch offices as they can. Building a relationship with someone—even if the relationship is based on an outside interest, like sports or children—makes it easier for that person to see you as an individual and to trust you.

When you don't yet have the credibility that comes from being expert, high-profile, or well known, build credibility by the language and strategy you use:

- *Be factual.* Don't exaggerate. If you can test your idea ahead of time, do so, and report the results. Facts about your test are more convincing than opinions about your idea.

- *Be specific.* If you say "X is better," show in detail *how* it is better. Show the audience exactly where the savings or other benefits come from so that it's clear the proposal really is as good as you say it is.

- *Be reliable.* If you suspect a project will take longer to complete, cost more money, or be less effective than you originally thought, tell your audience *immediately.* Negotiate a new schedule that you can meet.

Figure 11.2	Common Logical Fallacies

- *Hasty generalization.* Making general assumptions based on limited evidence. "Most of my friends agree that the new law is a bad idea. Americans do not support this law."

- *False cause.* Assuming that because one event follows another, the first event caused the second. "In the 1990s farmers increased their production of corn for ethanol. Soon after, more Americans began using ethanol fuel in their cars."

- *Weak analogy.* Making comparisons that don't work. "Outlawing guns because they kill people is like outlawing cars because they kill people."

- *Appeal to authority.* Quoting from a famous person who is not really an expert. "Hollywood actor Joe Gardner says this hand mixer is the best on the market today."

- *Appeal to popularity.* Arguing that because many people believe something, it is true. "Thousands of Americans doubt the reality of climate change, so climate change must not be happening."

- *Appeal to ignorance.* Using lack of evidence to support the conclusion. "There's nothing wrong in the plant; all the monitors are in the safety zone."

- *False dichotomy.* Setting up the situation to look like there are only two choices. "If you are not with us, you are against us."

Keep It Simple, Keep Your Customers

Companies can help keep customers by simplifying communications and building credibility. Both qualities are important now that technology gives consumers more options, sometimes more than they can deal with.

According to research from Corporate Executive Board, the most effective companies simplify consumer choices. Most do this by organizing relevant information and helping consumers navigate it, providing trustworthy sources of information, and providing tools to help weigh options.

Usually, companies excel in one of those actions, but not all. One company that is leading the pack is Intuit. The company has had great success with its software product, TurboTax, because it abides by these simplification components:

- Information and navigation: Any customer with a question can consult with other customers as well as TurboTax experts in large online support communities where the software will redirect them to the top five answers as rated by customers.

- Trust: The company holds itself accountable by publicly displaying more than 160,000 product reviews, including negative ones. Customers can even search based on reviews made by customers similar to themselves.

- Options: TurboTax presents product choices with clear, side-by-side visual comparisons and even features a quick question-and-answer activity to help customers determine which product best suits them.

Adapted from Patrick Spenner and Karen Freeman, "To Keep Your Customers, Keep It Simple." *Harvard Business Review* 90, no. 5 (May 2012): 109–14.

Emotional appeal means making the audience *want* to do what you ask. People don't make decisions—even business decisions—based on logic alone. As John Kotter and Holger Rathgeber, authors of the popular business book *Our Iceberg Is Melting,* found, "feelings often trump thinking."[3] Jonah Lehrer, author of *How We Decide,* goes a step further. He offers research that shows people make better decisions—ones that satisfy them better—about large purchases such as cars or homes when they followed their emotions: "The process of thinking requires feeling, for feelings are what let us understand all the information that we can't directly comprehend. Reason without emotion is impotent."[4]

Some of the most popular Super Bowl commercials use emotional appeals. Budweiser's Clydesdales frequently appear in emotional commercials: trainer and horse reunited or horse friends reunited were two that got much buzz. Yes, animals and emotions are an easy pairing, but good communicators can add emotional appeals to almost anything. Investment strategy? Retirement counselors do it all the time. Search engines? Google did it with the "Parisian Love" campaign, which takes a young man from searching "study abroad Paris France," through "how to impress a French girl," searching for churches, and finally searching for instruction on crib assembly.[5]

4. What Kind of Persuasion Is Best for the Situation?

Different kinds of people require different kinds of persuasion. What works for your boss may not work for your colleague. But even the same person may require different kinds of persuasion in different situations. Many people who make rational decisions at work do not do so at home, where they may decide to smoke and overeat even though they know smoking and obesity contribute to many deaths.

For years, companies have based their persuasion techniques on the idea that money is most people's primary motivator. And sometimes it is, of course. How many people buy an extra item to reach the $35 amount for free shipping at Amazon? But research in the last decade has shown that people are also motivated by other factors, including competition and social norms. Utility companies, for example, have found that people are more likely to conserve energy if they see how their use compares to their neighbors' use.[6] A hotel that posted signs saying that the majority of guests reused their towels increased the reusage rate 26%.[7] These factors, derived from behavioral economics, open up new ways to persuade people to act.

Even when money is the motivator, companies are beginning to use it differently, especially when trying to persuade their employees to lead healthier lives. Many of these new techniques stem from **behavioral economics,** a branch of economics that uses insights from sociology and psychology. It finds that people often behave irrationally, although still predictably, and not in their own best interests. Techniques include lotteries and short-term financial incentives. Employees who enroll in weight-loss or smoking-cessation programs and stick with them might be eligible for a daily lottery (people tend to give greater weight to the small probability of a lottery than to the much larger probability of long-term health improvements from a healthier lifestyle) or a regular series of payments (people tend to value short-term benefits over long-term health improvements). Capitalizing on the well-known aversion to loss, companies are also asking employees in such programs to put a dollar or two each day into the program. Employees who meet their goals get their money back plus matching funds.[8] Some companies are going even further and penalizing employees, sometimes by $1,000 or more, who fail to participate in health programs or assessments.[9]

Another kind of persuasion that is getting much attention is **choice architecture,** which involves changing the context in which people make decisions to encourage them to make specific choices.

examples ↓

- Companies that automatically enroll new employees in savings and retirement plans are using choice architecture. Instead of having to fill out forms to opt in to saving, employees have to fill out the forms to opt out. Since employees do not like to fill out voluntary forms, more of them remain in the savings programs.

- Asking people the day before the election if they intend to vote increases the probability of their voting by up to 25%.

- A study of 40,000 people that asked them if they intended to buy a car in the next six months increased car purchase rates 35%.

- Officials in Minnesota persuaded more residents to pay their taxes simply by telling them that 90% of their fellow residents obeyed the tax laws. (Neither threats nor information about the good causes funded by taxes had worked.)[10]

In *Drive: The Surprising Truth about What Motivates Us*, Daniel Pink summarizes decades of research that shows many businesses are using the wrong kinds of persuasion on their employees who do knowledge work, work that demands sophisticated understanding, flexible problem solving, and creativity. According to this research, once basic levels of financial fairness are reached, "carrot" motivators, such as financial ones, do not work for employees who are expected to be innovative. In fact, carrot motivators will actually decrease innovation; they turn creative work into drudgery.[11]

"Stick" motivators, in the form of ill-chosen goals, are also harmful and can lead to unethical and illegal behavior. Managers hit short-term goals to get performance bonuses, even when they know the short-term goals will cause long-term problems. Sears set sales quotas on its auto repair personnel, who then made national news by overcharging and performing unnecessary repairs. Mortgage issuers provided financial incentives for new mortgages, which got offered to people who could not afford them, contributing to a worldwide recession.

So what does motivate knowledge workers? Pink says it is three drives: "our deep-seated desire to direct our own lives, to expend and expand our abilities, and to live a life of purpose."[12]

5. What Kind of Persuasion Is Best for the Organization and the Culture?

Choosing the wrong kind of persuasion can have a deleterious effect on reaching your goals. In the '80s and '90s, the government spent almost a billion dollars on anti-drug campaigns, such as the famous "Just Say No" ads, directed at youth. The messages did not have the expected effect. Research showed that youths who had seen the ads were more likely to use drugs than those who had not. Why? The ads proved that lots of youth were using drugs, or all those ads wouldn't exist. The more people seem to be doing something, the more likely it is that other people think they should try it too.[13]

Bet You Watch This Safety Video

Most airline passengers ignore the preflight safety presentation, where the flight crew details important procedures in case of emergency. Even though the information is vital, the presentation is standard and routine.

New Zealand's national airline is uniquely persuading its passengers to watch the safety presentation: the company filmed its safety video with the crew members wearing nothing but skin-painted uniforms. The saucy video uses safety equipment to protect the actors' privacy.

The safety video is complemented by television commercials for the airline that feature a new slogan: "At Air New Zealand, our fares have nothing to hide."

New Zealand's approach got plenty of attention. In the first four days after its release, it had more than 1 million views on YouTube.

Adapted from "New Zealand Safety Video Bares Painted Plane Crew," *Des Moines Register*, July 4, 2009, 4A; and "Nude Safety Video: New Zealand Airline Issues In-Flight Safety Video Starring Naked Cabin Crew," Huffington Post, May 25, 2011, http://www.huffingtonpost.com/2009/07/03/nude-safety-video-new-zea_n_225459.html.

To persuade passengers to watch, Air New Zealand filmed its safety video with crew members wearing nothing but skin-painted uniforms.

Organizational Culture   In the business world, a strategy that works in one organization may not work somewhere else. One corporate culture may value no-holds-barred aggressiveness. In another organization with different cultural values, an employee who uses a hard-sell strategy for a request would antagonize people. Managers at Google, a culture where job titles do not come with power, have to learn to use ideas and persuasiveness to engage employees. Some businesses are willing to try creative means of persuasion. MGM Resorts produced a talent show starring employees for their corporate training program in diversity and sustainability. The show engaged the talents of 70 employees and ran for 10 performances.[14]

Organizational culture (see Chapter 4) isn't written down; it's learned by imitation and observation. What style do high-level people in your organization use to persuade? When you show a draft to your boss, are you told to tone down your statements or to make them stronger? Role models and advice are two ways organizations communicate their culture to newcomers.

Social Culture   Different kinds of persuasion also work for different social cultures. In North Carolina, police are using a new combination to persuade drug dealers to shut down. The combination includes iron-clad cases against the dealers, but also pressure from loved ones—mothers, grandmothers, mentors—along with a second chance.

Texas used a famous antilitter campaign based on the slogan "Don't Mess with Texas." Research showed the typical Texas litterer was 18 to 35 years old, male, a pickup driver, and a lover of sports and country music. He did not respond to authority (Don't litter) or cute owls (Give a hoot; don't pollute). Instead, the campaign aimed to convince this target audience that people like him did not pollute. Ads featured Texan athletes and musicians making the point that Texans don't litter. The campaign was enormously successful: during its first five years, Texas roadside litter decreased 72% and roadside cans 81%.[15] The campaign is still going 25 years later.[16]

What counts for "evidence" also varies by culture. People control the sample of information they absorb so it supports the conclusions they wish to draw. So someone who wishes to scoff at global warming, for instance, will tend to use sources and see information from a culture that negates the trend. When people do encounter information that counters their beliefs, they tend to ignore it or interpret it differently than other people. People also set the proof standards higher for information that counters their beliefs, both for quality and quantity.[17] In general, people count a scientist as an expert only when that scientist agrees with a position held by most of those who share their cultural values. This remains true even if the scientist got a degree from a major university, is on the faculty at another major university, and is a member of the National Academy of Sciences.[18]

National Cultures   Different native cultures also have different preferences for gaining compliance. In one study, students who were native speakers of American English judged direct statements ("Do this"; "I want you to do this") clearer and more effective than questions ("Could you do this?") or hints ("This is needed"). Students who were native speakers of Korean, in contrast, judged direct statements to be *least* effective. In the Korean culture, the clearer a request is, the ruder and therefore less effective it is.[19]

Researchers are studying the sale of counterfeit drugs, which is a huge business, both in the United States and abroad. They have found that the quality of the fakes matters only in the United States; people in other countries are willing to accept a price–quality trade-off. U.S. citizens harbor ill will toward big drug companies; people in other countries do not. U.S. citizens consider the consumption of counterfeit drugs unethical; people in China and Russia do not.

So what should drug companies do? In countries placing a low priority on drug quality, companies can highlight the dangers of such drugs, including the contaminants that are common in them. In cultures lacking ethical concerns, drug companies can stress social concerns. Diluted malaria drugs, for instance, can help the parasite causing the disease to develop drug resistance.[20]

Choosing a Persuasive Strategy LO 11-3

If your organization prefers a specific approach, use it. If your organization has no preference, or if you do not know your audience's preference, use the following guidelines to help you choose a strategy. These guidelines work in many cases but not all.

- Use the **direct request pattern** when
  - The audience will do as you ask without any resistance.
  - You need responses only from people who will find it easy to do as you ask.
  - The audience may not read all of the message.

- Use the **problem-solving pattern** when the audience may resist doing as you ask and you expect logic to be more important than emotion in the decision.

- Use the **sales pattern** when the audience may resist doing as you ask and you expect emotion to be more important than logic in the decision.

 WARNING: You always need to consider your audience and situation before choosing your persuasive strategy.

Why Threats and Punishment are Less Effective Than Persuasion

Sometimes people think they will be able to cause change by threatening or punishing subordinates. Actually, there is a reason for this belief: on a onetime basis, it is frequently true. Most people will not threaten or punish a subordinate unless the behavior is particularly bad. But it is also true of particularly bad behavior that it is out of the ordinary, i.e., that the next occurrence will be better no matter what the supervisor does. Much research shows that over the long run, persuasion is far more effective than threats or punishment. Threats are even less effective in trying to persuade people whose salaries you don't pay.

A **threat** is a statement—explicit or implied—that someone will be punished if he or she does (or doesn't do) something. Various reasons explain why threats and punishment don't work:

1. **Threats and punishment don't produce permanent change.** Many people obey the speed limit only when a marked police car is in sight.
2. **Threats and punishment won't necessarily produce the action you want.** If you punish whistle-blowers, you may stop hearing about problems you could be solving—hardly the response you'd want!
3. **Threats and punishment may make people abandon an action—even in situations where it would be appropriate.** Punishing workers for chatting with each other may reduce their overall collaboration.

Making Ethics Training Fun

BearingPoint, a management and technology consulting firm, has taken a different approach to its ethics training.

Russ Berland, BearingPoint's chief compliance officer, faced the problem of reworking the company's ethics and compliance program from a rarely used legal manual into a regularly consulted solution to ethics problems.

After interviewing associates from around the country, he found that many of them had experienced ethical dilemmas, and their stories were interesting and compelling.

Berland and his associates then came up with a brilliant idea: instead of simply reworking the manual, they decided to put the drama of real-life situations on television. They hired a director and filmed 10 episodes in a weekend, with the plan to release one episode each Monday. Using the format of NBC's hit sitcom *The Office*, the episodes talked about sticky ethics subjects with comic exaggeration.

The series was an instant hit. Employees not only watched the videos, but they also responded to them, talked about them, and searched for the next episodes before they were released. With humor and heart, BearingPoint helped persuade employees to "take" their ethics training.

Adapted from Dan Heath and Chip Heath, "How to Make Corporate Training Rock," *Fast Company*, accessed June 28, 2013, http://www.fastcompany.com/1460648/how-make-corporate-training-rock.

4. **Threats and punishment produce tension.** People who feel threatened put their energies into ego defense rather than into productive work.
5. **People dislike and avoid anyone who threatens or punishes them.** A supervisor who is disliked will find it harder to enlist cooperation and support on the next issue that arises.
6. **Threats and punishment can provoke counteraggression.** Getting back at a boss can run the gamut from complaints to work slowdowns to sabotage.

Making Persuasive Direct Requests LO 11-4

When you expect quick agreement, you can generally save your audience's time by presenting the request directly (see Figure 11.3). Also use the direct request pattern for busy people who do not read all the messages they receive and in organizations whose cultures favor putting the request first.

This pattern is also frequently used to persuade in dire situations. In 2008, at the height of the U.S. financial crisis, Fed Chairman Ben Bernanke and Henry Paulson, then treasury secretary, bluntly asked Congress for $700 billion to rescue the banks and prevent a deep, prolonged recession.[21]

In written direct requests, put the request, the topic of the request, or a question in the subject line.

Subject: Request for Updated Software

My copy of HomeNet does not accept the nicknames for Gmail accounts.

Subject: Status of Account #3548-003

Please get me the following information about account #3548-003.

Subject: Do We Need an Additional Training Session in October?

The two training sessions scheduled for October will each accommodate 20 people. Last month, you said that 57 new staff accountants had been hired. Should we schedule an additional training session in October? Or can the new hires wait until the next regularly scheduled session in February?

Figure 11.4 illustrates a direct request. Note that a direct request does not contain benefits and does not need to overcome objections: it simply asks for what is needed.

Figure 11.3	How to Organize a Persuasive Direct Request

1. **Consider asking immediately for the information or service you want.** Delay the request if it seems too abrupt or if you have several purposes in the message.
2. **Give your audience all the information they will need to act on your request.** Number your questions or set them off with bullets so readers can check to see that all have been answered.
3. **Ask for the action you want.** Do you want a check? A replacement? A catalog? Answers to your questions? If you need an answer by a certain time, say so. If possible, show why the time limit is necessary.

Figure 11.4 A Direct Request

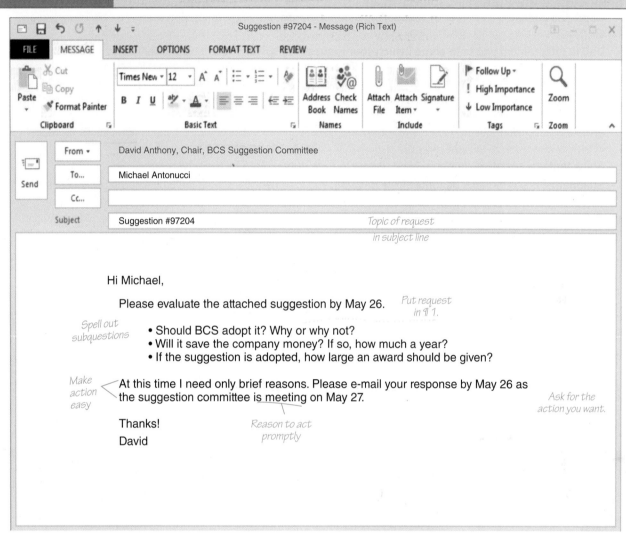

Direct requests should be clear. Don't make people guess what you want.

Indirect request: Is there a newer version of the 2003 *Chicago Manual of Style?*

Direct request: If there is a newer version of the 2003 *Chicago Manual of Style,* please send it to me.

In more complicated direct requests, anticipate possible responses. Suppose you're asking for information about equipment meeting certain specifications. Explain which criteria are most important so that the reader can recommend an alternative if no single product meets all your needs. You may also want to tell the reader what your price constraints are and ask whether the item is in stock or must be special-ordered.

Writing Persuasive Problem-Solving Messages LO 11-5

Generally, you will use an indirect approach and the problem-solving pattern of organization (see Figure 11.5) when you expect resistance from your audience but can show that doing what you want will solve a problem you and your audience share. This pattern allows you to disarm opposition by

11.5 How to Organize a Persuasive Problem-Solving Message

1. **Catch the audience's interest by mentioning a common ground.** Show that your message will be interesting or beneficial. You may want to catch attention with a negative (which you will go on to show can be solved).

2. **Define the problem you both share (which your request will solve).** Present the problem objectively: don't assign blame or mention personalities. Be specific about the cost in money, time, lost goodwill, and so on. You have to convince people that *something* has to be done before you can convince them that your solution is the best one.

3. **Explain the solution to the problem.** If you know that the audience will favor another solution, start with that solution and show why it won't work before you present your solution.

   Present your solution without using the words *I* or *my.* Don't let personalities enter the picture; don't let the audience think they should say *no* just because you've had other requests accepted recently.

4. **Show that any negative elements (cost, time, etc.) are outweighed by the advantages.**

5. **Summarize any additional benefits of the solution.** The main benefit—solving the problem—can be presented briefly since you described the problem in detail. However, if there are any additional benefits, mention them.

6. **Ask for the action you want.** Often your audience will authorize or approve something; other people will implement the action. Give your audience a reason to act promptly, perhaps offering a new benefit. ("By buying now, we can avoid the next quarter's price hikes.")

How to Write a Believable Persuasive Message

Daniel Kahneman, Nobel Prize winner in economics, Princeton psychology professor, and author of *Thinking, Fast and Slow*, notes that true messages are not necessarily believable and offers advice for achieving belief for written documents.

- Use bold type and high-quality paper to maximize the contrast between the print and its background.
- Use simple language. Pretentious diction lowers credibility.
- Use features to make the message memorable (he recommends rhyming verse).
- If you cite a source, make it one with an easy-to-pronounce name.

As strange as some of these suggestions seem (he offers experimental evidence for each), he says they contribute to a sense of "cognitive ease" that biases people toward belief.

Adapted from Daniel Kahneman, *Thinking, Fast and Slow* (New York: Farrar, Straus and Giroux, 2011), 62–64.

showing all the reasons in favor of your position before you give your audience a chance to say *no*. As always, you need to analyze your audience and situation before you choose this approach to ensure it is a good one for the occasion.

The message in Figure 11.6 uses the problem-solving pattern of organization. Benefits can be brief in this kind of message since the biggest benefit comes from solving the problem.

Subject Lines for Problem-Solving Messages

When you have a reluctant audience, putting the request in the subject line just gets a quick *no* before you've had a chance to give all your arguments. One option is to use a neutral subject line. In the following example, the first is the most neutral. The remaining two increasingly reveal the writer's preference.

Subject: A Proposal to Change the Formula for Calculating Retirees' Benefits

Subject: Arguments for Expanding the Marysville Plant

Subject: Why Cassano's Should Close Its West Side Store

Another option is to use common ground or a benefit—something that shows the audience that this message will help them.

> Subject: Reducing Energy Costs in the Louisville Office
>
> Energy costs in our Louisville office have risen 12% in the last three years, even though the cost of gas has remained constant and the cost of electricity has risen only 5%.

Although your first paragraph may be negative in a problem-solving message, your subject line should be neutral or positive.

Developing a Common Ground

A common ground avoids the me-against-you of some persuasive situations and suggests that both you and your audience have a mutual interest in solving the problems you face. To find a common ground, analyze the audience;

Figure 11.6   A Problem-Solving Persuasive Message

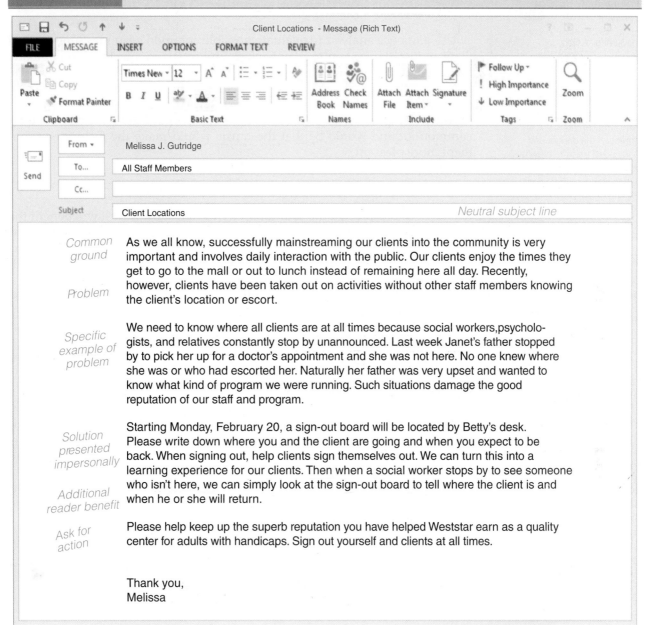

	Client Locations - Message (Rich Text)
	FILE MESSAGE INSERT OPTIONS FORMAT TEXT REVIEW

From ▾   Melissa J. Gutridge

To...   All Staff Members

Cc...

Subject   Client Locations   *Neutral subject line*

Common ground

Problem

As we all know, successfully mainstreaming our clients into the community is very important and involves daily interaction with the public. Our clients enjoy the times they get to go to the mall or out to lunch instead of remaining here all day. Recently, however, clients have been taken out on activities without other staff members knowing the client's location or escort.

Specific example of problem

We need to know where all clients are at all times because social workers, psychologists, and relatives constantly stop by unannounced. Last week Janet's father stopped by to pick her up for a doctor's appointment and she was not here. No one knew where she was or who had escorted her. Naturally her father was very upset and wanted to know what kind of program we were running. Such situations damage the good reputation of our staff and program.

Solution presented impersonally

Additional reader benefit

Starting Monday, February 20, a sign-out board will be located by Betty's desk. Please write down where you and the client are going and when you expect to be back. When signing out, help clients sign themselves out. We can turn this into a learning experience for our clients. Then when a social worker stops by to see someone who isn't here, we can simply look at the sign-out board to tell where the client is and when he or she will return.

Ask for action

Please help keep up the superb reputation you have helped Weststar earn as a quality center for adults with handicaps. Sign out yourself and clients at all times.

Thank you,
Melissa

---

understand their biases, objections, and needs; and identify with them to find common goals. This analysis should not be carried out in a cold, manipulative way; it should, rather, be based on a respect for and sensitivity to the audience's position.

Audiences are highly sensitive to manipulation. No matter how much you disagree with your audience members, respect their intelligence. Try to understand why they believe or do something and why they may object to your position. If you can understand your audiences' initial positions, you'll be more effective—and you won't alienate your audience by talking down to them.

The best common grounds are specific. Often a negative—a problem the audience will want to solve—makes a good common ground.

Persuasion for Responsible Behavior

In Mumbai, 6,000 people a year were dying by taking shortcuts across train tracks. FinalMile, a consulting firm called in to help, used behavioral economics to save lives. The firm hung graphic photos of the danger and persuaded trains to blow their whistles in sharp bursts that would stand out from background noise. Deaths declined drastically.

Given this success, FinalMile was hired to create similar persuasive campaigns for other problems related to other transportation safety issues as well as health ones such as tuberculosis. The firm plans to continue persuading with creative presentations of information. For example, the firm has ideas such as placing a patient's photo—taken when ill—on a medicine container to remind him or her why that medicine needs to be taken. The firm is also working on a campaign to increase toilet use and stop public defecation.

In one of its pro bono projects, FinalMile worked with a social worker to try to increase sanitation in one of New Delhi's many slums. Residents there believed the slum was just a temporary location and thus had no investment in keeping common spaces clean. In a test alley, FinalMile installed brackets to hold plastic grocery bags. Above each bracket were illustrations of trash being put in the bags and the bags being placed in a trash receptacle. The plan worked. In that alley, the path was swept clean and rotting garbage was gone.

Adapted from David Shaftel, "Scaring India to Save It," *Bloomberg Businessweek*, October 29, 2012, 18–19.

| Vague common ground: | We all want this plant to be profitable. |
| Improved specific common ground: | We forfeited a possible $1,860,000 in profits last month due to a 17% drop in productivity. |

Use audience analysis to evaluate possible common grounds. Suppose you want to install a system to play background music in a factory. To persuade management to pay for the system, a possible common ground would be increasing productivity. However, to persuade the union to pay for the system, you'd need a different common ground. Workers would see increasing productivity as a way to get them to do more work for the same pay. A better common ground would be that the music would make the factory environment more pleasant.

Explaining the Solution

If at all possible, present the solution in terms that show how it will benefit the audience. If the situation is complicated, you may need to provide background information and outline the steps of the solution. Don't present the solution as your solution; don't use *I* or *my*. If another solution is being favored, you will need to show why that solution is not as good.

Develop the positives of your solution (see Chapter 2 for a detailed discussion of audience benefits, and Chapter 3 for a discussion of positive tone). Research has shown that when people attempt to make lists of positives and negatives about a decision, whichever side they focus on first has the greatest impact on their choice.[22]

Dealing with Objections

If you know that your audience will hear other points of view, or if your audience's initial position is negative, you have to deal with the objections to persuade the audience. The stronger the objection is, the earlier in your message you should deal with it.

The best way to deal with an objection is to eliminate it. When hail damaged mail-order apples just before harvest, the orchard owner inserted a note in each crate being shipped:

> Note the hail marks which have caused minor skin blemishes in some of these apples. They are proof of their growth at a high mountain altitude where the sudden chills from hailstorms help firm the flesh, develop the natural sugars, and give these apples their incomparable flavor.

No one asked for a refund; in fact, some customers requested the hail-marked apples the next year.[23]

If an objection is false and is based on misinformation, give the response to the objection without naming the objection. (Repeating the objection gives it extra emphasis.) In some communications, you can present responses with a "question/answer" format.

When objections have already been voiced, you may want to name the objection so that your audience realizes that you are responding to that specific objection. However, to avoid solidifying the opposition, don't attribute the objection to your audience. Instead, use a less personal attribution: "Some people wonder . . ."; "Some citizens are afraid that. . . ."

If real objections remain, try one or more of the following strategies to counter objections:

1. Specify how much time and/or money is required—it may not be as much as the audience fears.

> Distributing flyers to each house or apartment in your neighborhood will probably take two afternoons.

2. Put the time and/or money in the context of the benefits they bring.

> The additional $252,500 will (1) allow the Essex Shelter to remain open 24 rather than 16 hours a day, (2) pay for three social workers to help men find work and homes, and (3) keep the Neighborhood Bank open, so that men don't have to cash Social Security checks in bars and so that they can save for the $800 deposit they need to rent an apartment.

3. Show that money spent now will save money in the long run.

> By buying a $1,000 safety product, we can avoid $5,000 in OSHA fines.

4. Show that doing as you ask will benefit some group or cause the audience supports, even though the action may not help the audience directly. This is the strategy used in fund-raising letters.

> By being a Big Brother or a Big Sister, you'll give a child the adult attention he or she needs to become a well-adjusted, productive adult.

5. Show the audience that the sacrifice is necessary to achieve a larger, more important goal to which they are committed.

> These changes will mean more work for all of us. But we've got to cut our costs 25% to keep the plant open and to keep our jobs.

6. Show that the advantages as a group outnumber or outweigh the disadvantages as a group.

> None of the locations is perfect. But the Backbay location gives us the most advantages and the fewest disadvantages.

Use the following steps when you face major objections:

1. **Find out why your audience members resist what you want them to do.** Sit down one-on-one with people and listen. Don't try to persuade them; just try to understand.
2. **Try to find a win–win solution.** People will be much more readily persuaded if they see benefits for themselves. Sometimes your original proposal may have benefits that the audience had not thought of, and explaining the benefits will help. Sometimes you'll need to modify your original proposal to find a solution that solves the real problem and meets everyone's needs.
3. **Let your audience save face.** Don't ask people to admit that they have been wrong. If possible, admit that the behavior may have been appropriate in

Hard Tests for Persuasion

How do you get your employees to agree to be tested for AIDS? This was a huge concern for SABMiller, a South African brewer that faced losing about 15% of its workforce within three years. The first step was to hire an outside testing firm to allay fears that a positive HIV test would become company gossip or hurt careers. Participants also joined raffles for free radios and TVs. The company paid for anti-retroviral treatment for infected employees.

How do you get employees to leave their jobs? France Telecom's need for a major workforce reduction inspired the company to be creative. In addition to traditional means such as early retirement plans and retirement bonuses, it developed a program to shift people to public-sector jobs at other institutions. The company also helped employees start their own businesses, offering assistance with writing business plans, applying for loans, and purchasing equipment. France Telecom paid for consultations with businesspeople and new educational courses.

What other hard tests for businesses can you identify? What persuasive solutions can you imagine?

Adapted from William Echikson and Adam Coher, "SABMiller's AIDS Test Program Gets Results: Effort Benefits Business, Saves Employee Lives; Building Confidence Is Key," *Wall Street Journal,* August 18, 2006, A7; and Leila Abboud, "At France Telecom, Battle to Cut Jobs Breeds Odd Tactics: Company Offers Money, Advice on Starting New Business if Employees Will Leave," *Wall Street Journal,* August 14, 2006, A1.

the past. Whether you can do that or not, always show how changed circumstances or new data call for new action.

4. **Ask for something small.** When you face great resistance, you won't get everything at once. Ask for a month's trial. Ask for one step that will move toward your larger goal. For example, if your ultimate goal is to eliminate prejudice in your organization, a step toward that goal might be to convince managers to make a special effort for one month to recognize the contributions of women or members of minorities in group meetings.

5. **Present your arguments from your audience's point of view.** Offer benefits that help the audience, not just you. Take special care to avoid words that attack or belittle your audience. Present yourself as someone helping your audience members achieve their goals, not someone criticizing or giving orders from above.

Organizational changes work best when the audience buys into the solution. And that happens most easily when they find it themselves. Management can encourage employees to identify problems and possible solutions. If that is not possible because of time, sensitive information, or organizational cultural constraints, a good second alternative is to fully explain to employees how the decision for organizational change was made, the reasons behind the change, what alternatives were considered, and why they were rejected. A study of over 100 employers found that workers who received such explanations were more than twice as likely to support the decision as those workers who did not.[24]

Offering a Reason for the Audience to Act Promptly

The longer people delay, the less likely they are to carry through with the action they had decided to take. In addition, you want a fast response so you can go ahead with your own plans.

Request action by a specific date. Try to give people at least a week or two: they have other things to do besides respond to your requests. Set deadlines in the middle of the month, if possible. If you say, "Please return this by March 1," people will think, "I don't need to do this till March." Ask for the response by February 28 instead. Similarly, a deadline of 5 p.m. Friday will frequently be seen as Monday morning. If such a shift causes you problems, if you were going to work over the weekend, set a Thursday deadline. If you can use a response even after the deadline, say so. Otherwise, people who can't make the deadline may not respond.

Your audience may ignore deadlines that seem arbitrary. Reveal why you need a quick response:

- **Show that the time limit is real.** Perhaps you need information quickly to use it in a report that has a due date. Perhaps a decision must be made by a certain date to catch the start of the school year, the Christmas selling season, or an election campaign. Perhaps you need to be ready for a visit from out-of-town or international colleagues.

- **Show that acting now will save time or money.** If business is slow and your industry isn't doing well, then your company needs to act now (to economize, to better serve customers) in order to be competitive. If business is booming and everyone is making a profit, then your company needs to act now to get its fair share of the available profits.

- **Show the cost of delaying action.** Will labor or material costs be higher in the future? Will delay mean more money spent on repairing something that will still need to be replaced?

Building Emotional Appeal

Emotional appeal helps make people care. Storytelling, audience focus, and psychological description are effective ways of building emotional appeal.

Storytelling Even when you need to provide statistics or numbers to convince the careful reader that your anecdote is a representative example, telling a story first makes your message more persuasive. In *Made to Stick*, Chip and Dan Heath report on research supporting the value of stories. After a survey (completing the survey for money ensured all participants had cash for the real experiment), participants received an envelope with a letter requesting they donate to Save the Children. Researchers tested two letters: One was full of grim statistics about starving Africans. The other letter told the story of seven-year-old Rokia. Participants receiving the Rokia letter gave more than twice as much money as those receiving the statistics letter. A third group received a letter with both sets of information: the story and the statistics. This group gave a little more than the statistics group, but far less than the group that had the story alone. The researchers theorized that the statistics put people in an analytical frame of mind, which canceled the emotional effect of the story.[25]

Audience Focus As with other appeals, the **emotional appeal** should focus on the audience. To customers who had fallen behind with their payments, one credit card company sent not the expected stern collection notice but a hand-addressed, hand-signed greeting card. The front of the card pictured a stream running through a forest. The text inside noted that sometimes life takes unexpected turns and asked people to call the company to find a collaborative solution. When people called the 800 number, they got credit counseling and help in creating a payment plan. Instead of having to write off bad debts, the company received payments—and created goodwill.[26]

Sometimes emotional appeals go too far and alienate audiences. Germany's Federal Constitutional Court ruled that a PETA ad campaign was an offense against human dignity and not protected by freedom of speech laws. The campaign compared factory farms and animal slaughterhouses to Jewish concentration camps and the Holocaust.[27]

Psychological Descriptions Sense impressions—what the reader sees, hears, smells, tastes, feels—evoke a strong emotional response. **Psychological description** means creating a scenario rich with sense impressions so readers can picture themselves using your product or service and enjoying its benefits. Restaurant menus are frequently good examples.

You can also use psychological description to describe the problem your product, service, or solution will ease. Psychological description works best early in the message to catch readers' attention.

Because our smokers take their breaks on the front patio, clients visiting our office frequently pass through a haze of acrid smoke—as well as through a group of employees who are obviously not working.

Love alone didn't save her.

Practicing fire safety did.

Children under the age of five are twice as likely to die in a fire than the rest of us. That's why parents and others who care for babies and toddlers need to pay special attention to fire safety. Keep matches and lighters out of reach, test your smoke alarms monthly, change the batteries at least once a year, and practice a home fire escape plan.

PREPARE. PRACTICE. PREVENT THE UNTHINKABLE.
A Fire Safety Campaign for Babies and Toddlers

For a free Parents' Guide, visit www.usfa.fema.gov

FEMA

Emotional appeal is often used in public service announcements. Here FEMA uses the emotional appeal of the young child to underscore a fire safety message.

Tone in Persuasive Messages

The best phrasing for tone depends on your relationship to your audience. When you ask for action from people who report directly to you, polite orders ("Please get me the Ervin file") and questions ("Do we have the third-quarter numbers yet?") will work. When you need action from co-workers, superiors, or people outside the organization, you need to be more polite. See Chapter 3 for a discussion of tone and politeness.

How you ask for action affects whether you build or destroy positive relationships with other employees, customers, and suppliers. Avoiding messages that sound parental or preachy is often a matter of tone. Adding "Please" is a nice touch. Tone will also be better when you give reasons for your request or reasons to act promptly.

Parental:	Everyone is expected to comply with these regulations. I'm sure you can see that they are commonsense rules needed for our business.
Better:	Even on casual days, visitors expect us to be professional. So please leave the gym clothes at home!

Writing to superiors is trickier. You may want to tone down your request by using subjunctive verbs and explicit disclaimers that show you aren't taking a *yes* for granted.

Arrogant:	Based on this evidence, I expect you to give me a new computer.
Better:	If department funds permit, I would like a new computer.

Passive verbs and jargon sound stuffy. Use active imperatives—perhaps with "Please" to create a friendlier tone.

Stuffy:	It is requested that you approve the above-mentioned action.
Better:	Please authorize us to create a new subscription letter.

It can be particularly tricky to control tone in e-mail messages, which tend to sound less friendly than paper documents or conversations. For important requests, compose your message off-line and revise it carefully before you send it.

Major requests that require great effort or changes in values, culture, or lifestyles should not be made in e-mail messages.

Varieties of Persuasive Messages

Performance reviews and letters of recommendation are two important kinds of persuasive messages.

Performance Reviews

Good supervisors give their employees regular feedback on their performances. The feedback may range from a brief "Good job!" to a hefty bonus. Blanchard and Johnson's *One Minute Manager* is a popular business guide for brief but effective performance feedback.

Companies are recognizing the need to lavish more praise on their workers, especially younger ones. Lands' End and Bank of America hired consultants to teach their supervisors how to compliment workers. The Scooter Store Inc.

hired a "celebrations assistant," whose duties included handing out 100 to 500 celebration balloons and tossing 25 pounds of confetti—per week. (The celebrations assistant became averse to confetti, so her praise came in the form of text messaging.) Computer-security software maker Symantec has software allowing employees to nominate colleagues for good-work rewards ranging from $25 for everyday good work to $1,000 for outstanding project work.[28] Such companies see the praise as a way to maintain work quality and keep good workers.

Companies are also recognizing the need for more frequent feedback, again especially for younger workers, who are used to instant feedback on Facebook and Twitter. Some companies, including Facebook, have their own "social" networks where employees seek and give continual feedback—after meetings, presentations, or projects. Other companies are turning to peer reviews, rather than manager reviews, for performance feedback. This system is particularly valuable in offices where employees switch teams frequently and no one leader has insight into all an employee's efforts.[29]

Performance review documents are more formal ways by which supervisors evaluate the performance of their subordinates. In most organizations, employees have access to their reviews; sometimes they must sign the document to show that they've read it. The superior normally meets with the subordinate to discuss the review.

Reviews need to both protect the organization and motivate the employee. Sometimes these two purposes conflict. Most of us will see a candid review as negative; we need praise and reassurance to believe that we're valued and can do better. But the praise that motivates someone to improve can come back to haunt the company if the person does not eventually do acceptable work. An organization is in trouble if it tries to fire someone whose evaluations never mention mistakes.

Problems with Performance Reviews Performance reviews have been getting a tarnished reputation lately. Academic studies have been showing they have no effect on the performance of the majority of employees.[30] Employees themselves may not want to be honest with their supervisor about their need for improvement or training. A supervisor who praises an employee may need to reward that person. On the other hand, a supervisor who criticizes a poor performance may then need to explain why this person wasn't managed more effectively. Supervisors of Army Major Nidal Hasan, who killed 13 people at Fort Hood, praised him in performance reviews, even though they knew he was often late for work, disappeared when on call, saw few patients, and pushed his religious views on those around him.[31]

Critics also complain about vague criteria and feedback, or stock phrases. They note that "not a team player" is being used to eliminate the need to give high achievers well-deserved promotions. Even widely touted techniques such as 360-degree feedback (anonymous input from supervisors, peers, and subordinates) have their critics. Some companies are suspending this form of review because of conflicting input with vague support.[32]

Another type of performance review now gathering criticism is the forced, or stack, ranking, a technique somewhat like grading on a curve. With forced rankings, most employees receive mediocre reviews. Only a small number of employees receive excellent, or in some cases even good, reviews, and some employees must receive poor reviews. Some companies go so far as to fire the bottom 10% of employees annually. Critics says this type of performance review instills behaviors that are highly detrimental to the good of the company: managers may deliberately hire weak performers so as not to have to

Put Positive Emphasis in Performance Reviews

Positive emotional appeal is a great tool for performance reviews and other "management moments" where you need to give motivating feedback to a co-worker, teammate, or employee.

Julia Stewart, the chair and CEO of the restaurant company DineEquity, describes how she uses positive emotional appeals when she gives feedback to employees. "I'd go behind the counter, get on the food prep line, and catch an employee doing something right. I'd say, 'Great job—that's the perfect way to portion that taco' and then turn to the next person down the line and ask, 'Did you see how well this was done?' Or I'd stand in the middle of the kitchen and half-shout, 'Who did the walk-in here today?' There would be silence, and then someone would confess, 'I did.' And I'd compliment him on the job and ask the people in the kitchen to gather around so they could see what had gone right and what could be done even better the next time."

This type of positive emphasis is a great persuasive tool: your audience associates your feedback with the positive emotional feeling of being praised, which makes them more likely to view your recommendations as positive and act on them.

Adapted from Daisy Wademan Dowling, "DineEquity Chairman and CEO Julia A. Stewart on Leaders as Teachers," *Harvard Business Review* 87, no. 3 (March 2009): 29.

dismiss team members, and employees compete against each other instead of other companies. In some instances, mediocre workers may strive to undercut top employees.[33]

Preparing for Your Own Performance Reviews   As a subordinate, you should prepare for the review interview by listing your achievements and goals.

- What have you accomplished during the review period?

- What evidence of your accomplishments will you need?

- Where do you want to be in a year or five years?

- What training and experience do you need to do your job most effectively and to reach your goals?

If you need training, advice, or support from the organization to advance, the review interview is a good time to ask for this help. As you prepare, choose the persuasive strategy that will best present your work.

Writing Performance Reviews   Performance reviews for good employees are usually easy to write: most supervisors enjoy giving their employees well-deserved praise. Even in these reviews, however, it is important that specifics about the good work be included to help good employees continue to shine and also to receive their well-deserved raises and promotions.

When you are writing performance reviews for employees who need to do better, you will need to document areas for improvement and avoid labels (*wrong, bad*) and inferences. Instead, cite specific observations that describe behavior.

Inference:	Sam is an alcoholic.
Vague observation:	Sam calls in sick a lot. Subordinates complain about his behavior.
Specific observation:	Sam called in sick a total of 12 days in the last two months. After a business lunch with a customer last week, Sam was walking unsteadily. Two of his subordinates have said that they would prefer not to make sales trips with him because they find his behavior embarrassing.

Sam might be an alcoholic. He might also be having a reaction to a physician-prescribed drug; he might have a mental illness; he might be showing symptoms of a physical illness other than alcoholism. A supervisor who jumps to conclusions creates ill will, closes the door to solving the problem, and may provide grounds for legal action against the organization.

Be specific in a review.

Too vague:	Sue does not manage her time as well as she could.
Specific:	Sue's first three weekly sales reports have been three, two, and four days late, respectively; the last weekly sales report for the month is not yet in.

Without specifics, Sue won't know that her boss objects to late reports. She may think that she is being criticized for spending too much time on sales calls or for not working 80 hours a week. Without specifics, she might change the wrong things in a futile effort to please her boss.

Reviews are more useful to subordinates if they make clear which areas are most important and contain specific recommendations for improvement. No one can improve 17 weaknesses at once. Which two should the employee work on this month? Is getting in reports on time more important than increasing sales?

Phrase goals in specific, concrete terms. The subordinate may think that "considerable progress toward completing" a report may mean that the project should be 15% finished. The boss may think that "considerable progress" means 50% or 85% of the total work.

Sometimes a performance review reflects mostly the month or week right before the review, even though it is supposed to cover six months or a year. Many managers record specific observations of subordinates' behavior two or three times a month. These notes jog the memory so that the review doesn't focus unduly on recent behavior.

A recent trend in performance reviews is attempting to make them objective. Instead of being subjectively evaluated on intangible qualities such as "works well with others," employees are monitored on how well they meet quantifiable goals. Nurses might be ranked on items such as low infection rates and high patient-satisfaction scores. Technical support personnel might be ranked on number of projects completed on time and customer-satisfaction scores.[34] If you will be evaluated by the numbers, try to have a say in setting your goals so you are not judged on items to which you only indirectly contribute. Make sure your goals stay updated so you are not judged on goals that are no longer a priority for your position or your efforts on new goals are not being measured.

Figure 11.7 shows a performance review for a member of a collaborative business communication student group.

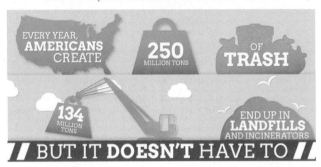

Many infographics provide persuasive arguments such as this one on recycling. See Chapter 6 for more information on infographics.

Source: Environmental Protection Agency, accessed August 24, 2013, http://www.epa.gov/wastes/nonhaz/municipal/infographic/pdfs/Infographic_full-060513-high.pdf.

Letters of Recommendation

You may write letters of recommendation when you want to recommend someone for an award or for a job. Letters of recommendation must be specific. General positives that are not backed up with specific examples and evidence are seen as weak recommendations. Letters of recommendation that focus on minor points also suggest that the person is weak.

Letters of recommendation frequently follow a standard organization:

■ Either in the first or the last paragraph, summarize your overall evaluation of the person.

■ Early in the letter, perhaps in the first paragraph, show how well and how long you've known the person.

■ In the middle of the letter, offer specific details about the person's performance.

■ At the end of the letter, indicate whether you would be willing to rehire the person and then repeat your overall evaluation.

Figure A.1 in Appendix A shows a sample letter of recommendation.

Figure 11.7 — A Performance Review for a Student Group Member

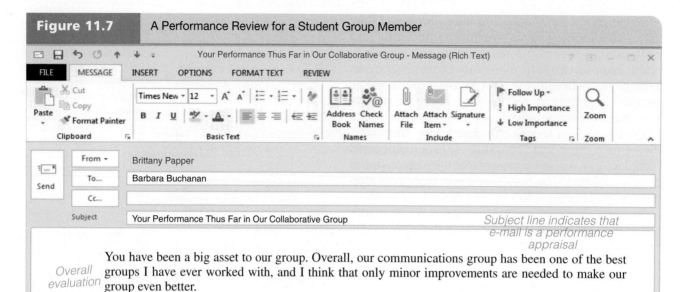

Subject line indicates that e-mail is a performance appraisal

Overall evaluation

You have been a big asset to our group. Overall, our communications group has been one of the best groups I have ever worked with, and I think that only minor improvements are needed to make our group even better.

These headings would need to be changed in a negative performance appraisal.

Strengths

Specific observations provide dates, details of performance

You demonstrated flexibility and compatibility at our last meeting before we turned in our proposal on February 9 by offering to type the proposal since I had to study for an exam in one of my other classes. I really appreciated this because I definitely did not have the time to do it. I will definitely remember this if you are ever too busy with your other classes and cannot type the final report.

Another positive critical incident occurred February 2. We had discussed researching the topic of sexual discrimination in hiring and promotion at Midstate Insurance. As we read more about what we had to do, we became uneasy about reporting the information from our source who works at Midstate. I called you later that evening to talk about changing our topic to a less personal one. You were very understanding and said that you agreed that the original topic was a touchy one. You offered suggestions for other topics and had a positive attitude about the adjustment. Your suggestions ended my worries and made me realize that you are a positive and supportive person.

Other strengths

Your ideas are a strength that you definitely contribute to our group. You're good at brainstorming ideas, yet you're willing to go with whatever the group decides. That's a nice combination of creativity and flexibility.

Areas for Improvement

Two minor improvements could make you an even better member.

Specific recommendations for improvement

The first improvement is to be more punctual to meetings. On February 2 and February 5 you were about 10 minutes late. This makes the meetings last longer. Your ideas are valuable to the group, and the sooner you arrive the sooner we can share in your suggestions.

Positive cast to suggestion

Specific behavior to be changed

The second suggestion is one we all need to work on. We need to keep our meetings positive and productive. I think that our negative attitudes were worst at our first group meeting February 3. We spent about half an hour complaining about all the work we had to do and about our busy schedules in other classes. In the future if this happens, maybe you could offer some positive things about the assignment to get the group motivated again.

Overall Compatibility

Positive, forward-looking ending

I feel that this group has gotten along very well together. You have been very flexible in finding times to meet and have always been willing to do your share of the work. I have never had this kind of luck with a group in the past, and you have been a welcome breath of fresh air. I don't hate doing group projects any more!

Although experts are divided on whether you should include negatives, the trend is moving away from doing so. Negatives can create legal liabilities, and many readers feel that any negative weakens the letter. Other people feel that presenting but not emphasizing honest negatives makes the letter more convincing. In either case, you must ensure that your recommendation is honest and accurate.

In many discourse communities, the words "Call me if you need more information" in a letter of recommendation mean "I have negative information that I am unwilling to put on paper. Call me and I'll tell you what I really think."

In an effort to protect themselves against lawsuits, some companies state only how long they employed someone and the position that person held. Such bare-bones letters have themselves been the target of lawsuits when employers did not reveal relevant negatives.

Sales and Fund-Raising Messages LO 11-6

Sales and fund-raising messages are a special category of persuasive messages. They are known as **direct marketing** because they ask for an order, inquiry, or contribution directly from the audience. Direct marketing, which includes printed (direct mail), verbal (telemarketing), and electronic (e-mails, social media, websites, infomercials) channels, is a $300 billion industry.[35]

This section focuses on two common channels of direct marketing: sales and fund-raising letters. Large organizations hire professionals to write their direct marketing materials. If you own your own business, you can save money by doing your firm's own direct marketing. If you are active in a local group that needs to raise money, writing the fund-raising letter yourself is likely to be the only way your group can afford to use direct mail. If you can write an equally effective e-mail message, you can significantly cut the costs of a marketing campaign or supplement the success of your direct mail with direct e-mail.

The principles in this chapter will help you write solid, serviceable letters and e-mails that will build your business and help fund your group.

Sales, fund-raising, and promotional messages have multiple purposes:

Primary purpose

To have the reader act (order the product, send a donation).

Secondary purpose

To build a good image of the writer's organization (to strengthen the commitment of readers who act, and make readers who do not act more likely to respond positively next time).

Organizing a Sales or Fund-Raising Message

Use the sales persuasion pattern to organize your message (see Figure 11.8).

Figure 11.8	How to Organize a Sales or Fund-Raising Message

1. Open by catching the audience's attention.
2. In the body, provide reasons and details.
3. End by telling the audience what to do and providing a reason to act promptly.

345

...bers"

...what we're

doing . . .

The conversational style of these subject lines made them the top three used for fund-raising during the 2012 Obama reelection campaign.

Daily Show host Jon Stewart poked fun at the campaign's subject lines, and some critics called them borderline creepy, but for all the mockery they received they pulled in much cash. "If you believe in what we're doing . . ." raked in $911,806, "Some scary numbers" delighted with $1,941,379, and "I will be outspent" ensured that Obama wasn't by garnering $2,540,866.

Toby Fallsgraff, the e-mail director for the campaign, thinks the friendliness factor made them work. The casual, informal tone of the subject lines helped them stand out, and Fallsgraff has the research to prove it. With a team of 20 writers, he tested subject lines with a number of variations—as many as 18 in one case—and the most effective ones were always casual. Many other conversational subject lines were created, tested, and sent, and in the end they brought in most of the $690 million in online earnings.

Adapted from Joshua Green, "Fund-raising: Hey. Read This," *Bloomberg Businessweek,* December 3, 2012, 31–32.

Opener   The opener of your message gives you a chance to motivate your audience to read the rest of the message.

A good opener will make readers want to read the message and provide a reasonable transition to the body of the message. A very successful subscription letter for *Psychology Today* started out,

> Do you still close the bathroom door when there's no one in the house?

The question was both intriguing in itself and a good transition into the content of *Psychology Today:* practical psychology applied to the quirks and questions we come across in everyday life.

It's essential that the opener not only get attention but also be something that can be linked logically to the body of the message. A sales letter started,

> Can You Use $50 This Week?

Certainly that gets attention. But the letter only offered the reader the chance to save $50 on a product. Readers may feel disappointed or even cheated when they learn that instead of getting $50, they have to spend money to save $50.

To brainstorm possible openers, use the four basic modes: questions, narration, startling statements, and quotations.

1. Questions

> Dear Subscriber,
>
> **ARE YOU NUTS?** Your subscription to PC Gamer is about to expire!
> **No reviews. No strategies. No tips.**
> *No PC Gamer. Are you willing to suffer the consequences?*

This letter urging the reader to renew *PC Gamer* is written under a large banner question: Do you want to get eaten alive? The letter goes on to remind its audience, mostly young males, of the magazine's gaming reviews, early previews, exclusive demo discs, and "awesome array of new cheats for the latest games"—all hot buttons for computer gaming fans.

Good questions are interesting enough that the audience want the answers, so they read the letter.

Poor question:	Do you want to make extra money?
Better question:	How *much* extra money do you want to make next year?

A series of questions can be an effective opener. Answer the questions in the body of the letter.

2. Narration, stories, anecdotes

> Dear Reader:
>
> She hoisted herself up noiselessly so as not to disturb the rattlesnakes snoozing there in the sun.
>
> To her left, the high desert of New Mexico. Indian country. To her right, the rock carvings she had photographed the day before. Stick people. Primitive animals.

> Up ahead, three sandstone slabs stood stacked against the face of the cliff. In their shadow, another carving. A spiral consisting of rings. Curious, the young woman drew closer. Instinctively, she glanced at her watch. It was almost noon. Then just at that moment, a most unusual thing happened.
>
> Suddenly, as if out of nowhere, an eerie dagger of light appeared to stab at the topmost ring of the spiral. It next began to plunge downward—shimmering, laser-like.
>
> It pierced the eighth ring. The seventh. The sixth. It punctured the innermost and last. Then just as suddenly as it had appeared, the dagger of light was gone. The young woman glanced at her watch again. Exactly twelve minutes had elapsed.
>
> Coincidence? Accident? Fluke? No. What she may have stumbled across that midsummer morning three years ago is an ancient solar calendar. . . .

This subscription letter for *Science84* argues that it reports interesting and significant discoveries in all fields of science—all in far more detail than do other media. The opener both builds suspense so that the reader reads the subscription letter and suggests that the magazine will be as interesting as the letter and as easy to read.

3. Startling statements

> I don't drink the water I use to flush.

This startling statement, accompanied by a picture of a toilet, was the catchphrase used by the French bottled water industry. It appeared in response to a campaign by public water companies touting tap water as equal to bottled water.[36]

Variations of this mode include special opportunities, twists, and challenges.

4. Quotations

> "If you are ever buried under a ton of rubble, trapped where no one can find you, or caught in the aftermath of a storm, I promise to sniff you out. I promise to go about my work with a wagging tail and a hero's heart. . . . I promise never to give up."[37]

This "quotation," printed with a photo of a dog paw raised in position to take an oath, is part of a fund-raising ad for the National Disaster Search Dog Foundation. The position of the paw, as well as the title of the ad, "The Pledge," helps support the quotation.

Body The body of the message provides the logical and emotional links that move the audience from a first flicker of interest to the action that is wanted. A good body answers the audience's questions, overcomes their objections, and involves them emotionally.

All this takes space. One industry truism is "The more you tell, the more you sell." Tests show that longer letters bring in more new customers or new donors than do shorter letters. A four-page letter is considered ideal for mailings to new customers or donors.

longer letters

Bricks-and-Mortar Persuasion

In a world of convenience, traditional stores are challenged to compete with online stores that offer faster browsing features, personally tailored purchasing recommendations, and frequently lower prices. Instead of giving up, though, stores are persuading customers to buy from them through creative persuasion techniques:

- E-mail deals catering to a shopper's individual shopping history.
- In-store deep discounts lasting for only several hours.
- Attractively lit shelves for items such as beauty products.
- Free promotions such as haircuts or family portraits.
- Extended layaway offers.
- Services such as snack bars or computer repair desks.
- Exclusive merchandise not found online.

Adapted from Sam Grobart, "Target Practice," *Bloomberg Businessweek,* January 7, 2013, 68–69; and Matt Townsend, "The War Over Christmas," *Bloomberg Businessweek,* November 5, 2012, 19–20.

THE PLEDGE

If you are ever buried under a ton of rubble, trapped where no one can find you, or caught in the aftermath of a storm, I promise to sniff you out.

I promise to go about my work with a wagging tail and a hero's heart.

I promise to ignore all the fascinating smells out there, and to concentrate on finding you.

I promise to never give up.

NATIONAL DISASTER SEARCH DOG FOUNDATION®
www.SearchDogFoundation.org

This National Disaster Search Dog Foundation ad presents a dog paw raised in a human vow to create a visual "startling statement."

Can short letters work? Yes, when you're writing to old customers or when the mailing is supported by other media. E-mail direct mail is also short—generally just one screen. The Direct Marketing Association says a postcard is the mailing most likely to be read.[38] The shortest message on record may be the two-word postcard that a fishing lake resort sent its customers: "They're biting!"

Content for the body of the message can include

- Information the audience will find useful even if they do not buy or give.
- Stories about how the product was developed or what the organization has done.
- Stories about people who have used the product or who need the organization's help.
- Word pictures of people enjoying the benefits offered.

Be careful not to give too much information, though. New research shows that giving people too much information hinders sales. Customers want sales information that provides "decision simplicity": they want easy access to trustworthy information and tools for quick sorting and easy weighing of options so they feel confident about their choice. Consider the complex and expensive decision of buying diamonds. For years De Beers has successfully used the "4Cs" (cut, color, clarity, and carat) to help consumers feel confident they have made a good selection.[39]

Because consumers are more likely to choose or favor the familiar, linking your sales message to the things people do or use every day is a good way to increase your message's perceived importance. Of course, that requires that you do a good job of audience analysis up front. Stanford University researchers showed that children given chicken nuggets and French fries preferred the taste of the food in McDonald's packaging, even though all the food came from the same source. The familiarity effect works on adults, too. In another study, adults tasting the same peanut butter from three different jars preferred the spread from the jar with a name brand label.[40]

Costs are generally mentioned near the end of the body and are connected to specific benefits. Sometimes costs are broken down to monthly, weekly, or daily amounts: "For less than the cost of a cup of coffee a day, you can help see that Erena is no longer hungry."

Action Close   The action close in the message must do four things:

1. **Tell the audience what to do.** Specify the action you want. Avoid *if* ("If you'd like to try . . .") and *why not* ("Why not send in a check?"). They lack positive emphasis and encourage your audience to say *no*.
2. **Make the action sound easy.** "Fill in the information on the reply card and mail it today." If you provide an envelope and pay postage, say so.
3. **Offer a reason for acting promptly.** People who think they are convinced but wait to act are less likely to buy or contribute. Reasons for acting promptly are easy to identify when a product is seasonal or there is a genuine limit on the offer—time limit, price rise scheduled, limited supply, and so on. Sometimes you can offer a premium or a discount if your audience acts quickly. When these conditions do not exist, remind readers that the sooner they get the product, the sooner they can benefit from it; the sooner they contribute funds, the sooner their dollars can go to work to solve the problem.
4. **End with a positive picture** of the audience enjoying the product (in a sales message) or of the audience's money working to solve the problem (in a fund-raising message). The last sentence should never be a selfish request for money.

The action close can also remind people of central selling points, and mention when the customer will get the product.

Using a P.S.   In a direct-mail letter or e-mail, the postscript, or P.S., occupies a position of emphasis by being the final part of the message. Direct mail often uses a deliberate P.S. after the signature block. It may restate the central selling point or some other point the letter makes, preferably in different words so that it won't sound repetitive when the reader reads the letter through from start to finish.

Here are four of the many kinds of effective postscripts.

Reason to act promptly:

> P.S. Once I finish the limited harvest, that's it! I do not store any SpringSweet Onions for late orders. I will ship all orders on a first-come, first-served basis and when they are gone they are gone. Drop your order in the mail today . . . or give me a call toll free at 800-531-7470! (In Texas: 800-292-5437)

Sales letter for Frank Lewis Alamo Fruit

Description of a premium the reader receives for giving:

> P.S. And . . . we'll be pleased to send you—as a new member—the exquisite, full-color Sierra Club Wilderness Calendar. It's our gift . . . absolutely FREE to you . . . to show our thanks for your membership at this critical time.

Fund-raising letter for Sierra Club

Reference to another part of the package:

> P.S. Photographs may be better than words, but they still don't do justice to this model. Please keep in mind as you review the enclosed brochure that your SSJ will look even better when you can see it firsthand in your own home.

Sales letter for the Danbury Mint's model of the Duesenberg SSJ

Restatement of central selling point:

> P.S. It is not easy to be a hungry child in the Third World. If your parents' crops fail or if your parents cannot find work, there are no food stamps . . . no free government-provided cafeteria lunches.
>
> Millions of hungry schoolchildren will be depending on CARE this fall. Your gift today will ensure that we will be there—that CARE won't let them down.

Fund-raising letter for CARE

Strategy in Sales Messages and Fund-Raising Appeals

In both sales messages and fund-raising appeals, the basic strategy is to help your audience see themselves using your products/services or participating in the goals of your charity. Too often, communicators stress the new features of their gadgets, rather than picturing the audience using it, or they focus on statistics about their cause, rather than stories about people helping that cause.

Sales Messages   The basic strategy in sales messages is satisfying a need. Your message must remind people of the need your product meets, prove that the product will satisfy that need, show why your product is better than similar products, and make people *want* to have the product. For years, V8 vegetable juice used the advertising slogan "Wow, I could've had a V8!" But in reality, most people prefer fruit juices. Then V8's makers realized that what they did better than those other juices was giving people a convenient way to get vegetable nutrients. Once the ad campaign focused on that fact, revenues quadrupled.[41]

Various techniques will help you build your case. Use psychological description (page 339) to show people how the product will help them. Details about how the product is made can carry the message of quality. Testimonials from other buyers can help persuade people that the product works. In fact, sales trainer and best-seller business author Jeffrey Gitomer cites customer testimonials as one of the best ways to overcome price resistance.[42]

Generally, the price is not mentioned until the last fourth of the mes-sage, after the content makes the audience *want* the product. People tend to make relative choices. If you offer various related choices, such as donation amounts or service packages, they will generally choose an option for a mid-dle amount. Similarly, a high-priced dish on a menu tends to help revenue, because although most people won't buy it, they will buy the second-most expensive dish.[43]

You can make the price more palatable with the following techniques:

- **Link the price to the benefit the product provides.** "Your piece of history is just $39.95."

- **Link the price to benefits your company offers.** "You can reach our customer service agents 24/7."

■ **Show how much the product costs each day, each week, or each month.** "You can have all this for less than the cost of a cup of coffee a day." Make sure that the amount seems small and that you've convinced people that they'll use this product sufficiently.

■ **Allow customers to charge sales or pay in installments.** Your bookkeeping costs will rise, and some sales may be uncollectible, but the total number of sales will increase.

Fund-Raising Appeals   In a fund-raising appeal, the basic emotional strategy is **vicarious participation.** By donating money, people participate vicariously in work they are not able to do personally. This strategy affects the pronouns you use. Throughout the appeal, use *we* to talk about your group. However, at the end, talk about what *you* the audience will be doing. End positively, with a picture of the audience's dollars helping to solve the problem.

Fund-raising appeals require some extra strategy. To achieve both your primary and secondary purposes, you must give a great deal of information. This information (1) helps to persuade people; (2) gives supporters evidence to use in conversations with others; and (3) gives people who are not yet supporters evidence that may make them see the group as worthwhile, even if they do not give money now.

In your close, in addition to asking for money, suggest other ways people can help: doing volunteer work, scheduling a meeting on the subject, writing letters to Congress or the leaders of other countries, and so on. By suggesting other ways to participate, you not only involve your audience but also avoid one of the traps of fund-raising appeals: sounding as though you are interested in your audience only for the money they can give.

Deciding How Much to Ask For   Most messages to new donors suggest a range of amounts, from $25 or $100 (for employed people) up to perhaps double what you *really* expect to get from a single donor. The **anchoring effect** says that when people consider a specific value for a quantity (like a donation) and then have to come up with their own value for that quantity, their value will be close to the specified value. Thus, contribution letters suggesting higher contributions draw more money than those suggesting lower contributions.[44]

One of the several reasons people give for not contributing is that a gift of $25 or $100 seems too small to matter. It's not. Small gifts are important both in themselves and to establish a habit of giving. The American Heart Association determined that first-time donors responding to direct mail give an average of $21.84 and give $40.62 over a lifetime. But multiplied by the 7.6 million donors who respond to the AHA's mailings, the total giving is large. Also, more than $20 million of the money that the AHA receives from estate settlements after a person's death comes from people who have a relationship as direct-mail donors.[45]

You can increase the size of gifts by using the following techniques:

■ **Link the gift to what it will buy.** Tell how much money it costs to buy a brick, a hymnal, or a stained-glass window for a church; a book or journal subscription for a college library; a meal for a hungry child. Linking amounts to specific gifts helps the audience feel involved and often motivates them to give more: instead of saying, "I'll write a check for $25," the person may say, "I'd like to give a ———" and write a check to cover it.

■ **Offer a premium for giving.** Public TV and radio stations have used this ploy with great success, offering books, CDs, DVDs, umbrellas, and totes for gifts at a certain level. The best premiums are things that people both want and will

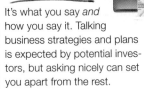

Etiquette for Asking

It's what you say *and* how you say it. Talking business strategies and plans is expected by potential investors, but asking nicely can set you apart from the rest.

Wall Street Journal staff surveyed experts at charities that thrive on investment support, and this is what they found.

Do:

■ Offer to educate donors with site visits or information packets.

■ Acknowledge young investors by providing children-centric learning opportunities.

■ Recognize shared values and passions.

■ Show strong leadership and fiscal responsibility.

■ Connect in a meaningful way by building relationships for the long-term and following up with investors.

Don't:

■ Overwhelm donors with too much information.

■ Offend by comparing them to other investors.

■ Beg or have continual "emergency" requests.

■ Give up on donors who may be interested in contributing later.

■ Ignore those who currently contribute.

Adapted from Veronica Dagher, "Ask Nicely, Please," *Wall Street Journal*, November 28, 2011, R5.

use or display, so that the organization will get further publicity when other people see the premium.

- **Ask for a monthly pledge.** People on modest budgets could give $15 or $25 a month; more prosperous people could give $100 a month or more. These repeat gifts not only bring in more money than the donors could give in a single check but also become part of the base of loyal supporters, which is essential to the continued success of any organization that raises funds.

Annual appeals to past donors often use the amount of the last donation as the lowest suggested gift, with other gifts 25%, 50%, or even 100% higher.

Always send a thank-you message to people who respond to your appeal, whatever the size of their gifts. By telling about the group's recent work, a thank-you message can help reinforce donors' commitment to your cause.

Logical Proof in Fund-Raising Messages   The body of a fund-raising message must prove that (1) the problem deserves attention, (2) the problem can be solved or at least alleviated, (3) your organization is helping to solve or alleviate it, (4) private funds are needed, and (5) your organization will use the funds wisely.

1. The problem deserves attention.   No one can support every cause. Show why your audience should care about solving this problem.

If your problem is life-threatening, give some statistics: Tell how many people are killed in the United States every year by drunken drivers, or how many children in the world go to bed hungry every night. Also tell about one individual who is affected.

If your problem is not life-threatening, show that the problem threatens some goal or principle your audience finds important. For example, a fund-raising letter to boosters of a high school swim team showed that team members' chances of setting records were reduced because timers relied on stopwatches. The letter showed that automatic timing equipment was accurate and produced faster times, since the timer's reaction time was no longer included in the time recorded.

2. The problem can be solved or alleviated.   People will not give money if they see the problem as hopeless—why throw money away? Sometimes you can reason by analogy. Cures have been found for other deadly diseases, so it's reasonable to hope that research can find a cure for cancer. Sometimes you can show that short-term or partial solutions exist. For example, UNICEF shows how simple changes—oral rehydration, immunization, and breastfeeding—could save the lives of millions of children. These solutions don't affect the underlying causes of poverty, but they do keep children alive while we work on long-term solutions.

3. Your organization is helping to solve or alleviate the problem.   Prove that your organization is effective. Be specific. Talk about your successes in the past. Your past success helps readers believe that you can accomplish your goals.

These are some of the specifics that the Charity: Water website gives about its efforts:

> Our Progress So Far: 8,661 water projects funded. 3,300,000 people will get clean water. 20 countries, 22 local partners.[46]

4. Private funds are needed to accomplish your group's goals.   We all have the tendency to think that taxes, or foundations, or church collections yield enough to pay for medical research or basic human aid. If your group does get some tax or foundation money, show why more money is needed. If the organization helps people who might be expected to pay for the service, show why they cannot pay, or why they cannot pay enough to cover the full cost. If some of the funds have been raised by the people who will benefit, make that clear.

5. Your organization will use the funds wisely. Prove that the money goes to the cause, not just to the cost of fund-raising. This point is becoming increasingly important as stories become more common of "charities" that give little money to their mission. One study of 80 professional fund-raisers serving over 500 charities found the median percentage of proceeds going to the charity was 24%; only five charities received more than 75%. In fact, one fund-raising company charged charities more money than the company raised.[47]

Emotional Appeal in Fund-Raising Messages Emotional appeal is needed to make people pull out their checkbooks. How strong should emotional appeal be? A mild appeal is unlikely to sway anyone who is not already committed, but your audience will feel manipulated by appeals they find too strong and reject them. Audience analysis may help you decide how much emotional appeal to use. If you don't know your audience well, use the strongest emotional appeal *you* feel comfortable with.

Emotional appeal is created by specifics. It is hard to care about, or even to imagine, a million people; it is easier to care about one specific person. Details and quotes help us see that person as real. Sensory details also help people connect to a cause. Covenant House, an organization that takes in homeless youth, does both. It provides vivid pictures both of children arriving at the door and of individuals who have turned their lives around. Covenant House also uses relevant sensory details: a child crawling into bed on a cold night, feeling warm and safe under soft blankets, versus a girl crawling into a cardboard box on the street to try to stay warm on a cold night.[48]

Sample Fund-Raising Letter The letter from UNICEF (see Figure 11.9) seeks aid for Third World children. It opens by catching interest and establishing common ground with the concept of keeping promises to children. It stresses the enormity of the problem—"millions of children," "perilous day-to-day existence." It moves on to list specific UNICEF programs and numbers helped—in the millions—for each program. Since this was a letter to someone who had donated before, the close refers to previous support.

Writing Style

Direct mail is the one kind of business writing where elegance and beauty of language matter; in every other kind, elegance is welcome but efficiency is all that finally counts. Direct mail imitates the word choice and rhythm of conversation. The best sales, fund-raising, and promotional writing is closer to the language of poetry than to that of academia: it shimmers with images, it echoes with sound, it vibrates with energy.

Many of the things that make writing vivid and entertaining *add* words because they add specifics or evoke an emotional response. Individual sentences should flow smoothly. The passage as a whole may be fun to read precisely because of the details and images that "could have been left out."

Make Your Writing Interesting If the style is long-winded and boring, the reader will stop reading. Eliminating wordiness is crucial. You've already seen ways to tighten your writing in Chapter 5. Direct mail goes further, breaking some of the rules of grammar. In the following examples, note how sentence

Enclosures in Fund-Raising Letters

Fund-raising letters sometimes use inexpensive enclosures to add interest and help carry the message.

Brochures are inexpensive, particularly if you photocopy them. Mailings to alumni might include "Why I Teach at State U" or letters from students who have received scholarships.

Reprints of newspaper or magazine articles about the organization or the problem it is working to solve add interest and credibility. Pictures of people the organization is helping build emotional appeal.

Seeds don't cost much. Mailings from both CARE and the New Forests Fund include four or five seeds of the leucaena, a subtropical tree that can grow 20 feet in a year. Its leaves feed cattle; its wood provides firewood or building materials; its roots reduce soil erosion. (Indeed, the enclosure easily becomes the theme for the letter.)

Major campaigns may budget for enclosures: pictures of people served, DVDs of activities, and maps of areas served.

Figure 11.9   Excerpts from a Fund-Raising Letter

Interest-grabbing picture

Dear Dr. Kienzler,

For more than 65 years, UNICEF has kept a promise to the world's children: no matter who you are, how poor you are, or what danger you are facing, UNICEF will do everything possible to help you survive.

Letter opens with a common ground: keeping promises to children.

As a committed supporter of the U.S. Fund for UNICEF, you know that millions of children face a perilous day-to-day existence, threatened by natural disasters, armed conflicts, malnutrition, exploitation, and disease. In fact, 21,000 children die every day from causes that are totally preventable.

Extent of problem

As we enter the New Year, I hope you'll join me in making a promise to the world's , most vulnerable children by vowing to give them the one thing they need the most: **the chance to survive**.

. . .

Children around the world are counting on your promise and your continued generosity to address the many challenges they confront every day. By sending a tax-drductible gift of $25, $35, $50 – or whatever amount you can afford – you will join with hundreds of thousands of other U.S. Fund for UNICEF supporters to help transport vital medicines and immunizations to prevent disease . . .

Fund-raising letters may use format features such as underlining and ellipses

Hundreds of thousands of people are also supporting this cause

. . .

UNICEF's efforts to reach children with basic health care, clean water and sanitation, better nutrition, and protection from exploitation and violence are paying real dividends in terms of young lives saved:

Sentence shows situation is not hopeless

- **More than six million** children's lives are saved each year through UNICEF's effective, low-cost survival programs.
- Over 75 percent of children in developing countries are now protected with immunizations, saving the lives of an estimated **2.5 million children annually**.
- **Polio is on the verge of being eradicated**.
- Today, 70 percent of all households in developing countries have access to iodized salt, **protecting 85 million newborns** each year from losses in learning ability.
- **Two million children's lives** are saved from diarrheal dehydration due to drinking unclean water through the provision of Oral Rehydration Salts.
- **More children are in school** than ever before.

Bulleted information shows past success, which promises future successes

Those young lives are living proof that your support for the U.S. Fund for UNCIEF makes a difference.

On behalf of the millions of children whose lives you have so profoundly affected, I extend our best wishes for the upcoming year to you and your loved ones, and I thank you for the generous spirit that is demonstrated in your continued support.

Sincerely,

Caryl M. Stren

Caryl M. Stren
President & CEO

Reference to donor's continued support

Source: Reprinted with permission from the U.S. Fund for UNICEF.

fragments and ellipses (spaced dots) are used in parallel structure to move the reader along:

> Dear Member-elect:
>
> If you still believe that there are nine planets in our solar system . . . that wine doesn't breathe . . . and that you'd recognize a Neanderthal man on sight if one sat next to you on the bus . . . check your score. There aren't. It does. You wouldn't.

Subscription letter for *Natural History*

Use Psychological Description Psychological description (page 339) means describing your product or service with vivid sensory details. In a sales letter, you can use psychological description to create a scenario so readers can picture themselves using your product or service and enjoying its benefits. You can also use psychological description to describe the problem your product or service will solve.

A *Bon Appétit* subscription letter used psychological description in its opener and in the P.S., creating a frame for the sales letter:

> Dear Reader:
>
> First, fill a pitcher with ice.
> Now pour in a bottle of ordinary red wine, a quarter cup of brandy, and a small bottle of Club soda.
> Sweeten to taste with a quarter to half cup of sugar, garnish with slices of apple, lemon, and orange. . . .
> . . . then *move your chair to a warm, sunny spot.* You've just made yourself Sangria—one of the great glories of Spain, and the perfect thing to sit back with and sip while you consider this invitation. . . .
> . . .
> P.S. One more thing before you finish your Sangria. . . .

It's hard to imagine any reader really stopping to follow the recipe before finishing the letter, but the scenario is so vivid that one can imagine the sunshine even on a cold, gray day.

Make Your Letter Sound Like a Letter, Not an Ad Maintain the image of one person writing to one other person that is the foundation of all letters. Use an informal style with short words and sentences, and even slang.

You can also create a **persona**—the character who allegedly writes the letter—to make the letter interesting and keep us reading. Use the rhythms of speech, vivid images, and conversational words to create the effect that the author is a "character."

The following opening creates a persona who fits the product:

> Dear Friend:
>
> There's no use trying. I've tried and tried to tell people about my fish. But I wasn't rigged out to be a letter writer, and I can't do it. I can close-haul a sail with the best of them. I know how to pick out the best fish of the catch, I know just which fish will make the tastiest mouthfuls, but I'll never learn the knack of writing a letter that will tell people why my kind of fish—fresh-caught prime-grades, right off the fishing boats with the deep-sea tang still in it—is lots better than the ordinary store kind.

Sales letter, Frank Davis Fish Company

This letter, with its "Aw, shucks, I can't sell" persona, with language designed to make you see an unassuming fisherman ("rigged out," "close-haul"), was written by a professional advertiser.[49]

Technology and Persuasion

Although a preferred channel for many big businesses that need to reach a wide audience is still television advertising, even big businesses are looking to websites and social media channels to supplement their ads as large prime-time television audiences continue to shrink. Super Bowl ads, which are now up to $3.8 million for 30 seconds, are supplemented with early web views, web contests, and ad character tweets.[50]

Most smaller businesses also use websites and social media channels to aid their sales. Sales reps follow potential clients on Facebook and Twitter; they find leads in Twitter complaints, LinkedIn questions, and Facebook posts. They maintain Facebook walls and LinkedIn profiles full of helpful information. Perhaps even more importantly, they use social tools for maintaining relationships with customers. So vital are these contacts that some companies are training their personnel, and not just sales personnel, to create posts with proper grammar, an appealing tone, useful information, and personalized messages.[51]

Many businesses are finding that some of their best "sales reps" are people outside the company, "influencers" whose posts and tweets help sales. They use tools such as Klout, Little Bird, and Tellagence to locate these influencers. Chevrolet gave about 900 people with good Klout scores a three-day loan of a Chevy Volt, an action that resulted in over 46,000 tweets and 20.7 million blog posts.[52]

Social media channels are good sources for information about products and services. And many consumers consult the wealth of information available on them before buying. Today's consumers are more informed than ever before; in fact, some consumers know more about what they are buying than the salespeople helping them. They also consult price comparison sites, rating sites, and complaint sites. The wealth of information available online has forced a new level of honesty and transparency in sales.

Most charities now also have at least a website, which allows them to expand both their emotional appeals and their logical proof. Good charity websites use both interesting text and colorful visuals to attract donors (see Chapter 6 for information on website design).

Websites alone, however, will be ineffective. Well-known charities, such as UNICEF or Doctors without Borders, can be confident their site will be visited. Smaller charities do not have that luxury and must use other publicity means to spread their message. And even large, well-known charities rely heavily on other channels of direct marketing.

Another problem with websites concerns visitors' browsing habits. Most visits to a website last only seconds; only 10% last longer than two minutes.[53] Furthermore, most first-time visitors do not scroll past the first screen. So the design of a charity's home page is crucial. The space offered by the first screen is less than even a letter, and much less than the usual multipage letter, so information selection is crucial.

Technologies wax and wane in popularity. QR (quick response) codes, those little squares with a dense grid of black and white boxes, began waning in popularity as consumers lost interest in connecting with corporate websites. The codes do not work in low lighting, and they work only for smartphone users in areas with cell reception. Research shows only 5% of Americans scan QR codes.[54]

On the other side of the coin, e-mail still hangs on. In fact, the Direct Marketing Association reports that e-mail still has the highest return on investment—$39.40 for every dollar spent—of any major marketing channel; social media return only $12.90 for every dollar spent. To be opened, a marketing e-mail must have an interest-catching subject line. The text of the e-mail must also be interesting, for most readers will stay for only a few seconds. It must also be easy to read on a cell phone screen.[55]

Solving a Sample Problem

Little things add up to big issues, especially where workplace quality of life is at stake.

Problem

FirstWest Insurance's regional office has 300 employees, all working the same 8-to-5 shift. Many of them schedule their lunch break during the noon hour, and that's where the problem started: there was only one microwave in the canteen. People had to wait up to 30 minutes to heat their lunches. As director of human resources, you implemented lunch shifts to break the gridlock. That program failed: people were used to their schedules and resisted the change. In your second attempt, you convinced FirstWest's operations vice president to approve a purchase order for a second microwave oven.

Now there's a new problem: fish. FirstWest recently recruited five new employees. They're from the Philippines, and fish is a prominent part of their diet. Each day at lunchtime, they heat their meals—usually containing fish—and each afternoon, the air-conditioning system in your closed-air building sends the aroma of fish wafting through the whole building.

Other employees have complained bitterly about the "foul odor." You've spoken to the new employees, and while they're embarrassed by the complaints, they see no reason to change. After all, they're just as disgusted by the smell of cooking beef: why haven't you asked the American employees not to reheat hamburger? And having just purchased a second oven, you know that management won't pay $1,000 for a new microwave with a filter system that will eliminate the odors. You need to solve the microwave problem.

Analysis of the Problem

Use the problem analysis questions in the first chapter to think through the problem.

1. Who is (are) your audience(s)?

    You'll be addressing all of the employees at this location. That's a broad audience, but they have certain characteristics in common, at least regarding this topic. They're all on a similar lunch schedule, and many of them use the canteen and the microwaves. They've also responded poorly to a previous attempt to change their lunch habits.

    Many members of your audience won't see this as their problem: only the new employees are doing something objectionable. The new employees will react poorly to being singled out.

2. What are your purposes in writing?

    To help eliminate cooking odors. To solve a minor issue before it begins to impact morale and cause ill will directed at new employees.

3. What information must your message include?

    The effects of the present situation. The available options and their costs (in money, and also in time, effort, and responsibility).

4. How can you build support for your position? What reasons or benefits will your audience find convincing?

   Improving the workplace environment—and eliminating a minor but persistent irritation—should improve morale. While expensive solutions exist, this is a matter that can, and should, be solved with cooperative behaviors.

5. What aspects of the total situation may be relevant?

   This issue is a minor one, and it may be difficult to get people to take it seriously. The easy solution—mandating what the new employees are allowed to bring for lunch—is discriminatory. For budgetary reasons, company management will not invest in a third (and much more expensive) microwave for the canteen.

Discussion of the Sample Solutions

The solution shown in Figure 11.10 is unacceptable. By formatting the communication as a notice designed to be posted in the canteen, the author invites the audience to publicly embarrass their co-workers: a form of threat. The subject line displays the author's biases in a way that discourages further discussion on the topic and eliminates the possibility of a broader consensus for any solution to the problem. The author uses emotional appeals to place blame on a

Figure 11.10	An Unacceptable Solution to the Sample Problem

ATTENTION!!!!

DON'T BRING DISGUSTING LUNCHES!!

Negative, biased subject line and clip art

Some of you (you KNOW!!! who you are) have been bringing in <u>foul-smelling</u> food and cooking it in the microwave at lunch. We've all smelled the result. It's not fair that everyone has to put up with your <u>stink</u>.

Negative diction

I'm writing to tell everyone that this is the END. As of today, no one is allowed to cook any food with a <u>strong smell</u> in the canteen microwave ovens.

Vague diction

The microwaves are a privilege and not a right. If you people continue to abuse company property, the microwaves will be removed from the canteen for good. ☹ *Don't use emoticons in serious communications*

Threatens

Thank you in advance for your cooperation in this matter.

Close does not sound sincere after threat

Clip art not appropriate for this serious communication

small segment of the audience, but the lack of logical observations or arguments (and the presence of clip art and emoticons) undermines the author's seriousness. The demand to stop cooking food with strong smells is vague: does this include pizza? popcorn? The author concludes with a threat, again eliminating the possibility of consensus-based actions.

Checklist

Checklist for Direct Requests

☐ If the message is an e-mail, does the subject line indicate the request? Is the subject line specific enough to differentiate this message from others on the same subject?

☐ Does the first paragraph summarize the request or the specific topic of the message?

☐ Does the message give all of the relevant information? Is there enough detail?

☐ Does the message answer questions or overcome objections that readers may have without introducing unnecessary negatives?

☐ Does the closing tell the reader exactly what to do? Does it give a deadline if one exists and a reason for acting promptly?

Originality in a direct request may come from

☐ Good lists and visual impact.

☐ Thinking about readers and giving details that answer their questions, overcome any objections, and make it easier for them to do as you ask.

☐ Adding details that show you're thinking about a specific organization and the specific people in that organization.

Ethics and Direct Mail

Deception in direct mail is all too easy to find.

Some mailers have sent "checks" to readers. But the "check" can only be applied toward the purchase of the item the letter is selling.

Some mailings now have yellow sticky notes with "hand-written" messages signed with initials or a first name only—to suggest that the mailing is from a personal friend.

Some messages offer a "free" membership "valued at, say, $800" (note the passive—who's doing the valuing?) but charge—up front—hundreds of dollars for "maintenance fees."

Such deception has no place in well-written direct mail.

The second solution, shown in Figure 11.11, is a more effective persuasive message. The author recognizes that this persuasive situation centers on goodwill and begins with a neutral subject line (as a more directed subject could detract from goodwill). The opening paragraph creates common ground by describing the problem in terms of group experience, rather than by assigning blame. It includes fish odors in with pleasant odors (brownies) and suggests that the e-mail's purpose is to propose a consensus-based solution.

The problem is spelled out in detail, balancing the emotional, goodwill-centered problem with rational arguments based on process and cost. The solution is presented as the recommendation of the Employee Council, rather than the administrators, and the cost is broken down into small increments. Until the new microwave arrives, small, easily accommodated, changes are recommended. The e-mail ends by linking cooperation with the audience benefit of group participation and identity.

Figure 11.11   A Good Solution to the Sample Problem

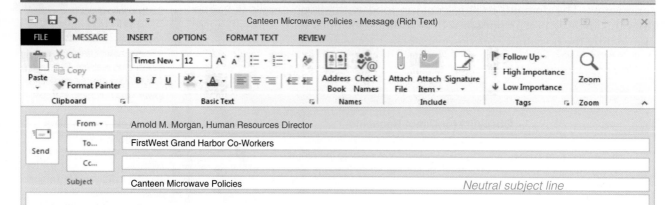

From ▾   Arnold M. Morgan, Human Resources Director

To...   FirstWest Grand Harbor Co-Workers

Cc...

Subject   Canteen Microwave Policies   *Neutral subject line*

Creates common ground
We all notice when someone uses the microwaves in the first-floor canteen to reheat strong-smelling food. These odors are distracting—whether they're the scent of burned popcorn, a fish lunch, or fresh-baked brownies—and none of us need any extra distractions in our busy days! Let's work together to "clear the air."

Cause of problem
How is it that we all smell food cooking in the first-floor canteen? Our building has a closed-air ventilation system: it's good for the environment, and it saves on heating and cooling costs by recirculating air throughout the building. It also circulates any odors in the air. That's why we can smell food from the first-floor canteen down in the basement archives and up in the third-floor conference rooms: we're all sharing the same air.

Long-term solution to problem
We're all sharing the same microwaves, too. Due to popular demand, we recently purchased a second microwave to relieve crowding at lunchtime. A third microwave—an odor-eliminating, air-filtration microwave—will cost $1,000, plus $20/month for filters. The Employee Council has recommended that we purchase this microwave by instituting a voluntary contribution of 25 cents per microwave use. At approximately 200 uses per day, the Council could collect enough money for the new microwave in about one month. Until then, there are simple things each of us can do to reduce problems with odors.

Short-term solution to problem
- **Use containers with lids** when you heat up your food. Not only will this help contain any odors, it will reduce the mess in the microwaves.

- **Clean up any mess you make** when you cook. If you cook something with a strong odor—or something that spatters!—take a minute when you're done and wipe the oven down with a damp paper towel.

- **Stay with your food** while it's cooking. When food overcooks or burns, it smells more strongly, so watching your food and removing it from the oven before it overcooks is the easiest way to avoid creating a distracting smell.

We work together as a team every day to serve our customers and succeed as an organization. Please take a little time to use the microwaves responsibly, and help us make sure that the only smell in our workplace is success!

Ends on positive note

Checklist

Checklist for Problem-Solving Persuasive Messages

☐ If the message is an e-mail, does the subject line indicate the writer's purpose or offer a benefit? Does the subject line avoid making the request?

☐ Does the first sentence interest the audience?

☐ Is the problem presented as a joint problem both communicator and audience have an interest in solving, rather than as something the audience is being asked to do for the communicator?

☐ Does the message give all of the relevant information? Is there enough detail?

☐ Does the message overcome objections that the audience may have?

☐ Does the message avoid phrases that sound dictatorial, condescending, or arrogant?

☐ Does the closing tell the audience exactly what to do? Does it give a deadline if one exists and a reason for acting promptly?

Originality in a problem-solving persuasive message may come from

☐ A good subject line and common ground.

☐ A clear and convincing description of the problem.

☐ Thinking about the audience and giving details that answer their questions, overcome objections, and make it easier for them to do as you ask.

☐ Adding details that show you're thinking about a specific organization and the specific people in that organization.

Get Involved

Getting involved with nonprofit work is a great opportunity to give back to your community while developing your professional and communication skills. Here are some online resources to get you started:

- http://www1.network forgood.org
- http://www.change.org
- http://www.dosomething.org
- http://firstgiving.org
- http://www.donorschoose .org
- http://www.kiva.org
- http://www. opportunity.org
- http://www.accion.org

Summary by Learning Objectives

LO 11-1 **Identify the purposes of persuasive messages.**

The primary purpose in a persuasive message is to have the audience act or change beliefs. Secondary purposes are to overcome any objections that might prevent or delay action, to build a good image of the communicator and the communicator's organization, to cement a good relationship between the communicator and audience, and to reduce or eliminate future communication on the same subject.

LO 11-2 **Analyze a persuasive situation.**

Use the questions in Figure 11.1 to analyze persuasive situations.

LO 11-3   Identify basic persuasive strategies.

You always need to consider your audience and situation before choosing your persuasive strategy. In general,

- Use the direct request pattern when the audience will do as you ask without any resistance. Also use the direct request pattern for busy readers in your own organization who do not read all the messages they receive. See Figure 11.3.

- Use the problem-solving pattern when the audience may resist doing what you ask and you expect logic to be more important than emotion in the decision. See Figure 11.5.

- Use the sales pattern when the audience may resist doing as you ask and you expect emotion to be more important than logic in the decision. See Figure 11.8.

LO 11-4   Write persuasive direct requests.

Use the information in Figure 11.3 to write persuasive direct requests.

LO 11-5   Write persuasive problem-solving messages.

- Use the information in Figure 11.5 to write persuasive problem-solving messages.

- Use one or more of the following strategies to counter objections that you cannot eliminate:

  - Specify how much time and/or money is required.
  - Put the time and/or money in the context of the benefits they bring.
  - Show that money spent now will save money in the long run.
  - Show that doing as you ask will benefit some group the audience identifies with or some cause the audience supports.
  - Show the audience that the sacrifice is necessary to achieve a larger, more important goal to which they are committed.
  - Show that the advantages as a group outnumber or outweigh the disadvantages as a group.
  - Turn the disadvantage into an opportunity.

- Threats don't produce permanent change. They won't necessarily produce the action you want, they may make people abandon an action entirely (even in situations where abandoning would not be appropriate), and they produce tension. People dislike and avoid anyone who threatens them. Threats can provoke counteraggression.

- To encourage people to act promptly, set a deadline. Show that the time limit is real, that acting now will save time or money, or that delaying action will cost more.

- Build emotional appeal with stories and psychological description.

LO 11-6   Write sales and fund-raising messages.

- A good opener makes readers want to read persuasion messages and provides a reasonable transition to the body of the message. Four modes for openers are questions, narration, startling statements, and quotations. A good body answers the audience's questions, overcomes their objections, and involves them emotionally. A good action close tells people what to do, makes the action sound easy, gives them a reason for acting promptly, and ends with a benefit or a picture of their contribution helping to solve the problem.

- In a fund-raising appeal, the basic strategy is vicarious participation. By donating money, people participate vicariously in work they are not able to do personally.

- The primary purpose in a fund-raising appeal is to get money. An important secondary purpose is to build support for the cause so that people who are not persuaded to give will still have favorable attitudes toward the group and will be sympathetic when they hear about it again.

LO 11-7   Use technology for persuasive messages.

- Most businesses use websites and social media channels to aid their persuasion.

- Many businesses are finding that some of their best "sales reps" are people outside the company, "influencers" whose posts and tweets boost sales.

- E-mail still remains one of the major channels of persuasion in business.

Continuing Case

The All-Weather Case, set in an HR department in a manufacturing company, extends through all 19 chapters and is available at www.mhhe.com/locker11e. The portion for this chapter asks students to write a persuasive message about a cross-cultural training program.

Exercises and Cases

Go to www.mhhe.com/locker11e for additional Exercises and Cases.

11.1 Reviewing the Chapter

1. What are the purposes of persuasive messages? (LO 11-1)
2. What are four questions you should answer when analyzing persuasive situations? Which question do you think is the most important? Why? (LO 11-2)
3. What are three basic persuasive strategies? In what kinds of situations is each preferred? (LO 11-3)
4. Why aren't threats effective persuasion tools? (LO 11-3)
5. How do you start the body of persuasive direct requests? Why? (LO 11-4)
6. How do you organize persuasive problem-solving messages? (LO 11-5)
7. How do you develop a common ground with your audience? (LO 11-5)
8. What are 10 ways to deal with objections? (LO 11-4 and LO 11-5)
9. What are ways to build emotional appeal? (LO 11-4 and LO 11-5)
10. What are four good beginnings for sales and fund-raising messages? (LO 11-6)
11. What are ways to de-emphasize costs or donation requests? (LO 11-6)
12. What kind of logical proof is used in fund-raising messages? (LO 11-6)
13. How are social media being used for persuasion? (LO 11-7)
14. How are websites being used for persuasion? What are some concerns relevant to their use for persuasion? (LO 11-7)

11.2 Reviewing Grammar

Persuasion uses lots of pronouns. Correct the sentences in Exercise B.4, Appendix B, to practice making pronouns agree with their nouns, as well as practicing subject–verb agreement.

11.3 Evaluating Subject Lines

Evaluate the following subject lines. Is one subject line in each group clearly best? Or does the "best" line depend on company culture, whether the message is a paper memo or an e-mail message, or on some other factor?

1. Subject: Request
   Subject: Why I Need a New Computer
   Subject: Increasing My Productivity
2. Subject: Who Wants Extra Hours?
   Subject: Holiday Work Schedule
   Subject: Working Extra Hours During the Holiday Season
3. Subject: Student Mentors
   Subject: Can You Be an E-Mail Mentor?
   Subject: Volunteers Needed
4. Subject: More Wine and Cheese
   Subject: Today's Reception for Japanese Visitors
   Subject: Reminder
5. Subject: Reducing Absenteeism
   Subject: Opening a Day Care Center for Sick Children of Employees
   Subject: Why We Need Expanded Day Care Facilities

11.4 Evaluating P.S.'s

Evaluate the following postscripts. Will they motivate readers to read the whole message if readers turn to them first? Do they create a strong ending for those who have already read the message?

1. P.S. It only takes <u>one</u> night's stay in a hotel you read about here, <u>one</u> discounted flight, <u>one</u> budget-priced cruise, or <u>one</u> low-cost car rental to make

mailing back your Subscription Certificate well worth it.

P.P.S. About your free gift! Your risk-free subscription to CONSUMER REPORTS TRAVEL LETTER comes with a remarkable 314-page book as a FREE GIFT.

2. P.S. Help spread the tolerance message by using your personalized address labels on all your correspondence. And remember, you will receive a free *Teaching Tolerance* magazine right after your tax-deductible contribution arrives.

3. P.S. Every day brings more requests like that of Mr. Agyrey-Kwakey—for our "miracle seeds." And it's urgent that we respond to the emergency in Malaysia and Indonesia by replanting those forests destroyed by fire. Please send your gift today and become a partner with us in these innovative projects around the world.

4. P.S. Even as you read this letter, a donated load of food waits for the ticket that will move it to America's hungry. Please give today!

11.5 Choosing a Persuasive Approach

For each of the following situations requiring a persuasive message, choose the persuasive approach that you feel would work best. Explain your reasoning; then give a short list of the types of information you'd use to persuade your audience.

1. Asking for an extension on a project.
2. Requesting a job interview.
3. Requesting a free trial of a service.
4. Inviting customers to a store demonstration.
5. Reporting a co-worker's poor work performance.
6. Asking your supervisor to reconsider a poor performance review.
7. Requesting a new office computer.
8. Requesting time off during your company's busy season.
9. Asking to be excused from the company service day, when all employees work on a community service project.

As your instructor directs,

a. Write a letter or e-mail that addresses one of the situations in this exercise, drawing on details from your personal experiences. (You might address a real problem that you've faced.)

b. Write an e-mail to your instructor listing the choices you've made and justifying your approach.

11.6 Identifying Observations

Susan has taken the following notes about her group's meetings. Which of the following are specific observations that she could use in a performance review of group members? If she had it to do over again, what kinds of details would turn the inferences into observations?

1. February 22: Today was very frustrating. Sam was totally out of it—I wonder if he's on something. Jim was dictatorial. I argued, but nobody backed me up. Masayo might just as well have stayed home. We didn't get anything done. Two hours, totally wasted.

2. February 24: Jim seems to be making a real effort to be less domineering. Today he asked Sam and me for our opinions before proposing his own. And he noticed that Masayo wasn't talking much and brought her into the conversation. She suggested some good ideas.

3. February 28: Today's meeting was OK. I thought Masayo wasn't really focusing on the work at hand. She needs to work on communicating her ideas to others. Sam was doing some active listening, but he needs to work at being on time. Jim was involved in the project. He has strong leadership skills. There were some tense moments, but we got a lot done, and we all contributed. I got to say what I wanted to say, and the group decided to use my idea for the report.

4. March 5: This week most of us had midterms, and Masayo had an out-of-town gymnastics trip. We couldn't find a time to meet. So we did stuff by e-mail. Sam and Jim found some great stuff at the library and on the web. Jim created a tentative schedule that he sent to all of us and then revised. I wrote up a draft of the description of the problem. Then Masayo and I put everything together. I sent my draft to her; she suggested revisions (in full caps so I could find them in the e-mail message). Then I sent the message to everyone. Masayo and Jim both suggested changes, which I made before we handed the draft in.

5. March 15: We were revising the proposal, using Prof. Jones's comments. When we thought we were basically done, Masayo noticed that we had not responded to all of the specific comments about our introductory paragraph. We then went back and thought of some examples to use. This made our proposal better and more complete.

As your instructor directs,

a. Based on Susan's notes, write a performance review addressed to Prof. Jones. For each group member, including Susan, note specific areas of good performance and make specific suggestions for improvement.

b.   Write an e-mail to your instructor describing the process you used to make your recommendations. Be sure to identify each of the observations you used to provide specific details, and each of the inferences that needed more information.

11.7   Revising a Persuasive E-mail

Your co-worker is concerned about the new computer software that IT just installed on everyone's office computers. She is not very familiar with the new program and has been struggling to figure it out. She wants to request a training session for those who still do not feel comfortable with the new system, but she is embarrassed to explain how much she is struggling with the software. She has written a draft of the e-mail to your supervisor and asks you for your feedback.

> Subject: Help!
>
> I am sorry to bother you, but I am really struggling with the new computer software that was installed last week. I am not sure, but I think there are a few of us in the office for whom this has been a struggle. I really miss the old one we used. This new software is so different; I am really struggling with entering some of my data.
>
> So, I was wondering if we could put together a training session sometime next week. We could ask IT if they would be willing to do a quick training seminar so we can make sure we are all on the same page. Maybe we could even do a follow-up session later on sometime just to check on our progress.
>
> If you could get back to me soon, I would really appreciate it. I think this learning curve is cutting into my productivity. I really don't want to be behind.
>
> Thanks,
>
> Joanie

Revise the e-mail and send it to your instructor. In a separate e-mail to your instructor, explain the changes you made to make this message more persuasive.

11.8   Creating Persuasive Videos

As they try to undo the harm from YouTube drinking videos starring their institutions, school officials are making their own YouTube videos. Some, such as deans lecturing on course offerings, are ludicrously bad. Other videos are slick promotional films. Still others, such as videos of classes, are somewhere in between.

Some schools are sponsoring contests to persuade students to create videos showing what they like about the school.

What would you put in a video to convince students—and parents who foot the bills—to consider your school? Share your ideas in small groups.

11.9   Creating Alternative Activities

You are residence director at Expensive Private University. Enrollment at your school has been declining because of repeated publicity about excessive drinking among the students. Last year 23 were treated for alcohol poisoning at the local hospital, and one died.

You have been ordered by the president of EPU to develop alcohol-free activities for the campus and ways to persuade students to participate. She wants your plans by the end of June so EPU can work on implementing them for the next academic year. Write the e-mail to her detailing your plans. Write a second e-mail to your instructor explaining your persuasive strategies.

Hints:

- Who are your audiences?
- Do they share any common ground?
- What objections will your audiences have?
- What are some ways you can deal with those objections?
- What pitfalls do you need to avoid?

11.10   Writing a Fundraiser Flyer

You have volunteered to create a flyer with detailed fundraising information for a local charity event. Your boss has given you the following information to include on the flyer:

- Shoes for kids—think of a clever title, please!
- All employees should bring children's shoes (any kind, any size) to the break room in the office by August 10th (before school starts).
- The shoes will go to children in need in the metro area.
- We are hoping to have enough shoes to fill up the back of one of our delivery vans.
- Shoes can be used, but they still have to be in good condition.

- Please do not bring dirty shoes.
- Please include some kind of graphic or picture.
- Please stress how important this is, and the fact that there are many children in our area who go without decent shoes.

Things to consider:

- How can you make this flyer persuasive?
- How will you grab employees' attention?
- Is there an emotional appeal you can use?
- Will there be objections you need to overcome?
- Is there more information you need to include?
- What audience benefits can you use?

Make the flyer.

11.11   Asking for More Time and/or Resources

Today, this message from your boss shows up in your e-mail inbox:

> Subject: Want Climate Report
>
> This request has come down from the CEO. I'm delegating it to you. See me a couple of days before the board meeting—the 4th of next month—so we can go over your presentation.
>
> I want a report on the climate for underrepresented groups in our organization. A presentation at the last board of directors' meeting showed that while we do a good job of hiring women and minorities, few of them rise to the top. The directors suspect that our climate may not be supportive and want information on it. Please prepare a presentation for the next meeting. You'll have 15 minutes.

Making a presentation to the company's board of directors can really help your career. But preparing a good presentation and report will take time. You can look at exit reports filed by Human Resources when people leave the company, but you'll also need to interview people—lots of people. And you're already working 60 hours a week on three major projects, one of which is behind schedule. Can one of the projects wait? Can someone else take one of the projects? Can you get some help? Should you do just enough to get by? Ask your boss for advice—in a way that makes you look like a committed employee, not a shirker.

11.12   Persuading Employees Not to Share Files

Your computer network has been experiencing slowdowns, and an investigation has uncovered the reason. A number of employees have been using the system to download and share songs and vacation photos. You are concerned because the bulky files clog the network, and downloading files opens the network to computer viruses and worms. In addition, management does not want employees to spend work time and resources on personal matters. Finally, free downloads of songs are often illegal, and management is worried that a recording firm might sue the company for failing to prevent employees from violating its copyrights.

As director of management information systems (MIS), you want to persuade employees to stop sharing files unrelated to work. You are launching a policy of regularly scanning the system for violations, but you prefer that employees voluntarily use the system properly. Violations are hard to detect, and increasing scanning in an effort to achieve system security is likely to cause resentment as an intrusion into employees' privacy.

Write an e-mail message to all employees, urging them to refrain from downloading and sharing personal files.

11.13 Persuading Employees to Join a Competition

Your supervisor has decided the employees of the company should participate in a weight-loss program and compete against the business across the street. Your supervisor isn't sure how to begin the program and is asking you for some ideas. She wants to know:

- How can we get employees interested in the weight-loss program?
- Will a competition get more employees to sign up?
- How long should we run the program?
- Should we have a goal?
- What should the program be called?
- Should there be a prize at the end for the person who lost the most weight?

- Should we get rid of Friday morning doughnuts during the program?
- Should we have some healthy eating and healthy living seminars to encourage our employees to be healthier?

Write an e-mail to your supervisor answering her questions. Then write an e-mail that will go to all employees. Include all the information they will need and use persuasion to get them to join the weight-loss program. Write a third e-mail to your instructor explaining the differences between the e-mails to your supervisor and your fellow employees.

11.14 Handling a Sticky Recommendation

As a supervisor in a state agency, you have a dilemma. You received this e-mail message today:

> From: John Inoye, Director of Personnel, Department of Taxation
>
> Subject: Need Recommendation for Peggy Chafez
>
> Peggy Chafez has applied for a position in the Department of Taxation. On the basis of her application and interview, she is the leading candidate. However, before I offer the job to her, I need a letter of recommendation from her current supervisor.
>
> Could you please let me have your evaluation within a week? We want to fill the position as quickly as possible.

Peggy has worked in your office for 10 years. She designed, writes, and edits a monthly statewide newsletter that your office puts out; she designed and maintains the department website. Her designs are creative; she's a very hard worker; she seems to know a lot about computers.

However, Peggy is in many ways an unsatisfactory staff member. Her standards are so high that most people find her intimidating. Some find her abrasive. People have complained to you that she's only interested in her own work; she seems to resent requests to help other people with projects. And yet both the newsletter and the web page are projects that need frequent interaction. She's out of the office a lot. Some of that is required by her job (she takes the newsletters to the post office, for example), but some people don't like the fact that she's out of the office so much. They also complain that she doesn't return voice mail and e-mail messages.

You think managing your office would be a lot smoother if Peggy weren't there. You can't fire her: state employees' jobs are secure once they get past the initial six-month probationary period. Because of budget constraints, you can hire new employees only if vacancies

are created by resignations. You feel that it would be pretty easy to find someone better.

If you recommend that John Inoye hire Peggy, you will be able to hire someone you want. If you recommend that John hire someone else, you may be stuck with Peggy for a long time.

As your instructor directs,

a. Write an e-mail message to John Inoye.

b. Write an e-mail to your instructor listing the choices you've made and justifying your approach.

Hints:

- Polarization may make this dilemma more difficult than it needs to be. What are your options? Consciously look for more than two.
- Is it possible to select facts or to use connotations so that you are truthful but still encourage John to hire Peggy? Is it ethical? Is it certain that John would find Peggy's work as unsatisfactory as you do? If you write a strong recommendation and Peggy doesn't do well at the new job, will your credibility suffer? Why is your credibility important?

11.15 Using Public Accountability as Persuasion

During the 2012 presidential election, some political action committees sought increased voter participation by sending eligible voters mailings indicating whether or not they voted in previous elections as well as whether or not their neighbors did. Although the mailings did not reveal how the neighbors voted, people receiving them reported feeling pressure to vote in the upcoming election because their past voting behaviors had become public knowledge.

Researchers have conducted studies on the psychology of social influence and found that when voters were held publicly accountable, the likelihood of them voting in the next election increased.[56] Some consider this a form of modern-day shaming, others dismiss it as harmless peer influence.

- How do you feel about having your voting record mailed to your neighbors?

- How do you feel about public accountability in other situations?

- Can you think of a business that uses public accountability to sell its products or services? If so, what language do they use in their advertisements? Do you think it is effective? Do you think it is ethical?

- Can you think of a way a specific charitable organization might utilize public accountability as a persuasive strategy? What might be some of the drawbacks of this strategy? Benefits?

- How would you feel about your electric company sharing your electricity usage with your neighbors? Would such an action cause you to use less electricity?

Discuss your answers in small groups.

11.16 Asking an Instructor for a Letter of Recommendation

You're ready for the job market, transfer to a four-year college, or graduate school, and you need letters of recommendation.

As your instructor directs,

a. Assume you've orally asked an instructor for a recommendation, and he or she has agreed to write one, but asks, "Why don't you write up something to remind me of what you've done in the class? Tell me what else you've done, too. And tell me what they're looking for. Be sure to tell me when the letter needs to be in and to whom it goes." Write the e-mail.

b. Assume you've been unable to talk with the instructor whose recommendation you want. When you call, no one answers the phone; you stopped by

once and no one was in. Write asking for a letter of recommendation.

c. Assume the instructor is no longer on campus. Write him or her asking for a recommendation.

Hints:

- Be detailed about what the organization is seeking and the points you'd like the instructor to mention.

- How well will this instructor remember you? How much detail about your performance in his or her class do you need to provide?

- Specify the name and address of the person to whom the letter should be written; specify when the letter is due.

11.17 Writing a Performance Review for a Member of a Collaborative Group

During your collaborative writing group meetings, keep a log of events. Record specific observations of both effective and ineffective things that group members do. Then evaluate the performance of the other members of your group. (If there are two or more other people, write a separate review for each of them.)

In your first paragraph, summarize your evaluation. Then in the body of your message, give the specific details that led to your evaluation by answering the following questions:

- What specifically did the person do in terms of the task? Brainstorm ideas? Analyze the information? Draft the text? Suggest revisions in parts drafted by others? Format the document or create visuals? Revise? Edit? Proofread? (In most cases, several people will have done each of these activities together. Don't overstate what any one person did.) What was the quality of the person's work?

- What did the person contribute to the group process? Did he or she help schedule the work? Raise

or resolve conflicts? Make other group members feel valued and included? Promote group cohesion? What roles did the person play in the group?

Support your generalizations with specific observations. The more observations you have and the more detailed they are, the better your review will be.

As your instructor directs,

a. Write a midterm performance review for one or more members of your collaborative group. In each review, identify the two or three things the person should try to improve during the second half of the term.

b. Write a performance review for one or more members of your collaborative group at the end of the term. Identify and justify the grade you think each person should receive for the portion of the grade based on group process.

c. Give a copy of your review to the person about whom it is written.

11.18 Writing a Self-Assessment for a Performance Review

Your company privileges good communication skills. In fact, during their second year, all employees are sent to a four-month communication course. As part of your annual review, you must prepare a self-assessment that includes your assessment of your progress in the communication course. Assume that your business communication course is the company's communication course and prepare the communications part of your self-assessment. The company expects this portion to be a page long.

11.19 Evaluating Sales and Fund-Raising Messages

Collect the sales and fund-raising messages that come to you, your co-workers, landlord, neighbors, or family. Use the following questions to evaluate each message:

- What mode does the opener use? Is it related to the rest of the message? How good is the opener?
- What central selling point or common ground does the message use?
- What kinds of proof does the message use? Is the logic valid? What questions or objections are not answered?
- How does the message create emotional appeal?
- Is the style effective?
- Does the close tell people what to do, make action easy, give a reason for acting promptly, and end with a positive picture?
- Does the message use a P.S.? How good is it?
- Is the message visually attractive? Why or why not?
- What other items besides the letter or e-mail are in the package?

As your instructor directs,

a. Share your analysis of one or more messages with a small group of your classmates.

b. Analyze one message in a presentation to the class. Make a copy of the message to use as a visual aid in your presentation.

c. Analyze one message in an e-mail to your instructor. Provide a copy of the message along with your e-mail.

d. With several other students, write a group e-mail or report analyzing one part of the message (e.g., openers) or one kind of letter (e.g., political messages, organizations fighting hunger, etc.). Use at least 10 messages for your analysis if you look at only one part; use at least 6 messages if you analyze one kind of message. Provide copies as an appendix to your report.

11.20 Comparing Persuasive Apology Letters

Soon after the iPhone 5 went on sale, Apple customers publicly aired grievances with the company for releasing a product with so many technical glitches in its mapping application. Within a week, Apple CEO Tim Cook issued an apology letter to disgruntled customers regarding these glitches. Many critics have compared Cook's apology to letters written by his predecessor, Steve Jobs. Others have argued that Cook's persuasive style is different in that he uses more persuasive strategies to build an intimate feeling of connectedness with his audience, something Jobs did not do.

Compare Cook's apology letter with Job's pricing apology. Make a list of similar strategies that both writers employ as well as a list of the different strategies each uses.

- What differences do you see in the salutations? The first paragraphs?
- How does each handle the explanation of the problem? The apology?
- How does the tone differ in the two letters?
- What differences do you see in the endings of each letter?

Discuss your lists in small groups. Together, decide which letter you found more persuasive and why. Write an e-mail to your instructor persuading him or her that your choice is the correct one.

To our customers,

At Apple, we strive to make world-class products that deliver the best experience possible to our customers. With the launch of our new Maps last week, we fell short on this commitment. We are extremely sorry for the frustration this has caused our customers and we are doing everything we can to make Maps better.

We launched Maps initially with the first version of iOS. As time progressed, we wanted to provide our customers with even better Maps including features such as turn-by-turn directions, voice integration, Flyover and vector-based maps. In order to do this, we had to create a new version of Maps from the ground up.

There are already more than 100 million iOS devices using the new Apple Maps, with more and more joining us every day. In just over a week, iOS users with the new Maps have already searched for nearly half a billion locations. The more our customers use our Maps the better it will get and we greatly appreciate all of the feedback we have received from you.

While we're improving Maps, you can try alternatives by downloading map apps from the App Store like Bing, MapQuest and Waze, or use Google or Nokia maps by going to their websites and creating an icon on your home screen to their web app.

Everything we do at Apple is aimed at making our products the best in the world. We know that you expect that from us, and we will keep working non-stop until Maps lives up to the same incredibly high standard.

Tim Cook

Apple's CEO

To all iPhone Customers:

I have received hundreds of emails from iPhone customers who are upset about Apple dropping the price of iPhone by $200 two months after it went on sale. After reading every one of these emails, I have some observations and conclusions.

First, I am sure that we are making the correct decision to lower the price of the 8GB iPhone from $599 to $399, and that now is the right time to do it. iPhone is a breakthrough product, and we have the chance to 'go for it' this holiday season. iPhone is so far ahead of the competition, and now it will be affordable by even more customers. It benefits both Apple and every iPhone user to get as many new customers as possible in the iPhone 'tent.' We strongly believe the $399 price will help us do just that this holiday season.

Second, being in technology for 30+ years I can attest to the fact that the technology road is bumpy. There is always change and improvement, and there is always someone who bought a product before a particular cutoff date and misses the new price or the new operating system or the new whatever. This is life in the technology lane. If you always wait for the next price cut or to buy the new improved model, you'll never buy any technology product because there is always something better and less expensive on the horizon. The good news is that if you buy products from companies that support them well, like Apple tries to do, you will receive years of useful and satisfying service from them even as newer models are introduced.

Third, even though we are making the right decision to lower the price of iPhone, and even though the technology road is bumpy, we need to do a better job taking care of our early iPhone customers as we aggressively go after new ones with a lower price. Our early customers trusted us, and we must live up to that trust with our actions in moments like these.

Therefore, we have decided to offer every iPhone customer who purchased an iPhone from either Apple or AT&T, and who is not receiving a rebate or any other consideration, a $100 store credit towards the purchase of any product at an Apple Retail Store or the Apple Online Store. Details are still being worked out and will be posted on Apple's website next week. Stay tuned.

We want to do the right thing for our valued iPhone customers. We apologize for disappointing some of you, and we are doing our best to live up to your high expectations of Apple.

Steve Jobs Apple CEO

Sources: Letter from Tim Cook, accessed June 14, 2013, http://www.apple.com/letter-from-tim-cook-on-maps/; and Letter from Steve Jobs, accessed September 30, 2012, http://opnlttr.com/letter/all-iphone-customers.

Notes

1. Daniel H. Pink, *To Sell Is Human: The Surprising Truth about Moving Others* (New York: Riverhead Books, 2012), 21.

2. Jay A. Conger, "The Necessary Art of Persuasion," *Harvard Business Review* 76, no. 3 (May–June 1998): 88.

3. John Kotter and Holger Rathgeber, *Our Iceberg Is Melting: Changing and Succeeding under Any Conditions* (New York: St. Martin's Press, 2005), 140.

4. Jonah Lehrer, *How We Decide* (New York: Houghton Mifflin Harcourt, 2009), 26, 235; and Jonah Lehrer, "Attention, Shoppers: Go with Your Gut," *Wall Street Journal*, October 1, 2011, C12.

5. Jonah Berger, *Contagious: Why Things Catch On* (New York: Simon & Schuster, 2013), 113–15.

6. Michael Sanserino, "Peer Pressure and Other Pitches," *Wall Street Journal*, September 14, 2009, B6.

7. Steve Martin, "98% of HBR Readers Love This Article: Businesses Are Just Beginning to Understand the Power of 'Social Norms,'" *Harvard Business Review* 90, no. 10 (October 2012): 23–25.

8. Vanessa Fuhrmans, "Training the Brain to Choose Wisely," *Wall Street Journal*, April 28, 2009, D1.

9. Leslie Kwoh, "Shape Up or Pay Up: Firms Put in New Health Penalties," *Wall Street Journal*, April 6, 2013, A1, A10.

10. Richard H. Thaler and Cass R. Sunstein, *Nudge: Improving Decisions about Health, Wealth, and Happiness* (New Haven, CT: Yale University Press, 2008), 65–70.

11. Daniel H. Pink, *Drive: The Surprising Truth about What Motivates Us* (New York: Riverhead Books, 2009); and Tomas Chamorro-Premuzic, "Does Money Really Affect Motivation? A Review of the Research," *HBR Blog Network*, April 10, 2013, http://blogs.hbr.org/cs/2013/04/does_money_really_affect_motiv.html.

12. Pink, *Drive*, 145.

13. Berger, *Contagious*, 151–53.

14. Joseph Walker, "Google's Algorithms for Talent," *Wall Street Journal*, July 5, 2012, B1; and Claire Suddath, "Let's Put on a Show!" *Bloomberg Businessweek*, January 7, 2013, 66–67.

15. Chip Heath and Dan Heath, *Made to Stick: Why Some Ideas Survive and Others Die* (New York: Random House, 2007), 195–98; and Mark Schoofs, "Novel Police Tactic Puts Drug Markets out of Business: Confronted by the Evidence, Dealers in High Point, N.C., Succumb to Pressure," *Wall Street Journal*, September 27, 2006, A1, A16.

16. "'Don't Mess with Texas' Anti-Litter Ad Features Strait," *Des Moines Register*, May 11, 2010, 2A.

17. Daniel Gilbert, *Stumbling on Happiness* (New York: Alfred A. Knopf, 2006), 165, 168–70.

18. National Science Foundation, "Why 'Scientific Consensus' Fails to Persuade," news release, September 13, 2010, http://www.nsf.gov/news/news_summ.jsp?cntn_id5117697.

19. Min-Sun Kim and Steven R. Wilson, "A Cross-Cultural Comparison of Implicit Theories of Requesting," *Communication Monographs* 61, no. 3 (September 1994): 210–35; and K. Yoon, C. H. Kim, and M. S. Kim, "A Cross-Cultural Comparison of the Effects of Source Credibility on Attitudes and Behavior Intentions," *Mass Communication and Society* 1, nos. 3 and 4 (1998): 153–73.

20. Peggy E. Chaudhry and Stephen A. Stumpf, "Getting Real about Fakes," *Wall Street Journal*, August 17, 2009, R4.

21. David Wessel, "Inside Dr. Bernanke's E.R.," *Wall Street Journal*, July 18, 2009, W3.

22. Karen Blumenthal, "Fraud Doesn't Always Happen to Someone Else," *Wall Street Journal*, August 12, 2009, D1.

23. Ray Considine and Murray Raphael, *The Great Brain Robbery* (Los Angeles: Rosebud Books, 1980), 95–96.

24. Phred Dvorak, "How Understanding the 'Why' of Decisions Matters," *Wall Street Journal*, March 19, 2007, B3.

25. Heath and Heath, *Made to Stick*, 165–68.

26. Scott Robinette, "Get Emotional," *Harvard Business Review* 79, no. 5 (May 2001): 24–25.

27. "Around the World," *Washington Post*, March 27, 2009, A14.

28. Jeffrey Zaslow, "The Most-Praised Generation Goes to Work," *Wall Street Journal*, April 20, 2007, W1, W7; and Rachel Emma Silverman, "Performance Reviews, Facebook Style," *Wall Street Journal*, August 1, 2012, B6.

29. Rachel Emma Silverman, "Yearly Reviews? Try Weekly," *Wall Street Journal*, September 6, 2011, B6; and Silverman, "Performance Reviews, Facebook Style."

30. Silverman, "Yearly Reviews? Try Weekly."

31. "Fort Hood Suspect's Personnel File Filled with Praise, Despite Problems," *Des Moines Register*, January 20, 2010, 5A.

32. Samuel A. Culbert, "Get Rid of the Performance Review! It Destroys Morale, Kills Teamwork, and Hurts the Bottom Line. And That's Just for Starters," *Wall Street Journal*, June 21, 2012, http://online.wsj.com/article/SB122426318874844933.html; and Jared Sandberg, "Performance Reviews Need Some Work, Don't Meet Potential," *Wall Street Journal*, November 20, 2007, B1.

33. "Microsoft's Downfall: Inside the Executive E-Mails and Cannibalistic Culture that Felled a Tech Giant," *VanityFair.com*, July 3, 2012, http://www.vanityfair.com/online/daily/2012/07/microsoft-downfall-emails-steve-ballmer.

34. Joe Light, "Performance Reviews by the Numbers," *Wall Street Journal*, June 29, 2010, D4.

35. Steve Salerno, "As Seen on TV: But Wait . . . There's More!" *Wall Street Journal*, March 25, 2009, A11.

36. David Gauthier-Villars, "Water Fight in France Takes a Dirty Turn," *Wall Street Journal*, February 1, 2007, B7.

37. "The Pledge," National Disaster Search Dog Foundation, accessed June 12, 2013, http://www.searchdogfoundation.org/images/3_pledge.jpg.

38. "How to Launch a Direct-Mail Campaign," *BusinessWeek SmallBiz*, August/September 2008, 28.

39. Patrick Spenner and Karen Freeman, "To Keep Your Customers, Keep It Simple," *Harvard Business Review* 90, no. 5 (May 2012): 108–14.

40. Barbara Kiviat, "Why We Buy: Consumers Tend to Go with What (Little) They Know," *Time*, August 27, 2007, 50–51.

41. Clayton M. Christensen, James Allworth, and Karen Dillon, *How Will You Measure Your Life?* (New York: Harper Business, 2012), 109–10.

42. Jeffrey Gitomer, *Little Red Book of Sales Answers: 99.5 Real World Answers That Make Sense, Make Sales, and Make Money* (Upper Saddle River, NJ: Prentice Hall, 2006), 112.

43. Dan Ariely, *Predictably Irrational: The Hidden Forces that Shape Our Decisions*, rev. ed. (New York: Harper Perennial, 2008), 4.

44. Daniel Kahneman, *Thinking, Fast and Slow* (New York: Farrar, Straus and Giroux, 2011), 119, 124.

45. Beth Negus Viveiros, "Gifts for Life," *Direct*, July (2004): 9.

46. Charity: Water home page, accessed June 15, 2013, http://www.charitywater.org.

47. Lee Rood, "Little Raised over Phone Goes to Charity," *Des Moines Register*, December 14, 2008, 1A.

48. Fund-raising letter from Kevin M Ryan. Undated correspondence.

49. Maxwell Sackheim, *My First Sixty-Five Years in Advertising* (Blue Ridge Summit, PA: Tab Books, 1975), 97–100.

50. Suzanne Vranica, "Chrysler, Taco Bell Win in Ad Bowl," *Wall Street Journal,* February 4, 2013, B1.

51. Barbara Giamanco and Kent Gregoire, "Tweet Me, Friend Me, Make Me Buy," *Harvard Business Review* 90, no. 7–8, (July–August 2012): 88–93.

52. Olga Kharif, "Social Media: Finding a Haystack's Most Influential Needles," *Bloomberg Businessweek,* October 22, 2012, 46–48.

53. Harald Weinreich et al., "Not Quite the Average: An Empirical Study of Web Use," *ACM Transactions on the Web* 2, no. 1 (2008): 18.

54. Mark Milian, "How Ridiculous Are QR Codes? Scan This One to Find Out," *Bloomberg Businessweek,* July 2, 2012, 28–29.

55. "Despite Advancements in Social Communication, Email Is Far from Dead," *Business2Community.com,* April 29, 2013, http://www.business2community.com/sponsored/despite-advancements-in-social-communication-email-is-far-from-dead-0479236; and Elizabeth Holmes, "Dark Art of Store Emails," *Wall Street Journal,* December 19, 2012, D1.

56. Gregory Korte, "Shaming Voters to Vote: How Groups Use Peer Pressure," *USA Today,* November 2, 2012, http://www.usatoday.com/story/news/politics/2012/11/02/peer-pressure-and-voting/1675019/.

12 Building Résumés

Chapter Outline

Dishonesty Hurts

When Yahoo Inc. hired Scott Thompson in January 2012, the company believed it was getting a great leader. Thompson had a strong history of success leading companies and an impeccable résumé that included dual bachelor's degrees in accounting and computer science.

But the résumé was a lie. Thompson did have more than 30 years of industry experience and was known for his technical prowess. But he graduated from Stonehill College in 1979 with only a degree in business administration. The school didn't even have a computer science program until the early 1980s. At some point in his career, the extra degree was added to his résumé through what Yahoo terms "an inadvertent error." Thompson resigned from Yahoo shortly after the mistake was revealed.

Résumé dishonesty is unfortunately all too common, even among high-profile executives. Here are a few of the most public from the past several years:

■ British chef Robert Irvine lost his job on Food Network's *Dinner Impossible* after overstating his contributions to Princess Diana's wedding cake.

■ Wall Street analyst Jack Grubman was fired from his $20 million per year job for saying that he attended MIT when he never did.

■ Notre Dame's head football coach George O'Leary was fired five days after being hired when it was revealed he didn't get a master's degree or play college football, despite claims to the contrary on his résumé.

Hiring managers can easily check the claims you make on your résumé, and lying can keep you from getting a job or cause you to lose your job.

Sources: Amir Efrati and Joann S. Lublin, "Résumé Trips Up Yahoo's Chief," *Wall Street Journal*, May 5, 2012, A1; and Vivian Giang and Jhaneel Lockhart, "Busted: This Is What Happened to 10 Executives Who Lied About Their Résumés," *Business Insider*, May 7, 2012, http://www.businessinsider.com/9-people-who-were-publicly-shamed-for-lying-on-their-resumes-2012-5?op=1.

Learning Objectives

After studying this chapter, you will know how to

LO 12-1 Prepare a detailed time line for your job search.

LO 12-2 Conduct an effective job search.

LO 12-3 Prepare a résumé that makes you look attractive to employers.

LO 12-4 Deal with common difficulties that arise during job searches.

LO 12-5 Handle the online portion of job searches.

LO 12-6 Keep your résumé honest.

Job Hunt Organization

The amount of information you gather during a job search can be overwhelming. Here are some tips for staying organized:

- Bookmark important websites, such as job postings, company HR sites, and industry information sites.
- Save jobs on online job sites, so you don't have to begin with a new search each day.
- Track your progress. Use a spreadsheet, physical or virtual folders, and your calendar to keep application deadlines and progress organized.
- Use online tools such as JibberJobber, StartWire, or ones provided on the job listing sites to manage your deadlines and information.

Adapted from Debra Auerbach, "Keep Organized During Job Hunt," *Des Moines Register*, November 4, 2012, 1K.

You will probably change jobs many times during your career. The U.S. Bureau of Labor Statistics' National Longitudinal Survey of Youth shows that the average person held an average of 11 jobs from age 18 to age 44. Even in middle age, when job changing slows down, 69% of jobs ended in fewer than five years. This means you should always keep your résumé up to date.[1]

A **résumé** is a persuasive summary of your qualifications for a job with a specific employer. If you're on the job market, having a résumé is a basic step in the job hunt. When you're employed, having an up-to-date résumé makes it easier to take advantage of opportunities that may come up for even better jobs. If you're several years away from job hunting, preparing a résumé now will help you become more conscious of what to do in the next two or three years to make yourself an attractive candidate.

This chapter covers paper and electronic résumés. Job application letters (sometimes called cover letters) are discussed in Chapter 13. Chapter 14 discusses interviews and communications after the interview. All three chapters focus on job hunting in the United States. Conventions, expectations, and criteria differ from culture to culture; different norms apply in different countries.

All job communications should be tailored to your unique qualifications and the specifications of the job you want. Adopt the wording or layout of an example if it's relevant to your own situation, but don't be locked into the forms in this book. You've got different strengths; your résumé will be different, too.

A Time Line for Job Hunting LO 12-1

Many employers consider the way you do your job hunt to be evidence of the way you will work for them. Therefore, you should start preparing yourself several years ahead of your formal applications.

Informal preparation for job hunting should start soon after you arrive on campus. Check out the services of your college placement and advising offices. Join extracurricular organizations on campus and in the community to increase your knowledge and provide a network for learning about jobs. Find a job that gives you experience. Note which courses you like—and why you like them. If you like thinking and learning about a subject, you're more likely to enjoy a job in that field. Select course projects and paper topics that will help you prepare for a job—and look good on your résumé.

Keep track of your classes, papers, and work experiences. Make notes in an electronic file or working résumé of skills and lessons you learned, along with stories about your successes and even your failures. Documenting your experiences as you have them will help you when you are ready to look for a job: you will have a trove of information for your résumé, cover letter, and job interviews.

Once you have selected a major, start reading job ads, particularly those posted on your professional organization's website. What kinds of jobs are available? Do you need to change your course selections to better fit them? What kinds of extras are employers seeking? Do they want communication skills? Extra statistics courses? International experience? Learn this information early while you still have time to add to the knowledge and skill sets you are acquiring. Attend job seminars and job fairs. Join your professional association and its Listserv.

Formal preparation for job hunting should begin a full year *before you begin interviewing.* Enroll for the services of your campus placement office. Ask friends who are on the job market about their experiences in interviews; find out what kinds of job offers they get. Check into the possibility of getting an internship or a co-op job that will give you relevant experience before you interview.

If you are already working, make sure your job search does not interfere with your current employment. Even if you hate your job, acting professionally and searching for a new job outside of work hours or on lunch breaks will help you keep your job and, more importantly, the good reference of your current employer.

The year you interview, register with your placement office early. An active job search takes significant chunks of time, so plan accordingly. If you plan to graduate in the spring, prepare your résumé and plan your interview strategy early in the fall. Initial campus interviews occur from October to February for May or June graduation. In January or February, write to any organization you'd like to work for that hasn't interviewed on campus. From February to April, you're likely to visit one or more offices for a second interview.

Try to have a job offer lined up *before* you get the degree. People who don't need jobs immediately are more confident in interviews and usually get better job offers. If you have to job-hunt after graduation, plan to spend at least 30 hours a week on your job search. The time will pay off in a better job that you find more quickly.

Evaluating Your Strengths and Interests

A self-assessment is the first step in producing a good résumé. Each person could do several jobs happily. Richard Bolles, a nationally recognized expert in career advising for over a third of a century and author of the *What Color Is Your Parachute?* books, says most people who don't find a job they like fail because they lack information about themselves.[2] Personality and aptitude tests can tell you some of your strengths, but you should still answer for yourself questions such as these:

■ What skills and strengths do you have?

■ What achievements have given you the most satisfaction? *Why* did you enjoy them? What jobs would offer these kinds of satisfactions?

■ What work conditions do you like? Would you rather have firm deadlines or a flexible schedule? Do you prefer working independently or with other people? Do you prefer specific instructions and standards for evaluation or freedom and uncertainty? How comfortable are you with pressure? How much challenge do you want?

What Employers Want

Hiring managers look for a range of qualities in a job candidate. Here are a few of the most common:

1. **Fit.** Will the candidate fit in with the company and fill current needs?

2. **Longevity.** Will the candidate stay with the company long-term?

3. **Professionalism.** Does the candidate communicate professionally in written documents and the interview?

4. **Relevant experience.** Can the candidate make his/her job or volunteer experience relevant to the company?

5. **Collaboration.** Will the candidate be able to work with other employees *and* provide leadership?

6. **Learning ability.** Will the candidate be able to learn the job quickly and to continue learning on the job?

7. **Cross-cultural experience.** Does the candidate have international experiences that would help in the new position?

8. **Enthusiasm.** Is the candidate clearly interested in the job? Does he or she show the energy necessary for the work?

Sources: Robert Half International, "What Employers Think When They Read Your Résumé," *CareerBuilder,* September, 23, 2008, http://www.careerbuilder.com/Article/CB-427-Resumes-Cover-Letters-What-Employers-Think-When-They-Read-Your-R%C3%A9sum%C3%A9/; and Chana R. Schoenberger, "Help Wanted . . . But in a Whole New Way," *Wall Street Journal,* October 29, 2012, B10.

- What kind of work/life balance do you want? Are you willing to take work home? To work weekends? To travel? How important is money to you? Prestige? Time to spend with family and friends?

- How fast do you want to move up? Are you willing to pay your dues for several years before you are promoted?

- Where do you want to live? What features in terms of weather, geography, cultural and social life do you see as ideal?

- Is it important to you that your work achieve certain purposes or values, or do you see work as just a way to make a living? Are an organization's culture and ethical standards important to you? If so, what values will you look for?

Once you know what is most important to you, check to see what businesses are looking for (see the sidebar "What Employers Want" on page 377). Then analyze the job market to see where you could find what you want. Each possibility will require somewhat different training and course selection, underscoring the need for you to begin considering your job search process early in your college career.

Conducting a Job Search   LO 12-2

Most people think they know how to conduct a job search. You prepare a résumé, look through a few job ads, send your application in, interview, and get the job, right? According to most experts, that's wrong. Successful job searches rely on much more than putting the right things on résumés. In fact, according to Richard Bolles, employers look for employees in the exact opposite way from the way most people look for jobs.[3] Employers prefer to hire people in the following order:

1. From within their organization.
2. With proof of expertise, through a job portfolio.
3. With a reference from a trusted friend.
4. From a trusted recruiting agency.
5. From a job advertisement.
6. From a résumé.

A simple résumé is the last on the list for a reason: it is very difficult to tell from a résumé what kind of worker a person will be. Some employers are now moving away from placing job ads in favor of searching for new employees through personal and online networks.

To be successful in your job search, you should

- Use the Internet effectively.

- Build relationships through internships and networking.

- Establish a reputation online through wise use of social media.

- Be prepared with excellent traditional résumés and cover letters.

Using the Internet Effectively in Your Job Search

The Internet is a crucial tool for job seekers as well as employers. There are thousands of pages of information about job searches and preparing yourself for a career. The key during your search is to use the Internet effectively.

Figure 12.1	Job Listings on the Web

America's Job Bank	**Monster.com**
www.jobbankinfo.org	www.monster.com
CareerBuilder.com	**MonsterTrak**
www.careerbuilder.com	college.monster.com
Careers.org	
www.careers.org	Job listings from the *Chicago Tribune*, *Detroit News*, *Los Angeles Times*, *Miami Herald*, *Philadelphia Inquirer*, *San Jose Mercury News*, and other city newspapers' websites.
EmploymentGuide.com	
www.employmentguide.com	
Federal Jobs Career Central	
www.fedjobs.com	
Indeed.com	
www.indeed.com	

Probably the most common use of the Internet for job candidates is to search for openings (see Figure 12.1). In addition to popular job boards such as Monster and CareerBuilder, job candidates typically search for jobs posted on organizations' Facebook pages, LinkedIn sites, and Twitter (TwitJobSearch .com). Many successful companies are reducing their postings on job boards in favor of recruiting through social networking sites.

Job candidates also check electronic listings in local newspapers and professional societies. However, you do need to be careful when responding to online ads. Some of them turn out to be pitches from career or financial services firms, or even phishing ads—ploys from identity thieves seeking your personal information.

Phishing ads often look like real postings; many have company names and logos nearly identical to those of real employers. People behind phishing ads may even e-mail job candidates to build trust. Privacy experts caution job candidates to be particularly careful with job postings that lack details about the hiring company or job description, and ads that list a large salary range.[4]

In addition to searching for ads, every job candidate should check the Internet for information about writing résumés and application letters, researching specific companies and jobs, and preparing for interviews. Many comprehensive sites give detailed information that will help you produce more effective documents and be a better-prepared job candidate.

As you search the web, remember that not all sites are current and accurate. In particular, be careful of .com sites: some are good, others are not. And even good sources can have advice that is bad for you. Check your school's career site for help. Check the sites of other schools: Stanford, Berkeley, and Columbia have particularly excellent career sites. Figure 12.2 lists some of the best sites.

A relatively new use of the Internet for job searchers is online job fairs. At online fairs, you can browse through virtual booths, leave your résumé at promising ones, and sometimes even apply on the spot, all without leaving your home. Other advantages of online job fairs are their wide geographic range and 24-hour access.

As you do all this research for your job hunt, you will probably begin to find conflicting advice. When evaluating suggestions, consider the age of the advice; what was true five years ago may not be true today, because the job search process is changing so much. Also consider your industry; general

Figure 12.2	Comprehensive Websites Covering the Entire Job Search Process

About.com (Part of New York Times Company) http://jobsearch.about.com	Monster.com http://www.monster.com
Campus Career Center http://www.campuscareercenter.com	MonsterCollege http://college.monster.com
CareerBuilder http://www.careerbuilder.com	OWL (Purdue Online Writing Lab) http://owl.english.purdue.edu
Career Rookie http://www.careerrookie.com	Quintessential Careers http://www.quintcareers.com
College Central http://www.collegecentral.com	The Riley Guide http://www.rileyguide.com
College Grad Job Hunter http://www.collegegrad.com	Spherion Career Center http://www.spherion.com/job-seekers
The Five O'Clock Club http://www.fiveoclockclub.com	Wetfeet http://www.wetfeet.com
JobHuntersBible.com (Dick Bolles) http://www.jobhuntersbible.com	Vault http://www.vault.com

advice that works for most may not work for your industry. Above all, consider what advice helps you present yourself as favorably as possible.

Building Relationships through Networking

Many experts now consider networking to be THE most important factor in finding a job. It is important for entry-level work and becomes even more crucial as you advance in your career.

Networking starts with people you know—friends, family, friends of your parents, classmates, teammates, gym mates, colleagues—and quickly expands to your electronic contacts in social media. Let people know you are looking for a job, and what your job assets are. Use social media to emphasize your field knowledge and accomplishments. Join your school's alumni association to find alumni in businesses that interest you.

Begin early in your job time line to contact people in your chosen field. Your professors likely have friends in your industry. Job fairs, special lectures, and field trips give you opportunities to meet people and begin building your network. Be prepared for these opportunities and don't be afraid to introduce yourself and ask questions.

The secret to successful networking is reciprocity. Too many people network just for themselves, and they quickly gain a "one-way" reputation that hurts further networking. Good networkers work for a "two-way" reputation; to earn it, they look for ways to reciprocate. They help their contacts make fruitful connections. They share useful information and tips. Successful networks are not just for finding jobs: they are vital for career success.

Building Relationships through Internships

Internships are becoming increasingly important as ways to build relationships and to find out about professions, employers, and jobs. Many companies use their internships to find full-time employees. GE, for example, makes about 80% of its new-graduate hires from students who held summer

Figure 12.3	Percentage of Interns Offered Full-Time Jobs
Industry	**Percentage**
Entertainment/media	85
Oil and gas extraction	81
Construction	80
Accounting	75
Food and beverage	71
Retail	70
Finance/insurance/real estate	67
Engineering	67
Computer and electronics	64
Chemical/pharmaceutical	61

Source: Joe Walker, "Getting Creative to Land an Internship," *Wall Street Journal,* June 8, 2010, D7.

internships with the company. A *Wall Street Journal* survey of college recruiters found 25% reporting that more than 50% of their new-graduate hires came from their intern pools. The National Association of Colleges and Employers found in a survey of internships that 57% of interns became full-time hires (see Figure 12.3). In fact, some industry experts are predicting that within the next few years intern recruiting will largely replace entry-level recruiting.[5]

Even if your internship does not lead to a full-time job, it can still give you valuable insight into the profession, as well as contacts you can use in your job search. An increasingly important side benefit is the work you do in your internship, which can become some of the best items in your professional portfolio.

Establishing a Reputation Online

When you are searching for a job, a good reputation is vital to your success. According to one recent survey, nearly all employers use social media to find new employees. Of those, 98% use LinkedIn, 42% use Twitter, and 33% use Facebook.[6] Even more use social networking sites to learn about job candidates who have already applied. Using social media wisely can help you build your reputation and become visible to employers.

A specialized use of the Internet is **personal branding**, a popular term for marketing yourself, including job searching. It covers an expectation that you will use various options, from the traditional résumé and cover letter to social media, to market your expertise. As has always been true of job searches, you will use these tools to show your value (what do you offer employers?) and quality (why should they hire you instead of other candidates?). These are some of the most popular tools:

- **LinkedIn:** This site allows you to include useful information beyond your résumé, and, unlike your web page, it has a powerful search engine behind it.

- **Personal web page:** Your web page allows you to connect to examples of your professional work. You should invest in a domain name that includes your name. This helps you control how you will show up in online searches, since most search algorithms favor URLs that include the search term.[7]

- **Blogs:** A blog can contribute to your professional image if it focuses on your professional specialty and current issues in your field. However, keeping a blog up to date is time-consuming work during an already stressful period. An out-of-date, irrelevant, or poorly written blog can hurt your online branding.

- **Facebook:** If you keep your Facebook profile up to date with your education, employment, and interests, it can serve as an attractive informal résumé. Manage your privacy settings to make only those things that would be important for an employer to see public. But remember that Facebook has a history of making personal information public. Keep all of your content professional. Avoid inappropriate language and all content involving alcohol, other drugs, and incomplete attire.

- **Google Plus:** Use a Google Plus account to connect with other people in your field, engage with employers, and develop your professional image. As you should do with Facebook, keep your profile up-to-date and be professional in all of your posts, photos, and communications.

- **Twitter:** Share useful information such as thoughtful comments about news in your field as you work to build up your Twitter network. Aim for quality, not numbers. Also, follow companies you would like to work for and people throughout your profession.

- **Professional forums:** Participate thoughtfully; doing so enables people to recognize your name favorably when your application arrives.

However you develop your personal brand using these tools, remember that consistency matters. Use your résumé, cover letter, personal website, and social networking to create a consistent, professional image that demonstrates the qualities you want your potential employer to see. This consistency includes seemingly small details such as your profile photo you include on LinkedIn or Facebook and large details like your samples of professional work and blog posts. When you develop a consistent personal brand, employers are more likely to view your profiles, interview you, and hire you.[8]

WARNING: Select your tools carefully; you probably do not have time to use successfully all the tools on this list. Stay professional in all venues; avoid negative comments about people, your school, and your employers. In addition to content, writing (grammar, coherence, style, logic, spelling) will be judged by potential employers. The list of candidates rejected after a basic web search grows daily.

A Caution about Blogs, Social Networking Sites, and Internet Tracking

Most employers routinely search the Internet for information about job candidates, and many report they are turned off by what they find—especially on personal blogs and web pages and social networking sites such as Facebook.

Use the "Grandma Test" when you are posting anything online. If you wouldn't want her to see it, you won't want an employer to, either. See the "Cleanup Assistance" sidebar on this page.

One international survey found that 1 in 10 job applicants from the ages 16 to 34 had been rejected for a job because of their Facebook activities.[9] If you have a personal blog, web page, or other electronic presence, check your sites carefully before you enter the job market.

- Remove any unprofessional material such as pictures of you at your computer with a beer in your hand or descriptions of your last party.

- Remove negative comments about current or past employers and teachers. People who spread dirt in one context will probably do so in others, and no one wants to hire such people.

- Remove political and social rants. While thoughtful, supported opinions can show both education and logic, emotional or extreme statements will turn off most employers.

- Remove any personal information that will embarrass you on the job. If you blog about romance novels, but don't want to be teased about your choice in literature on your new job, make ruthless cuts on your blog.

- Remove inappropriate material posted by friends, relatives, and colleagues.

- Check your blog for writing aptitude. Many employers will consider your blog an extended writing sample. If yours is full of grammatical and spelling errors, obviously you are not a good writer.

Even if you take your blog off-line while you are job searching, employers may still find it in cached data on search engines. The best advice is to plan ahead and post nothing unprofessional on the web.

 WARNING: According to a 2012 survey conducted by CareerBuilder.com, 40% of recruiters also check photo- and video-sharing sites, gaming sites, virtual world sites, and classifieds and auction sites such as Craigslist, Amazon, and eBay.[10]

Innovative Uses of the Internet in Job Searches

Your best bet in establishing a good online reputation is to stick with standard uses of websites and social media. While there are opportunities for innovative job applications and résumés on the Internet, many employers will shy away from flashy displays in favor of more conventional professional materials. Unless you are in advertising, design, or another creative field, be very careful how you use the following tools:

- **Video and multimedia.** Some job applicants will post videos of themselves talking about their expertise or experience. While videos do give employers an opportunity to see your personality and make a connection, they also open up doors to possible discrimination. Additionally, employers may judge you by the production quality of your videos.

- **Social media résumés.** As noted above, Twitter, Facebook, and Google+ all offer opportunities to connect with employers and showcase your education, experience, and professionalism. Some users take social media a step further, however, and focus their profiles and posts entirely on getting a job. While this may draw attention, it may also make you appear desperate instead of confident. Employers turn to social media to get a more complete picture of applicants. Balance your posts and your information

great idea

to show off the best information about yourself rather than simply your desire for a job.

- **Imitation product websites.** In 2013, one enterprising web product manager named Philippe Dubost created his résumé as an imitation of an Amazon .com product page, complete with user reviews. His website drew millions of visitors and inspired profiles on news sites.[11] Others have imitated different sites for their résumés. While this certainly draws attention if it is done well, it may not necessarily lead to employment.

- **Prezumes.** A growing number of people are creating interactive résumés using the online presentation tool Prezi. These "prezumes" include animation, narration, and music to show employers the applicants' skills and personalities. Like the other innovative uses of the Internet, prezumes can be successful, but you should use this tool only if you can produce it well and it makes sense for your future career.

Innovative uses of the Internet may draw attention, but you are more likely to be successful in your job search if you are continually building a solid online reputation through your wise use of social media.

Be Prepared with an Excellent Traditional Résumé and Cover Letter

Although all of your searching online, building relationships, and using social media will be important in your job search, when you apply for a job you will most likely need to have a traditional cover letter and résumé ready to present to the potential employer. Even when an employer contacts you to recruit you, the first request will most likely be to send a copy of your documents to the company.

The best strategy is to create and maintain your résumé so you don't need to scramble when an employer contacts you. You should be able to respond with your materials almost immediately. The remainder of this chapter will discuss how to produce an effective résumé. Cover letters will be discussed in Chapter 13.

How Employers Use Résumés LO 12-3

Understanding how employers use résumés will help you create a résumé that works for you.

1. **Employers use résumés to decide whom to interview.** (The major exceptions are on-campus interviews, where the campus placement office has policies that determine who meets with the interviewer.) Résumés are examined for relevant experience and skills such as those in Figure 12.4. Since résumés are also used to screen out applicants, omit anything that may create a negative impression.

2. **Résumés are scanned or skimmed.** At many companies, especially large ones, résumés are scanned electronically. Only résumés that match key words are skimmed by a human being. A human may give a résumé 10 to 30 seconds before deciding to keep or toss it. You must design your résumé to pass both the "scan test" and the "skim test" by emphasizing crucial qualifications and using the diction of the job ad.

Figure 12.4	Percentage of Employers Who Want Colleges to Place More Emphasis on These Skills	
Skill		**Percent**
Effective communication, both oral and written		89
Critical thinking and analytical reasoning		81
Application of knowledge to the work world, through internships and other hands-on experiences		79
Ability to analyze and solve complex problems		75
Teamwork		71
Innovation and creativity		70
Understanding of basic concepts and new developments in science and technology		70
Ability to locate, organize, and evaluate information from multiple sources		68
Understanding of global contexts and developments		67
Ability to work with numbers and understand statistics		63

Source: From *Raising the Bar: Employers' Views on College Learning in the Wake of the Economic Downturn: A Survey among Employers Conducted on Behalf of the Association of American Colleges and Universities,* January 20, 2010. Reprinted with permission.

3. **Employers assume that your letter and résumé represent your best work.** Neatness, accuracy, and freedom from typographical errors are essential. Spelling errors will probably cost you your chance at a job, so proofread carefully.

4. **After an employer has chosen an applicant, he or she submits the applicant's résumé to people in the organization who must approve the appointment.** These people may have different backgrounds and areas of expertise. Spell out acronyms. Explain awards, Greek-letter honor societies, unusual job titles, or organizations that may be unfamiliar to the reader.

Guidelines for Résumés

Writing a résumé is not an exact science. What makes your friend look good does not necessarily help you. If your skills are in great demand, you can violate every guideline here and still get a good job. But when you must compete against many applicants, these guidelines will help you look as good on paper as you are in person.

Length

A one-page résumé is sufficient, but you must fill the page. Less than a full page suggests that you do not have much to say for yourself.

If you have more good material than will fit on one page, use a second page. A common myth is that all résumés must fit on one page. According to surveys conducted by international staffing firm Accountemps of executives at the 1,000 largest companies in this country, approval of the two-page résumé is increasing *if* candidates have sufficient good material that relates to the posted job.[12] An experiment that mailed one- or two-page résumés to

How Coca-Cola Hires

Coca-Cola is a huge company, with 146,000 corporate employees and another 550,000 employees who work for its bottling partners.

To maintain its level of success, Coca-Cola strives to attract and keep the best employees. Its most successful method of hiring is through current employees referring people in their networks to the company.

As the company considers applicants, however, it looks for a combination of the right skills and intangible qualities. These include

1. Teamwork.
2. Innovation.
3. Ability to get results.
4. Sharing common values.
5. Caring for the environment.
6. Appreciating the Coca-Cola brand.

Getting the right employees in place keeps Coca-Cola a world leader.

Adapted from Damian Ghigliotty, "Coke's Secret Hiring Formula," *HR Insider,* May 30, 2012, http://sales-jobs.fins.com/Articles/SBB0001424052702304840904577424442684831730/Coke-s-Secret-Hiring-Formula?reflink=djm_emailfinshouse_061512_wsjpa.

recruiters at major accounting firms showed that even readers who said they preferred short résumés were more likely to want to interview the candidate with the longer résumé.[13] The longer résumé gives managers a better picture of how you will fit in.

If you do use more than one page, the second page should have at least 10 to 12 lines. Use a second sheet of paper; do not print on the back of the first page. Leave less important information for the second page. Put your name and "Page 2" on the page. If the pages are separated, you want the reader to know that the qualifications belong to you and that the second page is not your whole résumé.

Emphasis

Emphasize the things you've done that (a) are most relevant to the position for which you're applying, (b) show your superiority to other applicants, and (c) are recent (in the past three to five years). Whatever your age at the time you write a résumé, you want to suggest that you are now the best you've ever been.

Show that you're qualified by giving relevant details on course projects, activities, and jobs where you've done similar work. Be brief about low-level jobs that simply show dependability. To prove that you're the best candidate for the job, emphasize items that set you apart from other applicants: promotions, honors, achievements, experience with computers or other relevant equipment, statistics, foreign languages, and so on.

You can emphasize material by putting it at the top or the bottom of a page, by giving it more space, and by setting it off with white space. The beginning and end—of a document, a page, a list—are positions of emphasis. When you have a choice (e.g., in a list of job duties), put less important material in the middle, not at the end, to avoid the impression of "fading out." You can also emphasize material by presenting it in a vertical list, by using informative headings, and by providing details. Headings that name skills listed in the job ad, or skills important for the job (e.g., Managerial Experience), also provide emphasis and help set you apart from the crowd.

Details

Details provide evidence to support your claims, convince the reader, and separate you from other applicants. Numbers make good details. Tell how many people you trained or supervised, how much money you budgeted or saved. Describe the interesting aspects of the job you did.

Too vague:	Sales Manager, *The Daily Collegian*, University Park, PA, 2012–2014. Supervised staff; promoted ad sales.
Good details:	Sales Manager, *The Daily Collegian*, University Park, PA, 2012–2014. Supervised 22-member sales staff; helped recruit, interview, and select staff; assigned duties and scheduled work; recommended best performers for promotion. Motivated staff to increase paid ad inches 10% over previous year's sales.

Omit details that add nothing to a title, that are less impressive than the title alone, or that suggest a faulty sense of priorities (e.g., listing hours per week spent filing). Either use strong details or just give the office or job title without any details.

Almost certainly, you can create a better résumé by adapting a basic style you like to your own unique qualifications. Experiment with layout, fonts, and spacing to get an attractive résumé. Consider creating a letterhead that you use for both your résumé and your application letter.

Determine your best selling points and promote them early. Since most résumés will be put into electronic formats (discussed later), make sure the first screen of information about you is strong, tempting readers to look further.

One of the major decisions you will make is how to treat your **headings**. Do you want them on the left margin, with text immediately below them, as in Figure 12.5? Do you want them alone in the left column, with text in a column to the right, as in Figure 12.8? Generally, people with more text on their résumés use the first option. Putting headings in their own column on the left takes space and thus helps spread a thinner list of accomplishments over the page. But be careful not to make the heading column too wide, or it will make your résumé look unbalanced and empty.

Work with **fonts**, bullets, and spacing to highlight your information. Be careful, however, not to make your résumé look "busy" by using too many fonts. Generally, you should use only two fonts in a document, and you should avoid unusual fonts. Keep fonts readable by using at least 10-point type for large fonts such as Arial and 11-point for smaller fonts such as Times New Roman. Use enough white space to group items and make your résumé easy to read, but not so much that you look as if you're padding.

Use **color** sparingly, if at all. Colored text and shaded boxes can prevent accurate scanning. Similarly, white 8½- by 11-inch paper is standard, but do use a good-quality paper. Contrary to some popular myths, using brightly colored paper or cardstock-weight paper to get noticed by employers will more likely hurt your prospects than help you get an interview.

All of these guidelines are much more flexible for people in creative fields such as advertising and design. As you prepare your résumé, consult with advisers, professors, professionals, and other job seekers to discover the best strategies for your field.

Kinds of Résumés

Two basic categories of résumés are chronological and skills. A **chronological résumé** summarizes what you did in a time line (starting with the most recent events, and going backward in **reverse chronology**). It emphasizes degrees, job titles, and dates and is the traditional résumé format. Figures 12.5 and 12.6 show chronological résumés.

Use a chronological résumé when

- Your education and experience are a logical preparation for the position for which you're applying.

- You have impressive job titles, offices, or honors.

A **skills résumé**, also called a functional résumé, emphasizes the skills you've used, rather than the job in which you used them or the date of the experience. Figure 12.8 shows a skills résumé. Use a skills résumé when

- Your education and experience are not the usual route to the position for which you're applying.

- You're changing fields.

- You want to combine experience from paid jobs, activities, volunteer work, and courses to show the extent of your experience in administration, finance, public speaking, and so on.

James Jiang

jianj@wccc.edu

Vary font sizes. Use larger size for name and main headings.

Campus Address
1524 E. Main St
Portland, OR 97231
503-403-5718

Using both addresses ensures continuous contact information.

Permanent Address
2526 Prairie Lane
Portland, OR 97233
503-404-7793

Education
West Coast Community College
A.A. in Financial Management, June 2014
GPA: 3.0/4.0 *Give your grade average if it's 3.0 or higher.*

Summary of Qualifications

Use key words employers might seek.

- Self-motivated, detail-minded, results-oriented
- Consistently successful track record in sales
- Effectively developed and operated entrepreneurial business

List 3–7 qualifications.

Sales Experience
Financial Sales Representative, ABC Inc., Portland, OR, February 2012–present
- Establish client base
- Develop investment strategy plans for clients
- Research and recommend specific investments

Other Experience
Entrepreneur, A-Plus T-Shirt Company, Portland, OR, September 2010–January 2013

One way to handle self-employment.

- Created a saleable product (Graphic T-shirts)
- Secured financial support
- Located a manufacturer
- Supervised production
- Sold t-shirts to high school students
- Realized a substantial profit to pay for college expenses

Cook, Hamburger Shack, Portland, OR, Summers 2008–2010
- Learned sales strategies
- Ensured customer satisfaction
- Collaborated with a team of 25

Collector and Repair Worker, ACN, Inc., Portland, OR, Summer 2006–2008
- Collected and counted approximately $10,000 a day *Specify large sums of money.*
- Assisted technicians with troubleshooting and repairing coin mechanisms

Other Skills
Computer: Word, Excel, InDesign, WordPress, Outlook
Language: Fluent in Spanish *Many employers appreciate a second language.*

The two kinds differ in what information is included and how that information is organized. You may assume that the advice in this chapter applies to both kinds of résumés unless there is an explicit statement that the two kinds of résumés would handle a category differently.

What to Include in a Résumé

Although the résumé is a factual document, its purpose is to persuade. In a job application form or an application for graduate or professional school, you answer every question even if the answer is not to your credit. In a résumé, you cannot lie, but you can omit some information that does not work in your favor.

Résumés commonly contain the following information. The categories marked with an asterisk are essential.

- Name and Contact Information*
- Career Objective
- Summary of Qualifications
- Education*
- Honors and Awards
- Experience*
- Other skills
- Activities
- Portfolio

You may choose other titles for these categories and add categories that are relevant for your qualifications, such as computer skills or foreign languages.

Education and Experience always stand as separate categories, even if you have only one item under each heading. Combine other headings so that you have at least two long or three short items under each heading. For example, if you're in one honor society and two social clubs, and on one athletic team, combine them all under Activities and Honors.

If you have more than seven items under a heading, consider using subheadings. For example, a student who participated in many activities might divide them into Campus Activities and Community Service.

Put your strongest categories near the top and at the bottom of the first page. If you have impressive work experience, you might want to put that category first and Education second.

Name and Contact Information

Use your full **name**, even if everyone calls you by a nickname. You may use an initial rather than spelling out your first or middle name. Put your name in big type.

If you use only one **address**, consider centering it under your name. If you use two addresses (office and home, campus and permanent, until_____ / after_____) set them up side by side to balance the page visually. Use either

What Happens to Your Résumé?

Each year, technology giant Siemens Global hires more than 10,000 employees from over 780,000 applicants. One civil engineering position had 187 applications, but only three made it to the face-to-face interview.

How does Siemens find the right people? *CNNMoney* found four key steps:

1. Hire internally. Like many corporations, Siemens advertises positions both internally and externally, but hires 40% of open positions from inside the company.

2. Use the web. Siemens posts jobs on Monster and CareerBuilder. Recruiters also use LinkedIn both to eliminate candidates and to recruit people who may not be looking for a job.

3. Use computers to scan applications and find applicants who match job requirements.

4. Conduct initial interviews by phone. Only after applicants pass this step can they be sent on to the hiring manager.

For large corporations, using technology and recruiters to screen applicants is vital to finding the right people for jobs.

Adapted from Tami Luhby, "The Secret Life of a Résumé," *CNNMoney*, May 18, 2011, http://money.cnn.com/fdcp?unique 51305728467379.

A résumé is your most important document at career fairs.

post office (two-letter, full caps, no period) abbreviations for the state or spell out the state name, but do be consistent throughout your résumé.

Urbana, IL 61801

Wheaton, Illinois 60187

Give a complete **phone number**, including the area code. Some job candidates give both home and cell phone numbers. Do provide a phone number where you can be reached during the day. Employers usually call during business hours to schedule interviews and make job offers. Do not give lab or dorm phone numbers unless you are sure someone there will take an accurate message for you at all times. Also, be sure your voice mail has a professional-sounding message.

If you have a **web page**, and you are sure it looks professional (both content and writing), you may wish to include its URL. Be sure your web page does not reveal personal information—such as marital status, ethnicity, religious beliefs, or political stance—that could work against you. Be particularly careful of photographs.

Provide an **e-mail address**. Some job candidates set up a new e-mail address just for job hunting. Your e-mail address should look professional; avoid sexy, childish, or illicit addresses. List your **LinkedIn** site, if you have one. You may also list your Google+ page, Facebook profile, or Twitter stream if you use them professionally or if social networking is required or desired in your profession.

Career Objective

Career objective statements should sound like the job descriptions an employer might use in a job listing. Keep your statement brief—two lines at most. Tell what you want to do, what level of responsibility you want to hold. The best career objectives are targeted to a specific job at a specific company.

Ineffective career objective:	To offer a company my excellent academic foundation in hospital technology and my outstanding skills in oral and written communication
Better career objective:	Hospital and medical sales for Rand Medical requiring experience with state-of-the-art equipment

Good career objectives are hard to write. If you talk about entry-level work, you won't sound ambitious; if you talk about where you hope to be in 5 or 10 years, you won't sound as though you're willing to do entry-level work. When you're applying for a job that is a natural outgrowth of your education and experience, you may omit this category and specify the job you want in your cover letter.

Often you can avoid writing a career objective statement by putting the job title or field under your name:

Joan Larson Ooyen	Terence Edward Garvey	David R. Lunde
Marketing	Technical Writer	Corporate Fitness Director

Note that you can use the field you're in even if you're a new college graduate. To use a job title, you should have some relevant work experience.

If you use a separate heading for a career objective, put it immediately after your contact information, before the first major heading (see Figure 12.6). The résumé in Figure 12.5 does not use a Career Objective because it is being used for various jobs offered at a career fair. If you were particularly interested in several jobs there, you would make targeted résumés for those companies. More and more experts are advising that objectives be clarified in the cover letter rather than wasting valuable space at the top of the résumé.

Summary of Qualifications

A section summarizing the candidate's qualifications seems to have first appeared with scannable résumés, where its key words helped increase the number of matches a résumé produced. But the section proved useful for human readers as well and now is a standard part of many résumés. The best summaries show your knowledge of the specialized terminology of your field and offer specific, quantifiable achievements.

Weak:	Staff accountant
Better:	Experience with accounts payable, accounts receivable, audits, and month end closings. Prepared monthly financial reports.
Weak:	Presentation skills
Better:	Gave 20 individual and 7 team presentations to groups ranging from 5 to 100 people.

Some career advisers believe a summary is too repetitious of other sections on a one-page résumé. They believe the space is better used by listing your achievements that set you apart from other candidates.

Education

Education can be your first major category if you've just earned (or are about to earn) a degree, if you have a degree that is essential or desirable for the position you're seeking, or if you can present the information briefly. Put your

Objectionable Objectives

[These job objectives did not help their writers:]

- "A job." Any one will do.
- "To obtain a position that will allow me to utilize my strengths and reinforce my weaknesses." Are you sure that's a good idea?
- "To become a billionier." A candidate who's not on the money.
- "I am seeking a permanent position to get out of debt." Will we get anything out of the deal?
- "To obtain a position that will enable me to utilize my professional skills and knowledge in a capacity that demonstrates me intelligence." My, oh, my.
- "To work for XYZ Company." We'll forward your résumé to them.
- "My dream job would be as a professional baseball player, but since I can't do that, I'll settle on being an accountant." Your enthusiasm is overwhelming.
- "To learn new skills and gain training which will help me develop my new business." Your dedication is touching.

From Robert Half International, "Resumania Archive," accessed June 26, 2013, http://www.resumania .com/arcindex.html. Reprinted with permission of Robert Half International.

Figure 12.6   A One-Page Chronological Résumé

Jeff Moeller

831.503.4692
51 Willow Street
San José, CA 95112
jmoeller@csmb.edu

Use job title and company name in Career Objective.

Career Objective

To bring my attention to detail and love for computer/video games to Telltale Games as a Game Tester

Qualifications

- Experienced in JavaScript, Lua, and Python
- Intermediate proficiency with Visual Studio; high proficiency with Source Safe
- Excellent communication, interpersonal, and collaboration skills
- Advanced knowledge of computers
- Love of video games

Highlights qualifications specific to the job.

Education

California State University—Monterey Bay
August 2010–May 2014 (expected)
Bachelor of Science in Computer Science and Information Technology

Keeps Education section simple to emphasize experience.

Experience

Online Marketing Consultant—Self-Employed
October 2011–present

Lists job titles on separate lines.

- Manage multiple client Google Adwords accounts
- Install web software and implement designs for fast turnarounds
- Interface with clients using Basecamp

Editor-in-Chief—Point Network LLC
June 2009–present

Use present tense verbs when you are doing the job now.

- Write and edit for several LucasArts-related gaming news websites
- Design and code websites using Wordpress
- Manage and administrate the LucasForums.com community

Online Marketing Assistant—Hayfield Group
May 2012–August 2012; May 2013–August 2013

Use past tense for jobs that are over.

- Managed all client Google Adwords accounts
- Assisted in or managed planning and executing PPC and SEO campaigns
- Coded the company website and integrated the Drupal CMS
- Prepared website analytics reports using Google Analytics and other analytics suites

Community Manager—Praise Entertainment, Inc.
April 2011–September 2013

- Managed the community at AdminFusion.com, a website geared toward online forum owners
- Organized and ran a monthly contest for community members

Close with strong section.

Honors and Activities

- Member of the gaming press for E3 2012 and 2013
- Member of second place team in 2013 National STEM Video Game challenge
  (see demo, "Parrot Villa" at www.STEMChallenge.gov/2013_winners)

Include activities that employer might value.

Education section later if you need all of page 1 for another category or if you lack a degree that other applicants may have (see Figure 12.8).

Under Education, provide information about your undergraduate and graduate degrees, including the location of institutions and the year you received or expect your degree, if these dates are within the last 10 years.

Use the same format for all schools. List your degrees in reverse chronological order (most recent first).

Master of Accounting Science, May 2014, Arizona State University, Tempe, AZ
Bachelor of Arts in Finance, May 2012, New Mexico State University, Las Cruces, NM

BS in Industrial Engineering, May 2014, Iowa State University, Ames, IA
AS in Business Administration, May 2012, Des Moines Area Community College, Ankeny, IA

When you're getting a four-year degree, include community college only if it will interest employers, such as by showing an area of expertise different from that of your major. You may want to include your minor, emphasis, or concentration and any graduate courses you have taken. Include study abroad, even if you didn't earn college credits. If you got a certificate for international study, give the name and explain the significance of the certificate. Highlight proficiency in foreign or computer languages by using a separate category.

To punctuate your degrees, do not space between letters and periods:

A.S. in Office Administration

B.S. in Accounting

Ed.D. in Business Education

Current usage also permits you to omit the periods (BS, MBA), but be consistent with the usage you choose.

Professional certifications can be listed under Education or in a separate category.

If your GPA is good and you graduated recently, include it. If your GPA is under 3.0 on a 4.0 scale, use words rather than numbers: "B– average." If your GPA isn't impressive, calculate your average in your major and your average for your last 60 hours. If these are higher than your overall GPA, consider using them. If you do use your major GPA or upper class GPA, make sure you label them as such so you can't be accused of dishonesty. The National Association of Colleges and Employers, in its Job Outlook survey, found that more than 78% of employers do screen job applicants by GPA. In some industries, such as management consulting and computer manufacturing, more than 90% of employers screen by GPA.[15] If you leave your GPA off your résumé, most employers will automatically assume that it is below a 3.0. If yours is, you will need to rely on internships, work experience, and skills acquired in activities to make yourself an attractive job candidate.

After giving the basic information (degree, field of study, date, school, city, state) about your degree, you may wish to list courses, using short descriptive titles rather than course numbers. Use a subhead such as "Courses Related to Major" or "Courses Related to Financial Management" that will allow you to list all the courses (including psychology, speech, and business communication) that will help you in the job for which you're applying. Don't say "Relevant Courses," as that implies your other courses were irrelevant.

Bachelor of Science in Management, May 2014, Illinois State University, Normal, IL
GPA: 3.8/4.0
Courses Related to Management:
  Personnel Administration   Business Decision Making
  Finance   International Business
  Management I and II   Marketing
  Accounting I and II   Legal Environment of Business
  Business Report Writing   Business Speaking

Listing courses is an unobtrusive way to fill a page. You may also want to list courses or the number of hours in various subjects if you've taken an unusual combination of courses that uniquely qualify you for the position for which you're applying.

BS in Marketing, May 2014, California State University at Northridge
  30 hours in marketing
  15 hours in Spanish
  9 hours in Chicano studies

If your course list is similar to that of others in your major, you should use the space for material that better shows your uniqueness. In that case, another way to fill the page is to include a Projects section, in which you highlight some course projects relevant to the jobs you are seeking.

As you advance in your career, your education section will shrink until finally it probably will include only your degrees and educational institutions.

Honors and Awards

It's nice to have an Honors and Awards section, but not everyone can do so. If you have fewer than three and therefore cannot justify a separate heading, consider a heading Honors and Activities to get that important word in a position of emphasis.

Include the following kinds of entries in this category:

- Academic honor societies. Specify the nature of Greek-letter honor societies (i.e., journalism honorary) so the reader doesn't think they're just social clubs.

- Fellowships and scholarships, including honorary scholarships for which you received no money and fellowships you could not hold because you received another fellowship at the same time.

- Awards given by professional societies.

- Major awards given by civic groups.

- Varsity letters; selection to all-state or all-America teams; finishes in state, national, or Olympic meets. (These could also go under Activities but may look more impressive under Honors. Put them under one category or the other—not both.)

Identify honor societies ("national journalism honorary," "campus honorary for top 2% of business majors") for readers who are not in your discipline.

If your fellowships or scholarships are particularly selective or remunerative, give supporting details:

Clyde Jones Scholarship:	four-year award covering tuition, fees, room, and board.
Marilyn Terpstra Scholarship:	$25,000 annually for four years.
Heemsly Fellowship:	50 awarded nationally each year to top Information Science juniors.

Be careful of listing Dean's List for only one or two semesters. Such a listing reminds readers that in these days of grade inflation you were off the list many more times than you were on it. Omit honors such as "Miss Congeniality" or "Muscle Man Star" that work against the professional image you want your résumé to create.

As a new college graduate, try to put Honors on page 1. In a skills résumé, put Honors on page 1 if they're major (e.g., Phi Beta Kappa, Phi Kappa Phi). Otherwise, save them until page 2—Experience will probably take the whole first page.

Experience

You may use other headings if they work better: Work Experience, Summer and Part-Time Jobs, Military Experience, Marketing Experience. In a skills résumé, headings such as "Marketing Experience" allow you to include accomplishments from activities and course projects. Headings that reflect skills mentioned in the job ad are particularly effective.

What to Include   Under this section in a chronological résumé, include the following information for each job you list: position or job title, organization, city and state (no zip code), dates of employment for jobs held during the last 10 to 15 years, and other details, such as full- or part-time status, job duties, special responsibilities, or the fact that you started at an entry-level position and were promoted. Use strong verbs such as the ones in Figure 12.7 to brainstorm what you've done. Try to give supporting details for highly valued attributes such as communication skills and leadership experience. Include any internships and co-ops you have had. Also, include unpaid jobs and self-employment if they provided relevant skills (e.g., supervising people, budgeting, planning, persuading). Experience information for skills résumés is discussed on page 399.

If you went to college right after high school, it is common to go back as far as the summer after high school. Include earlier jobs only if you started working someplace before graduating from high school but continued working there after graduation, or if the job is pertinent to the one you are applying for. If you worked full-time after high school, make that clear. More experienced workers generally go back no more than 10 years.

The details you give about your experience are some of the most vital information on your résumé. As you provide these details, use bulleted lists (easy to read) rather than paragraphs, which are harder to read and may be skipped over. Remember that items in lists need to have parallel structure; see Appendix B for a refresher. Focus on results rather than duties; employers are far more interested in what you accomplished than in what you had to do. Use numbers to support your results wherever possible:

Supervised crew of 15.

Managed $120,000 budget; decreased expenses by 19%.

Wrote monthly electronic newsletter; increased hits by 12%.

Emphasize accomplishments that involve money, customers, teamwork, leadership, computer skills, and communication.

Fast-Food Roots

If you've got experience working in fast food, you are in good company. According to *Bloomberg Businessweek*, these famous people all worked at McDonald's:

- Paul Ryan, 2012 vice presidential candidate.
- Jeff Bezos, CEO of Amazon.
- Sharon Stone, actress.
- Jay Leno, late-night TV host.
- Seal, singer.
- Carl Lewis, Olympic athlete.
- Andrew Card, chief of staff for President George W. Bush.

Any work experience can be good for your résumé if you learn new skills, develop leadership, and network.

Adapted from Kate Abbot, "McDonald's Famous Former Burger Flippers," *Bloomberg Businessweek*, August 17, 2012, http://images.businessweek.com/slideshows/ 2012-08-17/mcdonalds-famous-former-burger-flippers.

Figure 12.7	Action Verbs for Résumés		
analyzed	directed	led	reviewed
budgeted	earned	managed	revised
built	edited	motivated	saved
chaired	established	negotiated	scheduled
coached	evaluated	observed	simplified
collected	examined	organized	sold
conducted	helped	persuaded	solved
coordinated	hired	planned	spoke
counseled	improved	presented	started
created	increased	produced	supervised
demonstrated	interviewed	recruited	trained
designed	introduced	reported	translated
developed	investigated	researched	wrote

Use past tense verbs for jobs you held in the past, and present tense verbs for jobs you still have. Do not list minor duties such as distributing mail or filing documents. If your duties were completely routine, say, at your summer job at McDonald's, do not list them. If the jobs you held in the past were low-level ones, present them briefly or combine them:

> 2010–2014 Part-time and full-time jobs to finance education

If as an undergraduate you've earned a substantial portion of your college expenses with jobs and scholarship, say so in a separate statement under either Experience or Education. (Graduate students are expected to support themselves.)

> These jobs paid 40% of my college expenses.

> Paid for 65% of expenses with jobs, scholarships, and loans.

Paying for school expenses just with loans is generally not considered noteworthy.

Formats for Experience Section   There are two basic ways to set up the Experience section of your résumé. In **indented format**, items that are logically equivalent begin at the same space, with carryover lines indented. Indented format emphasizes job titles. It provides work information in this order:

Job title, name of organization, city, state, dates. Other information.

> Experience
> **Engineering Assistant,** Sohio Chemical Company, Lima, Ohio, Summers 2013 and 2014.
> - Tested wastewater effluents for compliance with Federal EPA standards
> - Helped chemists design a test to analyze groundwater quality and seepage around landfills
> - Presented weekly oral and written progress reports to Director of Research and Development
>
> **Animal Caretaker,** Animal care, Worthington, Ohio, Summers 2010–2012.

Two-margin or **block format** frequently can be used to emphasize *when you worked*, if you've held only low-level jobs. Don't use two-margin format if your work history has gaps.

EXPERIENCE	
Summers, 2012–14	Repair worker, Bryant Heating and Cooling, Providence, RI
2010–11	Library Clerk, Boston University Library, Boston, MA. Part-time during school year
2008–10	Food Service Worker, Boston University, Boston, MA. Part-time during school year
Summer, 2009	Delivery person, Domino's Pizza, Providence, RI

The left column can also emphasize steadily increasing job titles.

Experience at Gene Elton, Miami, Florida
Intern
Computer Programmer
Systems Analyst

The right column would list duties and dates.
Use a dash to join inclusive dates:

March–August 2014 (or write out March to August 2014)

2011–2014 or 2011–14

If you use numbers for dates, do not space before or after the slash:

10/12–5/14

Skills Résumés Skills résumés stress the skills you have acquired rather than specific jobs you have held. They show employers that you do have the desired skill set even if you lack the traditional employment background. They allow you to include skills acquired from activities and course projects in addition to jobs. On the other hand, they are also a clue to employers that you do lack that traditional background, or that you have gaps in your job history, so you will need to make your skill set convincing.

In a skills résumé, the heading of your main section usually changes from "Experience" to "Skills." Within the section, the subheadings will be replaced with the skills used in the job you are applying for, rather than the title or the dates of the jobs you've held (as in a chronological résumé). For entries under each skill, combine experience from paid jobs, unpaid work, classes, activities, and community service.

Use headings that reflect the jargon of the job for which you're applying: *logistics* rather than *planning* for a technical job; *procurement* rather than *purchasing* for a job with the military. Figure 12.8 shows a skills résumé for someone who is changing fields.

A job description can give you ideas for headings. Possible headings and subheadings for skills résumés include

Administration	**Communication**
Budgeting	Editing
Coordinating	Fund-Raising
Evaluating	Interviewing
Implementing	Negotiating
Negotiating	Persuading
Planning	Presenting
Supervising	Writing

Figure 12.8   A Skills Résumé for Someone Changing Fields

Mandy Shelly
www.wisc.edu/~Shelly88/home.htm

If you have a professional web page, include its URL.

266 Van Buren Drive
Madison, WI 53706
shellym@wisc.edu
608-897-1534 (home)
608-842-4242 (cell)

Objective   To contribute my enthusiasm for writing as a Technical Writer at PDF Productions

Job objective includes the position and name of the company.

Skills

Largest section on skills résumé; allows you to combine experiences from work and class.

Computer
- Designed a web page using Dreamweaver
  www.madisonanimalshelter.com
- Used a variety of Macintosh and PC platform programs and languages:

Aspects (online discussion forum)	Adobe Professional
Dreamweaver CS5	HTML
PageMaker	Java Script
XML	Photoshop CS5

Specify computer programs you know well.

Design and Writing

Use parallel structure for bulleted lists.

- Designed a quarterly newsletter for local animal shelter
- Developed professional brochures
- Wrote a variety of professional documents: letters, memos, and reports
- Edited internal documents and promotional materials
- Proofread seven student research papers as a tutor

Organization and Administration
- Coordinated program schedules
- Developed work schedules for five employees
- Led a ten-member team in planning and implementing sorority philanthropy program
- Created cataloging system for specimens
- Ordered and handled supplies, including live specimens

Employment History

Condensed to make room for skills.

Technical Writer, Madison Animal Shelter, Madison, WI 2012–present
Undergraduate Lab Assistant, Department of Biology, University of Wisconsin–Madison, Madison, WI, 2012–present
Tutor, University of Wisconsin–Madison, Madison, WI, 2011–2012

Uses reverse chronology.

Education   Bachelor of Arts, May 2014
University of Wisconsin–Madison, Madison, WI
Major: Animal Ecology
Minor: Chemistry
GPA 3.4/4.0

Give minor when it can be helpful.

Honors   Phi Kappa Phi Honor Society
Alpha Lambda Delta Honor Society, Ecology Honorary
Dean's List, 2010 to present
Raymond Hamilton Scholarship, 2012–2013
          ($5000 to a top ecology student in Wisconsin)

Explain honors your reader may not know.

End with strong items at the bottom of your page, a position of emphasis.

Many jobs require a mix of skills. Try to include the skills that you know will be needed in the job you want. You need at least three subheadings in a skills résumé; six or seven is not uncommon. Give enough detail under each subheading so the reader will know what you did. Begin with the most important category from the reader's point of view.

In a skills résumé, list your paid jobs under Work History or Employment Record near the end of the résumé (see Figure 12.8). List only job title, employer, city, state, and dates. Omit details that you have already used under Skills.

Other Skills

You may want a brief section in a chronological résumé where you highlight skills not apparent in your work history. These skills may include items such as foreign languages or programming languages. You might want to list software you have used or training on expensive equipment (electron microscopes, NMR machines). As always on your résumé, be completely honest: "two years of high school German," or "elementary speaking knowledge of Spanish." Any knowledge of a foreign language is a plus. It means that a company desiring a second language in its employees would not have to start from scratch in training you. Figure 12.6 lists skills in its Qualifications section.

Activities

Employers may be interested in your activities if you're a new college graduate because they can demonstrate leadership roles, management abilities, and social skills as well as the ability to juggle a schedule. If you've worked for several years after college or have an advanced degree (MBA, JD), you can omit Activities and include Professional Activities and Affiliations or Community and Public Service. If you went straight from college to graduate school but have an unusually strong record demonstrating relevant skills, include this category even if all the entries are from your undergraduate days.

Include the following kinds of items under Activities:

- Volunteer work. Include important committees, leadership roles, communication activities, and financial and personnel responsibilities.

- Membership in organized student activities. Include leadership and financial roles as well as important subcommittees. Include minor offices only if they're directly related to the job for which you're applying or if they show growing responsibility (you held a minor office one year, a bigger office the following year). Include so-called major offices (e.g., vice president) even if you did very little. Provide descriptive details if (but only if) they help the reader realize how much you did and the importance of your work, or if they demonstrate usable job skills.

- Membership in professional associations. Many of them have special low membership fees for students, so you should join one or more, particularly the ones directly associated with your major.

- Participation in varsity, intramural, or independent athletics. However, don't list so many sports that you appear not to have had adequate time to study.

- Social clubs, if you held a major leadership role or if social skills are important for the job for which you're applying.

As you list activities, add details that will be relevant for your job. Did you handle a six-figure budget for your Greek organization? Plan all the road trips

Job Skills Checklist

Having trouble identifying your skills? OWL, Purdue's Online Writing Lab, has an excellent list to help get you going. Connect the skills you identify to experiences in your life that demonstrate the skills; then put the best material into your résumé and cover letter. See this website: http://owl.english.purdue.edu/owl/resource/626/1/.

for your soccer club? Coordinate all the publicity for the campus blood drive? Design the posters for homecoming? Major leadership, financial, and creative roles and accomplishments may look more impressive if they're listed under Experience instead of under Activities.

Portfolio

If you have samples of your work available, you may want to end your résumé by stating "Portfolio (or writing samples) available on request." or by giving the URL for your work.

References

References are generally no longer included on résumés. Nor do you say "References Available on Request," since no job applicant is going to refuse to supply references. However, you will probably be asked for references at some point in your application process, so it is wise to be prepared.

You will need at least three, usually no more than five, never more than six. As a college student or a new graduate, include at least one professor and at least one employer or adviser—someone who can comment on your work habits and leadership skills. If you're changing jobs, include your current superior. For a skills résumé, choose references who can testify to your abilities in the most important skills areas. Omit personal or character references, who cannot talk about your work. Don't use relatives, friends, or roommates, even if you've worked for them, because everyone will believe they are biased in your favor.

Always ask permission to use the person as a reference. Doing so is not only polite, but ensures the person will remember you when contacted. Instead of the vague "May I list you as a reference?" use, "Can you speak specifically about my work?" Jog the person's memory by taking along copies of work you did for him or her and a copy of your current résumé. Tell the person what qualifications a specific employer is seeking. Keep your list of references up-to-date. If it's been a year or more since you asked someone, ask again—and tell the person about your recent achievements.

On your list of references, provide name, title or position, organization, city, state, phone number, and e-mail for each of your references. If their connection to you is not clear, add an identifying line (former academic adviser; former supervisor at Careltons) so they do not look like personal references. You could also give the full mailing address if you think people are more likely to write than to call. Use courtesy titles (*Dr., Mr., Ms.*) for all or for none. By convention, all faculty with the rank of assistant professor or above may be called *Professor*.

References that the reader knows are by far the most impressive. In fact, employers may ask about you among people they already know: a former classmate may now work for them; a professor in your major department may consult for them. Through these routes, employers can get references about you even in companies whose formal human resources policy provides only dates of employment. Therefore, you should be well thought of by as many people as possible.

Some employers are also checking contacts on social networking sites such as LinkedIn and Facebook to find people who may know you. When you are on the job market, you may want to consider adjusting your privacy settings so that your contacts are visible to only a select few. On sites without such adjustments, you need to be careful with your contact list. Remember that Facebook has a history of making personal information public.

Include the name and address of your placement office if you have written recommendations on file there; that contact information will be all you need.

What Not to Include in a Résumé

Certain items do not belong on résumés used in the United States (standards differ in other countries). These include age, ethnicity, marital status, number of children, and health. Photographs also do not belong on résumés unless you are applying for jobs such as entertainment positions. Although interested parties can frequently find your picture on Facebook, for instance, pictures have long been excluded from résumés because they can enable discrimination. For security reasons, résumés should never include your Social Security number.

Including these kinds of information shows you have not researched the job-hunting process. Since many employers take your performance on the job hunt as an indication of the quality of work you will do for them, résumé lapses indicate that you may not be the best employee.

Because résumés are used to eliminate a large pool of job candidates down to the handful that will be interviewed, do not include controversial activities or associations. This category generally includes work for specific religious or political groups. (If the work is significant, you can include it generically: Wrote campaign publicity for state senator candidate.)

High school facts are generally omitted once you are a junior in college unless you have good reasons for keeping them. These reasons might include showing you have local connections or showing skill in a needed area not covered by college activities (perhaps you are applying for coaching jobs where a variety of team sports will help you, and you played basketball in high school and volleyball in college). The fact that you have good high school activities but few if any college activities is not a good reason. In this case, listing high school activities will show you are on a downward trend at a very early age!

Do not pad your résumé with trivial items; they are easily recognized as padding and they devalue the worth of your other items. For instance, except under the most unusual circumstances, graduate students should not list grants for travel to conferences as honors, since such travel grants are ubiquitous. Some community groups, especially religious organizations, list all college graduates in their group-specific "honorary." Since everyone who graduates will belong, these are not considered honors.

As you advance in your career, you will continually cut information from earlier stages of your life, as well as from outside activities, to focus on your recent career achievements.

Dealing with Difficulties   `LO 12-4`

Some job hunters face special problems. This section gives advice for six common problems.

"I Don't Have Any Experience."

If you have a year or more before you job hunt, you can get experience in several ways:

- **Seek an internship.**   Your college career center or professors in your major can direct you toward opportunities. Internships provide solid experience in your field, and many lead to full-time jobs.

- **Take a fast-food job—and keep it.**   If you do well, you'll be promoted to a supervisor within a year. Use every opportunity to learn about management and financial aspects of the business.

- **Sign on with agencies that handle temporary workers.**   As an added bonus, some of these jobs become permanent.

- **Join a volunteer organization that interests you.**   If you work hard, you'll quickly get an opportunity to do more: manage a budget, write fund-raising materials, and supervise other volunteers.

- **Freelance.**   Design brochures, create web pages, do tax returns for small businesses. Use your skills—for free, if you have to at first.

- **Write.**   Create a portfolio of ads, instructions, or whatever documents are relevant for the field you want to enter. Ask a professional—an instructor, a local businessperson, someone from a professional organization—to critique them.

If you're on the job market now, think carefully about what you've really done. Complete sentences using the action verbs in Figure 12.7 to help jog your memory. Think about what you've done in courses, volunteer work, and unpaid activities. Focus on skills in problem solving, critical thinking, teamwork, and communication. Solving a problem for a hypothetical firm in an accounting class, thinking critically about a report problem in business communication, working with a group in a marketing class, and communicating with people at the senior center where you volunteer are good experiences, even if no one paid you.

"All My Experience Is in My Family's Business."

In your résumé, simply list the company you worked for. For a reference, instead of a family member, list a supervisor, client, or vendor who can talk about your work. Since the reader may wonder whether "Jim Clarke" is any relation to the owner of "Clarke Construction Company," be ready to answer interview questions about why you're looking at other companies. Prepare an answer that stresses the broader opportunities you seek but doesn't criticize your family or the family business.

"I Want to Change Fields."

Have a good reason for choosing the field in which you're looking for work. "I want a change" or "I need to get out of a bad situation" does not convince an employer that you know what you're doing.

Think about how your experience relates to the job you want. Sam wants a new career as a pharmaceutical sales representative. He has sold woodstoves, served subpoenas, and worked on an oil rig. A chronological résumé makes his work history look directionless. But a skills résumé could focus on persuasive ability (selling stoves), initiative and persistence (serving subpoenas), and technical knowledge (courses in biology and chemistry).

Learn about the skills needed in the job you want: learn the buzzwords of the industry. Figure 12.8 shows a skills résumé of someone changing fields from animal ecology to technical writing. Her reason for changing could be that she found she enjoyed the writing duties of her jobs more than she enjoyed the ecology work.

"I've Been Out of the Job Market for a While."

You need to prove to a potential employer that you're up-to-date and motivated. Try the following:

- Create a portfolio of your work to show what you can do for the employer.
- Do freelance work.
- Be active in professional organizations. Attend meetings.
- Look for volunteer work where you can use and expand relevant work skills.
- Attend local networking events.

- Read the journals and trade publications of your field.

- Learn the software that professionals use in your field.

- Be up-to-date with electronic skills such as text messaging, Internet searches, and social networking.

- Take professional training to expand your skill set.

Employment counselors advise that you not leave a gap on your résumé; such a gap makes employers speculate about disasters such as nervous breakdowns or jail time. They suggest you matter-of-factly list an honorable title such as Parent or Caregiver; do not apologize. Better yet is to fill in the gap with substantial volunteer experience. Heading a $75,000 fund-raising drive for a new playground looks good for almost any employer. A side benefit of volunteer work, in addition to new career skills, is networking. Boards of directors and executives of nonprofit organizations are frequently well-connected members of the community.

"I Was Laid Off."

In times of large layoffs, this is not an overwhelming obstacle. You do not need to point out the layoff in your application materials; the end date of your last employment will make the point for you. Instead, use your documents to highlight your strengths.

Do be prepared to be asked about the layoff in an interview. Why were you laid off when other employees were retained? It helps if you can truthfully give a neutral explanation: the accounting work was outsourced; our entire lab was closed; the company laid off everyone who had worked fewer than five years. Be sure you do not express bitterness or self-pity; neither emotion will help you get your new job. On the other hand, do not be overly grateful for an interview; such excess shows a lack of self-confidence. Be sure to show you are keeping yourself current by doing some of the items in the bulleted list in the previous section.

"I Was Fired."

First, deal with the emotional baggage. You need to reduce negative feelings to a manageable level before you're ready to job-hunt.

Second, take responsibility for your role in the termination.

Third, try to learn from the experience. You'll be a much more attractive job candidate if you can show that you've learned from the experience—whether your lesson is improved work habits or that you need to choose a job where you can do work you can point to with pride.

Fourth, collect evidence showing that earlier in your career you were a good worker. This evidence could include references from earlier employers, good performance evaluations, and a portfolio of good work.

Some common strategies may also give you some help for references. You should check with the Human Resources Department to understand the company's reference policy. Some companies now give no references other than verification of job title and work dates. Others do not give references for employees who worked only a short time.[16] Another option is to ask someone other than your former boss for a reference. Could you ask a supplier or vendor? A different department head?

A different tactic is suggested by Phil Elder, an interviewer for an insurance company. He suggests calling the person who fired you and saying something like this: "Look, I know you weren't pleased with the job I did at _____. I'm applying for a job at _____ now and the personnel director may call you to ask about me. Would you be willing to give me the chance to get this job so that

Résumé Blasting

Résumé blasting is the process of distributing your résumé to dozens, hundreds, or thousands of résumé sites and databases. Résumé blasting services will do the work for you, for a price. But don't yield to the temptation.

ResumeDoctor.com surveyed more than 5,000 recruiters and hiring managers about online job postings. Top complaints were

1. Large numbers of irrelevant responses (92%). Most participants indicated that they receive hundreds of responses per online job posting.

2. Résumés not matching the job description (71%).

3. Job candidates "blasting out" résumés (63%).

Adapted from WetFeet, "Tailoring Résumés and Cover Letters to Fit Employers," June 16, 2011, https://www.wetfeet.com/articles/tailoring-resumes-and-cover-letters-to-fit-employers.

Beware of Spam Filters

Employers are using filters to keep out spam and computer viruses. Unfortunately, legitimate e-mails, including résumés, are also getting blocked. Applicants who send résumés with an e-mail may be rejected by spam filters for various reasons such as "foul" language (B.S.) or overused phrases (*responsible for* or *duties included*).

What can you do to avoid spam filters?

- Avoid acronyms or titles that may be considered "foul" language.
- Watch overusing words or phrases.
- Avoid words like *free, extend, unbelievable, opportunity, trial, mortgage.*
- Avoid using unusual colors.
- Be careful of using all capitals, exclamation points, or dollar amounts in subject lines.

What preventative steps can you take to avoid being caught by spam filters?

- Set your personal spam filter to high; then send your résumé to your own e-mail account.
- Send your résumé to a spam checker.

Adapted from Michael Trust, "How to Stop Your Résumé from Becoming Spam," *Careerealism,* October 11, 2010, http://www.careerealism.com/stop-resume-spam.

I can try to do things right this time?" All but the hardest of heart, says Elder, will give you one more chance. You won't get a glowing reference, but neither will the statement be so damning that no one is willing to hire you.[17]

Above all, be honest. Do not lie about your termination at an interview or on a job application. The application usually requires you to sign a statement that the information you are providing is true and that false statements can be grounds for dismissal.

Electronic Résumés `LO 12-5`

In addition to a paper résumé for job fairs, interviews, and potential contacts, you will need electronic versions of your résumé. With a few exceptions noted below, these résumés will have the same content but will be formatted differently so they can be "read" by both software and humans.

Sending Your Résumé Electronically

Many employers are asking to have résumés posted on their organizations' websites. When doing so, be sure you follow the directions exactly. You may also be asked by some employers to send your résumé by e-mail.

Here are some basic guidelines of e-mail job-hunting etiquette:

- Don't use your current employer's e-mail system for your job search. You'll leave potential employers with the impression that you spend company time on writing résumés and other nonwork-related activities.

- Set up a free, Internet-based e-mail account using services such as Gmail or Yahoo! to manage correspondence related to your job hunt.

- Avoid using silly or cryptic e-mail addresses. Instead of bubbles@aol.com, opt for something businesslike: yourname@yahoo.com. If you have a common name, try using combinations like "firstname.lastname@yahoo.com" or "firstname_lastname@yahoo.com" rather than using strings of numbers after your name.

- Write a simple subject line that makes a good first impression: Résumé—Kate Sanchez. A good subject line will improve the chances that your résumé is actually read, since e-mail from unknown senders is often deleted without being opened. If you are responding to an ad, use the job title or job code listed.

- Before sending your résumé into cyberspace, test to see how it will look when it comes out on the other end. E-mail it to yourself and a friend, then critique and fix it.

- Send only one résumé, even if the firm has more than one position for which you qualify. Most recruiters have negative reactions to multiple résumés.

- Experts differ on whether candidates should phone to follow up. Phoning once to be sure your résumé arrived is probably fine.

It's important to heed the specific directions of employers that you are e-mailing. Many do not want attachments because of viruses. While a few may want a Microsoft Word or PDF attachment of your résumé, others may specify that you paste your résumé directly into the body of your e-mail message.

If you are sending your résumé in the text of an e-mail,

- Start all lines at the left margin.
- Eliminate decorative elements such as boxes or vertical or horizontal lines.
- Do not use bold, underlining, bullets, tabs, or unusual fonts. Instead use keys such as asterisks. You can also put some headings in all capital letters, but use this device sparingly.

- To avoid awkward line breaks for your readers, shorten line lengths to 65 characters and spaces.

Your résumé will look plain to you, but the employers receiving it are used to the look of in-text résumés.

If you are sending your résumé as an attachment, name the document appropriately: Smith Robyn Résumé.docx. Never name it Résumé.docx; you do not want it to get lost in a long directory of documents.

With your résumé include a brief e-mail message that will make the receiver want to look at your résumé. In it, mention the types of files you've included. (See Figure 13.8.) Remember, it takes only an instant for readers to delete your e-mail. Do not give them reasons to trash your résumé.

Some people confuse electronic and scannable résumés. The former are résumés you send in or attached to an e-mail. The latter are paper résumés specially formatted for older software. Software programs have greatly improved recently and most can now scan regular résumés posted on websites. Guidelines for scannable résumés can be found on the web.

Posting Your Résumé on the Web

You will probably want to post your résumé online. Be selective when you do: stick with well-known sites for data security reasons. Choose one or two of the large popular sites such as Monster or CareerBuilder. Also choose one or two smaller sites, preferably ones specific to your desired occupation or location. A well-chosen niche site can show employers that you know your field. Studies are still showing that about 25% of external hires are made through job boards.[18]

Many responsible career sites recommend that you should not succumb to **résumé blasting**—posting your résumé widely on the web. Many employers consider such blasting to be akin to spam, and they respond negatively to job candidates who do it.

If the websites you choose have you place your information into their résumé form, cut and paste from your résumé to avoid typos. Do not use résumé templates unless you are asked to do so; they will rarely present you as well as the layout you have designed for yourself.

For safety reasons, use your e-mail address as contact information instead of your address and phone number. Make sure your e-mail address looks professional; you should not be HotLips@gmail.com. To foil identity thieves, some web consultants also recommend that you remove all dates from your résumé, and that you replace employer names with generic descriptions (statewide information technology company). Identity thieves can take information directly from online résumés, or they can call employers and, claiming to be conducting background checks, get additional information.

Since many databases sort résumés by submission date, renew your résumé by making small changes to it at least every two weeks. If you don't get any response to your résumé after a month or two, post it on a different site.

If you post your résumé on your personal website, be sure that all the links go to professional-looking pages, such as documents you have created. Now is not the time to link to pictures of you partying. Also, make sure the first screen includes a current job objective and Summary of Qualifications. One study found that résumés on personal websites were particularly useful for self-employed workers, for whom they attracted clients.[19]

When you have your new job, remove your résumé from all sites. Your new employer will probably take a dim view of finding your résumé on job sites and it is virtually impossible to block your online résumé from people at your current place of employment.

The Cost of a Typo

Typos can cost you a job. Many employers say they will not consider résumés with spelling mistakes or typographical errors.

Why? Employers consider your job documents to be examples of your finest work. If you are careless on them, they assume you will be even more careless in the work you do for them.

A spell-check is not enough. Too many "mangers" (managers) with great ability "to to" attend to detail are seeking work in the "pubic area" (public arena). You get the point. Proofread your documents carefully. Get your friends and family to proof them also, but remember, no one cares as much about your documents as you do. If English is not your first language, or your strong suit, consider paying for a professional editor. The success of your career starts with these documents.

Honesty   LO 12-6

Be absolutely honest on your résumé—and in the rest of your job search. Just ask Marilee Jones, former dean of admissions at Massachusetts Institute of Technology (MIT). In 1979, when she applied for an admissions job at MIT, her résumé listed bachelor's and master's degrees from Rensselaer Polytechnic Institute. In reality, she attended there only one year as a part-time student. By 1997, when she was promoted to the deanship, she did not have the courage to correct her résumé. In April 2007, she was forced to resign, even though she was a nationally recognized leader in admissions, after an anonymous tip.[20]

Most businesses now conduct some kind of background check on job applicants. Even graduate schools, particularly business schools, are checking applicants. A survey of over 3,000 hirers conducted for CareerBuilder reported that 49% had caught lies on résumés.[21]

Background checks on job candidates can include a credit check, legal and criminal records, complete employment history, and academic credentials. Such checks turn up some incredible whoppers. Résumés have been found using someone else's photo, listing degrees from nonexistent schools, listing fake Mensa memberships, and even claiming false connections to famous people.[22]

You can omit some material on your résumé, because obviously you cannot include everything about your life to date. For instance, it's still ethical to omit a low GPA, although most employers will assume it is very low indeed to be omitted. But what you do include must be absolutely honest.

Some of the most frequent inaccuracies on résumés are inflated job titles and incorrect dates of employment. While these data are easy to fudge, they are also easy to catch in background checks. It is also possible that some of these particular inaccuracies come from careless records kept by job candidates. Do you remember the exact job title of that first job you held as a sophomore in high school? Keep careful records of your employment history!

If employers do an employment history check, and many do, they will have a complete work history for you. They will be able to spot inaccurate company names and work dates. If you left a company off your résumé, they may wonder why; some may assume your performance at that company was not satisfactory.

Other areas where résumés are commonly inaccurate are

- Degrees: many people conveniently forget they were a few hours short of a degree.

- GPAs: inflating one's grade point seems to be a big temptation. If you are using the classes in your major or the last 60 hours of coursework to calculate your GPA, label them as such so you won't appear to be inflating your overall GPA.

- Honors: people list memberships in fake honoraries, or fake memberships in real honoraries.

- Fake employers.

- Job duties: many people inflate or embellish them.

- Salary increases.

- Fake addresses: people create these to have the "local" advantage.

- Fake contact information for references: this information frequently leads to family members or friends who will give fake referrals.

- Technical abilities.

- Language proficiency.

All dishonesty on a résumé is dangerous, keeping you from being hired if discovered early, and causing you to be fired if discovered later. However, the last two bullets listed above are particularly dangerous because your chances are good of being asked at an interview to demonstrate your listed proficiencies.

Checklist for Résumés

Content

☐ Does the résumé target the specific employer and position?

☐ Are the résumé sections clearly, correctly, and consistently labeled?

☐ Does the order of the headings highlight the strongest qualifications?

☐ Does the résumé need a career objective? If so, is it targeted to a specific job at a specific company? Is it concise and accurate?

☐ Are experience and education listed in reverse chronological order?

☐ Does the résumé provide details for your best qualifications?

☐ Does the résumé use numbers to support accomplishments?

☐ Does the résumé use key words? Action verbs?

☐ Is the information provided relevant to the position?

☐ Does the information flow logically and easily?

☐ Do the bulleted lists use parallel structure?

☐ Are grammar, punctuation, and spelling correct?

☐ Does the information support your claim that you are qualified and the best person for this position?

☐ Does the résumé address possible audience concerns with your application?

☐ Is all information on the résumé accurate and honest?

Design

☐ Does the page look balanced?

☐ Does the résumé look original, not based on a template?

☐ Does the length of the résumé fit the situation and position?

☐ Does the résumé include clear headings, bullets, and white space?

☐ Does the résumé use fonts appropriate for the career level and industry?

☐ Does the résumé use consistent font sizes and spacing throughout the document?

☐ Does the design reflect your career ambitions?

Summary by Learning Objectives

LO 12-1 **Prepare a detailed time line for your job search.**

Informal preparation for job hunting should start soon after you arrive on campus. Formal preparation for job hunting should begin a full year before you begin interviewing. The year you interview, register with your placement office early.

LO 12-2 **Conduct an effective job search.**

- The Internet has many tools for job searching. Choose the ones that will be best for you and your career.
- Networking and internships help you build relationships in your profession.
- When you are searching for a job, your online reputation is vital. Use social networking like Twitter, Facebook, LinkedIn, and Google+ wisely to build and maintain your online personal brand.
- With your online job search efforts, always be prepared to give a traditional cover letter and résumé to an interested employer.

LO 12-3 **Prepare a résumé that makes you look attractive to employers.**

- Employers skim résumés to decide whom to interview. Employers assume that the letter and résumé represent your best work.
- Emphasize information that is relevant to the job you want, is recent (last three years), and shows your superiority to other applicants.
- To emphasize key points, put them in headings, list them vertically, and provide details.
- Résumés use sentence fragments punctuated like complete sentences. Items in the résumé must be concise and parallel. Verbs and gerunds create a dynamic image of you.
- A chronological résumé summarizes what you did in a time line (starting with the most recent events, and going backward in reverse chronology). It emphasizes degrees, job titles, and dates. Use a chronological résumé when
  - Your education and experience are a logical preparation for the position for which you're applying.
  - You have impressive job titles, offices, or honors.

- A skills résumé emphasizes the skills you've used, rather than the job in which or the date when you used them. Use a skills résumé when
  - Your education and experience are not the usual route to the position for which you're applying.
  - You're changing fields.
  - You want to combine experience from paid jobs, activities, volunteer work, and courses to show the extent of your experience in administration, finance, speaking, etc.
  - Your recent work history may create the wrong impression (e.g., it has gaps, shows a demotion, shows job-hopping, etc.).

- Résumés contain the applicant's contact information, education, and experience. Career objectives, summary of qualifications, honors and awards, other skills, activities, and a portfolio reference may also be included.

LO 12-4 **Deal with common difficulties that arise during job searches.**

- Remove any unprofessional material from your personal web page, blog, and social networking sites.
- If you have gaps in your employment history, low experience, or if you were laid off or fired, address those problems honestly in both your résumé and your interview.
- Seek opportunities, such as internships and volunteer work, to fill in or expand your employment history and to reinforce your skills.

LO 12-5 **Handle the online portion of job searches.**

Many résumés are now sent electronically and are posted on the Internet or the organization's website. Prepare your résumé to send both electronically and in print.

LO 12-6 **Keep your résumé honest.**

Always be completely honest in your résumé and job search. Dishonesty can keep you from being hired or cause you to lose your job later.

Continuing Case

The All-Weather Case, set in an HR department in a manufacturing company, extends through all 19 chapters and is available at www.mhhe.com/locker11e. The portion for this chapter provides a job posting and asks students to evaluate the résumés of two candidates.

Exercises and Cases

*Go to www.mhhe.com/locker11e for additional Exercises and Cases.

12.1   Reviewing the Chapter

1. What should you do soon after starting college to prepare for your job search? (LO 12-1)
2. What should you do a full year before your job search? (LO 12-1)
3. How can you use the Internet effectively in your job search? (LO 12-2)
4. What is the role of networking and internships when you are looking for a job? (LO 12-2)
5. What is the role of social networking in your job search? (LO 12-2)
6. How can you use writing components such as emphasis and details to help set yourself apart from other candidates? (LO 12-3)
7. What are factors you should consider when preparing your contact information? (LO 12-3)
8. Why are career objectives hard to write? (LO 12-3)
9. What are key words? How do you use them in your summary of qualifications? In electronic résumés? (LO 12-3)
10. What kinds of details make your experience look most attractive to potential employers? (LO 12-3)
11. How can activities help make you look attractive to potential employers? (LO 12-3)
12. What can you do to help get the best references possible? (LO 12-3)
13. Pick one of the common problems job hunters may face and explain how you would deal with it if it happened to you during your career. (LO 12-4)
14. What safety precautions do you need to take when you post your résumé online? (LO 12-5)
15. Why is it more important now than ever before to be completely honest on your résumé? (LO 12-5)

12.2   Reviewing Grammar

Most résumés use lists, and items in lists need to have parallel structure. Polish your knowledge of parallel structure by revising the sentences in Exercise B.7, Appendix B.

12.3   Analyzing Your Accomplishments

List the 10 achievements that give you the most personal satisfaction. These could be things that other people wouldn't notice. They can be accomplishments you've achieved recently or things you did years ago.

Answer the following questions for each accomplishment:

1. What skills or knowledge did you use?
2. What personal traits did you exhibit?
3. What about this accomplishment makes it personally satisfying to you?

As your instructor directs,

a. Share your answers with a small group of other students.
b. Summarize your answers in an e-mail to your instructor.
c. Present your answers orally to the class.

12.4   Remembering What You've Done

Use the following list to jog your memory about what you've done. For each item, give three or four details as well as a general statement.

Describe a time when you

1. Used facts and figures to gain agreement on an important point.

2. Identified a problem that a group or organization faced and developed a plan for solving the problem.
3. Made a presentation or a speech to a group.
4. Won the goodwill of people whose continued support was necessary for the success of some long-term project or activity.
5. Interested other people in something that was important to you and persuaded them to take the actions you wanted.
6. Helped a group deal constructively with conflict.
7. Demonstrated creativity.
8. Took a project from start to finish.
9. Created an opportunity for yourself in a job or volunteer position.
10. Used good judgment and logic in solving a problem.

As your instructor directs,

a. Identify which job(s) each detail is relevant for.
b. Identify which details would work well on a résumé.
c. Identify which details, further developed, would work well in a job letter.

12.5   Developing Action Statements

Use 10 of the verbs from Figure 12.7 to write action statements describing what you've done in paid or volunteer work, in classes, in extracurricular activities, or in community service.

12.6   Evaluating Career Objective Statements

The following career objective statements are not effective. What is wrong with each statement as it stands? Which statements could be revised to be satisfactory? Which should be dropped?

1. To use my acquired knowledge of accounting to eventually own my own business.
2. A progressively responsible position as a MARKETING MANAGER where education and ability would have valuable application and lead to advancement.
3. To work with people responsibly and creatively, helping them develop personal and professional skills.
4. A position in international marketing which makes use of my specialization in marketing and my knowledge of foreign markets.
5. To bring Faith, Hope, and Charity to the American workplace.
6. To succeed in sales.
7. To design and maintain web pages.

12.7   Deciding How Much Detail to Use

In each of the following situations, how detailed should the applicant be? Why?

1. Ron Oliver has been steadily employed for the last six years while getting his college degree, but the jobs have been low-level ones, whose prime benefit was that they paid well and fit around his class schedule.
2. Adrienne Barcus was an assistant department manager at a clothing boutique. As assistant manager, she was authorized to approve checks in the absence of the manager. Her other duties were ringing up sales, cleaning the area, and helping mark items for sales.
3. Lois Heilman has been a clerk-typist in the Alumni Office. As part of her job, she developed a schedule for mailings to alumni, set up a merge system, and wrote two of the letters that go out to alumni. The merge system she set up has cut in half the time needed to produce letters.
4. As a co-op student, Stanley Greene spends every other term in a paid job. He now has six semesters of job experience in television broadcasting. During his last co-op he was the assistant producer for a daily "morning magazine" show.

12.8   Taking Advantage of Volunteer Opportunities

Volunteer work can improve your skills and enhance your résumé. With a partner, seek volunteer opportunities on your campus or in your city. Make a list of volunteer groups that may need help. Here are a few organizations that might help you get started:

- Big Brothers Big Sisters
- ASPCA
- Your local library or art center
- A local food pantry
- Ronald McDonald House

Present your findings to the class and encourage your friends to join you in volunteering.

12.9   Evaluating Yourself

Using the questions under "Evaluating Your Strengths and Interests" on pages 377–78, determine what is important to you in a career. Write your answers to the questions. Are you taking the necessary steps to align with your strengths and interests? What kinds of careers line up with your strengths and interests?

12.10   Writing a Job Description

Write a job description for your "dream position." Include the following:
- Position title.
- Position description including tasks, special requirements.
- Location.
- Work hours.
- Working conditions (for example, office space, scheduling, amount of supervision).
- Company culture.
- Pay.

- Experience and education requirements.
- Personal competencies (for example, ability to communicate, work in teams, problem solve, etc.).
- Amount of travel.
- Social, political, and ethical issues that may be involved.
- Opportunities for on-the-job learning and personal growth.

In small groups, share your descriptions. Did you get some ideas from the dream jobs of other students?

12.11   Performing a Needs Analysis

Identify a specific job posting you are interested in and list its requirements. Analyze the needs of the job and identify your personal strengths and qualifications to obtain it.

As your instructor directs,
a.   Work on incorporating your list into a résumé.

b.   Compose bullet entries for each qualification using action verbs.
c.   Identify areas in which you still need to improve. Brainstorm a list of ways in which you can achieve what you need.

12.12   Evaluating Your Online Reputation

Your online reputation is vital to your successful job search. Evaluate your reputation online using the following steps.

a.   Search for your name on Google. What are the results on the first page? Do you see a positive online presence?
b.   Search for your name on Google and click on the Images search tab. What pictures come up? Is there anything that could embarrass you?

c.   Check your privacy settings on Facebook. What can employers see? What can your friends see?
d.   Review your Twitter, Facebook, and Google+ posts for the past several months. What do they say about you? Do they pass the "Grandma Test"?
e.   Review and update your LinkedIn profile. Do you think it will be attractive to potential employers?

12.13   Editing a Résumé

Below are a job ad and a résumé applying for that job. Using the information you have about Jennifer's two jobs (given below the résumé), critique Jennifer's résumé. Her job letter is Exercise 13.18, if you wish to look at it, too. Redo her résumé to improve it. Then write an e-mail to your instructor discussing the strengths and weaknesses of the résumé and explaining why you made the changes you did.

Account Manager

Location: Aurora, IL
Job Category: Business/Strategic Management
Career Level: Entry-Level Manager (Manager/Supervisor of Staff)

Quantum National is the market leader in providing research, sales and marketing, health care policy consulting, and health information management services to the health care industry. Quantum has more than 20,000 employees worldwide and offices in 15 countries in Central and South America. Medical Innovation Communications, a division of Quantum National, currently has an opportunity for an Account Manager in our Aurora, IL, office. Medical Innovation Communications provides comprehensive product commercialization at all stages of product development: from phase 2, through national and international product launches to ongoing support.

The Account Manager has global responsibility for managing the client's marketing communications programs, assuring that the client's objectives are met in terms of program quality and on-time delivery.

Responsibilities include:

- Day-to-day client contact to identify and translate marketing objectives into strategic medical communications/education programs.

- Develop proposals, budgets, estimates of job cost, and profitability.

- Lead a team of Project Managers and Marketing Associates through guidance, delegation, and follow-up; and significant interaction with the client.

- Work with New Business Development Teams to develop proposals, budgets, and presenting company capabilities/business pitches to clients.

- Schedule the workflow of a 30-person demonstration and marketing team.

Requirements:

- Bachelor's degree.

- Ability to define and respond to client needs, working effectively under tight deadlines.

- Proven client management experience.

- Proven team management experience.

- Superior written and spoken communication skills.

E-mail applications and résumés to pattersj@micquant.com, and direct inquiries to J. Pattersen.

Jennifer Stanton	8523 8th Street	125 A S. 27th Ave
wildechilde@gmail.com	Ames, IA 50011	Omaha, NE 68101
cell: 515-668-9011	515-311-8243	402-772-5106

Objective
To get a job as an account manager.

Education
Iowa State University, Ames, IA—Business
May 2014, maybe December 2014
Minor: Botany
Cumulative GPA: 2.63 / 4.0

Mid-Plains Community College, North Platte, NE—Associate of Arts
May 2010

Bryan High School, Omaha, NE
May 2007

Work Experience
May 2013–August 2013—Summer Internship at FirstWest Insurance, Des Moines, IA

- Worked with a senior account manager to oversee some medical and EAP accounts.

- Made her phone calls to customers.

- Organized meetings with customers.

- I had to write some training "how-to's" for the new billing database.

2000–2012—*Worked in family business*
Worked weekends and summers in my parents' used-book store.

Skills

Microsoft Office
Fluent in Spanish

When you ask, Jennifer tells you about her two jobs:

> At her internship this summer, the person she worked with was pretty much an absentee supervisor: Jennifer had to do all the work alone (and she's still a little bitter about that). Her department managed five Employee Assistance Provider accounts with a total of about 36,000 individual policyholders in five Midwestern states. She had to set up and maintain work schedules for 12 employees, and manage the expense reports for the entire group. Four of those employees traveled a lot, so there were lots of expense reports to manage; there were so many that Jennifer had to revise the department's budget twice. She spent about four hours of every day returning customer phone calls and linking customers on conference calls with her department's employees. And those training how-to's? That turned into a 20-page how-to manual, which she wrote up and then had FirstWest's IT department turn into a website for the department to use.

> Her parents' family bookstore in Omaha is actually a franchise of a national chain of aftermarket bookstores: Booktopia. The store generates about $450,000 in gross sales per year, and stocks about 100,000 titles (not counting Internet sales and special orders); it employs 5 full-time and 17 part-time employees. In addition to filling in as a floor clerk, stocker, and cashier—all jobs that put her customer-service,

cash-handling, and "people skills" to the test—Jennifer has been handling all of the paperwork between the store and the Booktopia corporate office. (Her parents are great salespeople but they're not good at paying attention to details. That's created friction between them and the corporate office.) That paperwork includes all of the store's quarterly and yearly budget, staffing, and marketing reports since 2000.

Note: This exercise was written by Matthew Search.

12.14   Analyzing Job Applicants Based on Their Résumés

Based on your reading of Chapter 12, the following job description, and the two résumés below, analyze the two applicants for the position. What are their strengths and weaknesses as highlighted by their résumés? Which of the two candidates would you select? Why?

Job description for Cost Accountant

The position of Cost Accountant is responsible for budgeting, reviewing, analyzing, controlling, and forecasting costs involving different cost centers throughout the production process, including raw material procurement, inventory management, manufacturing, warehousing, and shipping. Other responsibilities include analyzing G/L reports; ensuring compliance with Generally Accepted Accounting Principles (GAAP) and Cost Accounting Standards (CAS); conducting breakeven (BE), contribution margin, and variance analyses; and preparing periodic reports for upper management. The position requires a bachelor's degree in accounting. A certification in management accounting from the Institute of Management Accountants (IMA) will be a plus. The position also requires a minimum of two years of work experience in cost accounting at a manufacturing company.

SAM PORTER

1010, Buck St., Fairfax, VA
sporter@bestwebsite.com

OBJECTIVE
_____

Cost Accountant position in which I can effectively utilize my skills in budgeting, accounting, costing, forecasting, reporting, and teamworking

EXPERIENCE
_____

2009–2010   Abacus Engineering   Portland, OR.

Cost Accounting Trainee
- Calculated cost variance for different cost centers.
- Prepared quarterly budget reports
- Coodinated with employees at different levels for data collection

2011–till date   Bourke Winodws   Fairfax, VA

Costing Manager
- Monitored 12 cost centers
- Implemented policies that reduced costs by 25%
- Supervised a staff of three, including one cost accountant.
- I also produced multiple G/L reports for the production department as well as upper management

EDUCATION

2005–2009   Edward Young University, Perry, OH
- B.A., accounting.
- Currently pursuing CMA of Institute of Management Accounting

INTERESTS

Country music, computers, fishing, golf

Jose Cortez

1212 S. E. Avenue, Earl, PA
(111) 112-1121-jc8@pearlnews.com

Qualification Summary

Skills in **controling** and reucing costs, experience with GAAP and CAS, skills in cost analyses, project management, CMA (IMA), member of the Financial Management Association International, well-versd with ERP software

Education

- **Certification in Management Accounting**
  Graduation—2014
  Institute of Management Accountants
- True Blue University, Roald, PA
  Graduation—2013
  Degree—Bachelor of Sciences (BS)
  Major—Accounting, G.P.A. 3.55

Experience

Silverstein Windows and Doors, Earl, PA   2014-Till date

Cost Accountant

- Estimate, review, budget, analyze, and forecast direct / indirect and variable and fixed costs for all stages of production
- Work on the ERP system to genrate reports and data sheets giving cost analyses
- Suggested a procedure in a contract that saved the company $35,000
- Worked with the Marketing Department on the costing / pricing of lower-priced vinyl casement windows

Achievements

- Volunteered more than 100 hours for the Habitat for Humnity Award 2012–2013
- Visted door and widow manufacturing plants in Argentina, Belgium, and Japan
- Received the best employee of the month award at Silverstein Windows and Doors
- Wrote articles for *Financial Control Weekly,* a publication of Costing Professionals Association

References

Available upon request

Note: This exercise was written by Anish Dave.

12.15 Preparing a Résumé

Write a résumé that you could use in your job search.

As your instructor directs,

a. Write a résumé for the field in which you hope to find a job.

b. Write two different résumés for two different job paths you are interested in pursuing. Write an e-mail to your instructor explaining the differences.

c. Adapt your résumé to a specific company you hope to work for. Write an e-mail to your instructor explaining the specific adaptations you made and why.

d. Write a résumé for the dream job you developed in Exercise 12.10.

12.16 Critiquing Your Résumé

Answer the Résumé Checklist questions (see page 409) for your résumé:

Variation: Review a class member's résumé using the same checklist questions.

12.17 Critiquing Prezumés

Some job seekers are now using online resources such as Prezi (a modern presentation tool) to create and present résumés to employers. Go to the Prezi website at http://prezi.com/explore/prezumes-and-portfolios/ and look through five or six of the submissions. In a small group answer the following questions about the Prezumés you viewed:

- Do they include all of the necessary information?

- Do they include any unnecessary or distracting information?
- How does the Prezi format affect how you view or think about the person and the information?
- In which fields would this kind of résumé be useful?
- Which employers would not be impressed by this kind of résumé?
- What problems do you see with this type of résumé?

12.18 Creating a Web or Paper Portfolio

Create a web or paper portfolio highlighting your professional and academic accomplishments. Include course projects, workplace samples, and other documents that support your professional accomplishments and goals.

Write an e-mail to your instructor listing each item in your portfolio and explaining why you chose it.

12.19 Evaluating Visual Résumés

Working individually, in pairs, or in small groups, as your instructor directs,

a. Look at five of the example student résumés on VisualCV.com. What features do you like? Why? What features would you change or omit? Why?

What are the advantages of VisualCV over your own web page? Disadvantages?

b. Discuss strengths and weaknesses of two résumés in an e-mail to your teacher, a posting on the class website, or an oral presentation.

12.20 Evaluating LinkedIn Profiles

Working individually, in pairs, or in small groups, as your instructor directs, look at six profiles on LinkedIn. You could use those of your classmates, family members, or local businesspeople.

- Which one has the best résumé? Why?
- How do the profiles and résumés differ?

- Which one has the best recommendations? Why?
- Overall, which one has the best profile? Why?

Discuss your conclusions in an e-mail to your teacher, a posting on the class website, or an oral presentation.

Notes

1. U.S. Department of Labor Bureau of Labor Statistics, "Number of Jobs Held, Labor Market Activity, and Earnings Growth among the Youngest Baby Boomers: Results from a Longitudinal Survey," news release, July 25, 2012, USDL-12-1489, http://www.bls.gov/news.release/pdf/nlsoy.pdf.

2. Richard Nelson Bolles, *What Color Is Your Parachute? 2013: A Practical Manual for Job-Hunters and Career-Changers* (Berkeley: Ten Speed Press, 2013), 57.

3. Ibid., 15.

4. Sarah E. Needleman, "It Isn't Always a Job behind an Online Job Posting: Employment Ads on the Web Can Lead You to Marketing Pitches, or Worse: Ways to See Which Ones Are Sincere," *Wall Street Journal*, February 17, 2009, B14.

5. Teri Evans, "Penn State, Texas A&M Top the List: Recruiters Like One-Stop Shopping for Grads with Solid Academics, Job Skills, Record of Success," *Wall Street Journal*, September 13, 2010, B1; and Alexandra Cheney, "Firms Assess Young Interns' Potential: Businesses Look to Pools for Full-Time Hires, Tracking Future Employees as Early as Freshman Year," *Wall Street Journal*, September 13, 2010, B10.

6. Julie Strickland, "The Good Hires? They're in Your Network," *Inc.*, May 2013, 24.

7. Geoffrey James, "Online Personal Branding Increases Your Hireability," *FINS Sales & Marketing*, July 18, 2012, http://sales-jobs.fins.com/Articles/SBB0001424052702304070304577394374201618012/Online-Personal-Branding-Increases-Your-Hireability.

8. Cheryl Lu-Lien Tan, "The Art of Online Portraiture," *Wall Street Journal*, October 20, 2011, D6.

9. "Facebook Costing 16–34s Jobs in Tough Economic Climate," *OnDeviceResearch.com*, May 29, 2013, http://ondeviceresearch.com/blog/facebook-costing-16-34s-jobs-in-tough-economic-climate#sthash.Yvmg7k4T.5wuXCgt6.dpbs.

10. Leslie Kwoh, "Beware: Potential Employers Are Watching You," *Wall Street Journal*, October 29, 2012, B8.

11. Dean Irvine, "Fake Amazon Resume Proves the Power of Personal Branding," *CNN.com*, February 1, 2013, http://edition.cnn.com/2013/01/31/business/fake-amazon-resume-cv-philippe-dubost.

12. Accountemps: A Robert Half Company, "Résumés Inching Up: Survey Shows Longer Résumés Now More Acceptable," news release, March 20, 2010, http://accountemps.rhi.mediaroom.com/index.php?s5189&item5210.

13. Elizabeth Blackburn-Brockman and Kelly Belanger, "One Page or Two? A National Study of CPA Recruiters' Preferences for Résumé Length," *The Journal of Business Communication* 38 (2001): 29–45.

14. CareerBuilder.com, "Nearly Half of Employers Have Caught a Lie on a Résumé, CareerBuilder.com Survey Shows," press release, July 30, 2008, http://www.careerbuilder.com/share/aboutus/pressreleasesdetail.aspx?id5pr448&sd57%2f30%2f2008&ed512%2f31%2f2008; and Dennis Nishi, "'Keywords' May Unlock a New Job," *Wall Street Journal*, February 24, 2013, http://online.wsj.com/article/SB10001424127887323949404578314220242353956.html.

15. National Association of Colleges and Employers, "Job Outlook 2013," November 2012, http://www.unco.edu/careers/assets/documents/NACEJobOutlookNov2013.pdf.

16. Roni Noland, "It's Not a Disaster if Your Old Boss Won't Provide a Reference," *Boston Globe*, March 8, 2009, 5.

17. Phil Elder, "The Trade Secrets of Employment Interviews," paper presented at the Association for Business Communication Midwest Convention, Kansas City, MO, May 2, 1987.

18. Joe Light, "For Job Seekers, Company Sites Beat Online Boards, Social Media," *Wall Street Journal*, April 4, 2011, B8.

19. John B. Killoran, "Self-Published Web Résumés: Their Purposes and Their Genre Systems," *Journal of Business and Technical Communication* 20, no. 4 (2006): 425–59.

20. Keith J. Winstein and Daniel Golden, "MIT Admissions Dean Lied on Résumé in 1979, Quits," *Wall Street Journal*, April 27, 2007, B1.

21. CareerBuilder.com, "Nearly Half of Employers Have Caught a Lie on a Résumé."

22. Dan Fastenberg, "The Most Common Lies on Résumés," *AOL Jobs*, April 1, 2013; and Alison Doyle, "Employment Background Checks," *About.com Job Searching*, accessed June 21, 2013, http://jobsearch.about.com/cs/backgroundcheck/a/background.htm.

13 Writing Job Application Letters

Chapter Outline

NEWSWORTHY COMMUNICATION

Viral Cover Letters

College students who are seeking employment on Wall Street face a difficult path. With little or no experience, they have to rely on cover letters to set them apart. In letters that were widely forwarded among Wall Street executives, two college students tried different approaches.

Consider this excerpt from an "ambitious undergraduate at NYU": "I am unequivocally the most unflaggingly hard worker I know, and I love self-improvement. I have always felt that my time should be spent wisely, so I continuously challenge myself; I left [my job] because the work was too easy. Once I realized I could achieve a perfect GPA while holding a part-time job at NYU, I decided to redouble my effort by placing out of two classes, taking two honors classes, and holding two part-time jobs. That semester I achieved a 3.93, and in the same time I managed to bench double my bodyweight and do 35 pull-ups."

Compare this excerpt from another student: "I am aware it is highly unusual for undergraduates from average universities like [mine] to intern at [your company], but nevertheless I was hoping you might make an exception. I am extremely interested in investment banking and would love nothing more than to learn under your tutelage. I have no qualms about fetching coffee, shining shoes, or picking up laundry, and will work for next to nothing. In all honesty, I just want to be around professionals in the industry and gain as much knowledge as I can."

Which of these applicants would *you* hire?

Sources: Eric Platt, "Here's the Full Summer Analyst Application Cover Letter That Went Viral on Wall Street," *Business Insider*, February 8, 2012, http://www.businessinsider.com/heres-the-full-summer-analyst-application-cover-letter-that-went-viral-on-wall-street-2012-2; and Maseena Ziegler, "Wall Street Bosses Are Calling This 'The Best Cover Letter Ever'—But Not Everyone Agrees," *Forbes*, January 16, 2013, http://www.forbes.com/sites/crossingborders/2013/01/16/wall-street-bosses-are-calling-this-the-best-cover-letter-ever-but-not-everyone-agrees/.

LO 13-1 Find the information you need to write a good job letter to a specific employer.

LO 13-2 Write a job letter that makes you look attractive to employers.

LO 13-3 Use social networking and a personal website to create a virtual cover letter.

The purpose of a job application letter is to get an interview. If you get interviews arranged by your campus placement office or through contacts, you may not need to write a letter. Similarly, if you apply electronically through a company's website, a letter may not be part of the materials you submit. However, if you want to work for an organization that isn't interviewing on campus, or later when you change jobs, you may need a letter. A survey conducted by Robert Half International, the world's largest specialized staffing firm, found 86% of executives said cover letters were still valuable components of job applications in the electronic age.[1]

The co-founder of one software firm says,

> We ignore résumés. . . . Résumés reduce people to bullet points, and most people look pretty good as bullet points.
>
> What we do look at are cover letters. Cover letters say it all. They immediately tell you if someone wants this job or just any job. And cover letters make something else very clear: They tell you who can and who can't write. . . . When in doubt, always hire the better writer.[2]

Job letters can play an important role in your personal branding (see pages 381–83). They can show your personality and, through careful reference to well-chosen details about the organization, interest in a particular job.

Job letters are frequently seen as evidence of your written communication skills, so you want to do your best work in them. Flaws in your letter may well be seen as predicting shoddy job performance in the future.

How Content Differs in Job Letters and Résumés

The job application letter accompanies your résumé and serves as its cover letter. Make the most of your letter; it is your chance to showcase the features that set you apart from the crowd. Here you bring to life the facts presented in your résumé; here you can show some personality (but don't overdo it). The cover letter is your opportunity to "sell" yourself into an interview.

Although résumés and job letters overlap somewhat, they differ in three important ways:

- The résumé summarizes *all* your qualifications. The letter expands your *best* qualifications to show how you can help the organization meet its needs, how you differ from other applicants, and how much knowledge of the organization you possess.

- The résumé avoids controversial material. The job letter can explain in a positive way situations such as career changes or gaps in employment history. If you have one of the difficulties described in Chapter 12, a cover letter may help you overcome it.

- The résumé uses short, parallel phrases and sentence fragments. The letter uses complete sentences in well-written paragraphs.

How to Find Out about Employers and Jobs LO 13-1

To adapt your letter to a specific organization, you need information both about the employer and about the job itself. You'll need to know

- **The name and address of the person who should receive the letter.** To get this information, check the ad, call the organization, check its website, or check with your job search contacts. An advantage of calling is that you can find out what courtesy title (Chapter 3) the individual prefers and get current information.

- **What the organization does, and some facts about it.** Knowing the organization's larger goals enables you to show how your specific work will help the company meet its goals. Useful facts can include market share, new products or promotions, the kind of computer or manufacturing equipment it uses, plans for growth or downsizing, competitive position, challenges the organization faces, and the corporate culture (Chapter 4).

- **What the job itself involves.** Campus placement offices and web listings often have fuller job descriptions than appear in ads. Talk to friends who have graduated recently to learn what their jobs involve. Conduct information interviews to learn more about opportunities that interest you.

The websites listed in Figure 13.1 provide a wide range of information. For instance, the *Forbes* and *Money* sites have good financial news stories; the Public Register (prars.com) is a good source for annual reports. As a consumer, you may have used the Better Business Bureau (bbb.org) site.

More specific information about companies can be found on their websites. To get specific financial data (and to see how the organization presents itself to the public), get the company's annual report from your library or the web. (Note: Only companies whose stock is publicly traded are required to

Figure 13.1	Web Sources for Facts about Companies

Company Facts

http://www.jobbankinfo.org
http://www.wetfeet.com
http://www.forbes.com
http://www.irin.com
http://www.corporateinformation.com
http://www.vault.com
http://www.stockmarketyellowpages.com
http://www.prars.com
http://money.cnn.com
http://www.inc.com/inc5000

http://www.bbb.org
http://legacy.www.nypl.org/research/sibl/company/c2index.htm
http://www.lib.berkeley.edu/BUSI
http://online.wsj.com/public/page/news-career-jobs.html

Salary Calculators

http://salaryexpert.com
http://www.indeed.com/salary
http://www.payscale.com

Multiple Career Changes

You will probably need a cover letter as you change careers during your lifetime. A study from the U.S. Bureau of Labor Statistics shows that young people hold an average of 11 jobs between the ages of 18 and 44. But what are these jobs? Are people changing careers?

The answer can be complex. If a worker takes a company promotion to move from being an active engineer to becoming a manager, is that a career change? Just a promotion? The work being done will certainly change. If someone laid off from her financial career takes a landscaping job for six months to pay bills before her next financial job comes along, is that a career change? Will it count as a double career change when she returns to finance?

One thing is certain: in a job market that is constantly shifting, having an up-to-date cover letter and résumé will prepare you for any sort of job change or promotion.

Adapted from U.S. Department of Labor Bureau of Labor Statistics, "Frequently Asked Questions: Does BLS Have Information on the Number of Times People Change Careers in their Lives?" National Longitudinal Surveys, last modified June 12, 2013, http://www.bls.gov/nls/nlsfaqs.htm; and U.S. Department of Labor Bureau of Labor Statistics, "Number of Jobs Held, Labor Market Activity, and Earnings Growth among the Youngest Baby Boomers: Results from a Longitudinal Survey," news release, July 25, 2012, USDL-12-1489, http://www.bls.gov/news.release/pdf/nlsoy.pdf.

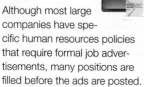
issue annual reports. In this day of mergers and buyouts, many companies are owned by other companies. The parent company may be the only one to issue an annual report.) Recruiting notebooks at your campus placement office may provide information about training programs and career paths for new hires. Many companies also have this information on their websites. To learn about new products, plans for growth, or solutions to industry challenges, read business newspapers such as the *Wall Street Journal*, business magazines such as *Fortune* or *Bloomberg Businessweek*, and trade journals.

Tapping into the Hidden Job Market

Many jobs are never advertised—and the number rises the higher on the job ladder you go. In fact, some authorities put the percentage of jobs that are not advertised as high as 80%.[3] Many new jobs come not from responding to an ad but from networking with personal contacts. Some of these jobs are created especially for a specific person. These unadvertised jobs are called the **hidden job market.** Information and referral interviews are two organized methods of networking.

Information Interviews

In an **information interview** you talk to someone who works in the area you hope to enter to find out what the day-to-day work involves and how you can best prepare to enter that field. An information interview can let you know whether or not you'd like the job, give you specific information that you can use to present yourself effectively in your résumé and application letter, and create a good image of you in the mind of the interviewer. If you present yourself positively, the interviewer may remember you when openings arise.

In an information interview, you might ask the following questions:

- How did you get started in this field?
- What have you been working on today?
- How do you spend your typical day?
- Have your duties changed a lot since you first started working here?
- What do you like best about your job? What do you like least?
- What do you think the future holds for this kind of work?
- What courses, activities, or jobs would you recommend as preparation for this kind of work?

To set up an information interview, you can phone or write an e-mail like the one in Figure 13.2. If you do e-mail, phone the following week to set up a specific time.

Referral Interviews

Referral interviews are interviews you schedule to learn about current job opportunities in your field. Sometimes an interview that starts out as an information interview turns into a referral interview.

| Figure 13.2 | E-mail Requesting an Information Interview |

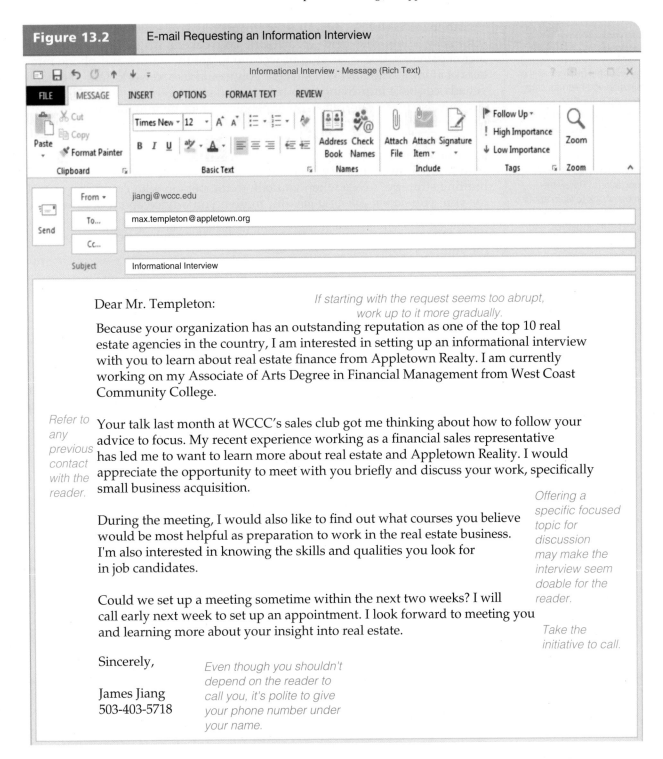

Dear Mr. Templeton:

If starting with the request seems too abrupt, work up to it more gradually.

Because your organization has an outstanding reputation as one of the top 10 real estate agencies in the country, I am interested in setting up an informational interview with you to learn about real estate finance from Appletown Realty. I am currently working on my Associate of Arts Degree in Financial Management from West Coast Community College.

Refer to any previous contact with the reader.

Your talk last month at WCCC's sales club got me thinking about how to follow your advice to focus. My recent experience working as a financial sales representative has led me to want to learn more about real estate and Appletown Reality. I would appreciate the opportunity to meet with you briefly and discuss your work, specifically small business acquisition.

During the meeting, I would also like to find out what courses you believe would be most helpful as preparation to work in the real estate business. I'm also interested in knowing the skills and qualities you look for in job candidates.

Offering a specific focused topic for discussion may make the interview seem doable for the reader.

Could we set up a meeting sometime within the next two weeks? I will call early next week to set up an appointment. I look forward to meeting you and learning more about your insight into real estate.

Take the initiative to call.

Sincerely,

Even though you shouldn't depend on the reader to call you, it's polite to give your phone number under your name.

James Jiang
503-403-5718

A referral interview should give you information about the opportunities currently available in the area you're interested in, refer you to other people who can tell you about job opportunities, and enable the interviewer to see that you could make a contribution to his or her organization. Therefore, the goal of a referral interview is to put you face-to-face with someone who has the power to hire you: the president of a small company, the division vice president or branch manager of a big company, the director of the local office of a state or federal agency.

http://www.google
.com/about/

Many websites give you all the information you need to write a good job letter. Google's About page, for example, has links to jobs, news, company information, and investor relations, where you will find financial information and annual reports. Follow the "Company" link to learn about topics such as Google's history, initiatives, and philosophy.

Start by scheduling interviews with people you know who may know something about that field—professors, co-workers, neighbors, friends, former classmates. Use your alumni website to get the names and phone numbers of alumni who now work where you would like to work. Talk to them to get advice about improving your résumé and about general job-hunting strategy, but also to get referrals to other people. In fact, go into the interview with the names of people you'd like to talk to. If the interviewer doesn't suggest anyone, say, "Do you think it would be a good idea for me to talk to ——?"

Armed with a referral from someone you both know, you can call people with hiring power, and say, "So-and-so suggested I talk with you about job-hunting strategy." Even when you talk to the person who could create a job for you, you *do not ask for a job*. But to give you advice about your résumé, the person has to look at it. If there's a match between what you can do and what the organization needs, that person has the power to create a position for you.

> **⚠ WARNING:** Many businesspeople are cynical about information and referral interviewing; they know the real purpose of such interviews, and they resent the time needed. Therefore you need to prepare carefully for these interviews. Prepare a list of good questions; know something about the general field or industry; research the specific company.

Always follow up information and referral interviews with personal thank-you letters. Use specifics to show that you paid attention during the interview, and enclose a copy of your revised résumé.

Content and Organization for Job Application Letters LO 13-2

Job letters help show employers why they should interview you instead of other—sometimes hundreds of others—qualified applicants. In your letter, focus on

- Your qualifications to meet major requirements of the job.

- Points that separate you from other applicants.

- Points that show your knowledge of the organization.

- Qualities that every employer is likely to value: the ability to write and speak effectively, to solve problems, to work well with people.

Two different hiring situations call for two different kinds of application letters. Write a **solicited letter** when you know that the company is hiring: you've seen an ad, you've been advised to apply by a professor or friend, you've read in a trade publication that the company is expanding. This situation is similar to a direct request in persuasion (see Chapter 11): you can indicate immediately that you are applying for the position. Sometimes, however, the advertised positions may not be what you want, or you may want to work for an organization that has not announced openings in your area. Then you write a **prospecting letter.** (The metaphor is drawn from prospecting for gold.) The prospecting letter is like a problem-solving persuasive message (see Chapter 11).

Prospecting letters help you tap into the hidden job market. In some cases, your prospecting letter may arrive at a company that has decided to hire but has not yet announced the job. In other cases, companies create positions to get a good person who is on the market. Even in a hiring freeze, jobs are sometimes created for specific individuals.

In both solicited and prospecting letters you should

- Address the letter to a specific person (a must for a prospecting letter).

- Indicate the specific position for which you're applying.

- Be specific about your qualifications.

- Show what separates you from other applicants.

- Show knowledge of the company and the position.

- Refer to your résumé (which you would enclose with the letter).

- Ask for an interview.

The following discussion follows the job letter from beginning to end. The two kinds of letters are discussed separately where they differ and together where they are the same. Letters for internships follow the same patterns: use a solicited letter to apply for an internship that has been advertised and a prospecting letter to create an internship with a company that has not announced one.

How to Organize Solicited Letters

When you know the company is hiring, use the pattern of organization in Figure 13.3. A sample solicited letter for a graduating senior is shown in Figure 13.4. A solicited letter following up from a career fair and requesting an internship is shown in Figure 13.7. The job ad for the letter in Figure 13.4 is printed in Exercise 13.20.

Figure 13.3	How to Organize a Solicited Job Application Letter

1. State that you're applying for the job (phrase the job title as your source phrased it). Tell where you learned about the job (ad, referral, etc.). Include any reference number mentioned in the ad. Briefly show that you have the major qualifications required by the ad: a college degree, professional certification, job experience, etc. Summarize your other qualifications briefly in the same order in which you plan to discuss them in the letter.

2. Develop your major qualifications in detail. Be specific about what you've done; relate your achievements to the work you'd be doing in this new job.

3. Develop your other qualifications, even if the ad doesn't ask for them. Show what separates you from the other applicants who will also answer the ad. Demonstrate your knowledge of the organization.

4. Ask for an interview; tell when you'll be available to be interviewed and to begin work. Thank recipient for considering your application. End on a positive, forward-looking note.

Figure 13.4 A Solicited Letter from a Graduating Senior

Jeff Moeller

831.503.4692
51 Willow Street
San José, CA 95112
jmoeller@csmb.edu

April 4, 2014

Mr. Richard Grove
Telltale Games
P.O. Box 9737
San Rafael, CA 94912

Dear Mr. Grove:

Tell where you learned about the job.
If the job has a reference number, provide it.

In paragraph 1, show you have the qualifications the ad lists.

I am applying for your Game Designer position posted on your website. As an avid player of Telltale games, I believe that I have all the qualifications to do a great job. With my degree in Computer Science and Information Technology and my experience creating game content, I will be able to apply many skills to the Game Designer position. My passion for becoming part of the gaming industry, combined with my oral and written communication skills, makes me a great fit for the Telltale team.

This summary sentence forecasts the structure of the rest of the letter.

Shows enthusiasm for the profession and picks up on the programming experience emphasis in the job ad.

Since I was five, I have had a strong interest in computers and video games, and my interest and knowledge have only increased in recent years. Not only do I play video games, I discuss them with others, read news articles about them online, and consider ways to improve or change a specific game. I have also used game editors to create my own content in games. When it comes to computers, I have a keen interest in staying current with the latest technology, and I apply my knowledge hands-on by building systems. These experiences give me an understanding of how modern computers and video game systems function. I also have experience with several programming languages, from both taking courses and learning them on my own. This has increased my eye for detail, a necessary ability for any game designer.

My passion for creating video games was recognized this year in President Obama's National STEM video game challenge. With a team of students in Professor Kent Olbernath's game development class at California State University, I produced "Parrot Villa," the first level of an immersive game where players solve mysteries on a unique jungle world. The programming quality and detailed story line helped my team earn second place in the nationwide competition. You can see a demo of "Parrot Villa" at www.STEMChallenge.gov/2013_Winners.

Provides evidence for his achievements in the profession.

Relates what he has done to what he could do for the company.

Evidence of communication skills is a plus for almost any job.

Along with my enthusiasm for games, I have strong oral and written communication skills. I am a confident public speaker, and I have an ability to relay information in a clear and concise manner. More importantly, though, I have developed the ability in my creative writing courses to create engaging and coherent narratives, which will be a large component of developing new games. In addition to my coursework and experience, I have honed my skills online by writing articles about games. In covering the video game industry for Point Network, I have reviewed Telltale's own *Tales of Monkey Island*.

Shows familiarity with company's products.

Working in the video game industry is my goal, and I would be a great asset to Telltale Games. I would love to come in for an interview to discuss the position and the contributions I can make. I have always enjoyed playing Telltale's games, and I look forward to the possibility of working on them one day soon.

Sincerely,

Jeff Moeller

Jeff Moeller

Figure 13.5	How to Organize a Prospecting Letter

1. Catch the reader's interest.

2. Create a bridge between the attention-getter and your qualifications. Focus on what you know and can do. Since the employer is not planning to hire, he or she won't be impressed with the fact that you're graduating. Summarize your qualifications briefly in the same order in which you plan to discuss them in the letter. This summary sentence or paragraph then covers everything you will talk about and serves as an organizing device for your letter.

3. Develop your strong points in detail. Be specific. Relate what you've done in the past to what you could do for this company. Show that you know something about the company. Identify the specific niche you want to fill.

4. Ask for an interview and tell when you'll be available for interviews. (Don't tell when you can begin work.) Thank the recipient for considering your application. End on a positive, forward-looking note.

How to Organize Prospecting Letters

When you don't have any evidence that the company is hiring, you cannot use the pattern for solicited letters. Instead, use the pattern of organization in Figure 13.5. A sample prospecting letter for an applicant desiring to change fields is shown in Figure 13.6.

First Paragraphs of Solicited Letters

When you know that the firm is hiring, announcing that you are applying for a specific position enables the firm to route your letter to the appropriate person, thus speeding consideration of your application. Identify where you learned about the job: "the position of junior accountant announced in Sunday's *Dispatch*," "William Paquette, our placement director, told me that you are looking for. . . ."

Note how the following paragraph picks up several of the characteristics of the ad:

Ad: Business Education Instructor at Shelby Adult Education. Candidate must possess a Bachelor's degree in Business Education. Will be responsible for providing in-house training to business and government leaders. . . . Candidate should have at least one year teaching experience.

Letter: I am applying for your position in Business Education that is posted on your school website. In December, I will receive a Bachelor of Science degree from North Carolina A & T University in Business Education. My work has given me two years' experience teaching word processing and computer accounting courses to adults plus leadership skills developed in the North Carolina National Guard.

Your **summary sentence** or **paragraph** covers everything you will talk about and serves as an organizing device for your letter.

Through my education, I have a good background in standard accounting principles and procedures and a working knowledge of some of the special accounting practices of the oil industry. This working knowledge is enhanced by practical experience in the oil fields: I have pumped, tailed rods, and worked as a roustabout.

My business experience, familiarity with DeVilbiss equipment, and communication skills qualify me to be an effective part of the sales staff at DeVilbiss.

Unconventional Tactics

In a competitive job market, you may be tempted to try an unconventional approach to getting attention from employers.

Nathan Schwagler tried to get past the traditional hiring process at Ingram Micro. He dressed up as a deliveryman, complete with a clipboard, a bouquet of flowers, and a Candygram. He got through security and to the office of Jessica, the company's recruiter. When he finally met her, Schwagler stripped off his coveralls to reveal his business suit underneath and presented Jessica with his résumé, in addition to the flowers and candy.

Did it work? When Schwagler followed up a week later, he found he had been barred from entering the office or calling again.

According to surveys, only 9% of hiring managers have hired someone who used unconventional tactics to get noticed. The other 91% hired candidates who had a strong cover letter and a well-designed résumé.

Adapted from Rachel Zupek, "Unusual Job Search Tactics," CareerBuilder, accessed June 20, 2013, http://www.careerbuilder .com/article/cb-1076-job-search-unusual-job-search-tactics/.

Mandy Shelly
www.wisc.edu/~Shelly88/home.htm

Mandy uses a "letterhead" that hamonizes with her résumé. (see Figure 12.7)

266 Van Buren Drive
Madison, WI 53706
shellym@wisc.edu
608-897-1534 (home)
608-842-4242 (cell)

March 29, 2014

Mr. Franklin Kohl
PDF Productions
3232 White Castle Road
Minneapolis, MN 85434

Dear Mr. Kohl:

In a prospecting letter, open with a sentence which (1) will seem interesting and true to the reader and (2) provides a natural bridge to talking about yourself.

The Wall Street Journal says that PDF Productions is expanding operations into Wisconsin, Minnesota, and Nebraska. My experience in technical writing, design, and computers would be an asset to your expanding organization.

Shows knowledge of the organization.

Briefly shows a variety of technical writing and computer skills.

While working at a local animal shelter, I used my technical writing skills to create a website that allows users to easily access information. To improve the website, I conducted usability tests which provided useful feedback that I incorporated to modify the overall design. In addition, I was also responsible for writing and editing the shelter's monthly newsletter, which was distributed to roughly 1,200 "Friends of the Shelter." I have extensive computer and design skills, which I am anxious to put to use for PDF Productions.

Relates what she's done to what she could do for this company.

Coursework has also prepared me well for technical writing. I have written technical material on a variety of levels ranging from publicity flyers for the animal shelter to scientific reports for upper-level science courses. My course work in statistics has shown me how to work with data and present it accurately for various audiences. Because of my scientific background, I also have a strong vocabulary in both life sciences and chemistry. This background will help me get up to speed quickly with clients such as ChemPro and Biostage. My background in science has also taught me just how important specific details can be.

Shows how her course-work is an asset.

Names specific clients, showing more knowledge of company.

In May, I will complete my degree from the University of Wisconsin and will be most interested in making a significant contribution to PDF Productions. I am available every Monday, Wednesday, and Friday for an interview (608-897-1534). I look forward to talking with you about technical writing I can do for PDF Productions.

Sincerely,

Mandy Shelly

Mandy Shelly

Figure 13.7 Letter Following Up from a Career Fair and Requesting an Internship

James Jiang
jiangj@wccc.edu

Campus Address
1524 E. Main St
Portland, OR 97231
503-403-5718

Letterhead matches his résumé.

Permanent Address
2526 Prairie Lane
Portland, OR 97233
503-404-7793

January 23, 2014

Ms. Deborah Pascel, HR Department
Prime Financial
401 Prime Park Place
Beaverton, OR 97007

Dear Ms. Pascel:

Uses his contact immediately.

Mary Randi at the West Coast Community College Career Fair suggested I send you my résumé for the Sales Advisor internship. My education, combined with my past work experiences, makes me a strong candidate for Prime Financial.

Shows he has been getting full value from his schooling.

While working toward my Associate of Arts degree in Financial Management from West Coastal Community College, I have learned the value of fiscal responsibility. For example, in my social financial planning course, I developed a strategic plan to eliminate credit card debt for a one-income household with two children. Moreover, in my business communication course, I improved my oral communication ability so that I could effectively communicate my plans to potential clients. This ability will be an asset to Prime Financial as the organization works to maintain the strong relationship with the community and small business owners that Ms. Randi informed me about.

Refers to knowledge gained at career fair.

Paragraphs 2 and 3 show he has skills he can use immediately as an intern.

My financial education, combined with my previous work experiences in sales, will allow me to thoroughly analyze investment opportunities and establish a strong client base for Prime Financial. For example, I started the A-Plus T-Shirt Company that sold graphic T-shirts to high school students; it had a routine client base of over 150 customers. From managing this business, I know what it takes to be reliable and responsive to customer needs. I am looking forward to learning new approaches from Prime Financial's internship, particularly new ways to work with small businesses.

Provides details about his sales experience to interest his reader.

With my education and experience, I can provide the innovative and competitive edge necessary to be part of your team. I would welcome an interview to discuss your internship and the contributions I could make at Prime Financial.

Sincerely,

James Jiang

James Jiang

First Paragraphs of Prospecting Letters

In a prospecting letter, asking for a job in the first paragraph is dangerous: unless the company plans to hire but has not yet announced openings, the reader is likely to throw the letter away. Instead, catch the reader's interest. Then in the second paragraph you can shift the focus to your skills and experience, showing how they can be useful to the employer and specifying the job you are seeking.

Here are some effective first and second paragraphs that provide a transition to the writer's discussion of his or her qualifications.

First two paragraphs of a letter to the director of publications at an oil company:

> If scarcity of resources makes us use them more carefully, perhaps it would be a good idea to ration words. If people used them more carefully, internal communications specialists like you would have fewer headaches because communications jobs would be done right the first time.
>
> For the last six years I have worked on improving my communications skills, learning to use words more carefully and effectively. I have taught business communication at a major university, worked for two newspapers, completed a Master's degree in English, and would like to contribute my skills to your internal communications staff.

First two paragraphs of a letter applying to be a computer programmer for an insurance company:

> As you know, merging a poorly written letter with a database of customers just sends out bad letters more quickly. But you also know how hard it is to find people who can both program computers and write well.
>
> My education and training have given me this useful combination. I'd like to put my associate's degree in computer technology and my business experience writing to customers to work in State Farm's service approach to insurance.

Notice how the second paragraph provides a transition to a discussion of qualifications.

Questions work well only if the answers aren't obvious. The computer programmer above should *not* ask this question:

> Do you think that training competent and motivated personnel is a serious concern in the insurance industry?

If the reader says *yes,* the question will seem dumb. If the reader says *no,* the student has destroyed his or her common ground. The computer programmer, however, could pose this question:

> How often do you see a programmer with both strong programming skills and good communication skills?

This question would give him or her an easy transition into paragraphs about his/her programming and communication skills.

Showing a Knowledge of the Position and the Company

If you could substitute another inside address and salutation and send out the letter without any further changes, it isn't specific enough. A job application letter is basically a claim that you could do a specific job for a particular company. Use your knowledge of the position and the company to choose relevant evidence from what you've done to support your claims that you could help the company. (See Figures 13.4 and 13.6.)

The following paragraphs show the writer's knowledge of the company.

A letter to PricewaterhouseCoopers's Minneapolis office uses information the student learned in a referral interview with a partner in an accounting firm. Because the reader will know that Herr Wollner is a partner in the Berlin office, the student does not need to identify him.

> While I was studying in Berlin last spring, I had the opportunity to discuss accounting methods for multinational clients of PricewaterhouseCoopers with Herr Fritz Wollner. We also talked about communication among PricewaterhouseCoopers's international offices.
>
> Herr Wollner mentioned that the increasing flow of accounting information between the European offices—especially those located in Germany, Switzerland, and Austria—and the U.S. offices of PricewaterhouseCoopers makes accurate translations essential. My fluency in German enables me to translate accurately; and my study of communication problems in Speech Communication, Business and Professional Speaking, and Business and Technical Writing will help me see where messages might be misunderstood and choose words which are more likely to communicate clearly.

A letter to KMPG uses information the student learned in a summer job.

> As an assistant accountant for Pacific Bell during this past summer, I worked with its computerized billing and record-keeping system, BARK. I had the opportunity to help the controller revise portions of the system, particularly the procedures for handling delinquent accounts. When the KMPG audit team reviewed Pacific Bell's transactions completed for July, I had the opportunity to observe your System 2170. Several courses in computer science allow me to appreciate the simplicity of your system and its objective of reducing audit work, time, and costs.

One or two specific details about the company usually are enough to demonstrate your knowledge. Be sure to use the knowledge, not just repeat it. Never present the information as though it will be news to the reader. After all, the reader works for the company and presumably knows much more about it than you do.

Showing What Separates You from Other Applicants

Your knowledge of the company can separate you from other applicants. You can also use coursework, an understanding of the field, and experience in jobs and extracurricular events to show that you're unique. Stress your accomplishments, not your job responsibilities. Be specific but concise; usually three to five sentences will enable you to give enough specific supporting details.

This student uses both coursework and summer jobs to set herself apart from other applicants. Her research told her Monsanto had recently adopted new accounting methods for fluctuations in foreign currencies. Therefore, she mentions relevant simulations from her coursework.

Unfortunate Cover Letter Statements

- "Please find my résumé." Did you look under the couch?
- "I have integrity so I will not steal office supplies and take them home." Good to know.
- "Please, please, please hire me for this job. I will be waiting by the phone." Don't wait too long.
- "What interested me about this job is that it's with a prestigious company." Glad to hear it.
- "After perusing my résumé, I am looking forward to hearing from you soon." If you don't mind, we'd appreciate the opportunity to peruse it ourselves before we get back to you.
- "I'm submitting the attached copy of my résumé for your consumption." Yum.
- "I perform my job with effortless efficiency, effectiveness, efficacy, and expertise." And an awful lot of alliteration, apparently.
- "The interview you schedule will undoubtedly reveal my unmatched talent and suitability for the position." Uh, don't count your chickens. . . .
- "But wait . . . there's more. You get all this business knowledge plus a grasp of finance that is second nature." If I act now, will you throw in a set of kitchen knives?

Quoted from "Resumania Archive," Resumania, 2013, http://www.resumania.com/ResumaniaArchive.

My college courses have taught me the essential accounting skills required to contribute to the growth of Monsanto. In two courses in international accounting, I compiled simulated accounting statements of hypothetical multinational firms in countries experiencing different rates of currency devaluation. Through these classes, I acquired the skills needed to work with the daily fluctuations of exchange rates and at the same time formulate an accurate and favorable representation of Monsanto.

Both my summer jobs and my coursework prepare me to do extensive record keeping as well as numerous internal and external communications. As Office Manager for the steamboat *Julia Belle Swain*, I was in charge of most of the bookkeeping and letter writing for the company. I kept accurate records for each workday, and I often entered over 100 transactions in a single day. In business communication I learned how to write persuasive messages and how to present extensive data in reports in a simplified style that is clear and easy to understand.

In your résumé, you may list activities, offices, and courses. In your letter, give more detail about what you did and show how those experiences will help you contribute to the employer's organization more quickly.

When you discuss your strengths, don't exaggerate. No employer will believe that a new graduate has a "comprehensive" knowledge of a field. Indeed, most employers believe that six months to a year of on-the-job training is necessary before most new hires are really earning their pay. Specifics about what you've done will make your claims about what you can do more believable and ground them in reality.

Writing the Last Paragraph

In the last paragraph, indicate when you'd be available for an interview. If you're free anytime, you can say so. But it's likely that you have responsibilities in class and work. If you'd have to go out of town, there may be only certain days of the week or certain weeks that you could leave town for several days. Use a sentence that fits your situation.

November 5–10 I'll be attending the Oregon Forestry Association's annual meeting and will be available for interviews then.

Any Monday or Friday I could come to Memphis for an interview.

Should you wait for the employer to call you, or should you call the employer to request an interview? In a solicited letter, it's safe to wait to be contacted: you know the employer wants to hire someone, and if your letter and résumé show that you're one of the top applicants, you'll get an interview. In a prospecting letter, call the employer. Because the employer is not planning to hire, you'll get a higher percentage of interviews if you're assertive.

If you're writing a prospecting letter to a firm that's more than a few hours away by car, say that you'll be in the area the week of such-and-such and could stop by for an interview. Companies pay for follow-up visits, but not for first interviews. A company may be reluctant to ask you to make an expensive trip when it isn't yet sure it wants to hire you.

End the letter on a positive note that suggests you look forward to the interview and that you see yourself as a person who has something to contribute, not as someone who just needs a job.

I look forward to discussing with you ways in which I could contribute to The Limited's continued growth.

Do not end your letter with a variation of the negative cliché "Please do not hesitate to contact me." Why do you think the reader would hesitate? Also avoid this other tired cliche: "Thank you for your time." Using an overworked ending dumps you right back in the pool with all the other applicants.

Oh yes, one more thing. Don't forget to sign your letter—with blue or black ink—legibly.

E-mail Application Letters

You will probably e-mail most of your applications. If your application is solicited, you can paste your traditional letter into your e-mail. If your application is prospecting, you need a shorter letter that will catch the reader's attention within the first screen (see Figure 13.8). In both solicited and prospecting applications, your first paragraph is crucial; use it to hook the reader.

As with any letter, what you write depends on your audience. For solicited applications, your e-mail will most likely be read initially by someone in Human Resources rather than the hiring manager. The HR staff member is reading your letter to see what job you are applying for and whether you meet the basic qualifications. In some cases, you will send a transmission e-mail to Human Resources with only basic information (the job number and your contact information) and an attached cover letter for the hiring manager. Pay close attention to the instructions in the job ad on how to submit your application.

For prospecting applications, your e-mail will more likely go directly to a hiring manager, who is not expecting it. You therefore need to do more to convince him or her to read your letter and look at your résumé. Do not make the mistake of treating a prospecting e-mail like a transmission e-mail. The recipient is unlikely to look at an unsolicited cover letter or résumé without a persuasive e-mail message.

If you don't know who will receive your e-mail, use a traditional cover letter format for your e-mail. Some experts are starting to recommend a shorter letter for both situations, but many caution that you need to include enough information to make you, not one of the numerous other applicants, the person for the job. Frequently that is hard to do in one screen.

When you submit an e-mail letter with your résumé,

Be Specific

Employers often read hundreds of cover letters each year. They know all the tricks and have seen all of the buzzwords. The best way for you to stand out is to be specific. Here are some tips for improving your cover letter:

1. If you are reusing text from cover letters to different companies, watch for errors like including the wrong company name, using "his" when you mean "hers," or extra or missing words.

2. Using vague language tells an employer you are either unsure about your own experience or you are inflating some facts.

3. Buzzwords can hurt more than they help, unless you link the buzzwords to specific experiences and examples.

4. Don't make jokes, include personal asides, or talk about your family or personal connections to the company.

Adapted from John Lopez, "The Recommendation Letter Employers Don't Want," *Bloomberg Businessweek*, June 11–17, 2012, 86.

- Include your name as part of the subject line. Many companies will also request the job number or title in the subject line.

- Repeat the job number or title for which you're applying in the first paragraph.

- Prepare your letter in a word-processing program. Use the spell checker to edit and proof the document.

- Use standard business letter features: salutation, standard closing, single-spacing with double-spacing between paragraphs.

- Use standard business language, without abbreviations or acronyms. Use standard, correct punctuation.

- Don't put anything in all capital letters.

- Don't use smiley faces or other emoticons.

- Put your name at the end of the message.

- Include contact information (at least your e-mail address and phone number) below your name.

Follow all guidelines posted by the company. Do not add attachments unless you know doing so is OK. Test your e-mail by sending it to a friend; have your friend check it for appearance and correctness.

Figure 13.8   An E-mail with Application Letter and Résumé

From ▾   jiangj@wccc.edu

To...   pascel@prime.com

Cc...

Subject   Résumé—James Jiang

Dear Ms. Pascel: *Uses contact immediately*

Tell what format the attached résumé is in. At the West Coast Community College Fair, Ms. Mary Randi said to e-mail you my résumé for the Sales Advisor internship. I have pasted my résumé below and have also attached it as a PDF. My degree in Financial Management, combined with my past work experiences, makes me a strong candidate for Prime Financial.

My course work honed professional skills. For example, in my social financial planning course, I developed a strategic plan to eliminate credit card debt for a one-income household with two children. In my business communication course, I improved my oral communication ability so that I could effectively communicate my plans to potential clients.   *See James's longer letter in Figure 13.7.*

Pick your most impressive information for the shortened version. My understanding of clients and their needs derives from my own work experiences. I started the A-Plus T-shirt Company that sold graphic T-shirts to high school students; it had a routine client base of over 150 customers. From managing this business, I know what it takes to be reliable and responsive to customer needs. I can provide the innovative and competitive edge necessary to be part of your team. I would welcome an interview to discuss your internship and the contributions I could make at Prime Financial.

Thank you,

Send a Word document or PDF file only if requested. May employers will not open them because of viruses. James Jiang

[Electronic résumé would be pasted here. PDF of résumé would be attached.]

Creating a Professional Image

Every employer wants businesslike employees who understand professionalism. To make your application letter professional,

- Create your letter in a word-processing program so you can use features such as a spell-checker. Use a standard font such as Times New Roman, Arial, or Helvetica in 12-point type.

- Address your letter to a specific person. If the reader is a woman, call the office to find out what courtesy title she prefers.

- Don't mention relatives' names. It's OK to use names of other people if the reader knows those people and thinks well of them, if they think well of you and will say good things about you, and if you have permission to use their names.

- Omit personal information not related to the job.

- Unless you're applying for a creative job in advertising, use a conservative style: few contractions; no sentence fragments, clichés, or slang.

- Edit the letter carefully and proof it several times to make sure it's perfect. Errors suggest that you're careless or inept. Double-check the spelling of the receiver's name.

- Print on the same paper (both shade and weight) you used for your résumé. Envelopes should match, too.

- Use a computer to print the envelope address.

Writing Style

Use a smooth, concise writing style (Chapter 5). Use the technical jargon of the field to show your training, but avoid businessese and stuffy words like *utilize*, *commence*, and *transpire* (for *happen*). Use a lively, energetic style that makes you sound like a real person.

Avoid words that can be interpreted sexually. A model letter distributed by the placement office at a Midwestern university included the following sentence:

> I have been active in campus activities and have enjoyed good relations with my classmates and professors.

Sentences like this get shared for laughs; that's not the kind of attention you want to get!

Be sure your letter uses the exact language of the job ad and addresses all items included in the ad. If the ad mentions teamwork, your letter should give examples of teamwork; don't shift the vocabulary to collaboration. Many readers expect their job ad language in applicants' letters. If the language is not there, they may judge the applicant as not fitting the position. And so may their computer, since the vocabulary of the job ad probably contains crucial key words for the computer to find.

Positive Emphasis

Be positive. Don't plead ("Please give me a chance") or apologize ("I cannot promise that I am substantially different from the lot"). Most negatives should be omitted from the letter.

You(r) Attitude Matters

If you find getting a job difficult, your attitude may be the reason. Here are four common career-blocking attitudes and responses to them:

Attitude: I deserve a good job because I went to school for four years.

Response: Employers are looking for who is best for a job, not who "deserves" a job.

Attitude: I am open to any job. I have no idea what I want to do.

Response: Employers want workers who are focused.

Attitude: I don't have experience because no one will give me a chance.

Response: Employers do not employ people to give them a "chance." Employers are concerned with what an applicant can do for them.

Attitude: I am so down on myself that it's hard to keep looking for a job.

Response: Get professional help, because this attitude is poisonous to your life as well as your career.

Adapted from Peter Vogt, "Self-Defeating Attitudes Will Stop Your Job Search Cold," Monster.com, accessed June 21, 2013, http://career-advice.monster.com/job-search/getting-started/self-defeating-attitudes-job-search/article.aspx.

Avoid word choices with negative connotations (see Chapter 3). Note how the following revisions make the writer sound more confident.

Negative: I have learned an excessive amount about writing through courses in journalism and advertising.

Positive: Courses in journalism and advertising have taught me to recognize and to write good copy. My profile of a professor was published in the campus newspaper; I earned an "A+" on my direct mail campaign for the American Dental Association to persuade young adults to see their dentist more often.

Excessive suggests that you think the courses covered too much—hardly an opinion likely to endear you to an employer.

Negative: You can check with my references to verify what I've said.

Positive: Professor Hill can give you more information about my work on his national survey.

Verify suggests that you expect the employer to distrust what you've said.

You-Attitude

Unsupported claims may sound overconfident, selfish, or arrogant. Create you-attitude (Chapter 3) by describing accomplishments and by showing how they relate to what you could do for this employer.

Lacks you-attitude: An inventive and improvising individual like me is a necessity in your business.

You-attitude: Building a summer house-painting business gave me the opportunity to find creative solutions to challenges. At the end of the first summer, for example, I had nearly 10 gallons of exterior latex left, but no more jobs. I contacted the home economics teacher at my high school. She agreed to give course credit to students who were willing to give up two Saturdays to paint a house being renovated by Habitat for Humanity. I donated the paint and supervised the students. I got a charitable deduction for the paint and hired the three best students to work for me the following summer. I could put these skills in problem solving and supervising to work as a personnel manager for Burroughs.

Show what you can do for them, not what they can do for you.

Lacks you-attitude: A company of your standing could offer the challenging and demanding kind of position in which my abilities could flourish.

You-attitude: Omit sentence.

Remember that the word *you* refers to your reader. Using *you* when you really mean yourself or "all people" can insult your reader by implying that he or she still has a lot to learn about business:

Lacks you-attitude: Running my own business taught me that you need to learn to manage your time.

You-attitude: Running my own business taught me to manage my time.

Beware of telling readers information they already know as though they do not know it. This practice can also be considered insulting.

Lacks you-attitude: Your company has just purchased two large manufacturing plants in France.

You-attitude: My three college French courses would help me communicate in your newly acquired French manufacturing facilities.

Since you're talking about yourself, you'll use *I* in your letter. Reduce the number of *I*'s by revising some sentences to use *me* or *my*.

Under my presidency, the Agronomy Club. . . .

Courses in media and advertising management gave me a chance to. . . .

My responsibilities as a summer intern included. . . .

In particular, avoid beginning every paragraph with *I*. Begin sentences with prepositional phrases or introductory clauses:

As my résumé shows, I. . . .

In my coursework in media and advertising management, I. . . .

As a summer intern, I. . . .

While I was in Italy. . . .

Paragraph Length and Unity

Keep your first and last paragraphs fairly short—preferably no more than four or five typed lines. Vary paragraph length within the letter; it's OK to have one long paragraph, but don't use a series of eight-line paragraphs.

When you have a long paragraph, check to be sure that it covers only one subject. If it covers two or more subjects, divide it into two or more paragraphs.

Use topic sentences at the beginning of your paragraphs to make your letter more readable.

Letter Length

Have at least three paragraphs. A short letter throws away an opportunity to be persuasive; it may also suggest that you have little to say for yourself or that you aren't very interested in the job.

Without eliminating content, tighten each sentence (Chapter 5) to be sure that you're using words as efficiently as possible. If your letter is a bit over a page, use slightly smaller margins or a type size that's one point smaller to get more on the page.

If you have excellent material that will not fit on one page, use it—as long as you have at least 6 to 12 lines of body text on the second page. The extra space gives you room to be more specific about what you've done and to add details about your experience that will separate you from other applicants. Employers don't *want* longer letters, but they will read them *if* the letter is well written and *if* the applicant establishes early in the letter that he or she has the credentials the company needs. Remember, however, that the trend is toward shorter letters.

Editing and Proofreading

Be sure you edit and proofread your cover letter. Failure to do so can undo all the work you put into it. The web abounds with humorous examples of spelling errors making unintended statements (I'm excellent at spelling and grammer). In fact, some companies post the best bloopers on their websites. For example, Robert Half International maintains Resumania (resumania.com); Killian Branding, an advertising agency, has "Cover Letters from Hell" on its website (www.killianbranding.com/cover-letters-from-hell/): the "poetic" Night-before-Christmas cover letter is amazing.

Check your content one last time to ensure that everything presents you as a hardworking professional. Make sure you are not revealing any frustration with the job search process in your content or diction. Check your tone to see that it is positive about your previous experiences and yourself. Don't beg or show too much gratitude for commonplaces such as reading your letter.

Follow-Up

Follow up with the employer once if you hear nothing after two or three weeks. It is also OK to ask once after one week if e-mail materials were received. If your job letter was prospecting, it is fine to follow up two or three times. Do not make a pest of yourself, however, by calling or e-mailing too often; doing so could eliminate you from further consideration.

Application Essays

Some jobs and internships, and many scholarship and graduate school applications, ask for an application essay. In a sense, this essay is an extended cover letter, but one written in an essay format rather than letter format. It will detail your strengths for the job/internship/scholarship/graduate school slot and show why you should be chosen instead of other applicants.

The essay offers you a chance to expand on your best points in more detail than does a cover letter. In so doing, you need to capture your readers' attention and show that you are exceptional. Frequently this means you need to put some of your personality into your essay. Here you can spell out with more interesting details skills you have already acquired from previous experiences and will bring to the new job or internship. Here you can elaborate on your academic achievements so you seem worthy of a scholarship or able to thrive in the rigors of graduate school. You can also expand more on general skills such as communication, critical thinking, and teamwork. Show that you are capable, hardworking, and interesting.

The essay also gives you room to include content that you would not put in a cover letter. For instance, you might want to include an anecdote that shows something about you as a developing professional (hint: make it interesting but not melodramatic). Or you might talk some about future goals. How did you arrive at these goals? How would this internship advance your career goals? Why do you want to go to graduate school? What do you want to do after the internship, scholarship, or graduate career is over?

 WARNING: Be careful when giving goals for job application essays. You do not want your goals to make the job seem like a quick stepping-stone to better opportunities.

Remember to use the good writing techniques you have learned in this course and your other communication classes.

- Follow the directions, especially word and page limits, precisely. If the essay is to respond to a question, make sure it answers the question.

- Have a focal point for your essay, a unifying theme. This will help prevent you from merely listing accomplishments (your résumé did that).

- Start your essay with an interesting paragraph to catch attention. Do not summarize your essay, or your reader may go no further.

- Remember your audience. Show what you can do for this company, or why you want to go to this particular graduate school. But most of all, show what's in it for the readers if they accept you.

- Use vivid details in the body of the essay. They don't have to be wildly creative for a job essay; showing how you cut production time for the department newsletter by 15% will be interesting to your reader if the job is a good fit for you.

- Use some unique details. If your sentence could be used in many other applications, it is not showing why *you* should get the internship/job/scholarship/graduate school slot.

- Avoid unsupported generalities and clichés.

- Use topic sentences at the beginnings of your paragraphs. Remember these essays are frequently read quickly.

- Let your word choice reveal your personal voice. Since the essay is about you, it's fine to use some first person. Avoid thesaurus diction.

- End with a strong concluding paragraph. Remember, this is the reader's last impression of you. Do not waste it on a boring summary of a one-page essay.

Social Networking and Personal Websites

Many employers are no longer finding their employees through job ads and applications. Rather, they are searching LinkedIn, Facebook, Twitter, and Google+ for qualified, interesting people to recruit. In these cases, you will not get a chance to submit a cover letter until after the employer has seen what you have posted online. In addition to the tips on personal branding from Chapter 12, you can also use your online presence to create a virtual cover letter—an introduction to employers who may be searching for you.

Here are some ideas for creating a virtual cover letter:

- **Manage your social networking profiles.** Employers will likely find you by your profile. Keep your education and employment up-to-date on all of your profiles. Include professional interests with your personal interests to give employers a well-rounded picture of who you are and how you could fit into their company.

- **Use key words.** In a competitive marketplace, where employers could see millions of profiles, using key words will at least get you on the radar. If you use key words and tie them into your experiences, you are more likely to stand out.

- **Keep your profile pictures professional.** When an employer searches for you, your profile picture will be one of the first things he or she sees. If it shows you making a funny face or partying with friends, it may be a red flag to an employer. The best bet is to keep your profile pictures simple and professional.

- **Manage your posts to social networks.** While a potential employer may not read through all your posts, you do need to show that you are professional and interesting. If you use key words in your posts, you are more likely to be found by an employer.

- **Create an effective personal website.** Your personal website can be your cover letter, résumé, and portfolio of work samples all in one place. Use the space effectively. Write a short introduction on the main page that talks about your goals and professional interests. On a different page or pages, include the stories and experiences that you would include in your cover letter. Show that your experience is real and interesting. Provide context and explanation for your portfolio items.

Using electronic resources well can help you stand out to potential employers.

Summary by Learning Objectives

LO 13-1 **Find the information you need to write a good job letter to a specific employer.**

Use some of the good websites mentioned in this chapter. Information and referral interviews can help you tap into the hidden job market—jobs that are not advertised. In an information interview you find out what the day-to-day work involves and how you can best prepare to enter that field. Referral interviews are interviews you schedule to learn about current job opportunities in your field.

LO 13-2 **Write a job letter that makes you look attractive to employers.**

- When you know that a company is hiring, send a solicited job letter. When you want a job with a company that has not announced openings, send a prospecting job letter. In both letters, you should
  - Address the letter to a specific person.
  - Indicate the specific position for which you're applying.
  - Be specific about your qualifications.
  - Show what separates you from other applicants.
  - Show knowledge of the company and the position.

- Refer to your résumé (which you would enclose with the letter).
- Ask for an interview.

- Use your knowledge of the company, your coursework, your understanding of the field, and your experience in jobs and extracurricular activities to show that you're unique.

- Don't repeat information that the reader already knows; don't seem to be lecturing the reader on his or her business.

- Use positive emphasis to sound confident. Use you-attitude by supporting general claims with specific examples and by relating what you've done to what the employer needs.

- Have at least three paragraphs in your letter. Most job letters are only one page.

- Application essays give you a chance to expand on your best points and show your personality.

LO 13-3 **Use social networking and a personal website to create a virtual cover letter.**

Your social networking and personal website can function as a virtual cover letter to reach those employers searching for people to recruit.

Continuing Case

The All-Weather Case, set in an HR department in a manufacturing company, extends through all 19 chapters and is available at www.mhhe.com/locker11e. The portion for this chapter provides a job posting and asks students to evaluate the letters of two candidates.

Exercises and Cases

*Go to www.mhhe.com/locker11e for additional Exercises and Cases.

13.1   Reviewing the Chapter

1. What are three ways that job letters differ from résumés? (LO 13-2)

2. What are some ways to research specific employers? (LO 13-1)

3. What is the difference between information and referral interviews? (LO 13-1)

4. What are the differences between solicited and prospecting letters? (LO 13-2)

5. What are five tips for writing a job letter that makes you look attractive to employers? (LO 13-2)

6. What are 10 ways to create a professional image with your letter? (LO 13-2)

7. How can you improve your online presence to make a virtual cover letter? (LO 13-3)

13.2 Reviewing Grammar

As you have read, it is crucial that your job letter be error-free. One common error in job letters, and one that spell-checker programs will not catch, is confusing word pairs like *affect/effect*. Practice choosing the correct word with Exercises B.12, B.13, and B.14 in Appendix B.

13.3 Analyzing First Paragraphs of Prospecting Letters

All of the following are first paragraphs in prospecting letters written by new college graduates. Evaluate the paragraphs on these criteria:

- Is the paragraph likely to interest readers and motivate them to read the rest of the letter?
- Does the paragraph have some content that the student can use to create a transition to talking about his or her qualifications?
- Does the paragraph avoid asking for a job?

1. Redeccer just added three new stores in Ohio. They also got voted best hardware store in Denton. This is where I want to start my career in supply-chain management.

2. From the time I was old enough to walk, my father involved me with the many chores and decisions that happen on a successful family farm. He taught me to work, to manage employees, and to handle large amounts of money. I believe my lifelong experience has prepared me to contribute to the continued success of your company.

3. Two years ago, my right leg was crushed in a car accident in the middle of my second semester of college. Although I had to have two surgeries and was on heavy painkillers, I successfully completed the semester with a 3.4. I know that this experience shows I have what it takes to succeed in your law firm.

4. For the past two and one-half years I have been studying turf management. On August 1, I will graduate from ——— University with a BA in Ornamental Horticulture. The type of job I will seek will deal with golf course maintenance as an assistant superintendent.

5. Ann Gibbs suggested that I contact you.

6. Each year, the Christmas shopping rush makes more work for everyone at Nordstrom's, especially for the Credit Department. While working for Nordstrom's Credit Department for three Christmas and summer vacations, the Christmas sales increase is just one of the credit situations I became aware of.

7. Whether to plate a two-inch eyebolt with cadmium for a tough, brilliant shine or with zinc for a rust-resistant, less expensive finish is a tough question. But similar questions must be answered daily by your salespeople. With my experience in the electroplating industry, I can contribute greatly to your constant need of getting customers.

8. What a set of tractors! The new 9430 and 9630 diesels are just what is needed by today's farmer with his ever-increasing acreage. John Deere has truly done it again.

9. Prudential Insurance Company did much to help my college career as the sponsor of my National Merit Scholarship. Now I think I can give something back to Prudential. I'd like to put my education, including a BS degree in finance from ——— University, to work in your investment department.

10. Since the beginning of Delta Electric Construction Co. in 1993, the size and profits have grown steadily. My father, being a stockholder and vice president, often discusses company dealings with me. Although the company has prospered, I understand there have been a few problems of mismanagement. I feel with my present and future qualifications, I could help ease these problems.

13.4 Improving You-Attitude and Positive Emphasis in Job Letters

Revise each of these sentences to improve you-attitude and positive emphasis. You may need to add information.

1. I got laid off at Barlons three months ago when they down-sized.

2. Your company needs someone like me, who has the experience and knowledge to take your department to new heights.

3. I may not be the most qualified candidate you will see, but with your location and financial struggles, I am certainly the best you will get.

4. I understand that your company has had problems due to the mistranslation of documents during international ad campaigns.

5. Included in my résumé are the courses in Finance that earned me a fairly attractive grade average.

6. I am looking for a position that gives me a chance to advance quickly.

7. Although short on experience, I am long on effort and enthusiasm.

8. I have been with the company from its beginning to its present unfortunate state of bankruptcy.

9. I wish to apply for a job at Austin Electronics. I will graduate from Florida State in May. I offer you a degree in electrical engineering and part-time work at Best Buy.

10. I was so excited to see your opening. This job is perfect for me.

11. You will find me a dedicated worker, because I really need a job.

13.5   Evaluating Letter Content

Improve the content of these passages from job cover letters. You may need to add content.

1. I am a very hard worker. In fact, I am known for finishing the jobs of my co-workers.

2. I have always worked hard, even when most of my co-workers and my boss were hardly working.

3. I have received a 4.0 in every semester at my university. This shows my dedication to perfection.

4. My internship gave me lots of experience for this job.

5. My job duties at Saxon Sport were to create displays, start an employee newsletter, and on weekends I was part of the sales staff.

6. While at San Fernando State, I participated in lots of activities. I played intramurals in baseball, football, basketball, hockey, and volley ball. I was treasurer and then president of the Marketing Club. I was in the Gaffers' Guild, where I made blown-glass creations. I was also in Campus Democrats.

7. I will be in Boston for a family reunion June 23–25 and will drop by your office then for an interview.

8. I feel any of my bosses would tell you that I try hard and pay attention to to detail.

9. I wish to apply for your job as a computer programmer. I have a computer science minor and two summers of sales experience at Best Buy in their computer department.

13.6   Evaluating Rough Drafts

Evaluate the following drafts. What parts should be omitted? What needs to be changed or added? What parts would benefit from specific supporting details?

1.
Dear_____:

There is more to a buyer's job than buying the merchandise. And a clothing buyer in particular has much to consider.

Even though something may be in style, customers may not want to buy it. Buyers should therefore be aware of what customers want and how much they are willing to pay.

In the buying field, request letters, thank-you letters, and persuasive letters are frequently written.

My interest in the retail field inspired me to read The Gap's annual report. I saw that a new store is being built. An interview would give us a chance to discuss how I could contribute to this new store. Please call me to schedule an interview.

Sincerely,

2.
Dear Sir or Madam:

I am taking the direct approach of a personnel letter. I believe you will under stand my true value in the areas of practical knowledge and promotional capabilities.

I am interested in a staff position with Darden in relation to trying to improve the operations and moral of the Olive Garden Restaurants, which I think that I am capable of doing. Please take a minute not to read my résumé (enclosed) and call to schedule an interview.

Sincerely,

3.

Dear_____:

Hello, my name is Dave. I am very interested in the position of marketing guy for Applicious Applesauce. I have recently graduated from Iowa State University, with a Bachelor's Degree in Marketing and Finance. I graduated with a 2.0 GPA, and took many classes in Marketing and Finance. I believe these classes will help me to grow your company to where it needs to be.

I did some marketing work for my friend, Aaron, who is starting his own business. I helped promote his new business and came up with a clear marketing plan for him to follow. He is doing really well with it so far.

I have no problem relocating for this job. I really want it.

Thank you for your time.

Sincerely,

13.7   Gathering Information about an Industry

Use six recent issues of a trade journal to report on three or four trends, developments, or issues that are important in an industry.

As your instructor directs,

a.   Share your findings with a small group of other students.

b.   Summarize your findings in an e-mail to your instructor. Include a discussion of how you could use this information in your job letter and résumé.

c.   Present your findings to the class.

d.   Join with a small group of other students to write a report summarizing the results of this research.

13.8   Gathering Information about Companies in Your Career Field

Use five different websites, such as those listed in Figure 13.1, to investigate three companies in your career field. Look at salary guides for your level of qualifications, product/service information, news articles about the companies, mission/vision statements, main competitors, annual reports, and financial reports.

As your instructor directs,

a.   Share your findings with a small group of other students.

b.   Summarize your findings in an e-mail to your instructor. Include a discussion of how you could use this information in your job letter and résumé.

c.   Present your findings to the class.

d.   Join with a small group of other students to write a report summarizing the results of this research.

13.9   Gathering Information about a Specific Organization

Gather information about a specific organization, using several of the following methods:

- Check the organization's website.
- Read the company's annual report.
- Pick up relevant information at the Chamber of Commerce.
- Read articles in trade publications and the *Wall Street Journal* or that mention the organization (check the indexes).
- Read recruiting literature provided by the company.

As your instructor directs,

a.   Share your findings with a small group of other students.

b.   Summarize your findings in an e-mail to your instructor. Include a discussion of how you could use this information in your job letter and résumé.

c.   Present your findings orally to the class.

d.   Write a paragraph for a job letter using (directly or indirectly) the information you found.

13.10 Conducting an Information Interview

Interview someone working in a field you're interested in. Use the questions listed on page 424 or the shorter list here:

- How did you get started in this field?
- What do you like about your job?
- What do you dislike about your job?
- What courses and jobs would you recommend as preparation for this field?

As your instructor directs,

a. Share the results of your interview with a small group of other students.

b. Write an e-mail to your instructor containing the results of your interview. Include a discussion of how you could use this information in your job letter and résumé.

c. Present the results of your interview orally to the class.

d. Write to the interviewee thanking him or her for taking the time to talk to you.

13.11 Conducting a Referral Interview

a. Write to a friend who is already in the workforce, asking about one or more of the following topics:

- Are any jobs in your field available in your friend's organization? If so, what?
- If a job is available, can your friend provide information beyond the job listing that will help you write a more detailed, persuasive letter? (Specify the kind of information you'd like to have.)
- Can your friend suggest people in other organizations who might be useful to you in your job search? (Specify any organizations in which you're especially interested.)

b. List possible networking contacts from your co-workers, classmates, fraternity/sorority members, friends, family friends, former employers and co-workers, neighbors, faculty members, and local businesspeople. Who would be the most valuable source of information for you? Who would you feel most comfortable contacting?

13.12 Writing a Solicited Letter

Write a letter of application in response to an announced opening for a full-time job (not an internship) you would like.

Turn in a copy of the listing. If you use option (a) below, your listing will be a copy. If you choose option (b), you will write the listing.

a. Respond to an ad in a newspaper, in a professional journal, in the placement office, or on the web. Use an ad that specifies the company, not a blind ad. Be sure that you are fully qualified for the job.

b. If you have already worked somewhere, assume that your employer is asking you to apply for full-time work after graduation. Be sure to write a fully persuasive letter.

13.13 Writing a Prospecting Letter

Pick a company you'd like to work for and apply for a specific position that is not being advertised. The position can be one that already exists or one that you would create if you could to match your unique blend of talents.

Address your letter to the person with the power to create a job for you: the president of a small company, or the area vice president or branch manager of a large company.

Create a job description; give your instructor a copy of it with your letter.

13.14 Critiquing a Job Letter

After you have written your job letter for Exercise 13.12 or 13.13, bring it to class and share it with a classmate.

- Read your cover letter aloud to your classmate noting any changes you would like to make and any areas that may not sound appropriate.

- Have your classmate reread your job letter and make suggestions to enhance it.

- Swap letters and go through the exercise again.

Write an e-mail to your instructor discussing the changes you will make to your job letter on the basis of this exercise.

13.15 Writing a Rhetorical Analysis of Your Job Letter

a. Examine the job letter you wrote for Exercise 13.12 or 13.13 and answer the following questions in an e-mail to your instructor:

- Who is your audience? Identify them beyond their name. What will they be looking for?
- How did you consider this audience when selecting information and the level of detail to use? What information did you exclude? How did you shape the information about you to address your audience's needs?
- How did you organize your information for this audience?

- How did you adapt your tone and style for this audience? How did you balance your need to promote yourself without bragging? Where did you use you-attitude, positive tone, and goodwill?
- How did you show knowledge of the company and the position without telling your audience what they already know?

b. Review a class member's cover letter using the same questions.

13.16 Applying Electronically

Write an e-mail application letter with a résumé in the text of the message.

13.17 Creating a Virtual Cover Letter

Using a cover letter you have written, review your online presence. What key words do you see in your social networking profiles? What job experience, education, and skills are highlighted? How can you make your online profiles more attractive to potential employers? Write an e-mail to your instructor detailing what you found and what changes you are going to make to your online presence.

13.18 Editing a Cover Letter

In Chapter 12, Exercise 12.13, you critiqued the résumé of Jennifer Stanton. Below is her cover letter. Using the information about Jennifer from Exercise 12.13, redo her letter to improve it. Then write an e-mail to your instructor discussing the strengths and weaknesses of the letter and explaining why you made the changes you did.

From: wildechilde@gmail.com

To: pattersj@micquant.com

Date: 13 February, 2014

Re: Job!

Dear Ms. Patterson:

My name is Jennifer Stanton and I really want to work with you at Quantum National! Your job looks a whole lot like the one I had at my internship this past summer, so I'm pretty sure I'd be great at it.

I can't start until this Summer, because I'm finishing up my degree at Iowa State. I'm currently working on a degree in Buisness Management, so I'd be a great manager at your business. The one thing I've learned for sure in college is how to balance deadlines to get everything done on time. I've had a few classes where we had to work in teams, and I've been the team leader every time: once I step in, people just want to follow where I lead.

I think my work experience is exactly what you're looking for, too. At my internship last summer, I was basically unsupervised, so I had to learn fast! I managed cliet and department needs, I did the budgets—twice!—and I worked with a sales and marketing team to put together client information packages. I also did the scheduling for the team the whole time, which was my supervisor's job but she delegated it to me, because I am trustworthy. I also worked for years at my family's bookstore, which shows I can hold down a job.

Like I said, I'm really interested in this job. I think that this would be a great place to start my career, and I know I can do the job! Give me a call on my cell when you decide who you're interviewing!

Thanks,

Jennifer Stanton

13.19   Reviewing Cover Letters

All-Weather, Inc., invited applications for the position of sales representative (Residential Sales). To be based in Nebraska, this person will be mainly responsible for sales of All-Weather's vinyl windows in local markets, including single- and double-hung windows and casement windows. The job description for the position reads as follows:

> The Sales Representative (Residential Sales) will be responsible for successful market penetration of identified market segments. Specifically, the duties include achieving targeted sales, conducting product demonstrations, contacting customers and other stakeholders, gathering market intelligence, preparing market and sales reports, communicating with internal customers, coordinating between customers and the Service and Installation Group, participating in meetings of trade associations and government agencies, attending company training events, and performing other duties assigned by managers. The ideal candidate will be someone with a BS degree, preferably with a technical major. Additionally, the candidate must have at least one year of sales experience, preferably in industrial products. Candidates with experience in brand marketing will also be considered. Among skills for the job, the candidate must possess computer skills, PR and communication skills, teamwork skills, and the ability to perform basic mathematical computations.

Below are two cover letters received from applicants. In an e-mail to your instructor, discuss the strengths and weaknesses of both. Judging just from their cover letter, which applicant would you prefer to hire? Why?

Antonio Ramirez aramirez@bestmail.com 164 Beet St. Houston, TX

October 12, 2014
Ms. Erin Lenhardt
1210 Polaroid Av.
St. Paul, MN

Dear Ms. Lenhardt:

Please consider this letter as my application for the post of Sales Representative (Residential Sales). I learned about your job from the journal *Plastics US* (September issue). I have a bachelor's degree in chemistry from the University of Austin, Texas, and have two years of experience selling PVC resin.

The last two years I have been a Sales Executive in Goodman Petrochemicals in Houston, TX. My responsibilities include selling Goodman's PVC resin to Houston-based PVC processors of rigid and flexible applicatons.

As you suggest in your advertisement, my degree in chemistry will help me explain to customers the important technical attributes of your vinyl windows. My focus during my bachelor's degree was inorganic chemistry, especially hydrocarbons and its practical applications. Apart from my coursework, I also interned at Bright Fenestration Products in Austin, TX.

I look forward to discussing my experience and interst in your organization with you in a face-to-face interview. I'm available for the interview anytime in the next two weeks at a day's notice. I'm confident I will meet—and exceed—all your expetations for this important front line position.

Sincerely,

Antonio Ramirez

Michelle Chang
4334, Sunset Boulevard, Lincoln, NE
mchang@myemail.com

October 14, 2014
Ms. Erin Lenhardt
HR Manager
1210 Polaroid Av.
St. Paul, MN

Dear Ms. Lenhardt:

I wish to apply for the position of Sales Representative (Residential Sales) advertised through Monster.com. After acquiring a bachelor's degree in design, I joined Albatross Advertising in November, 2010, as a trainee in the Accounts Department. Currently, I'm an Account Representative handling three of our most promising brands: *LiteWait* vacuum cleaners, Nebraska Furniture Mart, and Chimney Rock Art Gallery.

My bachelor's degree in design with a major in community and regional planning not only familiarized me with demands of buildings and landscapes in our 21st century living but also acquainted me with concepts of media and design. I joined Albatross because I wanted to see if my education has equipped me to inform, persuade, and help customers with regard to products and brands.

During my nearly two-year tenure at Albatross as Account Representative, I have created and given insightful presentations to clients. As a result of my performance, the agency has entrusted me with three of its most promising accounts, the ones that I mention above.

I would be delighted at an opportunity for a personal interview to further make my case for the job. You can contact me at my e-mail address mentioned above.

Sincerely,

Michelle Chang

13.20 Reviewing a Cover Letter

In the cover letter in Figure 13.4, Jeff Moeller is responding to the following job advertisement from Telltale Games. Using the ad, evaluate Jeff's letter to see how well he shows he is qualified for the job.

Game Designer

Telltale is searching for game designers to work on our growing library of unique episodic games. The game designer will be responsible for generation of detailed concepts covering all aspects of gameplay and story, as well as for prototyping, implementation and polish. Creative writing skills are a plus.

- Responsibilities
  - Work with lead designer to conceive fresh, innovative storytelling games, consistent with company game philosophy and vision
  - Design and implement gameplay-related functionality including controls, dialogs, puzzles, and mini-games using Lua
  - Implement front end and menu systems, NPC interactions and various other scripted events
  - Implement character behaviors in various game scenarios according to story specifications and gameplay needs
  - Test and refine gameplay features throughout the development cycle of the project
- Essential Skills and Experience
  - Demonstrated ability to work with artists and other designers
  - Good communication and interpersonal skills
  - Proven experience and proficiency with high-level scripting languages (examples: JavaScript, Lua, Python, Perl)
  - Demonstrated ability to write clear, maintainable code
- Preferred Skills and Experience
  - Game industry experience in a design or programming position
  - Experience with Lua
  - Experience with Visual Studio and Source Safe
  - Creative writing skills
  - B.S. in Computer Science, Literature or Creative Writing

Principals only. Sorry, no unsolicited agencies, please!

Notes

1. "Importance of the Cover Letter," *Robert Half International*, 2013, http://www.roberthalf.com/coverletter.
2. Jason Fried, "Never Read Another Résumé," *Inc.*, June 2010, 37.
3. Katharine Hansen and Randall Hansen, "The Basics of a Dynamic Cover Letter," in *Cover Letter Resources for Job-Seekers*, accessed June 21, 2013, http://www.quintcareers.com/cover_letter_basics.html.

14 Interviewing, Writing Follow-Up Messages, and Succeeding in the Job

Chapter Outline

Interview Channels
- Campus Interviews
- Phone Interviews
- Video Interviews

Interview Strategy

Interview Preparation
- Final Research
- Elevator Speech
- Travel Planning
- Attire
- Professional Materials
- Interview Practice

Interview Customs
- Behavior
- Meal Etiquette
- Note-Taking
- Interview Segments

Traditional Interview Questions and Answers

Kinds of Interviews
- Behavioral Interviews
- Situational Interviews
- Stress Interviews
- Group Interviews
- Multiple Interviews

Final Steps for a Successful Job Search
- Following Up with Phone Calls and Written Messages
- Negotiating for Salary and Benefits
- Deciding Which Offer to Accept
- Dealing with Rejection

Starting Your Career
- Your First Full-Time Job
- A Long-Term Strategy

Summary by Learning Objectives

NEWSWORTHY COMMUNICATION

The Twitter Interview

Many companies are working to improve how they handle their social networking presence. Sites such as Facebook, Twitter, and even Instagram have become vital parts of many companies' marketing and public relations strategies. It's no longer enough to assign someone to pay attention to social media; now companies are hiring specialized social media experts to design organized marketing campaigns.

But where do companies find a social media expert? How do they determine who will succeed in this relatively new field?

When Pizza Hut was looking for an expert, the company decided to do something different: hold interviews that tested the candidates' abilities to communicate in short formats. Rather than conducting traditional job interviews, each candidate was given 140 seconds (inspired by Twitter's 140-character message limit) to say why they would be best for the position.

According to Caroline Masullo, Pizza Hut's director of digital and social marketing, "We're specifically looking for people who are quick on their feet, know who they are, [and are] passionate about pizza and [about] Pizza Hut specifically." She says that the super-short interview allows Pizza Hut to find someone who can communicate in "the way [consumers] communicate with brands."

The Twitter-style interview is not appropriate for every job, of course. But more and more, job interviews are designed to test candidates' abilities to succeed in actually doing the job, not just talking about it.

Source: Laurel Nakkas, "Pizza Hut Takes on Interviewing, Twitter-Style," *QSR Magazine*, March 8, 2013, http://www.qsrmagazine.com/news/pizza-hut-takes-interviewing-twitter-style.

After studying this chapter, you will know

LO 14-1 What interview channels you may encounter.

LO 14-2 How to create a strategy for successful interviewing.

LO 14-3 What preparations to make before you start interviewing.

LO 14-4 What to do during an interview.

LO 14-5 How to answer common interview questions.

LO 14-6 How to prepare for less common interview types.

LO 14-7 What to do after an interview.

LO 14-8 How to plan for a successful career.

Job interviews are an important part of the hiring process. A survey of 600 managers found that they overwhelmingly preferred evaluating job candidates in person, either by interviews or temporary work performance.[1] Because they are so important, job interviews are scary, even when you've prepared thoroughly. Surveys show that, according to hiring managers, job candidates are more likely to make mistakes during their interviews than at any other point of their job search.[2] But when you are prepared, you can reduce the number of missteps so that you put your best foot forward and get the job you want. The best way to prepare is to know as much as possible about the process and the employer. The following steps will help you prepare well for the interview process:

- Learn the kinds of interview channels you may encounter.

- Create a strategy for interviewing.

- Prepare for your interview.

- Be aware of the customs and expectations of interviews.

- Be prepared to answer common interview questions.

- Prepare to accept an offer and succeed in your career.

Interview Channels LO 14-1

Although you may picture a job interview in a traditional office setting, modern interviews use other channels as well. Knowing about different interview channels can help you prepare for a successful interview. As a college student, you may well find yourself being interviewed on campus. You may also find you have a phone interview or videoconference, as more and more companies use technology to keep hiring costs in check. Most of the interview advice in this chapter applies to all settings, but some channels do have unique particulars you should consider.

Campus Interviews

Most campus career offices have written protocols and expectations for campus interviews arranged through them. Be sure to follow these expectations so that you look informed.

Remember that campus job fairs are the first places to make an impression on recruiters and interviewers (see Chapter 12 for more information). As you approach the booths at a job fair, show interest, be engaged, and be prepared with a résumé, business card, or other professional materials. If you make a good impression at a job fair, you already have an advantage when you enter the formal campus interview later.

Because campus interviewers will see so many students who are all following the same protocols, it is important that you have good details and professional stories about your work to help you stand out from the crowd. Focus on three to four selling points you most want the interviewer to remember about you. If you have a choice, do not schedule your interview late in the day when interviewers are getting tired.

Phone Interviews

Your job search will involve a lot of time on the phone. You should place special emphasis on developing your phone skills for before the interview, during the interview, and when you are following up. Be polite to everyone with whom you speak, including administrative assistants and secretaries. Find out the person's name on your first call and use it on subsequent calls. Be considerate, both on the phone and when leaving voice mail messages. Keep your messages concise, and make sure to give both your name and your phone number slowly and distinctly.

Some organizations use phone interviews to narrow the list of candidates they bring in for office visits. Phone interviews give you some advantages. Obviously, you do not have to dress up for them, or find an office. You can use all the materials you want as you speak. You can also take all the notes you want, although copious note-taking will probably impact your speaking quality, and you certainly don't want the sound of keyboard clicking to be heard by your interviewer.

On the other hand, phone interviews obviously deny you the important component of visual feedback. To compensate for this loss, you can ask your interviewer for verbal feedback (e.g., Is this sufficient detail? Would you like more on this topic?).

Here are some additional tips for a good phone interview:

- **Speak distinctly.** Although you always want to speak distinctly at an interview, doing so is even more crucial for a phone interview.

- **Treat the interview like an in-person interview.** Although you don't need to dress up, doing so may help you focus and be appropriately formal. Speech experts recommend that you smile, lean forward, and gesture, even though no one can see you. Such activities add warmth and personality to your words.

- **Find a quiet, private location.** Don't interview in a room where people are coming and going. Be sure to eliminate all background noise such as music or TV.

- **Make sure your phone works.** If you are using your cell phone, make sure it is fully charged before the interview *and* that you can get good reception in the room where you will be speaking. If possible, use a landline instead to get a better, clearer, and more consistent connection.

- **Focus on your selling points.** Just as you did for a campus interview, focus on three to four selling points you most want the interviewer to remember about you.

Video Interviews

Video interviews are becoming more common. You may experience two different kinds. In one, the organization sends you a list of questions and you prepare a video to send back to them. In the other, the organization conducts live interviews using videoconferencing equipment or programs such as Skype.

If you are preparing a video,

- **Practice your answers so you are fluent.** You don't want to stumble over your responses, but you also don't want to sound like you have memorized the answers.

- **Be thorough.** Since the employer can't ask follow-up questions, you want to consider what those questions could be and then be sure to answer them.

- **Pay attention to your surroundings.** Make sure you choose a location for your video with a background that is not visually distracting. If you choose a background with objects, make it someplace interesting and, if possible, related to your field (for example, a laboratory or a set of bookshelves). But take care that the background is not cluttered or distracting and that it does not include objects or pictures that could hurt the professional image you are trying to establish.

If you are participating in a videoconference,

- **Do a practice video ahead of time.** Listen to your pronunciation and voice qualities. Watch your video with the sound turned off: check your posture, gestures, facial expressions, and clothing. Do you have nervous mannerisms you need to control?

- **During the actual interview, keep your answers under two minutes.** Then ask if interviewers want more information. People are generally more reluctant to interrupt a speaker in another location, and body language cues are limited, so ask for feedback ("Would you like to hear about that?").

- **Treat the interview as if you are in the same room.** Remember that even though you are not in the same room with the interviewers, they are still judging your appearance and mannerisms as if you were sitting in front of them. Use the tips for an in-person interview to help your videoconference interview go well.

- **Be prepared for a technology failure.** While the technologies that support videoconferencing are improving quickly, they still may have glitches. Be prepared for a technology failure by providing your telephone number in a polite e-mail before the interview and having your phone handy and charged just in case.

Interview Strategy **LO 14-2**

One of the most important steps in preparing for your interview is to have a successful interview strategy. Develop an overall strategy based on your answers to these three questions:

1. **What about yourself do you want the interviewer to know?** Pick two to five points that represent your strengths for that particular job and that show how you will add value to the organization. These facts are frequently character traits (such as enthusiasm), achievements, and experiences that qualify you for the job and separate you from other applicants, or unique abilities such as fluency in Spanish. For each strength, think of a specific accomplishment to support it. For instance, be ready to give an

example to prove that you're hardworking. Be ready to show how you helped an organization save money or serve customers better with specific numbers and details: "I saved my department $250,000 over three years with my redesigned training program."

Then at the interview, listen to every question to see if you could make one of your key points as part of your answer. If the questions don't allow you to make your points, bring them up at the end of the interview.

2. **What disadvantages or weaknesses do you need to minimize?** Expect that you may be asked to explain weaknesses or apparent weaknesses in your record such as lack of experience, so–so grades, and gaps in your record.

    Plan how to deal with these issues if they arise. Decide if you want to bring them up yourself, particularly disadvantages or weaknesses that are easily discoverable. If you bring them up, you can plan the best context for them during the interview. Many students, for example, have been able to get good jobs after flunking out of school by explaining that the experience was a turning point in their lives and pointing out that when they returned to school they maintained a B or better grade point average. Although it is illegal to ask questions about marital status, married candidates with spouses who are able to move easily sometimes volunteer that information: "My husband is a dentist and is willing to relocate if the company wants to transfer me." See the suggestions later in this chapter under "Traditional Interview Questions and Answers," "Behavioral Interviews," and "Situational Interviews."

3. **What do you need to know about the job and the organization to decide whether you want to accept this job if it is offered to you?** Plan *in advance* the criteria on which you will base your decision (you can always change the criteria). Use "Deciding Which Offer to Accept" below to plan questions to elicit the information you'll need to rank each offer.

Interview Preparation   LO 14-3

With your strategy in place, you can prepare for a specific interview. Preparing for your interviews is vital in these days of intense competition for jobs. It can also help you to feel more confident and make a better impression.

Final Research

Research the company interviewing you. Read its web pages, Facebook page, Twitter page, company newsletters, and annual reports. Many companies now have YouTube videos and employee blogs to give you insight into the company and its culture. Some of them even offer interview tips. Read about the company in trade journals and newspapers. Search the Internet. Ask your professors, classmates, friends, family, and co-workers about the firm. If possible, find out who will interview you and research them, too.

Also research salaries for the job: What is average? What is the range? Use web tools like those found at indeed.com/salary or salary.com to find salary information by job title and location.

Elevator Speech

After you have finished your research, prepare your elevator speech, a short—60–90 seconds—powerful statement of why you are a good candidate for this particular job. (The name comes from the scenario of being alone with the recruiter for a multifloor elevator ride. What can you say in that short period to convince the recruiter to consider you?) Even though it is short, your elevator speech will need some carefully selected details to be convincing. It will come in handy for questions like "Tell me about yourself" or "Why should I hire you?" It is useful in a variety of situations, including group interviews and receptions where you meet a variety of the company's employees in brief, one-on-one conversations.

Travel Planning

Before your interview, make sure you can find the building and the closest parking. Plan how much time you will need to get there. Leave time cushions for stressors such as traffic jams or broken elevators. If you are fortunate enough to be flown to an interview, don't schedule too tightly. Allow for flight delays and cancellations. Plan how you will get from the airport to the interview site. Take enough cash and credit cards to cover emergencies.

Attire

First impressions are important; employers start judging you from the first second they see you. A major part of that first impression is your appearance.

The outfit you wear to an interview should meet your interviewer's expectations. The most conservative choice is the traditional dark business suit with a light blouse or shirt plus tie, shoes with matching dark socks for men and close-toed pumps with nude, unpatterned hose for women. Although this outfit is probably still the most common choice, you cannot count on it being the right choice. Many companies now expect more casual attire: sport jackets for men, coordinated jackets for women. Skirts should come at least to the knee; tight or low-cut tops should be avoided. Sneakers and sandals are inappropriate.

For campus interviews, you should still be professional in your attire. Although recruiters and interviewers on campus know they are interviewing students, you shouldn't dress like a student. Treat the interview like an off-campus interview and dress up (within the guidelines and dress code of your campus career center). If possible, leave your backpack, laptop, and other items you would take to class at home or in a safe location. Take only those things that you need, like a pen or pencil, some paper, your résumé, and any work samples or other materials you may need during the interview.

For office interviews, you should show that you understand the organization's culture. Try to find out from your career contacts what is considered appropriate attire. While some interviewers do not mind if you ask them what you should wear to the interview, others do, so be careful. Use your other contacts first before you ask the interviewer. Find out what other employees wear each day, and dress a little nicer.[3]

No matter what outfit you choose, make sure it fits well (especially important if it has been a few months since you wore it), is comfortable, and does not show too much cleavage or chest. Avoid casual items such as skintight pants, shorts, or sandals.

Choose comfortable shoes. You may do a fair amount of walking during an onsite interview. Check your heels to make sure they aren't run down; make sure your shoes are shined.

Make conservative choices. Have your hair cut or styled conservatively. Jewelry and makeup should be understated; face jewelry, such as eyebrow and nose studs, should be removed. If possible, cover tattoos. Personal hygiene must be impeccable, with close attention paid to fingernails and breath. Make sure your clothes are clean and pressed. Avoid cologne and perfumed aftershave lotions.

You can wear a wide range of apparel to interviews. Find out what is appropriate—and inappropriate—for each interview. Which of these outfits would you wear?

Professional Materials

Take extra copies of your résumé. If your campus placement office has already given the interviewer a data sheet, present the résumé at the beginning of the interview: "I thought you might like a little more information about me."

Take something to write on and something to write with. It's OK to carry a small notepad with the questions you want to ask on it.

Take copies of your work or a portfolio: an engineering design, a copy of a letter you wrote on a job or in a business writing class, an article you wrote for the campus paper. You don't need to present these unless the interview calls for them, but they can be very effective: "Yes, I have done a media plan. Here's a copy of a plan I put together in my advertising seminar last year. We had a fixed budget and used real figures for cost and rating points, just as I'd do if I joined Toth and Rawlins."

Take the names, street addresses, e-mail addresses, and phone numbers of references. Take complete details about your work history and education, including dates and street addresses, in case you're asked to fill out an application form.

If you can afford it, buy a briefcase in which to carry these items. At this point in your life, an inexpensive vinyl briefcase is acceptable. Women should let the briefcase replace a purse.

Interview Practice

Rehearse everything you can: Put on the clothes you'll wear and practice entering a room, shaking hands, sitting down, and answering questions. Ask a friend to interview you. Saying answers out loud is surprisingly harder than saying them in your head. If your department or career center offers practice interviews, take advantage of them.

Some campuses have videotaping facilities so that you can watch your own sample interview. Videotaping is particularly valuable if you can do it at least twice, so you can modify behavior the second time and check the tape to see whether the modification works.

Your interviewing skills will improve with practice. If possible, schedule a few interviews with other companies before your interview with your first choice company. However, even if you're just interviewing for practice, you must still do all the research on that company. If interviewers sense that you aren't interested, they won't take you seriously and you won't learn much from the process. Also, interviewers talk to each other, sharing impressions and stories, sometimes with names attached.

Interview Customs   LO 14-4

Strategy, preparation, and practice help you get ready for your interviews. But you also need to be aware of what will be expected of you during the interview. Not all interviews are question-and-answer sessions. More employers are starting to use other screening devices; they are asking candidates to provide on-the-spot writing samples, or to take critical thinking, intelligence, writing, skills, personality, emotional intelligence, and drug tests. Some also use complicated computer algorithms to screen their applicants.[4]

Behavior

How you act at the interview is as important as what you say, and first impressions of behavior are as important as they are for appearance.

Employers start judging you from the first second they see you. If you meet multiple people, first impressions will begin anew with each encounter. Always act professionally. Have a firm, pleasant handshake; avoid the limp, dead-fish handshake or the overly aggressive knuckle-crusher. Be polite to everyone, including people such as security agents, receptionists, and people in the restroom. Learn names and introduce yourself whenever possible. Their input about you may be sought.

Politeness extends to the interview itself.

- Be punctual, but not too early (no more than 10 minutes early). Many recruiters don't like someone hanging around their reception area.

- Practice active listening (see Chapter 4); it makes speakers feel appreciated and you will likely pick up clues you can use effectively during your interview.

- Do not monopolize the interview time with lengthy monologues. Generally your interviewer will have many questions to cover and will not appreciate an undue amount of time wasted on just one. Check the interviewer's verbal cues and body language for the amount of detail and depth desired. After two to three minutes, ask if the interviewer wants more detail. The best interviews are conversations in which you and your interviewer enjoy your interactions.

- Never say anything bad about current and former employers, a category that includes schools. Candidates who snipe about their employers and instructors will likely continue to do so on their new job and thus appear to be unattractive colleagues.

Be enthusiastic about the job. **Enthusiasm** helps convince people you have the energy to do the job well. Show how you are a good choice for their job by clearly presenting your carefully chosen accomplishments and strengths. If you are attending an onsite interview, where you could well be asked the same questions by different people, prepare to repeat yourself—with enthusiasm.

Should you be yourself? There's no point in assuming a radically different persona. If you do, you run the risk of getting into a job that you'll hate (though the persona you assumed might have loved it). Furthermore, as interviewers point out, you have to be a pretty good actor to come across convincingly if you try to be someone other than yourself. Yet keep in mind that all of us have several selves: we can be lazy, insensitive, bored, slow-witted, and tongue-tied, but we can also be energetic, perceptive, interested, intelligent, and articulate. Be your best self at the interview.

Interviews can make you feel vulnerable and defensive; to counter this, review your accomplishments—the things you're especially proud of having done. You'll make a better impression if you have a firm sense of your own self-worth.

Every interviewer repeats the advice that you've probably heard: sit up straight, don't mumble, look at people when you talk. It's good advice for interviews. Be aware that many people respond negatively to smoking. Remember to turn off your cell phone.

As much as possible, avoid **nervous mannerisms:** playing with your hair, jingling coins in your pocket, clicking your pen, or repeating verbal spacers such as "like" and "uh." These mannerisms distract your audience and detract from your interview. It's OK to be a little nervous, however; it shows that you care.

Sometimes you will be asked to visit the company for a day or more of interviews. Because they may last longer, sometimes site interviews will present you with **minor problems** such as being brought back late from lunch, or being kept overtime with one interviewer so you are late for your appointment with another. Don't let these minor problems throw you. Think of them as a new opportunity to show that you can roll with the punches; move forward calmly.

If you have any **expenses,** be sure you keep all receipts for reimbursement. Many people forget to get taxi or shuttle receipts and thus are not reimbursed for those expenses.

The interview is also a time for you to see if you want to work for this organization. Look for signs of organizational culture (see Chapter 4). How do people treat each other? Are offices or cubbies personalized? How many hours a week do the newest employees work? Is this the place where you want to become another new employee?

Meal Etiquette

Site visits that involve meals and semi-social occasions call for sensible choices. Remember that as long as you are with any person from the company, you are in an interview. They are evaluating how you behave in different situations.

Body Language Mistakes

CareerBuilder surveyed over 2,500 hiring managers and found that body language mistakes can lessen the chances of being hired. Managers reported that poor eye contact (67%), no smile (38%), and fidgeting too much (33%) would lessen hiring chances.

Other negative mannerisms listed by hiring managers were

- Poor posture.
- Weak handshake.
- Crossed arms over the chest.
- Repeated hair or face touching.
- Too many hand gestures.

Videotaping a practice interview is a good way to check body language.

Adapted from CareerBuilder, "New CareerBuilder Survey Reveals Top Body Language Mistakes Candidates Make in Job Interviews," press release, July 28, 2010, http://www.careerbuilder.com/share/aboutus/pressreleases detail.aspx?id=pr581&sd=7/29/2010&ed=7/29/2099.

Meals may be an important part of the interview process. Be sure your manners measure up.

The meals during a site visit are more relaxed, but do not make the mistake of relaxing too much. Here are some tips:

- When you order, choose something that's easy to eat without being messy.

- Watch your table manners. Sit up straight, keep your arms off the table, and use your napkin. Silverware is used from the outside in. So you grab the correct glass or bread plate, remember BMW for table settings: bread on the left, meal in the center, water on the right.

- Take small bites that allow you to maintain the conversation—you are still answering interview questions.

- Eat a light lunch, so that you'll be alert during the afternoon.

- Do not drink alcohol at lunch. At dinner or an evening party, accept only one drink, if any. A survey by the Society for Human Resource Management found that 96% of human resources professionals believe job candidates should not drink at interview meals.[5] Your best bet is to decline alcohol during your site visit, even if everyone else is drinking. You're still being evaluated, and you can't afford to have your guard down.

Note-Taking

During or immediately after the interview, write down

- The name of the interviewer (or all the people you talked to, if it's a group interview or an onsite visit).

- Tips the interviewer gave you about landing the job and succeeding in it.

- What the interviewer seemed to like best about you.

- Any negative points or weaknesses that came up that you need to counter in your follow-up messages or phone calls.

- Answers to your questions about the company.

- When you'll hear from the company.

The easiest way to get the interviewer's name is to ask for his or her card. You may be able to make all the notes you need on the back of the card.

Some interviewers say they respond negatively to applicants who take notes during the interview. However, if you have several interviews back-to-back or if you know your memory is terrible, do take brief notes during the interview. That's better than forgetting which company said you'd be on the road every other week and which interviewer asked that *you* get in touch with him or her. Try to maintain eye contact as much as possible while taking notes.

Interview Segments

Every interview has an opening, a body, and a close.

In the **opening** (two to five minutes), most good interviewers will try to set you at ease. Some interviewers will open with easy questions about your major or interests. Others open by telling you about the job or the company. If this happens, listen so you can answer questions later to show that you can do the job or contribute to the company that's being described.

The **body** of the interview (10 to 25 minutes) is an all-too-brief time for you to highlight your qualifications and find out what you need to know to decide if you want to accept a site trip. Expect questions that give you an opportunity to showcase your strong points and questions that probe any weaknesses evident from your résumé. (You were neither in school nor working last fall. What were you doing?) Normally the interviewer will also try to sell you on the company and give you an opportunity to raise questions.

You need to be aware of time so that you can make sure to get in your key points and questions: "We haven't covered it yet, but I want you to know that I . . ." "I'm aware that it's almost 10:30. I do have some more questions that I'd like to ask about the company."

In the **close** of the interview (two to five minutes), the interviewer will usually tell you what happens next: "We'll be bringing our top candidates to the office in February. You should hear from us in three weeks." Make sure you know who to contact if the next step is not clearly spelled out or you don't hear by the stated time.

The close of the interview is also the time for you to summarize your key accomplishments and strengths and to express enthusiasm for the job. Depending on the circumstances, you could say: "I've certainly enjoyed learning more about Zappos." "I hope I get a chance to visit your Las Vegas office. I'd really like to see the new computer system you talked about."

Traditional Interview Questions and Answers LO 14-5

One of the best ways to prepare for an interview is to practice answering specific common interview questions. As Figure 14.1 shows, successful applicants use different communication behaviors when answering questions than do unsuccessful applicants. Successful applicants are more likely to use the company name, show they have researched the company, support their claims with specific details, use appropriate technical language, and ask specific questions about the company and industry. In addition to practicing the content of questions, try to incorporate these tactics.

The ultimate questions in your interviewers' minds are probably these three: What can you do for us? Why should we hire you instead of another candidate? Will you fit in our company/division/office? However, many interviewers do not ask these questions directly. Instead, they ask other questions to get their answers more indirectly. Some of the more common questions

Figure 14.1	The Communication Behaviors of Successful Interviewees	
Behavior	**Unsuccessful Interviewees**	**Successful Interviewees**
Statements about the position	Have only vague ideas of what they want to do.	Specific and consistent about the position they want; are able to tell why they want the position.
Use of company name	Rarely use the company name.	Refer to the company by name.
Knowledge about company and position	Make it clear that they are using the interview to learn about the company and what it offers.	Make it clear that they have researched the company; refer to specific website, publications, or people who have given them information.
Level of interest, enthusiasm	Respond neutrally to interviewer's statements: "OK," "I see." Indicate reservations about company or location.	Express approval nonverbally and verbally of information provided by the interviewer; "That's great!" Explicitly indicate desire to work for this particular company.
Nonverbal behavior	Make little eye contact; smile infrequently.	Make eye contact often; smile.
Picking up on interviewer's cues	Give vague or negative answers even when a positive answer is clearly desired ("How are your writing skills?").	Answer positively and confidently; and back up the claim with a specific example.
Use of industry terms and technical jargon	Use almost no technical jargon.	Use appropriate technical jargon.
Use of specifics in answers	Give short answers—10 words or less, sometimes only one word; do not elaborate. Give general responses: "fairly well."	Support claims with specific personal experiences.
Questions asked by interviewee	Ask a small number of general questions.	Ask specific questions based on knowledge of the industry and the company. Personalize questions: "What would my duties be?"

are discussed below. Do some preparation before the interview so that you'll have answers that are responsive, honest, and positive. Choose answers that fit your qualifications and the organization's needs.

Initial interviews often seek to screen out less qualified candidates rather than to find someone to hire. Negative information will hurt you less if it comes out in the middle of the interview and is preceded and followed by positive information. If you blow a question near the end of the interview, don't leave until you've said something positive—perhaps restating one of the points you want the interviewer to know about you.

Check your answers for hidden negatives. If you say you are the kind of person who is always looking for challenges, your interviewer may wonder about hiring you for this entry-level position, which needs someone who does mostly routine work with care. Similarly, if you say you want lots of responsibility, your interviewer may again not see you as a good fit for entry-level positions, which are not known for providing lots of responsibility.

Rehearse your answers mentally, so you feel confident you have good answers. Then get family and friends to interview you. You may be surprised at how much work good mental answers still need when you give them out loud.

1. **Tell me about yourself.** Focus on several strengths that show you are a good candidate. Give examples with enough specifics to prove each strength. Don't launch into an autobiography, which will have too many details the interviewer will not care about. Provide professional, not personal, information. This is often one of the first questions asked in an interview; be prepared for it. Use it to set the tone of the interview and to establish your selling points.

2. **Walk me through your résumé.** Highlight your best features and offer reasons for major decisions. Why did you choose this college? Why did you take that job? Have professional reasons: You went to State U because it has a top-ranked accounting department, not because it is close to home; you took that summer job because it allowed some interaction with the company's accounting department, not because it was the only one you could find.

   Don't try to cover too much; your résumé walk-through should be no longer than three minutes. Tie your résumé into your selling points, and add some interesting details that are not on your résumé. Above all, do maintain eye contact; do not read your résumé.

3. **What makes you think you're qualified to work for this company? Or, I'm interviewing 120 people for two jobs. Why should I hire you?** This question may feel like an attack. Use it as an opportunity to state (or restate) your strong points. Remember, though, that most of the candidates who are interviewing meet the basic qualifications. Your focus should be on the qualities that separate you from other applicants.

4. **What two or three accomplishments have given you the greatest satisfaction?** Pick accomplishments that you're proud of, that create the image you want to project, and that enable you to share one of the things you want the interviewer to know about you. Focus not just on the end result, but on the problem-solving, thinking, and innovation skills that made the achievement possible.

5. **Why do you want to work for us? What is your ideal job?** Even if you're interviewing just for practice, make sure you have a good answer—preferably two or three reasons you'd like to work for that company. If you don't seem to be taking the interview seriously, the interviewer won't take you seriously, and you won't even get good practice.

   If your ideal job is very different from the ones the company has available, the interviewer may simply say there isn't a good match and end the interview. If you're interested in this company, do some research so that what you ask for is in the general ballpark of the kind of work the company offers.

6. **What college subjects did you like best and least? Why?** This question may be an icebreaker; it may be designed to discover the kind of applicant they're looking for. If your favorite class was something outside your major, prepare an answer that shows that you have qualities that can help you in the job you're applying for: "My favorite class was a seminar in the American novel. We got a chance to think on our own, rather than just regurgitate facts; we made presentations to the class every week. I found I really like sharing my ideas with other people and presenting reasons for my conclusions about something."

7. **What is your class rank? Your grade point? Why are your grades so low?** If your grades aren't great, be ready with a nondefensive explanation. If possible, show that the cause of low grades now has been solved or isn't relevant to the job you're applying for: "My father almost died last year, and my schoolwork really suffered." "When I started, I didn't have any

Tell Me a Story

One effective way to stand out from the hordes of people being interviewed is to tell a memorable story about yourself.

- Choose a story that shows your personality as well as professional abilities.
- Use a story highly relevant for the particular job.
- Use colorful details, including sensory ones.
- Keep it short—two minutes at the very most.
- Your story is to be an honest anecdote about your professional self, not a fiction.

firm goals. Once I discovered the field that was right for me, my grades have all been B's or better." "I'm not good at multiple-choice tests. But I am good at working with people."

8. **What have you read recently? What movies have you seen recently?** These questions may be icebreakers; they may be designed to probe your intellectual depth. The term you're interviewing, read at least one book or magazine (multiple issues) and see at least one serious movie that you could discuss at an interview. Make thoughtful selections.

9. **Show me some samples of your writing.** Many jobs require the ability to write well. Employers no longer take mastery of basic English for granted, even if the applicant has a degree from a prestigious university.

    The year you're interviewing, go through your old papers and select a few of the best ones, editing them if necessary, so that you'll have samples to present at the interview if you're asked for them.

10. **Describe a major problem you have encountered in your work and how you dealt with it.** Choose a problem that was not your fault: a customer's last-minute change to a large order, a flu outbreak during Christmas rush. In your solution, stress skills you know the company will be seeking.

11. **What are your interests outside work? What campus or community activities have you been involved in?** While it's desirable to be well-rounded, naming 10 interests is a mistake: the interviewer may wonder when you'll have time to work. Select activities that show skills and knowledge you can use on the job: "I have polished my persuasion skills by being a cabin counselor at a camp for troubled preteens."

    If you mention your fiancé, spouse, or children in response to this question ("Well, my fiancé and I like to go sailing"), it is perfectly legal for the interviewer to ask follow-up questions ("What would you do if your spouse got a job offer in another town?"), even though the same question would be illegal if the interviewer brought up the subject first.

12. **What have you done to learn about this company?** An employer may ask this to see what you already know about the company (if you've read the recruiting literature and the website, the interviewer doesn't need to repeat them). This question may also be used to see how active a role you're taking in the job search process and how interested you are in this job.

13. **What adjectives would you use to describe yourself?** Use only positive ones. Be ready to illustrate each with a specific example of something you've done.

14. **What are your greatest strengths?** Employers ask this question to give you a chance to sell yourself and to learn something about your values. Pick strengths related to work, school, or activities: "I'm good at working with people." "I really can sell things." "I'm good at solving problems." "I learn quickly." "I'm reliable. When I say I'll do something, I do it." Be ready to illustrate each with a specific example of something you've done. It is important to relate your strengths to the specific position.

15. **What is your greatest weakness?** Use a work-related negative, even if something in your personal life really is your greatest weakness. Interviewers won't let you get away with a "weakness" like being a workaholic or just not having any experience yet. Instead, use one of these strategies:

    a. Discuss a weakness that is not related to the job you're being considered for and will not be needed even when you're promoted. (Even if you won't work with people or give speeches in your first job, you'll need those skills later in your career, so don't use them for this question.) End your answer with a positive that *is* related to the job.

> [For a creative job in advertising:] I don't like accounting. I know it's important, but I don't like it. I even hire someone to do my taxes. I'm much more interested in being creative and working with people, which is why I find this position interesting.

> [For a job in administration:] I don't like selling products. I hated selling cookies when I was a Girl Scout. I'd much rather work with ideas—and I really like selling the ideas that I believe in.

    b.   Discuss a weakness that you are working to improve.

> In the past, I wasn't a good writer. But last term I took a course in business writing that taught me how to organize my ideas and how to revise. I may never win a Pulitzer Prize, but now I can write effective reports and letters.

    c.   Describe advice you received, and how that advice helped your career.

> The professor for whom I was an undergraduate assistant pointed out to me that people respond well to liberal praise, and that I was not liberal with mine. As I have worked on providing more positive feedback, I have become a better manager.

16. **What are your career goals? Where do you want to be in five years? Ten years?** This question is frequently a test to see if you fit with this company. Are your goals ones that can be met at this company? Or will the company have the expense of training you only to see you move on promptly to another company?

17. **Why are you looking for another job?** Do not answer this with a negative—"My boss didn't like me," "I didn't like the work"—even if the negative is true. Stress the new opportunities you're looking for in a new job, not why you want to get away from your old one: "I want more opportunity to work with clients."

    Also be careful of hidden negatives: "I couldn't use all my abilities in my last job" sounds like you are complaining. It also suggests that you don't take the initiative to find new challenges. If you are looking for a job with a bigger salary, it is better to use other points when answering this question.

    If you were fired, say so. There are various acceptable ways to explain why you were fired:

    a. It wasn't a good match. Add what you now know you need in a job, and ask what the employer can offer in this area.

    b. You and your supervisor had a personality conflict. Make sure you show that this was an isolated incident, and that you normally get along well with people.

    c. You made mistakes, but you've learned from them and are now ready to work well. Be ready to offer a specific anecdote proving that you have indeed changed.

18. **Why do you have a gap in your employment history?** Answer briefly and positively; do not apologize for family decisions.

> I cared for an ill family member. Because of the time it took, it wasn't fair to an employer to start a new job.

> I stayed home with my children while they were young. Now that they are both in school, I can devote myself to top performance in your company.

If you were laid off, be prepared to explain why you were one of the people let go. It helps if you can truthfully say that all new employees with less than three years' experience at the firm were laid off, or that legal services were outsourced, or that the entire training department was disbanded. Be careful you do not display bitter, angry feelings; they will not help you get a new job. It may help you to realize that in tight economies, being laid off is not an issue for many interviewers.

19. **What questions do you have?** This question gives you a chance to cover things the interviewer hasn't brought up; it also gives the interviewer a sense of your priorities and values. Almost all interviewers will ask you for questions, and it is crucial that you have some. A lack of questions will probably be interpreted as a lack of interest in the company and a lack of preparation for the interview. Figure 14.2 lists some questions you might want to ask.

Do not ask these questions:

- Questions about information you can easily find (and should have found) on the company's website.
- Questions that indicate dissatisfaction with the job for which you are being interviewed (How soon can I get promoted?).
- Questions about salary and benefits (wait until you have a job offer).

Not all questions asked by interviewers are proper. Various federal, state, and local laws prohibit questions that would allow employers to discriminate

Figure 14.2	Questions to Ask about a Potential Job

- What would I be doing on a day-to-day basis?
- What's the top challenge I would face in this job?
- What kind of training program do you have?
- How do you evaluate employees? How often do you review them?
- What will a good employee have done by the time of his or her first evaluation?
- Where would you expect a new trainee (banker, staff accountant) to be three years from now? Five years? Ten years?
- What happened to the last person who had this job?
- How would you describe the company's culture?
- This sounds like a great job. What are the drawbacks?
- How are interest rates (new products from competitors, imports, demographic trends, government regulations, etc.) affecting your company? Questions like these show that you care enough to do your homework and that you are aware of current events.
- What do you like best about working for this company? Ending with a question like this closes your interview on an upbeat note.

on the basis of protected characteristics such as race, sex, age, disability, and marital status. If you are asked an improper or illegal question during an interview, you have several options:

- You can answer the question, but you may not get hired if you give the "wrong" answer.

- You can refuse to answer the question. Doing so is within your rights, but it may make you look uncooperative or confrontational, so again you may not get hired.

- You can look for the intent behind the question and provide an answer related to the job. For example, if you were asked who would care for your children when you had to work late on an urgent project, you could answer that you can meet the work schedule a good performance requires.

Keep in mind in each situation that legal and illegal questions can be very similar. It is legal to ask if you are over 18, but illegal to ask you how old you are. It is legal to ask you which languages you speak (if that talent is relevant for the job), but it is illegal to ask you what your native language is. Also be careful of variants of illegal questions. Asking when you graduated from high school gives the interviewer a pretty good idea of your age.

You won't be able to anticipate every question you may get. Check with other people at your college or university who have interviewed recently to find out what questions are currently being asked in your field. Search the Internet for the most common interview questions.

Kinds of Interviews   LO 14-6

Although traditional interviews are still the most popular form of interview, many companies are turning to alternative kinds of interviews that may help them find the best employees. Many companies will inform you about what to expect during the interview, but you should be prepared for these less common interview types. Some of the other kinds of interviews include behavioral, situational, stress, group, and multiple interviews.

Behavioral Interviews

Using the theory that past behaviors predict future performance, **behavioral interviews** ask applicants to describe actual past behaviors, rather than future plans. Thus instead of asking "How would you motivate people?" the interviewer might ask, "Tell me what happened the last time you wanted to get other people to do something." Follow-up questions might include, "What exactly did you do to handle the situation? How did you feel about the results? How did the other people feel? How did your superior feel about the results?"

Additional behavioral questions may ask you to describe a situation in which you

- Created an opportunity for yourself in a job or volunteer position.

- Used writing to achieve your goal.

- Went beyond the call of duty to get a job done.

- Communicated successfully with someone you disliked.

- Had to make a decision quickly.
- Took a project from start to finish.
- Used good judgment and logic in solving a problem.
- Worked under a tight deadline.
- Worked with a tough boss.
- Worked with someone who wasn't doing his or her share of the work.

In your answer, describe the situation, tell what you did, and explain what happened. Think about the implications of what you did and be ready to talk about whether you'd do the same thing next time or if the situation were slightly different. For example, if you did the extra work yourself when a team member didn't do his or her share, does that fact suggest that you prefer to work alone? If the organization you're interviewing with values teams, you may want to go on to show why doing the extra work was appropriate in that situation but that you can respond differently in other situations.

A good way to prepare for behavioral interviews is to make a chart. Across the top list jobs, accomplishments, and projects. Down the left side, list qualities employers will want in candidates for the jobs you seek. These qualities should include skills such as communication, teamwork, critical thinking, networking, influencing people, and leadership; traits such as honesty, reliability, and a developed ethical sense; and the ability to meet situations such as those in the list above. Then you fill in the boxes. How does that presentation you made to skeptical administrators demonstrate your communication skills? Your ethics? Your ability to perform under pressure? Make sure each item in your boxes casts you in a favorable light: the ability to work under pressure is generally valued, but if you had to pull three all-nighters to finish your marketing project, employers might see you as a procrastinator.

Situational Interviews

Situational interviews put you in situations similar to those you will face on the job. They test your problem-solving skills, as well as your ability to handle problems under time constraints and with minimal preparation. While behavioral interviews asked how you handled something in the past, situational interviews focus on the future. For instance, for jobs with strong service components you could expect to be asked how you would handle an angry client. For jobs with manufacturing companies, you might be asked to imagine a new product.

Frequently situational interviews contain actual tasks candidates are asked to perform. You may be asked to fix some computer coding, sell something to a client, prepare a brochure, or work with an actual spreadsheet. Two favorite tasks are to ask candidates to prepare and give a short presentation with visuals or to work through an online in-box. Both of these tasks test communication and organization skills, as well as the ability to perform under time constraints.

Stress Interviews

Obviously, if the task is complex, performing it at a job interview, particularly with time constraints, is stressful. Thus situational interviews can easily move

Stress interviews can use physical conditions and people placement to see how candidates respond to uncomfortable situations. You have the option to change some uncomfortable conditions, such as lights shining in your eyes.

into stress interviews. The higher you move in your career, the more likely it is that you will have situational or stress interviews. **Stress interviews** deliberately put applicants under stress to see how they handle the pressure. The key is to stay calm; try to maintain your sense of humor.

Sometimes the stress is physical: for example, you're given a chair where the light is in your eyes. Speak up for yourself: ask if the position of the blind can be changed, or move to another chair.

Usually the stress is psychological. Panel interviews, such as those for many political appointments, may be stressful (see "The Four-Day Interview" sidebar on page 472). The group of interviewers may fire rapid questions. However, you can slow the pace with deliberate answers. In another possibility, a single interviewer may probe every weak spot in your record and ask questions that elicit negatives. If you get questions that put you on the defensive, rephrase them in less inflammatory terms, if necessary, and then treat them as requests for information.

Q: Why did you major in physical education? That sounds like a pretty Mickey Mouse major.

A: Are you wondering whether I have the academic preparation for this job? I started out in physical education because I've always loved team sports. I learned that I couldn't graduate in four years if I officially switched my major to business administration because the requirements were different in the two programs. But I do have 21 hours in business administration and 9 hours in accounting. And my sports experience gives me practical training in teamwork, motivating people, and management.

Respond assertively. The candidates who survive are those who stand up for themselves and who explain why indeed they *are* worth hiring.

Sometimes the stress comes in the form of unusual questions: Why are manhole covers round? How many tennis balls would fit inside a school bus? If

---

STAR: An Interviewing Technique

"One strategy for preparing for behavioral interviews is to use the STAR technique, as outlined below. (This technique is also referred to as the SAR and PAR techniques.)

Situation or Task
Describe the situation that you were in or the task that you needed to accomplish. You must describe a specific event or situation, not a generalized description of what you have done in the past. Be sure to give enough detail for the interviewer to understand. This situation can be from a previous job, from a volunteer experience, or any relevant event.

Action You Took
Describe the action you took and be sure to keep the focus on you. Even if you are discussing a group project or effort, describe what you did—not the efforts of the team. Don't tell what you might do, tell what you did.

Results You Achieved
What happened? How did the event end? What did you accomplish? What did you learn?"

Quoted from "STAR Interviewing Response Technique for Success in Behavioral Job Interviews," Quint-Careers, accessed June 27, 2013, http://www.quintcareers .com/STAR_interviewing.html. Reprinted with permission.

The Four-Day Panel Interview

When President Barack Obama nominated Elena Kagan to fill a place on the United States Supreme Court, she had to perform well in a four-day panel interview with the 16 members of the Senate Judiciary Committee, which was split between the two political parties.

Here are some techniques she used during her interview that may help during yours:

- Kagan answered the most difficult questions candidly and thoughtfully, with occasional humor.

- She acknowledged the complexities of the questions and explained her positions without apologizing.

- When she was grilled about her past, she held her ground politely and professionally.

By the end of the hearings, she had won over some of her harshest critics. In fact, Senator Tom Coburn, who had criticized her answers early in the process, said at the end that her hearings had been some of the best in his experience.

Adapted from Ariane De Vogue and Ann H. Sloan, "The Kagan Hearings: Were They Necessary and Worthwhile?" ABC News, July 2, 2010, http://abcnews.go.com/Politics/Supreme_Court/elena-kagan-hearings-worthwhile/story?id=11068199&page=1.

you were a cookie/car/animal, what kind would you be? If you could be any character from a book, who would you be? How you handle the question will be as important as your answer, maybe more important. Can you think creatively under pressure?

Silence can also create stress. One woman walked into her scheduled interview to find a male interviewer with his feet up on the desk. He said, "It's

Supreme Court Justice Elena Kagan survived a four-day, highly publicized interview to win her position. See "The Four-Day Interview" sidebar on this page.

been a long day. I'm tired and I want to go home. You have five minutes to sell yourself." Since she had planned the points she wanted to be sure interviewers knew, she was able to do this. "Your recruiting brochure said that you're looking for someone with a major in accounting and a minor in finance. As you may remember from my résumé, I'm majoring in accounting and have had 12 hours in finance. I've also served as treasurer of a local campaign committee and have worked as a volunteer tax preparer through the Accounting Club." When she finished, the interviewer told her it was a test: "I wanted to see how you'd handle it."

Group Interviews

In group interviews, sometimes called "cattle calls," multiple candidates are interviewed at a time. While many interview tips still apply to these interviews, successful candidates will also practice other techniques. Researching the job and company becomes even more important, because your time to show how you fit the job will be so limited. Have a two-minute summary of your education and experience that shows how you fit this job. Practice it so you can share it during the interview.

Arrive early so you have time to meet as many interviewers and interviewees as possible. Get business cards from the interviewers if you can. This pre-interview time may be part of the test, so make the most of it.

During the interview, listen carefully to both interviewers and interviewees. Make eye contact with both groups as well. Participate in the discussion, and look engaged even when you aren't. Watch your body language (see Chapter 4) so you don't give off unintended signals.

Some group interviews are organized around tasks. The group may be asked to solve a problem. Another scenario is that the group will be split into teams, with each team performing a task and then presenting to the whole group. Remember that your participation in these activities is being watched. You will be judged on skills such as communication, persuasion, leadership, organization, planning, analysis, and problem solving. Do you help move the action forward? Are you too assertive? Too shy? Do you praise the contributions of others? Do you help the group achieve consensus? Are you knowledgeable?

Many group interviews particularly test how you interact with other people. Talking too much may work against you. Making an effort to help quiet people enter the discussion may work in your favor. Connecting your comments to previous comments shows you are a good listener as well as a team player. Be careful not to get caught up in a combative situation.

At the end of the interview, thank each interviewer. Follow up with a written thank-you to each interviewer.

Multiple Interviews

Some companies, dissatisfied with hires based on one interview, are turning to multiple interviews. Geoff Smart and Randy Street, in their business best seller *Who: The A Method for Hiring,* present a four-interview system for finding the best employees:

1. Screening interview, which culls the list (done by phone).
2. "Topgrading" interview, which walks job candidates through their careers so far.
3. Focused interview, which focuses on one desired aspect of the candidate's career.
4. Reference interview, which checks in with candidates' references.[6]

Granted, this system is not for hiring entry-level people, but you won't be entry level very long, even if you are now. If you are scheduled for multiple interviews, you need to pay extra attention to your interview strategy so you provide the interviewers with a consistent view of you and your qualifications. Be prepared to answer some of the same questions multiple times with the same level of enthusiasm each time. Multiple interviews will likely draw on traditional interview questions in the early stages and some of the more focused types of interview questions in the later stages.

Final Steps for a Successful Job Search `LO 14-7`

What you do after the interview can determine whether you get the job. Many companies expect applicants to follow up on their interviews within a week. If they don't, the company assumes they wouldn't follow up with clients.

If the employer sends you an e-mail query, answer it promptly. You're being judged not only on what you say but on how quickly you respond. Have your list of references (see page 402) and samples of your work ready to send promptly if requested to do so.

Following Up with Phone Calls and Written Messages

After a first interview, make a follow-up phone call to show enthusiasm for the job, to reinforce positives from the first interview, to overcome any negatives, and to provide information to persuade the interviewer to hire you. Do not stalk the recruiter. Call only once unless you have excellent reasons for multiple calls. If you get voice mail, leave a message. Remember that caller ID will tell the recruiter that you were the person making the multiple hang-ups.

A thank-you note, written within 24 hours of an interview, is essential. Some companies consider the thank-you note to be as important as the cover letter. Figure 14.3 lists what a good thank-you note does.

Interview Bloopers

A recent survey asked executives for the most embarrassing interview moments they had encountered. Here are some examples.

- Candidate brought a "how to interview book" with him to the interview.
- Candidate asked, "What company is this again?"
- Candidate put the interviewer on hold during a phone interview. When she came back on the line, she told the interviewer that she had a date set up for Friday.
- Candidate wore a Boy Scout uniform and never told interviewers why.
- Candidate talked about promptness as one of her strengths after showing up 10 minutes late.
- On the way to the interview, candidate passed, cut off, and flipped the middle finger to a driver who happened to be the interviewer.
- Candidate referred to himself in the third person.
- Candidate took off his shoes during interview.
- Candidate asked for a sip of the interviewer's coffee.
- A mature candidate told the interviewer she wasn't sure if the job offered was worth "starting the car for."

Bullets quoted from The WorkBuzz, "10 Unusual Interview Mistakes, and 6 That Are All Too Common," *TheWorkBuzz.com*, February 22, 2012, http://www.theworkbuzz.com/get-the-job/interviews/unusual-interview-mistakes. Copyright 2012, CareerBuilder LLC. Reprinted with permission.

Figure 14.3	Steps for a Good Thank-You Note

- Thank the interviewer for useful information and any helpful action.
- Remind the interviewer of what he or she liked in you.
- Use the jargon of the company and refer to specific things you learned during your interview or saw during your visit.
- Be enthusiastic about the position.
- Refer to the next move, whether you'll wait to hear from the employer or whether you want to call to learn about the status of your application.
- Thank your hosts for their hospitality if the note is for a site visit. In the postscript, mention enclosed receipts for your expenses.
- Use your best writing skills, and correct grammar, capitalization, punctuation, and spelling. Double-check the spelling of all names.

The note can be an e-mail, but many employers are still impressed by paper thank-you notes. In either case, do not use text messaging abbreviations or emoticons. Figure 14.4 is an example of a follow-up letter after a site visit.

Negotiating for Salary and Benefits

The best time to negotiate for salary and benefits is after you have the job offer. Try to delay discussing salary early in the interview process, when you're still competing against other applicants.

Prepare for salary negotiations by finding out what the going rate is for the work you hope to do. Ask friends who are in the workforce to find out what they're making. Ask the campus placement office for figures on what last year's graduates got. Check trade journals and the web.

This research is crucial. The White House Report on the status of women shows that women earn about 75% as much as men, at all levels of education. Even when compared to direct male counterparts, the difference is substantial.[7] Knowing what a job is worth will give you the confidence to negotiate more effectively.

The best way to get more money is to convince the employer that you're worth it. During the interview process, show that you can do what the competition can't.

After you have the offer, you can begin negotiating salary and benefits. You're in the strongest position when (1) you've done your homework and know what the usual salary and benefits are and (2) you can walk away from this offer if it doesn't meet your needs. Avoid naming a specific salary. Don't say you can't accept less. Instead, say you would find it difficult to accept the job under the terms first offered.

Remember that you're negotiating a package, not just a starting salary. A company that truly can't pay any more money now might be able to review you for promotion sooner than usual, or pay your moving costs, or give you a better job title. Some companies offer fringe benefits that may compensate for lower taxable income: use of a company car, reimbursements for education, child care or elder care subsidies, or help in finding a job for your spouse or partner. And think about your career, not just the initial salary. Sometimes a low-paying job at a company that will provide superb experience will do more for your career (and your long-term earnings prospects) than a high salary now with no room to grow.

Work toward a compromise. You want the employer to be happy that you're coming on board and to feel that you've behaved maturely and professionally.

Figure 14.4   Follow-Up Letter after a Site Visit

405 West College, Apt. 201   *Single-space your address and the date*
Thibodaux, LA 70301   *when you don't use letterhead.*
April 2, 2014

Mr. Robert Land, Account Manager
Sive Associates
378 Norman Boulevard
Cincinnati, OH 48528

Dear Mr. Land:

After visiting Sive Associates last week, I'm even more sure that writing direct mail is the career for me.

Refers to things she saw and learned during the interview.

I've always been able to brainstorm ideas, but sometimes, when I had to focus on one idea for a class project, I wasn't sure which idea was best. It was fascinating to see how you make direct mail scientific as well as creative by testing each new creative package against the control. I can understand how pleased Linda Hayes was when she learned that her new package for *Smithsonian* beat the control.

Seeing Kelly, Luke, and Gene collaborating on the Sesame Street package gave me some sense of the tight deadlines you're under. As you know, I've learned to meet deadlines, not only for my class assignments but also in working on Nicholls' newspaper. The award I won for my feature on the primary election suggests that my quality holds up even when the deadline is tight!

Reminds interviewer of her strong points.

Thank you for your hospitality while I was in Cincinnati. You and your wife made my stay very pleasant. I especially appreciate the time the two of you took to help me find information about apartments that are accessible to wheelchairs. Cincinnati seems like a very livable city.

I'm excited about a career in direct mail and about the (possibility) of joining Sive Associates. I look forward to hearing from you soon!

Be positive, not pushy. She doesn't assume she has the job.

Refers to what will happen next.

Sincerely,

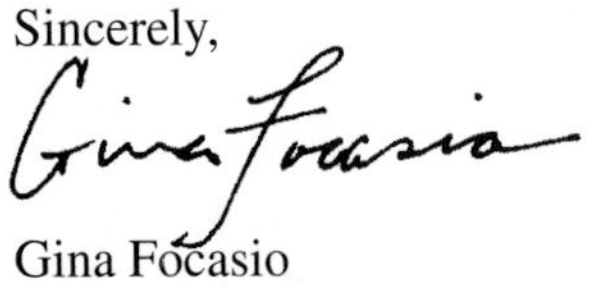

Gina Focasio

Gina Focasio
(504) 555-2948

Writer's phone number.

Puts request for reimbursement in P.S. to de-emphasize it; focuses on the job, not the cost of the trip.

P.S. My expenses totaled $454. Enclosed are receipts for my plane fare from New Orleans to Cincinnati ($367), the taxi to the airport in Cincinnati ($30), and the bus from Thibodaux to New Orleans ($57).

Encl.: Receipts for Expenses

Deciding Which Offer to Accept

The problem with choosing among job offers is that you're comparing apples and oranges. The job with the most interesting work pays peanuts. The job that pays best is in a city where you don't want to live. The secret of professional happiness is taking a job where the positives are things you want and the negatives are things that don't matter as much to you.

To choose among job offers, you need to know what is truly important to *you*. Start by answering questions like the following:

- Are you willing to work after hours? To take work home? To travel? How important is money to you? Prestige? Time to spend with family and friends?

- Would you rather have firm deadlines or a flexible schedule? Do you prefer working alone or with other people? Do you prefer specific instructions and standards for evaluation or freedom and uncertainty? How comfortable are you with pressure? How much variety and challenge do you want?

- What kinds of opportunities for training and advancement are you seeking?

- Where do you want to live? What features in terms of weather, geography, cultural and social life do you see as ideal?

- Is it important to you that your work achieve certain purposes or values, or do you see work as "just a way to make a living"? Are the organization's culture and ethical standards ones you find comfortable? Will you be able to do work you can point to with pride?

No job is perfect but some jobs will fulfill more of your major criteria than will others.

Some employers offer jobs at the end of the office visit. In other cases, you may wait for weeks or even months to hear. Some employers may offer jobs orally. In those instances you must say something in response immediately, so it's good to plan some strategies in advance.

If your first offer is not from your first choice, express your pleasure at being offered the job, but do not accept it on the phone. "That's great! I assume I have two weeks to let you know?" Then *call* the other companies you're interested in. Explain, "I've just gotten a job offer, but I'd rather work for you. Can you tell me what the status of my application is?" Nobody will put that information in writing, but almost everyone will tell you over the phone. With this information, you're in a better position to decide whether to accept the original offer.

Companies routinely give applicants two weeks to accept or reject offers. Some students have been successful in getting those two weeks extended to several weeks or even months. Certainly if you cannot decide by the deadline, it is worth asking for more time: The worst the company can do is say *no*. If you do try to keep a company hanging for a long time, be prepared for weekly phone calls asking you if you've decided yet.

Make your acceptance contingent upon a written job offer confirming the terms. That letter should spell out not only salary but also fringe benefits and any special provisions you have negotiated. If something is missing, call the interviewer for clarification: "You said that I'd be reviewed for a promotion and higher salary in six months, but that isn't in the letter." Even well-intentioned people can forget oral promises. You have more power to resolve misunderstandings now than you will after six months or a year on the job. Furthermore, the person who made you the promise may no longer be with the company a year later.

When you've accepted one job, notify the other places you visited. Then they can go to their second choices. If you're second on someone else's list, you'll appreciate other candidates' removing themselves so the way is clear for you.

Dealing with Rejection

Because multiple people usually apply for each job opening, most job seekers get far more rejections than job offers. Learn to live with this fact of the job hunt. Form support groups with your friends who are also on the job market. Try to keep an upbeat attitude; it will show in job interviews and make you a more attractive candidate. Remember that candidate selection can be a political process. You may have been competing with the boss's daughter, an inside candidate, or a candidate who was recommended by a respected employee.

Starting Your Career   LO 14-8

Your successful job interview is just the first step toward your career. Once you have landed the job, you need to succeed in the job so it can be a path to your professional goals. Remember that your end goal is not to just have any job; your goal should be to continue to develop your skills and to see a clear path to promotion. Planning a career successfully involves two steps: starting out in the right way in your first full-time job and creating a strategy to achieve your long-term goals.

Your First Full-Time Job

Just like the step from high school to college, the step from college to your first full-time job brings changes that you must negotiate. The new business environment is exhilarating, with many opportunities, but it also contains pitfalls. As you go to being the new kid on the block yet again, remember all the coping strategies you have developed as a newbie in middle school, high school, and college.

- Reread all your materials on the organization, its competition, and the industry.

- Get to know your new colleagues, but also keep networking with people in the field.

- Talk to recent hires in the organization. Ask them what they found to be helpful advice when they were starting.

- Fit into the corporate culture by being observant. Watch what people wear, how they act, how they talk. Watch how they interact during meetings and in the break room. Look at the kinds of e-mails and letters people send. Discover who people go to when they need help.

- Use your breaks effectively. Stop by the coffee station, water cooler, or break room occasionally to plug into the grapevine.

- Find a successful person who is willing to mentor you. Even better, find a support network.

- Ask lots of questions. It may feel embarrassing, but it will feel even worse to still be ignorant several months down the road.

- Seek early opportunities for feedback. What you hear may not always be pleasant, but it will help you become a valued employee more quickly.

- Learn the jargon, but use it sparingly.

- Be pleasant and polite to everyone, including support personnel.

- Be punctual. Arrive for work and meetings on time.

- Be dependable. Do what you say you will do—and by the deadline.

- Be organized. Take a few minutes to plan your daily work. Keep track of papers and e-mails.

- Be resourceful. Few work projects will come to you with the detailed instructions provided by your professors. Think projects through. Ask for suggestions from trusted colleagues. Have a plan before you go to your boss with questions.

- Use technology professionally. Keep your cell phone on vibrate, or turn it off. Resist the temptation to send text messages during meetings. Don't visit inappropriate websites; remember that all computer activity can be tracked. Learn the company's Internet policies.

- Be discreet. Be careful what you say, and where you say it. Above all, be careful what you put in e-mails!

- Proofread all your written messages, including tweets and texts, before you send them. At rushed times, such as the end of the day or week, proofread them twice.

- Go the extra mile. Help out even when you are not asked. Put in extra hours when your help is needed.

- Do your share of grunt work—making coffee or refilling the paper tray.

- Take advantage of company social events, but always act professionally at them. Seriously limit your intake of alcohol.

- Document your work. Collect facts, figures, and documents. You will need this information for your performance reviews.

- Enjoy yourself. Enthusiasm for your new job and colleagues will have you part of the team in short order.

A Long-Term Strategy

The *Harvard Business Review* suggests planning for your career in the same way that presidential candidates plan for a campaign: begin early, calculate how to win, and plan a detailed time line of tasks to achieve the goal.[8] These tasks usually include the following:

- Continue to network. The people you know are not just there to help you get a job. Build real relationships that are productive and reciprocal.

- Continue seeking mentors for different aspects of your work.

- Take advantage of voluntary training opportunities.

- Plan where you want to be. Look ahead in your career, not just to your next promotion but to your goals for the next 10 to 20 years.

- Collect work for your professional portfolio.

- Prewrite your future résumé. As you plan your career, write a résumé that you may use in 10 years' time. What jobs do you have on it? What other activities? What is missing from your experience or education that would help you achieve your goals?

- Look for opportunities. Some of the advances in your career will happen by luck or because of chance encounters. Be prepared to take advantage of opportunities by always working hard, talking with people, and keeping your focus on your ultimate goals.

- Read. Read the *Wall Street Journal*, business magazines, trade journals, trade blogs. When Wharton business students asked Warren Buffett where he got his ideas, he replied that he just reads—all day.[9]

Summary by Learning Objectives

LO 14-1 What interview channels you may encounter.

- Phone and video interviews may precede face-to-face interviews.
- Campus interviews and job fairs provide you with opportunities to impress recruiters.

LO 14-2 How to create a strategy for successful interviewing.

Develop an overall strategy based on your answers to these three questions:

1. What two to five facts about yourself do you want the interviewer to know?
2. What disadvantages or weaknesses do you need to overcome or minimize?
3. What do you need to know about the job and the organization to decide whether or not you want to accept this job if it is offered to you?

LO 14-3 What preparations to make before you start interviewing.

- Conduct research about the company; spend time on its website.
- Check on dress expectations before the interview.
- Rehearse everything you can. In particular, practice answers to common questions. Ask a friend to interview you. If your campus has practice interviews or videotaping facilities, use them so that you can evaluate and modify your interview behavior.
- Prepare professional materials, including copies of your résumé, a list of references, a work portfolio, and detailed work and education histories in case you are asked to fill out an application form.

LO 14-4 What to do during an interview

- Bring an extra copy of your résumé, something to write on and write with, and copies of your work to the interview.
- Record the name of the interviewer, tips the interviewer gave you, what the interviewer liked about you, answers to your questions about the company, and when you'll hear from the company.
- Behave professionally; show enthusiasm for the job.

LO 14-5 How to answer common interview questions.

Successful applicants know what they want to do, use the company name in the interview, have researched the company in advance, back up claims with specifics, use appropriate technical jargon, ask specific questions, and talk more of the time.

LO 14-6 How to prepare for less common interview types.

- **Behavioral interviews** ask the applicant to describe actual behaviors, rather than plans or general principles. To answer a behavioral question, describe the situation, tell what you did, and tell what happened. Think about the implications of what you did and be ready to talk about what you'd do the next time or if the situation were slightly different.
- **Situational interviews** put you in a situation that allows the interviewer to see whether you have the qualities the company is seeking.
- **Stress interviews** deliberately create physical or psychological stress. Change the conditions that create physical stress. Meet psychological stress by rephrasing questions in less inflammatory terms and treating them as requests for information.

- **Group interviews** involve several candidates at one time. You will need to make sure you are prepared and focused to take advantage of opportunities to stand out.
- **Multiple interviews** involve several tiers of interviews. Prepare to answer questions multiple times and to maintain your enthusiasm through a long process.

LO 14-7   **What to do after an interview.**

- Use follow-up phone calls and written messages to reinforce positives from the first interview, and to provide information to persuade the interviewer to hire you.

- The best time to negotiate for salary and benefits is after you have the job offer.
- If your first offer isn't from your first choice, call the other companies you're interested in to ask the status of your application.

LO 14-8   **How to plan for a successful career.**

- Begin your new job well. Work hard, contribute, ask questions, and build your professional network.
- Keep your career goals in mind. Find mentors, network effectively, and plan for 10 years in the future.

Continuing Case

The All-Weather Case, set in an HR department in a manufacturing company, extends through all 19 chapters and is available at www.mhhe.com/locker11e. The portion for this chapter asks students to evaluate the interviews of two candidates and recommend one for the position.

Exercises and Cases

14.1   Reviewing the Chapter

1. Name four interview channels. What special considerations do you have to make for them? (LO 14-1)
2. How can you create an effective strategy for your interview? (LO 14-2)
3. What preparations should you make before an interview? (LO 14-3)
4. What are some behavior tips you should keep in mind during an interview? (LO 14-4)
5. What should you accomplish in the close of an interview? (LO 14-4)

6. What are some common interview questions? What are effective answers for you? (LO 14-5)
7. What are three special kinds of interviews you may encounter? What are tips to succeed in them? (LO 14-6)
8. What do you need to do after an interview? (LO 14-7)
9. When do you negotiate for salary? Why? (LO 14-7)
10. What are some tips to help you succeed at your first full-time job? (LO 14-8)
11. How can you plan for a successful career? (LO 14-8)

14.2   Interviewing Job Hunters

Talk to students at your school who are interviewing for jobs this term. Possible questions to ask them include the following:

- What field are you in? How good is the job market in that field this year?
- How long is the first interview with a company, usually?
- What questions have you been asked at job interviews? Were you asked any stress or sexist questions? Any really oddball questions?

- What answers seemed to go over well? What answers bombed?
- At an office visit or plant trip, how many people did you talk to? What were their job titles?
- Were you asked to take any tests (skills, physical, drugs)?
- How long did you have to wait after a first interview to learn whether you were being invited for an office visit? How long after an office visit did it take to

learn whether you were being offered a job? How much time did the company give you to decide?

- What advice would you have for someone who will be interviewing next term or next year?

14.3   Interviewing an Interviewer

Talk to someone who regularly interviews candidates for entry-level jobs. Possible questions to ask include the following:

- How long have you been interviewing for your organization? Does everyone on the management ladder at your company do some interviewing, or do people specialize in it?
- Do you follow a set structure for interviews? What are some of the standard questions you ask?
- What are you looking for? How important are (1) good grades, (2) leadership roles in extracurricular groups, or (3) relevant work experience? What advice would you give to someone who lacks one or more of these?
- What are the things you see students do that create a poor impression? Think about the worst candidate you've interviewed. What did he or she do (or not do) to create such a negative impression?

- What are the things that make a good impression? Recall the best student you've ever interviewed. Why did he or she impress you so much?
- How does your employer evaluate and reward your success as an interviewer?
- What advice would you have for someone who still has a year or so before the job hunt begins?

As your instructor directs,

a. Summarize your findings in an e-mail to your instructor.
b. Report your findings orally to the class.
c. Join with a small group of students to write a group report describing the results of your interviews.
d. Write to the interviewer thanking him or her for taking the time to talk to you.

14.4   Analyzing a Video Interview

Analyze a video clip of an interview session.

As your instructor directs,

a. In groups of four, search on a video-based website such as Google video or YouTube for terms such as "interview" or "student interview."
b. Watch a video clip of an interview and note the strengths and weaknesses of the interviewee.

c. Discuss your observations with your group and explain why you considered certain responses as strengths and weaknesses.
d. Share your video and analysis with your class.

14.5   Analyzing a Panel Interview

Watch some of the videos of the confirmation hearings (e.g., job interviews) for Elena Kagan. What good interview behaviors do you notice? What interview behaviors do you think could be improved? How does she handle difficult questions?

As your instructor directs,

a. Share your findings with a small group of other students.
b. Describe your findings in an e-mail to your instructor.
c. Present your findings orally to the class.

14.6   Preparing an Interview Strategy

Prepare your interview strategy.

1. List two to five things about yourself that you want the interviewer to know before you leave the interview.
2. Identify any weaknesses or apparent weaknesses in your record and plan ways to explain them or minimize them.

3. List the points you need to learn about an employer to decide whether to accept an office visit or plant trip.

As your instructor directs,

a. Share your strategy with a small group of other students.
b. Describe your strategy in an e-mail to your instructor.
c. Present your strategy orally to the class.

As your instructor directs,

a. Summarize your findings in an e-mail to your instructor.
b. Report your findings orally to the class.
c. Join with a small group of students to write a group report describing the results of your survey.

14.7   Preparing Questions to Ask Employers

Prepare a list of questions to ask at job interviews.

1.   Prepare a list of three to five general questions that apply to most employers in your field.
2.   Prepare two to five specific questions for the three companies you are most interested in.

As your instructor directs,

a.   Share the questions with a small group of other students.
b.   List the questions in an e-mail to your instructor.
c.   Present your questions orally to the class.

14.8   Analyzing Answers to Interview Questions

What might be problematic about these responses to interview questions? How might the answers be improved?

a.   Q: Tell me about yourself.
     A: I'm really easy-going and casual.
b.   Q: I noticed that you had a pretty large break between your last two jobs. What can you tell us about that?
     A: Oh, it wasn't a big deal. I just wanted to take some time for myself.
c.   Q: Tell me about a collaborative project that you've worked on.
     A: I usually work better by myself. I'm very independent.
d.   Q: What was your least favorite class in college?
     A: Business communication.
e.   Q: Tell me about your last boss.
     A: He was a real jerk. I couldn't stand him, but neither could anyone else. He always expected us to stay late to finish up projects. It was annoying.

f.   Q: Tell me about a weakness that you have.
     A: I always help people when they ask for it. I just love to help.
g.   Q: Tell me about a book you have read and enjoyed that wasn't a textbook.
     A: We read *To Kill a Mockingbird* in 10th-grade English.
h.   Q: What are your interests outside work?
     A: Partying.
i.   Q: What are some of your strengths?
     A: I never give up; I am really stubborn. I like to get my work done really quickly and I hate to waste time on little things.
j.   Q: Tell me about a group project that had problems.
     A: Our marketing team had a real deadbeat on it. But I saved our asses by going to the teacher and getting her to take him off.
k.   Q: Why do you want this job?
     A: This is a great job for me. It will really increase my skills set.

14.9   Preparing for the Worst Interview Questions

In small groups, discuss the worst or most difficult interview questions you have ever received. Add to your list by searching the Internet for weird or unusual questions. Review your list and discuss how you would answer these questions in an interview. Use the questions to conduct practice interviews and analyze the answers. Share your best two examples with the class.

14.10   Preparing Answers to Questions You May Be Asked

Prepare answers to each of the interview questions listed in this chapter and to any other questions that you know are likely to be asked of job hunters in your field or on your campus.

As your instructor directs,

a.   Write down the answers to your questions and turn them in.
b.   Conduct mini-interviews in a small group of students. In the group, let student A be the interviewer and ask five questions from the list. Student B will play the job candidate and answer the questions, using real information about student B's field and qualifications.

Student C will evaluate the content of the answer. Student D will observe the nonverbal behavior of the interviewer (A); student E will observe the nonverbal behavior of the interviewee (B).

After the mini-interview, let students C, D, and E share their observations and recommend ways that B could be even more effective. Then switch roles. Let another student be the interviewer and ask five questions of another interviewee, while new observers note content and nonverbal behavior. Continue the process until everyone in the group has had a chance to be "interviewed."

14.11   Writing a Follow-Up Message after an Onsite Visit

Write a follow-up e-mail message or letter after an office visit or plant trip. Thank your hosts for their hospitality; relate your strong points to things you learned about the company during the visit; allay any negatives that may remain; be enthusiastic about the company; and submit receipts for your expenses so you can be reimbursed.

14.12   Revising a Follow-Up Message after an Onsite Visit

Revise the follow-up message below to be more professional and effective, based on the principles in this chapter.

May 2, 2014
Ms. Charlotte LeCliare
Pebble Creek Publishing Inc.
New York, NY

Dear Ms. LeClaire:

I wanted to thank you for taking time out of your busy schedule to show me around Pebble Creek Publishing. I really enjoyed it.

I've always wanted to join the publishing field, and Pebble Creek just seemed right to me. I loved watching how all of your employees work together to create the best possible product. They were quite a friendly bunch, especially the guys in the break room.

As you know, I have had extensive editing experience in my English courses that I took here at ISU. I also took a Grammatical Analysis class through the Linguistics program here, which was really helpful for me. I really love making sure things are right, and I would love to do that for your company.

I enjoyed my stay in New York very much. I am so looking forward to moving there very soon!

Thank you so, so much,

Terese Mart
(515) 888-1212

P.S. I did have a few expenses from my stay, so will I be reimbursed for those? That would be awesome.

14.13   Clarifying the Terms of a Job Offer

Last week, you got a job offer from your first-choice company, and you accepted it over the phone. Today, the written confirmation arrived. The letter specifies the starting salary and fringe benefits you had negotiated. However, during the office visit, you were promised a 5% raise in six months. The job offer says nothing about the raise. You do want the job, but you want it on the terms you thought you had negotiated.

Write to your contact at the company, Damon Winters.

14.14   Researching a Geographic Area

Research a geographic area where you would like to work. Investigate the cost of living, industrial growth in the area, weather and climate, and attractions in the area you could visit. The local Chamber of Commerce is a good place to start your research.

As your instructor directs,

a.   Share your findings with a small group of other students.

b.   Describe your findings in an e-mail to your instructor.

c.   Present your findings orally to the class.

Notes

1. Accountemps, "The Personal Connection: Survey Shows That in Hiring Process, There's No Substitute for Being There," 2013, http://accountemps.rhi.mediaroom.com/PersonalConnection.

2. Accountemps, "Hiring Manager to Applicant: 'What Is Your Greatest Weakness?': Accountemps Survey Finds Job Seekers Make Most Mistakes During Interview," news release, September 23, 2010, http://accountemps.rhi.mediaroom.com/interview_mistakes.

3. Alison Doyle, "How to Dress for an Interview: Dress Code for Job Interviews," *About.com Careers*, accessed June 27, 2013, http://jobsearch.about.com/od/interviewattire/a/interviewdress.htm.

4. Joseph Walker, "Meet the New Boss: Big Data: Companies Trade in Hunch-Based Hiring for Computer Modeling," *Wall Street Journal*, September 20, 2012, B1.

5. Dana Mattioli, "Sober Thought: How to Mix Work, Alcohol: Taking Cues from Bosses and Clients Can Keep Parties or Meals under Control," *Wall Street Journal*, December 5, 2006, B10.

6. Geoff Smart and Randy Street, *Who: The A Method for Hiring* (New York: Ballantine, 2008).

7. U.S. Department of Commerce Economics and Statistics Administration and Executive Office of the President, Office of Management and Budget, White House Council on Women and Girls, *Women in America: Indicators of Social and Economic Well-Being*, March 2011, 32, http://www.whitehouse.gov/sites/default/files/rss_viewer/Women_in_America.pdf.

8. Dorie Clark, "A Campaign Strategy for Your Career, "*Harvard Business Review* 90, no. 11 (November 2012): 131–34.

9. Carol Loomis, ed., *Tap Dancing to Work: Warren Buffett on Practically Everything, 1966–2012: A Fortune Magazine Book* (New York: Portfolio/Penguin, 2012), 275.

15 Researching Proposals and Reports

Chapter Outline

NEWSWORTHY COMMUNICATION

Dangerous Research

In May 2013, the United Nations issued a nearly 50-page report on how children are affected by war. Like any extensive report, the UN report *Children and Armed Conflict* involved months of careful research and planning. Unlike most reports, however, the research involved in this report was life-threatening.

Children and Armed Conflict documents incidents where children were imprisoned, wounded, killed, tortured, or assaulted in 22 current armed conflicts around the world, including those in Syria, Lebanon, Sudan, and Afghanistan. To create the report, the authors consulted various UN committees, ambassadors from the member states involved with the conflicts, UN country teams, and nongovernmental organizations.

Since every war involves at least two sides, the UN teams also collected information from rebels, insurgents, and opposition groups in war-torn countries. This research involved personal visits to war zones; interviews with leaders, soldiers, and affected children and families; and inspection of camps and battle sites. Since the goal of the report was to create further protections for children during war, not to take sides in the conflicts, each reported incident was verified for accuracy.

For this UN report, careful research was essential. Overreporting or underreporting the number of children harmed by war could hurt the organization's credibility and harm efforts to protect children. By conducting its research carefully—with all the effort and risks involved—the UN could present a powerful case to make the world safer for children, even during wars.

Source: UN General Assembly, 67th Session, *Children and Armed Conflict: Report of the Secretary General*, May 15, 2013, http://childrenandarmedconflict.un.org/annual-report-of-the-secretary-general-on-children-and-armed-conflict.

After studying this chapter, you will know how to

LO 15-1 Recognize varieties of reports.

LO 15-2 Define report problems.

LO 15-3 Employ various research strategies.

LO 15-4 Use and document sources.

Businesses use carefully planned research all the time. Corporations such as Procter & Gamble constantly research their products to keep market share. Grocery stores use data from store loyalty cards to tweak inventory and prices. Money lenders sift data on applicants' car payments, rent, child care, and insurance records as well as phone and utility bills before making loans.[1]

Proposals and reports also depend on research. The research may be as simple as pulling up data with a computer program or as complicated as calling many different people, conducting focus groups and surveys, or even conducting experiments. Care in planning and researching proposals and reports is needed to produce effective documents.

In writing any report, there are five basic steps:

1. Define the problem.
2. Gather the necessary data and information.
3. Analyze the data and information.
4. Organize the information.
5. Write the report.

After reviewing the varieties of reports, this chapter focuses on the first two steps. Chapter 18 discusses the last three steps. You can find tips for creating visuals and data displays in Chapter 16. Chapter 17 covers guidelines for writing proposals.

Varieties of Reports LO 15-1

Many kinds of documents are called reports. In some organizations, a report is a long document or one that contains numerical data. In others, one- and two-page memos are called reports. In still others, reports consist of Power-Point slides delivered orally or printed and bound together. A short report to a client may use letter format. **Formal reports** contain formal elements such as a title page, a transmittal, a table of contents, and a list of illustrations. **Informal reports** may be letters and e-mails or even computer printouts of production or sales figures. But all reports, whatever their length or degree of formality, provide the information that people in organizations need to make plans and solve problems.

Reports can provide just information, both information and analysis alone, or information and analysis to support a recommendation (see Figure 15.1). Reports can be called **information reports** if they collect data for the reader, **analytical reports** if they interpret data but do not recommend action, and **recommendation reports** if they recommend action or a solution.

Figure 15.1 Variety of Information Reports Can Provide

Information only

Sales reports (sales figures for the week or month).

Quarterly reports (figures showing a plant's productivity and profits for the quarter).

Information plus analysis

Annual reports (financial data and an organization's accomplishments during the past year).

Audit reports (interpretations of the facts revealed during an audit).

Make-good or payback reports (calculations of the point at which a new capital investment will pay for itself).

Information plus analysis plus a recommendation

Recommendation reports evaluate two or more alternatives and recommend which alternative the organization should choose.

Feasibility reports evaluate a proposed action and show whether or not it will work.

Justification reports justify the need for a purchase, an investment, a new personnel line, or a change in procedure.

Problem-solving reports identify the causes of an organizational problem and recommend a solution.

The following reports can be information, analytical, or recommendation reports, depending on what they provide:

- **Accident reports** can simply list the nature and causes of accidents in a factory or office. These reports can also analyze the data and recommend ways to make conditions safer.

- **Credit reports** can simply summarize an applicant's income and other credit obligations. These reports can also evaluate the applicant's collateral and creditworthiness and recommend whether or not to provide credit.

- **Progress and interim reports** can simply record the work done so far and the work remaining on a project. These reports can also analyze the quality of the work and recommend that a project be stopped, continued, or restructured.

- **Trip reports** can simply share what the author learned at a conference or during a visit to a customer or supplier. These reports can also recommend action based on that information.

- **Closure reports** can simply document the causes of a failure or possible products that are not economically or technically feasible under current conditions. They can also recommend action to prevent such failures in the future.

The Report Production Process

When you write a report, you know the actual writing will take a significant chunk of time. But you should also plan to spend significant time analyzing your data, revising drafts, and preparing visuals.

When you write a report for a class project, plan to complete at least one-fourth of your research before you write the proposal. Begin analyzing your

E-Readers Research

Amazon, Apple, and Google are researching your e-reading habits. Not only do they know what you read, but they also know how long you spent reading it, if you finished it, and if you didn't finish, where you stopped.

Now retailers and publishers are beginning to use that data to learn how readers of particular genres engage with their books. Readers of science fiction, romance, and crime fiction tend to read more books more quickly and more completely than readers of more literary fiction. Readers of nonfiction tend to work in fits and starts. They frequently quit long books, so some publishers are acquiring shorter nonfiction works. Scholastic, publisher of the *Harry Potter* series and *The Hunger Games*, took its research a step further by creating online message boards and games for its *39 Clues* series. Data from both venues were used to shape characters and plots and have helped turn the series into a global success, with over 15 million copies in print.

Adapted from Alexandra Alter, "Your E-Book Is Reading You," *Wall Street Journal*, June 29, 2012, D1, D2.

data as you collect it; prepare your list of sources and drafts of visuals as you go along. Start writing your first draft before the research is completed. An early draft can help clarify where you need more research. Save at least one-fourth of your time at the end of the project to think and write after all your data are collected. For a collaborative report, you'll need even more time to write and revise.

Up-front planning helps you use your time efficiently. Start by thinking about the whole report process. Talk to your readers to understand how much detail and formality they want. Look at reports that were produced earlier (sample reports in this text are in Chapter 18). List all the parts of the report you'll need to prepare. Then articulate—to yourself or your team members—the purposes, audiences, and generic constraints for each part. The fuller idea you have of the final product when you start, the fewer drafts you'll need to write and the better your final product will be.

Report Problems LO 15-2

Good reports grow out of real problems: disjunctions between reality and the ideal, choices that must be made. When you write a report as part of your job, the organization may define the problem. To brainstorm problems for class reports, think about issues that face your college or university; housing units on campus; social, religious, and professional groups on campus and in your city; local businesses; and city, county, state, and federal governments and their agencies. Read your campus and local papers and newsmagazines; read the news on the Internet, watch it on TV, or listen to it on National Public Radio.

A good report problem in business meets the following criteria:

1. The problem is
   - Real.
   - Important enough to be worth solving.
   - Narrow but challenging.
2. The audience for the report is
   - Real.
   - Able to implement the recommended action.
3. The data, evidence, and facts are
   - Sufficient to document the severity of the problem.
   - Sufficient to prove that the recommendation will solve the problem.
   - Available to *you*.
   - Comprehensible to *you*.

Often problems need to be narrowed. For example, "improving the college experiences of international students studying in the United States" is far too broad. First, choose one college or university. Second, identify the specific problem. Do you want to increase the social interaction between U.S. and international students? Help international students find housing? Increase the number of ethnic grocery stores and restaurants? Third, identify the specific audience that would have the power to implement your recommendations. Depending on the specific topic, the audience might be the Office of International Studies, the residence hall counselors, a service organization on campus or in town, a store, or a group of investors.

Some problems are more easily researched than others. If you have easy access to the Chinese Student Association, you can survey its members about their experiences at the local Chinese grocery. However, if you want to recommend ways to keep the Chinese grocery in business, but you do not have access to the store's financial records, you will have a much more difficult time solving the problem. Even if you have access, if the records are written in Chinese, you will have problems unless you read the language or have a willing translator.

Pick a problem you can solve in the time available. Six months of full-time (and over-time) work and a team of

Hasbro does extensive research to keep developing games people will play.

colleagues might allow you to look at all the ways to make a store more profitable. If you're doing a report in 6 to 12 weeks for a class that is only one of your responsibilities, limit the topic. Depending on your interests and knowledge, you could choose to examine the prices and brands carried, its inventory procedures, its overhead costs, its layout and decor, or its advertising budget.

Look at the following examples of report problems in the category of technology use:

Too broad:	Texting in class and its effects on college students.
Too time-consuming:	What are the effects of in-class texting on college students?
Better:	What are texting habits of students in XYZ University's Business School?
Better:	How can texting be integrated in XYZ University's business courses?

The first problem is too broad because it covers all college students. The second one is too time-consuming. Scholars are only starting to study the effects, and for you to do a report on this topic, you would need to do your own longitudinal project. The third and fourth problems would both be possibilities. You would select one over the other depending on whether you wanted to focus on students or courses.

How you define the problem shapes the solutions you find. For example, suppose that a manufacturer of frozen foods isn't making money. If the problem is defined as a marketing problem, the researcher may analyze the product's price, image, advertising, and position in the market. But perhaps the problem is really that overhead costs are too high due to poor inventory management, or that an inadequate distribution system doesn't get the product to its target market. Defining the problem accurately is essential to finding an effective solution.

Once you've defined your problem, you're ready to write a purpose statement. The purpose statement goes both in your proposal and in your final report. A good **purpose statement** makes three things clear:

- The organizational problem or conflict.

- The specific technical questions that must be answered to solve the problem.

- The rhetorical purpose (to explain, to recommend, to request, to propose) the report is designed to achieve.

A Newspaper Explains Its Research

Students aren't the only ones who need to sift through mountains of conflicting information; journalists do too. How do professionals do it? The *Des Moines Register* offers four strategies:

- **Use documents.** Original documents, including public documents, e-mails, and videos, tell you what really happened or was said, not what people say they said.

- **Understand context.** Expand your research to include how the information fits into the big picture. What you may see as important data may look different in the larger pattern.

- **Use credible sources.** Make sure the sources you use have good track records of accuracy and fair treatment of both sides of an issue.

- **Present opinions as opinions.** Forecasts of the future are almost always opinions.

Adapted from Carolyn Washburn, "How Register Journalists Work to Bring You the Facts," *Des Moines Register*, October 31, 2010, OP1.

The following purpose statement for a report to the superintendent of Yellowstone National Park has all three elements:

> Current management methods keep the elk population within the carrying capacity of the habitat but require frequent human intervention. Both wildlife conservation specialists and the public would prefer methods that controlled the elk population naturally. This report will compare the current short-term management techniques (hunting, trapping and transporting, and winter feeding) with two long-term management techniques, habitat modification and the reintroduction of predators. The purpose of this report is to recommend which techniques or combination of techniques would best satisfy the needs of conservationists, hunters, and the public.

To write a good purpose statement, you must understand the basic problem and have some idea of the questions that your report will answer. Note, however, that you can (and should) write the purpose statement before researching the specific alternatives the report will discuss.

Research Strategies for Reports   LO 15-3

Research for a report may be as simple as getting a computer printout of sales for the last month; it may involve finding published material or surveying or interviewing people. **Secondary research** retrieves information that someone else gathered. Library research and online searches are the best known kinds of secondary research. **Primary research** gathers new information. Surveys, interviews, and observations are common methods for gathering new information for business reports.

Finding Information Online and in Print

You can save time and money by checking online and published sources of data before you gather new information. Many college and university libraries provide workshops and handouts on research techniques, as well as access to computer databases and research librarians.

Categories of sources that may be useful include

- Specialized encyclopedias for introductions to a topic.

- Indexes to find articles. Most permit searches by key word, by author, and often by company name.

- Abstracts for brief descriptions or summaries of articles. Sometimes the abstract will be all you'll need; almost always, you can tell from the abstract whether an article is useful for your needs.

- Citation indexes to find materials that cite previous research. Citation indexes thus enable you to use an older reference to find newer articles on the topic. The *Social Sciences Citation Index* is the most useful for researching business topics.

- Newspapers for information about recent events.

- U.S. Census reports, for a variety of business and demographic information.

To use a computer database efficiently, identify the concepts you're interested in and choose key words that will help you find relevant sources.

Good research uses multiple media and sources.

Key words are the terms that the computer searches for. If you're not sure what terms to use, check the ABI/Inform Thesaurus for synonyms and the hierarchies in which information is arranged in various databases.

Specific commands allow you to narrow your search. For example, to study the effect of the minimum wage on employment in the restaurant industry, you might use a Boolean search (see Figure 15.2):

> (minimum wage) *and* (restaurant *or* fast food) *and*
> (employment rate *or* unemployment).

This descriptor would give you the titles of articles that treat all three of the topics in parentheses. Without *and*, you'd get articles that discuss the minimum wage in general, articles about every aspect of *restaurants*, and every article that refers to *unemployment*, even though many of these would not be relevant to your topic. The *or* descriptor calls up articles that use the term *fast food* or the term *restaurant*. Many web search engines, including Bing and Google, allow you also to specify words that cannot appear in a source.

Many words can appear in related forms. To catch all of them, use the database's **wild card** or **truncated code** for shortened terms and root words. To find this feature and others, go to the Advanced Search screen for the search engine you are using. Search engines vary in the symbols they use for searches, so be sure to check for accurate directions.

When you do a computer search, be aware that Google now personalizes your search results, as Eli Pariser explains in *The Filter Bubble: What the*

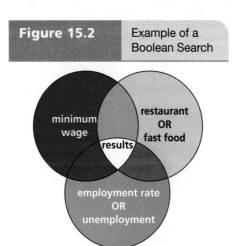

| Figure 15.2 | Example of a Boolean Search |

Researching and Reporting at Reuters

Thomson Reuters is the largest business-to-business information services company in the world. Some years ago, it reinvented itself by learning more about clients who use its products and services: tax professionals, investment managers, brokers, lawyers, accountants, financial analysts, and researchers.

Thomson Reuters began by identifying eight market segments and exploring each of them in greater detail. It employed both quantitative (surveys) and qualitative (interviews) research methods to collect information. Thomson Reuters even filmed users as they performed their job duties.

The comprehensive approach to research paid off. After thoroughly investigating the eight market segments, Thomson Reuters created a list of product attributes that needed improvement to yield better customer satisfaction. Based on its exhaustive market research, Thomson Reuters redesigned its product portfolio, beginning with what could be done most easily and moving to advanced features.

Today, nearly 70% of Thomson Reuter's products have undergone improvements based on its user-oriented market research process, adding both to the company's bottom line and customer satisfaction.

Adapted from Richard J. Harrington and Anthony K. Tjan, "Transforming Strategy One Customer at a Time," *Harvard Business Review* 86, no. 3 (March 2008): 62–72.

Research for Developing Countries

Procter & Gamble researchers found that 60% of shoppers at tiny stores in developing countries already know what they want, so they do not spend time browsing. But they do gaze at the cashier's area for five seconds as they wait for their purchase or change. So P&G is thinking of ways to persuade store owners to put more P&G products in these areas.

Because running water is in short supply for many low-income Mexican consumers, P&G researchers developed a fabric softener that, when added to the laundry load along with the detergent, can eliminate a rinse cycle in the kinds of washing machines being used.

Through research, P&G learned that women in developing countries are particularly interested in removing stains when they wash their clothing. P&G then developed a new stain removal formula for detergent.

Adapted from Ellen Byron, "P&G's Global Target: Shelves of Tiny Stores: It Woos Poor Women Buying Single Portions; Mexico's 'Hot Zones,'" *Wall Street Journal*, July 16, 2007, A1; and P&G, "Consumer Focused Innovation: Latest Innovations," June 27, 2011, http://www.pgscience.com/files/pdf/Internal_Research/latest_innovations/Ariel.pdf.

Internet is Hiding from You. This means that someone with environmental concerns, say a member of the Sierra Club, who Googles "global warming" will be led to widely different sources than someone with big oil connections. To get a more complete picture, you will have to dig deeper.[2]

Web search engines are particularly effective for words, people, or phrases that are unlikely to have separate pages devoted to them. For general topics or famous people, directories like Yahoo or Google may be more useful. Figure 15.3 lists a few of the specialized sources available.

Figure 15.3   Sources for Web Research

Subject matter directories

SmartPros (accounting and corporate finance)
    http://ecampus.smartpros.com/pages/index.aspx?pageId=1
Rutgers Accounting Web (RAW)
    http://raw.rutgers.edu
Education Index
    http://www.educationindex.com
Resources for Economists on the Internet
    http://www.aeaweb.org/RFE
Human Resource Management Resources
    http://www.hrmguide.co.uk/buscon1.html
Global Edge
    http://www.globaledge.msu.edu
Management and Entrepreneurship
    http://www.lib.lsu.edu/sp/subjects/management
Mergent Online
    http://www.mergentonline.com
KnowThis: Knowledge Source for Marketing
    http://www.knowthis.com
Internet Marketing Resources
    http://www.lib.lsu.edu/sp/subjects/guide.php?subject=marketing

News sites

Bloomberg Businessweek
    http://www.businessweek.com
CNN
    http://www.cnn.com (news)
    http://money.cnn.com/ (financial news)
National Public Radio
    http://www.npr.org
New York Times
    http://www.nytimes.com
Wall Street Journal
    http://online.wsj.com/home-page
Washington Post
    http://www.washingtonpost.com

Figure 15.3	Sources for Web Research (Concluded)

U.S. government information

FedStats (links from over 100 federal agencies)
   http://www.fedstats.gov

U.S. Government Printing Office (free electronic access to government documents)
   http://www.gpo.gov/fdsys

Bureau of Economic Analysis
   http://www.bea.gov

Bureau of Labor Statistics
   http://www.bls.gov

Census Bureau (including a link to the *Statistical Abstract of the United States*)
   http://www.census.gov

Securities and Exchange Commission Filings and Forms (EDGAR)
   http://sec.gov/edgar.shtml

Small Business Administration
   http://www.sbaonline.sba.gov

White House Briefing Room (presidential events and public statements)
   http://www.whitehouse.gov/briefing_room

Reference collections

Hoover's Online (information about businesses)
   http://www.hoovers.com

My Virtual Reference Desk
   http://www.refdesk.com

Tile.Net (reference guide to e-mail newsletters and discussion lists)
   http://tile.net/lists

Evaluating Web Sources

Some of the material on the web is excellent, but some of it is wholly unreliable. With print sources, the editor or publisher serves as a gatekeeper, so you can trust the material in good journals. To put up a web page, all one needs is access to a server.

Use the criteria in Figure 15.4 to evaluate websites for your research project.

Answers to those questions may lead you to discard some of the information you find. A recurring example concerns travel and product reviews: some authors of positive reviews are connected to the companies providing the goods and services, while some authors of negative reviews are connected to competitors.

Figure 15.4	Criteria for Evaluating Websites

Authors: What person or organization sponsors the site? What credentials do the authors have?

Objectivity: Does the site give evidence to support its claims? Does it give both sides of controversial issues? Is the tone professional?

Information: How complete is the information? What is it based on?

Currency: How current is the information?

Audience: Who is the intended audience?

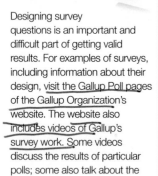

http://www
.publicagenda.org/
pages/20-questions-
journalists-should-
ask-about-poll-results

Public Agenda provides 20
     questions to ask about
     poll results when you are
     reading the findings.

http://www
.gallup.com

Designing survey
questions is an important and
difficult part of getting valid
results. For examples of surveys,
including information about their
design, visit the Gallup Poll pages
of the Gallup Organization's
website. The website also
includes videos of Gallup's
survey work. Some videos
discuss the results of particular
polls; some also talk about the
poll's audience and purpose,
important factors in a survey's
design. Watch several videos
and examine several polls for the
     ways in which audience
     and purpose shape the
     questions in the survey.

Many students start their research with Wikipedia, the largest, most popular encyclopedia ever. It has over 26 million articles in 286 languages and is the seventh most visited website in the world.[3] So, while it may be acceptable as a starting place, be aware that many instructors and other professionals do not accept Wikipedia—or any encyclopedia, frequently—as an authoritative source. These are some of their reasons:

- Many remember the beginnings of Wikipedia when it was full of errors.

- Because not all entries are written by experts on the topic, some entries still contain errors.

- Wikipedia makes the news when pranksters maliciously alter entries.

- Thanks to WikiScanner, some editors have been shown to have self-interest. For instance, Diebold deleted paragraphs criticizing its electronic voting machines, and PepsiCo deleted paragraphs on negative health effects in the Pepsi entry. All edits from IP addresses owned by the Church of Scientology have been banned by Wikipedia.[4]

- Because Wikipedia is constantly changing, information you cite may be changed or eliminated if someone goes to check it.

- One final, growing concern is that the volunteers who edit and police Wikipedia are declining at a much faster rate than new contributors are joining.[5]

Analyzing and Designing Surveys

A **survey** questions a group of people. The easiest way to ask many questions is to create a **questionnaire,** a written list of questions that people fill out. An **interview** is a structured conversation with someone who will be able to give you useful information. Organizations use surveys and interviews to research both internal issues such as employee satisfaction and external issues such as customer satisfaction.

Even professional survey organizations can have trouble with their surveys. After the 2012 U.S. presidential election, Gallup called in outside help to investigate why its polls consistently favored Mitt Romney.[6]

Another survey that has been the target of much questioning in the press is the one behind the annual college rankings of *U.S. News & World Report.* Critics charge that the rankings are based far too heavily on opinion (peer evaluations from other schools), uncorroborated data supplied by the schools themselves, and irrelevant data (such as rates of alumni giving). Critics also charge schools with gaming the system through practices such as heavy solicitation of students who have almost no chance of being accepted (low acceptance rates help schools' rankings). Critics find constant ammunition in the news with reports of financial aid to high-scoring students who don't need the money, paying accepted students to retake the SAT, and even outright falsifying SAT exam scores (high SAT scores also help rankings).[7]

Because surveys can be used to show almost anything, people need to be careful about using the results of surveys or designing their own. In many cases, if you lack information about how a survey was done, you should question the results. Figure 15.5 lists questions to ask about surveys.

1. Who Did the Survey and Who Paid for It?   Unfortunately, it is far too easy to introduce bias into surveys. Thus, a good place to start when examining survey results is with the survey producers. Who are they? How were

Figure 15.5	Questions to Ask about Surveys
	1. Who did the survey and who paid for it?
	2. How many people were surveyed and how were they chosen?
	3. How was the survey conducted?
	4. What was the response rate?
	5. What questions were asked?

[handwritten margin note: ✓ Independent 3rd party college]

they financed? How comfortable should you be with the results of a survey about a medical device when the survey was financed by the maker of the device? Was a survey about auto model satisfaction financed by the maker of the auto?

2. How Many People Were Surveyed and How Were They Chosen?   To keep research costs reasonable, usually only a sample of the total population is polled. How that sample is chosen and the attempts made to get responses from nonrespondents will determine whether you can infer that what is true of your sample is also true of the population as a whole.

A **sample** is a subset of the population. The **sampling units** are those actually sampled. Frequently, the sampling unit is an individual. If a list of individuals is not available then a household can be the sampling unit. The list of all sampling units is the **sampling frame.** For interviews, this could be a list of all addresses, or for companies a list of all Fortune 500 CEOs.[8] The **population** is the group you want to make statements about. Depending on the purpose of your research, your population might be all Fortune 1000 companies, all business students at your college, or all consumers of tea in the mid-Atlantic states.

A **convenience sample** is a group of subjects who are easy to get: students who walk through the union, people at a shopping mall, workers in your own unit. Convenience samples are useful for a rough pretest of a questionnaire and may be acceptable for some class research projects. However, you cannot generalize from a convenience sample to a larger group. If, for instance, you survey people entering your local library about their opinion of the proposed library bond (which has to be voter approved), you are taking a convenience sample, and one that will not tell you what non-library users think.

A purposive or **judgment sample** is a group of people whose views seem useful. Someone interested in surveying the kinds of writing done on campus might ask each department for the name of a faculty member who cared about writing and then send surveys to those people.

In a **random sample,** each person in the population theoretically has an equal chance of being chosen. When people say they did something *randomly* they often mean *without conscious bias.* However, unconscious bias exists. Someone passing out surveys in front of the library will be more likely to approach people who seem friendly and less likely to ask people who seem intimidating, in a hurry, much older or younger, or of a different race, class, or sex. True random samples rely on random digit tables, published in texts and online.

If you take a true random sample, you can generalize your findings to the whole population from which your sample comes. Consider, for example, a random phone survey that shows 65% of respondents approve of a presidential policy. Measures of variability should always be attached to survey-derived estimates like this one. Typically, a **confidence interval** provides this measure of variability. Using the confidence interval, we might conclude it is likely that between 58% and 72% of the population approve of the presidential policy when the margin of error is 6 to 7%. The confidence interval is based on the size of the sample and the expected variation within the population. Statistics texts tell you how to calculate measures of variability.

For many kinds of research, a large sample is important for giving significant results. In addition to its electronic data, Nielsen Media Research collects about 2 million television viewing diaries annually to gather viewing data. The large numbers also allow it to provide viewing information for local stations and advertisers.[9]

Do not, however, confuse **sample size** with randomness. A classic example is the 1936 *Literary Digest* poll that predicted Republican Alf Landon would beat Democrat incumbent President Franklin Roosevelt. *Literary Digest* sent out 10 million ballots to its magazine subscribers as well as people who owned cars and telephones, most of whom in 1936 were richer than the average voter—and more Republican.[10]

Many people mistakenly believe any survey provides information about the general population. One famous incident with a biased sample that got huge publicity involved Dear Abby, who asked her readers, "If you had it to do over, would you have children?" Thousands of *No* answers poured in, making national news broadcasts and newspaper headlines. Only later were more knowledgeable people able to explain that such questions are more attractive to people with extreme experiences and that the results were not a random survey.

3. How Was the Survey Conducted?   **Face-to-face surveys** are convenient when you are surveying a fairly small number of people in a specific location. In a face-to-face survey, however, the interviewer's sex, race, and nonverbal cues can bias results. Most people prefer not to say things they think their audience will dislike. For that reason, women will be more likely to agree that sexual harassment is a problem if the interviewer is also a woman. Members of a minority group are more likely to admit that they suffer discrimination if the interviewer is a member of the same minority.

Telephone surveys are popular because they can be closely supervised. Interviewers can read the questions from a computer screen and key in answers as the respondent gives them. The results can then be available just a few minutes after the last call is completed.

Phone surveys also have limitations. First, they reach only people who have phones and thus underrepresent some groups such as poor people. Voice mail, caller ID, and cell phones also make phone surveys more difficult. Most people do not answer or return calls from unknown sources, nor are their cell phone numbers readily available in most cases.

Since a survey based on a phone book would exclude people with unlisted numbers, professional survey-takers use automatic random-digit dialing.

To increase the response rate for a phone survey, call at a time respondents will find convenient. Avoid calling between 5 and 7 p.m., a time when many families have dinner.

Mail surveys can reach anyone who has an address. Some people may be more willing to fill out an anonymous questionnaire than to give sensitive information to a stranger over the phone. However, mail surveys are not effective for respondents who don't read and write well. Further, it may be more difficult to get a response from someone who doesn't care about the survey or who sees the mailing as junk mail. Over the phone, the interviewer can try to persuade the subject to participate.

Online surveys deliver questions over the Internet. The researcher can contact respondents with an e-mail containing a link to a web page with the survey or can ask people by mail or in person to log on and visit the website with the survey.

Another alternative is to post a survey on a website and invite the site's visitors to complete the survey. This approach does not generate a random sample, so the results probably do not reflect the opinions of the entire population. Mattel, maker of Barbie, conducted an online poll to see what young girls wanted for the doll's next career. Results of the poll surprised Mattel. Although young girls wanted Barbie to be a TV anchorwoman, the career winning the most votes was computer engineer, because various computer organizations for women asked their members to vote.[11]

In general, volunteers for online surveys are more educated, more likely to be white, and more likely to be at the ends of the age spectrum than the general population.[12]

Nevertheless, with online surveys costing about one-tenth of phone surveys, they are increasing their acceptance among experts and growing in popularity as response rates for phone surveys continue to drop. The American Customer Satisfaction Index, a phone survey conducted for years by the University of Michigan, began incorporating online polling in 2010. YouGov, which tracks opinions of corporate brands, has a panel of 1 million U.S. adults. Daily it sends enough surveys to receive back 5,000 completed ones. Although not random, the survey tries to be representative; YouGov ensures respondents reflect the overall population by factors such as age and gender.[13]

4. What Was the Response Rate? A major concern with any kind of survey is the **response rate,** the percentage of people who respond. People who refuse to answer may differ from those who respond, and you need information from both groups to be able to generalize to the whole population. Low response rates pose a major problem, especially for phone surveys. Answering machines and caller ID are commonly used to screen incoming calls resulting in decreased response rates.

Widespread use of cell phones in recent years has also negatively affected the ability of telephone surveyors to contact potential respondents. Because U.S. laws prevent autodialing of cell phones in most situations, including cell phones in a survey adds significantly to both the cost and the complexity. For survey firms that rely on recordings to conduct polls automatically, the cost of a cell phone call is 10 times more. Nevertheless, to protect their reputation, some survey firms are requiring clients to include a set percentage of cell phone calls.[14]

Relying on just landlines or cell phones will probably bias a phone survey. The National Center for Health Statistics reports that 38% of households have only cell phone service; for adults age 25–29 that number rises to 62%. Many adults having only cell phones are in the lowest household income categories; they also tend to be minorities, single, and less well educated.[15] Adults 50 and older are significantly overrepresented in landline phone surveys, where they account for 66% of the average sample.[16] These figures show that phone surveys that are landline only, as is true for most, may have significant biases built into their samples.

The problem of nonresponse has increased dramatically in recent years. The mail response rate for the *mandatory* U.S. Census was only 65%, even with the $370.6 million spent promoting response.[17] The response rate for random phone surveys is 9%; the rate for cell phone surveys is 7%.[18] Organizations such as the Pew Research Center and the American Association for Public Opinion Research are stressing the necessity for all phone surveys to include both cell phone and landline calls.[19]

To get as high a response rate as possible, good researchers follow up, contacting nonrespondents at least once and preferably twice to try to persuade them to participate in the survey. Sometimes money or other rewards are used to induce people to participate.

5. What Questions Were Asked?   Surveys and interviews can be useful only if the questions are well designed. Good questions have these characteristics:

- They ask only one thing.
- They are phrased neutrally.
- They are asked in an order that does not influence answers.
- They avoid making assumptions about the respondent.
- They mean the same thing to different people.

At a telecommunications firm, a survey asked employees to rate their manager's performance at "hiring staff and setting compensation." Although both tasks are part of the discipline of human resource management, they are different activities. A manager might do a better job of hiring than of setting pay levels, or vice versa. The survey gave respondents—and the company using the survey—no way to distinguish performance on each task.[20]

Phrase questions in a way that won't bias the response, either positively or negatively. Respondents tend to agree more than disagree with statements. If a survey about managers asks employees whether their manager is fair, ethical, intelligent, knowledgeable, and so on, they are likely to assign all of these qualities to the manager—and to agree more and more as the survey goes along. To correct for this, some questions should be worded to generate the opposite response. For example, a statement about ethics can be balanced by a statement about corruption, and a statement about fairness can be balanced by a statement about bias or stereotypes.[21]

The order in which questions are asked may matter. Asking about the economy—and its impact on families—before asking about the president will lower opinions of the president during bad economic times; the opposite is true for good economic times.[22]

Avoid questions that make assumptions about your subjects. The question "Does your spouse have a job outside the home?" assumes that your respondent is married.

Use words that mean the same thing to you and to the respondents. If a question can be interpreted in more than one way, it will be. Words like *often* and *important* mean different things to different people. When a consulting firm helped Duke Energy assess the leadership skills of its managers, an early draft of the employee survey asked employees to rate how well their manager "understands the business and the marketplace." How would employees know what is in the manager's mind? Each respondent would have to determine what is reasonable evidence of a manager's understanding. The question was rephrased to identify behavior the employees could observe: "resolves complaints from customers quickly and thoroughly." The wording is still subjective ("quickly and thoroughly"), but at least all employees will be measuring the same category of behavior.[23]

As discussed in Chapter 5, **bypassing** occurs when two people use the same words or phrases but interpret them differently. To catch questions that can be misunderstood and to reduce bypassing, avoid terms that are likely to mean different things to different people and pretest your questions with several people who are like those who will fill out the survey. Even a small pretest with 10 people can help you refine your questions.

Survey questions can be categorized in several ways. **Closed questions** have a limited number of possible responses. **Open questions** do not lock the subject into any sort of response. Figure 15.6 gives examples of closed and open questions. The second question in Figure 15.6 is an example of a Likert-type scale.

Figure 15.6	Closed and Open Questions

Closed questions

Are you satisfied with the city bus service? (yes/no)

How good is the city bus service?

Excellent 5 4 3 2 1 Terrible

Indicate whether you agree (A) or disagree (D) with each of the following statements about city bus service.

    A   D   The schedule is convenient for me.

    A   D   The routes are convenient for me.

    A   D   The drivers are courteous.

    A   D   The buses are clean.

Rate each of the following improvements in the order of their importance to you
(1 = most important and 5 = least important).

____ Buy new buses.

____ Increase non-rush-hour service on weekdays.

____ Increase service on weekdays.

____ Provide earlier and later service on weekdays.

____ Buy more buses with wheelchair access.

____ Provide unlimited free transfers.

Open questions

How do you feel about the city bus service?

Tell me about the city bus service.

Why do you ride the bus? (or, Why don't you ride the bus?)

What do you like and dislike about the city bus service?

How could the city bus service be improved?

Closed questions are faster for subjects to answer and easier for researchers to score. However, since all answers must fit into pre-chosen categories, they cannot probe the complexities of a subject. You can improve the quality of closed questions by conducting a pretest with open questions to find categories that matter to respondents. Analyzing the responses from open questions is usually less straightforward than analyzing responses from closed questions.

Use closed multiple-choice questions for potentially embarrassing topics. Seeing their own situation listed as one response can help respondents feel that it is acceptable. However, very sensitive issues are perhaps better asked in an interview, where the interviewer can build trust and reveal information about himself or herself to encourage the interviewee to answer.

Use an "Other, Please Specify" category when you want the convenience of a closed question but cannot foresee all the possible responses. These responses can be used to improve choices if the survey is to be repeated.

What is the single most important reason that you ride the bus?

____ I don't have a car.

____ I don't want to fight rush-hour traffic.

____ Riding the bus is cheaper than driving my car.

____ Riding the bus conserves fuel and reduces pollution.

____ Other (please specify): ____

When you use multiple-choice questions, make the answer categories mutually exclusive and exhaustive. This means you make sure that any one answer fits in only one category and that a category is included for all possible answers. In the following example of overlapping categories, a person who worked for a company with exactly 25 employees could check either *a* or *b*. The resulting data would be hard to interpret.

Overlapping categories: Indicate the number of full-time employees in your company on May 16:

    ____ a. 0–25
    ____ b. 25–100
    ____ c. 100–500
    ____ d. over 500

Discrete categories: Indicate the number of full-time employees on your payroll on May 16:

    ____ a. 0–25
    ____ b. 26–100
    ____ c. 101–500
    ____ d. more than 500

Branching questions direct different respondents to different parts of the questionnaire based on their answers to earlier questions.

> 10. Have you talked to an academic adviser this year?   yes   no
>   (If "no," skip to question 14.)

Generally, put early in the questionnaire questions that will be easy to answer. Put questions that are harder to answer or that people may be less willing to answer (e.g., age and income) near the end of the questionnaire. Even if people choose not to answer such questions, you'll still have the rest of the survey filled out.

If subjects will fill out the questionnaire themselves, pay careful attention to the physical design of the document. Use indentations and white space effectively; make it easy to mark and score the answers. Label answer scales frequently so respondents remember which end is positive and which is negative. Include a brief statement of purpose if you (or someone else) will not be available to explain the questionnaire or answer questions. Pretest the questionnaire to make sure the directions are clear. One researcher mailed a two-page questionnaire without pretesting it. One-third of the respondents didn't realize there were questions to answer on the back of the first page.

See Figure 15.7 for an example of a questionnaire for a student report.

Conducting Research Interviews

Schedule interviews in advance; tell the interviewee about how long you expect the interview to take. A survey of technical writers (who get much of their information from interviews) found that the best days to interview subject matter experts are Tuesdays, Wednesdays, and Thursday mornings.[24] People are frequently swamped on Mondays and looking forward to the weekend, or trying to finish their week's work on Fridays.

Interviews can be structured or unstructured. In a **structured interview,** the interviewer uses a detailed list of questions to guide the interview. Indeed, a structured interview may use a questionnaire just as a survey does.

In an **unstructured interview,** the interviewer has three or four main questions. Other questions build on what the interviewee says. To prepare for an

Figure 15.7 | Questionnaire for a Student Report Using Survey Research

An interesting title can help.

In your introductory ¶,
①tell how to return the survey
②tell how the information will be used

Survey: Why Do Students Attend Athletic Events?

The purpose of this survey is to determine why students attend sports events, and what might increase attendance. All information is to be used solely for a student research paper. Please return completed surveys to Elizabeth or Vicki at the Union help desk. Thank you for your assistance!

Start with easy–to–answer questions

1. Gender (Please circle one) ,   M   F

2. What is your class year? (Please circle)   1   2   3   4   Grad   Other

Seeing a response in a survey can make respondents more willing to admit to feelings they may be embarrassed to volunteer.

3. How do you feel about women's sports? (Please circle)

The words below each number anchor responses, while still allowing you to average the data.

1	2	3	4	5
I enjoy watching women's sports		I'll watch, but it doesn't really matter		Women's sports are boring/ I'd rather watch men's sports

4. Do you like to attend MSU men's basketball games? (Please circle)
   Y   N

5. How often do you attend MSU women's basketball games? (Please circle)

1	2	3	4	5
All/most games	Few games a season	Once a season	Less than once a year	Never

6. If you do not attend all of the women's basketball games, why not? (Please check all that apply. If you attend all the games, skip to #7.)

__I've never thought to go.
__I don't like basketball.
__I don't like sporting events.
__The team isn't good enough.
__My friends are not interested in going.
__I want to go, I just haven't had the opportunity.
__The tickets cost too much ($10).
__Other (please specify) _____

Think about factors that affect the problem you're studying, and write survey questions to get information about them.

7. To what extent would each of the following make you more likely to attend an MSU women's basketball game? (please rank all)

1	2	3
Much more likely to attend	Possibley more likely	No effect

__Increased awareness on campus (fliers, chalking on the Oval, more articles in the *Gazette*)
__Marketing to students (give-aways, days for residence halls or fraternities/sororities)
__Student loyalty program (awarding points towards free tickets, clothing, food for attending games)
__Education (pocket guide explaining the rules of the game provided at the gate)
__Other (please specify) _____

Thank you!
Please return this survey to Elizabeth or Vicki at the Union help desk.

Repeat where to turn in or mail completed surveys.

unstructured interview, learn as much as possible about the interviewee and the topic. Go into the interview with three or four main topics you want to cover.

Interviewers sometimes use closed questions to start the interview and set the interviewee at ease. The strength of an interview, however, is getting at a person's attitudes, feelings, and experiences. **Situational questions** let you probe what someone does in a specific circumstance. **Hypothetical questions** that ask people to imagine what they would do generally yield less reliable answers than questions about **critical incidents** or key past events.

Situational question:	How do you tell an employee that his or her performance is unsatisfactory?
Hypothetical question:	What would you say if you had to tell an employee that his or her performance was unsatisfactory?
Critical incident question:	You've probably been in a situation where someone who was working with you wasn't carrying his or her share of the work. What did you do the last time that happened?

A **mirror question** paraphrases the content of the last answer: "So you confronted him directly?" "You think that this product costs too much?" Mirror questions are used both to check that the interviewer understands what the interviewee has said and to prompt the interviewee to continue talking.

Probes follow up an original question to get at specific aspects of a topic:

Question:	What do you think about the fees for campus parking?
Probes:	Would you be willing to pay more for a reserved space? How much more? Should the fines for vehicles parked illegally be increased? Do you think fees should be based on income?

Probes are not used in any definite order. Instead, they are used to keep the interviewee talking, to get at aspects of a subject that the interviewee has not yet mentioned, and to probe more deeply into points that the interviewee brings up.

If you read questions to subjects in a structured interview, use fewer options than you might in a written questionnaire.

> I'm going to read a list of factors that someone might look for in choosing a restaurant. After I read each factor, please tell me whether that factor is Very Important to you, Somewhat Important to you, or Not Important to you.

If the interviewee hesitates, reread the scale.

Always record the interview. Test your equipment ahead of time to make sure it works. If you think your interviewee may be reluctant to be recorded, offer to give a copy of the recording to the interviewee.

Well-done interviews can yield surprising results. When the owners of Kiwi shoe polish interviewed people about what they wanted in shoe care products, they learned that shiny shoes were far down on the list. What people cared most about was how fresh and comfortable their shoes were on the inside. So Kiwi developed a new line of products, including Fresh'ins (thin, lightly scented shoe inserts) and Smiling Feet (cushioning and nonslip pads and strips).[25]

Using Focus Groups

A **focus group,** yet another form of qualitative research, is a small group of people convened to provide a more detailed look into some area of interest—a product, service, process, concept, and so on. Because the group setting allows members to build on each other's comments, carefully chosen focus groups can provide detailed feedback; they can illuminate underlying attitudes and emotions relevant to particular behaviors.

Focus groups also have some problems. The first is the increasing use of professional respondents drawn from databases, a practice usually driven by cost and time limitations. The *Association for Qualitative Research Newsletter* labeled these respondents as a leading industry problem.[26] To get findings that are consistent among focus groups, the groups must accurately represent the target population. A second problem with focus groups is that such groups sometimes aim to please rather than offering their own evaluations.

Using Online Networks

An updated version of the focus group is the online network. Del Monte, for instance, has an online community, called "I Love My Dog," of 400 handpicked dog enthusiasts that it can query about dog products. These networks, first cultivated as research tools by technology and video game companies, are being employed by various producers of consumer products and services, including small companies. The networks are often cheaper and more effective than traditional focus groups because they have broader participation and allow for deeper and ongoing probing. Companies can use them for polls, real-time chats with actual consumers, and product trials.[27]

Some of the better online panels include experts as well as users. One small-scale automaker has design engineers and transportation experts on its panel. Although larger than focus groups, these panels carry some of the same drawbacks. They are not necessarily representative, either of current or future customers. Studies have also shown that they tend to discourage innovation.[28] On the other hand, they tend to give responses that members see as positive for the sponsor. Procter & Gamble repeatedly got go-aheads for product development from its online panels, only to see the new products fail field tests.[29]

A still larger online community comes from Twitter and online blogs. These communities are the least controllable of feedback groups, but are becoming more important all the time. Many companies are hiring employees or technology services to monitor comments on social networks and respond quickly. They also use data from Twitter and Facebook to track trends and preferences.

Observing Customers and Users

Answers to surveys and interviews may differ from actual behavior—sometimes greatly. To get more accurate consumer information, many marketers observe users. Before designing new ketchup packets, Heinz watched fast-food customers in their vehicles wrestle with traditional packets. The new packets allow users to dip or squeeze.[30] Intuit, a leader in observation studies, sends employees to visit customers and watch how they use Intuit products such as QuickBooks. Watching small businesses struggle with QuickBooks Pro told the company of the need for a new product, QuickBooks Simple Start.[31]

Observation can also be used for gathering in-house information such as how efficiently production systems operate and how well employees serve customers. Some businesses use "mystery shoppers." For instance, McDonald's has used mystery shoppers to check cleanliness, customer service, and food

Looking with the Customers' Eyes

IDEO, an internationally famous design firm, uses observational research to design work processes that improve the customer's experience.

IDEO requires its clients to participate in the research so that they can see how it feels to be one of their own customers. Clients may try using the company's product or go on shopping trips, or they may quietly observe customers.

Following an initial observation phase, IDEO works with clients to use the observation data for brainstorming. IDEO then prepares and tests prototypes of the redesigned service, refines the ideas, and puts the revisions into action.

IDEO helped Kaiser Permanente revise its long-term growth plan to be more focused on clients' experiences with the health system. IDEO employees had Kaiser nurses, doctors, and managers observe patients and role-play patient experiences. Based on these observations, Kaiser realized that it needed to focus more on improving patient experiences than on the original plan of modernizing buildings. The company created more comfortable areas in which patients could wait with family and friends, as well as examination rooms large enough to accommodate two people in addition to the patient.

Expanding its collaborative nature, IDEO has created OpenIDEO, a social platform where over 45,000 people from more than 170 countries use the IDEO process to help solve social problems.

Adapted from Bruce Nussbaum, "The Power of Design," *Business-Week*, May 17, 2004, 86; and Nathan Waterhouse, "Nine Ways Business Can Improve Health in the Workplace and Beyond," *Guardian*, March 15, 2013, http://www.guardian.co.uk/sustainable-business/improving-health-workplace-society-nine-ways.

Procter & Gamble, maker of a variety of household products, researches shopping patterns for both in-store and online customers.

quality. The company posts store-by-store results online, giving store operators an incentive and the information they need to improve quality on measures where they are slipping or lagging behind the region's performance.[32]

Even health care facilities use mystery "shoppers." After they give their reports, the most common changes are improved estimates of waiting times and better explanations of medical procedures. So many organizations use mystery shoppers that there is a Mystery Shopping Providers Association.

Observation is often combined with other techniques to get the most information. **Think-aloud protocols** ask users to voice their thoughts as they use a document or product: "First I'll try. . . ." These protocols are recorded and later analyzed to understand how users approach a document or product. **Interruption interviews** interrupt users to ask them what's happening. For example, a company testing a draft of computer instructions might interrupt a user to ask, "What are you trying to do now? Tell me why you did that." **Discourse-based interviews** ask questions based on documents that the interviewee has written: "You said that the process is too complicated. Tell me what you mean by that."

Using Technology for Research

Technology has been routinely used in research. We do our Google searches, read web pages, and consult our online networks. But technology is playing an ever-increasing role in business research. Frequently it provides better and cheaper data than older research methods. For example, one problem with asking consumers about their television-watching behavior is that they sometimes underreport the number of hours they watch and the degree to which they watch programs they aren't proud of liking.

Researchers have tried to develop a variety of measurement methods that collect viewing data automatically. Arbitron introduced the Portable People Meter (PPM), which receives an inaudible electronic signal from radio stations and broadcast and cable TV stations. Consumers simply carry the PPM, and it records their media exposure. One of the first results showed that consumers listened to radio more than they had indicated in diaries.[33]

Nielsen Media Research added commercial viewings to its famous TV show numbers; advertisers are naturally eager to know how many people actually watch commercials instead of leaving to get a snack or fast-forwarding through them on digital video recorders.[34] Nielsen also started tracking college students' viewing, installing its people meters in commons areas such as dorms. The new data boosted ratings for some shows, such as *Grey's Anatomy* and *America's Next Top Model*, by more than 35%.[35]

Within the past few years, social media are also playing a larger role in research. Businesses are using cell phone feedback to get more immediate, realistic information about products and marketing. Medical researchers use websites such as PatientsLikeMe, where patients post personal medical information so it can be used for research. Biotechnology firm 23andMe is using social media to collect tens of thousands of DNA samples to use in Parkinson's disease research.[36]

Twitter is also beginning to play a larger role in research:

- Businesses use Twitter to track opinions about products, marketing, and employee morale.

- Researchers can use Twitter data to track outbreaks of flu or food poisoning; in fact, Twitter is usually faster than information from the Centers for Disease Control and Prevention.

- The U.S. Geological Survey is experimenting with Twitter as an earthquake tracking method that is faster and cheaper than its seismometers.

- Hedge funds and investment firms are using Twitter data in their investment formulas.

Twitter information is not cheap. Twitter is becoming protective of its data and is charging companies a base rate of up to $360,000 annually.[37]

One major limitation of Twitter data mining is that Twitter users are not a representative sample, let alone a random sample, of the population. They tend to be younger, more educated, more urban, more affluent, and less likely to have children than nonusers. Another significant limitation is that thanks to language complexity, it is not always obvious, even to human researchers let alone data-mining programs, what opinion is being expressed in a tweet.[38]

One notable outcome of all this data collection is that the job of data scientist—composed of a combination of mathematician, statistician, computer scientist, and business guru—is predicted to be one of the hottest jobs of the decade.[39]

Data Scientist

Source Citation and Documentation LO 15-4

In effective proposals and reports, sources are cited and documented smoothly and unobtrusively. **Citation** means attributing an idea or fact to its source in the body of the text: "According to the 2010 Census. . . ," "Jane Bryant Quinn

Researching Emotional Purchasing

Research told Campbell Soup that people did not have logical reasons for their soup-eating habits. Furthermore, even when surveys showed ads were successful and memorable, that reaction didn't translate to additional sales. Words were not capturing people's unconscious soup responses.

To improve the results, Campbell's turned to a new method, "neuromarketing," using advanced biometrics such as eye tracking and measurements of changes in pupil diameter, heart rate, skin moisture, and body temperature to learn how customers feel about product packaging.

Campbell's revised its packaging based on the research, putting greater emphasis on the image of the soup and adding steam to the photograph to make it appear warm and comforting. It also removed or changed elements that did not get an emotional response.

Biometrics may be the marketing research of the future, testing not only what customers say, but also what they truly feel.

Adapted from Ilan Brat, "The Emotional Quotient of Soup Shopping," *Wall Street Journal*, February 17, 2010, B6.

The Cost of Plagiarism

Copying from other articles or online sources may seem like a small thing, but it is dishonest and can cost you much more than a poor grade on a school paper.

In 2012, Hungary's president, Pat Schmitt, resigned from his post after being accused of plagiarism in his doctoral thesis. Semmelweis University revoked his degree after investigators found large chunks of material copied from sources.

In another high-stakes case, Karl-Theodor zu Guttenberg, a German politician, was forced to resign in 2011 after revelations that he plagiarized large sections of his doctoral thesis. As Germany's defense minister, zu Guttenberg was one of the country's most powerful and popular politicians and seemed to be on track to become chancellor someday.

In a more recent German scandal, at the end of 2012, Education Minister Annette Schavan was also accused of plagiarizing portions of her doctoral dissertation. After the University of Dusseldorf investigated the claims, it withdrew her degree in early 2013.

Schmitt's, zu Guttenberg's, and Schavan's downfalls can serve as a warning to business communicators. Plagiarism is not only dishonest, it is costly. And, with Internet research tools, plagiarism is becoming much easier to detect.

Adapted from Gordon Fairclough, "Hungary President Quits in Scandal," *Wall Street Journal*, April 3, 2012, A10; and Soraya Sarhaddi Nelson, "A Wave of Plagiarism Cases Strikes German Politics," *NPR.org*, November 24, 2012, http://www.npr.org/2012/11/24/165790164/a-wave-of-plagiarism-cases-strikes-german-politics

argues that. . . ." In-text citations provide, in parentheses in the text, the source where the reference was found. Citing sources demonstrates your honesty and enhances your credibility.

Documentation means providing the bibliographic information readers would need to go back to the original source. The two usual means of documentation are notes and lists of references.

Failure to cite and document sources is **plagiarism,** the passing off of the words or ideas of others as one's own. Plagiarism can lead to nasty consequences. The news regularly showcases examples of people who have been fired or sued for plagiarism. For example, Fareed Zakaria, a foreign policy commentator, was suspended from both *Time* magazine and his CNN show after he was accused of copying a paragraph from a *New Yorker* article on gun control.[40] In another case, Jonah Lehrer, best-selling author of *Imagine: How Creativity Works,* was disgraced and had his book recalled after he fabricated quotations and combined previous quotations from Bob Dylan in his writing.[41]

Now that curious people can type sentences into Google and find the sources, plagiarism is easier than ever to catch. Plagiarism is both unethical and illegal.

Another unethical practice that may occur when using sources is taking material out of context in such a way that the meaning of the material used is counter to the meaning of the material within its full context. An example of this practice discussed in national news occurred when Shirley Sherrod, the Agriculture Department's director of rural development in Georgia, was asked to resign because of a comment that became racist when taken out of context. (See "A Costly Comment out of Context" sidebar on the next page.)

Incorporating Quotations

If you quote someone in your writing, you will need to use citation and documentation in addition to quotation marks. If you use the source's exact words, you'll use the name of the person you're citing in the body of the proposal or report; you'll put quotation marks around the quote; and you'll indicate the source in parentheses and a list of references, or in an endnote. If you put the source's idea into your own words (**paraphrasing**), or if you condense or synthesize information, you don't need quotation marks, but you still need to tell whose idea it is and where you found it. See Appendix C for examples of quoting and paraphrasing using both APA and MLA formats.

Long quotations (four typed lines or more) are used sparingly in business proposals or reports. Since many readers skip quotes, always summarize the main point of the quotation in a single sentence before the quotation itself. End the sentence with a colon, not a period, since it introduces the quote. Indent long quotations on the left to set them off from your text. Indented quotations do not need quotation marks; the indentation shows the reader that the passage is a quote.

To make a quotation fit the grammar of your writing, you may need to change one or two words. Sometimes you may want to add a few words to explain something in the longer original. In both cases, use square brackets to indicate words that are your replacements or additions. Omit any words in the original source that are not essential for your purposes. Use ellipses (spaced dots) to indicate your omissions.

Document every fact and idea that you take from a source except facts that are common knowledge. Historical dates and facts are considered common knowledge. Generalizations are considered common knowledge ("More and more women are entering the workforce") even though specific statements about the same topic (such as the percentage of women in the workforce in 1975 and in 2000) would require documentation.

Using Common Formats

The three most widely used formats for footnotes, endnotes, and bibliographies in reports are those of the American Psychological Association (APA), the Modern Language Association (MLA), and the University of Chicago *Manual of Style* format, which this book uses. Some technical materials use IEEE or CBE formats.

Internal documentation provides in parentheses in the text the source where the reference was found. (See Appendix C for a complete explanation and example.)

For a portion of a report in APA and MLA formats, see Appendix C. Appendix C also outlines the APA and MLA formats for the sources most often used in proposals and reports.

If you use a printed source that is not readily available, consider including it as an appendix in your report. For example, you could copy an ad or include an organization's promotional brochure.

A Costly Comment out of Context

Shirley Sherrod was the Agriculture Department's director of rural development in Georgia. Then conservative activist Andrew Breitbart posted video excerpts of her speech at an NAACP event. The excerpts seemed to say that she did not give the white farmer who came to her for bankruptcy help the same help she would give to black farmers, in other words, racial discrimination. Fox News and CBS reported on the excerpts the same day they were posted, and Sherrod was asked to resign by government officials, which she did.

In the full video, posted later on other websites, it became clear that the white farmer was an example of a time when she could have discriminated but didn't; he was the person who taught her that white people didn't always have advantages. In fact, the farmer in question told CNN that he and Sherrod were still friends, 20 years later.

Adapted from Marcus K. Garner and Christian Boone, "USDA Reconsiders Firing of Ga. Official over Speech on Race," *Atlanta Journal Constitution*, July 21, 2010, http://www.ajc .com/news/usda-recon siders-firing-of-574027.html.

Summary by Learning Objectives

LO 15-1   Recognize varieties of reports.

- Information reports collect data for the reader.
- Analytical reports present and interpret data.
- Recommendation reports recommend action or a solution.

LO 15-2   Define report problems.

- A good report problem in business meets the following criteria:
  - The problem is real, important enough to be worth solving, and narrow but challenging.
  - The audience for the report is real and able to implement the recommended action.

- The data, evidence, and facts are sufficient to document the severity of the problem, sufficient to prove that the recommendation will solve the problem, available to *you*, and comprehensible to *you*.

- A good purpose statement must make three things clear:
  - The organizational problem or conflict.
  - The specific technical questions that must be answered to solve the problem.
  - The rhetorical purpose (to explain, to recommend, to request, to propose) that the report is designed to achieve.

LO 15-3 **Employ various research strategies.**

- Use indexes and directories to find information about a specific company or topic.

- To decide whether to use a website as a source in a research project, evaluate the site's authors, objectivity, information, audience, and revision date.

- A survey questions a large group of people, called respondents or subjects. A questionnaire is a written list of questions that people fill out. An interview is a structured conversation with someone who will be able to give you useful information.

- Because surveys can be used to show almost anything, people need to be careful when analyzing the results of surveys or designing their own. These are questions commonly asked about surveys:
  - Who did the survey and who paid for it?
  - How many people were surveyed and how were they chosen?
  - How was the survey conducted?

- What was the response rate?
- What questions were asked?

- Good questions ask just one thing, are phrased neutrally, avoid making assumptions about the respondent, and mean the same thing to different people.

- A convenience sample is a group of subjects who are easy to get. A judgment sample is a group of people whose views seem useful. In a random sample, each object in the population theoretically has an equal chance of being chosen. A sample is random only if a formal, approved random sampling method is used. Otherwise, unconscious bias can exist.

- Qualitative research may also use interviews, focus groups, online networks, and technology.

LO 15-4 **Use and document sources.**

- Citation means attributing an idea or fact to its source in the body of the report.

- Documentation means providing the bibliographic information readers would need to go back to the original source.

Continuing Case

The All-Weather Case, set in an HR department in a manufacturing company, extends through all 19 chapters and is available at www.mhhe.com/locker11e. The portion for this chapter asks students to revise a questionnaire about the cross-cultural training program.

Exercises and Cases

*Go to www.mhhe.com/locker 11e for additional Exercises and Cases.

15.1   Reviewing the Chapter

1. What are three different varieties of reports? (LO 15-1)
2. What are some criteria for defining report problems? (LO 15-2)
3. What are four criteria for evaluating web sources? (LO 15-3)
4. What questions should you use to analyze a survey? (LO 15-3)
5. What are some criteria for good survey questions? (LO 15-3)
6. What is a random sample? (LO 15-3)
7. What are some disadvantages of focus groups and online networks? (LO 15-3)
8. What is the different between citation and documentation? (LO 15-4)

15.2   Reviewing Grammar

Reports use lots of numbers. Test your knowledge about writing numbers by doing Exercise B.10 in Appendix B.

15.3 Defining and Evaluating Report Problems

In small teams, turn the following categories into specific report problems you could research for a business communication course. Write three possible report problems for each category.

1. Social media sites
2. Global warming or climate change
3. Globalization
4. Marketing to younger audiences
5. Career planning
6. Technology/cell phone use
7. Credit card debt
8. Campus-based organizations
9. Tuition
10. Housing/parking on campus

Once you have defined three possible problems for each category, evaluate the problems using the following questions:

- Which problem(s) could you address satisfactorily in the time allotted for your course project?

- Which problem(s) are real?
- Which problem(s) are important enough to be worth researching?
- Are the problem(s) narrow enough?
- Who will be able to implement recommended action from your research?
- For which problem(s) could you find adequate resources to create sound solutions?

As your instructor directs,

a. Write an e-mail to your instructor that shares your evaluation of the problems.

b. Pick two of the categories and present to the class your evaluation of the problems in an oral presentation.

c. Write a preliminary purpose statement for each of the three problems you have identified for a category.

15.4 Identifying the Weaknesses in Problem Statements

Identify the weaknesses in the following problem statements:

- Is the problem narrow enough?
- Can a solution be found in a semester or quarter?
- What organization could implement any recommendations to solve the problem?
- Could the topic be limited or refocused to yield an acceptable problem statement?

1. I want to explore how many Twitter users subscribe to repeat news organizations' Twitter feeds.
2. How can smartphone apps influence driving habits?
3. One possible report topic I would like to investigate would be the differences in women's intercollegiate sports in our athletic conference.

4. How to market products effectively to college students.
5. Should web banners be part of a company's advertising?
6. How can U.S. and Canadian students get jobs in Europe?
7. We want to explore ways our company can help raise funds for the Open Shelter. We will investigate whether collecting and recycling glass, aluminum, and paper products will raise enough money to help.
8. How can XYZ University better serve students from traditionally underrepresented groups?
9. What are the best investments for the next year?

15.5 Writing a Preliminary Purpose Statement

Answer the following questions about a topic on which you could write a formal report.

As your instructor directs,

a. Be prepared to answer the questions orally in a conference.

b. Bring written answers to a conference.

c. Submit written answers in class.

d. Give your instructor a photocopy of your statement after it is approved.

1. What problem will you investigate or solve?
   a. What is the name of the organization facing the problem?

b. What is the technical problem or difficulty?

c. Why is it important to the organization that this problem be solved?

d. What solution or action might you recommend to solve the problem?

e. Who (name and title) is the person in the organization who would have the power to accept or reject your recommendation?

2. Will this report use information from other classes or from work experiences? If so, give the name and topic of the class and/or briefly describe the job. If you will need additional information (that you have

not already gotten from other classes or from a job), how do you expect to find it?

3. List the name, title, and business phone number of a professor who can testify to your ability to handle the expertise needed for this report.

4. List the name, title, and business phone number of someone in the organization who can testify that you have access to enough information about that organization to write this report.

15.6   Choosing Research Strategies

For each of the following reports, indicate the kinds of research that might be useful. If a survey is called for, indicate the most efficient kind of sample to use.

1. How can Twitter and Facebook users on campus be more connected to school events?
2. Is it feasible to send all XYZ organization's communication through e-mail?
3. How can XYZ store increase sales?
4. What is it like to live and work in [name of country]?
5. Should our organization have a dress code?
6. Is it feasible to start a monthly newsletter for students in your major?
7. How can we best market to mature adults?
8. Can compensation programs increase productivity?
9. What skills are in demand in our area? Of these, which could the local community college offer courses in?

15.7   Comparing Search Results

Do a Google search on these three terms:

- Global warming
- Immigration
- Gun control

Print off the first 10 sources Google gives you for each. In small groups, compare your listings. How do they differ? Pick one of the three topics and present the differences you found to your classmates.

15.8   Evaluating Websites

Choose five websites that are possible resources for a report. Evaluate them on the credibility and trustworthiness of their information. Consider the following questions and compare and contrast your findings.

- What person or organization sponsors the site? What credentials do the authors have?
- Does the site give evidence to support its claims? Does it give both sides of controversial issues?
- Is the tone professional?
- How complete is the information? What is it based on?

- How current is the information?

Based on your findings, which sites are best for your report and why?

As your instructor directs,

a. Write an e-mail to your instructor summarizing your results.
b. Share your results with a small group of students.
c. Present your results to the class in an oral presentation.

15.9   Choosing Samples for Surveys and Interviews

For the following topics, indicate the types of sample(s) you would use in collecting survey data and in conducting interviews.

1. How can your school improve the usability of its website?
2. How can your school use social media to increase communication with students?
3. How can your school save money to limit tuition increases?
4. How can your favorite school organization attract more student members?
5. How can your school improve communication with international students?
6. How should your school deal with hate speech?
7. How can instructors at your school improve their electronic presentations for students?

15.10 Evaluating Survey Questions

Evaluate each of the following questions. Are they acceptable as they stand? If not, how can they be improved?

a. Survey of clerical workers:
   Do you work for the government? ☐
   or the private sector? ☐

b. Questionnaire on grocery purchases:
   1. Do you *usually* shop at the same grocery store?
      a. Yes
      b. No
   2. Do you use credit cards to purchase items at your grocery store?
      a. Yes
      b. No
   3. How much is your average grocery bill?
      a. Under $25
      b. $25–50
      c. $50–100
      d. $100–150
      e. Over $150

c. Survey on technology:

   1. Would you generally welcome any technological advancement that allowed information to be sent and received more quickly and in greater quantities than ever before?
   2. Do you think that all people should have free access to all information, or do you think that information should somehow be regulated and monitored?

d. Survey on job skills:

   How important are the following skills for getting and keeping a professional-level job in U.S. business and industry today?

	Low				High
Ability to communicate	1	2	3	4	5
Leadership ability	1	2	3	4	5
Public presentation skills	1	2	3	4	5
Selling ability	1	2	3	4	5
Teamwork capability	1	2	3	4	5
Writing ability	1	2	3	4	5

15.11 Designing Questions for an Interview or Survey

Submit either a one- to three-page questionnaire or questions for a 20- to 30-minute interview AND the information listed below for the method you choose.

Questionnaire
1. Purpose(s), goal(s).
2. Subjects (who, why, how many).
3. How and where to be distributed.
4. Any changes in type size, paper color, etc., from submitted copy.
5. Rationale for order of questions, kinds of questions, wording of questions.
6. References, if building on questionnaires by other authors.

Interview
1. Purpose(s), goal(s).
2. Subjects (who, and why).
3. Proposed site, length of interview.
4. Rationale for order of questions, kinds of questions, wording of questions, choice of branching or follow-up questions.
5. References, if building on questions devised by others.

As your instructor directs,

a. Create questions for a survey on one of the following topics:
   - Survey students on your campus about their knowledge of and interest in the programs and activities sponsored by a student organization.
   - Survey workers at a company about what they like and dislike about their jobs.
   - Survey people in your community about their willingness to pay more to buy products using recycled materials and to buy products that are packaged with a minimum of waste.
   - Survey two groups on a topic that interests you.

b. Create questions for an interview on one of the following topics:
   - Interview an international student about the forms of greetings and farewells, topics of small talk, forms of politeness, festivals and holidays, meals at home, size of families, and roles of family members in his or her country.
   - Interview a TV producer about what styles and colors work best for people appearing on TV.
   - Interview a worker about an ethical dilemma he or she faced on the job, what the worker did and why, and how the company responded.
   - Interview the owner of a small business about problems the business has, what strategies the owner has already used to increase sales and profits and how successful these strategies were, and the owner's attitudes toward possible changes in product line, decor, marketing, hiring, advertising, and money management.
   - Interview someone who has information you need for a report you're writing.

15.12 Comparing Online Survey Sites

Visit these online survey websites and analyze their features. What kinds of services do they offer? How useful are they? What are their limitations?

http://www.surveymonkey.com
http://www.polldaddy.com
http://web-online-surveys.com

http://www.surveygizmo.com
http://www.survs.com
http://freeonlinesurveys.com

Discuss your findings in small groups.

15.13 Comparing an Online Survey with a Face-to-Face Survey

Surveymonkey.com is an online survey website whose basic features are available free for those who sign up. Design a small survey using the website for a course project or something else. Administer the survey. The website compiles and analyzes the results for you.

Now, distribute the same survey in the form of a questionnaire to the same number of people, but choose new respondents.

Compare the results of the online survey with those of the survey that respondents filled out manually. What similarities and differences do you find in the two results? What might account for these similarities and differences? Do this exercise individually or in a group. Share the results with the class.

15.14 Reviewing a Scholarly Survey

In professional journals in your discipline, find an article based on a survey. Analyze the survey according to the criteria in this chapter.

As your instructor directs,

a. Share your results orally with a small group of students.

b. Present your results to the class.

c. Write an e-mail to your instructor explaining your findings.

15.15 Reviewing Corporate Reports

As companies become increasingly socially and environmentally conscious, they document their social and environmental contributions in reports such as corporate citizenship reports, corporate responsibility reports, corporate sustainability reports, sustainability progress reports, and so on. These reports are available on the companies' websites, often on pages that contain company information.

Go to www.fortune.com, which creates lists of the top 500 and 100 companies as well as the most admired

companies. Select a company related to your major and future career field. Visit its website and access one of the reports mentioned above or a report similar to the ones mentioned above. Study the nature and structure of the report; find out whether it informs, analyzes, recommends, or does all three. What kinds of evidence does it use? How well supported are the conclusions? Share your findings in small groups.

15.16 Citing Sources

As your instructor directs,

a. Revise the following list of sources using MLA format.

b. Revise the following list of sources using APA format. For help, see Appendix C.

1. Shirley S. Wang

    Wall Street Journal

    Doubling Up on Research Using a Database of Twins

    November 6, 2012

    D1

2. Michelle Leder and Michael J. de la Merced

    The New York Times

    Businesses Take a Cautious Approach to Disclosures Using Social Media

    http://dealbook.nytimes.com/2013/04/25/businesses-take-a-wary-approach-to-disclosures-using-social-media/

    April 25, 2013

    Accessed May 28, 2013

3. Dorie Clark

   Reinventing Your Personal Brand

   Harvard Business Review

   Volume 89, Issue No. 3

   March 2011

   78-81

4. Jakob Nielsen

   Nielsen Norman Group: Jakob Nielsen's Alertbox

   Seniors as Web Users

   http://www.nngroup.com/articles/
   usability-for-senior-citizens/

   May 28, 2013

   Accessed March 29, 2013

5. Rebecca Hagen and Kim Golombisky

   White Space is Not Your Enemy: A Beginners Guide to Communicating Visually Through Graphic, Web, and Multimedia Design

   2nd edition

   2013

   Focal Press

   New York

15.17 Writing a Report Based on a Survey

As your instructor directs,

a. Survey 40 to 50 people on some subject of your choice.

b. Team up with your classmates to conduct a survey and write it up as a group. Survey 50 to 80 people if your group has two members, 75 to 120 people if it has three members, 100 to 150 people if it has four members, and 125 to 200 people if it has five members.

c. Keep a journal during your group meetings and submit it to your instructor.

d. Write an e-mail to your instructor describing and evaluating your group's process for designing, conducting, and writing up the survey.

For this assignment, you do *not* have to take a random sample. Do, however, survey at least two different groups so that you can see if they differ in some way. Possible groups are men and women, business majors and English majors, Greeks and independents, first-year students and seniors, students and townspeople.

As you conduct your survey, make careful notes about what you do so that you can use this information when you write up your survey. If you work with a group, record who does what.

In an e-mail, write up your survey. Your subject line should be clear and reasonably complete. Omit unnecessary words such as "Survey of." Your first paragraph serves as an introduction, but it needs no heading. The rest of the body of your e-mail will be divided into four sections with the following headings: Purpose, Procedure, Results, and Discussion.

In your first paragraph, briefly summarize (not necessarily in this order) who conducted the experiment or survey, when it was conducted, where it was conducted, who the subjects were, what your purpose was, and what you found out. You will discuss all of these topics in more detail in the body of your e-mail.

In your Purpose section, explain why you conducted the survey. What were you trying to learn? What hypothesis were you testing? Why did this subject seem interesting or important?

In your Procedure section, describe in detail *exactly* what you did. "The first 50 people who came through the Union on Wed., Feb. 2" is not the same as "The first 50 people who came through the south entrance of the Union on Wed., Feb. 2, after 8 am, and agreed to answer my questions." Explain any steps you took to overcome possible sources of bias.

In your Results section, first tell whether your results supported your hypothesis. Use both visuals and words to explain what your numbers show. (See Chapter 16 on how to design visuals.) Process your raw data in a way that will be useful to your reader.

In your Discussion section, evaluate your survey and discuss the implications of your results. Consider these questions:

1. What are the limitations of your survey and your results?

2. Do you think a scientifically valid survey would have produced the same results? Why or why not?

3. Were there any sources of bias either in the way the questions were phrased or in the way the subjects were chosen? If you were running the survey again, what changes would you make to eliminate or reduce these sources of bias?

4. Do you think your subjects answered honestly and completely? What factors may have intruded? Is the fact that you did or didn't know them, were or weren't of the same sex relevant? If your results seem to contradict other evidence, how do you account for the discrepancy? Were your subjects shading the truth? Was your sample's unrepresentativeness the culprit? Or have things changed since earlier data were collected?

5. What causes the phenomenon your results reveal? If several causes together account for the phenomenon, or if it is impossible to be sure of the cause, admit this. Identify possible causes and assess the likelihood of each.

6. What action should be taken?

The Discussion section gives you the opportunity to analyze the significance of your survey. Its insight and originality lift the otherwise well-written e-mail from the ranks of the merely satisfactory to the ranks of the above-average and the excellent.

The whole assignment will be more interesting if you choose a question that interests you. It does not need to be "significant" in terms of major political or philosophic problems; a quirk of human behavior that fascinates you will do nicely.

15.18   Analyzing Annual Reports

Locate two annual reports either in paper or electronic form. Use the following questions to analyze both reports:

- Who is (are) the audience(s)?
- What is (are) the purpose(s) of the report?
- How is the report organized and what does the order of information reflect about the company?
- How does the report validate/support the claims it makes? What type of evidence is used more often—textual or visual? What kinds of claims are used—logical, emotional, or ethical?
- How does the text establish credibility for the report?
- What can you tell about the company's financial situation from the report?

- What role do visuals play in the report? What image do they portray for the company? How do the visuals help establish credibility for the report? What do they imply about power distribution in the company?
- Does the report deal with any ethical issues?

As your instructor directs,

a. Write an e-mail to your instructor comparing and contrasting the two reports according to your analysis answers. Explain which report you find more effective and why.

b. Share your results orally with a small group of students.

c. Present your results to the class.

Notes

1. Karen Weise, "In Search of High-Definition Credit Scores," *Bloomberg Businessweek,* August 13, 2012, 43–44.
2. Eli Pariser, *The Filter Bubble: What the Internet Is Hiding from You* (New York: Penguin, 2011).
3. "Wikipedia," *Wikipedia,* last modified June 13, 2013, http://en.wikipedia.org/wiki/Wikipedia.
4. Katie Hafner, "Seeing Corporate Fingerprints in Wikipedia Edits," *New York Times,* August 19, 2007, http://www.nytimes.com/2007/08/19/technology/19wikipedia.html?_r51; and Jonathan Zittrain, Robert McHenry, Benjamin Mako Hill, and Mike Schroepfer, "Ten Years of Inaccuracy and Remarkable Detail: Wikipedia," *Bloomberg Businessweek,* January 10, 2011, 57–61.
5. Julia Angwin and Geoffrey A. Fowler, "Volunteers Log Off as Wikipedia Ages," *Wall Street Journal,* November 23, 2009, A1, A17.
6. Carrie Johnson, "After Tough 2012, Gallup Enlists Polling Expert to Investigate," *NPR.org,* February 7, 2013, http://www.npr.org/blogs/itsallpolitics/2013/02/07/171413008/after-tough-2012-gallup-enlists-polling-expert-to-investigate.
7. "United States: The Ladder of Fame; College Education," *The Economist,* August 26, 2006, 35; and Associated Press, "Many Colleges Obsess over National Rankings," *Des Moines Register,* February 6, 2012, 10A.
8. Sharon L. Lohr, *Sampling: Design and Analysis* (Pacific Grove, CA: Duxbury Press, 1999), 3.
9. "TV Measurement," *Nielsen,* accessed June 22, 2013, http://www.nielsen.com/us/en/measurement/television-measurement.html.
10. Cynthia Crossen, "Fiasco in 1936 Survey Brought 'Science' to Election Polling," *Wall Street Journal,* October 2, 2006, B1.

11. Ann Zimmerman, "Revenge of the Nerds: How Barbie Got Her Geek On," *Wall Street Journal,* April 9, 2010, A1.
12. Andrew O'Connell, "Reading the Public Mind," *Harvard Business Review* 88, no. 10 (October 2010): 28.
13. Carl Bialik, "Online Polling, Once Easily Dismissed, Burnishes Its Image," *Wall Street Journal,* August 7, 2010, A2.
14. Carl Bialik, "Survey Says: Cellphones Annoy Pollsters," *Wall Street Journal,* December 3, 2011, A2.
15. Stephen J. Blumberg and Julian V. Luke, "Wireless Substitution: Early Release of Estimates from the National Health Interview Survey, July–December 2012," National Center for Health Statistics, June 2013, http://www.cdc.gov/nchs/data/nhis/earlyrelease/wireless201306.pdf.
16. Lean Christian, Scott Keeter, Kristen Purcell, and Aaron Smith, "Assessing the Cell Phone Challenge," Pew Research Center, May 20, 2010, http://pewresearch.org/pubs/1601/assessing-cell-phone-challenge-in-public-opinion-surveys.
17. Carl Bialik, "Making It Count: Alternative Ways to Gather Census Data," *Wall Street Journal,* July 31, 2010, A2; and Paul J. Lavrakas, "Nonresponse Issues in U.S. Cell Phone and Landline Telephone Surveys," National Research Council, February 17, 2011, http://www7.nationalacademies.org/cnstat/Lavrakas%20Pres.pdf.
18. Pew Research Center for the People & the Press, "Assessing the Representativeness of Public Opinion Surveys," Pew Research Center, May 15, 2012, http://www.people-press.org/2012/05/15/section-1-survey-comparisons-and-benchmarks/.
19. Pew Research Center for the People & the Press, "Assessing the Representativeness of Public Opinion Surveys;" and AAPOR Cell Phone Task Force, "New Considerations for Survey Researchers When Planning and Conducting

RDD Telephone Surveys in the U.S. with Respondents Reached Via Cell Phone Numbers," American Association for Public Opinion Research, 2010, http://www.aapor .org/Cell_Phone_Task_Force_Report.htm.

20. Palmer Morrel-Samuels, "Getting the Truth into Workplace Surveys," *Harvard Business Review* 80, no. 2 (February 2002): 111–18.

21. Ibid.

22. Sheldon R. Gawiser and G. Evans Witt, "20 Questions Journalists Should Ask about Poll Results," *Public Agenda Archives*, accessed June 25, 2013, http://www .publicagendaarchives.org/pages/20-questions-journalists-should-ask-about-poll-results.

23. Morrel-Samuels, "Getting the Truth into Workplace Surveys," 116.

24. Earl E. McDowell, Bridget Mrolza, and Emmy Reppe, "An Investigation of the Interviewing Practices of Technical Writers in Their World of Work," in *Interviewing Practices for Technical Writers*, ed. Earl E. McDowell (Amityville, NY: Baywood Publishing, 1991), 207.

25. Julie Jargon, "Kiwi Goes Beyond Shine in Effort to Step Up Sales," *Wall Street Journal*, December 20, 2007, B1.

26. Peter Noel Murray, "Focus Groups Are Valid When Done Right," *Marketing News*, September 1, 2006, 21, 25.

27. Emily Steel, "The New Focus Groups: Online Networks: Proprietary Panels Help Consumer Companies Shape Products, Ads," *Wall Street Journal*, January 14, 2008, B6.

28. Kelly K. Spors, "The Customer Knows Best," *Wall Street Journal*, July 13, 2009, R5.

29. Andrew O'Connell, "Reading the Public Mind," *Harvard Business Review* 88, no. 10 (October 2010): 28.

30. Sarah Nassauer, "Old Ketchup Packet Heads for Trash," *Wall Street Journal*, September 9, 2012, B1.

31. Christopher Meyer and Andre Schwager, "Understanding Customer Experience," *Harvard Business Review* 85, no. 2 (February 2007): 116–26.

32. Daniel Kruger, "You Want Data with That?" *Forbes* 173, no. 6 (2004): 58.

33. Louise Witt, "Inside Intent," *American Demographics* 26, no. 2 (2004): 34.

34. Nielsen, "C3 TV Ratings Show Impact of DVR Ad Viewing," *Newswire*, October 14, 2009, http://www.nielsen.com/ us/en/newswire/2009/c3-tv-ratings-show-impact-of-dvr-ad-viewing.html.

35. Emily Steel, "TV Networks Launch Big Campus Push; New Nielsen System Makes College Students Coveted Ratings Draw," *Wall Street Journal*, March 5, 2007, B3.

36. Emma K. Macdonald, Hugh N. Wilson, and Unut Konus, "Better Customer Insight—In Real Time," *Harvard Business Review* 90, no. 9 (September 2012): 102–08; "About PatientsLikeMe," *PatientsLikeMe*, accessed May 17, 2013, http:// www.patientslikeme.com/about; and Getchen Cuda-Kroen, "Search for Parkinson's Genes Turns to Online Social Networking," *NPR.org*, August 20, 2012, http:// www.npr.org/blogs/health/2012/08/20/158943097/ search-for-parkinsons-genes-turns-to-online-social-networking.

37. Robert Lee Hotz, "Decoding Our Chatter," *Wall Street Journal*, October 1, 2011, C1, C2.

38. Ibid; and Carl Bialik, "Tweets As Poll Data? Be Careful," *Wall Street Journal*, February 11, 2012, A2.

39. Jessi Hempel, "The Hot Tech Gig of 2022: Data Scientist," *Fortune*, January 16, 2012, 62.

40. Eyder Peralta, "Time, CNN Suspend Fareed Zakaria's Column after Plagiarism Claim," *NPR.org*, August 10, 2012, http://www.npr.org/blogs/thetwo-way/2012/08/ 10/158589006/time-magazine-suspends-fareed-zakarias-column-after-plagiarism-claim.

41. Jeffrey A. Trachtenberg, "Best-Selling Author Lehrer Admits Fabricating Dylan Quotes for Book," *Wall Street Journal*, July 21, 2012, B3.

16 Creating Visuals and Data Displays

Chapter Outline

When to Use Visuals and Data Displays

Guidelines for Creating Effective Visuals and Data Displays

1. Check the Quality of the Data.
2. Determine the Story You Want to Tell.
3. Choose the Right Visual or Data Display for the Story.
4. Follow Conventions.
5. Use Color and Decoration with Restraint.
6. Be Accurate and Ethical.

Integration of Visuals and Data Displays into Your Text

Software Programs for Creating Visuals and Data Displays

Conventions for Specific Visuals and Data Displays

- Tables
- Pie Charts
- Bar Charts
- Line Graphs
- Gantt Charts
- Photographs
- Drawings
- Maps
- Infographics
- Dynamic Displays

Summary by Learning Objectives

NEWSWORTHY COMMUNICATION

Discouraging Smoking through Visuals

Smoking causes more than 5 million deaths worldwide each year and costs governments billions of dollars in health care expenses. While most governments attempt to curb smoking through taxes and regulations, Australia is leading the way with a different approach: changing the visual design of cigarette packaging to include photographs of the consequences of smoking.

Despite appeals by the tobacco industry, Australia has required all tobacco sold in the country since 2012 to be packaged in the same dark, plain designs. Instead of prominent company logos and bright colors, each package comes with a large picture of an effect of smoking such as rotten teeth, cancerous lungs, or sick babies.

The graphic pictures are designed to discourage people from smoking by changing the message of the packaging. But are they working? According to a 14-country study conducted by the Centers for Disease Control and Prevention, the prominent warnings do work: in most countries, more than 90% of the people who purchased cigarettes noticed the warnings, and many of those reported a substantial interest in quitting smoking. According to CDC Director Thomas R. Frieden, "Warning labels motivate smokers to quit and discourage nonsmokers from starting."

Other countries are following Australia's lead in changing the package design of cigarettes. By including powerful visuals in the design, Australia is changing the behavior of smokers and saving lives.

Sources: Tom Watkins and Elizabeth Yuan, "Ruling Shows 'Big Tobacco Can Be Taken On and Beaten,' Australia Says," *CNN*, August 17, 2012, http://www.cnn.com/2012/08/15/world/asia/australia-tobacco-packaging; and Centers for Disease Control and Prevention, "Report Finds Global Smokers Consider Quitting Due to Graphic Health Warnings on Packages," Press Release, May 26, 2011, http://www.cdc.gov/media/releases/2011/p0526_cigarettewarnings.html.

NEWSWORTHY COMMUNICATION

Learning Objectives

After studying this chapter, you will know

LO 16-1 When to use visuals and data displays.

LO 16-2 How to create effective visuals and data displays.

LO 16-3 How to integrate visuals and data displays into text.

LO 16-4 How to use conventions for specific visuals and data displays.

Visuals of Fallen Heroes

After only a few weeks in office, President Obama reversed a controversial policy dealing with visuals. His administration overturned a policy that prohibited the media from photographing caskets of fallen soldiers returning to the United States.

Under the new policy, the families of fallen soldiers have the right to choose whether the media can be present at the Dover Air Force Base in Delaware, the place where all deceased soldiers are brought.

Former President George H. W. Bush started the policy in 1991 during the Gulf War. Critics suggest the policy was enacted to prevent the public from seeing the horrors of war and the number of people who had died. On the other hand, critics of the new policy argue that allowing the press to be present creates a spectacle out of a private family matter.

Supporters of the new policy believe the photos are a reminder to all Americans of the sacrifices made by our troops and of the high price of freedom.

How ethical do you believe it is to show the final ceremony of fallen soldiers? If you had a family member who died in war, would you want the press to be present?

Adapted from Julian E. Barnes, "U.S. to Allow Photos of War Dead's Coffins," *The Seattle Times: Politics & Government*, February 27, 2009, http://seattletimes.nwsource.com/html/politics/2008791894_wardead27.html.

Visuals and data displays are design elements that help make data meaningful and support arguments in your proposals and reports. They can also help communicate your points in documents such as brochures, e-mails, newsletters, reports, social media postings, and other business messages, where they can add color and emotional appeal, as well as new information. Visuals are often used to enhance oral presentations, which are discussed in Chapter 19.

Visuals and data displays are particularly useful for presenting numbers dramatically. Suppose you want to give investors information about various stocks' performances. They would not want to read paragraph after paragraph of statements about which stocks went up and which went down. Organizing the daily numbers into tables is much more useful.

Tables of stock prices have been the norm until recently. Now, the Internet offers options such as Map of the Market, www.smartmoney.com/map-of-the-market, a dynamic display tool that helps investors see the top performers. Map of the Market displays visual information for 1,000 U.S. and international stocks, providing details about each company's performance. Each company is shown as a rectangle, and companies are clustered into industry groups. The blocks are color-coded to signify the size of the stock price change or other criteria selected by the user. Size and color provide easy cues for spotting the best and worst performers.

When to Use Visuals and Data Displays **LO 16-1**

The ease of creating visuals and data displays by computer may make people use them uncritically. Use visuals and data displays only to achieve a specific purpose. Never include them in your documents just because you have them; instead, use them to convey information the audience needs or wants.

In your rough draft, use visuals and data displays

- **To see that ideas are presented completely.** A table, for example, can show you whether you've included all the items in a comparison.

- **To find relationships.** Charting sales on a map may show that the sales representatives who made quota all have territories on the East or the West Coast. Is the central United States suffering a recession? Is the product one that appeals to coastal lifestyles? Is advertising reaching the coasts but not the central states? Even if you don't use the visual in your final document, creating the map may lead you to questions you wouldn't otherwise ask.

In the final presentation or document, use visuals and data displays

- **To make points vivid.** Audiences skim reports and websites; a visual catches the eye. The brain processes visuals immediately. Understanding words—written or oral—takes more time.

- **To emphasize material** that might be skipped if it were buried in a paragraph. The beginning and end are places of emphasis. However, something has to go in the middle, especially in a long document. Visuals allow you to emphasize important material, wherever it logically falls.

- **To present material more compactly and with less repetition** than words alone would require. Words can call attention to the main points of the visual, without repeating all of the visual's information.

The number of visuals and data displays you will need depends on your purposes, the kind of information, and the audience. You'll use more when you want to show relationships and to persuade, when the information is complex or contains extensive numerical data, and when the audience values visuals and data displays. Some audiences expect presentations and reports to use lots of visuals and data displays. Other audiences may see them as frivolous and time spent making them as time wasted. For these audiences, sharply limit the number of visuals and data displays you use— but you should still use them when your own purposes and the information call for them.

Guidelines for Creating Effective Visuals and Data Displays [LO 16-2]

Use these six steps to create effective visuals and data displays:

1. Check the quality of the data.
2. Determine the story you want to tell.
3. Choose the right visual or data display for the story.
4. Follow conventions.
5. Use color and decoration with restraint.
6. Be accurate and ethical.

Let's discuss each of these in more detail.

1. Check the Quality of the Data.

Your data display is only as good as the underlying data. Check to be sure that your data come from a reliable source. See "Evaluating the Source of the Data" in Chapter 18.

Also check that you have data for all factors you should consider. Are some factors missing data from key locations or demographic areas? When Nielsen Media Research, the TV audience measuring organization, switched from paper diaries of TV viewing to "people meters," electronic recording devices, it discovered a marked rise in TV viewing by children and young adults.[1]

If the data may not be reliable, you're better off not using visuals. The visual picture will be more powerful than verbal disclaimers, and the audience will be misled.

2. Determine the Story You Want to Tell.

Every visual should tell a story. Stories can be expressed in complete sentences that describe something that happens or changes. The sentence can also serve as the title of the visual.

One Visual; Two Audiences and Two Messages

How do you address two distinctive audiences with different messages in one static visual?

Well, a new bus stop advertisement from Spain made big news because it did just that. The ad is from the Foundation for Aid to Children and Adolescents at Risk, whose mission is to combat child abuse. The foundation faced a conundrum: how does it encourage help for abused children when the children's parent standing next to them may be the abuser?

The advertisement uses lenticular printing, a special type that allows different images on the same display based on viewing angles. Adults see a picture of a boy and the words "Sometimes, child abuse is only visible to the child suffering it." Children observing the advertisement from a lower viewing angle will see the same boy but with bruises on his face, a phone number to call, and the words, "If somebody hurts you, phone us and we'll help you."

Follow this YouTube link to see the advertisement come to life: http://www.youtube.com/watch?v=6zoCDyQSH0o

What other types of advertisements could benefit from this type of printing that can aim messages at different audiences?

Adapted from Betsy Isaacson, "Child Abuse Hotline Ad Uses Photographic Trick That Makes It Visible Only to Children," *Huffington Post*, May 6, 2013, http://www.huffingtonpost.com/2013/05/06/child-abuse-ad_n_3223311.html.

Not a story:	U.S. Sales, 2007–2014
Possible stories:	Forty Percent of Our Sales Were to New Customers.
	Growth Was Highest in the South.
	Sales Increased from 2009 to 2014.
	Sales Were Highest in the Areas with More Sales Representatives.

Stories that tell us what we already know are rarely interesting. Instead, good stories may

- Support a hunch.
- Surprise you or challenge so-called common knowledge.
- Show trends or changes the audience didn't know existed.
- Have commercial or social significance.
- Provide information needed for action.
- Be personally relevant to the audience.

To find stories,

1. Focus on a topic (where are the most SUVs bought, who retweets the most, etc.).
2. Simplify the data on that topic and convert the numbers to simple, easy-to-understand units.
3. Look for relationships and changes. For example, compare two or more groups: do men and women have the same attitudes? Look for changes over time. Look for items that can be seen as part of the same group. To find stories about entertainers' incomes, for example, you might compare the incomes of writers, actors, and musicians.
4. Process the data to find more stories. Find the average and the median. Calculate the percentage change from one year to the next.

When you think you have a story, test it against all the data to be sure it's accurate.

Some stories are simple straight lines: "Computer Sales Increased." But other stories are more complex, with exceptions or outlying cases. Such stories will need more nuanced titles to do justice to the story. And sometimes the best story arises from the juxtaposition of two or more stories. Figure 16.1 uses three grouped visuals to tell a complex story about flu outbreaks.

Almost every data set allows you to tell several stories. You must choose the story you want to tell. Dumps of uninterpreted data confuse and frustrate your audience; they undercut the credibility and goodwill you want to create.

Sometimes several stories will be important. When that's the case, you'll need a separate visual for each.

3. Choose the Right Visual or Data Display for the Story.

Visuals and data displays are not interchangeable. Good writers choose the one that best matches the purpose of the communication. Follow these guidelines to choose the right visuals and data displays:

Figure 16.1	A Complex Story about Influenza Outbreaks Using Grouped Visuals

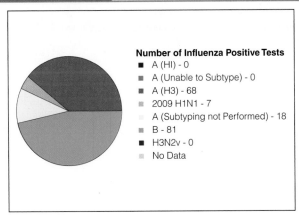

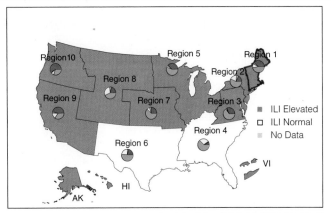

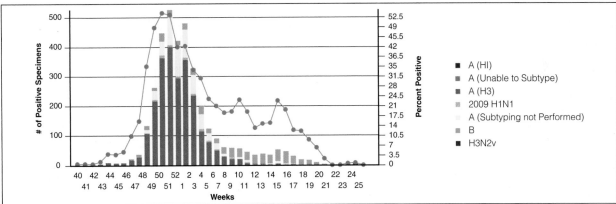

Source: Centers for Disease Control and Prevention, "National and Regional Outpatient Illness and Viral Surveillance," *Fluview,* accessed July 3, 2013, http://gis .cdc.gov/grasp/fluview/fluportaldashboard.html.

- Use a **table** when the audience needs to be able to identify exact values. (See Figure 16.2a.)

- Use a chart or graph when you want the audience to focus on relationships.

  - To compare a part to the whole, use a **pie chart.** (See Figure 16.2b.)
  - To compare one item to another item, use a **bar chart.** (See Figure 16.2c.)
  - To compare items over time, use a bar chart or a **line graph.** (See Figure 16.2d.)
  - To show frequency or distribution, use a line graph or bar chart. (See Figure 16.2e.)
  - To show correlations, use a bar chart, a line graph, or a **dot chart.** (See Figure 16.2f.)

- Use **Gantt charts** to show time lines for proposals or projects.

- Use **photographs** to create a sense of authenticity or show the item in use.

- Use **drawings** to show dimensions, show processes, emphasize detail, or eliminate unwanted detail.

- Use **maps** to emphasize location or compare items in different locations.

- Use **infographics** to show quantitative and qualitative material in a visually interesting way that informs and educates an audience.

- Use **dynamic displays** to allow users control over their visual experience.

Figure 16.2	Choose the Visual to Fit the Story

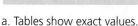

US sales reach $44.5 million.

	Millions of dollars		
	2010	2012	2014
Northeast	10.2	10.8	11.3
South	7.6	8.5	10.4
Midwest	8.3	6.8	9.3
West	11.3	12.1	13.5
Totals	37.4	38.2	44.5

a. Tables show exact values.

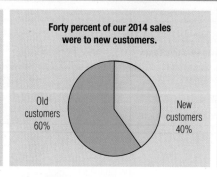

b. Pie charts compare a component to the whole.

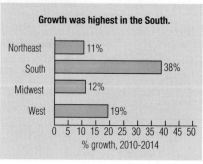

c. Bar charts compare items or show distribution or correlation.

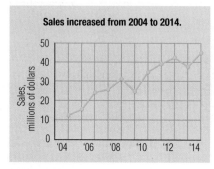

d. Line charts compare items over time or show distribution or correlation.

e. Bar charts can show frequency.

f. Dot charts show correlation.

4. Follow Conventions.

Follow conventions when creating visuals and data displays. When you stray from conventions, you may confuse or alienate your audience.

Proposals and reports use formal visuals and data displays, which are typically divided into tables and figures. **Tables** are numbers or words arrayed in rows and columns. **Figures** are everything that isn't a table and may include graphs, charts, maps, drawings, infographics, and photographs.

Formal visuals and data displays use both numbers and titles: "Figure 1. The Falling Cost of Computer Memory, 1994–2014." In an oral presentation, the title is usually used without the number: "The Falling Cost of Computer Memory, 1994–2014." The title should tell the story so the audience knows what to look for in the visual and why it is important.

Other types of documents use informal visuals and data displays, which are inserted directly into the text; they do not have numbers or titles.

Visuals and data displays usually contain the components listed in Figure 16.3.

5. Use Color and Decoration with Restraint.

Color makes visuals more dramatic, but it also creates some problems. Colors may be interpreted positively or negatively depending on their context and the unique experiences of the people viewing them. Figure 16.4 lists some common positive and negative associations found in Western cultures. A good use of color occurs in the weather maps printed daily in many newspapers. Blue seems to fit cold; red seems to fit hot temperatures.

Figure 16.3	Common Components of Visuals and Data Displays

- A title telling the story that the visual or data display shows.
- A clear indication of what the data are. For example, what people *say* they did is not necessarily what they really did. An estimate of what a number will be in the future differs from numbers in the past that have already been measured.
- Clearly labeled units.
- Labels or legends identifying axes, colors, symbols, and so forth.
- The source of the data, if you created the visual from data someone else gathered and compiled.
- The source of the visual or data display, if you reproduce one someone else created.

Figure 16.4	Colors and Their Common Connotations in Western Culture

Color	**Positive**	**Negative**
White	Clean, innocent, pure	Cold, empty, sterile
Red	Strong, brave, passionate	Dangerous, aggressive, domineering
Yellow	Happy, friendly, optimistic	Cowardly, annoying, brash
Brown	Warm, earthy, mature	Dirty, sad, cheap
Green	Natural, tranquil, relaxing	Jealous, inexperienced, greedy
Blue	Strong, trustworthy, authoritative	Cold, depressing, gloomy

Source: Katherine Nolan, "Color It Effective: How Color Influences the User," in *Microsoft Office Online, FrontPage 2003 Help and How-to: Working with Graphics,* accessed May 29, 2013, http://office.microsoft.com/en-us/frontpage-help/color-it-effective-how-color-influences-the-user-HA001042937.aspx.

Meanings assigned to colors differ depending on the audience's national background and profession. Blue suggests masculinity in the United States, religion in many Latin American countries, and femininity in China. Red is sometimes used to suggest danger or *stop* in the United States; it means *go* and is associated with festivities in China. Orange suggests courage and love in Japan, while many Middle Eastern countries associate it with mourning and loss. Purple is associated with royalty or honor in the United States, with mourning and death in Brazil, and symbolizes wealth in many Middle Eastern counties.[2]

These general cultural associations may be replaced by corporate, national, or professional associations. Some people associate blue with IBM or Facebook and red with Coca-Cola, communism, or Japan. People in specific professions learn other meanings for colors. Blue suggests *reliability* to financial managers, *water* or *coldness* to engineers, and *death* to health care professionals. Red means *losing money* to financial managers, *danger* to engineers, but *healthy* to health care professionals. Green usually means *safe* to engineers, but *infected* to health care professionals.

Try to avoid graphs that contrast red and green, because the colors will be indistinguishable to people with red–green color blindness. Almost 10% of men and 2% of women are color-blind. Furthermore, as people get older, their ability to perceive colors also decreases.[3] New smartphone apps, such as Colorblind Avenger, HueVue, and Colorblind Helper help vision-impaired persons to identify colors or highlight difficult colors.[4]

The Power of Color and Penalties

How much can jersey color influence a sporting team's penalties?

A researcher from the University of Florida, Gregory Webster, says quite a lot. His research team discovered that National Hockey League teams wearing darker colored jerseys are more likely to be penalized compared to teams in white jerseys. The most penalties were awarded to teams wearing black jerseys.

To reach his finding, Webster and his team analyzed more than 50,000 NHL games over 30 seasons. They even had a before and after set of data to analyze because the NHL changed rules for uniform colors for home and away games in 2003.

The link between darker colored jerseys and penalties is not entirely clear. But Webster offers three possibilities. First, it could be because white jerseys are less visible on the ice and therefore less likely to be penalized. Second, the darker colors somehow make the players seem more aggressive. Third, referees just have an unconscious bias against darker colored jerseys from cultural associations of good and bad.

A similar study was conducted at Cornell University on National Football League teams, and the color trend held true for penalties in football.

What do you think? Have you noticed this color phenomenon while watching your favorite team? If you had the say, would you encourage your favorite team to change the uniform color?

Adapted from Shankar Vedantam, "Power (Dis)Play? Teams in Black Draw More Penalties," *NPR*, April 26, 2012, http://www.npr.org/2012/04/26/151383136/power-dis-play-teams-in-black-draw-more-penalties.

Remember that color preferences change over time. In the 1970s, avocado green and harvest gold were standard colors for kitchen appliances, but today these colors seem retro to most U.S. audiences.

These various associations suggest that color is safest with a homogenous audience that you know well. In an increasingly multicultural workforce, color may send signals you do not intend.

In any visual, use as little shading and as few lines as are necessary for clarity. Don't clutter the visual with extra marks. When you design black-and-white graphs, use shades of gray rather than stripes, wavy lines, or checks to indicate different segments or items.

Resist the temptation to make your visual "artistic" or "relevant" by turning it into a picture or adding **clip art**, images that you can import into your document or visual. A small drawing of a car in the corner of a line graph showing the number of miles driven is acceptable in an oral presentation but out of place in a written report. Turning a line graph into a highway to show miles driven makes it harder to read: it's hard to separate the data line from lines that are merely decorative. Visuals authority Edward Tufte uses the term **chartjunk** for decorations that at best are irrelevant to the visual and at worst mislead the reader.[5]

6. Be Accurate and Ethical.

To be a trustworthy communicator and to avoid misleading your audience, strive to be ethical in your choice of visuals or data displays and ensure their accuracy. Always double-check them to be sure the information is accurate. In some cases, visuals or data displays have accurate labels but misleading visual shapes. Visuals or data displays communicate quickly; audiences remember the shape, not the labels. If the audience has to study the labels to get the right picture, the visual or data display is unethical even if the labels are accurate.

Two-dimensional figures, such as multisized school buildings used to show increasing school costs, distort data by multiplying the apparent value by the width as well as by the height—four times for every doubling in value. Three-dimensional graphs are especially hard to interpret accurately and should be avoided.[6]

Even simple bar and line graphs may be misleading if part of the scale is missing, or truncated; small changes may seem like major ones. **Truncated graphs** are most acceptable when the audience knows the basic data set well. For example, graphs of the stock market almost never start at zero; they are routinely truncated. This omission is acceptable for audiences who follow the market closely.

Data can also be distorted when the context is omitted. As Tufte suggests, a drop may be part of a regular cycle, a correction after an atypical increase, or a permanent drop to a new, lower plateau.[7]

To make your data displays more accurate,

- Differentiate between actual and estimated or projected values.
- When you must truncate a scale, do so clearly with a break in the bars or in the background.
- Avoid perspective and three-dimensional graphs.
- Avoid combining graphs with different scales.
- Use images of people carefully in histographs to avoid sexist, racist, or other exclusionary visual statements.

Photographs in particular have received close attention for accuracy and ethics concerns. With the proliferation of social media, be especially careful about the accuracy of photos, which are easily shared while divorced from their original source. A NASA satellite photo supposedly of India during Diwali, the festival of lights, showed the country lit in brightly colored lights. The photo was shared or liked hundreds of thousands of times on Facebook. But when the accuracy was verified, the photo was actually from the National Oceanic and Atmospheric Administration showing population growth over time and had nothing to do with Diwali.[8]

Photographers have always been able to frame their pictures in ways that cut objects they do not want. Pictures of homes for real estate sales can omit the collapsing garage; shots of collapsed homeless people can omit the image of social workers standing by to give aid.

Adobe Photoshop and similar photo-editing software have added a new dimension to the problem with their easy photo-altering aids. After major worldwide occurrences, handfuls of fabricated pictures appear on the Internet. Some have been so convincing that even the Associated Press was fooled and sent them across the newswire.[9]

Not long after the oil spill in the Gulf of Mexico, BP faced another scandal when a photo posted on its website was discovered to be altered. The photo showed BP's Houston Deepwater Horizon command center with control operators closely monitoring live video feeds on large screens. The three fake underwater images were inserted to cover blank screens.[10]

Other controversies have involved the use of digital alterations to increase the beauty of ad models to unnatural degrees. The Advertising Standards Authority (ASA) in the UK banned Maybelline and L'Oreal makeup advertisements featuring Julia Roberts and Christy Turlington. The ASA said the ads were too digitally altered to be real and therefore misleading.[11]

In his discussion of photography ethics, John Long notes that it's easy to think of small changes to photographs as harmless. He argues that any change to the picture is deceptive, because when people see a photo, they assume that it's a true record of a real event. When you change a photo, you use that assumption to deceive.[12]

Integration of Visuals and Data Displays into Your Text LO 16-3

Refer in your text to every visual and data display. Normally the text gives the table or figure number but not the title. Put the visual as soon after your reference as space and page design permit. If the visual must go on another page, tell the reader where to find it:

As Figure 3 shows (page 10), . . .

(See Table 2 on page 14.)

Summarize the main point of a visual or data display *before* you present it. Then when readers get to it, they'll see it as confirmation of your point.

Weak: Listed below are the results.

Better: As Figure 4 shows, sales doubled in the last decade.

How much discussion a visual or data displays needs depends on the audience, the complexity of the visual, and the importance of the point it makes. Use these guidelines:

Finding the Fakes

With the growing trend of altered photos, a researcher set out to find an easy way to spot them. Hany Farid, a computer scientist and forensic imagine specialist at Dartmouth College, developed a system to spot manipulated images and tell what kind of camera snapped the original picture.

Since most photo-editing software programs leave a digital signature, his system can tell if manipulation occurred by cross-checking it with a database of more than 10,000 digital camera models. One drawback to the program, however, is that it tells only if a photo has been altered, not what has been edited.

When the program is available for public use, Farid hopes the system will help law enforcement agencies and the newspaper industry.

Adapted from Oliver Staley, "Innovator: Hany Farid," *Bloomberg Businessweek*, January 3, 2011, 37.

Visuals That Translate Well

When preparing visuals, keep in mind cultural differences:

- Make sure any symbols in the visual will have the correct meaning in the culture of your audience. For example, a red cross symbolizes first aid in North America, but in Muslim countries the symbol with that meaning is typically a green crescent.

- If you use punctuation marks as symbols, be sure they are meaningful to your audience. A question mark in English and certain other languages might signal a help function or answers to questions. But in languages without this symbol, it has no meaning.

- In showing humans, respect the cultural norms of your audience. Europeans tend to accept images of nudity, but some cultures can be offended by images of even a bare leg or other body part.

- Organize the information according to the reading customs of the audience. North American and European audiences will tend to read visual information as they do text: from left to right. Middle Easterners view from right to left.

- Learn your audience's conventions for writing numbers. In the United States, a period indicates the decimal point, and commas separate groups of three digits. In much of Europe, a comma represents the decimal point, and a space goes between each group of three digits. For U.S. and French readers, 3,333 would have different values.

Adapted from Gerald J. Alred, Charles T. Brusaw, and Walter E. Oliu, *The Business Writer's Handbook*, 10th ed. (New York: St. Martin's Press, 2012), 244–46; and *The Chicago Manual of Style*, 16th ed. (Chicago: University of Chicago Press, 2010), 471.

- If the material is new to the audience, provide a fuller explanation than if similar material is presented to this audience every week or month.

- If the visual is complex, help the reader find key points.

- If the point is important, discuss its implications in some detail.

In contrast, one sentence about a visual or data display may be enough when the audience is already familiar with the topic and the data, when the visual is simple and well designed, and when the information in the visual is a minor part of your proof.

When you discuss visuals and data displays, spell out numbers that fall at the beginning of a sentence. If spelling out the number or year is cumbersome, revise the sentence so that it does not begin with a number.

Forty-five percent of the cost goes to pay wages and salaries.

In 2012, employers scaled back insurance coverage.

Put numbers in parentheses at the end of the clause or sentence to make the sentence easier to read:

Hard to read: As Table 4 shows, teachers participate (54%) in more community service groups than do members of the other occupations surveyed; dentists (20.8%) participate in more service groups than do members of five of the other occupations.

Better: As Table 4 shows, teachers participate in more community service groups than do members of the other occupations surveyed (54%); dentists participate in more service groups than do five of the other occupations (20.8%).

Software Programs for Creating Visuals and Data Displays

Many software programs enable you to create the specific types of visuals and data displays described in the next section of this chapter. For creating tables, pie charts, bar charts, line graphs, or Gantt charts, you could use Excel, Numbers, or open source programs such as OpenOffice or Google Spreadsheets.

For editing photographs or creating drawings, maps, or infographics, you might use programs such as Photoshop, Publisher, PowerPoint, InDesign, or Illustrator, or open source programs like OpenOffice Draw, Gimp, Paint, or Google Drawing.

These software programs are just a sampling; many more programs are available. Each of these will range in functionality and price. And each will come with advantages and disadvantages based on your visual and data display needs. However, even the simplest programs will get you started.

Proficiency in one or more of these software programs can make your employer view you more favorably. Gaining software proficiencies can also give you an advantage over other job seekers if you list them on your résumé when you're on the job market.

Figure 16.5	Table Shows Exact Values for FitWorld Gym Average Weekly Client Visits by Age Group in 2013			
Day	**Total Avg Client Visits**	**Ages 18–34**	**Ages 35–54**	**Ages 55–older**
Monday	2072	1212	763	97
Tuesday	2062	1132	827	103
Wednesday	2331	909	811	611
Thursday	1777	889	794	94
Friday	1213	168	778	267
Saturday	1198	389	395	414
Sunday	1126	135	376	615

Conventions for Specific Visuals and Data Displays LO 16-4

Once you know your story—what you're saying, how you're saying it, and how you want text and visuals to combine to say it—then you're in a position to choose and create visuals and data displays. Each type of visual can do different things for you. Here are some of the most common types of visuals and data displays and when, where, and how they're most effective.

Tables

Use tables only when you want the audience to focus on specific numbers. Graphs convey less specific information but are more memorable. Figure 16.5 illustrates a table. The **header row** presents the labels for column information at the top. When constructing tables,

- Use common, understandable units. Round off to simplify the data (e.g., 35% rather than 35.27%; 44.5 million rather than 44,503,276).

- Provide column and row totals or averages when they're relevant.

- Put the items you want audiences to compare in columns rather than in rows to facilitate mental subtraction and division.

- When you have many rows, shade alternate rows (or pairs of rows) or double-space after every five rows to help audiences line up items accurately.

Pie Charts

Pie charts force the audience to measure area. However, people can judge position or length (which a bar chart uses) more accurately than they judge area, thus making information in pie charts more difficult for an audience to understand accurately. The data in any pie chart can be put in a bar chart. Therefore, use a pie chart only when you are comparing one segment to the whole. When you are comparing one segment to another segment, use a bar chart, a line graph, or a map—even though the data may be expressed in percentages. In Figure 16.6, notice how it's nearly impossible to tell the difference in graduation rates between the two pie charts.

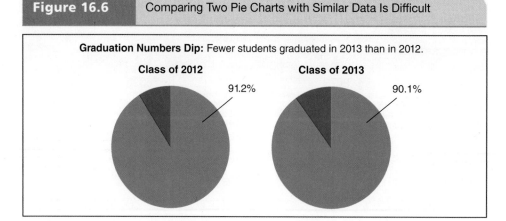

Figure 16.6 | Comparing Two Pie Charts with Similar Data Is Difficult

Graduation Numbers Dip: Fewer students graduated in 2013 than in 2012.

Class of 2012   91.2%   Class of 2013   90.1%

When constructing pie charts,

- Make the chart a perfect circle. Avoid 3-D circles; they distort the data.

- Express data as percentages.

- Start at 12 o'clock with the largest percentage or the percentage you want to focus on. Go clockwise to each smaller percentage or to each percentage in some other logical order.

- Limit the number of segments to no more than seven. If your data have more divisions, combine the smallest or the least important into a single "miscellaneous" or "other" category.

- Label the segments outside the circle. Internal labels are hard to read.

Bar Charts

Bar charts are easy to interpret because they ask people to compare distance along a common scale, which most people judge accurately. Bar charts are useful in a variety of situations: to compare one item to another, to compare items over time, and to show correlations. Use horizontal bars when your labels are long; when the labels are short, either horizontal or vertical bars will work. When constructing bar charts,

- Order the bars in a logical or chronological order.

- Put the bars close enough together to make comparison easy.

- Label both horizontal and vertical axes.

- Put all labels inside the bars or outside them. When some labels are inside and some are outside, the labels carry the visual weight of longer bars, distorting the data.

- Make all the bars the same width.

- Use different colors for different bars only when their meanings are different: estimates as opposed to known numbers, negative as opposed to positive numbers.

- Avoid using 3-D perspective; it makes the values harder to read and can make comparison difficult.

Several varieties of bar charts exist. See Figure 16.7 for examples.

Figure 16.7	Varieties of Bar Charts

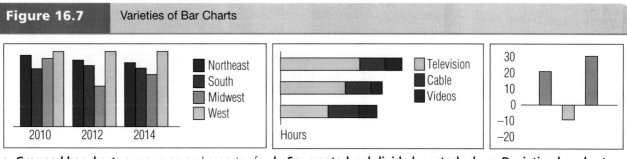

a. Grouped bar charts compare several aspects of each item or several items over time.

b. Segmented, subdivided, or **stacked bars** sum the components of an item.

c. Deviation bar charts identify positive and negative values.

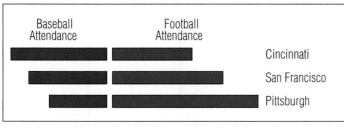

d. Paired bar charts show the comparison between two items.

e. Histograms or **pictograms** use images to create the bars.

- **Grouped bar charts** allow you to compare either several aspects of each item or several items over time. Group the items you want to compare. Figure 16.7a shows that sales were highest in the West each year. If we wanted to show how sales had changed in each region, the bars should be grouped by region, not by year.

- **Segmented, subdivided, or stacked bars** sum the components of an item. It's hard to identify the values in specific segments; grouped bar charts are almost always easier to use.

- **Deviation bar charts** identify positive and negative values, or winners and losers.

- **Paired bar charts** show the comparison between two items.

- **Histograms or pictograms** use images to create the bars.

Line Graphs

Line graphs are also easy to interpret. Use line graphs to compare items over time, to show frequency or distribution, and to show possible correlations. When constructing line graphs,

- Label both horizontal and vertical axes. When time is a variable, it is usually put on the horizontal axis.

- Avoid using more than three different lines on one graph. Even three lines may be too many if they cross each other.

- Avoid using perspective. Perspective makes the values harder to read and can make comparison difficult.

Figure 16.8   Gantt Charts Show the Schedule for Completing a Project

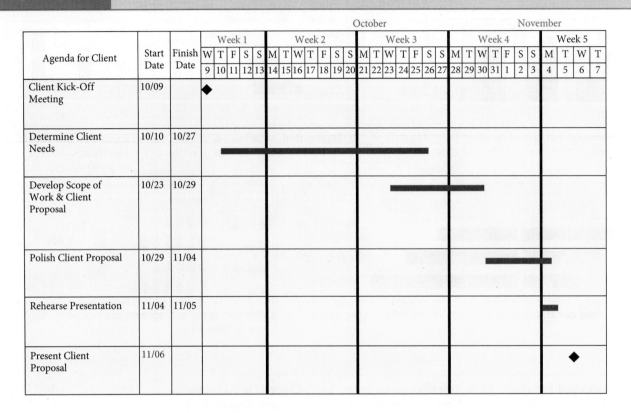

Agenda for Client	Start Date	Finish Date	October Week 1					Week 2							Week 3							Week 4						November Week 5			
			W 9	T 10	F 11	S 12	S 13	M 14	T 15	W 16	T 17	F 18	S 19	S 20	M 21	T 22	W 23	T 24	F 25	S 26	S 27	M 28	T 29	W 30	T 31	F 1	S 2	S 3	M 4	T 5	W 6	T 7
Client Kick-Off Meeting	10/09		◆																													
Determine Client Needs	10/10	10/27		▬																												
Develop Scope of Work & Client Proposal	10/23	10/29																▬														
Polish Client Proposal	10/29	11/04																						▬								
Rehearse Presentation	11/04	11/05																												▬			
Present Client Proposal	11/06																														◆	

Gantt Charts

Gantt charts are bar charts used to show schedules. They're most commonly used in proposals to show when elements of a project will be completed. Figure 16.8 is a Gantt chart for a marketing plan. From the chart, it is easy to see which activities must be completed first to finish the total plan on time. When using Gantt charts,

- Color-code bars to indicate work planned and work completed.
- Outline **critical activities,** which must be completed on time if the project is to be completed by the due date.
- Indicate progress reports, major achievements, or other accomplishments.

Photographs

Photographs convey a sense of authenticity. The photo of a devastated area can suggest the need for government grants or private donations. The photo of a prototype helps convince investors that a product can be manufactured. If the item is especially big or small, include something in the photograph that can serve as a reference point: a dime, a person.

Make sure to use high-quality professional photos, especially on websites where audiences may have the ability to zoom if they're viewing on smartphones. Be sure also to keep the photographs on a website consistent, whether it be the background, colors, or overall tone.

Figure 16.9	Drawings Can Show Process

A SHIRT'S JOURNEY

Dry cleaners are making changes to get rid of the solvent known as perc. Here's how the cleaning process generally works.

TICKETING, ID TAGGING: Items are checked in and ticketed with a tag designed to withstand the cleaning process. Some cleaners staple tags on, while others use plastic fasteners.

SORTING: Garments are arranged and sorted, generally by fabric type, color or stain.

PRE-TREATING: Some items under go'spot' cleaning by hand to treat stains.

RE-TAGGING: New ID tags are attached for customers. The items are hung on a conveyer and placed in garment bags for pickup.

SPOT CLEANING: Additional spot cleaning removes stains that didn't come out earlier.

IRONING: Garments are pressed, typically with an industrial steam press. Certain items are pressed by hand with a small iron.

DRUM CLEANING: A dry-cleaning machine is much like a big washing machine, but solvents are used instead of water. Soaps are added to aid in stain removal. Some machines can hold 60 to 80 pounds of garments.

HEATING: At the end of the 40-to-50-minute cycle, high temperatures evaporate the solvents.

BUTTON CATCH, INSPECTION: A contraption in the rear of the machine catches button or embellishments that come off during cleaning. They are sewn on before the garment is returned.

Source: From Ray A. Smith, "The New Dirt on Dry Cleaners, *Wall Street Journal,* July 28, 2011. Reproduced with permission of Dow Jones, Inc. via Copyright Clearance Center.

Smartphone Photo or Advertisement?

As Americans spend more time on social media such as Facebook, Instagram, and Pinterest, and less time on TV and magazines, advertisers are adapting. Lifestyle advertising captures the look of pictures consumers shoot with their own smartphones and then share online.

- Brands such as Burberry, Coach, and Tiffany used a street-style photographer for their ad campaigns, and those images got shared on sites like Facebook and YouTube.
- The web page of Rent the Runway, a rental dress company, now features its clothes on real women, not models.
- Taco Bell got permission from Instagram to use its name, logo, and app design in its commercials for Doritos Locos Tacos.

Photography that looks like social media is no cheaper than traditional photography, but it has an added bonus. Viewers "like" it and share it, giving it new coverage at no extra cost.

Adapted from Katherine Rosman, "Why Ads Are Imitating the Photos in Your Smartphone," *Wall Street Journal,* September 27, 2012, D1.

You may need to **crop,** or trim, a photo for best results. However, make sure to be ethical with any cropping you do. A growing problem with photos is that they may be edited or staged, purporting to show something as reality even though it never occurred. See the discussion of ethics and accuracy earlier in this chapter.

On the other hand, sometimes photos are obviously edited to serve a purpose. The consulting, technology, and outsourcing company Accenture got much publicity from its advertisement showing an elephant surfing on its hind legs. The ad's text said, "Who says you can't be big and nimble?"[13]

Drawings

The richness of detail in photos makes them less effective than drawings for focusing on details or showing a process. With a drawing, the artist can provide as much or as little detail as is needed to make the point; different parts of the drawing can show different layers or levels of detail. Drawings are also better for showing structures underground, undersea, or in the atmosphere.

The drawing in Figure 16.9 shows the process a shirt experiences once it is dropped off at the dry cleaners.

Figure 16.10 | Maps Help Compare Information in Different Locations

Prevalence of Binge Drinking among Adults,† 2010

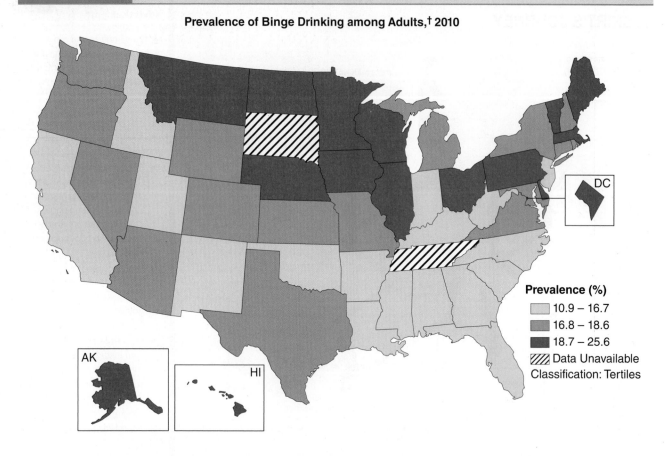

Prevalence (%)

☐	10.9 – 16.7
☐	16.8 – 18.6
☐	18.7 – 25.6
▨	Data Unavailable

Classification: Tertiles

†Age-adjusted to the 2000 U.S. Census standard population.

Source: Centers for Disease Control and Prevention, "Prevalence of Binge Drinking among Adults, 2010," accessed May 29, 2013, http://www.cdc.gov/alcohol/data-stats.htm.

Maps

Use maps to emphasize location or to compare items in different locations. Figure 16.10 shows the prevalence of binge drinking among adults by state. A map is appropriate because the emphasis is on the distribution of binge drinking in various regions. Several computer software packages now allow users to generate local, state, national, or global maps, adding color or shadings, and labels. When using maps,

- Label states, provinces, or countries if it's important that people be able to identify levels in areas other than their own.

- Avoid using perspective. Perspective makes the values harder to read and can make comparison difficult.

Infographics

Information graphics, or infographics, are best used to inform and educate an audience about a specific topic using a mixture of numbers, text, color, and drawings or images. They often present both qualitative and quantitative research studies in an easily digestible format. Many infographics present a sophisticated combination of the types of data displays already discussed in this section. Because of their visual nature, the information contained in infographics is likely to stick with a viewer longer. Infographics exist on nearly any business-related topic you can image. For a more in-depth discussion on infographics, complete with guidelines for creating your own, see Chapter 6.

Dynamic Displays

Technology is expanding the possibilities of data displays. Unlike infographics that are static once published, dynamic displays found on the Internet can be updated on the fly. These displays are interactive, allowing users to adapt them to personal needs or interests. At BabyNameWizard.com, you can see the popularity of various names over the years, or you can track the popularity of one name. Some displays are animated. At CReSIS, the Center for Remote Sensing of Ice Sheets, you can see the effects of global warming on coastal areas around the world as coasts flood while you watch. During presidential elections, many news websites such as *CNN*, the *New York Times*, and the *Wall Street Journal* offer audiences the ability to manipulate what-if scenarios for electoral college votes.

Summary by Learning Objectives

LO 16-1   **When to use visuals and data displays.**

- Visuals and data displays help make data meaningful for your audience and support your arguments.

- In the rough draft, use visuals and data displays to see that ideas are presented completely and to see what relationships exist. In the final presentation or document, use visuals and data displays to make points vivid, to emphasize material that the reader might skip, and to present material more compactly and with less repetition than words alone would require.

- Use visuals and data displays when you want to show relationships and to persuade, when the information is complex or contains extensive numerical data, and when the audience values visuals.

LO 16-2   **How to create effective visuals and data displays.**

- Check the quality of the data.

- Determine the story you want to tell.

- Choose the right visual or data display for the story. Visuals and data displays are not interchangeable. The best selection depends on the kind of data and the point you want to make with the data.

- Follow conventions to avoid alienating your audience.

- Use color and decoration with restraint.

- Be accurate and ethical. Chartjunk, truncated graphs, 3-D graphs, and altered or doctored photos all mislead audiences.

LO 16-3   **How to integrate visuals and data displays into text.**

- Refer in your text to every visual and data display.

- Summarize the main point of a visual or data display before it appears in the text.

- Determine how much discussion a visual or data display needs by considering the audience, the complexity, and the importance of the point it makes.

LO 16-4   **How to use conventions for specific visuals and data displays.**

- Each type of visual or data display can do different things. You should pick the one that best matches your purposes, audiences, and contexts.

- Visuals and data displays rely on conventions. The most common types of visuals and data displays include tables, pie charts, bar charts, line graphs, Gantt charts, photographs, drawings, maps, infographics, and dynamic displays.

Continuing Case

The All-Weather Case, set in an HR department in a manufacturing company, extends through all 19 chapters and is available at www.mhhe.com/locker11e. The portion for this chapter asks students to revise the visuals for a presentation on employee benefits.

Exercises and Cases

Go to www.mhhe.com/locker 11e for additional Exercises and Cases.

16.1   Reviewing the Chapter

1. When should you use visuals and data displays? (LO 16-1)

2. What are some specific ways to create effective visuals and data displays? (LO 16-2)

3. What are some concerns that must be addressed to keep your visuals and data displays accurate and ethical? (LO 16-2)

4. What are some guidelines for integrating visuals and data displays into your text? (LO 16-3)

5. What are some guidelines for constructing bar charts? (LO 16-4)

6. What is the difference between a pie chart and a Gantt chart? (LO 16-4)

7. How do infographics differ from dynamic displays? (LO 16-4)

16.2   Evaluating the Ethics of Design Choices

Indicate whether you consider each of the following actions ethical, unethical, or a gray area. Which of the actions would you do? Which would you feel uncomfortable doing? Which would you refuse to do?

1. Using photos of Hawaiian beaches in advertising for Bermuda tourism, without indicating the location of the beaches.

2. Editing a photo by inserting an image of a young black person into a picture of an all-white group, and using that photo in a recruiting brochure designed to attract minority applicants to a university.

3. Altering people in your photographs so that they look skinnier and younger.

4. Modifying real estate photos by changing the physical appearance of houses or stores.

5. Including pictures in restaurant menus that are exaggerated in presentation quality, color appearance, and portion size.

16.3   Evaluating Visuals

Evaluate each of the following visuals by answering the following questions.

Is the visual's message clear?

Is it the right visual for the story?

Is the visual designed appropriately? Is color, if any, used appropriately?

Is the visual free from chartjunk?

Does the visual distort data or mislead the reader in any way?

1.

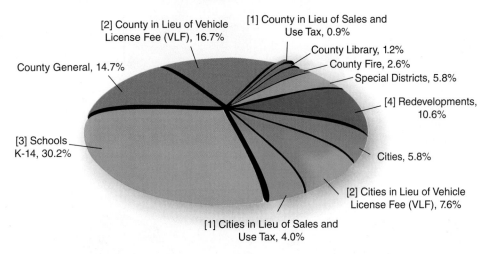

1% Property Tax Revenue Allocation - Fiscal Year 2012–2013
Total Revenue $268,278,928

[2] County in Lieu of Vehicle License Fee (VLF), 16.7%

[1] County in Lieu of Sales and Use Tax, 0.9%

County Library, 1.2%

County General, 14.7%

County Fire, 2.6%

Special Districts, 5.8%

[4] Redevelopments, 10.6%

[3] Schools K-14, 30.2%

Cities, 5.8%

[2] Cities in Lieu of Vehicle License Fee (VLF), 7.6%

[1] Cities in Lieu of Sales and Use Tax, 4.0%

[1] Represents the exchange of Property Tax for Cities and County Sales and Use Tax as authorized under Assembly Bill 1766, chaptered August 2, 2003.

[2] Represents the exchange of Property Tax for Cities and County Vehicle License Fees as authorized under Senate Bill 1096, chaptered August 5, 2004.

[3] Revenue for Schools has been reduced by the ERAF deficit as authorized under Senate Bill 1096, chaptered August 5, 2004.

[4] Effective February 1, 2012, Redevelopment agencies were dissolved and related revenue will be allocated as provided by Assembly Bill X1 26, chaptered June 29, 2011.

Source: http://www.tularecounty.ca.gov/treasurertaxcollector/index.cfm/property-tax-accounting/faqs/where-do-property-taxes-go

2.

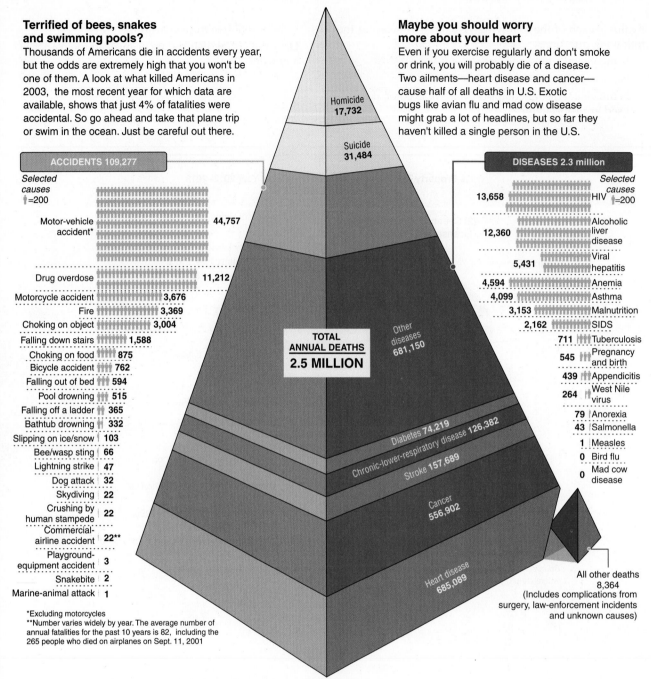

Terrified of bees, snakes and swimming pools?

Thousands of Americans die in accidents every year, but the odds are extremely high that you won't be one of them. A look at what killed Americans in 2003, the most recent year for which data are available, shows that just 4% of fatalities were accidental. So go ahead and take that plane trip or swim in the ocean. Just be careful out there.

Maybe you should worry more about your heart

Even if you exercise regularly and don't smoke or drink, you will probably die of a disease. Two ailments—heart disease and cancer—cause half of all deaths in U.S. Exotic bugs like avian flu and mad cow disease might grab a lot of headlines, but so far they haven't killed a single person in the U.S.

Homicide 17,732

Suicide 31,484

ACCIDENTS 109,277

Selected causes = 200

Motor-vehicle accident*	44,757
Drug overdose	11,212
Motorcycle accident	3,676
Fire	3,369
Choking on object	3,004
Falling down stairs	1,588
Choking on food	875
Bicycle accident	762
Falling out of bed	594
Pool drowning	515
Falling off a ladder	365
Bathtub drowning	332
Slipping on ice/snow	103
Bee/wasp sting	66
Lightning strike	47
Dog attack	32
Skydiving	22
Crushing by human stampede	22
Commercial-airline accident	22**
Playground-equipment accident	3
Snakebite	2
Marine-animal attack	1

*Excluding motorcycles
**Number varies widely by year. The average number of annual fatalities for the past 10 years is 82, including the 265 people who died on airplanes on Sept. 11, 2001

DISEASES 2.3 million

Selected causes = 200

13,658	HIV
12,360	Alcoholic liver disease
5,431	Viral hepatitis
4,594	Anemia
4,099	Asthma
3,153	Malnutrition
2,162	SIDS
711	Tuberculosis
545	Pregnancy and birth
439	Appendicitis
264	West Nile virus
79	Anorexia
43	Salmonella
1	Measles
0	Bird flu
0	Mad cow disease

TOTAL ANNUAL DEATHS 2.5 MILLION

Other diseases 681,150

Diabetes 74,219
Chronic-lower-respiratory disease 126,382
Stroke 157,689

Cancer 556,902

Heart disease 685,089

All other deaths 8,364 (Includes complications from surgery, law-enforcement incidents and unknown causes)

Source: Centers for Disease Control and Prevention; National Transportation Safety Board.

3.

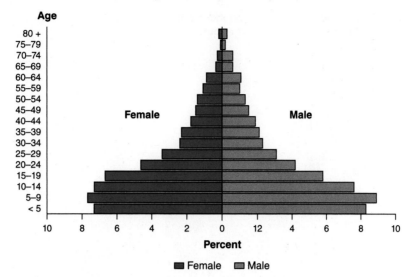

Afghanistan Population Pyramid

Source: MEASURE Demographic and Health Surveys/ICF International, www.measuredhs.com. Reprinted with permission.

4.

Burden of disease attributable to: ALCOHOL (% DALYs in each subregion)

Proportion of DALYs
- <0.5%
- 0.5–0.9%
- 1–1.9%
- 2–3.9%
- 4–7.9%
- 8–15.9%

Worldwide alcohol causes 1.8 million deaths (3.2% of total) and 58.3 million (4% of total) of Disability-Adjusted Life Years (DALYs). Unintentional injuries alone account for about one-third of the 1.8 million deaths, while neuro-psychiatric conditions account for close to 40% of the 58.3 million DALYs. The burden is not equally distributed among the countries, as is shown on the map.

Source: World Health Organization, "Alcohol," in *Management of Substance Abuse,* http://www.who.int/substance_abuse/facts/alcohol/en (accessed May 5, 2009).

5.

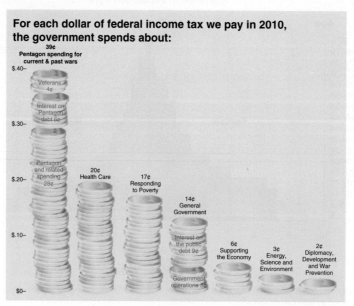

Source: Friends Committee on National Legislation, "Where Do Our Income Tax Dollars Go?" October 2010, *http://fcnl.org/assets/issues/budget/Taxes10coin_chart.pdf.*

16.4   Visualizing Healthy Eating Habits

With soaring obesity rates in the United States, the government continues to produce visuals that encourage healthy eating habits. While the food pyramids have been the norm, their messages have been largely ignored by U.S. citizens. The newest version of the visual to encourage healthy eating uses a plate with various portion sizes for fruits, grains, vegetables, protein, and dairy.

Evaluate each of the visuals by answering the following questions.

Which version of the visual is right for the story?

Which healthy eating visual is clearest?

Which is most informative?

Which visual will most likely encourage healthy eating habits?

Which visuals contain chartjunk?

Which did you prefer? Why?

1.

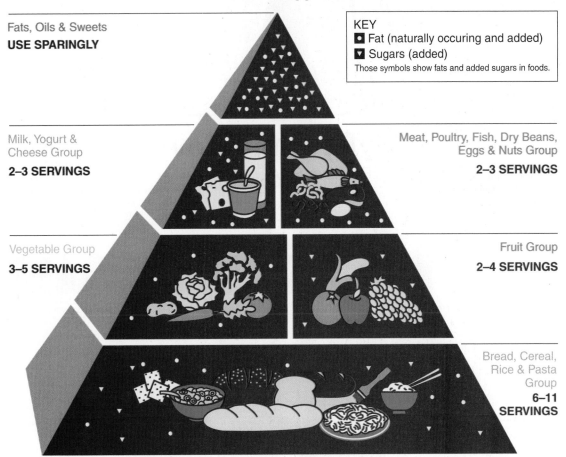

Former food pyramid

Fats, Oils & Sweets
USE SPARINGLY

KEY
◘ Fat (naturally occuring and added)
▼ Sugars (added)
Those symbols show fats and added sugars in foods.

Milk, Yogurt & Cheese Group
2–3 SERVINGS

Meat, Poultry, Fish, Dry Beans, Eggs & Nuts Group
2–3 SERVINGS

Vegetable Group
3–5 SERVINGS

Fruit Group
2–4 SERVINGS

Bread, Cereal, Rice & Pasta Group
6–11 SERVINGS

Source: United States Department of Agriculture, "Food Pyramid," accessed July 4, 2013, http://www.cnpp.usda.gov/Publications/MyPyramid/OriginalFoodGuidePyramids/FGP/FGPPamphlet.pdf.

2.

Anatomy of MyPyramid

One size doesn't fit all

USDA's new MyPyramid symbolizes a personalized approach to healthy eating and physical activity. The symbol has been designed to be simple. It has been developed to remind consumers to make healthy food choices and to be active every day. The different parts of the symbol are described below.

Activity

Activity is represented by the steps and the person climbing them, as a reminder of the importance of daily physical activity.

Moderation

Moderation is represented by the narrowing of each food group from bottom to top. The wider base stands for foods with little or no solid fats or added sugars. These should be selected more often. The narrower top area stands for foods containing more added sugars and solid fats. The more active you are, the more of these foods can fit into your diet.

Personalization

Personalization is shown by the person on the steps, the slogan and the URL. Find the kinds and amounts of food to eat each day at Mypyramid.gov.

Current Food Pyramid

MyPyramid.gov
STEPS TO A HEALTHIER YOU

Proportionality

Proportionality is shown by the different widths of the food group bands. The widths suggest how much food a person should choose from each group. The widths are just a general guide, not exact proportions. Check the Web site for how much is right for you.

Variety

Variety is symbolized by the 6 color bands representing the 5 food groups of the Pyramid and oils. This illustrates that foods from all groups are needed each day for good health.

Gradual Improvement

Gradual improvement is encouraged by the slogan. It suggests that individuals can benefit from taking small steps to improve their diets and lifestyle each day.

U.S. Department of Agriculture
Center for Nutrition Policy
and Promotion
April 2005 CNPP-16
USDA is an equal opportunity provider and employer

GRAINS	VEGETABLES	FRUITS	OILS	MILK	MEAT& BEANS

Source: United States Department of Agriculture, "Steps to a Healthier You," in MyPyramid.gov, accessed June 10, 2013, http://www.choosemyplate.gov/food-groups/downloads/MyPyramid_Getting_Started.pdf.

3.

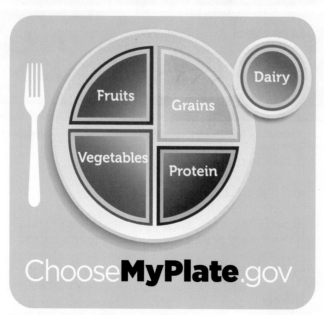

Source: United States Department of Agriculture, "Choose My Plate," in ChooseMyPlate.gov, accessed June 10, 2013, http://www.choosemyplate.gov/downloads/GettingStartedWithMyPlate.pdf.

16.5 Creating a Web Guide to Graphs

Create a web page explaining how to create effective visuals and data displays. Offer principles to a specific audience. Your web page should also provide at least seven links to examples of good and poor visuals and data displays. (More is better.) At the top of your web page, offer an overview of what the page contains. At the bottom of the page, put the creation/update date and your name and e-mail address.

As your instructor directs,

a. Turn in one copy of your page(s). On another page, give the URLs for each link.

b. Electronically submit your web page files.

c. Write an e-mail to your instructor (1) identifying the audience for which the page is designed and explaining (2) the search strategies you used to find material on this topic, (3) why you chose the pages and information you've included, and (4) why you chose the layout and graphics you've used.

d. Present your page orally to the class.

Hints:

- Searching for words (*graphs, maps, Gantt charts, data*) will turn up only pages with those words. Check pages on topics that may use data displays to explain information: finance, companies' performance, sports, labor statistics, cost of living, exports, and so forth.

- In addition to finding good and bad visuals and data displays on the web, you can also scan in examples you find in newspapers, magazines, and textbooks.

- If you have more than nine links, chunk them in small groups under headings.

16.6 Creating Visuals

As your instructor directs,

a. Identify visuals that you might use to help analyze each of the following data sets.

b. Identify and create a visual or data display for one or more of the stories in each set.

c. Identify additional information that would be needed for other stories related to these data sets.

1. Daily Change in Traffic to NCAA-Related Sports Websites, during "March Madness" (U.S., Home and Work).

Site	Wed: 3/15 UA (000)	Thurs: 3/16 UA (000)	Fri: 3/17 UA (000)	Wed Fri Growth
CBS Sportsline.com Network	1,958	3,603	3,135	84%
AOL Sports (web-only)	761	999	1,006	31%
FOX Sports on MSN	1,510	1,953	2,237	29%
Yahoo! Sports	2,121	2,601	2,377	23%
SI.com	724*	819*	773*	13%*
ESPN	3,074	3,312	2,941	8%
Total Unduplicated UA (Unique Audience)	**8,005**	**9,659**	**9,573**	**21%**

*These estimates are calculated on smaller sample sizes and are subject to increased statistical variability as a result.
Source: Enid Burns, "March Madness Invades Office Life," *Trends & Statistics: The Web's Richest Resource.* Reprinted with permission.

2. Customer Satisfaction with Airlines.

Airlines	Base-line	01	02	03	04	05	06	07	08	09	10	11	12	13	Previous Year % Change	First Year % Change
Airlines	**72**	**61**	**66**	**67**	**66**	**66**	**65**	**63**	**62**	**64**	**66**	**65**	**67**	**69**	**3.0**	**-4.2**
Southwest Airlines	78	70	74	75	73	74	74	76	79	81	79	81	77	81	5.2	3.8
All Others	NM	64	72	74	73	74	74	75	75	77	75	76	74	72	-2.7	2.9
Continental Airlines	67	67	68	68	67	70	67	69	62	68	71	64	#		N/A	N/A
American Airlines	70	62	63	67	66	64	62	60	62	60	63	63	64	65	1.6	-7.1
Delta Air Lines (Delta)	77	61	66	67	67	65	64	59	60	64	62	56	65	68	4.6	-11.7
US Airways	72	60	63	64	62	57	62	61	54	59	62	61	65	64	-1.5	.11.1
Northwest Airlines (Delta)	69	56	65	64	64	64	61	61	57	57	61	#	N/A		N/A	N/A
United Airlines	71	59	64	63	64	61	63	56	56	56	60	61	62	62	0.0	-12.7

NA Not available
Company merger
† Company defunct
NM Not measured
^ Industry aggregated

Source: "Airlines" in *The American Customer Satisfaction Index: Scores by Industry*, accessed June 4, 2013, http://www.theacsi.org/?option=com_content&view=article&id=149&catid=14:acsi-results&itemid=214&i=Airlines&c=Delta&sort=ChangeAnual.

16.7 Interpreting Education Data

As your instructor directs,

a. Identify at least five stories in one or more of the following data sets.

b. Create visuals or data displays for three of the stories.

c. Write an e-mail to your instructor explaining why you chose these stories and why you chose these visuals or data displays to display them.

d. Write an e-mail to some group that might be interested in your findings, presenting your visuals or data displays as part of a short report. Possible groups include career counselors, radio stations, advertising agencies, and local school boards.

e. Brainstorm additional stories you could tell with additional data. Specify the kind of data you would need.

Statistics on high school graduates:

1. Curriculum levels completed

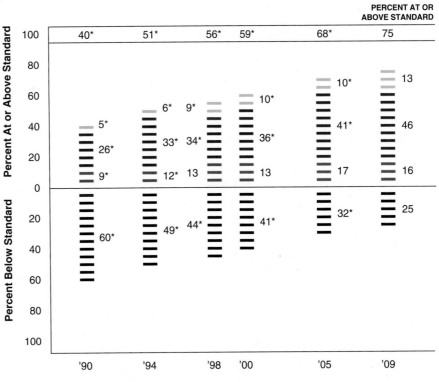

*Significantly different from 2009.

Source: C. Nord, S. Roey, R. Perkins, M. Lyons, N. Lemanski, J. Brown, and J. Schuknecht, *The Nation's Report Card: America's High School Graduates* (NCES 2011-462), U.S. Department of Education, National Center for Education Statistics (Washington, DC: U.S. Government Printing Office, 2011), 8, Figure 2.

2. Trend in grade point average by gender

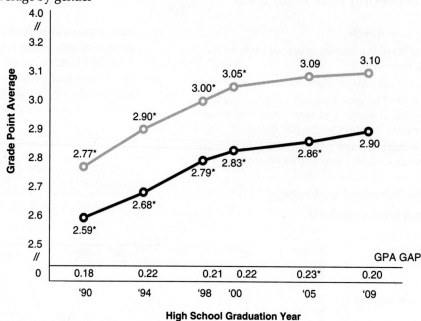

Significantly different from 2009.

Source: C. Nord, S. Roey, R. Perkins, M. Lyons, N. Lemanski, J. Brown, and J. Schuknecht, *The Nation's Report Card: America's High School Graduates* (NCES 2011-462), U.S. Department of Education, National Center for Education Statistics (Washington, DC: U.S. Government Printing Office, 2011), 29, Figure 22.

3. Trend in average course credits earned by graduates, by race/ethnicity

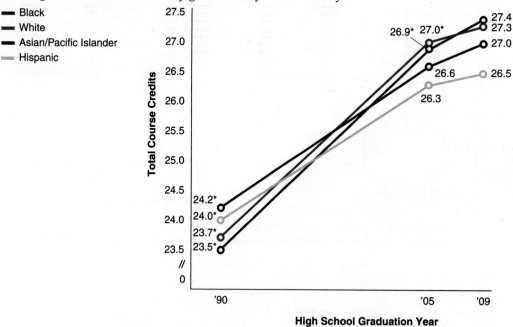

Significantly different from 2009.

Source: C. Nord, S. Roey, R. Perkins, M. Lyons, N. Lemanski, J. Brown, and J. Schuknecht, *The Nation's Report Card: America's High School Graduates* (NCES 2011-462), U.S. Department of Education, National Center for Education Statistics (Washington, DC: U.S. Government Printing Office, 2011), 32, Figure 24.

16.8   Creating Data Displays for a Client

You are volunteering for a local food bank and the director has asked for your assistance. The food bank may be able to receive some state funding if the director can assemble a persuasive proposal about the need for the food bank. The director gives you the following information and asks if you can create data displays for it.

■   Food bank is open four days a week.
■   One director and four volunteers.
■   Food bank feeds 100–150 families per week.
■   Of those families, 95% have children under 18.
■   Often, food will run out by the end of Thursday.
■   If given more support, the food bank could feed many more families in need (the goal would be 250), and could hire more staff members.

As your instructor directs,

a.   In a small group, identify and discuss possible data displays for the proposal.

b.   Individually, create one (or more) data display using the given data. Write an e-mail to your instructor where you justify your design choices.

c.   With a small group, create three data displays that persuade the state agency of the need for funding. Present the data displays to the class in an informal presentation where you justify your design choices.

16.9   Graphing Data from the Web

Find data on the web about a topic that interests you. Sites with data include the following:

Catalyst (women in business)
     http://www.catalyst.org/page/64/
     browse-research-knowledge
ClickZ (digital marketing)
     http://www.clickz.com/showPage
     .html?page=stats
FEDSTATS (links to 70 U.S. government agencies)
     http://www.fedstats.gov
United Nations Environment Program
     http://na.unep.net
U.S. Congress Joint Economic Committee
     http://www.jec.senate.gov/public/index
     .cfm?p=Charts

As your instructor directs,

a.   Identify at least five stories in the data.

b.   Create visuals or data displays for three of the stories.

c.   Write an e-mail to your instructor explaining why you chose these stories and why you chose these visuals or data displays to display them.

d.   Write an e-mail to a group that might be interested in your findings, presenting your visuals as part of a short report.

e.   Print out the data and include them with a copy of your e-mail or report.

16.10   Creating a Visual Argument

With a partner, research one of the following topics:
■   Having English-only laws in the workplace.
■   Introducing new technology into the marketplace.
■   Laying off employees during economic downturns.
■   Requiring employers to offer insurance plans.
■   Banning smoking in the workplace for insurance purposes.
■   Integrating social media and branding into an organization.
■   Hiring/recruiting and diversity in the workplace.
■   Current hot business topic.

Then, prepare a four-minute slide show presentation to share with your peers. The presentation should include only visual elements and contain no words. With the visuals, you should take a stand and present an argument about one of the topics. Recall the guidelines outlined in this chapter about effectively using visuals.

Remember that your presentation needs to be captivating to the audience and effectively convey your purpose. Finally, don't forget to cite all source material.

As your instructor directs,

a.   Submit a copy of your slide show presentation to your instructor.

b.   Write a brief e-mail in which you explain in words the argument you were trying to make.

c.   Submit a works cited page that lists each visual you used.

Notes

1. Monica M. Clark, "Nielsen's 'People Meters' Go Top 10: Atlanta Debut Is Milestone for Device That's Redefining Local TV Audiences' Image," *Wall Street Journal,* June 30, 2006, B2.

2. Gerald J. Alred, Charles T. Brusaw, and Walter E. Oliu, *The Business Writer's Handbook,* 10th ed. (New York: St. Martin's Press, 2012), 246; and Carrie Cousins, "Color and Cultural Design Association," *Webdesigner Depot,* June 11, 2012, http://www.webdesignerdepot.com/2012/06/color-and-cultural-design-considerations/.

3. Eric Kenly and Mark Beach, *Getting It Printed: How to Work with Printers & Graphic Imaging Services to Assure Quality, Stay on Schedule, and Control Costs,* 4th ed. (Cincinnati, OH: HOW Design Books, 2004), 68.

4. Melinda Beck, "New Outlook on Colorblindness," *Wall Street Journal,* November 6, 2012, D1.

5. Edward R. Tufte, *The Visual Display of Quantitative Information,* 2nd ed. (Cheshire, CT: Graphics Press, 2001), 107–21.

6. Charles Kostelnick, "The Visual Rhetoric of Data Displays: The Conundrum of Clarity," *IEEE Transactions on Professional Communication* 51, no. 1 (2008): 116–30.

7. Tufte, *The Visual Display of Quantitative Information,* 74–75.

8. "Some Photos on Facebook Not What They Seem," *Des Moines Register,* November 5, 2011, 5E.

9. Richard B. Woodward, "Debatable 'Evidence,'" *Wall Street Journal,* May 4, 2011, D5.

10. Steven Mufson, "Altered BP Photo Comes into Question," *Washington Post,* July 20, 2010, http://www.washingtonpost.com/wp-dyn/content/article/2010/07/19/AR2010071905256.html.

11. Kathryn Kattalia, "Julia Roberts, Christy Turlington Makeup Ads Banned in U.K.; L'Oreal, Maybelline Ads Cited," *New York Daily News,* July 27, 2011, http://www.nydailynews.com/life-style/fashion/julia-roberts-christy-turlington-makeup-ads-banned-u-oreal-maybelline-ads-cited-article-1.155892.

12. John Long, "Ethics in the Age of Digital Photography," in *National Press Photographers Association,* accessed June 2, 2013, https://nppa.org/page/5127.

13. Accenture advertisement, *Fortune,* August 16, 2010, 17.

17

Writing Proposals and Progress Reports

Chapter Outline

NEWSWORTHY COMMUNICATION

A Modest Financial Proposal

For the past several years, the largest banks in the United States have had a difficult relationship with the U.S. government.

Since the global financial crisis of 2008, the federal government has been pressing the banks for better plans on how to deal with future financial problems. Specifically, the government wants to avoid bailing out the banks again. Some lawmakers are pressing for more regulations on banks, to break up some of the larger institutions and to prevent the banks from causing future instability in the economy.

In response to the lawmakers, some of the largest U.S. banks have submitted their own proposal on how to pay for any restructuring in the future. Rather than another bailout, the banks are proposing a "bail-in," where the burden of debt falls on creditors rather than taxpayers, even while the government provides executive oversight to fix the banks' problems.

While the details of the banks' proposal are complicated, involving the specific terms of long-term debt-equity ratios, the basic message of the proposal was clear: The banks want

to be in control of their future, rather than allowing the government to make decisions that will affect their current business and future profitability. But the proposal the banks have submitted balances their desire for independence with the government's demands for oversight.

Most proposals involve creating a balance between what the other person or company wants and what you have to offer. Writing a proposal with detailed consideration of what that balance involves makes the proposal much more likely to be accepted.

Source: Dan Fitzpatrick, Shayndi Raice, and Michael R. Crittenden, "Banks Present Own Crisis Plan to Fed," *Wall Street Journal*, June 23, 2013, http://online .wsj.com/article/SB10001424127887323300004578555463649746982.html.

Learning Objectives

After studying this chapter, you will know how to

LO 17-1 Define proposals.

LO 17-2 Brainstorm for writing proposals.

LO 17-3 Organize proposals.

LO 17-4 Prepare budget and costs sections.

LO 17-5 Write different proposal varieties.

LO 17-6 Write progress reports.

Proposals and progress reports are two documents that frequently are part of larger, longer projects. **Proposals** argue for the work that needs to be done and who will do it. **Progress reports** let people know how you are coming on the project.

Defining Proposals LO 17-1

In the workplace, much work is routine or specifically assigned by other people. But sometimes you or your organization will want to consider new opportunities, and you will need to write a proposal for that work. Generally, proposals are created for projects that are longer or more expensive than routine work, that differ significantly from routine work, or that create larger changes than does normal work. Another way to view proposals is as tools for managing change.[1]

Proposals argue for work that needs to be done; they offer a method to find information, evaluate something new, solve a problem, or implement a change (see Figure 17.1). Proposals have two major goals: to get the project accepted and to get you or your organization accepted to do the work. To accomplish these goals, proposals must stress benefits for all affected audiences. A proposal for an organization to adopt flex hours would offer benefits for both employees and management, as well as for key departments such as finance.

Proposals may be competitive or noncompetitive. **Competitive proposals** compete against each other for limited resources. Applications for research funding are often highly competitive. Many companies will bid for corporate or government contracts, but only one will be accepted. In fiscal year 2012, the National Science Foundation spent $7 billion supporting research. The National Institutes of Health support almost 50,000 research projects at a cost of $30.9 billion annually.[2] These funds are awarded mainly through competitive proposals.

Noncompetitive proposals have no real competition. For example, a company could accept all of the internal proposals it thought would save money or improve quality. And often a company that is satisfied with a vendor asks for a noncompetitive proposal to renew the contract. Noncompetitive proposals can be as enormous as competitive ones: the proposal for the last U.S. census was $1 billion.

Brainstorming for Writing Proposals LO 17-2

As is true for all forms of business communication, you should begin the brainstorming process by considering your audience, context, and purposes. After you determine these key components, use the proposal questions in the

Figure 17.1	Relationship among Situation, Proposal, and Final Report	
Company's current situation	**The proposal offers to**	**The final report will provide**
We don't know whether we should change.	Assess whether change is a good idea.	Insight, recommending whether change is desirable.
We need to/want to change, but we don't know exactly what we need to do.	Develop a plan to achieve desired goal.	A plan for achieving the desired change.
We need to/want to change, and we know what to do, but we need help doing it.	Implement the plan, increase (or decrease) measurable outcomes.	A record of the implementation and evaluation process.

Source: Adapted from Richard C. Freed, Shervin Freed, and Joseph D. Romano, *Writing Winning Business Proposals*, 3rd ed. (New York: McGraw-Hill, 2010).

next section to brainstorm the content you are going to include. In addition, follow the guidelines in the proposal style section to make sure you're meeting the audience's expectations with your writing choices. These guidelines may also lead to additional content choices.

Proposal Questions

To write a good proposal, you need to have a clear view of the opportunity you want to fill or the problem you hope to solve and the kind of research or other action needed to solve it. A proposal must answer the following questions convincingly:

- **What problem are you going to solve or what opportunity do you hope to fill?** Show that you understand the problem or the opportunity and the organization's needs. Define the problem or opportunity as the audience sees it, even if you believe it is part of a larger problem that must first be solved. Sometimes you will need to show that the problem or opportunity exists. For instance, management might not be aware of subtle discrimination against women that your proposal will help eliminate.

- **Why does the problem need to be solved now or the opportunity explored immediately?** Show that money, time, health, or social concerns support solving the problem or exploring the opportunity immediately. Provide the predicted consequences if the problem is not solved now or if the opportunity is not explored immediately.

- **How are you going to solve it?** Prove that your methods are feasible. Show that a solution can be found in the time available. Specify the topics you'll investigate. Explain how you'll gather data. Show your approach is effective and desirable.

- **Can you do the work?** Show that you, or your organization, have the knowledge, means, personnel, and experience to do the work well. For larger projects, you will have to show some evidence such as preliminary data, personnel qualifications, or similar projects in the past.

- **Why should you be the one to do it?** Show why you or your company should do the work. For many proposals, various organizations could do the work. Why should the work be given to you? Discuss the benefits—direct and indirect—you and your organization can provide.

■ **When will you complete the work?** Provide a detailed schedule showing when each phase of the work will be completed.

■ **How much will you charge?** Provide a detailed budget that includes costs for items such as materials, salaries, and overhead. Give careful thought to unique expenses that may be part of the work. Will you need to travel? Pay fees? Pay benefits in addition to salary for part-time workers?

■ **What exactly will you provide for us?** Specify the tangible products you'll produce; develop their benefits. If possible, include benefits for all levels of audience.

Since proposals to outside organizations are usually considered legally binding documents, get expert legal and financial advice on the last two bullets. Even if the proposal will not be legally binding (perhaps it is an internal proposal), safeguard your professional reputation. Be sure you can deliver the promised products at the specified time using resources and personnel available to you.

Proposal Style

Good proposals are clear and easy to read. Remember that some of your audience may not be experts in the subject matter. Highly statistical survey and data analysis projects may be funded by finance people; medical and scientific studies may be approved by bureaucrats. This means you should use the language your readers understand and expect to see. Some style choices will also add content. How much detail does your audience expect? How much background?

As you write, anticipate and answer questions your readers may have. Support generalizations and inferences with data and other information. Stress benefits throughout the proposal, and make sure you include benefits for all elements of your audience.

Watch your word choice. Avoid diction that shows doubt.

Weak: "*If* we can obtain X. . . ."

"We *hope* we can obtain X."

"We will *try* to obtain X."

Better: "We plan to obtain X."

"We expect to obtain X."

Avoid bragging diction: "huge potential," "revolutionary process." Be particularly careful to avoid bragging diction about yourself. Also avoid "believing" diction: "we believe that . . ." Use facts and figures instead.

Use the expected format for your proposal. Shorter proposals (one to four pages) are generally in letter or e-mail format; longer proposals are frequently formal reports. Depending on the context, you may be asked to mail in a paper proposal, send it as an e-mail attachment, upload a pdf version to a website, or deliver the proposal as an oral presentation. Make sure if you're asked to submit an electronic proposal, you don't send in a paper copy or vice versa. If the proposal is electronic, include a clickable table of contents and other hyperlinks that will provide your audience with an easy way to search your document, especially if your proposal is long.

Government agencies and companies often issue **requests for proposals,** known as **RFPs.** Follow the RFP's specified format in every detail. Use the exact headings, terminology, and structure of the RFP when responding to one. Competitive proposals are often scored by giving points in each category. Evaluators look only under the headings specified in the RFP. If information isn't there, the proposal may get no points in that category.

Beginnings and endings of proposals are important. If you are not following an RFP, your proposal should begin with a clear statement of what you propose doing, why you propose doing it, and what the implications are of the proposed action, or why the action is important. Proposals should end with a brief but strong summary of major benefits of having you do the work. In some circumstances, an urge to action is appropriate:

> If I get your approval before the end of the month, we can have the procedures in place in time for the new fiscal year.

Allow a generous amount of time before the due date for polishing and finishing your proposal:

- Edit carefully.

- Make a final check that you have included all sections and pieces of information requested in the RFP. Many RFPs call for appendixes with items such as résumés and letters of support. Do you have all of yours?

- Ensure that your proposal's appearance will create a good impression. This step includes careful proofreading.

- Make sure you have chosen the correct media channel for your proposal submission.

- Allow enough time for production, reproduction, and administrative approvals before the deadline for receipt of the proposal. If multiple signatures are needed, it may take more than a day to get them all. If you are submitting a government grant proposal, the government server may be clogged with heavy usage on the final due date, or even the day before, so don't wait until the last minute.

Organizing Proposals   LO 17-3

Once you have brainstormed for your proposal, you'll need to select a proposal organization schema that is most appropriate for your purpose. If you're writing a proposal that your instructor has assigned for an in-class assignment, follow the guidelines for proposals for class research projects. See Figure 17.2, pages 558–61, for an example of this variety of proposal. If you're seeking to raise capital for new business ventures, follow the guidelines for business proposals.

Proposals for Class Research Projects

You may be asked to submit a proposal for a report that you will write for a class. Your instructor wants evidence that your problem is meaningful but not too big to complete in the allotted time, that you understand it, that your method will give you the information you need, that you have the knowledge and resources to collect and analyze the data, and that you can produce the report by the deadline.

A proposal for a student report usually has the following sections:

1. In your first paragraph (no heading), summarize in a sentence or two the topic and purposes of your report.

2. **Problem/Opportunity.** What problem or opportunity exists? Why does it need to be solved or explored? Is there a history or background that is relevant?

3. **Feasibility.** Are you sure that a solution can be found in the time available? How do you know? (This section may not be appropriate for some class projects.)

4. **Audience.** Who in the organization would have the power to implement your recommendation? What secondary audiences might be asked to evaluate your report? What audiences would be affected by your recommendation? Will anyone in the organization serve as a gatekeeper, determining whether your report is sent to decision makers? What watchdog audiences might read the report? Will there be other readers?

   For each of these audiences give the person's name and job title and answer the following questions:

   - What is the audience's major concern or priority? What "hot buttons" must you address with care?

   - What will the audience see as advantages of your proposal? What objections, if any, is the audience likely to have?

   - How interested is the audience in the topic of your report?

   - How much does the audience know about the topic of your report?

   List any terms, concepts, or assumptions that one or more of your audiences may need to have explained. Briefly identify ways in which your audiences may affect the content, organization, or style of the report.

5. **Topics to investigate.** List the questions you will answer in your report, the topics or concepts you will explain, the aspects of the problem or opportunity you will discuss. Indicate how deeply you will examine each of the aspects you plan to treat. Explain your rationale for choosing to discuss some aspects of the problem or opportunity and not others.

6. **Methods/procedure.** How will you get answers to your questions? Whom will you interview or survey? What questions will you ask? What published sources will you use? Give the full bibliographic references. Your methods section should clearly indicate how you will get the information needed to answer questions posed in the other sections of the proposal.

7. **Qualifications/facilities/resources.** Do you have the knowledge and skills needed to conduct this study? Do you have adequate access to the organization? Is the necessary information available to you? Are you aware of any supplemental information? Where will you turn for help if you hit an unexpected snag?

   You'll be more convincing if you have already scheduled an interview, checked out books, or printed online sources.

8. **Work schedule.** For each activity, list both the total time you plan to spend on it and the date when you expect to finish it. Some possible activities you might include could be gathering information, analyzing information, preparing a progress report, writing the report draft, revising the draft, preparing visuals, editing and proofreading the report, and preparing the oral presentation. Think of activities needed to complete your specific project.

   These activities frequently overlap. Many writers start analyzing and organizing information as it comes in. They start writing pieces of the final document and preparing visuals early in the process.

Organize your work schedule in either a chart or calendar. A good schedule provides realistic estimates for each activity, allows time for unexpected snags, and shows that you can complete the work on time.

9. **Call to action.** In your final section, indicate that you'd welcome any suggestions your instructor may have for improving the research plan. Ask your instructor to approve your proposal so that you can begin work on your report.

Figure 17.2 shows a student proposal for a long report.

Proposals for Businesses

Many business proposals recommend new programs, offer ways to solve problems, sell goods or services, request funds, or outline a new business idea. Writing such proposals often requires considerable research, including reading articles in trade and professional journals, looking up data online, talking to employees or customers, and even gathering data from outside the organization. All this information requires careful organization.

Any time you are asked to write a proposal for non-classroom purposes, you will want to follow the organization that is most routinely used in business settings.

Proposals for businesses usually employ the following organization scheme:

1. **Introduction.** Summarize the subject and purposes of your proposal. You should also discuss the significance of the project and any relevant background information.

2. **Current situation.** Describe the problem that needs to be solved or the opportunity to be explored, its causes, and the outcome if it is not resolved.

3. **Project plan.** Outline the steps you will follow to solve the problem or explore the opportunity you've identified in the previous section. You should also indicate the final deliverables of your project.

4. **Qualifications.** State the knowledge and skills you possess necessary to complete the project you're proposing. Some proposals include résumés in this section.

5. **Costs and benefits.** Briefly outline the costs associated with your project and then state all the benefits it will bring. Make sure the benefits outweigh the costs. (More details on preparing the costs and budget sections are included in the next section.)

Preparing the Budget and Costs Sections LO 17-4

For a class research project, you may not be asked to prepare a budget. However, many business proposals do require budgets, and a good budget is crucial to making the winning bid. In fact, your budget may be the most scrutinized part of your business proposal.

Ask for everything you need to do a quality job. Asking for too little may backfire, leading the funder to think that you don't understand the scope of the project. Include less obvious costs, such as overhead. Also include costs that will be paid from other sources. Doing so shows that other sources also have confidence in your work. Pay particular attention to costs that may appear to benefit you more than the sponsor such as travel and equipment. Make sure they are fully justified in the proposal.

Tapping into the Research Experts

Where else can you go besides Google to find the information you need for your next proposal? You might try your local library.

While you can find a wealth of information on Google, libraries subscribe to commercial databases, such as Mergent Online and Business Source Premier, that can give you access to powerful tools for writing your company's business or marketing plan. Often, these databases have much better search optimization abilities than a routine Google search. An added bonus is that librarians are experts at navigating those databases and can probably help you find exactly what you need.

Both students and small-business owners, in particular, can benefit. Many libraries even hold classes and provide networking opportunities with other local agencies and organizations geared to help the small businesses. So the next time you are working on a business proposal, visit your local library.

Figure 17.2	Proposal for a Student Team Report

Month Day, Year *Enter current date*

To: Professor Christopher Toth

From: JASS LLC (Jordan Koole, Alex Kuczera,   *In the subject line* ① *indicate that this is a proposal*
            Shannon Jones, Sean Sterling)   ② *specify the kind of report*
                                                              ③ *specify the topic.*

Subject: Proposal to Research and Make Recommendations on the Feasibility
            of Expanding RAC Inc. to South Korea

Summarize RAC Inc. has recently approached our company to determine the possibility of expanding
topic and internationally. We believe South Korea could be suitable for this expansion based on our initial
purpose of investigation of technology in the country. This proposal provides a brief look at South Korea
report. and gives an overview of our research topics and procedures in preparation for the formal
research report.

Problem
  If the "Problem" section is detailed and well-written, you may be able to use it unchanged in your report.
After establishing a solid consumer base in the U.S., RAC Inc. is looking to expand their
business internationally so that they do not fall behind their competitors. They have asked us to
research South Korea as a possible alternative site for the manufacturing of their slate tablets.

Country Overview   *This section is a "Background" section for this*
                          proposal. Not all proposals include background.

After some initial research, we believe that South Korea is a suitable country to research for
RAC's international manufacturing of new technology. South Korea has a population of
48.3 million, with 27% of the population located in the capital city Seoul and in Busan. They
have a labor force of 24.62 million, ranking as the 25th highest workforce in the world (CIA
Factbook, 2011). The official language is Korean, but English, Chinese, and Japanese are
taught as second languages (U.S. Department of State, 2010). *Proposal uses in-text citations.*

In 1950, North Korea invaded South Korea, beginning the Korean War. After three years of
fighting and pushing troops across both borders, North and South Korea signed an armistice
and agreed to a demilitarized zone (DMZ), which currently serves as the border between the
two countries and is protected by both countries' military (U.S. Department of State, 2010).
While relations between the two countries are still tense and a few minor skirmishes along the
border have occurred, we are not concerned about South Korea's stability.

In fact, since the devastation of the Korean War, the economy of South Korea has recovered
and has joined the ranks of the most economically prosperous nations. They have risen to the
13th highest GDP in the world and have the 45th highest GDP per capita at the equivalent of
$30,200. They have a very low unemployment rate that has dropped in the last year to 3.3%
(CIA Factbook, 2011).

South Korea is now ranked the 7th largest exporter in the world and the 9th largest importer.
Their economic policy has emphasized exporting products, explaining why their exports are so
high (U.S. Department of State, 2010). Their main exports include computers and component
parts, semiconductors, and wireless telecommunication equipment. South Korea is known for
making excellent products in these areas. They export mainly to the U.S., China, and Japan,
and import primarily from the same countries. As one of the most economically healthy
countries in the world, South Korea is situated as a prime country for RAC Inc.'s possible
expansion.

Not all class reports
will need a
"Feasibility" section.

Figure 17.2   Proposal for a Student Team Report (*Continued*)

RAC Inc. Proposal
Month Day, Year   *Enter current date*
Page 2

List your major audiences. Identify their knowledge, interests, and concerns.

Audience

Our formal report will have multiple layers of audiences.

- *Gatekeeper*: Professor Toth has the power to accept or reject our proposal for the formal report before it is passed on to Ms. Katie Nichols from RAC Inc.

- *Primary*: Ms. Katie Nichols, CEO of RAC Inc., and the board of directors are our primary audiences, along with other influential members of RAC Inc. They will decide whether to accept the recommendation found in the formal report.

- *Secondary*: Employees of RAC Inc., the legal department of RAC Inc., as well as current RAC Inc. employees who may be transferred to South Korea may all be affected by the primary audience's decision. In addition, the potential employees in South Korea who would work for RAC Inc. also make up this audience.

- *Auxiliary*: Other employees not involved with the expansion effort into South Korea and any Americans or South Koreans who will read about the expansion in the news serve this role.

- *Watchdog*: Stockholders of RAC Inc., the South Korean government, the Securities and Exchange Commission (SEC), the U.S. Department of Commerce, and other companies that may want to expand internationally to South Korea all have economic, social, and political power. Competitors of RAC Inc. already in South Korea (Samsung and LG) may also pay close attention.

Indicate what you'll discuss briefly and what you'll discuss in more detail. This list should match your audiences' concerns.

Topics to Investigate

We plan to answer the following questions in detail:

1. What information does RAC Inc. need to know about South Korean culture, politics, economy, and workforce to be succesful?

All items in list must be grammatically parallel. Here, all are questions.

- Culture—What differences exist between Korean and American cultures that might influence the move?
- Politics—How will relationships between North and South Korea and relationships between the U.S. and South Korea affect business with South Korea?
- Economics—What is the current economic state of the country? How could free trade between the U.S. and South Korea affect business?
- Workforce—What is the availabe workforce? How will the economy of the country affect the overall workforce?

2. How should RAC Inc. adapt their business practices to successfully expand into the South Korean market?

- Competition—Who is the competition in South Korea? How could they affect the business?
- Location—What city could RAC Inc. expand to for production of the slate tablet? Where should they locate the headquarters? Where should they host the initial product launch?
- Slate Tablet—What changes, if any, are needed to market and sell the product in South Korea?

Include a header on all additional pages.

Figure 17.2	Proposal for a Student Team Report (*Continued*)

RAC Inc. Proposal
Month Day, Year
Page 3

3. What other issues may RAC Inc. have by introducing their product into South Korea?

If it is well written, "Topics to Investigate" section will become the "Scope" section of the report—with minor revisions.

- Business Culture—How will the differences in business culture influence the expansion to South Korea?
- Technology—To what extent will the advanced state of South Korean technology influence marketing the tablet?
- Marketing—How will competitors' similar products sold in South Korea influence business?
- Integration—How receptive are the people of South Korea to new products from different companies and countries?

Methods and Resources

If you'll administer a survey or conduct interviews, tell how many subjects you'll have, how you'll choose them, and what you'll ask them. This group does not use a survey.

We expect to obtain our information from: (1) various websites, (2) articles, and (3) interviews with a native South Korean. The following websites and articles appear useful.

If you're using library or web research, list sources you hope to use. Use full bibliographic citations.

Central Intelligence Agency. (2011). *The world factbook: South Korea*. Retrieved March 18, 2011, from https:/ /www.cia.gov/library/publications/the-world-factbook/geos/ks.html#.

Fackler, M. (2011, January 6). Lessons learned, South Korea makes quick economic recovery. *The New York Times*. Retrieved from http:/ /www.nytimes.com/2011/01/07/world/asia/07seoul.html?_r=2.

Jeon, Kyung-Hwan. (2010, September 7). Why your business belongs in South Korea. Retrieved from http:/ /www.openforum.com/articles/why-your-business-belongs-in-south-korea-kyung-hwan-jeon.

This list uses APA format.

Life in Korea. (n.d.). Cultural spotlight. Retrieved March 31, 2011, from http:/ /www.lifeinkorea.com/Culture/spotlight.cfm.

Your list of sources should convince your instructor that you have made initial progress on the report.

Ogg, E. (2010, May 28). What makes a tablet a tablet? *CNet News*. Retrieved March 19, 2011, from http:/ /news.cnet.com/8301-31021_3-20006077-260.html?tag=newsLeadStoriesArea.1.

Settimi, C. (2010, September 1). Asia's 200 best under a billion. *Forbes*. Retrieved from http://www.forbes.com/2010/09/01/ bub-200-intro-asia-under-billion-10-small-companies.html.

UK Trade & Investment. (2011). 100 opportunities for UK companies in South Korea. Retrieved March 19, 2011, from http:/ /www.ukti.gov.uk/export/countries/asiapacific/fareast/koreasouth/item/119500.html.

U.S. Deparment of State. (2010, December 10). Background note: South Korea. Retrieved March 18, 2011, from http:/ /www.state.gov/r/pa/ei/bgn/2800.htm.

World Business Culture. (n.d.). Doing business in South Korea. Retrieved March 19, 2011, from http:/ /www.worldbusinessculture.com/Business-in-South-Korea.html.

Figure 17.2   Proposal for a Student Team Report (*Concluded*)

RAC Inc. Proposal
Month Day, Year
Page 4

Qualifications   *Cite knowledge and skills from other classes, jobs, and activities that will enable you to conduct the research and interpret your data.*

We are all members of JASS LLC who have backgrounds in finance, accounting, computer science, and technology. These diverse backgrounds in the business and technology world give us a good perspective and insight for this project. In addition, we are all enrolled in a business communication course that provides us with knowledge on producing high-quality documents. We are dedicated to producing a thoroughly researched report that will provide solid evidence on the feasibility of an international expansion for RAC Inc. into South Korea.

Work Schedule

The following schedule will enable us to finish this report on time.

Good reports need good revision, editing, and proofreading as well as good research.

Activity	Total Time	Completion Date
Gathering information	12 hours	March 30
Analyzing information	8 hours	April 2
Organizing information	4 hours	April 7
Writing draft/creating visuals	8 hours	April 10
Revising draft	3 hours	April 12
Preparing presentation slides	3–4 hours	April 14
Editing draft	3 hours	April 17
Proofreading report	3 hours	April 18
Rehearsing presentation	2 hours	April 20
Delivering presentaion	1 hour	April 21

Allow plenty of time

Time will depend on the length and topic of your report, your knowledge of the topic, and your writing skills.

Call to Action

We are confident that JASS LLC can complete the above tasks as scheduled. We would appreciate any suggestions for improving our project plan. Please approve our proposal so that we may begin work on the formal report.

It's tactful to indicate you'll accept suggestions. End on a positive, forward-looking note.

Do some research. Read the RFP to find out what is and isn't fundable. Talk to the program officer (the person who administers the funding process) and read successful past proposals to find answers to the following questions:

- What size projects will the organization fund in theory?
- Does the funder prefer making a few big grants or many smaller grants?
- Does the funder expect you to provide in-kind or cost-sharing funds from other sources?

Think about exactly what you'll do and who will do it. What will it cost to get that person? What supplies or materials will he or she need? Also think about indirect costs for using office space, about retirement and health benefits as well as salaries, about office supplies, administration, and infrastructure. Make the basis of your estimates specific.

Weak:	75 hours of transcribing interviews	$1,500
Better:	25 hours of interviews; a skilled transcriber can complete 1 hour of interviews in 3 hours; 75 hours @ $20/hour	$1,500

Figure your numbers conservatively. For example, if the going rate for skilled transcribers is $20 an hour, but you think you might be able to train someone and pay only $12 an hour, use the higher figure. Then, even if your grant is cut, you'll still be able to do the project well.

Writing Proposal Varieties LO 17-5

This section offers advice for writing two of the most common varieties of business proposals: sales proposals and business plans.

Sales Proposals

To sell expensive goods or services, you may be asked to submit a proposal.

To write a good sales proposal, be sure that you understand the buyer's priorities. A phone company lost a $36 million sale to a university because it assumed the university's priority would be cost. Instead, the university wanted a state-of-the-art system. The university accepted a higher bid.

Make sure your proposal presents your goods or services as solving the problem your audience perceives. Don't assume that the buyer will understand why your product or system is good. For everything you offer, show the benefits of each feature. Be sure to present the benefits using you-attitude.

Use language appropriate for your audience. Even if the buyers want a state-of-the-art system, they may not want the level of detail that your staff could provide; they may not understand or appreciate technical jargon.

Sales proposals, particularly for complicated systems costing millions of dollars, are often long. Provide a one-page cover letter to present your proposal succinctly. The best organization for this letter is usually a modified version of the sales pattern in Chapter 11:

1. Catch the reader's attention and summarize up to three major benefits you offer.
2. Discuss each of the major benefits in the order in which you mentioned them in the first paragraph.
3. Deal with any objections or concerns the reader may have. In a sales proposal, these objections probably include costs. Connect costs with benefits.

4. Mention other benefits briefly.
5. Ask the reader to approve your proposal and provide a reason for acting promptly.

Business Plans and Other Proposals for Funding

Proposals for funding include both **business plans** (documents written to raise capital for new business ventures) and proposals submitted to foundations, corporations, and government agencies to seek money for public service projects. In a proposal for funding, stress the needs your project will meet and show how your project helps fulfill the goals of the organization you are asking for funds. Every funding agency has a mission, so be sure to align your idea to fit the agency's needs in obvious ways. Try to weave the agency's mission throughout your proposal's content. Remember effective you-attitude—write for the needs of your audience, not yourself.

Since venture capitalists and other investors are not known for their patience, business plans in particular need to have a concise, compelling beginning describing exactly what you plan to do and what need it will fill. Pay careful attention to the "Executive Summary." This overview section is one of the most important places in any proposal. After reading this opening, the reviewer will make initial decisions about you, your writing, your idea, and your logic. Therefore, it must spark enthusiasm for your idea; the reviewer's interest will never increase later in your proposal. This section should also provide an overview of all of the major topics you will cover in the body.

Your business plan should answer the questions listed in Figure 17.3 with sufficient detail to be convincing and supporting evidence where applicable.

Financial information is important in any proposal, but it is even more crucial in a business plan. You will need to show how much of your own money you are investing, what investors are already supporting you, and how you plan to use the money you get. Many investors want to see a five-year financial forecast. Explain with convincing detail how you expect to make money. What is your time frame for financial success? What is your estimated monthly income the first year?

Anticipate problems (investors will already know them; this shows you do, too); show how you plan to solve them. Use details to help convince your audience. Many business plans are too general to convince investors. Details show you have done your homework; they can also show your business acumen.

Proposals are also a major part of nonprofits' fund-raising activity; they write grant proposals to governmental organizations, foundations, and individuals

Figure 17.3	Questions Business Plans Should Answer

- What is your product or service?
- How well developed is it? Is a mock-up or demo available?
- Who is your market? How large is it? Why does this market need your product or service?
- How will you promote your product or service?
- Who are your competitors? How will you be better? What other problems and challenges will you have to face on your path to profit?
- Who is also providing support for your business?
- Who will be working with you? How many more employees will you need? What will you pay them? What benefits will you give them?

to raise money for their organization. The writing process involves considerable research and planning, and often is preceded by informal conversations and formal presentations to potential funders. The funding process is often seen as a relationship-building process that involves researching, negotiating with, and persuading funders that the proposal not only meets their guidelines, but also is a cause worthy of a grant.

Every funding source has certain priorities; some have detailed lists of the kind of projects they fund. Be sure to do research before applying. Check recent awards to discover foundations that may be interested in your project. See Figure 17.4 for additional resources.

When you write proposals for funding, be sure you follow all format criteria. Be particularly obedient to specifications about page count, type size, margins, and spacing (single or double spacing). When flooded with applications, many funders use these criteria as preliminary weeding devices.

Finally, pay close attention to deadlines by reading the fine print. Turn your materials in early. The National Endowment for the Humanities encourages fund seekers to submit drafts six weeks before the deadline to allow time for their staff to review materials.[3]

Writing Progress Reports LO 17-6

When you're assigned to a single project that will take a month or more, you'll probably be asked to file one or more progress reports. A progress report reassures the funding agency or employer that you're making progress and allows you and the agency or employer to resolve problems as they arise. Different readers may have different concerns. An instructor may want to know whether you'll have your report in by the due date. A client may be more interested in what you're learning about the problem. Adapt your progress report to the needs of the audience.

Poor writers of progress reports tend to focus on what they have done and say little about the value of their work. Good writers, on the other hand, spend less space writing about the details of what they've done but much more space explaining the value of their work for the organization.

When you write progress reports, use what you know about emphasis, positive tone, and you-attitude. Don't present every detail as equally important.

Figure 17.4	Additional Resources for Writing Business Plans and Funding Proposals	
Organization	**URL**	**Description**
U.S. Small Business Administration	http://www.sba.gov/category/navigation-structure/starting-managing-business/starting-business	Offers detailed advice for writing a business plan.
Philanthropic Research Inc.	http://www.guidestar.org	Publishes free information about grants and grant makers.
Pivot—Community of Science	http://pivot.cos.com	Offers information on global funding opportunities, as well as tools to manage grants.
U.S. Department of Health and Human Services	http://www.grants.gov	Offers information on grant programs of all federal grantmaking agencies, as well as downloadable grant applications.
The Foundation Center	http://foundationcenter.org/	Indexes foundations by state and city as well as by field of interest.

Use emphasis techniques to stress the major ones. Readers will generally not care that Jones was out of the office when you went to visit him and that you had to return a second time to catch him. Trivial details like this should be omitted.

In your report, try to exceed expectations in at least some small way. Perhaps your research is ahead of schedule or needed equipment arrived earlier than expected. However, do not present the good news by speculating on the reader's feelings; many readers find such statements offensive.

Poor: You will be happy to hear the software came a week early.

Better: The software came a week early, so Pat can start programming earlier than expected.

Remember that your audience for your report is usually in a position of power over you, so be careful what you say to them. Generally it is not wise to blame them for project problems even if they are at fault.

Poor: We could not proceed with drafting the plans because you did not send us the specifications for the changes you want.

Better: Chris has prepared the outline for the plan. We are ready to start drafting as soon as we receive the specifications. Meanwhile, we are working on. . . .

Subject lines for progress reports are straightforward. Specify the project on which you are reporting your progress.

> Subject: Progress on Developing a Marketing Plan for Fab Fashions

If you are submitting weekly or monthly progress reports on a long project, number your progress reports or include the time period in your subject line. Include information about the work completed since the last report and work to be completed before the next report.

Make your progress report as positive as you *honestly* can. You'll build a better image of yourself if you show that you can take minor problems in stride and that you're confident of your own abilities.

> The preliminary data sets were two days late because of a server crash. However, Nidex believes they will be back on schedule by next week. Past performance indicates their estimate is correct, and data analysis will be finished in two weeks, as originally scheduled.

Focus on your solutions to problems rather than the problems themselves:

Negative: Southern data points were corrupted, and that problem set us back three days in our data analysis.

Positive: Although southern data points were corrupted, the northern team was able to loan us Chris and Lee to fix the data set. Both teams are currently back on schedule.

In the above example the problem with the southern data points is still noted, because readers may want to know about it, but the solution to the problem is emphasized.

http://www.hbs .edu/entrepreneur ship/resources/ businessplan.html

This website from the Harvard Business School offers many resources for creating a business plan. There are additional website links, articles, videos, and other tools to ensure your business plan is a success. Follow this advice and make sure your business plan uses a strong argument and is unique.

Other Uses of Progress Reports

Progress reports can do more than just report progress. You can use progress reports to

- **Enhance your image.** Details about the number of documents you've read, people you've surveyed, or experiments you've conducted create a picture of a hardworking person doing a thorough job.

- **Float trial balloons.** Explain, "I could continue to do X [what you approved]; I could do Y instead [what I'd like to do now]." The detail in the progress report can help back up your claim. Even if the idea is rejected, you don't lose face because you haven't made a separate issue of the alternative.

- **Minimize potential problems.** As you do the work, it may become clear that implementing your recommendations will be difficult. In your regular progress reports, you can alert your boss or the funding agency to the challenges that lie ahead, enabling them to prepare psychologically and physically to act on your recommendations.

Do remember to use judicious restraint with your positive tone. Without details for support, glowing judgments of your own work may strike readers as ill-advised bragging, or maybe even dishonesty.

Overdone positive tone, lack of support	Our data analysis is indicating some great new predictions; you will be very happy to see them.
Supported optimism:	Our data analysis is beginning to show that coastal erosion may not be as extensive as we had feared; in fact, it may be almost 10% less than originally estimated. We should have firm figures by next week.

Progress reports can be organized in three ways: by chronology, task, and recommendation support. Some progress reports may use a combination: they may organize material chronologically within each task section, for instance.

Chronological Progress Reports

The chronological pattern of organization focuses on what you have done and what work remains.

1. **Summarize your progress in terms of your goals and your original schedule.** Use measurable statements.

Poor:	Progress has been slow.
Better:	Analysis of data sets is about one-third complete.

2. **Under the heading "Work Completed," describe what you have already done.** Be specific, both to support your claims in the first paragraph and to allow the reader to appreciate your hard work. Acknowledge the people who have helped you. Describe any serious obstacles you've encountered and tell how you've dealt with them.

Poor:	I have found many articles about Procter & Gamble on the web. I have had a few problems finding how the company keeps employees safe from chemical fumes.
Better:	On the web, I found Procter & Gamble's home page, its annual report, and mission statement. No one whom I interviewed could tell me about safety programs specifically at P&G. I have found seven articles about ways to protect workers against pollution in factories, but none mentions P&G.

3. **Under the heading "Work to Be Completed," describe the work that remains.** If you're more than three days late (for school projects) or two weeks late (for business projects) submit a new schedule, showing how you will be able to meet the original deadline. You may want to discuss "Observations" or "Preliminary Conclusions" if you want feedback before writing the final report or if your reader has asked for substantive interim reports.

4. **Express your confidence in having the report ready by the due date.** If you are behind your original schedule, show why you think you can still finish the project on time.

Even in chronological reports you need to do more than merely list work you have done. Show the value of that work and your prowess in achieving it, particularly your ability at solving problems. The student progress report in Figure 17.5 uses the chronological pattern of organization.

Figure 17.5	A Student Chronological Progress Report

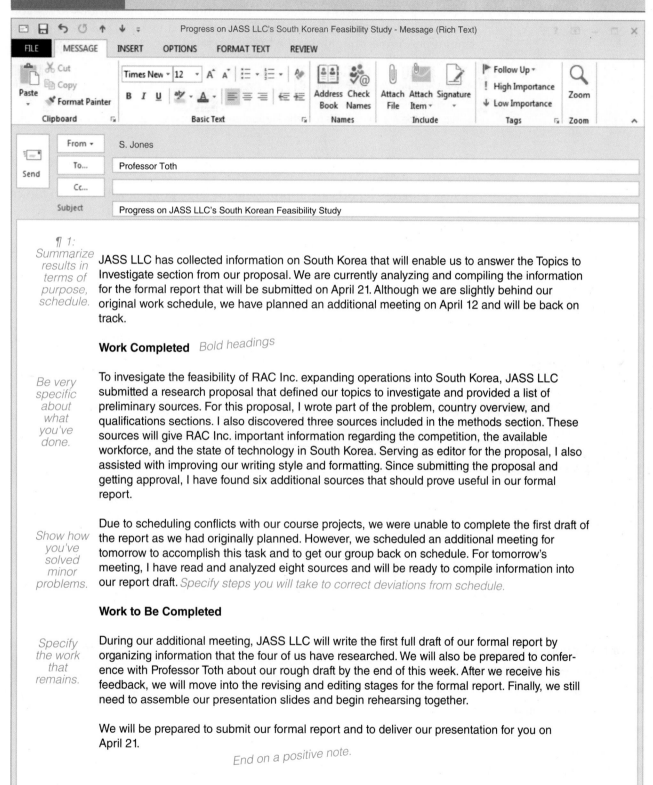

Progress on JASS LLC's South Korean Feasibility Study - Message (Rich Text)

From · S. Jones

To... Professor Toth

Cc...

Subject Progress on JASS LLC's South Korean Feasibility Study

¶ 1: Summarize results in terms of purpose, schedule.

JASS LLC has collected information on South Korea that will enable us to answer the Topics to Investigate section from our proposal. We are currently analyzing and compiling the information for the formal report that will be submitted on April 21. Although we are slightly behind our original work schedule, we have planned an additional meeting on April 12 and will be back on track.

Work Completed *Bold headings*

Be very specific about what you've done.

To invesigate the feasibility of RAC Inc. expanding operations into South Korea, JASS LLC submitted a research proposal that defined our topics to investigate and provided a list of preliminary sources. For this proposal, I wrote part of the problem, country overview, and qualifications sections. I also discovered three sources included in the methods section. These sources will give RAC Inc. important information regarding the competition, the available workforce, and the state of technology in South Korea. Serving as editor for the proposal, I also assisted with improving our writing style and formatting. Since submitting the proposal and getting approval, I have found six additional sources that should prove useful in our formal report.

Show how you've solved minor problems.

Due to scheduling conflicts with our course projects, we were unable to complete the first draft of the report as we had originally planned. However, we scheduled an additional meeting for tomorrow to accomplish this task and to get our group back on schedule. For tomorrow's meeting, I have read and analyzed eight sources and will be ready to compile information into our report draft. *Specify steps you will take to correct deviations from schedule.*

Work to Be Completed

Specify the work that remains.

During our additional meeting, JASS LLC will write the first full draft of our formal report by organizing information that the four of us have researched. We will also be prepared to conference with Professor Toth about our rough draft by the end of this week. After we receive his feedback, we will move into the revising and editing stages for the formal report. Finally, we still need to assemble our presentation slides and begin rehearsing together.

We will be prepared to submit our formal report and to deliver our presentation for you on April 21.

End on a positive note.

Task Progress Reports

In a task progress report, organize information under the various tasks you have worked on during the period. For example, a task progress report for a team report project might use the following headings:

Finding Background Information on the Web and in Print
Analyzing Our Survey Data
Working on the Introduction of the Report and the Appendixes

Under each heading, the team could discuss the tasks it has completed and those that remain.

Task progress reports are appropriate for large projects with distinct topics or projects.

Recommendation Progress Reports

Recommendation progress reports recommend action: increasing the funding or allotted time for a project, changing its direction, canceling a project that isn't working. When the recommendation will be easy for the reader to accept, use the direct request pattern of organization from Chapter 11. If the recommendation is likely to meet strong resistance, the problem-solving pattern, also in Chapter 11, may be more effective.

Summary by Learning Objectives

LO 17-1   Define proposals.

Proposals argue for the work that needs to be done and who will do it. Competitive proposals compete against each other for limited resources; noncompetitive proposals have no real competition.

LO 17-2   Brainstorm for writing proposals.

A proposal must answer the following questions:

- What problem are you going to solve or what opportunity do you hope to fulfill?
- Why does the problem need to be solved now or the opportunity explored immediately?
- How are you going to solve it?
- Can you do the work?
- Why should you be the one to do it?
- When will you complete the work?
- How much will you charge?
- What exactly will you provide for us?

LO 17-3   Organize proposals.

- In a proposal for a class research project, prove that your problem is the right size, that you understand it, that your method will give you

the information you need to solve the problem, that you have the knowledge and resources, and that you can produce the report by the deadline.

- In a proposal for business, introduce the problem or opportunity, explain its causes and what will happen if nothing is done, outline a project plan to solve the problem or opportunity, state your qualifications, and discuss the costs and benefits of accepting the project.

LO 17-4   Prepare budget and costs sections.

In a project budget, ask for everything you will need to do a good job. Research current cost figures so yours are in line. For costs that appear to benefit you more than the sponsor, give full justifications.

LO 17-5   Write different proposal varieties.

- Sales proposals are useful to sell expensive goods or services.
- Funding proposals should stress the needs your project will meet. Show how your project will help fulfill the goals of the organization you are asking for funds.

- Business plans need to pay particular attention to market potential and financial forecasts.

LO 17-6   **Write progress reports.**

- Progress reports let people know how you are coming on a project.

- Positive emphasis in progress reports creates an image of yourself as a capable, confident worker.

- Progress reports may be organized by chronology, task, or recommendation support.

Continuing Case

The All-Weather Case, set in an HR department in a manufacturing company, extends through all 19 chapters and is available at www.mhhe.com/locker11e. The portion for this chapter asks students to write a proposal to revise All-Weather's employee handbook.

Exercises and Cases

17.1   Reviewing the Chapter

1. What is the difference between a competitive and noncompetitive proposal? (LO 17-1)

2. What are six brainstorming questions to consider before starting your proposal? (LO 17-2)

3. How does the organization of proposals for class research projects and proposals for businesses differ? (LO 17-3)

4. What are some guidelines for preparing a budget for a proposal? (LO 17-4)

5. What are some tips for writing a sales proposal? (LO 17-5)

6. What is a business plan? (LO 17-5)

7. What are the differences between chronological and task progress reports? (LO 17-6)

17.2   Analyze a Real Proposal

Visit the following website: http://www.nyu.edu/nyu2031/nyuinnyc/. Click on "The Plan" link and read it. In groups, answer the following questions:

- What kind of proposal is this?
- What problems does it address?
- What solutions does it offer?

- What is the structure of the proposal?
- Who are the multiple audiences?
- What is the purpose of the proposal?
- Is there any information that is missing?
- What is the style of the proposal?

17.3   Revising a Progress Report

Read the following progress report.

Date: April 3, 2014

To: Prof. Keene

From: John

Subject: My Progress

So far my final project for this course has been slow. As you know, I am hoping to present my final report to my boss at the ice cream shop. He is actually very intentional in the idea of having an ice cream stand on campus.

Work Completed

So far I have interviewed a few people on campus and not found out a whole lot of anything. It has been very frustrating. I just handed out a few surveys on campus, but not very many students wanted to fill them out. I do have a little bit data, though. It seems as though several students are very interested in having an ice cream cart on campus, and would purchase ice cream items.

I have spoken to my boss, the owner of Super Duper Ice Cream, and he is looking forward to reading my final report on the campus ice cream stand. I have put together the numbers for the new stand and have already spoken to Dining Services on campus for permissions.

Work be Completed

During these last two weeks of class, I will have no problem geting this project done! I just have to interview more students, put together the information in the report, finish getting the permissions and information for my boss, and then compile all of the information. Oh, and I need to write a few more survey questions, too.

Then I will proofread everything, print it, and hand it to my boss!

Your favorite student,

John

Revise the progress report. Submit your revision, plus another document justifying your revisions, to your instructor.

17.4   Writing a Proposal for a Student Report

Write a proposal to your instructor to do the research for a formal or informal report.

The headings and the questions in the section titled "Proposals for Class Research Projects" are your RFP; be sure to answer every question and to use the headings exactly as stated in the RFP. Exception: where alternate heads are listed, you may choose one, combine the two ("Qualifications and Facilities"), or treat them as separate headings in separate categories.

17.5   Proposing a Change

No organization is perfect, especially when it comes to communication. Propose a change that would improve communication within your organization. The change can be specific to your unit or can apply to the whole organization; it can relate to how important information is distributed, who has access to important information, how information is accessed, or any other change in communication practices that you see as having a benefit. Direct your proposal to the person or committee with the power to authorize the change.

17.6   Proposing to Undertake a Research Project

Pick a project you would like to study whose results could be used by your organization. Write a proposal to your supervisor requesting time away from other duties to do the research. Show how your research (whatever its outcome) will be useful to the organization.

17.7   Writing a Proposal for Funding for a Nonprofit Group

Pick a nonprofit group you care about. Examples include professional organizations, a charitable group, a community organization, or your own college or university.

As your instructor directs,

a. Check the web or a directory of foundations to find one that makes grants to groups such as yours. Brainstorm a list of businesses that might be willing to give money for specific projects. Check to see whether state or national levels of your organization make grants to local chapters.

b. Write a proposal to obtain funds for a special project your group could undertake if it had the money. Address your proposal to a specific organization.

c. Write a proposal to obtain operating funds or money to buy something your group would like to have. Address your proposal to a specific organization.

17.8   Writing a Sales Proposal

Pick a project that you could do for a local company or government office. Examples include

- Establishing a social media presence.
- Creating a brochure, web page, or series of infographics.
- Revising form letters or other routine communications.
- Conducting a training program.
- Writing a newsletter or an annual report.
- Developing a marketing plan.

Write a proposal specifying what you could do and providing a detailed budget and work schedule.

As your instructor directs,

a. Phone or e-mail someone in the organization to talk about its needs and what you could offer.

b. Write an individual proposal.

c. Join with other students in the class to create a team proposal.

d. Present your proposal orally.

17.9   Presenting a Stockholder Proposal

Visit the websites of the following companies and locate their latest proxy statements or reports. These are generally linked from the "about us/company information–investor relations" or "investors" pages. Find shareholder proposals under the heading "proposals requiring your vote," "stockholder proposals," or "shareholder proposals."

- Facebook
- Ford Motor Company
- Citigroup
- AT&T
- JPMorgan Chase & Co.
- Delta Air Lines
- Home Depot
- Procter & Gamble
- Boeing
- Google
- Dow Chemical

As a team, select one proposal, and the management response following it, and give an oral presentation answering these questions:

1. What is the problem discussed in the proposal?

2. What is the rationale given for the urgency to solve the problem?

3. How does the proposal seek to solve it?

4. What benefits does the proposal mention that will accrue from the solution?

5. What is the management response to the proposal and what are the reasons given for the response? Does the management response strike you as justified? Why or why not?

Hint: It may help you to do some research on the topic of the proposal.

17.10   Writing a Progress Report to Your Superior

Describe the progress you have made this week or this month on projects you have been assigned. You may describe progress you have made individually or progress your unit has made as a team.

17.11   Writing a Progress Report

Write an e-mail to your instructor summarizing your progress on your report.

In the introductory paragraph, summarize your progress in terms of your schedule and your goals. Under a heading titled "Work Completed," list what you have already done. (This is a chance to toot your own horn: if you have solved problems creatively, say so. You can also describe obstacles you've encountered that you have not yet solved.) Under "Work to Be Completed," list what you still have to do. If you are more than two days behind the schedule you submitted with your proposal, include a revised schedule, listing the completion dates for the activities that remain.

17.12   Writing a Progress Report for a Team Report

Write an e-mail to your instructor summarizing your team's progress.

In the introductory paragraph, summarize the team's progress in terms of its goals and its schedule, your own progress on the tasks for which you are responsible, and your feelings about the team's work thus far.

Under a heading titled "Work Completed," list what has already been done. Be most specific about what you yourself have done. Describe briefly the chronology of team activities: number, time, and length of meetings; topics discussed and decisions made at meetings.

If you have solved problems creatively, say so. You can also describe obstacles you've encountered that you have not yet solved. In this section, you can also comment on problems that the team has faced and whether or not they've been solved. You can comment on things that have gone well and have contributed to the smooth functioning of the team.

Under "Work to Be Completed," list what you personally and other team members still have to do. Indicate the schedule for completing the work.

Notes

1. Richard Johnson-Sheehan, *Writing Proposals,* 2nd ed. (New York: Pearson/Longman Publishers, 2008), 1.
2. "NSF at a Glance," About the National Science Foundation, accessed July 6, 2013, http://www.nsf.gov/about/glance.jsp; and "NIH Budget," About NIH, accessed July 6, 2013, http://www.nih.gov/about/budget.htm.
3. "Grant Programs and Details," *National Endowment for the Humanities,* accessed June 24, 2013, http://www.neh.gov/grants.

18 Analyzing Information and Writing Reports

Chapter Outline

Using Your Time Efficiently

Analyzing Data and Information for Reports
- Evaluating the Source of the Data
- Choosing the Best Data
- Analyzing Numbers
- Analyzing Patterns
- Checking Your Logic

Choosing Information for Reports

Organizing Information in Reports
- Patterns for Organizing Information
- Patterns for Specific Varieties of Reports

Presenting Information Effectively in Reports
1. Use Clear, Engaging Writing.
2. Keep Repetition to a Minimum.

3. Introduce Sources and Visuals.
4. Use Forecasting, Transitions, Topic Sentences, and Headings.

Writing Formal Reports
- Title Page
- Letter or Memo of Transmittal
- Table of Contents
- List of Illustrations
- Executive Summary
- Introduction
- Background or History
- Body
- Conclusions and Recommendations
- Appendixes

Summary by Learning Objectives

NEWSWORTHY COMMUNICATION

Environmental Reporting

Large companies create a number of official reports each year to keep their boards, their investors, and the public aware of the health of the company and its major initiatives. Often, companies will also report their progress on social and environmental goals. Boeing, for example, releases an annual environmental report that discusses how the company is using energy and water and reducing waste.

In 2007, Boeing set goals for improving its operations and reducing its environmental footprint. In the 2013 report, the company highlighted its improvements, which included reducing

- Hazardous waste by 33%.
- Carbon-dioxide emissions by 26%.
- Energy use by 21%.
- Water intake by 20%.

In addition to providing these numbers (which are adjusted for revenue), Boeing used other strategies to show its successful environmental program. For example, "the reductions in carbon dioxide emissions . . . would be equal to taking 87,000 cars off the road for one year." This way of presenting information includes not only the percentage of improvement, but also a number that makes sense to readers and shows the real environmental impact of Boeing's programs.

In writing reports, whether they are designed for multinational company executives or the supervisor in the next cubicle, presenting the information effectively helps your audience understand your data and allows you to highlight the most important pieces.

Source: PR Newswire, "Boeing Reports Five-Year Environmental Improvements," *Market Watch*, June 20, 2013, http://www.marketwatch.com/story/boeing-reports-five-year-environmental-improvements-2013-06-20?reflink=MW_news_stmp.

After studying this chapter, you will know how to

LO 18-1	Use your time efficiently when writing reports.
LO 18-2	Analyze data, information, and logic.
LO 18-3	Choose information for reports.
LO 18-4	Organize reports.
LO 18-5	Present information effectively in reports.
LO 18-6	Prepare the different components of formal reports.

Careful analysis, smooth writing, and effective document design work together to make effective reports, whether you're writing a 2½ page memo report or a 250-page formal report complete with all the report components.

Chapter 15 covered the first two steps in writing a report:

1. Define the problem.
2. Gather the necessary data and information.

This chapter covers the last three steps:

3. Analyze the data and information.
4. Organize the information.
5. Write the report.

Using Your Time Efficiently LO 18-1

To use your time efficiently when writing a report, think about the parts before you begin writing. Much of the introduction can come from your proposal (see Chapter 17), with only minor revisions. You can probably write some sections even before you've finished your research: Purpose, Scope, Assumptions, Limitations, Methods, Criteria, and Definitions. Mock up visuals and data displays early using the guidelines in Chapter 16.

The background reading from your proposal can form the first draft of your list of references. Save a copy of your questionnaire or interview questions to use as an appendix. You can print appendixes before the final report is ready if you number their pages separately. Appendix A pages would be A-1, A-2, and so forth; Appendix B pages would be B-1, B-2, and so forth.

You can write the title page and the transmittal as soon as you know what your recommendation will be.

After you've analyzed your data, write the body, the conclusions and recommendations, and the executive summary. Prepare a draft of the table of contents and the list of illustrations.

When you write a long report, list all the sections (headings) that your report will have. Mark those that are most important to your reader and your logic, and spend most of your time on them. Write the important sections early. That way, you won't spend all your time on "Background" or "History of the Problem." Instead, you'll get to the heart of your report.

Technology can also help you manage your time more efficiently. For example, Google Drive, the home of Google Docs, will allow you and your teammates to work on different sections of the report simultaneously instead of e-mailing drafts back and forth. As an added bonus, a revision history is always saved so you can go back to an earlier version of your work if needed. Other features allow your team to have real-time instant message chats if your schedules don't permit you to all meet in the same physical location to work on the report.

Analyzing Data and Information for Reports LO 18-2

Good reports begin with good data. Analyzing the data you have gathered is essential to produce the tight logic needed for a good report. Analyze your data with healthy skepticism. Check to see that they correspond with expectations or other existing data. If they don't, check for well-supported explanations of the difference.

Be suspicious of all data, even from reputable sources. Ask yourself "How do they know?" or "What could prevent that data from being right?"

- If you read in the paper that 300,000 people attended a demonstration at the National Mall in Washington, D.C., ask yourself how they know. Unless they were able to get a photo, they are estimating, and such estimates have been known to vary by 100,000 or more, depending on whether the estimator wants a larger or smaller crowd.

- Want to know how many centenarians live in the United States? Surely the Census Bureau knows? Well, not exactly. An accurate count is obscured by lack of birth records, low literacy levels, cognitive disabilities, and the human desire to hit a milestone number.

- Did you read in a job-hunt article that U.S. workers average seven career changes during their working years? That number is a myth. It has been attributed to the U.S. Bureau of Labor Statistics so many times that the bureau now posts a disclaimer on its website. The bureau does not estimate lifetime career changes for a simple reason: no consensus exists for the definition of a career change. Is a promotion a career change? Is a layoff, a temporary subsistence job, and a return to work 0, 1, or 2 career changes?

- Have you heard that Thanksgiving is the busiest travel day of the year? Actually, no day in November has made the top 35 busiest airline days for years, according to the U.S. Department of Transportation (busiest days occur in the summer, when school is out). Even for those traveling by car, July 4, Labor Day, and Christmas are busier holidays.[1]

- Sometimes the discrepancies are not fun facts. Some states are meeting No Child Left Behind federal mandates for continued funding by lowering grade-level proficiency standards.[2]

Spreadsheets can be particularly troublesome (see "Amazing Spreadsheet Errors," the sidebar on this page). Cell results derived by formulas can be subtly, or grossly, wrong by incorrectly defining ranges, for example. It is easy to generate results that are impossible, such as sums that exceed known totals. Always have an estimate of the result of a calculation. Using spreadsheets, you can easily be wrong by a factor of 10, 100, or even 1,000. Studies have found up

Amazing Spreadsheet Errors

Studies have found up to 80% of spreadsheets have errors. Some of these errors are enormous:

- Fidelity's Magellan fund's dividend estimate spreadsheet was $2.6 billion off when a sign was wrongly transposed from minus to plus.

- Fannie Mae, the financer of home mortgages, once discovered a $1.136 billion error in total shareholder equity, again from a spreadsheet mistake.

- JPMorgan Chase's $6.2 billion trading loss was blamed in part on a model with spreadsheet errors.

Adapted from Thomas Wailgum, "Eight of the Worst Spreadsheet Blunders," *CIO*, August 17, 2007, http://www.cio.com/article/131500/Eight_of_the_Worst_Spreadsheet_Blunders; and Stephen Gandel, "Damn Excel! How the 'Most Important Software Application of All Time' is ruining the World," CNN Money, April 17, 2013, http://finance.fortune.cnn.com/2013/04/17/rogoff-reinhart-excel-errors/.

to 80% of spreadsheets have errors, such as misplaced decimal points, transposed digits, and wrong signs.[3]

Try to keep **ballpark figures**, estimates of what the numbers should be, in mind as you look at numerical data. Question surprises before accepting them.

Analyzing data can be hard even for experts. Numerous studies exist in scholarly journals challenging the data-based conclusions of earlier articles. One example is the fate of unmarried, college-educated women over 30. A famous *Newsweek* cover story, "Too Late for Prince Charming?" reported the Yale and Harvard study that suggested such women had only a 20% chance of finding husbands, and only a 2.6% chance by the time they reached 40. Twenty years later an economist at the University of Washington examined 30 years of census data. Her figures for the decade of the original study showed that women aged 40–44 with advanced degrees were only 25% less likely to be married than comparably aged women with just high school diplomas. Since then, those women with post-college education were slightly more likely to be married than those who had finished only high school.[4]

Evaluating the Source of the Data

When evaluating the source of your data, question the authors, objectivity, constituent data, and currency of the source.

Identify the Authors.   Which people or organization provided the data? What credentials do they have? If you want national figures on wages and unemployment, the U.S. Bureau of Labor Statistics would be a good source. But if you want the figures for your local town, your local Chamber of Commerce might be a more credible source. Use the strategies outlined in Chapter 15 to evaluate web sources.

Assess the Objectivity of the Source.   Ask yourself these questions:

- Does the source give evidence to support claims?

- Is the surrounding prose professional and unbiased?

- If the subject supports multiple viewpoints, are other opinions referenced or explained?

When the source has a vested interest in the results, scrutinize the data with special care. To analyze a company's financial prospects, use independent information as well as the company's annual report and press releases.

Drug and medical device companies, and the researchers funded by them, keep appearing in the news with reports of undue influence. Duke University researchers checked 746 studies of heart stents published in one year in medical journals. They found that 83% of the papers did not disclose whether authors were paid consultants for companies, even though many journals require that information. Even worse, 72% of the papers did not say who funded the research.[5] A study in the prestigious *New England Journal of Medicine* noted that positive studies of antidepressant trials got published and negative ones did not: "According to the published literature, it appeared that 94% of the trials conducted were positive. By contrast, the FDA analysis showed that 51% were positive."[6]

If your report is based upon secondary data from library and online research, look at the sample, the sample size, and the exact wording of questions to see what the data actually measure. (See Chapter 15 for more help on judging surveys.) Does the sample have a built-in bias? A survey of city library users may uncover information about users, but it may not find what keeps other people away from the library.

Assess the Constituent Data.   What is included? Omitted? What are the data based on? What assumptions are being made? Different retirement calculators give widely different estimates of how much savings is needed for retirement because of factors they include or omit (such as entertainment) and assumptions they make (such as inflation rate or healthiness of annuities and mutual funds) in the calculations.

Two reputable sources can give different figures because they take their data from different places. Suppose you wanted to know employment figures. The Labor Department's monthly estimate of nonfarm payroll jobs is the most popular, but some economists like Automatic Data Processing's monthly estimate, which is based on the roughly 20 million paychecks it processes for clients. Both survey approximately 400,000 workplaces, but the Labor Department selects employers to mirror the U.S. economy, while ADP's sample is skewed, with too many construction firms and too few of the largest employers. On the other hand, the government has trouble counting jobs at businesses that are opening and closing, and some employers do not return the survey. (Both organizations do attempt to adjust their numbers to compensate accurately.)[7]

Check the Currency of the Data.   Population figures should be from the 2010 census, not the 2000 one. Technology figures in particular need to be current. Do remember, however, that some large data sets are one to two years behind in being analyzed. Such is the case for some government figures, also. If you are doing a report in 2014 that requires national education data from the Department of Education, for instance, 2013 data may not even be fully collected. And even the 2012 data may not be fully analyzed, so indeed the 2011 data may be the most current available.

Choosing the Best Data

Sometimes even good sources and authorities can differ on the numbers they offer, or on the interpretations of the same data sets. Researchers from the United Nations and Johns Hopkins University differed on their estimates of Iraqi deaths in the war by 500% because of research design and execution flaws plus sampling error in the Hopkins report.[8] You will be best able to judge the quality of data if you know how it was collected.

In their books, *The Tipping Point* and *Freakonomics*, Malcolm Gladwell and Steven D. Levitt and Stephen J. Dubner reach different conclusions about the data on dropping crime rates for New York City. Gladwell attributes the drop to the crackdown by the new police chief on even minor crimes such as graffiti and public drunkenness. Levitt and Dubner first explain why the cause was not a crackdown on crime (the years don't match well; other cities also experienced the drop) and attribute it to the legalization of abortion (at the time of the crime drop the first wave of children born after *Roe v. Wade* was hitting late teen years and thus prime crime time; that group was short on the category most likely to become criminal: unwanted children). They also provide corroborating evidence from other countries.[9]

Another factor to consider when choosing data is that conditions change over time. Multiple studies have shown that people who cohabit with their future spouse are more likely to divorce than those who do not cohabit.

Hard to Quantify Sports Participation

How many people participate in sports, and which sports do they choose? Governments and equipment makers want to know, but the data are fuzzy. Multiple questions contribute to the lack of clarity.

- What is a sport? One survey includes bird-watching.
- Who should be counted? Do young children count?
- How often do you have to participate in a sport to be counted? Is once a year enough?
- How was the count made? Because younger and more active people tend to have only cell phones, a survey made through landlines probably won't be accurate.

In case you are curious, the National Sporting Goods Association survey says hiking is the most popular participation sport in the United States, with over 40 million people.

Adapted from Carl Bialik, "Sports Results that Leave Final Score Unclear," *Wall Street Journal*, June 9, 2012, A2.

Nicholas Felton displays a page from *The Feltron Annual Report*, a catalog of his life through custom charts and graph.

Now, that association seems to be weakening for younger people.[10] As another example, the number of patents held by a company frequently was used as a measure of that company's innovation, but with patents increasingly being used as defensive strategies for even the smallest design changes, patent citations may be a more accurate measure. A high number of patent citations may show that the company's patent truly represents innovation.

Analyzing Numbers

Many reports analyze numbers—either numbers from databases and sources or numbers from a survey you have conducted. The numerical information, properly analyzed, can make a clear case in support of a recommendation.

When you have multiple numbers for salaries or other items, an early analysis step is to figure the average (or mean), the median, and the range. The **average** or **mean** is calculated by adding up all the figures and dividing by the number of samples. The **mode** is the number that occurs most often. The **median** is the number that is exactly in the middle in a ranked list of observations. When you have an even number, the median will be the average of the two numbers in the center of the list. The **range** is the difference between the high and low figures for that variable.

Averages are particularly susceptible to a single extreme figure. Three different surveys reported the average cost of a wedding at nearly $30,000. Many articles picked up that figure because weddings are big business. However, the median cost in those three surveys was only about $15,000. And even that is probably on the high side, since the samples were convenience samples for a big wedding website, a bride magazine, and a maker of wedding invitations, and thus probably did not include smaller, less elaborate weddings.[11]

Often it's useful to simplify numerical data: rounding off, combining similar elements. Then you can see that one number is, for instance, about 2½ times another. Graphing can also help you see patterns in your data. (See Chapter 16 for a full discussion of tables and graphs as a way of analyzing and presenting numerical data.) Look at the raw data as well as at percentages. For example, a 50% increase in shoplifting incidents sounds alarming. An increase from two to three shoplifting incidents sounds less so but could be the same data, just stated differently.

Analyzing Patterns

Patterns can help you draw meaning from your data. If you have library sources, on which points do experts agree? Which disagreements can be explained by early theories or numbers that have now changed? Which disagreements are the result of different interpretations of the same data? Which are the result of having different values and criteria?

In your interviews and surveys, what patterns do you see?

- Have things changed over time?

- Does geography account for differences?

- Do demographics such as gender, age, or income account for differences?

- What similarities do you see?

- What differences do you see?

- What confirms your hunches?

- What surprises you?

Many descriptions of sales trends are descriptions of patterns derived from data.

Checking Your Logic

Check that your data actually measure what you want them to. What consumers say they will buy is not always what they actually do buy; what employees say they do at work does not always agree with objective studies.

A common belief is that satisfied customers will be repeat customers. But a *Harvard Business Review* study found little relationship between the two groups; customers who said on surveys they were satisfied did not necessarily make repeat purchases. (The best predictor of repeat purchases was that the customer would recommend the company to others.)[12]

Another common logic error is confusing causation with correlation. *Causation* means that one thing causes or produces another. *Correlation* means that two things happening at the same time are positively or negatively related. One might cause the other, but both might be caused by a third. For instance, consider a study that shows pulling all-nighters hurts grades: students who pull all-nighters get lower grades than those who do not pull all-nighters. But maybe it is not the all-nighter causing the poor grades; maybe students who need all-nighters are weaker students to begin with.

Correlation and causation are easy to confuse, but the difference is important. The Census Bureau publishes figures showing that greater education levels are associated with greater incomes. A widely held assumption is that more education causes greater earnings. But might people from richer backgrounds seek more education? Or might some third factor, such as intelligence, lead to both greater education and higher income?[13]

Consciously search for at least three possible causes for each phenomenon you've observed and at least three possible solutions for each problem. The more possibilities you brainstorm, the more likely you are to find good options. In your report, discuss in detail only the possibilities that will occur to readers and that you think are the real reasons and the best solutions.

When you have identified causes of the problem or the best solutions, check these ideas against reality. Can you find support in references or in numbers? Can you answer claims of people who interpret the data in other ways?

Cost-of-Living Comparison Patterns

Although popular with readers, cost-of-living rankings frequently are not very useful for various reasons, including the following:

- Currency fluctuations: Researchers use the exchange rate at the time they gather data, frequently several months before the report is issued.

- Items included: Generally items used by corporate executives who seek the same items everywhere. Adaptations to local products and lifestyles are not considered.

- Rankings are not percentages: Most people want to know how much more expensive New York is than San Antonio, for instance. Or the size of the gap between the fifth and sixth cities on a list. But this data, as well as actual price data, is usually only for sale.

Adapted from Carl Bialik, "Useful Cost-of-Living Data Don't Come Cheap," *Wall Street Journal*, February 9, 2013, A2.

Make the nature of your evidence clear to your reader. Do you have observations that you yourself have made? Or do you have inferences based on observations or data collected by others? Old data may not be good guides to future action.

If you can't prove the claim you originally hoped to make, modify your conclusions to fit your data. Even when your market test is a failure or your experiment disproves your hypothesis, you can still write a useful report.

- Identify changes that might yield a different result. For example, selling the product at a lower price might enable the company to sell enough units.

- Divide the discussion to show what part of the test succeeded.

- Discuss circumstances that may have affected the results.

- Summarize your negative findings in progress reports to let readers down gradually and to give them a chance to modify the research design.

- Remember that negative results aren't always disappointing to the audience. For example, the people who commissioned a feasibility report may be relieved to have an impartial outsider confirm their suspicions that a project isn't feasible.

A common myth associated with numbers is that numbers are more objective than words: "numbers don't lie." But as the previous discussion shows, numbers can be subject to widely varying interpretation.

Choosing Information for Reports LO 18-3

Don't put information in reports just because you have it or just because it took you a long time to find it. Instead, choose the information that your audience needs to make a decision. NASA received widespread criticism over the way it released results from an $11.3 million federal air safety study. NASA published 16,208 pages of findings with no guide to understanding them. Critics maintain the lapse was deliberate because the data contained hundreds of cases of pilot error.[14]

If you know your audience well, you may already know their priorities. For example, the supervisor of a call center knows that management will be looking for certain kinds of performance data including costs, workload handled, and customer satisfaction. To write regular reports, the supervisor could set up a format in which it is easy to see how well the center is doing in each of these areas. Using the same format month after month simplifies the audience's task.

If you don't know your audience, you may be able to get a sense of what is important by showing a tentative table of contents (a list of your headings) and asking, "Have I included everything?" When you cannot contact an external audience, show your draft to colleagues and superiors in your organization.

How much information you need to include depends on whether your audience is likely to be supportive, neutral, or skeptical. If your audience is likely to be pleased with your research, you can present your findings directly. If your audience will not be pleased, you will need to explain your thinking in a persuasive way and provide substantial evidence.

You must also decide whether to put information in the body of the report or in appendixes. Put material in the body of the report if it is crucial to your proof, if your most significant audience will want to see it there, or if it is short. (Something less than half a page won't interrupt the audience.) Frequently decision makers want your analysis of the data in the report body rather than the actual data itself. Supporting data that will be examined later by specialists such as accountants, lawyers, and engineers are generally put in an appendix.

Anything that a careful audience will want but that is not crucial to your proof can go in an appendix. Appendixes can include

- A copy of a survey questionnaire or interview questions.
- A tally of responses to each question in a survey.
- A copy of responses to open-ended questions in a survey.
- A transcript of an interview.
- Complex tables and visuals.
- Technical data.
- Previous reports on the same subject.

Organizing Information in Reports LO 18-4

Most sets of data can be organized in several logical ways. Choose the way that makes your information easiest for the audience to understand and use. If you were compiling a directory of all the employees at your plant, for example, alphabetizing by last name would be far more useful than listing people by height, Social Security number, or length of service with the company, although those organizing principles might make sense in lists for other purposes.

The following three guidelines will help you choose the arrangement that will be the most useful for your audience:

1. **Process your information before you present it to your audience.** The order in which you became aware of information usually is not the best order to present it to your audience.

2. **When you have lots of information, group it into three to seven categories.** The average person's short-term memory can hold only seven chunks, though the chunks can be of any size.[15] By grouping your information into seven categories (or fewer), you make your report easier to comprehend.

3. **Work with the audience's expectations, not against them.** Introduce ideas in the overview in the order in which you will discuss them.

Patterns for Organizing Information

Organize information in a way that will work best for your audience. Figure 18.1 lists common patterns for organizing information that are particularly useful in reports. Any of these patterns can be used for a whole report or for only part of it.

Comparison/Contrast Many reports use comparison/contrast sections within a larger report pattern. Comparison/contrast can also be the purpose of the whole report. Recommendation studies generally use this pattern. You can focus either on the alternatives you are evaluating or on the criteria you use. See Figure 18.2 for ways to organize these two patterns in a report.

Figure 18.1	**Ways to Organize Reports**
■ Comparison/contrast	■ General to particular or particular to general
■ Problem–solution	■ Geographic or spatial
■ Elimination of alternatives	■ Functional
■ SWOT analysis	■ Chronological

Figure 18.2	**Two Ways to Organize a Comparison/Contrast Report**
Focus on alternatives	
Alternative A	Opening a New Store on Campus
Criterion 1	Cost of Renting Space
Criterion 2	Proximity to Target Market
Criterion 3	Competition from Similar Stores
Alternative B	Opening a New Store in the Suburban Mall
Criterion 1	Cost of Renting Space
Criterion 2	Proximity to Target Market
Criterion 3	Competition from Similar Stores
Focus on criteria	
Criterion 1	Cost of Renting Space for the New Store
Alternative A	Cost of Campus Locations
Alternative B	Cost of Locations in the Suburban Mall
Criterion 2	Proximity to Target Market
Alternative A	Proximity on Campus
Alternative B	Proximity in the Suburban Mall
Criterion 3	Competition from Similar Stores
Alternative A	Competing Stores on Campus
Alternative B	Competing Stores in the Suburban Mall

Focus on the alternatives when

- One alternative is clearly superior.

- The criteria are hard to separate.

- The audience will intuitively grasp the alternative as a whole rather than as the sum of its parts.

Focus on the criteria when

- The superiority of one alternative to another depends on the relative weight assigned to various criteria. Perhaps Alternative A is best if we are most con-cerned about Criterion 1, cost, but worst if we are most concerned about Crite-rion 2, proximity to target market.

- The criteria are easy to separate.

- The audience wants to compare and contrast the options independently of your recommendation.

A variation of the comparison/contrast pattern is the **pro-and-con pattern.** In this pattern, under each specific heading, give the arguments for and against that alternative. A report recommending new plantings for a university quadrangle uses the pro-and-con pattern:

> Advantages of Monocropping
> > High Productivity
> > Visual Symmetry
> Disadvantages of Monocropping
> > Danger of Pest Exploitation
> > Visual Monotony

This pattern is least effective when you want to de-emphasize the disadvantages of a proposed solution, for it does not permit you to bury the disadvantages between neutral or positive material.

Problem–Solution   Identify the problem; explain its background or history; discuss its extent and seriousness; identify its causes. Discuss the factors (criteria) that affect the decision. Analyze the advantages and disadvantages of possible solutions. Conclusions and recommendation can go either first or last, depending on the preferences of your audience. This pattern works well when the audience is neutral.

A report recommending ways to eliminate solidification of a granular bleach during production uses the problem–solution pattern:

> Recommended Reformulation for Vibe Bleach
> Problems in Maintaining Vibe's Granular Structure
> > Solidification during Storage and Transportation
> > Customer Complaints about "Blocks" of Vibe in Boxes
> Why Vibe Bleach "Cakes"
> > Vibe's Formula
> > The Manufacturing Process
> > The Chemical Process of Solidification
> Modifications Needed to Keep Vibe Flowing Freely

Elimination of Alternatives   After discussing the problem and its causes, discuss the *impractical* solutions first, showing why they will not work. End with the most practical solution. This pattern works well when the solutions the audience is likely to favor will not work, while the solution you recommend is likely to be perceived as expensive, intrusive, or radical.

A report on toy commercials, "The Effect of TV Ads on Children," eliminates alternatives:

> Alternative Solutions to Problems in TV Toy Ads
> > Leave Ads Unchanged
> > Mandate School Units on Advertising
> > Ask the Industry to Regulate Itself
> > Give FCC Authority to Regulate TV Ads Directed at Children

SWOT Analysis   SWOT analysis is frequently used to evaluate a proposed project, expansion, or new venture. The analysis discusses **S**trengths, **W**eaknesses, **O**pportunities, and **T**hreats of the proposed action. Strengths and weaknesses are usually factors within the organization; opportunities and threats are usually factors external to the organization.

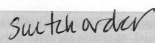
A report recommending an in-house training department uses a SWOT analysis to support its recommendation:

> Advantages of In-House Training
> Disadvantages of In-House Training
> Competitor Training Businesses
> Opportunities for Training Expansion

Switch order

This report switches the order of threats (Competitor Training Businesses) and opportunities to end with positive information.

General to Particular or Particular to General   General to particular starts with the problem as it affects the organization or as it manifests itself in general and then moves to a discussion of the parts of the problem and solutions to each of these parts. Particular to general starts with the problem as the audience defines it and moves to larger issues of which the problem is a part. Both are good patterns when you need to redefine the audience's perception of the problem to solve it effectively.

The directors of a student volunteer organization, VIP, have defined their problem as "not enough volunteers." After studying the subject, the writer is convinced that problems in training, supervision, and campus awareness are responsible for both a high dropout rate and a low recruitment rate. The general-to-particular pattern helps the audience see the problem in a new way:

> Why VIP Needs More Volunteers
> Why Some VIP Volunteers Drop Out
>   Inadequate Training
>   Inadequate Supervision
>   Feeling That VIP Requires Too Much Time
>   Feeling That the Work Is Too Emotionally Demanding
> Why Some Students Do Not Volunteer
>   Feeling That VIP Requires Too Much Time
>   Feeling That the Work Is Too Emotionally Demanding
>   Preference for Volunteering with Another Organization
>   Lack of Knowledge about VIP Opportunities
> How VIP Volunteers Are Currently Trained and Supervised
> Time Demands on VIP Volunteers
> Emotional Demands on VIP Volunteers
> Ways to Increase Volunteer Commitment and Motivation
>   Improving Training and Supervision
>   Improving the Flexibility of Volunteers' Hours
>   Providing Emotional Support to Volunteers
>   Providing More Information about Community Needs and VIP Services

Geographic or Spatial   In a geographic or spatial pattern, you discuss problems and solutions by units according to their physical arrangement. Move from office to office, building to building, factory to factory, state to state, region to region, etc.

A sales report might use a geographic pattern of organization.

> Sales Have Risen in the European Community
> Sales Are Flat in Eastern Europe
> Sales Have Fallen Sharply in the Middle East
> Sales Are Off to a Strong Start in Africa

Sales Have Risen Slightly in Asia
Sales Have Fallen Slightly in South America
Sales Are Steady in North America

Functional In functional patterns, discuss the problems and solutions of each functional unit. For example, a small business might organize a report to its venture capitalists by the categories of research, production, and marketing. A government report might divide data into the different functions an agency performed, taking each in turn.

Major Accomplishments FY 12
   Regulation
   Education
   Research
   International coordination

Chronological A chronological report records events in the order in which they happened or are planned to happen. Many progress reports are organized chronologically.

Work Completed in October
Work Planned for November

If you choose this pattern, be sure you do not let the chronology obscure significant points or trends.

Patterns for Specific Varieties of Reports

Informative, recommendation, and justification reports will be more successful when you work with the audience's expectations for that kind of report.

Informative and Closure Reports

Informative and **closure reports** summarize completed work or research that does not result in action or recommendation.

Informative reports often include the following elements:

- Introductory paragraph summarizing the problems or successes of the project.

- Purpose and scope section(s) giving the purpose of the report and indicating what aspects of the topic it covers.

- Chronological account outlining how the problem was discovered, what was done, and what the results were.

- Concluding paragraph offering suggestions for later action. The suggestions in a closure or informative report are not proved in detail.

Figure 18.3 presents an example of an informative report.

Closure reports also allow a firm to document the alternatives it has considered before choosing a final design.

Figure 18.3   An Informative Report Describing How a Company Solved a Problem

March 14, 2014

To: Donna S. Kienzler

From: Sara A. Ratterman *SAR*

Informal short reports use letter or memo format.

First paragraph summarizes main points.

Subject: Recycling at Bike Nashbar

Two months ago, Bike Nashbar began recycling its corrugated cardboard boxes. The program was easy to implement and actually saves the company a little money compared to our previous garbage pickup.

Purpose and scope of report.

In this report, I will explain how and why Bike Nashbar's program was initiated, how the program works and what it costs, and why other businesses should consider similar programs.

Bold headings.

The Problem of Too Many Boxes and Not Enough Space in Bike Nashbar

Cause of problem.

Every week, Bike Nashbar receives about 40 large cardboard boxes containing bicycles and other merchandise. As many boxes as possible would be stuffed into the trash bin behind the building, which also had to accommodate all the other solid waste the shop produces. Boxes that didn't fit in the trash bin ended up lying around the shop, blocking doorways, and taking up space needed for customers' bikes. The trash bin was emptied only once a week, and by that time, even more boxes would have arrived.

Triple space before heading.

The Importance of Recycling Cardboard Rather than Throwing It Away

Double space after heading.

Arranging for more trash bins or more frequent pickups would have solved the immediate problem at Bike Nashbar but would have done nothing to solve the problem created by throwing away so much trash in the first place.

Double space between paragraphs within heading.

Further seriousness of problem.

According to David Crogen, sales representative for Waste Management, Inc., 75% of all solid waste in Columbus goes to landfills. The amount of trash the city collects has increased 150% in the last five years. Columbus's landfill is almost full. In an effort to encourage people and businesses to recycle, the cost of dumping trash in the landfill is doubling from $4.90 a cubic yard to $9.90 a cubic yard next week. Next January, the price will increase again, to $12.95 a cubic yard. Crogen believes that the amount of trash can be reduced by cooperation between the landfill and the power plant and by recycling.

How Bike Nashbar Started Recycling Cardboard   *Capitalize first letter of major words in heading.*

Solution.

Waste Management, Inc., is the country's largest waste processor. After reading an article about how committed Waste Management, Inc., is to waste reduction and recycling, I decided to see whether Waste Management could recycle our boxes. Corrugated cardboard (which is what Bike Nashbar's boxes are made of) is almost 100% recyclable, so we seemed to be a good candidate for recycling.

Figure 18.3   An Informative Report Describing How a Company Solved a Problem   *(Continued)*

Donna S. Kienzler   *Reader's name,*
March 14, 2014   *date,*
Page 2   *page number.*

To get the service started, I met with a friendly sales rep, David Crogen, that same afternoon to discuss the service.

Waste Management, Inc., took care of all the details. Two days later, Bike Nashbar was recycling its cardboard.

How the Service Works and What It Costs   *Talking heads tell reader what to expect in each section.*

Details of solution. Waste Management took away our existing 8-cubic-yard garbage bin and replaced it with two 4-yard bins. One of these bins is white and has "cardboard only" printed on the outside; the other is brown and is for all other solid waste. The bins are emptied once a week, with the cardboard going to the recycling plant and the solid waste going to the landfill or power plant.

Double space between paragraphs. Since Bike Nashbar was already paying more than $60 a week for garbage pickup, our basic cost stayed the same. (Waste Management can absorb the extra overhead only if the current charge is at least $60 a week.) The cost is divided 80/20 between the two bins: 80% of the cost pays for the bin that goes to the landfill and power plant; 20% covers the cardboard pickup. Bike Nashbar actually receives $5.00 for each ton of cardboard it recycles.

Each employee at Bike Nashbar is responsible for putting all the boxes he or she opens in the recycling bin. Employees must follow these rules:

- The cardboard must have the word "corrugated" printed on it, along with the universal recycling symbol.

Indented lists provide visual variety.

- The boxes must be broken down to their flattest form. If they aren't, they won't all fit in the bin and Waste Management would be picking up air when it could pick up solid cardboard. The more boxes that are picked up, the more money that will be made.

- No other waste except corrugated cardboard can be put in the recycling bin. Other materials could break the recycling machinery or contaminate the new cardboard.

- The recycling bin is to be kept locked with a padlock provided by Waste Management so that vagrants don't steal the cardboard and lose money for Waste Management and Bike Nashbar.

(Continued)

Donna S. Kienzler
March 14, 2014
Page 3

Disadvantages of solution.

Minor Problems with Running the Recycling Program

The only problems we've encountered have been minor ones of violating the rules. Sometimes employees at the shop forget to flatten boxes, and air instead of cardboard gets picked up. Sometimes people forget to lock the recycling bin. When the bin is left unlocked, people do steal the cardboard, and plastic cups and other solid waste get dumped in the cardboard bin. I've posted signs where the key to the bin hangs, reminding employees to empty and fold boxes and relock the bin after putting cardboard in it. I hope this will turn things around and these problems will be solved.

Advantages of the Recycling Program

Advantages of solution.

The program is a great success. Now when boxes arrive, they are unloaded, broken down, and disposed of quickly. It is a great relief to get the boxes out of our way, and knowing that we are making a contribution to saving our environment builds pride in ourselves and Bike Nashbar.

Our company depends on a clean, safe environment for people to ride their bikes in. Now we have become part of the solution. By choosing to recycle and reduce the amount of solid waste our company generates, we can save money while gaining a reputation as a socially responsible business.

Why Other Companies Should Adopt Similar Programs

Argues that her company's experience is relevant to other companies.

Businesses and institutions in Franklin County currently recycle less than 4% of the solid waste they produce. David Crogen tells me he has over 8,000 clients in Columbus alone, and he acquires new ones every day. Many of these businesses can recycle a large portion of their solid waste at no additional cost. Depending on what they recycle, they may even get a little money back.

The environmental and economic benefits of recycling as part of a comprehensive waste reduction program are numerous. Recycling helps preserve our environment. We can use the same materials over and over again, saving natural resources such as trees, fuel, and metals and decreasing the amount of solid waste in landfills. By conserving natural resources, recycling helps the U.S. become less dependent on imported raw materials. Crogen predicts that Columbus will be on a 100% recycling system by the year 2020. I strongly hope that his prediction will come true.

Recommendation Reports Recommendation reports evaluate two or more alternatives and recommend one of them. (Doing nothing or delaying action can be one of the alternatives.)

Recommendation reports normally open by explaining the decision to be made, listing the alternatives, and explaining the criteria. In the body of the report, each alternative will be evaluated according to the criteria using one of the two comparison/contrast patterns. Discussing each alternative separately is better when one alternative is clearly superior, when the criteria interact, or when each alternative is indivisible. If the choice depends on the weight given to each criterion, you may want to discuss each alternative under each criterion.

Whether your recommendation should come at the beginning or the end of the report depends on your audience and the culture of your organization. Most audiences want the "bottom line" up front. However, if the audience will find your recommendation hard to accept, you may want to delay your recommendation until the end of the report when you have given all your evidence.

Justification Reports   **Justification reports** justify a purchase, investment, hiring, or change in policy. If your organization has a standard format for justification reports, follow that format. If you can choose your headings and organization, use this pattern when your proposal will be easy for your audience to accept:

1. **Indicate what you're asking for and why it's needed.** Since the audience has not asked for the report, you must link your request to the organization's goals.
2. **Briefly give the background of the problem or need.**
3. **Explain each of the possible solutions.** For each, give the cost and the advantages and disadvantages.
4. **Summarize the action needed to implement your recommendation.** If several people will be involved, indicate who will do what and how long each step will take.
5. **Ask for the action you want.**

If the reader will be reluctant to grant your request, use this variation of the problem-solving pattern described in Chapter 11:

1. **Describe the organizational problem (which your request will solve).** Use specific examples to prove the seriousness of the problem.
2. **Show why easier or less expensive solutions will not solve the problem.**
3. **Present your solution impersonally.**
4. **Show that the disadvantages of your solution are outweighed by the advantages.**
5. **Summarize the action needed to implement your recommendation.** If several people will be involved, indicate who will do what and how long each step will take.
6. **Ask for the action you want.**

How much detail you need to give in a justification report depends on the corporate culture and on your audience's knowledge of and attitude toward your recommendation. Many organizations expect justification reports to be short—only one or two pages. Other organizations may expect longer reports with much more detailed budgets and a full discussion of the problem and each possible solution.

Presenting Information Effectively in Reports   LO 18-5

The advice about style in Chapter 5 also applies to reports, with three exceptions.

1. **Use a fairly formal style, without contractions or slang.**
2. **Avoid the word** *you.* In a document with multiple audiences, it will not be clear who *you* is. Instead, use the company's name.
3. **Include in the report all the definitions and documents needed to understand the recommendations.** The multiple audiences for reports include people who may consult the document months or years from

The Importance of Annual Reports

A survey, conducted by WithumSmith+Brown and MGT Design Inc., found that the annual report is the most important publication a company produces. To understand the value of annual reports, the survey asked individual investors, portfolio managers, and securities analysts (the primary audiences for annual reports) about the ways that they read and use the reports to make decisions.

Here are some of their findings:

- 75% said the annual report is the most important publication that a company produces.
- 79% said the annual report is an important tool for investment decisions.
- 66% prefer photos and/ or illustrations in annual reports.
- 90% said that important concerns facing the industry, such as environment issues and corporate governance, should be addressed in the report.
- 81% prefer a print version over electronic versions. Respondents said the print documents were easier to read, highlight, annotate, and file.

Taken together, these findings suggest that the annual report is an important communication for organizations and well worth the time spent creating it.

Adapted from Kirk Holderbaum, "Survey Reveals Importance of Corporate Annual Reports," Commerce & Industry Association of New Jersey, accessed July 3, 2013, 66, http://www.withum .com/fileSave/Commerce_ Kirk_0207.pdf.

now; they will not share your inside knowledge. Explain acronyms and abbreviations the first time they appear. Explain as much of the history or background of the problem as necessary. Add as appendixes previous documents on which you are building.

The following points apply to any kind of writing, but they are particularly important in reports:

1. Use clear, engaging writing.
2. Keep repetition to a minimum.
3. Introduce sources and visuals.
4. Use forecasting, transitions, topic sentences, and headings to make your organization clear to your reader.

Let's look at each of these principles as they apply to reports.

1. Use Clear, Engaging Writing.

Most people want to be able to read a report quickly while still absorbing its important points. You can help them do this by using accurate diction. Not-quite-right word choices are particularly damaging in reports, which may be skimmed by readers who know little about the subject. Occasionally you can simply substitute a word:

Incorrect:	With these recommendations, we can overcome the solutions to our problem.
Correct:	With these recommendations, we can overcome our problem.
Also correct:	With these recommendations, we can solve our problem.

Sometimes you'll need to completely recast the sentence.

Incorrect:	The first problem with the incentive program is that middle managers do not use good interpersonal skills in implementing it. For example, the hotel chef openly ridicules the program. As a result, the kitchen staff fear being mocked if they participate in the program.
Better:	The first problem with the incentive program is that some middle managers undercut it. For example, the hotel chef openly ridicules the program. As a result, the kitchen staff fear being mocked if they participate in the program.

A strong writing style is especially important when you are preparing a report that relies on a wealth of statistics. Most people have difficulty absorbing number after number. To help your audiences, use text to highlight the message you want the statistics to convey. Examples and action-oriented details keep the audience engaged.

Warren Buffett says this about clear, engaging writing in annual reports, which can certainly present a wealth of statistics:

I really have a mental picture of my sisters in mind and it's Dear Doris and Birdie. And I envision them as people who have a very significant part of their net worth in the company, who are bright but who have been away for a year and who are not business specialists.

And once a year I tell them what's going on. . . . I think that should be the mental approach.[16]

2. Keep Repetition to a Minimum.

Some repetition in reports is legitimate. The conclusion restates points made in the body of the report; the recommendations appear in the transmittal, the abstract or executive summary, and in the recommendations sections of the report. However, repetitive references to earlier material ("As we have already seen") may indicate that the document needs to be reorganized. Read the document through at a single sitting to make sure that any repetition serves a useful purpose.

3. Introduce Sources and Visuals.

The first time you cite an author's work, use his or her full name as it appears on the work: "Thomas L. Friedman points out . . . " In subsequent citations, use only the last name: "Friedman shows . . . " Use active rather than passive verbs.

The verb you use indicates your attitude toward the source. *Says* and *writes* are neutral. *Points out, shows, suggests, discovers,* and *notes* suggest that you agree with the source. Words such as *claims, argues, contends, believes,* and *alleges* distance you from the source. At a minimum, they suggest that you know that not everyone agrees with the source; they are also appropriate to report the views of someone with whom you disagree.

Make sure you don't plagiarize from secondary sources; use in-text citations as well as full documentation on a "Works Cited" page. Be sure to use your own sentence structure to present information as well.

The report text should refer to all visuals before the audience encounters them:

As Table 1 shows, . . .
See Figure 4.

4. Use Forecasting, Transitions, Topic Sentences, and Headings

Forecasts are overviews that tell the audience what you will discuss in a section or in the entire report. Make your forecast easy to read by telling the audience how many points there are and using bullets or numbers (either words or figures). In the following example, the first sentence in the revised paragraph tells the reader to look for four points; the numbers separate the four points clearly. This overview paragraph also makes a contract with readers, who now expect to read about tax benefits first and employee benefits last.

Paragraph without numbers:	Employee stock ownership programs (ESOPs) have several advantages. They provide tax benefits for the company. ESOPs also create tax benefits for employees and for lenders. They provide a defense against takeovers. In some organizations, productivity increases because workers now have a financial stake in the company's profits. ESOPs are an attractive employee benefit and help the company hire and retain good employees.
Revised paragraph with numbers:	Employee stock ownership programs (ESOPs) provide four benefits. First, ESOPs provide tax benefits for the company, its employees, and lenders to the plan. Second, ESOPs help create a defense against takeovers. Third, ESOPs may increase productivity by giving workers a financial stake in the company's profits. Fourth, as an attractive employee benefit, ESOPs help the company hire and retain good employees.

[Handwritten margin notes: "Abstract = executive summary"; "citing"; "use of words to agree or distance from orig. author"]

Transitions are words, phrases, or sentences that tell audiences whether the discussion is continuing on the same point or shifting points.

> There are economic advantages, too.

(Tells audience that we are still discussing advantages but that we have now moved to economic advantages.)

> An alternative to this plan is. . . .

(Tells audience that a second option follows.)

> The second factor. . . .

(Tells audience that the discussion of the first factor is finished.)

> These advantages, however, are found only in A, not in B or C.

(Prepares audience for a shift from A to B and C.)

A **topic sentence** introduces or summarizes the main idea of a paragraph. Audiences who skim reports can follow your ideas more easily if each paragraph begins with a topic sentence.

Hard to read (no topic sentence):	Another main use of ice is to keep the fish fresh. Each of the seven kinds of fish served at the restaurant requires one gallon twice a day, for a total of 14 gallons. An additional 6 gallons a day are required for the salad bar.
Better (begins with topic sentence):	Twenty gallons of ice a day are needed to keep food fresh. Of this, the biggest portion (14 gallons) is used to keep the fish fresh. Each of the seven kinds of fish served at the restaurant requires one gallon twice a day. An additional 6 gallons a day are required for the salad bar.

Headings (see Chapter 6) are single words, short phrases, or complete sentences that indicate the topic in each section. A heading must cover all of the material under it until the next heading. For example, *Cost of Tuition* cannot include the cost of books or of room and board; *College Costs* could include all costs. You can have just one paragraph under a heading or several pages. If you do have several pages between headings you may want to consider using subheadings. Use subheadings only when you have two or more divisions within a main heading.

Topic headings focus on the structure of the report. As you can see from the following example, topic headings are vague and give little information.

> Recommendation
> Problem
>   Situation 1
>   Situation 2
> Causes of the Problem
>   Background
>   Cause 1
>   Cause 2
> Recommended Solution

Talking heads, in contrast, tell the audience what to expect. Talking heads, like those in the examples in this chapter, provide a specific overview of each section and of the entire report.

> Recommended Reformulation for Vibe Bleach
> Problems in Maintaining Vibe's Granular Structure
>   Solidification during Storage and Transportation
>   Customer Complaints about "Blocks" of Vibe in Boxes
> Why Vibe Bleach "Cakes"
>   Vibe's Formula
>   The Manufacturing Process
>   The Chemical Process of Solidification
> Modifications Needed to Keep Vibe Flowing Freely

Headings must be parallel (see Chapter 5); that is, they must use the same grammatical structure. Subheads must be parallel to each other but do not necessarily have to be parallel to subheads under other headings.

Not parallel:	Are Students Aware of VIP?
	Current Awareness among Undergraduate Students
	Graduate Students
	Ways to Increase Volunteer Commitment and Motivation
	We Must Improve Training and Supervision
	Can We Make Volunteers' Hours More Flexible?
	Providing Emotional Support to Volunteers
	Provide More Information about Community Needs and VIP Services
Parallel:	Campus Awareness of VIP
	Current Awareness among Undergraduate Students
	Current Awareness among Graduate Students
	Ways to Increase Volunteer Commitment and Motivation
	Improving Training and Supervision
	Improving the Flexibility of Volunteers' Hours
	Providing Emotional Support to Volunteers
	Providing More Information about Community Needs and VIP Services

In a complicated report, you may need up to three levels of headings. Figure 18.4 illustrates one way to set up headings. Follow these standard conventions for headings:

- Use a subheading only when you have at least two subsections under the next higher heading.

- Avoid having a subhead come immediately after a heading. Instead, some text should follow the main heading before the subheading. (If you have nothing else to say, give an overview of the division.)

- Avoid having a heading or subheading all by itself at the bottom of the page. Instead, have at least one line (preferably two) of type. If there isn't room for a line of type under it, put the heading on the next page.

- Don't use a heading as the antecedent for a pronoun. Instead, repeat the noun.

Figure 18.4   Setting Up Headings in a Single-Spaced Document

Center the title;
use bold and
a bigger font.

Typing Titles and Headings for Reports   *14-point type.*

For the title of a report, use a bold font two point sizes bigger than the largest size in the body of the report. You may want to use an even bigger size or a different font to create an attractive title page. Capitalize the first word and all major words of the title.

Two empty spaces (triple space)

Heading for main divisions

Typing Headings for Reports   *12-point type.*

One empty space (double space)

12-point type for body text

Center main headings, capitalize the first and all major words, and use bold. In single-spaced text, leave two empty spaces before main headings and one after. Also leave an extra space between paragraphs. You may also want to use main headings that are one point size bigger than the body text.

This example provides just one example of each level of heading. However, in a real document, use headings only when you have at least two of them in the document. In a report, you'll have several.

Two empty spaces (triple space)

Typing Subheadings   *Bold; left margin*

One empty space

Most reports use subheadings under some main headings. Use subheadings only if you have at least two of them under a given heading. It is OK to use subheadings in some sections and not in others. Normally you'll have several paragraphs under a subheading, but it's OK to have just one paragraph under some subheadings.

12-point type

Subheadings in a report use the same format as headings in letters and memos. Bold subheadings and set them at the left margin. Capitalize the first word and major words. Leave two empty spaces before the subheading and one empty space after it, before the first paragraph under the subheading. Use the same size font as the body paragraphs.

One empty space (normal paragraph spacing)

Period after heading

Typing Further Subdivisions. For a very long report, you may need further subdivisions under a subheading. Bold the further subdivision, capitalizing the first word and major words, and end the phrase with a period. Begin the text on the same line. Use normal spacing between paragraphs. Further subdivide a subheading only if you have at least two such subdivisions under a given subheading. It is OK to use divisions under some subheadings and not under others.

Writing Formal Reports   LO 18-6

Formal reports are distinguished from informal letter and memo reports by their length and by their components. A full formal report may contain the components outlined in Figure 18.5 in the left column.

As Figure 18.5 shows, not every formal report necessarily has all components. The components you need will depend on the audiences and purposes of your report. In addition, some organizations call for additional components or arrange these components in a different order. As you read each section below, you may want to turn to the corresponding sections of the report in Figure 18.6 to see how the component is set up and how it relates to the total report. The

Figure 18.5	The Components in a Report Can Vary

More formal ←——————————————→ **Less formal**

Cover	Title Page	Introduction
Title Page	Table of Contents	Body
Transmittal	Executive Summary	Conclusions
Table of Contents	Body	Recommendations
List of Illustrations	Introduction	
Executive Summary	Body	
Body	Conclusions	
Introduction	Recommendations	
Background		
Body		
Conclusions		
Recommendations		
References/Works Cited		
Appendixes		
Questionnaires		
Interviews		
Complex Tables		
Computer Printouts		
Related Documents		

http://www
.pewinternet.org/

To see examples of the ways in which reports are written and disseminated, visit the Pew Internet & American Life Project at the above website.

The project produces reports on the impact of the Internet on American lives, collecting and analyzing data on real-world developments as they intersect with the virtual world. Following data collection, the results are written into the reports and posted as pdfs to the website.

Visit the project's web pages to see examples of the ways in which reports are first presented and then rewritten by the press for their audience and purpose.

example in Figure 18.6 shows segments of a formal report for illustration purposes; the full report can be viewed on this book's companion website.

Title Page

The title page of a report usually contains four items: the title of the report, the person or organization for whom the report is prepared, the person or group who prepared the report, and the release date. Some title pages also contain a brief summary or abstract of the contents of the report; some title pages contain decorative artwork.

The title of the report should be as informative as possible. Like subject lines, report titles are straightforward.

Poor title:	New Plant Site
Better title:	Eugene, Oregon, Site for the New Kemco Plant

Large organizations that issue many reports may use two-part titles to make it easier to search for reports electronically. For example, U.S. government report titles first give the agency sponsoring the report, then the title of that particular report.

Small Business Administration: Management Practices Have Improved for the Women's Business Center Program

Figure 18.6   Segments of a Formal Report

Slated for Success

RAC Inc. Expanding to South Korea

Center all text on the title page.

Use a large font size for the main title.

Use a slightly smaller font size for the subtitle.

Prepared for

No punctuation.

Ms. Katie Nichols

CEO of RAC Inc.

Grand Rapids, Michigan, 49503

Name of audience, job title, organization, city, state, and zip code.

Prepared by

No punctuation.

JASS LLC

Jordan Koole

Alex Kuczera

Shannon Jones

Sean Sterling

Allendale, MI 49401

Name of writer(s), organization, city, state, and zip code.

Month Day, Year *Date report is released.*

Figure 18.6   Segments of a Formal Report   *(Continued)*

The students in this group designed their own letterhead, assuming they were doing this report as consultants.

This letter uses block format.

JASS LLC
1 Campus Drive
Allendale, MI 49401

Month Day, Year   *Enter current date*

Ms. Katie Nichols, CEO
RAC Inc.
1253 West Main Street
Grand Rapids, MI 49503

In paragraph 1, release the report. Note when and by whom the report was authorized. Note the report's purpose.

Dear Ms. Nichols:

In this document you will find the report that you requested in March. We have provided key information and made recommendations on a plan of action for the expansion of a RAC Inc. slate tablet manufacturing plant into South Korea.

Give recommendations or thesis of report.

Our analysis of expansion into South Korea covered several important areas that will help you decide whether or not RAC Inc. should expand and build a manufacturing plant in South Korea. To help us make our decision, we looked at the government, economy, culture, and most important, the competition. South Korea is a technologically advanced country and its economy is on the rise. Our research has led us to recommend expansion into South Korea. We strongly believe that RAC Inc. can be profitable in the long run and become a successful business in South Korea.

Note sources that were helpful.

JASS LLC used several resources in forming our analysis. The Central Intelligence Agency's *World Factbook*, the U.S. Department of State, World Business Culture, and Kwintessential were all helpful in answering our research questions.

Thank the audience for the opportunity to do the research.

Thank you for choosing JASS to conduct the research into South Korea. If you have any further questions about the research or recommendation please contact us (6l6-331-1100, info@jass.com) and we will be happy to answer any questions referring to your possible expansion into South Korea at no charge. JASS would be happy to conduct any further research on this issue or any other projects that RAC Inc. is considering. We look forward to building on our relationship with you in the future.

Sincerely,

Jordan Koole

Jordan Koole
JASS Team Member

Offer to answer questions about the report.

Center inital page numbers at the bottom of the page. Use a lowercase roman numeral for initial pages of report.

i

(Continued)

| Figure 18.6 | Segments of a Formal Report   *(Continued)* |

Main headings are parallel, as are subheadings within a section.

Table of Contents

Table of Contents does not list itself.

Use lowercase roman numerals for initial pages

Introduction begins on page 1.

Capitalize first letter of each major word in headings.

Indentions show level of heading at a glance.

Line up right margin (justify).

Add a "List of Illustrations" at the bottom of the page or on a separate page if the report has many visuals.

List of Illustrations

Figures and tables are numbered independently.

Figure 18.6 Segments of a Formal Report *(Continued)*

Report title. # Slated for Success

Many audiences read only the Executive Summary, not the report. Include enough information to give audiences the key points you make.

RAC Inc. Expanding to South Korea

Executive Summary

Start with recommendation or thesis.

To continue growth and remain competitive on a global scale, RAC Inc. should expand its business operations into South Korea. The country is a technologically advanced nation and would provide a strong base for future expansion. Slate tablet competitors of RAC Inc. in South Korea are doing quite well. Since RAC Inc. can compete with them in the United States, we are confident that RAC can remain on par with them in this new market.

The research we have done for this project indicates that this expansion will be profitable, primarily because the South Korean economy is flourishing. The workforce in South Korea is large, and finding talented employees to help set up and run the facility will be easy. In addition, the regulations and business structure are similar to those in the United States and will provide an easy transition into this foreign nation. The competition will be fierce; however, we believe that RAC Inc. will be profitable because of its track record with the Notion Tab in the United States.

Provide brief support for recommendations.

To ensure a successful expansion, JASS LLC recommends the following:

1. **RAC Inc. should establish its headquarters and manufacturing plant in Busan.**
   - Purchase a building to have a place to begin manufacturing the Notion Tab.
   - Educate RAC employees about South Korean culture and business practices before they begin working directly with South Koreans to avoid being disrespectful.
   - Explore hiring South Koreans; the available workforce is large.
   - Ensure that the Notion name is appropriate when translated into Korean. If not, change the name to better market the product.
   - Market and sell the product in both Busan and Seoul.

2. **After one year RAC should determine the acceptance and profitability of the expansion.**
   - Conduct a customer satisfaction survey with people who purchased the Notion Tab living in Seoul and Busan to determine the acceptance of the product.
   - Compare and contrast first-year sales with a competitor's similar product.

3. **If the tablet is competitive and profitable, RAC Inc. should expand its product line into all large cities in South Korea.**
   - To gain an edge on the competition, create a marketing plan that will offer the Notion Tab at some discount in the new cities.
   - Explore integrating other RAC Inc. products into South Korea. These products could also be manufactured at the new manufacturing plant in Busan.

Language in the Executive Summary can come from the report. Make sure any repeated language is well-written!

The Abstract or Executive Summary contains the logical skeleton of the report: the recommendation(s) and supporting evidence.

iii

(Continued)

Figure 18.6   Segments of a Formal Report   *(Continued)*

A running header is optional. This one includes the main title on the left and the page number on the right.

Slated for Success   1

Introduction   *Center main headings.*

To avoid getting left behind by competition in global expansion, RAC Inc. has contacted JASS LLC to perform an analysis about expanding into South Korea. JASS has researched South Korea to determine if RAC Inc. will be successful in expanding into this foreign market.

"Purpose" and "Scope" can be separate sections if either is long.

Purpose and Scope

RAC Inc. is a successful business in the United States and has had substantial growth over the last five years. With their competitors beginning to venture into foreign markets to gain more global market share, RAC Inc. is looking to expand into the international market as well. The purpose of our research is to decide whether or not RAC Inc. should expand its business into South Korea.

Give topics in the order you'll discuss them.

Tell what you discuss and how thoroughly you discuss each topic.

Topics in "Scope" section should match those in the report.

This report will cover several topics about South Korea including their government, economy, culture, technology market competition, and possible locations. Our research will not include any on-site research in South Korea. We are also not dealing directly with the South Korean people.

List any relevant topics you do not discuss.

Assumptions cannot be proved. But if they are wrong, the report's recommendation may no longer be valid.

Assumptions

The recommendations that we make are based on the assumption that the relationship between North and South Korea will remain the same as of the first part of 2011. We are also assuming that the technological state of South Korea will remain constant and not suffer from a natural disaster or an economic crash. In addition, we assume that the process of expansion into South Korea is the same with RAC Inc. as it has been with other American companies. Another assumption that we are making is that RAC Inc. has a good name brand and is competitive in the United States with Apple, Samsung, LG and other electronic companies.

If you collected original data (surveys, interviews, and observations), tell how you chose your subjects, what kind of sample you used, and when you collected the information. This report does not use original data; it just provides a brief discussion of significant sources.

Methods

The information in our report comes from online sources and reference books. We found several good sources, but the best information that we obtained came from The Central Intelligence Agency's *World Factbook*, the U.S. Department of State, World Business Culture, and Kwintessential. These resources have given us much useful information on which we have based our recommendation.

These limitations are listed because the students correctly assumed their teacher would want to know them. Limitations such as these would never be listed in a real consulting report, since they would disqualify the firm.

Limitations   *If your report has limitations, state them.*

The information in the report was limited to what we retrieved from our sources. We were not able to travel to South Korea to conduct on-site research. JASS was also limited by the language barrier that exists between the United States and South Korea. Other limitations exist because we have not been immersed in the Korean culture and have not gotten input from South Koreans on the expansion of companies into their country.

Definitions

There are a few terms that we use throughout the report that we would like to explain beforehand. The first term is slate tablet, an industry term, which from this point on is referred to as a tablet. Another term we would like to clarify is the city Busan. Some sources referred to it as Pusan. From this point forward, we use only Busan. An abbreviation we use is GDP, which stands for gross domestic product. The South Korean and United States Free Trade Agreement signed in 2007 is abbreviated as KORUS FTA, its official name in the United States government.

Define key terms your audience will need to read your report.

Figure 18.6	Segments of a Formal Report *(Continued)*

Slated for Success 2

This section outlines the criteria used to make the overall recommendation.

Criteria

JASS LLC has established criteria that need to be favorable before we give a positive recommendation about South Korea. The criteria include the government, economy, culture, and market competition. We have weighted our criteria by percentages:

- Government = 20%
- Economy = 20%
- South Korean culture = 20%
- Market possibilities and competitors = 40%

We will examine each separately and give each criterion a favorable or not favorable recommendation. Market competition is weighted the heaviest and must be favorable or somewhat favorable for us to give a positive recommendation. Market competition can be given a favorable, nonfavorable, or somewhat favorable recommendation based on various external factors in the marketplace. We need a minimum of a 70% total to give a positive recommendation overall.

Triple-space before major headings and double-space after them.

Government

Headings must cover everything under that heading until the next one.

Begin most paragraphs with topic sentences.

South Korea is recognized as a republic government by the rest of the world. A republic government is a democracy where the people have supreme control over the government (South Korea: Political structure, 2009). This foundation makes its similar to the United States' democracy. There is a national government as well as provincial-level governments (similar to state-level governments) with different branches. Larger cities, like Seoul and Busan, have their own city government as well. The government is considered multipartied and has multiple parties vying for positions (South Korea: Political structure, 2009). The Republic of South Korea shares its power among three branches of government, thus providing checks and balances inside the government. The three branches of the government are the presidential, legislative, and judicial (U.S. Department of State, 2010). In this section, we will discuss government control, business regulations, taxes, free trade, and concerns about North Korea.

List subtopics in the order in which they are discussed.

Capitalize all main words of headings and subheadings.

Government Control

It's OK to have subheadings under some headings and not others.

The Grand National Party (GNP) controls the major policy-making branches of the government. President Lee Myung-Bak and Prime Minister Kim Hwang-Sik are both members of the GNP. Winning control of the National Assembly in April 2008 (South Korea: Political structure, 2009), the GNP is considered the conservative party in South Korea and is similar to the Republican Party in the United States. Their policies favor conservatism and are considered pro-business (Grand National Party, 2011). RAC Inc. should not expect much interference from the government with their business venture into South Korea, unless the GNP loses control of the government in the next election.

Use subheadings only when you have two or more sections.

Period goes outside of parenthesis.

Business Regulations

South Korea ranks 16th on the ease of doing business index (World Bank Group, 2011a). This index measures the regulations that a government imposes on businesses and how easy it is to start and run a business in a given country. Factors this index measures include the ease of starting a business, doing taxes, and enforcing contracts. For comparison, the United States is ranked fifth on this list (World Bank Group, 2011b). While there are more regulations on business in South Korea, they are still near the top of the list. The relatively low rating on regulation can be due in part to the Grand National Party controlling the government. There are a few general regulations that RAC Inc. should know before going into South Korea. For more specific business regulations, RAC Inc. may need to do further research before expanding.

(Continued)

Figure 18.6   Segments of a Formal Report   *(Continued)*

Slated for Success   5

Since the 1960s, the GDP has had only one dip, a result of the Asian Economic crisis in the late 1990s that affected most Asian countries. In 2004, South Korea became a part of the trillion-dollar economy club, making them one of the world's top economies (Central Intelligence Agency, 2011).

However the economy faces challenges in maintaining steady growth in the future. These challenges include an aging population, inflexible workforce, and an overdependence on exports. Right now, though, South Korea's economy continues to grow. Their industrial production growth rate was 12.1% in 2010, making them the 11th fastest-growing nation in the production industry. In 2010, their GDP grew by 6.8%, the 28th largest growth of GDP in the world (Central Intelligence Agency, 2011). This growth makes South Korea a viable place of expansion.

Refer to figure in the text. Tell what main point it makes.

GDP and Other Important Economic Measures

The official GDP of South Korea was $1.467 trillion in 2010 (Central Intelligence Agency, 2011). This GDP is the 13th highest in the world. GDP measures the total value of goods produced by a country's economy. Figure 2 shows a comparison of GDP growth rates for top countries. GDP per capita in South Korea is $30,200, which is the 44th largest in the world. This measures the output of goods and services per person in the country. It is also an indicator of the average worker's

Number figures consecutively throughout the report; number tables and figures independently.

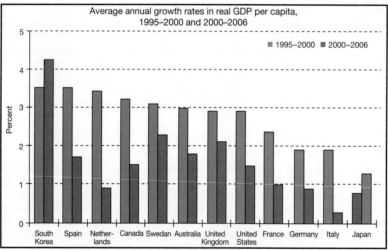

Label both axes of graphs. See Chapter 16 for more information on creating data displays.

Figure 2: Comparison of GDP Growth Rates
(Source: U.S. Bureau of Labor Statistics, 2008)

Cite source of data.

Figure captions need to be descriptive.

salary in the country. South Korea only has 15% of their population living in poverty. They have a labor force of 24.62 million which is the 25th largest labor force in the world, with an unemployment rate of 3.3% (Central Intelligence Agency, 2011). These numbers need to be considered when starting operations in South Korea. South Korea also has a service-driven economy with 57.6% of the country's GDP output in the service industry and 68.4% of the labor force employed in the service industry (Central Intelligence Agency, 2011). All of these numbers and high world rankings of the economic measures show that South Korea has a stable and healthy economy where a business could prosper.

Figure 18.6 Segments of a Formal Report *(Continued)*

Slated for Success

Conclusions repeat points made in the report. Recommendations are actions the audience should take.

11

Some companies ask for Conclusions and Recommendations at the beginning of the report.

Conclusions and Recommendations

All of the research that we have done supports the decision to expand into South Korea. The government, economy, and culture criteria all received favorable recommendations for a total of 60%. Market possibilities and competition received half support for an additional 20%. Together, South Korea has earned 80% based on our criteria.

Therefore, we believe that RAC Inc. could profitably expand into South Korea. The Notion Tab is a high-quality product, and it will be easily integrated into this technologically advanced county. In conclusion, we recommend that RAC Inc. should expand into South Korea.

To ensure a successful expansion, JASS LLC recommends the following:

1. **RAC Inc. should establish its headquarters and manufacturing plant in Busan.**
   - Purchase a building to have a place to begin manufacturing the Notion Tab.
   - Educate RAC employees about South Korean culture and business practices before they begin working directly with South Koreans to avoid being disrespectful.
   - Explore hiring South Koreans; the available workforce is large.
   - Ensure that the Notion name is appropriate when translated into Korean. If not, change the name to better market the product.
   - Market and sell the product in both Busan and Seoul.

Numbering points makes it easier for the audience to follow and discuss them.

2. **After one year RAC should determine the acceptance and profitability of the expansion.**
   - Conduct a customer satisfaction survey with people who purchased the Notion Tab living
   - in Seoul and Busan to determine the acceptance of the product.
   Compare and contrast first-year sales with a competitor's similar product.

Make sure all items in a list are parallel.

3. **If the tablet is competitive and profitable, RAC Inc. should expand its product line into all large cities in South Korea.**
   - To gain an edge on the competition, create a marketing plan that will offer the Notion Tab
   - at some discount in the new cities.
   Explore integrating other RAC Inc. products into South Korea. These products could also be manufactured at the new manufacturing plant in Busan.

Because many readers turn to the "Recommendations" first, provide enough information so that the reason is clear all by itself. The ideas in this section must be logical extensions of the points made and supported in the body of the report.

(Continued)

Figure 18.6   Segments of a Formal Report   *(Concluded)*

Slated for Success   12

References *This report uses APA citation style.*

Advameg, Inc. (2011). Culture of South Korea. *Countries and Their Cultures*.
   Retrieved April 2, 201l, from http://www.everyculture.com/Ja-Ma/South-Korea.html.

AFP. (2010, December 5). U.S., South Korea sign sweeping free-trade agreement. *Taipei Times*.
   Retrieved from http://www.taipeitimes.com/News/front/archives/2010/12/05/200349014.

Central Intelligence Agency. (2011). *The world factbook: South Korea*. Retrieved March 18, 2011,
   from https://www.cia.gov/library/publications/the-world-factbook/geos/ks.html#.

Grand National Party. (2011, April 1). In *Wikipedia*. Retrieved April 6, 2011, from
   http://en.wikipedia.org/wiki/Grand_National_Party.

iPad 2 specs. (2011). *OS X Daily*. Retrieved from http://osxdaily.com/2011/03/02/ipad-2-specs.

Koreans love their mobile phones. (2009, January 28). *Korean JoongAng Daily*. Retrieved from
   http://joongangdaily.joins.com/article/view.asp?aid=2900275.

KRWUS. (2011). *MSN Money*. Retrieved April 10, 201l, from
   http://investing.money.msn.com/investments/currency-exchange-rates/?symbol=%2fKRWUS.

KT. (2011, April 1). In *Wikipedia*. Retrieved April 2, 2011, from
   http://en.wikipedia.org/wiki/KT_%28telecommunication_company%29.

Kwintessential. (2010). *South Korea: Language, culture, customers and etiquette*. Retrieved from
   http://www.kwintessential.co.uk/resources/global-etiquette/south-korea-country-profile.html.

LG Corp. (2011, April 1). In *Wikipedia*. Retrieved April 2, 2011, from http://en.wikipedia.org/wiki/LG.

LG Slate full specifications and product details. (2011, February 2). *Gadgetian*. Retrieved
   April 3, 2011, from http: //gadgetian.com/7069/lg-g-slate-t-mobile-specs-price/.

LG Telecom. (2010, November 29). In *Wikipedia*. Retrieved April 2, 2011, from
   http://en.wikipedia.org/wiki/LG_Telecom.

Life in Korea. (n.d.). *Cultural spotlight*. Retrieved March 31, 2011, from
   http://www.lifeinkorea.com/Culture/spotlight.cfm.

Compare this list of sources with those in the proposal. Notice how the authors had to adjust the list as they completed research.

*List all the printed and online sources cited in your report.
Do not list sources you used for background but did not cite.*

Sources for this report continue onto a second page.

In many cases, the title will state the recommendation in the report: "Why the United Nations Should Establish a Seed Bank." However, the title should omit recommendations when

- The reader will find the recommendations hard to accept.

- Putting all the recommendations in the title would make it too long.

- The report does not offer recommendations.

If the title does not contain the recommendation, it normally indicates what problem the report tries to solve or the topic the report discusses. Eliminate any unnecessary words:

Wordy:	Report of a Study on Ways to Market Life Insurance to Urban Professional People Who Are in Their Mid-40s
Better:	Marketing Life Insurance to the Mid-40s Urban Professional

The identification of the receiver of the report normally includes the name of the person who will make a decision based on the report, his or her job title, the organization's name, and its location (city, state, and zip code). Government reports often omit the person's name and simply give the organization that authorized the report.

If the report is prepared primarily by one person, the "Prepared by" section will have that person's name, his or her title, the organization, and its location (city, state, and zip code). In internal reports, the organization and location are usually omitted if the report writer works at the headquarters office.

Government reports normally list the names of all people who wrote the report, using a separate sheet of paper if the group working on the report is large. Practices in business differ. In some organizations, all the names are listed; in others, the division to which they belong is listed; in still others, the name of the chair of the group appears.

The **release date,** the date the report will be released to the public, is usually the date the report is scheduled for discussion by the decision makers. The report is frequently due four to six weeks before the release date so that the decision makers can review the report before the meeting.

If you have the facilities and the time, try using type variations, color, and artwork to create a visually attractive and impressive title page. However, a plain typed page is acceptable. The format in Figure 18.6 will enable you to create an acceptable typed title page.

Letter or Memo of Transmittal

Use a letter of transmittal if you are not a regular employee of the organization for which you prepare the report; use a memo if you are a regular employee.

The transmittal has several purposes: to transmit the report, to orient the reader to the report, and to build a good image of the report and of the writer. An informal writing style is appropriate for a transmittal even when the style in the report is more formal. A professional transmittal helps you create a good image of yourself and enhances your credibility. Personal statements are appropriate in the transmittal, even though they would not be acceptable in the report itself.

Organize the transmittal in this way:

1. **Transmit the report.** Tell when and by whom it was authorized and the purpose it was to fulfill.

2. **Summarize your conclusions and recommendations.** If the recommendations will be easy for the audience to accept, put them early in the transmittal. If they will be difficult, summarize the findings and conclusions before the recommendations.

3. **Mention any points of special interest in the report. Show how you surmounted minor problems you encountered in your investigation. Thank people who helped you.** These optional items can build goodwill and enhance your credibility.

4. **Point out additional research that is necessary, if any.** Sometimes your recommendation cannot be implemented until further work is done. If you'd be interested in doing that research or if you'd like to implement the recommendations, say so.

5. **Thank the audience for the opportunity to do the work and offer to answer questions.** Provide contact information. Even if the report has not been fun to do, expressing satisfaction in doing the project is expected. Saying that you'll answer questions about the report is a way of saying that you won't charge the audience your normal hourly fee to answer questions (one more reason to make the report clear!).

The letter of transmittal on page i of Figure 18.6 uses this pattern of organization.

Table of Contents

In the table of contents, list the headings exactly as they appear in the body of the report. If the report is less than 25 pages, you'll probably list all the levels of headings. In a long report, pick a level and put all the headings at that level and above in the table of contents.

Some software programs, such as Microsoft Word, offer features that automatically generate a table of contents (and a list of illustrations) if you apply the style feature when you generate headings.

Page ii of Figure 18.6 shows the table of contents.

List of Illustrations

A list of illustrations enables audiences to refer to your visuals.

Report visuals comprise both tables and figures. *Tables* are words or numbers arranged in rows and columns. *Figures* are everything else: bar graphs, pie charts, flow charts, maps, drawings, photographs, computer printouts, and so on. Tables and figures may be numbered independently, so you may have both a Table 1 and a Figure 1. In a report with just two kinds of visuals, such as maps and graphs, the visuals are sometimes called Map 1 and Graph 1. Whatever you call the illustrations, list them in the order in which they appear in the report; give the name of each visual as well as its number.

See Chapter 16 for information about how to design and label visuals and data displays.

Executive Summary

An **executive summary** or **abstract** tells the audience what the document is about. It summarizes the recommendation of the report and the reasons for the recommendation or describes the topics the report discusses and indicates the depth of the discussion. It should be clear even to people who will read only the abstract.

A good abstract is easy to read, concise, and clear. Edit your abstract carefully to tighten your writing and eliminate any unnecessary words.

Wordy: The report describes two types of business jargon, *businessese* and *reverse gobbledygook.* It gives many examples of each of these and points out how their use can be harmful.

Tight: The report describes and illustrates two harmful types of business jargon, *businessese* and *reverse gobbledygook.*

Abstracts generally use a more formal style than other forms of business writing. Avoid contractions and colloquialisms. Try to avoid using the second-person *you.* Because reports may have many different audiences, *you* may become inaccurate. It's OK to use exactly the same words in the abstract and the report.

Summary abstracts present the logic skeleton of the report: the thesis or recommendation and its proof. Use a summary abstract to give the most useful information in the shortest space.

> To market life insurance to mid-40s urban professionals, Interstate Fidelity Insurance should advertise in upscale publications and use direct mail.
>
> Network TV and radio are not cost-efficient for reaching this market. This group comprises a small percentage of the prime-time network TV audience and a minority of most radio station listeners. They tend to discard newspapers and general-interest magazines quickly, but many of them keep upscale periodicals for months or years. Magazines with high percentages of readers in this group include *Architectural Digest, Bon Appetit, Forbes, Golf Digest, Metropolitan Home, Southern Living,* and *Smithsonian.*
>
> Any advertising campaign needs to overcome this group's feeling that they already have the insurance they need. One way to do this would be to encourage them to check the coverage their employers provide and to calculate the cost of their children's expenses through college graduation. Insurance plans that provide savings and tax benefits as well as death benefits might also be appealing.

One way to start composing an abstract is to write a sentence outline. A **sentence outline** not only uses complete sentences rather than words or phrases but also contains the thesis sentence or recommendation and the evidence that proves that point. Combine the sentences into paragraphs, adding transitions if necessary, and you'll have your abstract.

Descriptive abstracts indicate what topics the report covers and how deeply it goes into each topic, but they do not summarize what the report says about each topic. Phrases that describe the report ("this report covers," "it includes," "it summarizes," "it concludes") are marks of a descriptive abstract. An additional mark of a descriptive abstract is that the audience can't tell what the report says about the topics it covers.

> This report recommends ways Interstate Fidelity Insurance could market insurance to mid-40s urban professionals. It examines demographic and psychographic profiles of the target market. Survey results are used to show attitudes toward insurance. The report suggests some appeals that might be successful with this market.

Introduction

The **introduction** of the report always contains a statement of purpose and scope and may include all the parts in the following list:

- **Purpose.** The purpose statement identifies the problem the report addresses, the technical investigations it summarizes, and the rhetorical purpose (to explain, to recommend).

- **Scope.** The scope statement identifies how broad an area the report surveys. For example, Company XYZ is losing money on its line of computers. Does the report investigate the quality of the computers? The advertising campaign? The cost of manufacturing? The demand for computers? A scope statement allows the reader to evaluate the report on appropriate grounds.

- **Assumptions.** Assumptions in a report are like assumptions in geometry: statements whose truth you assume, and which you use to prove your final point. If they are wrong, the conclusion will be wrong too.

  For example, to plan cars that will be built five years from now, an automobile manufacturer commissions a report on young adults' attitudes toward cars. The recommendations would be based on assumptions both about gas prices and about the economy. If gas prices radically rose or fell, the kinds of cars young adults wanted would change. If there were a major recession, people wouldn't be able to buy new cars.

  Almost all reports require assumptions. A good report spells out its assumptions so that audiences can make decisions more confidently.

- **Methods.** If you conducted surveys, focus groups, or interviews, you need to tell how you chose your subjects, and how, when, and where they were interviewed. If the discussion of your methodology is more than a paragraph or two, you should probably make it a separate section in the body of the report rather than including it in the introduction. Reports based on scientific experiments usually put the methods section in the body of the report, not in the introduction.

  If your report is based solely on library or online research, provide a brief description of significant sources.

- **Limitations.** Limitations make your recommendations less valid or valid only under certain conditions. Limitations usually arise because time or money constraints haven't permitted full research. For example, a campus pizza restaurant considering expanding its menu may ask for a report but not have enough money to take a random sample of students and townspeople. Without a random sample, the writer cannot generalize from the sample to the larger population.

  Many recommendations are valid only for a limited time. For instance, a campus store wants to know what kinds of clothing will appeal to college men. The recommendations will remain valid for only a short time: two years from now, styles and tastes may have changed, and the clothes that would sell best now may no longer be in demand.

- **Criteria.** The criteria section outlines the factors or standards that you are considering and the relative importance of each. If a company is choosing a city for a new office, is the cost of office space more or less important than the availability of skilled workers? Check with your audience before you write the draft to make sure that your criteria match those of your audiences.

- **Definitions.** Many reports define key terms in the introduction. For instance, a report on unauthorized Internet use by employees might define what is meant by "unauthorized use." A report on the corporate dress code might define such codes broadly to include general appearance, so it could include items such as tattoos, facial piercings, and general cleanliness. Also, if you know that some members of your primary or secondary audience will not understand technical terms, define them. If you have only a few definitions, you can put them in the introduction. If you have many terms to define, put a **glossary** in an appendix. Refer to it in the introduction so that audiences know that you've provided it.

Background or History

Formal reports usually have a section that gives the background of the situation or the history of the problem. Even though the current audience for the report probably knows the situation, reports are filed and consulted years later. These later audiences will probably not know the background, although it may be crucial for understanding the options that are possible.

In some cases, the history section may cover many years. For example, a report recommending that a U.S. hotel chain open hotels in Romania may give the history of that country for at least several decades. In other cases, the background section is much briefer, covering only a few years or even just the immediate situation.

The purpose of most reports is rarely to provide a history of the problem. Do not let the background section achieve undue length.

Body

The body of the report is usually its longest section. Analyze causes of the problem and offer possible solutions. Present your argument with all its evidence and data. Data that are necessary to follow the argument are included with appropriate visuals, data displays, and explanatory text. Extended data sets, such as large tables and long questionnaires, are generally placed in appendixes. It is particularly important in the body that you use headings, forecasting statements, and topic sentences to help lead your audience through the text. Audiences will also appreciate clear, concise, and engaging prose. Remember to cite your sources (see Appendix C) and to refer in the text to all visuals and appendixes.

Conclusions and Recommendations

Conclusions summarize points you have made in the body of the report; **recommendations** are action items that would solve or ameliorate the problem. These sections are often combined if they are short: "Conclusions and Recommendations." No new information should be included in this section.

Many audiences turn to the recommendations section first; some organizations ask that recommendations be presented early in the report. Number the recommendations to make it easy for people to discuss them. If the recommendations will seem difficult or controversial, give a brief paragraph of rationale after each recommendation. If they'll be easy for the audience to accept, you can simply list them without comments or reasons. The recommendations will also be in the executive summary and perhaps in the title and the transmittal.

Appendixes

Appendixes provide additional materials that the careful audience may want. Common items are transcripts of interviews, copies of questionnaires, tallies of answers to questions, complex tables, printouts of original or difficult to find source material, and previous reports.

Summary by Learning Objectives

LO 18-1 **Use your time efficiently when writing reports.**

- Think about the parts of the report and what material can come from previous documents or research.

- When possible, even before finishing your research write some report sections: Purpose, Scope, Methods, Assumptions, Limitations, Criteria, and Definitions.

- Use technology tools to manage your time more efficiently.

LO 18-2 **Analyze data, information, and logic.**

- Good reports begin with good data. Make sure your data come from reliable sources.

- Analyze report numbers and text for accuracy and logic.

LO 18-3 **Choose information for reports.**

- Choose information to include that your audience needs to know to make a decision. Figuring out whether your audience is supportive, neutral, or skeptical will guide you on how much information you need to include.

- Determine what information to put in the body of the report or in appendixes.

LO 18-4 **Organize reports.**

Choose an appropriate organizational pattern for your information and purposes. The most common patterns are comparison/contrast, problem–solution, elimination of alternatives, SWOT analysis, general to particular, particular to general, geographic or spatial, functional, and chronological.

LO 18-5 **Present information effectively in reports.**

Reports use the same style as other business documents, with three exceptions:

1. Reports use a more formal style, without contractions or slang, than do many letters and memos.

2. Reports rarely use the word *you*.

3. Reports should include all the definitions and documents needed to understand the recommendations.

To create good report style,

1. Use clear, engaging writing.

2. Keep repetition to a minimum.

3. Introduce all sources and visuals.

4. Use forecasting, transitions, topic sentences, and headings.

Headings are single words short phrases, or complete sentences that describe all of the material under them until the next heading. Talking heads tell the audience what to expect in each section.

Headings must use the same grammatical structure. Subheads under a heading must be parallel to each other but do not necessarily have to be parallel to subheads under other headings.

LO 18-6 **Prepare the different components of formal reports.**

- The title page of a report usually contains four items: the title of the report, whom the report is prepared for, whom it is prepared by, and the date.

- If the report is 25 pages or less, list all the headings in the table of contents. In a long report, pick a level and put all the headings at that level and above in the contents.

- Organize the transmittal in this way:

  1. Release the report.

  2. Summarize your conclusions and recommendations.

  3. Mention any points of special interest in the report. Show how you surmounted minor problems you encountered in your investigation. Thank people who helped you.

  4. Point out additional research that is necessary, if any.

  5. Thank the reader for the opportunity to do the work and offer to answer questions.

- Summary abstracts present the logic skeleton of the article: the thesis or recommendation and its proof. Descriptive abstracts indicate what topics the article covers and how deeply it goes into each topic, but do not summarize what the article says about each topic. A good abstract or executive summary is easy to read, concise, and clear. A good abstract can be understood by itself, without the report or references.

- The "Introduction" of the report always contains a statement of purpose and scope. The purpose statement identifies the organizational problem the report addresses, the technical investigations it summarizes, and the rhetorical purpose (to explain, to recommend). The scope statement identifies how broad an area the report surveys. The introduction may also include limitations, problems or factors that limit the validity of your recommendations; assumptions, statements whose truth you assume, and which you use to prove your final point; methods, an explanation of how you gathered your data; criteria used to weigh the factors in the decision; and definitions of terms audiences may not know.

■ A "Background" or "History" section is usually included because reports are filed and may be consulted years later by people who no longer remember the original circumstances.

■ The body of the report, usually the longest section, analyzes causes of the problem and offers possible solutions. It presents your argument with all evidence and data.

■ "Conclusions" section summarizes points made in the body of the report; under "Recommendations" are action items that would solve or ameliorate the problem. These sections are often combined if they are short.

■ Appendixes provide additional materials that the careful audience may want.

Continuing Case

The All-Weather Case, set in an HR department in a manufacturing company, extends through all 19 chapters and is available at www.mhhe.com/locker11e. The portion for this chapter asks students to organize data from the cross-cultural training program and prepare an outline for a recommendation report based on the data.

Exercises and Cases

18.1   Reviewing the Chapter

1. What are some sections of the report you may be able to write even before finishing your research? (LO 18-1)

2. What are some criteria to check to ensure you have quality data? (LO 18-2)

3. What kinds of patterns should you look for in your data and text? (LO 18-2)

4. What are some guidelines for choosing information for reports? (LO 18-3)

5. Name seven basic patterns for organizing reports. For four of them, explain when they would be particularly effective or ineffective. (LO 18-4)

6. What are three ways that style in reports differs from conventional business communication style? (LO 18-5)

7. Name four good writing principles that are particularly important in reports. (LO 18-5)

8. How do you introduce sources in the text of the report? (LO 18-5)

9. Why should reports try to have a topic sentence at the beginning of each paragraph? (LO 18-5)

10. What are the characteristics of an effective report title? (LO 18-6)

11. What goes in the letter of transmittal? (LO 18-6)

12. What is the difference between summary and descriptive abstracts? (LO 18-6)

13. What goes in the introduction of a report? (LO 18-6)

14. What is the difference between conclusions and recommendations? (LO 18-6)

18.2   Identifying Assumptions and Limitations

Indicate whether each of the following would be an assumption or a limitation in a formal report.

a. Report on Ways to Encourage More Students to Join XYZ Organization's Twitter Feed

　1. I surveyed a judgment sample rather than a random sample.

　2. These recommendations are based on the attitudes of current students. Presumably, students in the next several years will have the same attitudes and interests.

b. Report on the Feasibility of Building Hilton Hotels in Romania

　1. This report is based on the expectation that the country will be politically stable.

2. All of my information is based on library research. The most recent articles were published two months ago; much of the information was published a year ago or more. Therefore, some of my information may be out of date.

c. Report on Car-Buying Preferences of Young Adults

　1. These recommendations may change if the cost of gasoline increases dramatically or if there is another deep recession.

　2. This report is based on a survey of adults ages 20 to 24 in California, Texas, Illinois, Ontario, and Massachusetts.

　3. These preferences are based on the cars now available. If a major technological or styling innovation occurs, preferences may change.

18.3   Revising an Executive Summary

The following executive summary is poorly organized and written. Revise it to make it more effective. Cut information that does not belong, and add any information that you feel is missing.

> This report will discuss the healthier food options for athletes at the University Gym. Currently, there are several vending machines that student athletes can buy snacks from, but all of the snacks are really unhealthy. Some of the vending machine options that they have are potato chips, candy bars, cookies, and fruit snacks. None of these are healthy options for athletes.
>
> I think there are a few options that can help this situation. Some of the options include setting up a snack bar. This snack bar could include items like fruits, vegetables, salads, and fruit smoothies. The University's Food Services would have to run this and hire several students to run it. This would cost quite a bit.
>
> Students need healthy food options, especially when they are athletes who are training for sports. Student athletes have very demanding schedules and may not have time to cook healthy foods for themselves.
>
> Another option that we could do would be to simply have a healthy, refrigerated vending machine, with healthy options in it, like fruits, ready-to-eat salads, veggies, and yogurts. This would be easier to install, but would have to be checked frequently to ensure that that items do not go bad.
>
> These are my recommendations for the problem.

18.4   Revising a Recommendation Section

A student has written the following recommendation section for a report for a local restaurant. The restaurant is called the American Grill and specializes in burgers and fries. The restaurant is new to the area and wants to increase its advertising in the local area to get the word out about their food.

Revise the recommendation section so it is well organized and clear. You may add any information that is needed.

> I recommend the following to expand the advertising for American Grill:
>
> American Grill should hand out flyers to people during the July 4th parade that goes through the downtown area. They could ask some of the servers to walk through the parade wearing their American Grill t-shirts to hand out the flyers. The flyers would contain lots of information, like hours, specials, and other important information.
>
> The American Grill should put a radio commercial on the local radio station with the drink specials and also hand out flyers. The radio commercial should also give location information for those who do not know where it is located.
>
> The American Grill should hand out coupons for appetizers and drink specials. These could also be handed out in a parade, or to college students when they first get to the University.

18.5   Comparing Report Formats

Locate five business or organizational reports (or white papers as they're sometimes called) on the Internet. A good online collection of organizational reports is the website of the Council on Library and Information Resources (CLIR) accessible at http://www.clir.org/pubs/reports/. Additionally, you can find reports linked from the websites of the Fortune 500 organizations, or you can search for them on Google using keywords such as "reports," "business reports," "company reports," or "organizational reports."

The reports you find could be about the organizations' environmental sustainability efforts, their products, or any other aspect of their operations.

Compare the organization of the five reports you select. What similarities and differences do you see in the formatting of all these reports? Make a table of your findings. Discuss your findings in small groups.

18.6 Comparing Style in Annual Reports

Locate two annual reports on the Internet. A good source is Report Watch, http://www.reportwatch.net/. Compare the style of the two reports. Here are some questions to get you started:

1. How do they use visuals to keep attention?
2. What differences do you see in the letters from the CEOs?
3. How do they present number-heavy information? Do they rely mainly on tables and graphs? Do they give prose summaries?
4. Is the writing easy to understand?
5. Do you see places where negative information is given a positive spin?
6. Is one report easier to understand than the other? Why?
7. Is one report more interesting than the other? Why?
8. Is one report more convincing than the other? Why?

As your instructor directs,

a. Work in small groups to do your comparison. Share your findings in a five-minute oral presentation to the class.
b. Work in small groups to do your comparison. Share your findings in an e-mail posted on the class website.
c. Work individually to do your comparison. Share your findings in an e-mail to your instructor.

18.7 Analyzing Business Reports

Visit the following collection of business reports: http://www.technologyreview.com/businessreports/. In small groups, choose a report and answer the following questions:

■ How many of the components of a report does it contain? (See Figure 18.5).
■ What is the style of the report? What kinds of language does it use? Try to find specific instances.
■ Is the writing clear and engaging?
■ Is it repetitive?

■ Does the report use sources and visuals? How are they used?
■ Does the report use forecasting, transitions, clear topic sentences, and/or headings?
■ What type of report is this?
■ These reports are *MIT Technology Review* business reports. Did that fact lessen your desire to read the report? Was the technology in the report understandable to you? Why or why not?

Share your findings with the class.

18.8 Evaluating a Report from Your Workplace

Consider the following aspects of a report from your workplace:

■ Content. How much information is included? How is it presented?
■ Emphasis. What points are emphasized? What points are de-emphasized? What verbal and visual techniques are used to highlight or minimize information?
■ Visuals and layout. Are visuals used effectively? Are they accurate and free from chartjunk? What image do the pictures and visuals create? Are color and white space used effectively? (See Chapter 16 on visuals.)

As your instructor directs,

a. Write an e-mail to your instructor analyzing the report.
b. Join with a small group of students to compare and contrast several reports. Present your evaluation in an informal group report.
c. Present your evaluation orally to the class.

18.9 Analyzing Information and Writing Reports

Reread the sidebar about the Pew Internet and American Life Project at http://www.pewinternet.org/ on page 597. Go to the website and browse through the reports. Select a report and answer the following questions:

■ Who is the report's audience?

■ What is its purpose?
■ How were the data collected?
■ What did the data collection measure?
■ Why was the data collection important?

Given your analysis of the report's audience, purpose, and data collection, consider the strategies used in the report to convey the information. Answer these questions:

- What tone did the writer adopt?
- How was the report organized and designed to meet the needs of the audience?
- What language choices did the writer make?

Finally, examine the press releases that are written about the report (the press releases for each report are included as links) for the ways the information in the report is adapted for a different audience and purpose. How do the content, organization, tone, and language choices differ from those of the original report? Do you see any ethical issues involved in condensing the report into a press release?

As your instructor directs,

- Write a report of your findings to your instructor.
- Present your findings to the class using presentation software.

18.10   Preparing an Information Report

Visit the website of the Global Reporting Initiative (https://www.globalreporting.org/Pages/default.aspx), a group of analysts from various industries and professions that is committed to advancing the cause of socially responsible reporting by organizations. Prepare an information report, either as an e-mail to your instructor or as a presentation for the class, describing the organization, the people behind it, their guidelines, their work, and their impact on the corporate world.

18.11   Recommending Action

Write a report recommending an action that your unit or organization should take. Possibilities include

- Developing a stronger social media presence online.
- Enhancing technology with smartphones, tablets, or laptops to accomplish work on the go.
- Buying more equipment for your department.
- Hiring an additional worker for your department.
- Making your organization more family-friendly.
- Making a change that will make the organization more environmentally sustainable.
- Making changes to improve accessibility for customers or employees with disabilities.

Address your report to the person who would have the power to approve your recommendation.

As your instructor directs,

a. Create a document or presentation to achieve the goal.
b. Write an e-mail to your instructor describing the situation at your workplace and explaining your rhetorical choices (medium, strategy, tone, wording, graphics or document design, and so forth).

18.12   Writing a Recommendation Report

Write a report evaluating two or more alternatives. Possible topics include the following:

1. Should your student organization start a Facebook page to promote events, speakers, etc.?
2. Should students in your major start a monthly newsletter? Would an electronic or paper version be more useful to the target audience?
3. Should your student organization write an annual report? Would doing so help the next year's officers?
4. Should your student organization create a wiki, blog, or newsletter to facilitate communication with a constituency?
5. Should your workplace create a newsletter to communicate internally?
6. Should a local restaurant open another branch? Where should it be?

In designing your study, identify the alternatives, define your criteria for selecting one option over others, carefully evaluate each alternative, and recommend the best course of action.

18.13   Writing an Informative or Closure Report

Write an informative report on one of the following topics.

1. What should a U.S. manager know about dealing with workers from _____ [you fill in the country or culture]? What factors do and do not motivate people in this group? How do they show respect and deference? Are they used to a strong hierarchy or to an egalitarian setting? Do they normally do one thing at once or many things? How important is clock time and being on time? What factors lead them to respect someone? Age? Experience? Education? Technical knowledge? Wealth? Or what? What conflicts or

miscommunications may arise between workers from this culture and other workers due to cultural differences? Are people from this culture similar in these beliefs and behaviors, or is there lots of variation?

2. What benefits do companies offer? To get information, check the web pages of three companies in the same industry. Information about benefits is usually on the page about working for the company.

3. Describe an ethical dilemma encountered by workers in a specific organization. What is the background of the situation? What competing loyalties exist? In the past, how have workers responded? How has the organization responded? Have whistle-blowers been rewarded or punished? What could the organization do to foster ethical behavior?

4. Describe a problem or challenge encountered by an organization where you've worked. Describe the

problem, show why it needed to be solved, tell who did what to try to solve it, and tell how successful the efforts were. Possibilities include

- How the organization is integrating a social media strategy.
- How the organization is implementing teams, downsizing, or changing organizational culture.
- How the organization uses e-mail or voice mail.
- How the organization uses telecommuting.
- How managers deal with stress, make ethical choices, or evaluate subordinates.
- How the organization is responding to changing U.S. demographics, the Americans with Disabilities Act, the Plain Writing Act, or international competition and opportunities.

18.14 Writing a Consultant's Report—Restaurant Tipping

Your consulting company has been asked to conduct a report for Diamond Enterprises, which runs three national chains: FishStix, The Bar-B-Q Pit, and Morrie's. All are medium-priced, family-friendly restaurants. The CEO is thinking of replacing optional tips with a 15% service fee automatically added to bills.

You read articles in trade journals, surveyed a random sample of 200 workers in each of the chains, and conducted an e-mail survey of the 136 restaurant managers. Here are your findings:

1. Trade journals point out that the Internal Revenue Service (IRS) audits restaurants if it thinks that servers underreport tips. Dealing with an audit is time-consuming and often results in the restaurant's having to pay penalties and interest.

2. Only one Morrie's restaurant has actually been audited by the IRS. Management was able to convince the IRS that servers were reporting tips accurately. No penalty was assessed. Management spent $5,000 on CPA and legal fees and spent over 80 hours of management time gathering data and participating in the audit.

3. Restaurants in Europe already add a service fee (usually 15%) to the bill. Patrons can add more if they choose. Local custom determines whether tips are expected and how much they should be. In Germany, for example, it is more usual to round up the bill (from 27 € to 30 €, for example) than to figure a percentage.

4. If the restaurant collected a service fee, it could use the income to raise wages for cooks and hosts and pay for other benefits, such as health insurance, rather than giving all the money to servers and bussers.

5. Morrie's servers tend to be under 25 years of age. FishStix employs more servers over 25, who are doing this for a living. The Bar-B-Q Pit servers are students in college towns.

6. In all three chains, servers oppose the idea. Employees other than servers generally support it.

	Retain tips	Change to service fee added to bill	Don't care
FishStix servers ($n = 115$)	90%	7%	3%
Bar-B-Q servers ($n = 73$)	95%	0%	5%
Morrie's servers ($n = 93$)	85%	15%	0%
Morrie's nonservers ($n = 65$)	25%	70%	5%
FishStix non servers ($n = 46$)	32%	32%	37%
Bar-B-Q nonservers ($n = 43$)	56%	20%	25%

(Numbers do not add up to 100% due to rounding.)

7. Servers said that it was important to go home with money in their pockets (92%), that their expertise increased food sales and should be rewarded (67%), and that if a service fee replaced tips they would be likely to look for another job (45%). Some (17%) thought that if the manager distributed service-fee income, favoritism rather than the quality of work would govern how much tip income they got. Most (72%) thought that customers would not add anything beyond the 15% service fee, and many (66%) thought that total tip income would decrease and their own portion of that income would decrease (90%).

8. Managers generally support the change.

	Retain tips	Change to service fee added to bill	Don't care
FishStix managers ($n = 44$)	20%	80%	0%
Bar-B-Q managers ($n = 13$)	33%	67%	0%
Morrie's managers ($n = 58$)	55%	45%	0%

9. Comments from managers include: "It isn't fair for a cook with eight years of experience to make only $12 an hour while a server can make $25 an hour in just a couple of months," and "I could have my pick of employees if I offered health insurance."

10. Morale at Bar-B-Q Pit seems low. This is seen in part in the low response rate to the survey.

11. In a tight employment market, some restaurants might lose good servers if they made the change.

However, hiring cooks and other non-servers would be easier.

12. The current computer systems in place can handle figuring and recording the service fee. Since bills are printed by computer, an additional line could be added. Allocating the service-fee income could take extra managerial time, especially at first.

Write the report.

18.15 Writing a Library Research Report

Write a library research report.

As your instructor directs,

Turn in the following documents:

a.   The approved proposal.

b.   The report, including

   Cover.

   Title Page.

   Letter or Memo of Transmittal.

   Table of Contents.

   List of Illustrations.

   Executive Summary or Abstract.

   Body (Introduction, all information, recommendations). Your instructor may specify a minimum length, a minimum number or kind of sources, and a minimum number of visuals.

   References or Works Cited.

c.   Your notes and at least one preliminary draft.

Choose one of the following topics.

1. **Selling to College Students.** Your car dealership is located in a university town, but the manager doubts that selling cars to college students will be profitable. You agree that college incomes are low to nonexistent, but you see some students driving late-model cars. Recommend to the dealership's manager whether to begin marketing to college students, suggesting some tactics that would be effective.

2. **Advertising on the Internet.** You work on a team developing a marketing plan to sell high-end sunglasses. Your boss is reluctant to spend money for online advertising because she has heard that the money is mostly wasted. Also, she associates the ads with spam, which she detests. Recommend whether the company should devote some of its advertising budget to online ads. Include samples of online advertising that supports your recommendation.

3. **Improving Job Interview Questions.** Turnover among the sales force has been high, and your boss believes the problem is that your company has been hiring the wrong people. You are part of a team investigating the problem, and your assignment is to evaluate the questions used in job interviews. Human resource personnel use tried-and-true questions like "What is your greatest strength?" and "What is your greatest weakness?" The sales manager has some creative alternatives, such as asking candidates to solve logic puzzles and seeing how they perform under stress by taking frequent phone calls during the interview. You are to evaluate the current interviewing approaches and propose changes that would improve hiring decisions.

4. **Selling to Walmart.** Your company has a reputation for making high-quality lamps and ceiling fans sold in specialty stores. Although the company has been profitable, it could grow much faster if it sold through Walmart. Your boss is excited about her recent discussions with that retailer, but she has heard from associates that Walmart can be a demanding customer. She asked you to find out if there is a downside to selling through Walmart and, if so, whether manufacturers can afford to say no to a business deal with the retail giant.

5. **Making College Affordable.** The senator you work for is concerned about fast-rising costs of a college education. Students say they cannot afford their tuition bills. Colleges say they are making all the cuts they can without compromising the quality of education. In order to propose a bill that would help make college affordable for those who are qualified to attend, the senator has asked you to research alternatives for easing the problem. Recommend one or two measures the senator could include in a bill for the Senate to vote on.

6. With your instructor's permission, investigate a topic of your choice.

18.16 Writing a Recommendation Report

Write an individual or a team report.

As your instructor directs,

Turn in the following documents:

1.   The approved proposal.

2.   The report, including

Cover.

Title Page.

Letter or Memo of Transmittal.

Table of Contents.

List of Illustrations.

Executive Summary or Abstract.

Body (Introduction, all information, recommendations). Your instructor may specify a minimum length, a minimum number or kind of sources, and a minimum number of visuals.

Appendixes if useful or relevant.

3.   Your notes and at least one preliminary draft.

Pick one of the following topics.

1.   **Improving Customer Service.** Many customers find that service is getting poorer and workers are getting ruder. Evaluate the service in a local store, restaurant, or other organization. Are customers made to feel comfortable? Is workers' communication helpful, friendly, and respectful? Are workers knowledgeable about products and services? Do they sell them effectively? Write a report analyzing the quality of service and recommending what the organization should do to improve.

2.   **Recommending Courses for the Local Community College.** Businesses want to be able to send workers to local community colleges to upgrade their skills; community colleges want to prepare students to enter the local workforce. What skills are in demand in your community? What courses at what levels should the local community college offer?

3.   **Improving Sales and Profits.** Recommend ways a small business in your community can increase sales and profits. Focus on one or more of the following:

the products or services it offers, its advertising, its decor, its location, its accounting methods, its cash management, or any other aspect that may be keeping the company from achieving its potential. Address your report to the owner of the business.

4.   **Increasing Student Involvement.** How could an organization on campus persuade more of the students who are eligible to join or to become active in its programs? Do students know that it exists? Is it offering programs that interest students? Is it retaining current members? What changes should the organization make? Address your report to the officers of the organization.

5.   **Evaluating a Potential Employer.** What training is available to new employees? How soon is the average entry-level person promoted? How much travel and weekend work are expected? Is there a "busy season," or is the workload consistent year-round? What fringe benefits are offered? What is the corporate culture? Is the climate nonracist and nonsexist? How strong is the company economically? How is it likely to be affected by current economic, demographic, and political trends? Address your report to the placement office on campus; recommend whether it should encourage students to work at this company.

6.   With your instructor's permission, choose your own topic.

Notes

1.   Carl Bialik, "Sizing Up Crowds Pushes Limits of Technology," *Wall Street Journal*, February 5, 2011, A4; Constance A. Krach and Victoria A. Velkoff, "Centenarians in the United States," *Current Population Reports, Series P23-199RV,* U.S. Bureau of the Census (Washington, DC: Government Printing Office, 1999), 14; "National Longitudinal Surveys Frequently Asked Questions: Number of Jobs Held in a Lifetime," Bureau of Labor Statistics, last modified June 12, 2013, http://www.bls.gov/nls/nlsfaqs .htm\#anch41; and Carl Bialik, "Claims of Thanksgiving Excess Fueled by Feast of Fuzzy Data," *Wall Street Journal,* November 25, 2009, A20.

2.   John Hechinger, "Some States Drop Testing Bar," *Wall Street Journal,* October 30, 2009, A3.

3.   Thomas Wailgum, "Eight   of the Worst Spreadsheet Blunders," *CIO,* August 17, 2007, http://www.cio.com/ article/131500/Eight_of_the_Worst_Spreadsheet_ Blunders.

4.   Jeffrey Zaslow, "An Iconic Report 20 Years Later: Many of Those Women Married After All," *Wall Street Journal,* May 25, 2006, D1.

5.   Arlene Weintraub, "What the Doctors Aren't Disclosing: A New Study Shows How Authors of Medical Journal Articles Flout Rules on Revealing Conflicts of Interest," *BusinessWeek,* May 26, 2008, 32.

6.   Erick H. Turner et al., "Selective Publication of Antidepressant Trials and Its Influence on Apparent Efficacy," *New England Journal of Medicine* 358, no. 3 (2008): 252.

7.   Scott Thurm, "Mind the Gap: Employment Figures Tell Different Stories," *Wall Street Journal,* October 2, 2010, A2.

8.   Stephen E. Moore, "655,000 War Dead?" *Wall Street Journal,* October 18, 2006, A20; and Neil Munro and Carl M.

Cannon, "Data Bomb," *National Journal,* January 4, 2008, http://www.freerepublic.com/focus/f-news/1948378/ posts.

9.   Malcolm Gladwell, *The Tipping Point: How Little Things Can Make a Big Difference* (New York: Little, Brown and Company, 2002), 146; Steven D. Levitt and Stephen J. Dubner, *Freakonomics: A Rogue Economist Explores the Hidden Side of Everything* (New York: William Morrow, 2005), 119–41.

10.   Casey E. Copen, et al., "First Marriages in the United States: Data from the 2006–2010 National Survey of Family Growth," *National Health Statistics Reports,* no. 49 (March 22, 2012): 1–22. Published by the National Center for Health Statistics, U. S. Centers for Disease Control and Prevention, http://198.246.98.21/nchs/data/nhsr/ nhsr049.pdf.

11.   Carl Bialik, "Weddings Are Not the Budget Drains Some Surveys Suggest," *Wall Street Journal,* August 24, 2007, B1.

12.   Frederick F. Reichheld, "The One Number You Need to Grow," *Harvard Business Review* 81, no. 12 (December 2003): 46–54.

13.   Jakob Nielsen, "Risks of Quantitative Studies," *Alertbox,* March 1, 2004, http://www.useit.com/alertbox/20040301 .html; and Dan Seligman, "The Story They All Got Wrong," *Forbes,* November 25, 2002, 124.

14.   "NASA Releases Information on Federal Survey of Pilots," *Des Moines Register,* January 1, 2008, 2A.

15.   Ellen Pastorino and Susann M. Doyle-Portillo, *What Is Psychology?: Essentials,* 2nd ed., (Stamford, CT: Cengage Learning, 2012), 208.

16.   Richard J. Connors, ed., *Warren Buffett on Business: Principles from the Sage of Omaha* (Hoboken, NJ: Wiley, 2010), 125.

19 Making Oral Presentations

Chapter Outline

NEWSWORTHY COMMUNICATION

Steve Jobs, Orator

When most company CEOs give presentations, the news media may provide a brief report in the business or technology sections. However, when Steve Jobs gave a presentation as CEO of Apple, Inc., he almost always got extra attention and often ended up as a lead news story. Part of the attention was directed at Apple's innovative products, of course, but the rest was devoted to Jobs himself: as a dynamic CEO, a technology innovator, and a master presenter.

Communications coach Carmine Gallo, like many other presentation experts, believes that Jobs was the epitome of the modern CEO presenter. So what made the difference? Gallo discusses some key techniques:

1. A simple catchphrase that carried over from the presentation to all marketing materials ("The World's Thinnest Laptop," for example).

2. An answer to the audience's primary questions: Why should I care?

3. A villain, who can motivate the audience to unite behind the hero (Apple).

4. Simple slides, focused on visuals and with few if any bulleted lists. Gallo found that Jobs once used only seven words on 10 slides.

5. A demonstration of the product. Jobs never talked about a product when he could show it off instead.

6. A holy smokes moment, where he wowed the audience with something new.

As an example of Jobs's effectiveness, Gallo uses a 10-minute "performance that revolutionized the music industry." In that short time, Jobs convinced many that it would be smart to pay for something they had been getting for free. He introduced villains—Napster and Kazaa, with slow downloads and unreliable quality—and a hero, iTunes, with fast downloads and high quality. The catchphrase was "only 99 cents."

The six techniques got much of their power from Jobs's careful attention to detail. He spent days preparing and rehearsing his presentations. And, most of all, he understood the audience in the room and prepared his presentation for them.

Anyone can incorporate some of the successful strategies used by Steve Jobs, particularly focusing on the audience, simplifying the message and the slides, and practicing the presentation.

Sources: Carmine Gallo, *The Presentation Secrets of Steve Jobs: How to Be Insanely Great in Front of Any Audience* (New York: McGraw-Hill, 2010); and "Presentation Skills: The 10-Minute Steve Jobs Performance that Revolutionized the Music Industry," *Forbes*, April 29, 2013, http://www.forbes.com/sites/carminegallo/2013/04/29/presentation-skills-the-10-minute-steve-jobs-performance-that-revolutionized-the-music-industry/.

After studying this chapter, you will know how to

LO 19-1   **Identify purposes of presentations.**

LO 19-2   **Plan a strategy for presentations.**

LO 19-3   **Organize effective presentations.**

LO 19-4   **Plan visuals for presentations.**

LO 19-5   **Deliver effective presentations.**

LO 19-6   **Handle questions during presentations.**

The power to persuade people to care about something you believe in is crucial to business success. Making a good oral presentation is more than just good delivery: it also involves developing a strategy that fits your audience and purpose, having good content, organizing material, planning visuals, and delivering effectively. The choices you make in each of these areas are affected by your purposes, audience, and situation.

Comparing Written and Oral Messages

Giving a presentation is in many ways similar to writing a message. All the chapters on using you-attitude and positive emphasis, developing audience benefits, analyzing your audience, and designing visuals remain relevant as you plan an oral presentation.

Oral messages make it easier to

- Use emotion to help persuade the audience.
- Focus the audience's attention on specific points.
- Answer questions, resolve conflicts, and build consensus.
- Modify a proposal that may not be acceptable in its original form.
- Get immediate action or response.

Written messages make it easier to

- Present extensive or complex data.
- Present many specific details of a law, policy, or procedure.
- Minimize undesirable emotions.

Oral and written messages have many similarities. In both, you should

- Adapt the message to the specific audience.
- Show the audience how they would benefit from the idea, policy, service, or product.
- Overcome any objections the audience may have.
- Use you-attitude and positive emphasis.

- Use visuals to clarify or emphasize material.
- Specify exactly what the audience should do.

Identifying Purposes in Presentations LO 19-1

Oral presentations have the same three basic purposes that written documents have: to inform, to persuade, and to build goodwill. Like written messages, most oral presentations have more than one purpose.

Informative presentations inform or teach the audience. Training sessions in an organization are primarily informative. Secondary purposes may be to persuade new employees to follow organizational procedures, rather than doing something their own way, and to help them appreciate the organizational culture.

Persuasive presentations motivate the audience to act or to believe. Giving information and evidence is an important means of persuasion. Stories and visuals are also effective. In addition, the speaker must build goodwill by appearing to be credible and sympathetic to the audience's needs. The goal in many presentations is a favorable vote or decision. For example, speakers making business presentations may try to persuade the audience to approve their proposals, to adopt their ideas, or to buy their products. Sometimes the goal is to change behavior or attitudes or to reinforce existing attitudes. For example, a speaker at a meeting of factory workers may stress the importance of following safety procedures.

Goodwill presentations entertain and validate the audience. In an after-dinner speech, the audience wants to be entertained. Presentations at sales meetings may be designed to stroke the audience's egos and to validate their commitment to organizational goals.

Make your purpose as specific as possible.

Weak: The purpose of my presentation is to discuss saving for retirement.

Better: The purpose of my presentation is to persuade my audience to put their 401k funds in stocks and bonds, not in money market accounts and CDs.

or: The purpose of my presentation is to explain how to calculate how much money someone needs to save in order to maintain a specific lifestyle after retirement.

Your purpose statement is the principle that guides your choice of strategy and content, so write it down before you start preparing your presentation. Note that the purpose is *not* the introduction of your talk; it may not be explicit in your presentation at all.

Planning a Strategy for Your Presentation LO 19-2

How will you reach your specific goals with the target audience? Think about the physical conditions in which you'll be speaking. Will the audience be tired at the end of a long day of listening? Sleepy after a big meal? Will the group be large or small? The more you know about your audience, the better you can adapt your message to them.

An oral presentation needs to be simpler than a written message to the same audience. If readers forget a point, they can reread it. Headings, paragraph indentation, and punctuation provide visual cues to help readers understand the message. Listeners, in contrast, must remember what the speaker says. Whatever they don't remember is lost. Even asking questions requires the audience to remember which points they don't understand.

Mastering Toasts and Public Speaking

To some, Toastmasters International still reflects its roots: helping nervous groomsmen prepare wedding toasts. But it has grown into an organization with over 280,000 members and 13,500 clubs in 116 countries. So what is it all about?

Toastmasters helps its members learn and practice public speaking. But the aim is not at high-stakes motivational speaking. Rather, "We help the new supervisor who just got promoted and doesn't feel comfortable talking to the five people working for him," says Daniel Rex, the executive director. "We teach people skills, but what we really teach is confidence."

The organization's success in teaching has been noticed. Official branches of Toastmasters can be found in many major corporations, and other companies sponsor Toastmasters classes for their employees. The principles taught—confidence, simplicity, personal branding, and audience engagement—are important for any presenter to learn.

Adapted from Joel Stein, "Making Every Word Count," *Bloomberg Businessweek,* January 24–30, 2011, 112–13; and "Welcome to Toastmasters International," Toastmasters International, 2013, http://www.toastmasters.org.

Oral presentation skills are a big asset in the business world.

In all presentations, simplify what you want to say. Identify the one idea you want the audience to take home. Simplify your supporting detail so it's easy to follow. Simplify visuals so they can be taken in at a glance. Simplify your words and sentences so they're easy to understand.

As you begin planning for your presentation, you'll need to determine what kind of presentation to deliver and how to adapt your ideas to the audience.

Choosing the Kind of Presentation

Choose one of three basic kinds of presentations: monologue, guided discussion, or interactive.

In a **monologue presentation,** the speaker talks without interruption; questions are held until the end of the presentation, at which time the speaker functions as an expert. The speaker plans the presentation and delivers it without deviation. This kind of presentation is the most common in class situations, but it's often boring for the audience. Good delivery skills are crucial, since the audience is comparatively uninvolved.

In a **guided discussion,** the speaker presents the questions or issues that both speaker and audience have agreed on in advance. Rather than functioning as an expert with all the answers, the speaker serves as a facilitator to help the audience tap its own knowledge. This kind of presentation is excellent for presenting the results of consulting projects, when the speaker has specialized knowledge, but the audience must implement the solution if it is to succeed. Guided discussions need more time than monologue presentations, but produce more audience response, more responses involving analysis, and more commitment to the result.

An **interactive presentation** is a conversation, even if the speaker stands in front of a group and uses charts and overheads. Most sales presentations are interactive presentations. The sales representative uses questions to determine the buyer's needs, probe objections, and gain provisional and then final commitment to the purchase. Even in a memorized sales presentation, the buyer will talk a significant portion of the time. Top salespeople let the buyer do the majority of the talking.

Adapting Your Ideas to the Audience

Analyze your audience for an oral presentation just as you do for a written message. If you'll be speaking to co-workers, talk to them about your topic or proposal to find out what questions or objections they have. For audiences inside the organization, the biggest questions are often practical ones: Will it work? How much will it cost? How long will it take? How will it impact me?

Measure the message you'd like to send against where your audience is now. If your audience is indifferent, skeptical, or hostile, focus on the part of your message the audience will find most interesting and easiest to accept.

Make your ideas relevant to your audience by linking what you have to say to their experiences and interests. Showing your audience that the topic affects them directly is the most effective strategy. When you can't do that, at least link the topic to some everyday experience.

http://www.
ted.com/

TED offers "riveting talks by remarkable people, free to the world." You can sort talks by categories such as business, technology, or science, or by tags such as persuasive, fascinating, funny, "most e-mailed this week," or "rated jaw-dropping."

Choosing Information to Include

Choose the information that is most interesting to your audience, that answers the questions your audience will have, and that is most persuasive for them. Limit your talk to three main points. In a long presentation (20 minutes or more) each main point can have subpoints. Your content will be easier to understand if you clearly show the relationship between each of the main points.

Think about colorful ways to present your information. What analogies or metaphors can you use to grab your audience's attention and help them remember your information? What props could you use? How can you entertain and inspire your audience with your presentation to increase its impact?

What pictures can you use to illustrate your ideas? Where could you use video clips? Research evidence is clear that people remember information far better and longer when its presentation involves pictures.

Turning your information into a **story** also helps. For example, a presentation about a plan to reduce scrap rates on the second shift can begin by setting the scene and defining the problem: Production expenses have cut profits in half. The plot unfolds as the speaker describes the facts that helped her trace the problem to scrap rates on the second shift. The resolution to the story is her group's proposal.

In an informative presentation, link the points you make to the knowledge your audience has. Show the audience members that your information answers their questions, solves their problems, or helps them do their jobs. When you explain the effect of a new law or the techniques for using a new machine, use specific examples that apply to the decisions they make and the work they do. If your content is detailed or complicated, give people a written outline or handouts. The written material both helps the audience keep track of your points during the presentation and serves as a reference after the talk is over.

Good presentations adapt their ideas to a particular audience.

To be convincing, you must answer the audience's questions and objections. However, don't bring up negatives or inconsistencies unless you're sure that the audience will think of them. If you aren't sure, save your evidence for the question phase. If someone does ask, you'll have the answer.

Choosing Data

As part of choosing what to say, you should determine what data to present. Any data you mention should be necessary for the points you are making and should start with decisions about what the audience needs to know.

Statistics and numbers can be convincing if you present them in ways that are easy to hear. Simplify numbers by reducing them to two significant digits and putting them in a context.

Hard to hear: Our 2010 sales dropped from $12,036,288,000 to $9,124,507,000.

Easy to hear: Our 2010 sales dropped from $12 billion to $9 billion. This is the steepest decline our company has seen in a quarter century.

Double-check your presentation statistics and numbers to ensure they are accurate. Mark Hurd, former chairman and CEO of Hewlett-Packard, gave as the best advice he ever got, "It's hard to look smart with bad numbers."[1]

Choosing Demonstrations

Demonstrations can prove your points dramatically and quickly. They offer an effective way to teach a process and to show what a product can do for the audience. Demonstrations can also help people remember your points.

Apple has become famous for using captivating demonstrations when it launches new versions of its products. Steve Jobs, in particular, was known for amazing presentations, and most of his finest involved a Wow! moment that had his audience standing and cheering.

When he introduced the MacBook Air, he picked up a manila envelope and pulled out his new notebook computer, holding it high for everyone to see how thin it was. When he introduced the Macintosh computer, he had the computer center stage, in a bag. He removed the Mac from the bag and had it show images while playing music. But the grand moment came when Jobs announced that he was going to let the Mac speak for itself—and it did, in a digitized voice.[2]

Wow! moments don't have to be announcements of world-class technological breakthroughs. In their book *Made to Stick: Why Some Ideas Survive and Others Die*, Chip Heath and Dan Heath say that ideas are remembered—and have lasting impact on people's opinions and behavior—when they have simplicity, are unexpected, are concrete, project credibility, stir emotions, and offer stories. The Heaths call the combination of these six factors stickiness.[3]

Organizing Your Information   LO 19-3

Unlike written documents where your audience can reread as many times as needed to understand your message, a presentation needs to be clear to the listener on the first (and only!) attempt. One way to achieve clarity with your message is to plan the organization of your information.

To develop an effective organization strategy for your presentation, plan a strong opening, structure the body, and plan a strong conclusion.

Planning a Strong Opening

The opening is the most important part of your presentation. Audience members are not going to decide halfway through your presentation that they should start listening; you need to grab their attention from the start and keep it.

The more you can do to personalize the opening for your audience, the better. Recent events are better than ones that happened long ago; local events are better than events at a distance; people they know are better than people who are only names.

Consider using one of four common modes for openers: startling statement, narration or anecdote, quotation, or question.

Startling Statement

> Twelve of our customers have canceled orders in the past month.

This presentation to a company's executive committee went on to show that the company's distribution system was inadequate and to recommend a third warehouse located in the Southwest.

Narration or Anecdote   The same presentation could also start with a relevant story.

> Last week Joe Murphy, purchasing agent for Westtrop's, our biggest client, came to see me. I knew something was wrong right away, because Joe was wearing a jacket instead of his usual cowboy shirt and smile. "Ajit," he said, "I have to tell you something. I didn't want to do it, but I had to change suppliers. We've been with you a long time, but it's just not working for us now."

Elements such as dialogue and sensory details will give stories more impact.

Quotation   A quotation could also start the presentation. This quotation came from Boyers, a major account for the company:

> "Faster and easier!" That's what Boyers said about their new supplier.

Quotations work best when they are directly connected to the audience, as opposed to quotes from famous people.

Question   Asking audience members to raise their hands or reply to questions gets them actively involved in a presentation. Tony Jeary skillfully uses this technique in sessions devoted to training the audience in presentation skills. He begins by asking the audience members to write down their estimate of the number of presentations they give per week:

> "How many of you said one or two?" he asks, raising his hand. A few hands pop up. "Three, four, six, eight?" he asks, walking up the middle of the aisle to the back of the room. Hands start popping up like targets in a shooting gallery. Jeary's Texas drawl accelerates and suddenly the place sounds like a cattle auction. "Do I hear 10? Twelve? Thirteen to the woman in the green shirt! Fifteen to the gentleman in plaid," he fires, and the room busts out laughing.[4]

Most presenters will not want to take a course in auctioneering, as Jeary did to make his questioning routine more authentic. However, Jeary's approach both engages the audience and makes the point that many jobs involve a multitude of occasions requiring formal and informal presentation skills.

Some speakers use humor to establish rapport. However, an inappropriate joke can turn the audience against the speaker. Never use humor that's directed against the audience or an inappropriate group. Humor directed at yourself or your team is safer, but even there, limit it. Don't make your audience squirm with too much self-revelation.

Humor isn't the only way to set an audience at ease. Smile at your audience before you begin; let them see that you're a real person and a nice one.

Structuring the Body

Most presentations use a direct pattern of organization, even when the goal is to persuade a reluctant audience. In a business setting, audience members are in a hurry and know that you want to persuade them. Be honest about your goal, and then prove that your goal meets the audience's needs too.

In a persuasive presentation, start with your strongest point, your best reason. If time permits, give other reasons as well and respond to possible objections. Put your weakest point in the middle so that you can end on a strong note.

Often one of five patterns of organization will work to structure the body of your presentation:

- ■ **Chronological.** Start with the past, move to the present, and end by looking ahead. This pattern works best when the history helps show a problem's complexity or magnitude, or when the chronology moves people to an obvious solution.

- ■ **Problem–causes–solution.** Explain the symptoms of the problem, identify its causes, and suggest a solution. This pattern works best when the audience will find your solution easy to accept.

- ■ **Excluding alternatives.** Explain the symptoms of the problem. Explain the obvious solutions first and show why they won't solve the problem. End by discussing a solution that will work. This pattern may be necessary when the audience will find the solution hard to accept.

- ■ **Pro–con.** Give all the reasons in favor of something, then those against it. This pattern works well when you want the audience to see the weaknesses in its position.

- ■ **1–2–3.** Discuss three aspects of a topic. This pattern works well to organize short informative briefings. "Today I'll review our sales, production, and profits for the last quarter."

Make your organization clear to your audience. Written documents can be reread; they can use headings, paragraphs, lists, and indentations to signal levels of detail. In a presentation, you have to provide explicit clues to the structure of your discourse.

Early in your talk—perhaps immediately after your opening—provide an **overview** of the main points you will make.

> First, I'd like to talk about who the homeless in Columbus are. Second, I'll talk about the services The Open Shelter provides. Finally, I'll talk about what you—either individually or as a group—can do to help.

An overview provides a mental peg that hearers can hang each point on. It also can prevent someone from missing what you are saying because he or she wonders why you aren't covering a major point that you've saved for later.

Offer a clear signpost as you come to each new point. A **signpost** is an explicit statement of the point you have reached. Choose wording that fits your style. The following statements are three different ways that a speaker could use to introduce the last of three points:

> Now we come to the third point: what you can do as a group or as individuals to help homeless people in Columbus.

> So much for what we're doing. Now let's talk about what you can do to help.

> You may be wondering, what can I do to help?

Planning a Strong Conclusion

The end of your presentation should be as strong as the opening. For your close, you could do one or more of the following:

- Restate your main point.
- Refer to your opener to create a frame for your presentation.
- End with a vivid, positive picture.
- Tell the audience exactly what to do to solve the problem you've discussed.

When Mike Powell described his work in science to an audience of nonscientists, he opened and then closed with words about what being a scientist feels like. He opened humorously, saying, "Being a scientist is like doing a jigsaw puzzle . . . in a snowstorm . . . at night . . . when you don't have all the pieces . . . and you don't have the picture you are trying to create." Powell closed by returning to the opening idea of "being a scientist," but he moved from the challenge to the inspiration with this vivid story:

> The final speaker at a medical conference [I] attended . . . walked to the lectern and said, "I am a thirty-two-year-old wife and mother of two. I have AIDS. Please work fast."[5]

When you write out your opener and close, be sure to use oral rather than written style. As you can see in the example above, oral style uses shorter sentences and shorter, simpler words than writing does. Oral style can even sound a bit choppy when it is read by eye. Oral style uses more personal pronouns, a less varied vocabulary, and more repetition.

Planning Visuals LO 19-4

Once you have planned a strategy for your presentation, you need to decide if you will use visuals to enhance the presentation. Visuals can give your

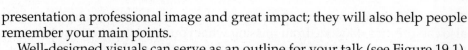

presentation a professional image and great impact; they will also help people remember your main points.

Well-designed visuals can serve as an outline for your talk (see Figure 19.1), eliminating the need for additional notes. Visuals can help your audience follow along with you, and help you keep your place as you speak. Your visuals should highlight your main points, not give every detail. Elaborate on your visuals as you talk; most people find it mind-numbing to have slide after slide read to them. **If the audience can read the entire presentation for themselves, why are you there?**

You can organize your presentation visuals and content with a software program such as PowerPoint, Keynote, Google Presentation, SlideRocket, and Prezi. Each has its own advantages and disadvantages. Two of the most common types of visual presentations in business settings, PowerPoint and Prezi, are discussed in the next sections.

In addition to choosing a presentation platform, you also need to consider how to appropriately use numbers and figures.

Designing PowerPoint Slides

When used well, PowerPoint can combine text, images, data, video, and audio into a powerful informative and persuasive message. But like any other form of communication, creating visuals requires careful thought, planning, and attention to the context, the message, and the audience.

As you design slides for PowerPoint and other presentation programs, keep the following guidelines in mind:

- Use a consistent background.

- Use a big font size: 44 or 50 point for titles, 32 point for subheads, and 28 point for examples. You should be able to read the smallest words easily when you print a handout version of your slides.

- Use bullet-point phrases rather than complete sentences. But don't go overboard with bullets because the result can become monotonous and dull.

- Use clear, concise language.

- Make only three to five points on each slide. If you have more, consider using two slides.

- Strive for creating slides that have more visuals than text. Add charts, pictures, screenshots, photos, and drawings.

- Customize your slides with your organization's logo for branding purposes.

Use **animation** to make words and images appear and move during your presentation—but only in ways that help you control information flow and build interest. Avoid using animation or sound effects just to be clever; they will distract your audience.

Use **clip art** in your presentations only if the art is really appropriate to your points. Internet sources have made such a wide variety of drawings and photos available that designers really have no excuse for failing to pick images that are both appropriate and visually appealing. See the web links in Chapter 6 for sites that offer public domain images.

Choose a consistent **template,** or background design, for your entire presentation. Make sure the template is appropriate for your subject matter and audience. For example, use a globe only if your topic is international business and palm

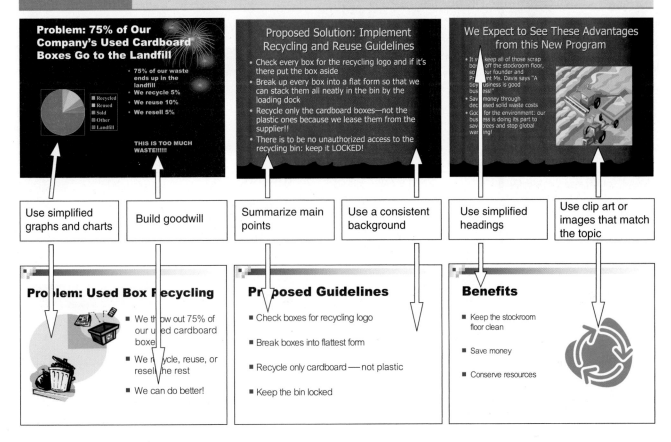

trees only if you're talking about tropical vacations. One problem with PowerPoint is that the basic templates may seem repetitive to people who see lots of presentations made with the program. For an important presentation, you may want to consider customizing the basic template. You can also find many professionally designed free templates online to help lend your presentation a more unique look. Make sure your template does not detract from your information.

Choose a light **background** if the lights will be off during your presentation. Slides will be easier to read if you use high contrast between the words and backgrounds. See Figure 19.2 for examples of effective and ineffective color combinations.

Not all presentations benefit from PowerPoint slides. Information design expert Edward Tufte wrote a famous essay blasting the slides. More recently, the U.S. Army came under harsh criticism for the now-infamous "spaghetti" PowerPoint slide, which was used in a daily briefing to show strategy complexity for the war in Afghanistan. (See Figure 19.3 and the "Visualizing in the Army" sidebar on the next page for more information.)

One final note about PowerPoint: because the program is so ubiquitous in the business world, audiences quickly become bored or annoyed and experience attention difficulties. One estimate suggests that 350 PowerPoint presentations are delivered in a given second around the globe.[6] Choose the program only after assessing the audience you'll be presenting to and understanding their expectations. You also might investigate alternative software programs to add more creativity and impact for your audience.

http://www
.authorstream
.com and http://
www.slideshare
.net

Created a great PowerPoint that you would like to share with the rest of the world? Interested in viewing some intricately crafted PowerPoint presentations? Well, Author Stream and SlideShare are just the places. You can join for free and upload your PowerPoint presentations on almost any topic. Both Author Stream and SlideShare also allow you to rate and comment on other users' PowerPoint presentations. An additional feature lets you keep track of people who embed your presentation on their website and the number of times it gets viewed.

Visualizing in the Army

The U.S. Armed Forces thrive on information. With the conflict in Afghanistan, generals, officers, and politicians received daily briefings on the complex situations in the war zone. And, like similar presentations in the business world, many of those briefings were conducted using PowerPoint.

For the U.S. Army, poor use of PowerPoint to present daily briefings has come under increasing criticism.

One particular slide, the "spaghetti slide" used in a daily briefing to show strategy complexity, received much attention. The slide was aptly named because the strategy looks like a pile of spaghetti with curling lines going in almost every direction (see Figure 19.3). The leader of the forces in Afghanistan, General McChrystal, reportedly responded, "When we understand that slide, we'll have won the war."

But it is not just this complicated slide that caused misunderstandings. Many of the PowerPoint slides used in daily briefings are bulleted lists that oversimplify the problems of war. For the U.S. Army, better visuals could ultimately result in fewer soldier deaths.

Adapted from Elisabeth Bumiller, "We Have Met the Enemy and He Is PowerPoint," *New York Times,* April 26, 2010, http://www.nytimes.com/2010/04/27/world/27powerpoint.html?_r=3; and "The PowerPoint Rant That Got a Colonel Fired," *Army Times,* December 6, 2010, http://www.armytimes.com/news/2010/09/army-colonel-fired-for-powerpoint-rant-090210w/.

Figure 19.2	Effective and Ineffective Colors for Presentation Slides

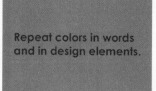

Effective

Use high contrast between words and the background.

Repeat colors in words and in design elements.

Ineffective

Limit the number of bright colors.

Dark colors disappear against a dark background.

Light colors disappear against a light background.

Figure 19.3	U.S. Army Spaghetti Slide

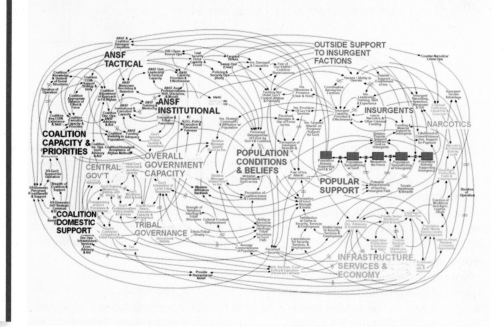

Creating a Prezi

Prezi, a free online tool, provides business communicators with another option when planning presentations. While PowerPoint's presentation philosophy is based on techniques of clicking through actual physical slides, Prezi uses modern technologies to create a different experience.

Rather than a series of consecutive slides, Prezi creates one large canvas. The presenter can place text and images anywhere on the canvas, and zoom in and out on areas or pan to different areas of the canvas. See Figure 19.4 for an example.

Figure 19.4 Screenshot of Prezi Canvas

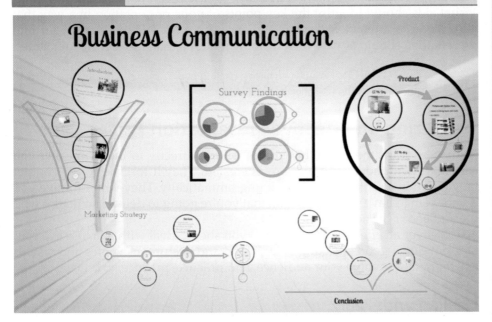

Source: Used with permission from Prezi Inc.

This approach allows presenters to display hierarchies and spatial relationships between items in ways that PowerPoint's linear progression does not allow.

Prezi's zooming and panning approach may be more engaging than PowerPoint, especially to viewers who are not familiar with it. But, just as with PowerPoint's transitions and animations, Prezi's movements can become distracting if used unwisely. Overuse of Prezi's movements can create a dizzying effect on the audience.

If you want to convert a PowerPoint into a Prezi, the program allows users to import PowerPoint slides one at a time or in a slide show. Finally, Prezi is cloud-based, meaning that you can access your presentation from any computer, tablet, or smartphone with an Internet connection.

Using Figures and Tables

Visuals for presentations need to be simpler than visuals the audience reads on paper. For example, to adapt a printed data table for a presentation, you might cut out one or more columns or rows of data, round off the data to simplify them, or replace the chart with a graph or other visual. If you have many data tables or charts in your presentation, consider including them on a handout for your audience.

Your presentation visuals should include titles, but don't need figure numbers. As you prepare your presentation, be sure to know where each visual is so that you can return to it easily if someone asks about it during the question period. Rather than reading from your slides, or describing visuals to your audience in detail, summarize the story contained on each slide and elaborate on what it means for your audience.

Using Technology Effectively

Projected visuals work only if the technology they depend on works. When you give presentations in your own workplace, plan ahead: check the equipment in advance. When you make a presentation in another location or for another organization, arrive early so that you'll have time to not only check the equipment but also track down a service worker if the equipment isn't functioning.

Avoiding Disastrous PowerPoints

Conference keynote presentations are notoriously boring, with long PowerPoint shows and droning presenters. Participants, bored, fiddle with smartphones and participate in electronic discussions. During one keynote presentation, bored audience members even designed a T-shirt and put it up for sale online. The shirt's message? "I survived the keynote disaster of 09."

How can you keep your presentations from ending up with their own T-shirts? Here are a few tips:

- *Use visuals and words together.* Your PowerPoint slides should augment and enhance your presentation, not distract from or displace it.

- *Keep your slides simple.* An audience should be able to completely understand each slide in two or three seconds.

- *Break complex ideas into multiple slides.* Don't try to get all the information on a single slide. Use several slides that add up to something more complex.

- *Use your slides as a mnemonic device.* Your slides should make your presentation emotionally appealing and memorable to your audience.

Adapted from Nancy Duarte, "Avoiding the Road to PowerPoint Hell," *Wall Street Journal,* January 27, 2011, C12.

How Not to Give a Presentation

John R. Brant has some excellent advice on how to give an awful presentation:

- Have a dull opening: If you really want to lose your audience in the first few minutes, read a prepared statement to them from a slide or a handout.

- Bury them in slides: Bore your audience with more slides than they'll be able to remember, or speed through your slides so quickly that your presentation turns into a blur.

- Use the wrong humor: Make everyone uncomfortable with self-deprecating humor.

- Show them your back: Demonstrate how disconnected you are with your audience by turning your back to them, and avoid the possibility of rapport-building eye contact by looking at the screen instead of at your audience.

Think about the uninspiring presentations you've seen from other students, or even from your instructors. What could the presenters have done to improve their work and gain your interest?

Adapted from John R. Brandt, "Missing the (Power) Point," *Industry Week*, January 2007, 48.

Keep in mind how you will use your visual aids. Most likely, they will provide support for a presentation in a face-to-face meeting or videoconference. Visual aids should identify the key points of your presentation in a way that allows you to interact with your audience. If you use PowerPoint, your oral presentation should always include more material than the text on your slides.

 WARNING: Be sure you have a backup plan in case of a technology failure that prevents the use of your visual aids.

Delivering an Effective Presentation LO 19-5

Audiences want the sense that you're talking directly to them and that you care that they understand and are interested. They'll forgive you if you get tangled up in a sentence and end it ungrammatically. They won't forgive you if you seem to have a "canned" talk that you're going to deliver no matter who the audience is or how they respond.

To deliver an effective presentation, you should deal with fear, use eye contact, develop a good speaking voice, stand and gesture, use notes and visuals appropriately, involve your audience, and practice, practice, practice.

Dealing with Fear

Feeling nervous about public speaking is normal; most people feel some fear about public speaking. But you can harness that nervous energy to help you do your best work. As various trainers have noted, you don't need to get rid of your butterflies. All you need to do is make them fly in formation.

To calm your nerves before you give an oral presentation,

- Be prepared. Analyze your audience, organize your thoughts, prepare visual aids, practice your opener and close, check out the arrangements.

- Have backup plans for various contingencies, including technical problems and likely questions.

- Use only the amount of caffeine you normally use. More or less may make you jumpy.

- Avoid alcoholic beverages.

- Relabel your nerves. Instead of saying, "I'm scared," try saying, "My adrenaline is up." Adrenaline sharpens our reflexes and helps us do our best.

Just before your presentation,

- Consciously contract and then relax your muscles, starting with your feet and calves and going up to your shoulders, arms, and hands.

- Take several deep breaths from your diaphragm; picture stress leaving your body as you exhale.

During your presentation,

- Pause and look at the audience before you begin speaking.

- Concentrate on communicating with your audience, not your feelings.

- Use body energy in strong gestures and movement.

Part of an effective presentation is its setting. Do you think this outdoor setting helps or hinders the presentation?

Using Eye Contact

Look directly at the people you're talking to. Make eye contact with individuals in different locations throughout the audience, because you want everyone to feel you are connecting with them. Do not stare at your computer screen or your notes. Researchers have found that observers were more than twice as likely to notice and comment on poor presentation features, like poor eye contact, than good features, and tended to describe speakers with poor eye contact as disinterested, unprofessional, and poorly prepared.[7]

The point in making eye contact is to establish one-on-one contact with the individual members of your audience. People want to feel that you're talking to them. Looking directly at individuals also enables you to be more conscious of feedback from the audience, so that you can modify your approach if necessary.

Developing a Good Speaking Voice

People will enjoy your presentation more if your voice is easy to listen to and your delivery is appropriate.

Voice Qualities To find out what your voice sounds like, record it using a digital voice recorder or video camera. Listen to your voice qualities, including tone, pitch, stress, and enunciation.

Tone of voice refers to the rising or falling inflection that tells you whether a group of words is a question or a statement, whether the speaker is uncertain or confident, whether a statement is sincere or sarcastic.

When tone of voice and the meaning of words conflict, people "believe" the tone of voice. If you respond to your friends' "How are you?" with the words "I'm dying, and you?" most of your friends will reply "Fine." If the tone of your voice is cheerful, they may not hear the content of the words.

Pitch measures whether a voice uses sounds that are low or high. Low-pitched voices are usually perceived as being more authoritative, sexier, and more pleasant to listen to than are high-pitched voices. Most voices go up in pitch when the speaker is angry or excited; some people raise pitch when they increase volume. Women whose normal speaking voices are high may need to practice projecting their voices to avoid becoming shrill when they speak to large groups.

Stress is the emphasis given to one or more words in a sentence. As the following example shows, emphasizing different words can change the meaning.

Developing Charisma

Charisma is an important skill for any leader to possess, but it's also a great trait to have when delivering presentations. Charisma allows you to communicate a vision or message that mesmerizes and moves your audience.

Some critics argue that people are born either with or without charisma. But new research suggests that anyone can develop "charismatic leadership tactics."

The 12 tactics are using metaphors and analogies, telling stories and anecdotes, offering contrasts, posing rhetorical questions, outlining three-part lists, expressing moral convictions, reflecting a group's sentiments, setting high goals, conveying confidence, using an animated voice, changing facial expressions, and gesturing.

The last three are most notable for delivering effective presentations. An animated voice helps spark interest about the topic and keeps the audience interested. Facial expressions reinforce a message as well as show passion. Gestures serve as signals to the audience about your message.

Of course, as with most things, developing charisma takes practice, practice, and more practice.

Adapted from John Antonakis, Marika Fenley, and Sue Liechti, "Learning Charisma: Transform Yourself Into the Person Others Want to Follow," *Harvard Business Review* 90, no. 6 (2012): 127-130.

I'll give you a raise.

> [Implication, depending on pitch and speed: "Another supervisor wouldn't" or "I have the power to determine your salary."]

I'll **give** you a raise.

> [Implication, depending on pitch and speed: "You haven't *earned* it" or "OK, all right, you win. I'm saying 'yes' to get rid of you, but I don't really agree," or "I've just this instant decided that you deserve a raise."]

I'll give **you** a raise.

> [Implication: "But nobody else in this department is getting one."]

I'll give you **a** raise.

> [Implication: "But just one."]

I'll give you a **raise.**

> [Implication: "But you won't get the promotion or anything else you want."]

I'll give **you** a **raise.**

> [Implication: "You deserve it."]

I'll give you a **raise!**

> [Implication: "I've just this minute decided to act, and I'm excited about this idea. The raise will please both of us."]

Enunciation is giving voice to all the sounds of each word. Words starting or ending with *f, t, k, v,* and *d* are especially hard to hear. "Our informed and competent image" can sound like "Our informed, incompetent image." The bigger the group is, the more carefully you need to enunciate.

Speakers who use many changes in tone, pitch, and stress as they speak usually seem more enthusiastic; often they also seem more energetic and more intelligent. Someone who speaks in a monotone may seem apathetic or unintelligent. When you are interested in your topic, your audience is more likely to be also.

Delivery   When you speak to a group, talk loudly enough so that people can hear you easily. If you're using a microphone, adjust your volume so you aren't shouting. When you speak in an unfamiliar location, try to get to the room early so you can check the size of the room and the power of the amplification equipment. If you can't do that, ask early in your talk, "Can you hear me in the back of the room?" Or another guideline: if you can hear your voice bouncing off the back wall of the room, usually everyone in the room can hear you.

Use your voice qualities as you would use your facial expressions: to create a cheerful, energetic, and enthusiastic impression for your audience. Doing so can help you build rapport with your audience and can demonstrate the importance of your material. If your ideas don't excite you, why should your audience find them exciting?

Standing and Gesturing

Stand with your feet far enough apart for good balance, with your knees flexed. Unless the presentation is very formal or you're on camera, you can walk if you want to. Some speakers like to come in front of the lectern to remove that barrier between themselves and the audience, or move about the room to connect with more people.

Build on your natural style for gestures. Gestures usually work best when they're big and confident. Avoid nervous gestures such as swaying on your feet, jingling coins in your pocket, twirling your hair, or twisting a button. These mannerisms distract the audience.

Using Notes and Visuals

If using PowerPoint, use the notes feature. If not using PowerPoint, put your notes on cards. Many speakers use 4-by-6-inch or 5-by-7-inch cards because they hold more information than 3-by-5-inch cards. Your notes need to be complete enough to help you if you go blank, so use key phrases. Avoid complete sentences on your notes because they can easily become a crutch, allowing you to read directly from them instead of delivering a presentation. Under each main point, you might list the evidence or illustration you'll use during that portion of the presentation.

Look at your notes infrequently. Most of your gaze time should be directed to members of the audience. If using paper note cards, hold them high enough so that your head doesn't bob up and down as you look from the audience to your notes and back again.

If you know your material well or have lots of visuals, you won't need notes.

If you use visuals, stand beside the screen so that you don't block it. Always stand facing the audience, not the screen. Remember that your audience can look at you or your visual, but not both at the same time. Direct attention to more complex visuals, such as figures and tables, and explain them or give your audience a few seconds to absorb them. Show the entire visual at once: don't cover up part of it. If you don't want the audience to read ahead, use animation or prepare several slides that build up.

Keep the room lights on if possible; turning them off makes it easier for people to fall asleep and harder for them to concentrate on you.

Involving Your Audience

Consider ways to involve your audience by stimulating curiosity, inviting questions, and building enthusiasm. For instance, instead of saying, "Sales grew 85% with this program," you could show a graph that shows sales declining up to the introduction of the program; invite the audience to consider what this program might do; and finally, after explaining the program, reveal the full sales graph with an animation that highlights the spike using a dramatic magenta line.

Just as when you're speaking with someone face-to-face, when you're presenting in front of a group it's important to involve your audience and look for feedback. Pay attention to body language, and ask your audience questions: the feedback that you get will help you build rapport with your audience so that you can express your message more clearly.

In some settings, such as when you're presenting to a large group, you might use other tools to gather audience feedback. For example, you could build a group discussion into your presentation: give your audience some questions to discuss in small groups, then invite them to share their answers with the room. Give questionnaires to your audience, either before your presentation or during a break. Have a member of your team tabulate audience responses, then build them into the remainder of your talk.

Technology also continues to offer new ways to involve your audience. Audience response devices (see the "Audience Feedback" sidebar on the next page) allow people to answer multiple-choice, true/false, and yes/no questions; software then quickly tabulates the responses into charts and graphs the audience can see. These response devices and other programs, such as Twitter, offer audiences a way to backchannel during your presentation.

Voice Leaves a Lasting Impression

Just how important is your voice when delivering a message?

New research suggests that your voice may actually be more important than the content of your message. In fact, research by Quantified Impressions showed that executives' voices were 12% more important than the content. The firm collected data from 1,000 study participants about their impressions of the executives' speeches.

In another study in the *Journal of Voice*, people whose voices were rough, strained, or breathy tended to be labeled negative, weak, and passive. Normal voices were perceived to be successful, smart, and social.

So what can be done about it when the way we hear our own voice is not the way an audience hears us? Most vocal issues that are not the result of medical concerns can be adjusted with voice therapy, which uses exercises to strengthen the voice muscles and improve breathing.

Try recording yourself with a digital voice recorder. How do you feel about the way you talk? How do you think others perceive your voice?

Adapted from Sue Shellenbarger, "Is That How You Really Talk?" *Wall Street Journal*, April 23, 2013, http://online.wsj.com/article/SB100014241 2788732373560457844408 510 83674898.html

Backchannel is the process of using online tools such as smartphones, tablets, or computers to hold concurrent conversations or disseminate information while a speaker presents. The audience of the backchannel can be physically in the same room as the presenter but does not have to be. For instance, Twitter audiences can follow multiple presentations at a single conference simply by following the hashtag of the event. The question for you will be how much such a system tempts your audience to send its own tweets instead of listening to you.

Practicing

Many presenters spend too much time thinking about what they will say and too little time rehearsing how they will say it. Presentation is important; if it weren't, you would just e-mail your text or PowerPoint to your audience.

Practice your speech over and over, out loud, in front of a mirror or to your family and friends. Jerry Weissman, a presentation coach for over 20 years, encourages every client to do verbalizations, the process of speaking your presentation aloud. He argues that practicing by looking at your slide show while thinking about what you'll say or mumbling through your slides are both ineffective methods. The best approach is to verbalize the actual words you will say.[8]

Other reasons to practice out loud are that doing so allows you

- To stop thinking about the words and to concentrate instead on emotions you wish to communicate to your audience.

- To work on your **transitions** that move your speech from one point to the next. Transitions are one of the places where speakers frequently stumble.

- To determine your pace and the overall amount of time that it takes you to deliver your message.

- To avoid unintentional negatives.

- To reduce the number of *uhs* you use. **Filler sounds,** which occur when speakers pause searching for the next word, aren't necessarily signs of nervousness. Searching takes longer when people have big vocabularies or talk about topics where a variety of word choices are possible. Practicing your talk makes your word choices automatic, and you'll use fewer *uhs*.[9]

As an added bonus, practicing your presentation out loud gives you reason to work on your voice qualities.

Handling Questions   LO 19-6

Prepare for questions by listing every fact or opinion you can think of that challenges your position. Put the questions into categories. Communication coach Carmine Gallo, who helps top executives with their presentations, says questions usually fall into no more than seven categories.[10] Then plan a good answer for each category. The answer should work no matter how the question is phrased. This bundling of questions helps reduce your preparation time and boost your confidence.

During your presentation, tell the audience how you'll handle questions. If you have a choice, save questions for the end. In your talk, answer the questions or objections that you expect your audience to have. Don't exaggerate your claims so that you won't have to back down in response to questions later.

During the question period, don't nod your head to indicate that you understand a question as it is asked. Audiences will interpret nods as signs that you agree with the questioner. Instead, look directly at the questioner. As you answer the question, expand your focus to take in the entire group. Don't say, "That's a good question." That response implies that the other questions have been poor ones.

If the audience may not have heard the question or if you want more time to think, repeat the question before you answer it. Link your answers to the points you made in your presentation. Keep the purpose of your presentation in mind, and select information that advances your goals.

If a question is hostile or biased, rephrase it before you answer it. Suppose that during a sales presentation, the prospective client exclaims, "How can you justify those prices?" A response that steers the presentation back to the service's benefits might be: "You're asking about our pricing. The price includes 24-hour, on-site customer support and . . ." Then explain how those features will benefit the prospective client.

Occasionally someone will ask a question that is really designed to state the speaker's own position. Respond to the question if you want to. Another option is to say, "That's a clear statement of your position. Let's move to the next question now." If someone asks about something that you already explained in your presentation, simply answer the question without embarrassing the questioner. No audience will understand and remember 100% of what you say.

If you don't know the answer to a question, say so. If your purpose is to inform, write down the question so that you can look up the answer before the next session. If it's a question to which you think there is no answer, ask if anyone in the room knows. When no one does, your "ignorance" is vindicated. If an expert is in the room, you may want to refer questions of fact to him or her. Answer questions of interpretation yourself.

At the end of the question period, take two minutes to summarize your main point once more. (This can be a restatement of your close.) Questions may or may not focus on the key point of your talk. Take advantage of having the floor to repeat your message briefly and forcefully.

Making Group Presentations

Plan carefully to involve as many members of the group as possible in speaking roles.

The easiest way to make a group presentation is to outline the presentation and then divide the topics, giving one to each group member. Another member can be responsible for the opener and the close. During the question period, each member answers questions that relate to his or her topic.

In this kind of divided presentation, be sure to

- Plan transitions.

- Coordinate individual talks to eliminate repetition and contradiction.

- Enforce time limits strictly.

- Coordinate your visuals so that the presentation seems a coherent whole.

- Practice the presentation as a group at least once; more is better.

How Do Experts Handle Tough Questions?

A CEO of a publicly traded company, when asked about negative comments from a competitor: "Our view on competition is different from many others. Our view is that you play with class. We compete by giving our customers superior service and sharing our vision for where we see this industry going. As we get more successful, we see more competitors entering the market. It's part of the process of being a leader."

Former Secretary of State Henry Kissinger, when asked how he handled media questions: "What questions do you have for my answers?"

Hillary Clinton, when asked about conflict of interest with her husband's global foundation and its donors: "I am very proud to be the president-elect's nominee for secretary of state, and I am very proud of what my husband and the Clinton Foundation and the associated efforts he's undertaken have accomplished, as well."

Quotes from Carmine Gallo, *The Presentation Secrets of Steve Jobs: How To Be Insanely Great in Front of Any Audience* (New York: McGraw Hill, 2010), 191–93.

Attack Responses

In their book, *Buy*In,*
John Kotter and Lorne
Whitehead suggest 24 common
attacks (A) on presentations.
They recommend that speakers
answer the attacks with brief
commonsense responses (R).
Here are some examples.

- A: We've never done this in
  the past, and things have
  always worked out okay. R:
  True. But surely we have all
  seen that those who fail to
  adapt eventually become
  extinct.

- A: Your proposal doesn't
  go nearly far enough. R:
  Maybe, but our idea will get
  us started moving in the
  right direction and will do
  so without further delay.

- A: You can't do A without
  first doing B, yet you can't
  do B without first doing A.
  So the plan won't work. R:
  Well, actually, you can do a
  little bit of A, which allows a
  little bit of B, which allows
  more A, which allows more
  of B, and so on.

Attacks and responses quoted
from John P. Kotter and Lorne A.
Whitehead, "Twenty-Four Attacks
and Twenty-Four Responses,"
chapter 7 in *Buy*In: Saving Your
Good Idea from Getting Shot Down*
(Boston: Harvard Business
Review Press, 2010).
Reprinted with permission.

Some group presentations are even more fully integrated: the group writes a detailed outline, chooses points and examples, and creates visuals together. Then, within each point, voices trade off. This presentation is effective because each voice speaks only a minute or two before a new voice comes in. However, it works only when all group members know the subject well and when the group plans carefully and practices extensively.

Whatever form of group presentation you use, be sure to introduce each member of the team to the audience and to pay close attention to each other. If other members of the team seem uninterested in the speaker, the audience gets the sense that that speaker isn't worth listening to.

Checklist
Points for Oral Presentations

☐ Is the presentation effective for the situation?

☐ Is the purpose clear, even if not explicitly stated? Is the purpose achieved?

☐ Does the presentation adapt to the audience's beliefs, experiences, and interests?

☐ Does the presentation engage the audience?

☐ Is the material vivid and specific?

☐ Does the material counter common objections without giving them undue weight?

☐ Is there an overview of the main points?

☐ Does the body contain signposts of the main points?

☐ Are there adequate transitions between points? Are the transitions smooth?

☐ Are the opening and closing strong and effective?

☐ Are there engaging visuals? Do they use an appropriate design or template?

☐ Are the visuals readable from a distance?

☐ Are visuals free of spelling, punctuation, and grammar mistakes?

☐ If the visuals contain data, are the data quickly assimilated?

☐ Did the speaker make good eye contact with the audience?

☐ Was the speaker positioned effectively? Did the speaker's body block the screen?

☐ Did the speaker use engaging vocal delivery?

☐ Could you hear and understand what the speaker was saying?

☐ Did the speaker use confident gestures?

☐ Did the speaker avoid nervous mannerisms?

☐ Did the speaker handle questions effectively?

☐ Did the presentation hold your attention? If it was a persuasive presentation, did it convince you?

Additional Points for Group Presentations

☐ Were team members introduced to the audience?

☐ Were all team members adequately involved in the presentation?

☐ Did the presentation transition smoothly among the team members?

☐ Did the individual presentation sections coordinate well?

☐ Did team members stay tuned in to the person speaking at the time?

Giving Feedback

Getting feedback from peers is one important part of preparing a presentation, and speakers can't get good feedback without peers who can give good feedback. Group presentations allow speakers to get feedback from peers who know the presentation well.

Too often peers comment just on simple things, like word choice or body posture, but the most important feedback is frequently about content.

- Help speakers adapt their material to the audience by asking questions about the people they expect to address.
- Note points that are unclear or need more support.
- Summarize the presenters' message as you understand it, and repeat it back. Doing so can help presenters see where they need to clarify.

No one likes to be criticized, so phrase your critiques in positive terms. Point out changes or suggestions that will make their presentation better, and if you can, back up your advice with tips from professionals.

Think about the way you prepare your own presentations. Do you practice them in front of an audience? What kind of feedback do you get? How could you encourage a practice audience to give you more helpful advice?

Summary by Learning Objectives

LO 19-1 **Identify purposes of presentations.**

- Informative presentations inform or teach the audience.
- Persuasive presentations motivate the audience to act or to believe.
- Goodwill presentations entertain and validate the audience. Most oral presentations have more than one purpose.

LO 19-2 **Plan a strategy for presentations.**

- An oral presentation needs to be simpler than a written message to the same audience.
- In a monologue presentation, the speaker plans the presentation and delivers it without deviation.
- In a guided discussion, the speaker presents the questions or issues that both speaker and

audience have agreed on in advance. Rather than functioning as an expert with all the answers, the speaker serves as a facilitator to help the audience tap its own knowledge.

- An interactive presentation is a conversation using questions to determine needs, probe objections, and gain provisional and then final commitment to the objective.

- Adapt your message to your audience's beliefs, experiences, and interests.

- Limit your talk to three main points. In a long presentation (20 minutes or more) each main point can have subpoints.

- Choose the information that is most interesting to your audience, that answers the questions your audience will have, and that is most persuasive for them.

LO 19-3   **Organize effective presentations.**

- Use the beginning and end of the presentation to interest the audience and emphasize your key point.

- Provide an overview of the main points you will make. Offer a clear signpost—an explicit statement of the point you have reached—as you come to each new point.

- Based on your audience and purposes, choose a pattern of organization for the

body: chronological, problem–cause–solution, excluding alternatives, pro–con, or 1-2-3.

LO 19-4   **Plan visuals for presentations.**

Use visuals to seem more prepared, more interesting, and more persuasive. As you prepare your visuals, determine the presentation platform you will use, use numbers and figures, and use technology effectively.

LO 19-5   **Deliver effective presentations.**

To deliver an effective presentation, you should deal with fear, use eye contact, develop a good speaking voice, stand and gesture, use notes appropriately, involve your audience, and practice.

LO 19-6   **Handle questions during presentations.**

- Tell the audience during your presentation how you'll handle questions.

- Treat questions as opportunities to give more detailed information than you had time to give in your presentation. Link your answers to the points you made in your presentation.

- Repeat the question before you answer it if the audience may not have heard it or if you want more time to think. Rephrase hostile or biased questions before you answer them.

Continuing Case

The All-Weather Case, set in an HR department in a manufacturing company, extends through all 19 chapters and is available at www.mhhe.com/locker11e. The portion for this chapter asks students to prepare a presentation for All-Weather employees.

Exercises and Cases

Go to www.mhhe.com/locker11e for additional Exercises and Cases.

19.1   Reviewing the Chapter

1. What are the different purposes for presentations? (LO 19-1)

2. What are three major components of planning effective presentations? (LO 19-2)

3. What three elements of a presentation should you focus on to organize your information? (LO 19-3)

4. What are four different kinds of presentation openers you can use? (LO 19-3)

5. Provide a suitable topic for each of the five common patterns of organization for presentations. (LO 19-3)

6. Name three guidelines for planning visuals for your presentation. (LO 19-4)

7. What are six ways to deliver an effective presentation? (LO 19-5)
8. What are some ways to deal with the common fear of public speaking? Which ways would work for you? (LO 19-5)

9. List some pointers for effectively handling questions during presentations. (LO 19-6)

19.2 Analyzing Openers and Closes

The following openers and closes came from class presentations on information interviews.

■ Does each opener make you interested in hearing the rest of the presentation?
■ Does each opener provide a transition to the overview?
■ Does the close end the presentation in a satisfying way?

    a. Opener: I interviewed Mark Perry at AT&T.
       Close: Well, that's my report.
    b. Opener: How many of you know what you want to do when you graduate?
       Close: So, if you like numbers and want to travel, think about being a CPA. Ernst & Young can take you all over the world.

    c. Opener: You don't have to know anything about computer programming to get a job as a technical writer at CompuServe.
       Close: After talking to Raj, I decided technical writing isn't for me. But it is a good career if you work well under pressure and like learning new things all the time.
    d. Opener: My report is about what it's like to work in an advertising agency.
       Middle: They keep really tight security; I had to wear a badge and be escorted to Susan's desk.
       Close: Susan gave me samples of the agency's ads and even a sample of a new soft drink she's developing a campaign for. But she didn't let me keep the badge.

19.3 Developing Points of Interest

One of the keys to preparing an engaging presentation is finding interesting points to share with your audience, either in the form of personal anecdotes to create rapport and build goodwill, or in the form of interesting facts and figures to establish your ethos as a presenter. For each of the following topics, prepare one personal anecdote based on your own experience, and research one interesting fact to share with your audience.

1. Why people need to plan.
2. Dealing with change.
3. The importance of lifelong learning.
4. The importance of effective communication.
5. The value of good customer service.
6. The value of listening.

As your instructor directs,

a. Share your points of interest with a small group of students, and critique each other's work.
b. Turn in your stories in an e-mail to your instructor.
c. Make a short (one- to two-minute) oral presentation featuring your story and fact(s) for one of the assignment topics.

19.4 Evaluating PowerPoint Slides

Evaluate the following drafts of PowerPoint slides.

■ Are the slides' background appropriate for the topic?
■ Do the slides use words or phrases rather than complete sentences?

■ Is the font big enough to read from a distance?
■ Is the art relevant and appropriate?
■ Is each slide free of errors?

a(1)

b(1)

c(1)

a(2)

b(2)

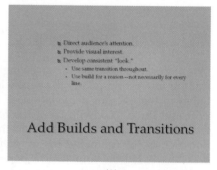

c(2)

a(3)

b(3)

c(3)

a(4)

b(4)

c(4)

19.5   Evaluating Speakers

Attend a lecture or public presentation on your campus. While the speaker is presenting, don't focus on the content of the message. Instead, focus only on his/her speaking ability and take notes. Pay attention to the speaker's abilities to deal with fear, use eye contact with the audience, project a clear speaking voice. In addition, notice how the speaker stands and gestures, uses notes, involves the audience, and handles questions.

As your instructor directs,

a.   Deliver your findings to the rest of the class in a two- to four-minute presentation.

b.   Write an e-mail to your instructor that discusses the presenter's speaking abilities, and how, if at all, they can be improved.

19.6   Evaluating Steve Jobs

On YouTube, watch clips of three different Steve Jobs presentations. What similarities do you see among them? What are some of his techniques you could use in a job you hope to have? Which ones do you think you would not use? Why not?

As your instructor directs,

a.   Discuss your findings in small groups.

b.   Write your findings in an e-mail to your instructor.

c.   Write your findings in an e-mail and post it on the class server.

19.7   Evaluating the Way a Speaker Handles Questions

Listen to a speaker talking about a controversial subject. (Go to a talk on campus or in town, or watch a speaker on a TV show like *Face the Nation* or *60 Minutes*.) Observe the way he or she handles questions.

■   About how many questions does the speaker answer?

■   What is the format for asking and answering questions?

■   Are the answers clear? Responsive to the question? Something that could be quoted without embarrassing the speaker and the organization he or she represents?

■   How does the speaker handle hostile questions? Does the speaker avoid getting angry? Does the speaker retain control of the meeting? How?

■   If some questions were not answered well, what (if anything) could the speaker have done to leave a better impression?

■   Did the answers leave the audience with a more or less positive impression of the speaker? Why?

As your instructor directs,

a.   Share your evaluation with a small group of students.

b.   Present your evaluation formally to the class.

c.   Summarize your evaluation in an e-mail to your instructor.

19.8   Presenting the News

Research a hot business communication topic from the news (ethics, the economy, job layoffs, communication technology, etc.). Find at least three sources for your topic. Then, make a two- to three-minute presentation where you share your findings with the class. Your presentation should invoke some effective communication strategies you learned in this course by discussing how the situation could have been handled more effectively.

As your instructor directs,

a.   Deliver your presentation to the class.

b.   Turn in a listing of your sources in APA or MLA format.

c.   Write an e-mail to your instructor that discusses the situation and explains how business communication principles would have helped improve the situation.

19.9   Making a Short Oral Presentation

Make a three- to five-minute presentation with Power-Point slides or a Prezi on one of the following topics:

1. Explain how what you've learned in classes, in campus activities, or at work will be useful to the employer who hires you after graduation.
2. Describe your boss's management style.
3. Describe how your co-workers employ teamwork on the job.
4. Explain a "best practice" in your organization.
5. Explain what a new hire in your organization needs to know to be successful.
6. Tell your boss about a problem in your unit.
7. Make a presentation to raise funds for a nonprofit organization.
8. Profile someone who is successful in the field you hope to enter and explain what makes him or her successful.

9. Describe a specific situation in an organization in which communication was handled well or badly.
10. Explain one of the challenges (e.g., technology, ethics, international competition) that the field you plan to enter is facing.
11. Profile a company that you would like to work for and explain why you think it would make a good employer.
12. Share the results of an information interview.
13. Share some advice for students currently on the job market.
14. Describe the way technology impacts the field you hope to enter.

19.10   Making a Longer Oral Presentation

Make a 5- to 12-minute presentation on one of the following. Use visuals to make your talk effective.

1. Persuade your supervisor to make a change that will benefit the organization.
2. Persuade your organization to make a change that will improve the organization's image in the community.
3. Describe the communication process of a person you've interviewed who is working in the field you plan to enter.
4. Evaluate a business document.
5. Evaluate the design of a corporate web page.

6. Present a web page you have designed.
7. Analyze rejection letters that students on your campus have received.
8. Persuade an organization on your campus to make a change.
9. Analyze international messages that your workplace has created or received.
10. Present the results of a survey you conduct.
11. Research an organization for which you would like to work.
12. Persuade classmates to donate time or money to a charitable organization.

19.11   Watching Yourself

One of the best ways to improve your presentation skills is to watch yourself present. After you have prepared a presentation on one of the topics listed in exercise 19.8 or 19.9, use a video camera to record your presentation. You should then review your presentation, noting what you did well and what you could improve.

As your instructor directs,

a. Write a two-page e-mail that discusses your strengths and weaknesses as a presenter.

Address how you could improve your weaknesses.

b. Prepare a two-minute oral summation for your peers about your strengths and weaknesses.

c. Record the presentation a second time to see if you have improved some of your weaknesses.

19.12   Making a Group Oral Presentation

Make an 8- to 12-minute presentation on one of the following. Use visuals to make your talk effective.

1. Explain the role of communication in one or more organizations.
2. Create and present a fund-raising strategy for a non-profit organization.

3. Report on the nonverbal customs of another country.
4. Report on the written communication styles of another country.
5. Report on the business outlook of another country.

6. Analyze print business materials of an organization and present your findings to the class.
7. Interview the employees of an organization about their teamwork strategies and present the information to the class.
8. Interview office members about their routine communication practices and present your findings to the class.

19.13   Evaluating Oral Presentations

Evaluate an oral presentation given by a classmate or a speaker on your campus. Use the following categories:

Strategy

1. Choosing an effective kind of presentation for the situation.
2. Adapting ideas to audience's beliefs, experiences, and interests.

Content

3. Providing a clear, unifying purpose.
4. Using specific, vivid supporting material and language.
5. Providing rebuttals to counterclaims or objections.

Organization

6. Using a strong opening and close.
7. Providing an overview of main points.
8. Signposting main points in body of talk.
9. Providing adequate transitions between points and speakers.

Visuals

10. Using visual aids or other devices to involve the audience.
11. Using an appropriate design or template.
12. Using standard edited English.
13. Being creative.

Delivery

14. Making direct eye contact with audience.
15. Using voice effectively.
16. Using gestures effectively.
17. Handling questions effectively.
18. Positioning (not blocking screen).

As your instructor directs,

a. Fill out a form indicating your evaluation in each of the areas.
b. Share your evaluation orally with the speaker.
c. Write an e-mail to the speaker evaluating the presentation. Forward a copy of the e-mail to your instructor.

19.14   Evaluating Team Presentations

Evaluate team presentations using the chapter checklist.

As your instructor directs,

a. Fill out a form indicating your evaluation in each of the areas.
b. Share your evaluation orally with the team.
c. Write an e-mail to the team evaluating the presentation. Send a copy of your e-mail to your instructor.

Notes

1. Jon Birger et al., "The Best Advice I Ever Got," *Fortune,* May 12, 2008, 70.
2. Carmine Gallo, *The Presentation Secrets of Steve Jobs: How to Be Insanely Great in Front of Any Audience* (New York: McGraw-Hill, 2010), 151–53.
3. Chip Heath and Dan Heath, *Made to Stick: Why Some Ideas Survive and Others Die* (New York: Random House, 2007), 16–18.
4. Julie Hill, "The Attention Deficit," *Presentations* 17, no. 10 (2003): 26.
5. Patricia Fripp, "Want Your Audiences to Remember What You Say? Learn the Importance of Clear Structure," Fripp and Associates, accessed June 25, 2011, http://www.fripp .com/art.clearstructure.html.
6. Bob Parks, "Death to PowerPoint!," *Bloomberg Businessweek,* August 30, 2012, http://www.businessweek.com/ articles/2012-08-30/death-to-powerpoint.
7. Ann Burnett and Diane M. Badzinski, "Judge Nonverbal Communication on Trial: Do Mock Trial Jurors Notice?" *Journal of Communication* 55, no. 2 (2005): 209–24.
8. Jerry Weissman, *Presentations in Action: 80 Memorable Presentation Lessons from the Masters* (Upper Saddle River, NJ: FT Press, 2011).
9. Michael Waldholz, "Lab Notes," *Wall Street Journal,* March 19, 1991, B1; and Dave Zielinski, "Perfect Practice," *Presentations* 17, no. 5 (2003): 30–36.
10. Gallo, *The Presentation Secrets of Steve Jobs,* 191.

APPENDIX

A

Formatting Letters and E-mail Messages

Appendix Outline

Formats for Letters

Formats for Envelopes

Formats for E-mail Messages

State and Province Abbreviations

After studying this appendix, you will know

LO A-1 Formats for letters.

LO A-2 Formats for envelopes.

LO A-3 Formats for e-mail messages.

Letters normally go to people outside your organization; **memos** go to other people in your organization. E-mails go to both audiences. More and more, paper memos are being replaced by e-mails, which are electronic memos.

Letters, memos, and e-mails do not necessarily differ in length, formality, writing style, or pattern of organization. However, letters, memos, and e-mails do differ in format. **Format** means the parts of a document and the way they are arranged on the page.

Formats for Letters   **LO A-1**

If your organization has a standard format for letters, use it.

Many organizations and writers choose one of two letter formats: **block format** (see Figure A.1) or the **simplified format** (see Figure A.2). Your organization may make minor changes from the diagrams in margins or spacing.

Use the same level of formality in the **salutation,** or greeting, as you would in talking to someone on the phone: *Dear Glenn* if you're on a first-name basis, *Dear Mr. Helms* if you don't know the reader well enough to use the first name.

Some writers feel that the simplified format is better since the reader is not *Dear.* Omitting the salutation is particularly good when you do not know the reader's name or do not know which courtesy title to use. (For a full discussion on nonsexist salutations and salutations when you don't know the reader's name, see Chapter 3.) However, readers like to see their names. Since the simplified format omits the reader's name in the salutation, writers who use this format but who also want to be friendly often try to use the reader's name early in the body of the letter.

The simplified letter format is good in business-to-business mail, or in letters where you are writing to anyone who holds a job (admissions officer, customer service representative) rather than to a specific person. It is too cold and distancing for cultures that place a premium on relationships.

Sincerely and *Yours truly* are standard **complimentary closes.** When you are writing to people in special groups or to someone who is a friend as well as a business acquaintance, you may want to use a less formal close. Depending on the circumstances, the following informal closes might be acceptable: *Cordially, Thank you,* or even *Cheers.*

In **mixed punctuation,** a colon follows the salutation and a comma follows the close.

A **subject line** tells what the message is about. Subject lines are required in memos and e-mails; they are optional in letters. Good subject lines are specific, concise, and appropriate for your purposes and the response you expect from your reader:

- When you have good news, put it in the subject line.

- When your information is neutral, summarize it concisely in the subject line.

- When your information is negative, use a negative subject line if the reader may not read the message or needs the information to act. Otherwise, use a neutral subject line.

- When you have a request that will be easy for the reader to grant, put either the subject of the request or a direct question in the subject line.

- When you must persuade a reluctant reader, use a common ground, a benefit, or a neutral subject line.

For examples of subject lines in each of these situations, see Chapters 9, 10, and 11.

A **reference line** refers the reader to the number used on the previous correspondence this letter replies to, or the order or invoice number this letter is about. Very large organizations use numbers on every piece of correspondence they send so that it is possible to find quickly the earlier document to which an incoming letter refers.

Both formats can use headings, lists, and indented sections for emphasis.

Each format has advantages. Both block and simplified can be typed quickly since everything is lined up at the left margin. Block format is the format most frequently used for business letters; readers expect it.

The examples of the two formats in Figures A.1 and A.2 show one-page letters on company letterhead. **Letterhead** is preprinted stationery with the organization's name, logo, address, phone number, and frequently e-mail.

When a letter runs two or more pages, use letterhead only for the first page. For the remaining pages, use plain paper that matches the letterhead in weight, texture, and color. Also include a heading on the second page to identify it (see Figure A.3).

> Reader's Name
> Date
> Page Number

Set side margins of 1 inch to 1½ inches on the left and ¾ inch to 1 inch on the right. If you are right justifying, use the 1 inch margin. If your letterhead extends all the way across the top of the page, set your margins even with the ends of the letterhead for the most visually pleasing page. The top margin should be three to six lines under the letterhead, or 1 to 2 inches down from the top of the page if you aren't using letterhead. If your letter is very short, you may want to use bigger side and top margins so that the letter is centered on the page.

The **inside address** gives the reader's name, title (if appropriate), and address. Always double check to see the name is spelled correctly. To eliminate typing the reader's name and address on an envelope, some organizations use envelopes with cutouts or windows so that the inside address on the letter shows and can be used for delivery. If your organization does this, adjust your margins, if necessary, so that the whole inside address is visible.

Many letters are accompanied by other documents. Whatever these documents may be—a multipage report or a two-line note—they are called **enclosures,** since they are enclosed in the envelope. The writer should refer to the enclosures in the body of the letter: "As you can see from my résumé, . . ." The enclosure notation (Encl.:) at the bottom of the letter lists the enclosures. (See Figures A.1 to A.3.)

Figure A.1	A Job Reference Letter in Block Format

151 Bayview Road • San Francisco, CA 81153 • (650) 405-7849 • www.baycity.com

2–6 spaces

September 15, 2014

2–6 spaces

1"–1½"

Ms. Mary E. Arcas
Personnel Director
Cyclops Communication Technologies
1050 South Sierra Bonita Avenue
Los Angeles, CA 90019   *Zip code on same line*

Dear Ms. Arcas: *Colon in mixed punctuation*

Do not indent paragraphs

I am responding to your request for an evaluation of Colleen Kangas. Colleen was hired as a clerk-typist by Bay City Information Systems on April 4, 2012, and was promoted to Administrative Assistant on August 1, 2013. At her review in June, I recommended that she be promoted again. She is an intelligent young woman with good work habits and a good knowledge of computer software.

1", because right margin is justified

Single-space paragraphs

As an Adminstrative Assistant, Colleen not only handles routine duties such as processing time sheets, ordering supplies, and entering data, but also screens calls for two marketing specialists, answers basic questions about Bay City Information Systems, compiles the statistics I need for my monthly reports, and investigates special assignments for me. In the past eight months, she has investigated freight charges, inventoried department hardware, and transferred files to archives. I need only to give her general directions: she has a knack for tracking down information quickly and summarizing it accurately.

Double-space between paragraphs (one blank line)

Although the department's workload has increased during the year, Colleen manages her time so that everything gets done on schedule. She is consistently poised and friendly under pressure. Her willingness to work overtime on occasion is particularly remarkable considering that she has been going to college part-time ever since she joined our firm.

At Bay City Information Systems, Colleen uses Microsoft Word, Excel, and Access software. She tells me that she also uses PowerPoint in her college classes.

If Colleen were staying in San Francisco, we would want to keep her. We would move her into staff work once she completed her degree. I recommend her highly.

1–2 spaces

Sincerely ,   *Comma in mixed punctuation*

3–4 spaces

Jeanne Cederlind

Jeanne Cederlind
Vice President, Marketing
jeanne_c@baycity.com

Line up signature block with date

1–4 spaces

Encl.: Evaluation Form for Colleen Kangas

Leave at least 6 spaces at bottom of page—more if letter is short

Figure A.2   Simplified Format on Letterhead

1500 Main Street   Iowa City, IA 52232   (319) 555-3113

↕ 2–6 spaces

Line up everything at left margin

August 24, 2014

↕ 2–6 spaces

←→ 1"–1½"

Melinda Hamilton
Medical Services Division
Health Management Services, Inc.
4333 Edgewood Road, NE
Cedar Rapids, IA 52401

Triple-space (two blank spaces)   *Subject line in full capital letters*

REQUEST FOR INFORMATION ABOUT COMPUTER SYSTEMS

←— No salutation

We're interested in upgrading our computer system and would like to talk to one of your marketing representatives to see what would best meet our needs. We will use the following criteria to choose a system:

1. Ability to use our current software and data files.

2. Price, prorated on a three-year expected life.

Double-space (one blank space) between items in list if any items are more than one line long

3. Ability to provide auxiliary services, e.g., controlling inventory of drugs and supplies, monitoring patients' vital signs, and processing insurance forms more quickly.

4. Freedom from downtime.

Triple-space (two blank spaces) between list, next paragraph

Do not indent paragraphs

McFarlane Memorial Hospital has 50 beds for acute care and 75 beds for long-term care. In the next five years, we expect the number of beds to remain the same while outpatient care and emergency room care increase.

←→ ¾"–1" when right margin is not justified

Could we meet the first or the third week in September? We are eager to have the new system installed by Christmas if possible.

Please call me to schedule an appointment.

Headings are optional in letters

No close.

HUGH PORTERFIELD   *Writer's name in full capital letters*
Controller

↕ 1–4 spaces

Encl.:   Specifications of Current System
          Databases Currently in Use

cc: Rene Seaburg

↕ Leave 6 spaces at bottom of page—more if letter is short

Figure A.3   A Two-Page Letter, Block Format

State
University

4302 Gateway Boulevard
Midland, TX 78013

August 11, 2014

↕ *2–6 spaces*

1"–1½" →

Ms. Stephanie Voght
Stephen F. Austin High School
1200 Southwest Blvd.
San Antonio, TX 78214

Dear Ms. Voght: *Colon in mixed punctuation.*

Enclosed are 100 brochures about State University to distribute to your students. The
brochures describe the academic programs and financial aid available. When you need
additional brochures, just let me know.

1" ↔

Further information about State University

You may also want your students to learn more about life at State University. You

*Plain paper
for page 2.*

↕ *½–1"*

Stephanie Voght ← *Reader's
name*
August 11, 2014
Page 2

campus life, including football and basketball games, fraternities and sororities, clubs and
organizations, and opportunities for volunteer work. It stresses the diversity of the student
body and the very different lifestyles that are available at State.

*Triple-space before
each new heading (two blank spaces).*

Scheduling a State Squad Speaker   *Bold or underline headings.*

*Same
margins
as p 1.*

To schedule one of the these dynamic speakers for your students, just fill out the
enclosed card with your first, second, and third choices for dates, and return it in the
stamped, self-addressed envelope. Dates are reserved in the order that requests arrive.
Send in your request early to increase the chances of getting the date you want.

Any one of our State Squad speakers will give your high school students a colorful
preview of the college experience. They are also great at answering questions.

1–2 spaces ↕

Sincerely,   *Comma in mixed punctuation.*

*3–4
spaces* ↕ *Michael J. Mahler*

Michael L. Mahler
Director of Admissions

↕ *1–4 spaces*

*Headings are
optional in
letters.*

Encl.: Brochures, Reservation Form

cc: R. J. Holland, School Superintendent
     Jose Lavilla, President, PTS Association

Sometimes you write to one person but send copies of your letter to other people. If you want the reader to know that other people are getting copies, list their names on the last page. The abbreviation *cc* originally meant *carbon copy* but now means *computer copy*. Other acceptable abbreviations include *pc* for *photocopy* or simply *c* for *copy*. You can also send copies to other people without telling the reader. Such copies, called **blind copies (*bcc*)**, are not mentioned on the original but are listed on the file copy.

Formats for Envelopes LO A-2

Business envelopes need to put the reader's name and address in the area that is picked up by the post office's optical character readers (OCRs). Use side margins of at least 1 inch. Your bottom margin must be at least ⅝ inch but no bigger than 2¼ inches.

Most businesses use envelopes that already have the return address printed in the upper left-hand corner. When you don't have printed envelopes, type your name (optional), your street address, and your city, state, and zip code in the upper left-hand corner. Since the OCR doesn't need this information to route your letter, exact margins don't matter. Use whatever is convenient and looks good to you.

Formats for E-mail Messages LO A-3

The "To" line on an e-mail provides the name and e-mail address of the receiver. Double check that the address is correct because even a one-character mistake will keep the receiver from getting your message. "Cc" denotes computer copies; the recipient will see that these people are getting the message. "Bcc" denotes blind computer copies; the recipient does not see the names of these people. Blind copies can cause hard feelings when they become known, so be sparing in their use. The computer program supplies the date and time automatically.

Most e-mail programs also allow you to attach documents from other programs, thus e-mails have attachments rather than enclosures.

Some aspects of e-mail format are still evolving. Even though the e-mail screen has a "To" line, many writers still use an informal salutation, as in Figure A.4. The writer in Figure A.4 also ends the message with a signature block. Signature blocks are particularly useful for e-mail recipients outside the organization who may not know your title or contact information. You can store a signature block in the e-mail program and set the program to insert the signature block automatically.

Sometimes writers omit both the salutation and their names, especially when writing to colleagues with whom they work closely.

Subject lines are important because most businesspeople receive large numbers of e-mails. Messages with vague subject lines may go unread. The advice for subject lines of letters (page 650) also applies to e-mails. Chapters 9 to 11 give more information on subject lines.

When you hit "reply," the e-mail program automatically uses "Re:" (Latin for *about*) and the previous subject line. The original message is set off, usually with one or more vertical lines in the left margin or with carats (see Figure A.5). You may want to change the subject line to make it more appropriate for your message.

Figure A.4   A Basic E-mail Message

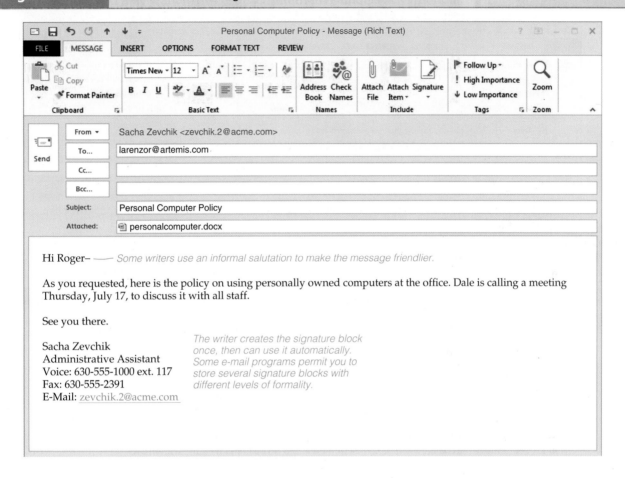

Hi Roger–——— *Some writers use an informal salutation to make the message friendlier.*

As you requested, here is the policy on using personally owned computers at the office. Dale is calling a meeting Thursday, July 17, to discuss it with all staff.

See you there.

Sacha Zevchik
Administrative Assistant
Voice: 630-555-1000 ext. 117
Fax: 630-555-2391
E-Mail: zevchik.2@acme.com

The writer creates the signature block once, then can use it automatically. Some e-mail programs permit you to store several signature blocks with different levels of formality.

Figure A.5   An E-mail Reply with Copies (response to a complaint)

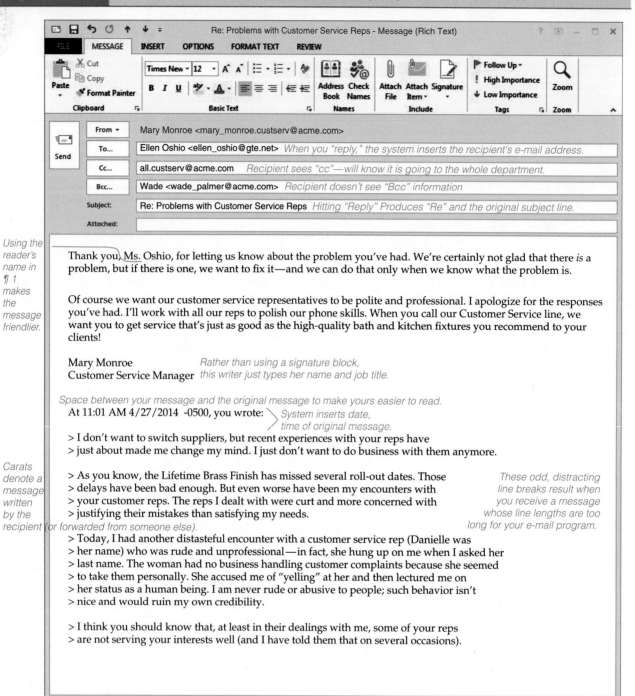

Using the reader's name in ¶ 1 makes the message friendlier.

Thank you, Ms. Oshio, for letting us know about the problem you've had. We're certainly not glad that there *is* a problem, but if there is one, we want to fix it—and we can do that only when we know what the problem is.

Of course we want our customer service representatives to be polite and professional. I apologize for the responses you've had. I'll work with all our reps to polish our phone skills. When you call our Customer Service line, we want you to get service that's just as good as the high-quality bath and kitchen fixtures you recommend to your clients!

Mary Monroe
Customer Service Manager   *Rather than using a signature block, this writer just types her name and job title.*

Space between your message and the original message to make yours easier to read.

At 11:01 AM 4/27/2014 -0500, you wrote: *System inserts date, time of original message.*

> I don't want to switch suppliers, but recent experiences with your reps have
> just about made me change my mind. I just don't want to do business with them anymore.

Carats denote a message written by the recipient (or forwarded from someone else).

> As you know, the Lifetime Brass Finish has missed several roll-out dates. Those
> delays have been bad enough. But even worse have been my encounters with
> your customer reps. The reps I dealt with were curt and more concerned with
> justifying their mistakes than satisfying my needs.

These odd, distracting line breaks result when you receive a message whose line lengths are too long for your e-mail program.

> Today, I had another distasteful encounter with a customer service rep (Danielle was
> her name) who was rude and unprofessional—in fact, she hung up on me when I asked her
> last name. The woman had no business handling customer complaints because she seemed
> to take them personally. She accused me of "yelling" at her and then lectured me on
> her status as a human being. I am never rude or abusive to people; such behavior isn't
> nice and would ruin my own credibility.

> I think you should know that, at least in their dealings with me, some of your reps
> are not serving your interests well (and I have told them that on several occasions).

State and Province Abbreviations

States with names of more than five letters are frequently abbreviated. The post office abbreviations use two capital letters with no punctuation, as listed in Figure A.6.

Figure A.6	Post Office Abbreviations for States, Territories, and Provinces		
State name	**Post office abbreviation**	**State name**	**Post office abbreviation**
Alabama	AL	Montana	MT
Alaska	AK	Nebraska	NE
Arizona	AZ	Nevada	NV
Arkansas	AR	New Hampshire	NH
California	CA	New Jersey	NJ
Colorado	CO	New Mexico	NM
Connecticut	CT	New York	NY
Delaware	DE	North Carolina	NC
District of Columbia	DC	North Dakota	ND
Florida	FL	Ohio	OH
Georgia	GA	Oklahoma	OK
Hawaii	HI	Oregon	OR
Idaho	ID	Pennsylvania	PA
Illinois	IL	Rhode Island	RI
Indiana	IN	South Carolina	SC
Iowa	IA	South Dakota	SD
Kansas	KS	Tennessee	TN
Kentucky	KY	Texas	TX
Louisiana	LA	Utah	UT
Maine	ME	Vermont	VT
Maryland	MD	Virginia	VA
Massachusetts	MA	Washington	WA
Michigan	MI	West Virginia	WV
Minnesota	MN	Wisconsin	WI
Mississippi	MS	Wyoming	WY
Missouri	MO		

Territory name	**Post office abbreviation**	**Province name**	**Post office abbreviation**
Guam	GU	Alberta	AB
Puerto Rico	PR	British Columbia	BC
Virgin Islands	VI	Manitoba	MB
		New Brunswick	NB
		Newfoundland and Labrador	NL
		Northwest Territories	NT
		Nova Scotia	NS
		Nunavut	NU
		Ontario	ON
		Prince Edward Island	PE
		Quebec	QC
		Saskatchewan	SK
		Yukon Territory	YT

APPENDIX

B

Writing Correctly

Appendix Outline

After studying this appendix, you will know

LO B-1 Common grammar usage.

LO B-2 Correct ways to use punctuation.

LO B-3 The right way to use words that are often confused.

Too much concern for correctness at the wrong stage of the writing process can backfire: writers who worry about grammar and punctuation when they're writing a first or second draft are more likely to get writer's block. Wait till you have your ideas on paper to check your draft for correct grammar, punctuation, typing of numbers and dates, and word use. Use the proofreading symbols at the end of this appendix to indicate changes needed in a printed copy.

Most writers make a small number of grammatical errors repeatedly. Most readers care deeply about only a few grammatical points. Keep track of the feedback you get (from your instructors now, from your supervisor later) and put your energy into correcting the errors that bother the people who read what you write. A command of standard grammar will help you build the credible, professional image you want to create with everything you write.

Using Grammar   **LO B-1**

With the possible exception of spelling, grammar is the aspect of writing that writers seem to find most troublesome. Faulty grammar is often what executives are objecting to when they complain that college graduates or MBAs "can't write."

Agreement

Subjects and verbs agree when they are both singular or both plural.

Incorrect:	The accountants who conducted the audit was recommended highly.
Correct:	The accountants who conducted the audit were recommended highly.

Subject–verb agreement errors often occur when other words come between the subject and the verb. Edit your draft by finding the subject and the verb of each sentence.

American usage treats company names and the words *company* and *government* as singular nouns. British usage treats them as plural:

Correct (U.S.):	State Farm Insurance trains its agents well.
Correct (Great Britain):	Lloyds of London train their agents well.

Use a plural verb when two or more singular subjects are joined by *and*.

Correct: Larry McGreevy and I are planning to visit the client.

Use a singular verb when two or more singular subjects are joined by *or, nor,* or *but.*

Correct: Either the shipping clerk or the superintendent has to sign the order.

Banished Words

Correct grammar and spelling are basic ways to signal careful, intelligent writing. Another fundamental is to choose words and phrases that say what you mean. Out of habit or carelessness, however, writers may sprinkle their work with meaningless words.

To highlight the problem, Lake Superior State University each January announces its "List of Words Banished from the Queen's English for Mis-Use, Over-Use and General Useless-ness." A sample from the lists:

- *Kick the can down the road*—"What's wrong with the word 'postpone'"?

- *Double down*—This phrase was adopted from blackjack, but now it means to repeat, reiterate, or rehash again and again repetitively.

- *YOLO*—Short for "you only live once," but it usually means "I'm about to do something stupid."

- *Spoiler alert*—What used to be an alert is now just "an obnoxious way to show one has trivial information."

- *Trending*—Social media trends are all the rage on the news. This overused word often signifies lazy reporting.

Adapted from "Lake Superior State University 2013 List of Banished Words," Lake Superior State University, accessed July 8, 2013, http://www.lssu.edu/banished/current.php.

When the sentence begins with *Here* or *There,* make the verb agree with the subject that follows the verb.

Correct: Here is the booklet you asked for.

Correct: There are the blueprints I wanted.

Note that some words that end in *s* are considered to be singular and require singular verbs.

Correct: A series of meetings is planned.

When a situation doesn't seem to fit the rules, or when following a rule produces an awkward sentence, revise the sentence to avoid the problem.

Problematic: The plant manager in addition to the sales representative (was, were?) pleased with the new system.

Better: The plant manager and the sales representative were pleased with the new system.

Problematic: None of us (is, are?) perfect.

Better: All of us have faults.

Errors in **noun–pronoun agreement** occur if a pronoun is of a different number or person than the word it refers to.

Incorrect: All drivers of leased automobiles are billed $300 if damages to his automobile are caused by a collision.

Correct: All drivers of leased automobiles are billed $300 if damages to their automobiles are caused by collisions.

Incorrect: A manager has only yourself to blame if things go wrong.

Correct: As a manager, you have only yourself to blame if things go wrong.

The following words require a singular verb and pronoun:

everybody	neither
each	nobody
either	a person
everyone	

Correct: Everyone should bring his or her copy of the manual to the next session on changes in the law.

If the pronoun pairs necessary to avoid sexism seem cumbersome, avoid the terms in this list. Instead, use words that take plural pronouns or use second-person *you.*

Each pronoun must refer to a specific word. If a pronoun does not refer to a specific term, add a word to correct the error.

Incorrect: We will open three new stores in the suburbs. This will bring us closer to our customers.

Correct: We will open three new stores in the suburbs. This strategy will bring us closer to our customers.

Hint: Make sure *this* and *it* refer to a specific noun in the previous sentence. If either refers to an idea, add a noun ("this strategy") to make the sentence grammatically correct.

Use *who* and *whom* to refer to people and *which* to refer to objects. *That* can refer to anything: people, animals, organizations, and objects.

Correct: The new executive director, who moved here from Boston, is already making friends.

Correct: The information, which she wants now, will be available tomorrow.

Correct: This confirms the price that I quoted you this morning.

Case

Case refers to the grammatical role a noun or pronoun plays in a sentence. Figure B.1 identifies the case of each personal pronoun.

Use **nominative case** pronouns for the subject of a clause.

Correct: Shannon Weaver and I talked to the customer, who was interested in learning more about integrated software.

Use **possessive case** pronouns to show who or what something belongs to.

Correct: Microsoft Office will exactly meet her needs.

Use **objective case** pronouns as objects of verbs or prepositions.

Correct: When you send in the quote, thank her for the courtesy she showed Shannon and me.

Hint: Use *whom* when *him* would fit grammatically in the same place in your sentence.

To (who/whom) do you intend to give this report?

You intend to give this report to him.

Whom is correct.

Have we decided (who, whom?) will take notes?

Have we decided he will take notes?

Who is correct.

Use **reflexive** pronouns to refer to or emphasize a noun or pronoun that has already appeared in the sentence.

Correct: I myself think the call was a very productive one.

Do not use reflexive pronouns as subjects of clauses or as objects of verbs or propositions.

Incorrect: Elaine and myself will follow up on this order.

Correct: Elaine and I will follow up on this order.

Incorrect: He gave the order to Dan and myself.

Correct: He gave the order to Dan and me.

Correcting Celebrity Tweets

Social media is quick communication, which means it is often rife with errors. Celebrities who tweet regularly are some of the worst abusers of the English language. But now, thanks to a school project at an elementary school in Brazil, the celebrities' grammar crimes are being corrected.

In a school project organized by Andrea Baena at the Red Balloon School in Brazil, children aged 8 to 13 find celebrity tweets with errors (which is not difficult) and share them with the class. They then respond to the celebrity tweets on a school Twitter account with corrections and examples of better usage.

While none of the celebrities have responded to the advice yet, the project has proven popular with the children in the school. After all, what better way to learn English as a second language than to correct the English of Americans?

Adapted from Shereen Dindar, "Brazilian School Kids Call Out Celebrity Grammar Errors on Twitter," *ShineOn,* June 28, 2013, http://ca.shine.yahoo.com/blogs/shine-on/brazilian-school-kids-call-celebrity-grammar-errors-twitter-185108137.html.

Figure B.1	The Case of the Personal Pronoun			
	Nominative (subject of clause)	**Possessive**	**Objective**	**Reflexive/ Intensive**
Singular				
1st person	I	my, mine	me	myself
2nd person	you	your, yours	you	yourself
3rd person	he/she/it	his/her(s)/its	him/her/it	himself/herself/ itself
	one/who	one's/whose	one/whom	oneself/(no form)
Plural				
1st person	we	our, ours	us	ourselves
2nd person	you	your, yours	you	yourselves
3rd person	they	their, theirs	them	themselves

Note that the first-person pronoun comes after names or pronouns that refer to other people.

Dangling Modifier

A **modifier** is a word or phrase that gives more information about the subject, verb, or object in a clause. A **dangling modifier** refers to a wrong word or word that is not actually in the sentence. The solution is to reword the modifier so that it is grammatically correct.

Incorrect:	Confirming our conversation, the truck will leave Monday. [The speaker is doing the confirming. But the speaker isn't in the sentence.]
Incorrect:	At the age of eight, I began teaching my children about American business. [This sentence says that the author was eight when he or she had children who could understand business.]

Correct a dangling modifier in one of these ways:

- Recast the modifier as a subordinate clause.

Correct:	As I told you, the truck will leave Monday.
Correct:	When they were eight, I began teaching my children about American business.

- Revise the main clause so its subject or object can be modified by the now-dangling phrase.

Correct:	Confirming our conversation, I have scheduled the truck to leave Monday.
Correct:	At the age of eight, my children began learning about American business.

Hint: Whenever you use a verb or adjective that ends in *-ing,* make sure it modifies the grammatical subject of your sentence. If it doesn't, reword the sentence.

Misplaced Modifier

A **misplaced modifier** appears to modify another element of the sentence than the writer intended.

Incorrect:	Customers who complain often alert us to changes we need to make. [Does the sentence mean that customers must complain frequently to teach us something? Or is the meaning that frequently we learn from complaints?]

Correct a misplaced modifier by moving it closer to the word it modifies or by adding punctuation to clarify your meaning. If a modifier modifies the whole sentence, use it as an introductory phrase or clause; follow it with a comma.

Correct:	Often, customers who complain alert us to changes we need to make.

Parallel Structure

Items in a series or list must have the same grammatical structure.

Not parallel:	In the second month of your internship, you will
	1. Learn how to resolve customers' complaints.
	2. Supervision of desk staff.
	3. Interns will help plan store displays.
Parallel:	In the second month of your internship, you will
	1. Learn how to resolve customers' complaints.

2. Supervise desk staff.

3. Plan store displays.

Also parallel: Duties in the second month of your internship include resolving customers' complaints, supervising desk staff, and planning store displays.

Hint: When you have two or three items in a list (whether the list is horizontal or vertical) make sure the items are in the same grammatical form. Put lists vertically to make them easier to see.

Predication Errors

The predicate of a sentence must fit grammatically and logically with the subject. Make sure that the verb describes the action done by or done to the subject.

Incorrect: Our goals should begin immediately.

Correct: Implementing our goals should begin immediately.

In sentences using *is* and other linking verbs, the complement must be a noun, an adjective, or a noun clause.

Incorrect: The reason for this change is because the SEC now requires fuller disclosure.

Correct: The reason for this change is that the SEC now requires fuller disclosure.

Understanding Punctuation LO B-2

Punctuation marks are road signs to help readers predict what comes next. (See Figure B.2.)

When you move from the subject to the verb, you're going in a straight line; no comma is needed. When you end an introductory phrase or clause, the comma tells readers the introduction is over and you're turning to the main clause. When words interrupt the main clause, like this, commas tell the reader when to turn off the main clause for a short side route and when to return.

Some people have been told to put commas where they'd take breaths. That's bad advice. How often you'd take a breath depends on how big your lung capacity is, how fast and loud you're speaking, and how much emphasis you want. Commas aren't breaths. Instead, like other punctuation, they're road signs.

Punctuating Sentences

A sentence contains at least one main clause. A **main or independent clause** is a complete statement. A **subordinate or dependent clause** contains both

Headline Problems

Charles Apple keeps a daily blog of some of the worst headline errors in newspapers, on the web, and on television. Here are a few of the howlers he found:

- HEADLINE WILL GO HERE BLAH BLAH BLAH BLAH BLAH BLAH. Nothing inspires readership more. (March 10, 2013)
- ALABAMA ROUTES NOTRE DAME. Perhaps they needed a better GPS. (January 8, 2013)
- FOR TOWNS HOLD ELECTIONS. Practice: one, two, three, FOUR, five . . . (June 20, 2011)
- [from a description of "The Martha Stewart Show"] CHILLED CRAP SALAD. I recommend you skip straight to the main course. (April 25, 2011)

Adapted from Charles Apple, "The Visual Side of Journalism," *American Copy Editors Society*, http://apple.copydesk.org/, accessed July 8, 2013.

Figure B.2	What Punctuation Tells the Reader
Mark	**Tells the reader**
Period	We're stopping.
Semicolon	What comes next is closely related to what I just said.
Colon	What comes next is an example of what I just said.
Dash	What comes next is a dramatic example of or a shift from what I just said.
Comma	What comes next is a slight turn, but we're going in the same basic direction.

a subject and a verb but is not a complete statement and cannot stand by itself. A phrase is a group of words that does not contain both a subject and a verb.

Main clauses

> Your order will arrive Thursday.
>
> He dreaded talking to his supplier.
>
> I plan to enroll for summer school classes.

Subordinate clauses

> if you place your order by Monday
>
> because he was afraid the product would be out of stock
>
> since I want to graduate next spring

Phrases

> With our current schedule
>
> As a result
>
> After talking to my advisor

A clause with one of the following words will be subordinate:

after	if
although, though	when, whenever
because, since	while, as
before, until	

Using the correct punctuation will enable you to avoid four major sentence errors: comma splices, run-on sentences, fused sentences, and sentence fragments.

Comma Splices

A **comma splice** or **comma fault** occurs when two main clauses are joined only by a comma (instead of by a comma and a coordinating conjunction).

> Incorrect: The contest will start in June, the date has not been set.

Correct a comma splice in one of the following ways:

- If the ideas are closely related, use a semicolon rather than a comma. If they aren't closely related, start a new sentence.

> Correct: The contest will start in June; the exact date has not been set.

- Add a coordinating conjunction.

> Correct: The contest will start in June, but the exact date has not been set.

- Subordinate one of the clauses.

> Correct: Although the contest will start in June, the exact date has not been set.

Remember that you cannot use just a comma with the following transitions:

however	nevertheless
therefore	moreover

Instead, either use a semicolon to separate the clauses or start a new sentence.

> Incorrect: Computerized grammar checkers do not catch every error, however, they may be useful as a first check before an editor reads the material.
>
> Correct: Computerized grammar checkers do not catch every error; however, they may be useful as a first check before an editor reads the material.

Run-on Sentences

A **run-on sentence** strings together several main clauses using *and, but, or, so,* and *for.* Run-on sentences and comma splices are "mirror faults." A comma splice *uses only* the comma and omits the coordinating conjunction, while a run-on sentence uses *only* the conjunction and omits the comma. Correct a short run-on sentence by adding a comma. Separate a long run-on sentence into two or more sentences. Consider subordinating one or more of the clauses.

Incorrect:	We will end up with a much smaller markup but they use a lot of this material so the volume would be high so try to sell them on fast delivery and tell them our quality is very high.
Correct:	Although we will end up with a much smaller markup, volume would be high since they use a lot of this material. Try to sell them on fast delivery and high quality.

Fused Sentences

A **fused sentence** results when two sentences or more are *fused,* or joined with neither punctuation nor conjunctions. To fix the error, add the punctuation, add punctuation and a conjunction, or subordinate one of the clauses.

Incorrect:	The advantages of Intranets are clear the challenge is persuading employees to share information.
Correct:	The advantages of Intranets are clear; the challenge is persuading employees to share information.
Also correct:	Although the advantages of Intranets are clear, the challenge is persuading employees to share information.

Sentence Fragments

In a **sentence fragment,** a group of words that is not a complete sentence is punctuated as if it were a complete sentence.

Incorrect:	Observing these people, I have learned two things about the program. The time it takes. The rewards it brings.

To fix a sentence fragment, either add whatever parts of the sentence are missing or incorporate the fragment into the sentence before it or after it.

Correct:	Observing these people, I have learned that the program is time-consuming but rewarding.

Remember that clauses with the following words are not complete sentences. Join them to a main clause.

after	if
although, though	when, whenever
because, since	while, as
before, until	

Incorrect:	We need to buy a new computer system. Because our current system is obsolete.
Correct:	We need to buy a new computer system because our current system is obsolete.

Punctuation within Sentences

The good business and administrative writer knows how to use the following punctuation marks: apostrophes, colons, commas, dashes, hyphens, parentheses, periods, and semicolons.

Apostrophe

1. Use an apostrophe in a contraction to indicate that a letter or symbol has been omitted.

   We're trying to renegotiate the contract.

   The '90s were years of restructuring for our company.

2. To indicate possession, add an apostrophe and an *s* to the word.

   The corporation's home office is in Houston, Texas.

   Apostrophes to indicate possession are especially essential when one noun in a comparison is omitted.

   This year's sales will be higher than last year's.

   When a word already ends in an *s*, add an apostrophe or an apostrophe and *s* to make it possessive.

   The meeting will be held at New Orleans' convention center.

   With many terms, the placement of the apostrophe indicates whether the noun is singular or plural.

   Incorrect: The program should increase the participant's knowledge. [Implies that only one participant is in the program.]

   Correct: The program should increase the participants' knowledge. [Many participants are in the program.]

   Hint: Use "of" in the sentence to see where the apostrophe goes.

   The figures of last year = last year's figures.

   The needs of our customers = our customers' needs.

   Note that possessive pronouns (e.g., *his, ours*) usually do not have apostrophes. The only exception is *one's*.

   The company needs the goodwill of its stockholders.

   His promotion was announced yesterday.

   One's greatest asset is the willingness to work hard.

3. Do not use an apostrophe to make plurals.

   Incorrect: Use the folder's above the cabinet to file these documents.

   Correct: Use the folders above the cabinet to file these documents.

Colon

1. Use a colon to separate a main clause and a list that explains the last element in the clause. The items in the list are specific examples of the word that appears immediately before the colon.

   Please order the following supplies:

   Printer cartridges

   Computer paper (20-lb. white bond)

   Bond paper (25-lb., white, 25% cotton)

   Company letterhead

   Company envelopes

   When the list is presented vertically, capitalize the first letter of each item in the list. When the list is run in with the sentence, you don't need to capitalize the first letter after the colon.

Please order the following supplies: printer cartridges, computer paper (20-lb. white bond), bond paper (25-lb., white, 25% cotton), company letterhead, and company envelopes.

Do not use a colon when the list is grammatically part of the main clause.

Incorrect: The rooms will have coordinated decors in natural colors such as: egg-plant, moss, and mushroom.

Correct: The rooms will have coordinated decors in natural colors such as egg-plant, moss, and mushroom.

Also correct: The rooms will have coordinated decors in a variety of natural colors: egg-plant, moss, and mushroom.

If the list is presented vertically, some authorities suggest introducing the list with a colon even though the words preceding the colon are not a complete sentence.

2. Use a colon to join two independent clauses when the second clause explains or restates the first clause.

Selling is simple: give people the service they need, and they'll come back with more orders.

Comma

1. Use commas to separate the main clause from an introductory clause, the reader's name, or words that interrupt the main clause. Note that commas both precede and follow the interrupting information.

R. J. Garcia, the new sales manager, comes to us from the Des Moines office.

A **nonrestrictive** (nonessential) **clause** gives extra information that is not needed to identify the noun it modifies. Because nonrestrictive clauses give extra information, they need extra commas.

Sue Decker, who wants to advance in the organization, has signed up for the company training program in sales techniques.

Do not use commas to set off information that restricts the meaning of a noun or pronoun. **Restrictive clauses** give essential, not extra, information.

Anyone who wants to advance in the organization should take advantage of on-the-job training.

The clause "who wants to advance in the organization" restricts the meaning of the pronoun *anyone*.

Do not use commas to separate the subject from the verb, even if you would take a breath after a long subject.

Incorrect: Laws requiring registration of anyone collecting $5,000 or more on behalf of another person, apply to schools and private individuals as well to charitable groups and professional fund-raisers.

Correct: Laws requiring registration of anyone collecting $5,000 or more on behalf of another person apply to schools and private individuals as well to charitable groups and professional fund-raisers.

2. Use a comma, with a conjunction, after the first clause in a compound sentence.

This policy eliminates all sick-leave credit of the employee at the time of retirement, and payment will be made only once to any individual.

Do not use commas to join independent clauses without a conjunction. Doing so produces comma splices.

3. Use commas to separate items in a series. Using a comma before the *and* or *or* is not required by some authorities, but using a comma always adds clarity. The comma is essential if any of the items in the series themselves contain the word *and*.

> The company pays the full cost of hospitalization insurance for eligible employees, spouses, and unmarried dependent children under age 23.

Dash

Use dashes to emphasize a break in thought.

> Ryertex comes in 30 grades—each with a special use.

To type a dash, use two hyphens with no space before or after.

Hyphen

1. Use a hyphen to indicate that a word has been divided between two lines.

> Attach the original receipts for lodging, meals, tips, trans-
> portation, and registration fees.

Divide words at syllable breaks. If you aren't sure where the syllables divide, look up the word in a dictionary. When a word has several syllables, divide it after a vowel or between two consonants. Don't divide words of one syllable (e.g., *used*); don't divide a two-syllable word if one of the syllables is only one letter long (e.g., *acre*).

Most computer software will take care of dividing words for you, but you should still check your final document for awkward breaks or breaks that could cause misreadings.

2. Use hyphens to join two or more words used as a single adjective.

> Order five 10- or 12-foot lengths.

> The computer-prepared income and expense statements will be ready next Friday.

The hyphen prevents misreading. In the first example, five lengths are needed, not lengths of 5, 10, or 12 feet. In the second example, without the hyphen, the reader might think that *computer* was the subject and *prepared* was the verb. If you are unsure whether two words should be joined by a hyphen, consult a dictionary or a usage guide.

Parentheses

1. Use parentheses to set off words, phrases, or sentences used to explain or comment on the main idea.

> For the thinnest Ryertex (.015″) only a single layer of the base material may be used, while the thickest (10″) may contain over 600 greatly compressed layers of fabric or paper. By varying the fabric used (cotton, asbestos, glass, or nylon) or the type of paper, and by changing the kind of resin (phenolic, melamine, silicone, or epoxy), we can produce 30 different grades.

Any additional punctuation goes outside the second parenthesis when the punctuation applies to the whole sentence. It goes inside when it applies only to the words in the parentheses.

> Please check the invoice to see if credit should be issued. (A copy of the invoice is attached.)

2. Use parentheses for the citations in a text. See Appendix C for examples.

Period

1. Use a period at the end of a sentence. Use only one space before the next sentence.

2. Use a period after some abbreviations. When a period is used with a person's initials, leave one space after the period before the next letter or word. In other abbreviations, no space is necessary.

R. J. Tebeaux has been named Vice President for Marketing.

The U.S. division plans to hire 300 new M.B.A.s in the next year.

The trend is to reduce the use of punctuation. It would also be correct to write

The US division plans to hire 300 new MBAs in the next year.

Semicolon

1. Use semicolons to join two independent clauses when they are closely related.

We'll do our best to fill your order promptly; however, we cannot guarantee a delivery date.

Using a semicolon suggests that the two ideas are very closely connected. Using a period and a new sentence is also correct but implies nothing about how closely related the two sentences are.

2. Use semicolons to separate items in a series when the items themselves contain commas.

The final choices for the new plant are El Paso, Texas; Albuquerque, New Mexico; Salt Lake City, Utah; Eureka, California; and Eugene, Oregon. ·

Hospital benefits are also provided for certain specialized care services such as diagnostic admissions directed toward a definite disease or injury; normal maternity delivery, Caesarean section delivery, or complications of pregnancy; and in-patient admissions for dental procedures necessary to safeguard the patient's life or health.

Hint: A semicolon could be replaced by a period and a capital letter. It has a sentence on both sides.

Special Punctuation Marks

Quotation marks, square brackets, ellipses, and underlining are necessary when you use quoted material.

Quotation Marks

1. Use quotation marks around the names of brochures, pamphlets, and magazine articles.

Enclosed are 30 copies of our pamphlet "Saving Energy."

You'll find articles like "How to Improve Your Golf Game" and "Can You Keep Your Eye on the Ball?" in every issue.

In U.S. punctuation, periods and commas go inside quotation marks. Colons and semicolons go outside. Question marks go inside if they are part of the material being quoted.

2. Use quotation marks around words to indicate that you think the term is misleading.

These "pro-business" policies actually increase corporate taxes.

3. Use quotation marks around words that you are discussing as words.

> Forty percent of the respondents answered "yes" to the first question.
>
> Use "Ms." as a courtesy title for a woman unless you know she prefers another title.

It is also acceptable to italicize words instead of using quotation marks.

4. Use quotation marks around words or sentences that you quote from someone else.

> "The Fog Index," says its inventor, Robert Gunning, is "an effective warning system against drifting into needless complexity."

Square Brackets

Use square brackets to add your own additions to or changes in quoted material.

Senator Smith's statement:	"These measures will create a deficit."
Your use of Smith's statement:	According to Senator Smith, "These measures [in the new tax bill] will create a deficit."

The square brackets show that Smith did not say these words; you add them to make the quote make sense in your document.

Ellipses

Ellipses are spaced dots. In typing, use three spaced periods for an ellipsis. When an ellipsis comes at the end of a sentence, use a dot immediately after the last letter of the sentence for a period. Then add three spaced dots, with another space after the last dot.

1. Use ellipses to indicate that one or more words have been omitted in the middle of quoted material. You do not need ellipses at the beginning or end of a quote.

> The *Wall Street Journal* notes that Japanese magazines and newspapers include advertisements for a "$2.1 million home in New York's posh Riverdale section . . . 185 acres of farmland [and] . . . luxury condos on Manhattan's Upper East Side."

2. In advertising and direct mail, use ellipses to imply the pace of spoken comments.

> If you've ever wanted to live on a tropical island . . . cruise to the Bahamas . . . or live in a castle in Spain . . .
>
> . . . you can make your dreams come true with Vacations Extraordinaire.

Italics and Underlining

1. Italicize the names of newspapers, magazines, and books.

> *Wall Street Journal*
>
> *Fortune*
>
> *The Wealth of Nations*

Titles of brochures and pamphlets are put in quotation marks.

2. Italicize words to emphasize them.

> Here's a bulletin that gives you, in handy chart form, *workable data* on over 50 different types of tubing and pipe.

You may also use underlining in place of italics, but italics are almost always preferred. For greater emphasis you may use bold to emphasize words. Bold type is better than either underlining or italics because it is easier to read, particularly on a computer screen.

Writing Numbers and Dates

Spell out **numbers** from one to nine. Use figures for numbers 10 and over in most cases. Always use figures for amounts of money (The new office costs $1.7 million). Large numbers frequently use a combination of numbers and words (More than 20 million people are affected by this new federal regulation).

Spell out any number that appears at the beginning of a sentence. If spelling it out is impractical, revise the sentence so that it does not begin with a number.

> Fifty students filled out the survey.

> In 2002, euro notes and coins entered circulation.

When two numbers follow each other, spell out the smaller number and use figures for the larger number.

In **dates,** use figures for the day and year. The month is normally spelled out. Be sure to spell out the month in international business communication. American usage puts the month first, so that 1/10/14 means *January 10, 2014.* European usage puts the day first, so that 1/10/14 means *October 1, 2014.* Modern punctuation uses a comma before the year only when you give both the month and the day of the month:

> May 1, 2014

but

> Summers 2011–14

> August 2014

> Fall 2014

No punctuation is needed in military or European usage, which puts the day of the month first: 13 July 2014. Do not space before or after the slash used to separate parts of the date: 10/07–5/14.

Use a hyphen to join inclusive dates.

> March–August 2014 (or write out: March to August 2014)

> '12–'14

> 2009–2014

Note that you do not need to repeat the century in the date that follows the hyphen: 2013–14.

Words That Are Often Confused   LO B-3

Here's a list of words that are frequently confused. Master them, and you'll be well on the way to using words correctly.

1. accede/exceed
   accede: to yield
   exceed: to go beyond, surpass
   > I accede to your demand that we not exceed the budget.

2. accept/except

accept: to receive; to agree to

except: to leave out or exclude; but

I accept your proposal except for point 3.

3. access/excess

access: the right to use; admission to

excess: surplus

As supply clerk, he had access to any excess materials.

4. adapt/adopt

adapt: adjust

adopt: to take as one's own

She would adapt her ideas so people would adopt them.

5. advice/advise

advice: (noun) counsel

advise: (verb) to give counsel or advice to someone

I asked him to advise me, but I didn't like the advice I got.

6. affect/effect

affect: (verb) to influence or modify

effect: (verb) to produce or cause; (noun) result

He hoped that his argument would affect his boss's decision, but so far as he could see, it had no effect.

The tax relief effected some improvement for the citizens whose incomes had been affected by inflation.

7. affluent/effluent

affluent: (adjective) rich, possessing in abundance

effluent: (noun) something that flows out

Affluent companies can afford the cost of removing pollutants from the effluents their factories produce.

8. a lot/allot

a lot: many (informal)

allot: divide or give to

A lot of players signed up for this year's draft. We allotted one first-round draft choice to each team.

9. among/between

among: (use with more than two choices)

between: (use with only two choices)

This year the differences between the two candidates for president are unusually clear.

I don't see any major differences among the candidates for city council.

10. amount/number

amount: (use with concepts or items that can be measured but that cannot be counted individually)

number: (use when items can be counted individually)

It's a mistake to try to gauge the amount of interest he has by the number of questions he asks.

11. attributed/contributed

attributed: was said to be caused by

contributed: gave something to

The rain probably contributed to the accident, but the police officer attributed the accident to driver error.

12. cite/sight/site

    cite: (verb) to quote

    sight: (noun) vision, something to be seen

    site: (noun) location, place where a building is or will be built

    She cited the old story of the building inspector who was depressed by the very sight of the site for the new factory.

13. complement/compliment

    complement: (verb) to complete, finish; (noun) something that completes

    compliment: (verb) to praise; (noun) praise

    The compliment she gave me complemented my happiness.

14. compose/comprise

    compose: make up, create

    comprise: consist of, be made up of, be composed of

    The city council is composed of 12 members. Each district comprises an area 50 blocks square.

15. confuse/complicate/exacerbate

    confuse: to bewilder

    complicate: to make more complex or detailed

    exacerbate: to make worse

    Because I missed the first 20 minutes of the movie, I didn't understand what was going on. The complicated plot exacerbated my confusion.

16. dependant/dependent

    dependant: (noun) someone for whom one is financially responsible

    dependent: (adjective) relying on someone else

    IRS regulations don't let us count our 27-year-old son as a dependant, but he is still financially dependent on us.

17. describe/prescribe

    describe: list the features of something, tell what something looks like

    prescribe: specify the features something must contain

    The law prescribes the priorities for making repairs. This report describes our plans to comply with the law.

18. different from/different than

    Almost always *different from* (try changing the adjective *different* to the verb *differs*)

    Bob's job description is different from mine.

    The most common exception is the indirect comparison.

    Susan has a different attitude than you and I [*do* is implied].

19. discreet/discrete

    discreet: tactful, careful not to reveal secrets

    discrete: separate, distinct

    I have known him to be discreet on two discrete occasions.

20. disinterested/uninterested

    Disinterested: impartial

    Uninterested: unconcerned

    Because our boss is uninterested in office spats, she makes a disinterested referee.

21. elicit/illicit

    elicit: (verb) to draw out

    illicit: (adjective) not permitted, unlawful

    > The reporter could elicit no information from the senator about his illicit love affair.

22. eminent/immanent/imminent

    eminent: distinguished

    immanent: existing in the mind or consciousness

    imminent: about to happen

    > The eminent doctor believed that death was imminent. The eminent minister believed that God was immanent.

23. farther/further

    farther: use for physical difference

    further: use for metaphoric difference; also use for *additional* or *additionally*

    > As I traveled farther from the destruction at the plant, I pondered the further evidence of sabotage presented to me today.

24. fewer/less

    fewer: (use for objects that can be counted individually)

    less: (use for objects that can be measured but not counted individually)

    > There is less sand in this bucket; there are probably fewer grains of sand, too.

25. forward/foreword

    forward: ahead

    foreword: preface, introduction

    > The author looked forward to writing the foreword to the book.

26. good/well

    good: (adjective, used to modify nouns; as a noun, means something that is good)

    well: (adverb, used to modify verbs, adjectives, and other adverbs)

    > Her words "Good work!" told him that he was doing well.

    > He spent a great deal of time doing volunteer work because he believed that doing good was just as important as doing well.

27. i.e./e.g.

    i.e.: (*id est*—that is) introduces a restatement or explanation of the preceding word or phrase

    e.g.: (*exempli gratia*—for the sake of an example; for example) introduces one or more examples

    > Although he had never studied Latin, he rarely made a mistake in using Latin abbreviations, e.g., i.e., and etc., because he associated each with a mnemonic device (i.e., a word or image used to help one remember something). He remembered *i.e.* as *in effect*, pretended that *e.g.* meant *example given*, and used *etc.* only when *examples to continue* would fit.

28. imply/infer

    imply: suggest, put an idea into someone's head

    infer: deduce, get an idea from something

She implied that an announcement would be made soon. I inferred from her smile that it would be an announcement of her promotion.

29. it's/its

   it's: it is, it has

   its: belonging to it

   It's clear that a company must satisfy its customers to stay in business.

30. lectern/podium

   lectern: raised stand with a slanted top that holds a manuscript for a reader or notes for a speaker

   podium: platform for a speaker or conductor to stand on

   I left my notes on the lectern when I left the podium at the end of my talk.

31. lie/lay

   lie: to recline; to tell a falsehood (never takes an object)

   lay: to put an object on something (always takes an object)

   He was laying the papers on the desk when I came in, but they aren't lying there now.

32. loose/lose

   loose: not tight

   lose: to have something disappear

   If I lose weight, this suit will be loose.

33. moral/morale

   moral: (adjective) virtuous, good; (noun: morals) ethics, sense of right and wrong

   morale: (noun) spirit, attitude, mental outlook

   Studies have shown that coed dormitories improve student morale without harming student morals.

34. objective/rationale

   objective: goal

   rationale: reason, justification

   The objective of the meeting was to explain the rationale behind the decision.

35. personal/personnel

   personal: individual, to be used by one person

   personnel: staff, employees

   All personnel will get personal computers by the end of the year.

36. possible/possibly

   possible: (adjective) something that can be done

   possibly: (adverb) perhaps

   It is possible that we will be able to hire this spring. We can choose from possibly the best graduating class in the past five years.

37. precede/proceed

   precede: (verb) to go before

   proceed: (verb) to continue; (noun: proceeds) money

   Raising the money must precede spending it. Only after we obtain the funds can we proceed to spend the proceeds.

38. principal/principle

principal: (adjective) main; (noun) person in charge; money lent out at interest

principle: (noun) basic truth or rule, code of conduct

The Prince, Machiavelli's principal work, describes his principles for ruling a state.

39. quiet/quite

quiet: not noisy

quite: very

It was quite difficult to find a quiet spot anywhere near the floor of the stock exchange.

40. regulate/relegate

regulate: control

relegate: put (usually in an inferior position)

If the federal government regulates the size of lettering on country road signs, we may as well relegate the current signs to the garbage bin.

41. respectfully/respectively

respectfully: with respect

respectively: to each in the order listed

When I was introduced to the queen, the prime minister, and the court jester, I bowed respectfully, shook hands politely, and winked, respectively.

42. role/roll

role: part in a play or script, function (in a group)

roll: (noun) list of students, voters, or other members; round piece of bread; (verb) move by turning over and over

While the teacher called the roll, George—in his role as class clown—threw a roll he had saved from lunch.

43. simple/simplistic

simple: not complicated

simplistic: watered down, oversimplified

She was able to explain the proposal in simple terms without making the explanation sound simplistic.

44. stationary/stationery

stationary: not moving, fixed

stationery: paper

During the earthquake, even the stationery was not stationary.

45. their/there/they're

their: belonging to them

there: in that place

they're: they are

There are plans, designed to their specifications, for the house they're building.

46. to/too/two

to: (preposition) function word indicating proximity, purpose, time, etc.

too: (adverb) also, very, excessively

two: (adjective) the number 2

> The formula is too secret to entrust to two people.

47. unique/unusual

    unique: sole, only, alone

    unusual: not common

    > I believed that I was unique in my ability to memorize long strings of numbers until I consulted *Guinness World Records* and found that I was merely unusual: someone else had equaled my feat in 1993.

48. verbal/oral

    verbal: using words

    oral: spoken, not written

    > His verbal skills were uneven: his oral communication was excellent, but he didn't write well. His sensitivity to nonverbal cues was acute: he could tell what kind of day I had just by looking at my face.

    Hint: Oral comes from the Latin word for mouth, *os.* Think of Oral-B Toothbrushes: for the mouth. Verbal comes from the Latin word for word, *verba.* Nonverbal language is language that does not use words (e.g., body language, gestures).

49. whether/weather

    whether: (conjunction) used to introduce possible alternatives

    weather: (noun) state of the atmosphere: wet or dry, hot or cold, calm or storm

    > We will have to see what the weather is before we decide whether to hold the picnic indoors or out.

50. your/you're

    your: belonging to you

    you're: you are

    > You're the top candidate for promotion in your division.

Proofreading Symbols

Use the proofreading symbols in Figure B.3 to make corrections on paper copies. Figure B.4 shows how the symbols can be used to correct a typed text.

Figure B.3	Proofreading Symbols		
ℒ	delete	⌐	move to left
ℰ	insert a letter	⌐	move to right
¶	start a new paragraph here	⌐	move up
(stet)	stet (leave as it was before the marked change)	⌐	move down
(tr) ⌐	transpose (reverse)	#	leave a space
(lc)	lower case (don't capitalize)	⌒	close up
≡	capitalize	‖	align vertically

Figure B.4	Marked Text

We could cut our travel bill by reimbursing employees only for the cost of a budget hotel or motel room.

A recent article from *The Wall Street Journal* suggests that many low-cost hotles and motels are tring to appeal to business travelers.   chains that are actively competing for the business market include

Motel 6
Hampton Inns
      Fairfield Inns
Econologde
Super 8

Comfort Inn
Travelodge.

To attract business travelers, some budget chains now offer free local phone calls, free in-room movies, free continental breakfasts and free Computer hookups.

By staying in a budget hotel, the business travelers can save at least $10 to $20 a night-- often much more. For a company whose employees travel frequently, The savings can be considerable. Last year Megacorp reimbursed employees for a total of 4,392 nights in hotels. If each employee had stayed in a budget hotel, our expenses for travel would be $44,000 to $88,000 lower. Budget hotels would not be appropriate for sales meetings since they lack photocopying facilities or meeting rooms. However, we could and should use budget hotels and motels for ordinary on-the-road travel.

Exercises and Cases

B.1   Diagnostic Test on Punctuation and Grammar

Identify and correct the errors in the following passages.

a.

Company's are finding it to their advantage to cultivate their suppliers. Partnerships between a company and it's suppliers can yield hefty payoffs for both company and supplier. One example is Bailey Controls an Ohio headquartered company. Bailey make control systems for big factories. They treat suppliers almost like departments of their own company. When a Bailey employee passes a laser scanner over a bins bar code the supplier is instantly alerted to send more parts.

b.
Entrepreneur Trip Hawkins appears in Japanese ads for the video game system his company designed. "It plugs into the future! he says in one ad, in a cameo spliced into shots of U.S kids playing the games. Hawkins is one of several US celebrities and business people whom plug products on Japanese TV. Jodie Foster, harrison ford, and Charlie Sheen adverstises canned coffee beer and cigarettes respectively.

c.
Mid size firms employing between 100 and 1000 peopole represent only 4% of companies in the U.S.; but create 33% of all new jobs. One observe attributes their success to their being small enough to take advantage of economic opportunity's agilely, but big enough to have access to credit and to operate on a national or even international scale. The biggest hiring area for midsize company's is wholesale and retail sales (38% of jobs), construction (20% of jobs, manufacturing (19% of jobs), and services (18 of jobs).

B.2   Providing Punctuation I

Provide the necessary punctuation in the following sentences. Note that not every box requires punctuation.

1. The system □ s □ user □ friendly design □ provides screen displays of work codes □ rates □ and client information.
2. Many other factors also shape the organization □ s □ image □ advertising □ brochures □ proposals □ stationery □ calling cards □ etc.
3. Charlotte Ford □ author of □ Charlotte Ford □ s □ Book of Modern Manners □ □ says □ □ Try to mention specifics of the conversation to fix the interview permanently in the interviewer □ s □ mind and be sure to mail the letter the same day □ before the hiring decision is made □ □
4. What are your room rates □ and charges for food service □
5. We will need accommodations for 150 people □ five meeting rooms □ one large room and four small ones □ □ coffee served during morning and afternoon breaks □ and lunches and dinners.
6. The Operational Readiness Inspection □ which occurs once every three years □ is a realistic exercise □ which evaluates the National Guard □ s □ ability to mobilize □ deploy □ and fight.
7. Most computer packages will calculate three different sets of percentages □ row percentages □ column percentages □ and table percentages □
8. In today □ s □ economy □ it □ s almost impossible for a firm to extend credit beyond it □ s regular terms.
9. The Department of Transportation does not have statutory authority to grant easements □ however □ we do have authority to lease unused areas of highway right □ of □ way.
10. The program has two goals □ to identify employees with promise □ and to see that they get the training they need to advance.

B.3   Providing Punctuation II

Provide the necessary punctuation in the following sentences. Note that not every box requires punctuation.

1. Office work □ □ especially at your desk □ □ can create back □ shoulder □ neck □ or wrist strain.
2. I searched for □ vacation □ and □ vacation planning □ on Google and Bing.
3. I suggest putting a bulletin board in the rear hallway □ and posting all the interviewer □ s □ photos on it.
4. Analyzing audiences is the same for marketing and writing □ you have to identify who the audiences are □ understand how to motivate them □ and choose the best channel to reach them.
5. The more you know about your audience □ □ who they are □ what they buy □ where they shop □ □ the more relevant and effective you can make your ad.
6. The city already has five □ two □ hundred □ bed hospitals.
7. Students run the whole organization □ and are advised by a board of directors from the community.
8. The company is working on three team □ related issues □ interaction □ leadership □ and team size.
9. I would be interested in working on the committee □ however □ I have decided to do less community work so that I have more time to spend with my family.
10. □ You can create you own future □ □ says Frank Montaño □ □ You have to think about it □ crystallize it in writing □ and be willing to work at it □ We teach a lot of goal □ setting and planning in our training sessions □ □

B.4   Creating Agreement

Revise the following sentences to correct errors in noun–pronoun and subject–verb agreement.

1. If there's any tickets left, they'll be $17 at the door.
2. A team of people from marketing, finance, and production are preparing the proposal.

3. Image type and resolution varies among clip art packages.
4. Your health and the health of your family is very important to us.
5. If a group member doesn't complete their assigned work, it slows the whole project down.
6. Baker & Baker was offended by the ad agency's sloppy proposal, and they withdrew their account from the firm.

7. To get out of debt you need to cut up your credit cards, which is hard to do.
8. Contests are fun for employees and creates sales incentives.
9. The higher the position a person has, the more professional their image should be.
10. A new employee should try to read verbal and non-verbal signals to see which aspects of your job are most important.

B.5   Correcting Case Errors

Revise the following sentences to correct errors in pronoun case.

1. I didn't appreciate him assuming that he would be the group's leader.
2. Myself and Jim made the presentation.
3. Employees which lack experience in dealing with people from other cultures could benefit from seminars in intercultural communication.

4. Chandra drew the graphs after her and I discussed the ideas for them.
5. Please give your revisions to Cindy, Tyrone, or myself by noon Friday.
6. Let's keep this disagreement between you and I.

B.6   Improving Modifiers

Revise the following sentences to correct dangling and misplaced modifiers.

1. Originally a group of four, one member dropped out after the first meeting due to a death in the family.
2. Examining the data, it is apparent that most of our sales are to people on the northwest side of the city.

3. As a busy professional, we know that you will want to take advantage of this special offer.
4. Often documents end up in files that aren't especially good.
5. By making an early reservation, it will give us more time to coordinate our trucks to better serve you.

B.7   Creating Parallel Structure

Revise the following sentences to create parallel structure.

1. To narrow a web search,
   • Put quotation marks around a phrase when you want an exact term.
   • Many search engines have wild cards (usually an asterisk) to find plurals and other forms of a word.
   • Reading the instructions on the search engine itself can teach you advanced search techniques.
2. Men drink more alcoholic beverages than women.
3. Each issue of *Hospice Care* has articles from four different perspectives: legislative, health care, hospice administrators, and inspirational authors.
4. The university is one of the largest employers in the community, brings in substantial business, and the cultural impact is also big.

5. These three tools can help competitive people be better negotiators:
   1. Think win–win.
   2. It's important to ask enough questions to find out the other person's priorities, rather than jumping on the first advantage you find.
   3. Protect the other person's self-esteem.
6. These three questions can help cooperative people be better negotiators:
   1. Can you developing a specific alternative to use if negotiation fails?
   2. Don't focus on the bottom line. Spend time thinking about what you want and why you need it.
   3. Saying "You'll have to do better than that because . . ." can help you resist the temptation to say "yes" too quickly.

B.8   Correcting Sentence Errors

Revise the following sentences to correct comma splices, run-on sentences, fused sentences, and sentence fragments.

1. Members of the group are all experienced presenters, most have had little or no experience using PowerPoint.

2. Proofread the letter carefully and check for proper business format because errors undercut your ability to sell yourself so take advantage of your opportunity to make a good first impression.

3. Some documents need just one pass others need multiple revisions.

4. Videoconferencing can be frustrating. Simply because little time is available for casual conversation.

5. Entrepreneurs face two main obstacles. Limited cash. Lack of business experience.

6. The margin on pet supplies is very thin and the company can't make money selling just dog food and the real profit is in extras like neon-colored leashes, so you put the dog food in the back so people have to walk by everything else to get to it.

7. The company's profits jumped 15%. Although its revenues fell 3%.

8. The new budget will hurt small businesses it imposes extra fees it raises the interest rates small businesses must pay.

9. Our phones are constantly being used. Not just for business calls but also for personal calls.

10. Businesses are trying to cut travel costs, executives are taking fewer trips and flying out of alternate airports to save money.

B.9   Editing for Grammar and Usage

Revise the following sentences to eliminate errors in grammar and usage.

1. The number of students surveyed that worked more than 20 hours a week were 60%.

2. Not everyone is promoted after six months some people might remain in the training program a year before being moved to a permanent assignment.

3. The present solutions that has been suggested are not adequate.

4. At times while typing and editing, the text on your screen may not look correct.

5. All employees are asked to cut back on energy waste by the manager.

6. The benefits of an online catalog are
   1. We will be able to keep records up-to-date;
   2. Broad access to the catalog system from any networked terminal on campus;
   3. The consolidation of the main catalog and the catalogs in the departmental and branch libraries;
   4. Cost savings.

7. You can take advantage of several banking services. Such as automatic withdrawal of a house or car payment and direct deposit of your pay check.

8. As a freshman, business administration was intriguing to me.

9. Thank you for the help you gave Joanne Jackson and myself.

10. I know from my business experience that good communication among people and departments are essential in running a successful corporation.

B.10   Writing Numbers

Revise the following sentences to correct errors in writing numbers.

1. 60% percent of the respondents hope to hold internships before they graduate.

2. 1992 marked the formal beginning of the European Economic Community.

3. In the year two thousand, twenty percent of the H-1B visas for immigrants with high-tech skills went to Indians.

4. More than 70,000,000 working Americans lack an employer-sponsored retirement plan.

5. The company's sales have risen to $16 million but it lost five million dollars.

B.11   Using Plurals and Possessives

Choose the right word for each sentence.

1. Many Canadian (companies, company's) are competing effectively in the global market.

2. We can move your (families, family's) furniture safely and efficiently.

3. The (managers', manager's) ability to listen is just as important as his or her technical knowledge.

4. A (memos, memo's) style can build goodwill.

5. (Social workers, social worker's) should tell clients about services available in the community.

6. The (companies, company's) benefits plan should be checked periodically to make sure it continues to serve the needs of employees.

7. Information about the new community makes the (families, family's) move easier.

8. The (managers, manager's) all have open-door policies.

9. (Memos, memo's) are sent to other workers in the same organization.

10. Burnout affects a (social workers', social worker's) productivity as well as his or her morale.

B.12   Choosing the Right Word I

Choose the right word for each sentence.

1. Exercise is (good, well) for patients who have had open-heart surgery.
2. This response is atypical, but it is not (unique, unusual).
3. The personnel department continues its (roll, role) of compiling reports for the federal government.
4. The Accounting Club expects (its, it's) members to come to meetings and participate in activities.
5. Part of the fun of any vacation is (cite, sight, site)-seeing.

6. The (lectern, podium) was too high for the short speaker.
7. The (residence, residents) of the complex have asked for more parking spaces.
8. Please order more letterhead (stationary, stationery).
9. The closing of the plant will (affect, effect) house prices in the area.
10. Better communication (among, between) design and production could enable us to produce products more efficiently.

B.13   Choosing the Right Word II

Choose the right word for each sentence.

1. The audit revealed a small (amount, number) of errors.
2. Diet beverages have (fewer, less) calories than regular drinks.
3. In her speech, she (implied, inferred) that the vote would be close.
4. We need to redesign the stand so that the catalog is eye-level instead of (laying, lying) on the desk.
5. (Their, There, They're) is some evidence that (their, there, they're) thinking of changing (their, there, they're) policy.

6. The settlement isn't yet in writing; if one side wanted to back out of the (oral, verbal) agreement, it could.
7. In (affect, effect), we're creating a new department.
8. The firm will be hiring new (personal, personnel) in three departments this year.
9. Several customers have asked that we carry more campus merchandise, (i.e., e.g.,) pillows and mugs with the college seal.
10. We have investigated all of the possible solutions (accept, except) adding a turning lane.

B.14   Choosing the Right Word III

Choose the right word for each sentence.

1. The author (cites, sights, sites) four reasons for computer phobia.
2. The error was (do, due) to inexperience.
3. (Your, You're) doing a good job motivating (your, you're) subordinates.
4. One of the basic (principals, principles) of business communication is "Consider the reader."
5. I (implied, inferred) from the article that interest rates would go up.
6. Working papers generally are (composed, comprised) of working trial balance, assembly sheets,

adjusting entries, audit schedules, and audit memos.

7. Eliminating time clocks will improve employee (moral, morale).
8. The (principal, principle) variable is the trigger price mechanism.
9. (Its, It's) (to, too, two) soon (to, too, two) tell whether the conversion (to, too, two) computerized billing will save as much time as we hope.
10. Formal training programs (complement, compliment) on-the-job opportunities for professional growth.

B.15   Tracking Your Own Mechanical Errors

Analyze the mechanical errors (grammar, punctuation, word use, and typos) in each of your papers.

- How many different errors are marked on each paper?
- Which three errors do you make most often?
- Is the number of errors constant in each paper, or does the number increase or decrease during the term?

As your instructor directs,

a.   Correct each of the mechanical errors in one or more papers.

b.   Deliberately write two new sentences in which you make each of your three most common errors. Then write the correct version of each sentence.

c.   Write an e-mail for your instructor discussing your increasing mastery of mechanical correctness during the semester or quarter.

d.   Briefly explain to the class how to avoid one kind of error in grammar, punctuation, or word use.

Citing and Documenting Sources

Appendix Outline

American Psychological Association (APA) Format   Modern Language Association (MLA) Format

After studying this appendix, you will know how to

LO C-1 Use APA format for citing and documenting sources.

LO C-2 Use MLA format for citing and documenting sources.

Citing and documenting sources is an important part of any research process. In effective business proposals and reports, sources are cited and documented smoothly and unobtrusively. **Citation** means attributing an idea or fact to its source in the body of the text: "Bill Gates argues that …" "According to the John Deere annual report…." **Documentation** means providing the bibliographic information readers would need to go back to the original source. The usual means of documentation are notes (endnotes or footnotes) and lists of references.

Failure to cite and document sources is **plagiarism,** the passing off of the words or ideas of others as one's own. Plagiarism can lead to serious consequences. The news regularly showcases examples of people who have been fired or sued for plagiarism. Now that curious people can type sentences into Google and other search engines and find the sources, plagiarism is easier than ever to catch.

Note that citation and documentation are used in addition to quotation marks. If you use the source's exact words, you'll use the name of the person you're citing and quotation marks in the body of the proposal or report; you'll indicate the source in parentheses and a list of references or in a footnote or endnote. If you put the source's idea into your own words (paraphrasing), or if you condense or synthesize information, you don't need quotation marks, but you still need to tell whose idea it is and where you found it.

Long quotations (four typed lines or more) are used sparingly in business proposals and reports. Since many readers skip quotes, always summarize the main point of the quotation in a single sentence before the quotation itself. End the sentence with a colon, not a period, because it introduces the quote. Indent long quotations on the left to set them off from your text. Indented quotations do not need quotation marks; the indentation shows the reader that the passage is a quote.

To make a quotation fit the grammar of your report, you may need to change one or two words. Sometimes you may want to add a few words to explain something in the longer original. In both cases, use square brackets to indicate words that are your replacements or additions. Omit any words in the original source that are not essential for your purposes. Use ellipses (spaced dots) to indicate your omissions.

Document every fact and idea that you take from a source except facts that are common knowledge. Historical dates and facts are considered common knowledge (e.g., Barack Obama is the 44th president of the United States, or the Twin Towers came down on September 11, 2001). Generalizations are considered common knowledge ("More and more women are entering the workforce") even though specific statements about the same topic (such as the percentage of women in the workforce in 1975 and in 2010) would require documentation.

Two widely used formats for citing and documenting sources in proposals and reports are those of the American Psychological Association (APA) and the Modern Language Association (MLA). Each will be discussed in this appendix.

American Psychological Association (APA) Format LO C-1

The APA format is a widely used documentation style, most notably in the natural and human sciences. *Publication Manual of the American Psychological Association,* 6th edition, second printing, 2009, is the official source for this type of documentation.

For APA in-text citations, the source is indicated by the author's last name and the date of the work in parentheses, unless those items are already in the text. A comma separates the author's name from the date: (Salt, 2009). Page numbers are given only for direct quotations or in cases where the reader may need help to find the location: (Salt, 2009, p. 20). If you have a source with two authors, use an ampersand in the citation: (Locker & Kienzler, 2014). If the author's name is used in the sentence, only the date is given in parentheses. Sec Figure C.1 for a portion of a report that uses APA format.

At the end of your document, include a **References** list that provides the full bibliographic citation for each source used. Arrange the entries alphabetically by the first author's last name. Use only initials for first and middle names. Figure C.2 shows APA format examples of the most often used sources in proposals and reports.

Modern Language Association (MLA) Format LO C-2

The MLA format is another widely used documentation style, most notably in the arts and humanities. *MLA Style Manual and Guide to Scholarly Publishing,* 3rd edition, 2008, is the official source for this type of documentation.

For MLA in-text citations, the source is indicated by the author's last name and page number in parentheses in the text for paraphrases and direct quotations. Unlike APA, the year is not given, unless you're using two or more works by the same author or if the dates are important. No comma separates the name and page number, and the abbreviation "p." is not used: (Salt 20). If you have a source with two authors, use "and" in the citation: (Locker and Kienzler 222). If the author's name is used in the sentence, only the page number is given in parentheses. See Figure C.3 for a portion of a report that uses MLA format and includes a Works Cited section.

At the end of your document, include a **Works Cited** list that provides the full bibliographic citation for each source you have cited. Arrange the entries alphabetically by the first author's last name. Use authors' names as they appear on the source. Note that the Works Cited list gives the medium (e.g., Web, Print, DVD). URLs for web sources are given only when the item may be otherwise hard to find. Figure C.4 shows MLA format examples of the most often used sources in proposals and reports.

Figure C.1   Report Paragraphs with APA Documentation

Headings and paragraph numbers help readers find material in a website without page numbers. If the source does not number the paragraphs, number the paragraphs yourself under each heading.

Square brackets indicate a change from the original to make the quote fit into the structure of your sentence.

Social media can be defined as "technology facilitated dialogue among individuals or groups, such as blogs, microblogs, forums, wikis," and other unofficial forms of electronic communication (Cone, 2008, What is social media? ¶. 1). In a 2008 study on social media, Cone found that 39% of Americans reported using social media websites at least once a week; 30% reported using them two or more times a week. Additionally, the study found that 34% believed that companies should have a presence on social media websites and use their presence to interact with their customers. Fifty-one percent of users believed that companies should be present on these websites but interact only if customers ask them to do so (Cone). "While the ultimate measure [of most companies' marketing efforts] is sales, social media expands that because of its focus on influencers," says Simon Salt (2009, p. 20), the CEO of Inc-Slingers, a marketing communication firm. For example, he says "cable provider Comcast utilizes social media to monitor existing customer issues. . . . Known on Twitter as @comcastcares, it quickly developed a reputation for engaging its customer base" (p. 20). *Use page number for direct quote. Author's name already in text, so not repeated here.*

Numbers at the beginning of sentences must be written out.

This citation for a direct quote uses only year and page number ("p." before number) since author is identified in sentence.

An ellipsis (three spaced dots) indicates some material has been omitted. An extra dot serves as the period of the sentence.

Because source is adequately identified in text, no parenthetical source citation is needed.

The Cone study also found that 25% of users of social media websites reported interacting with companies at least once a week. When asked what kind of role companies should play on these Web sites, 43% said giving virtual customer service, 41% said soliciting customer feedback. Among some of the most popular social media websites are Facebook, My Space, Twitter, Blogger, and Digg.

No need to provide a citation for facts that are general or common knowledge.

Basic APA citation: Place author and date in parentheses; separate with a comma. Use page numbers only for a direct quote.

Twitter, a microblogging website, asks its users a simple question: "What are you doing?" Users can post their own updates and follow others' updates. Twitter has grown at a breathtaking pace in the last few months. It registered a whopping 600% increase in traffic in the 12 months leading up to November 2008. It is estimated that the microblogging website has approximately 3 million registered account holders from across the globe (Salt, 2009). A message or post on Twitter, known as a "tweet," cannot be more than 140 characters long. Companies and organizations are increasingly taking to Twitter.

Visible Technologies, a Seattle-based market research firm, helps companies search for valuable market information from a virtual pool of millions of tweets. Some of the firm's clients include Hormel Foods and Panasonic. The computer manufacturer Dell, another customer, asks its customer representatives to interact with customers on Twitter. Recently, the company announced that it increased its sales by $500,000 through the use of Twitter (Baker, 2008, Promotional Tweets, para. 1). Zappos.com, an online shoe seller, encourages its employees to use Twitter to communicate about subjects as wide-ranging as politics to marketing plans (Vascellaro, 2008).

Date of publication (year, month day) for a weekly source.

Use URL of a specific web page; do not put period after URL. Break long URLs after a /.

Source by a corporate author.

Only initials for all names except last.

List all works (but only those works) cited in the text. List sources alphabetically.

References

Article titles use sentence capitalization and no quotation marks.

Retrieval date is month day, year.

Baker, S. (2008, May 15). Why Twitter matters. *BusinessWeek*. Retrieved April 15, 2009, from http://www.businessweek.com/technology/content/may2008/tc20080514_269697.htm

Cone. (2008). 2008 business in social media study [Fact sheet]. Retrieved April 15, 2009 from http://www.coneinc.com /stuff /contentmgr/ files/0/26ff8eb1d1a9371210502558013fe2a6/files / 2008_business_in_social_media_fact_sheet.pdf

Salt, S. (2009, February 15). Track your success. *Marketing News, 43*, 20.

Italicize volume number.

Vascellaro, J. (2008, October 27). Twitter goes mainstream. *Wall Street Journal*, p. R3.

Don't abbreviate month.

Figure C.2	APA Format for Sources Used Most Often in Proposals and Reports

In the examples below, headings in green identify the kind of work being referenced. The green headings are not part of the actual citation.

Put authors' last names first. Use only initials for first and middle names.

Note comma after initial, use of ampersand, period after parenthesis.

In titles of articles and books capitalize only (1) first word, (2) first word of subtitle, (3) proper nouns.

No quotation marks around title of article.

Article in a Periodical
Stowers, R. H., & Hummel, J. Y. (2011, June). The use of technology to combat plagiarism

Ampersands join names of coauthors, coeditors.

in business communication classes. *Business Communication Quarterly, 74,*

Use a DOI (Digital Object Identifier) when available because it is more stable than a URL.
164–169. doi:10.1177//1080569911404406
Give complete page numbers.
No "pp." when journal has a volume number

Volume number is italicized. Provide issue number in parentheses only if each issue begins with page 1.

Date is year, month day

Article in a Newspaper
Trottman, M. (2011, February 8). Facebook firing case is settled. *The Wall Street*

Journal, p. B3.

Use "p." for single page, "pp." for multiple pages.

Capitalize all major words in title of journal, magazine, or newspaper.

Author and editor names use initials for first and middle names.

Chapter in an Edited book
Blakeslee, A. M. (2010). Addressing audiences in a digital age. In R. Spilka (Ed.), *Digital*

Put editor before book title.

literacy for technical communication: 21st century theory and practice (pp. 199–229).

Editor names have last names last.

Give state abbreviation
New York, NY: Routledge.

Use full page numbers for article.

Publication date: year, month day.

Article from a Publication on the Web
Lowery, A. (2011, May 20). LinkedIn is worth $9 billion? How the year's hottest IPO is

fueling speculation about a new tech bubble. *Slate*. Retrieved from http://

www.slate.com/id/2295189/
No punctuation after URL

Only list retrieval date if the source is likely to change (i.e., wikis, blogs); the date would be inserted between "Retrieved" and "from".

Book
Baker, A. C. (2010). *Catalytic conversations: Organizational communication and*

innovation. New York, NY: M. E. Sharpe.

(Continued)

| Figure C.2 | APA Format for Sources Used Most Often in Proposals and Reports   *(Concluded)* |

Put in brackets information known to you but not printed in document.

Book or Pamphlet with a Corporate Author
American Cancer Society. (2011). *Cancer facts & figures 2010.* [Atlanta, GA:] Author.

Indicates organization authoring document also published it.

E-mail Message
[Identify e-mail messages in the text as personal communication. Give name of author

and specific date. Do not list in References.]

Abbreviate and use periods.

Government Document Available on the Web from the GPO Access Database
U.S. Government Accountability Office. (2011, May 19). *Banking regulation: Enhanced*

guidance on commerical real estate risks needed. (Publication No. GAO-11-489).

Retrieved from Government Accountability Office Reports Online via GPO Access:

Abbreviate Government Printing Office

http://www.gao.gov/htext/d11477r.html

Interview Conducted by the Researcher
[Identify interview in the text as personal communication. Give name of interviewee

and specific date. Do not list in References.]

Italicize titles of stand-alone works. An article that is part of a larger work is put in Roman type and quotation marks.

n.d. if no date is given

Website
Berry, T. (n.d.). *Getting started on your business plan.* Retrieved May 25, 2011, from

Retrieval dates: Month day, year

Break long URLs after a slash. No period after URL.

http://articles.bplans.com/writing-a-business-plan/getting-started-on-your-

business-plan/26

| **Figure C.3** | Report Paragraphs with MLA Documentation |

Do not list page or paragraph numbers if the source is unnumbered.

Square brackets indicate a change from the original to make the quote fit into the structure of your sentence.

Social media can be defined as "technology facilitated dialogue among individuals or groups, such as blogs, microblogs, forums, wikis" and other unofficial forms of electronic communication (Cone). In a 2008 study on social media, Cone found that 39% of Americans reported using social media websites at least once a week; 30% reported using them two or more times a week. Additionally, the study found that 34% believed that companies should have a presence on social media websites and use their presence to interact with their customers. Fifty-one percent of users believed that companies should be present on these websites but interact only if customers ask them to do so (Cone). "While the ultimate measure [of most companies' marketing efforts] is sales, social media expands that because of its focus on influencers," says Simon Salt, the CEO of Inc-Slingers, a marketing communication firm (20). For example, he says "cable provider Comcast utilizes social media to monitor existing customer issues. .... Known on Twitter as @comcastcares, it quickly developed a reputation for engaging its customer base" (20).

Numbers at the beginnings of sentences must be written out.

No "p." before page number; use only page number since author identified in sentence.

An ellipsis (three spaced dots) indicates some material has been omitted. An extra dot serves as the period of the sentence.

Use page number (no "p.") for direct quote. Author's name is already in text, so is not repeated here.

The Cone study also found that 25% of users of social media websites reported interacting with companies at least once a week. When asked what kind of role companies should play on these websites, 43% said giving virtual customer service, 41% said soliciting customer feedback. Among some of the most popular social media websites are Facebook, MySpace, Twitter, Blogger, and Digg.

Because source is identified in text and has no page numbers, no citation is needed.

No need to provide a citation for facts that are general or common knowledge.

Twitter, a microblogging website, asks its users a simple question: "What are you doing?" Users can post their own updates and follow others' updates. Twitter has grown at a breathtaking pace in the last few months. It registered a whopping 600% increase in traffic in the 12 months leading up to November 2008. It is estimated that the micro-blogging website has approximately 3 million registered account holders from across the globe (Salt 20). A message or post on Twitter, known as a "tweet," cannot be more than 140 characters long. Companies and organizations are increasingly taking to Twitter.

Basic MLA citation: author and page number. Give page number for facts as well as quotes. No comma or "p." between author and number.

Visible Technologies, a Seattle-based market research firm, helps companies search for valuable market information from a virtual pool of millions of tweets. Some of the firm's clients include Hormel Foods and Panasonic. The computer manufacturer Dell, another customer, asks its customer representatives to interact with customers on Twitter. Recently, the company announced that it increased its sales by $500,000 through the use of Twitter (Baker). Zappos.com, an online shoe seller, encourages its employees to use Twitter to communicate, about subjects as wide-ranging as politics to marketing plans (Vascellaro R3).

Do not list headings or paragraph numbers if the source is unnumbered.

Article titles use title capitalization and quotation marks.

Works Cited

List all works (but only those works) cited in the text. List sources alphabetically.

Baker, Stephen. "Why Twitter Matters." *BusinessWeek.* 15 May 2008. Web. 2 Apr. 2009.

Date of publication: day month (abbreviated) year.

Type of source (Print or Web).

Date you visited site: day month year. Abbreviate months.

Source by a corporate author.

Cone. "2008 Business in Social Media Study." 2008. Web. 2 Apr. 2009 <http://www.coneinc.com/stuff/contentmgr/files/ 0/26ff8eb1d1a9371210502558013fe2a6/files/ 2008_business_in_social_media_fact_sheet.pdf>.

All names typed as they appear in the source.

Salt, Simon. "Track Your Success." *Marketing News.* 2 Apr. 2009: 20. Print.

URL in angle brackets; period after angle brackets. Break long URLs after a slash. URLs are only given for sites that may be difficult to find otherwise.

Abbreviate months with five of more letters.

Vascellaro, Jessica. "Twitter Goes Mainstream." *Wall Street Journal.* 27 Oct. 2008: R3. Print.

Volume and issue number not listed for weekly magazines.

Figure C.4	MLA Format for Sources Used Most Often in Proposals and Reports

In the examples below, headings in green identify the kind of work being referenced. The green headings are not part of the actual citation.

Use authors' full names as printed in source. First name first for second author

Join authors' names with "and"

Put quotation marks around title of article

Capitalize all major words in titles of articles, books, journals, magazines, and newspapers

Article in a Periodical

Stowers, Robert H., and Julie Y. Hummel. "The Use of Technology to Combat Plagiarism in

Busniness Communication Classes." *Business Communication Quarterly* 74.2 (2011):

Use both volume and issue number; do not italicize

Omit "1" in "169"

164–69. Print.

Entries designated as Print or Web

Omit introductory articles (e.g. "The") for newspapers and journals.

Article in a Newspaper

Trottman, Melanie. "Facebook Firing Case Is Settled." *Wall Street Journal* 8 Feb. 2011: B3.

Print.

Date given as day month (abbreviated) year

Give author's or editor's full name as printed in the source.

Chapter in an Edited Book

Blakeslee, Ann M. "Addressing Audiences in a Digital Age." *Digital Literacy for Technical*

Communication: 21st Century Theory and Practice. Ed. Rachel Spilka.

Editor's first name goes first

New York: Routlege, 2010. 199–229. Print.

Put book title before editor's name.

City of publication but not state

Article from a Publication on the Web

Lowery, Annie. "LinkedIn Is Worth $9 Billion? How the Year's Hottest IPO Is Fueling

Speculation about a New Tech Bubble." *Slate.* Washington Post Co. 20 May 2011. Web.

Publication date

Access date   25 May 2011.

Publisher or sponsor of site.

URLS are given only for sites that may be difficult to find.

Book

Baker, Ann C. *Catalytic Conversations: Organizational Communication and Innovation.* New

Date after city and publisher

York: M. E. Sharpe, 2010. Print.

Figure C.4	MLA Format for Sources Used Most Often in Proposals and Reports *(Concluded)*

Book or Pamphlet with a Corporate Author

American Cancer Society. *Cancer Facts & Figures 2010*. [Atlanta, GA:] ACS Publishing, *Put in brackets information known to you but not printed in source.*

2011. Print.

E-mail Message

Kienzler, Donna S. "Re: Project Guidelines and New Criteria." Message to Abhijit Rao.

15 July 2011. E-mail.

Name of government, not abbreviated, then name of agency

Government Document Available on the Web from the GPO Access Database

United States. U.S. Government Accountability Office. *Banking Regulation: Enhanced*

Guidance on Commerical Real Estate Risks Needed. Rep GAO-11-489. Wahington: *Abbreviate Government Printing Office*

GPO, 19 May 2011. Web. 25 May 2011. <http://www.gao.gov/htext/d11477r.html>.

URL in angle brackets; period after angle brackets. Separate long URLs after a slash. URLs are given only for site that may be difficult to find.

Interview Conducted by the Researcher

Drysdale, Marissa. Telephone interview. 12 July 2011.

Italicize titles of stand-alone works. An article that is part of a larger work is put in Roman type and quotation marks.

Website

Berry, Tim. "Getting Started on Your Business Plan." *Bplans* Palo Alto Software, *Publisher or sponsor of site*

n.d. if no date is given

Inc., n.d. Web. 25 May 2011. <http://articles.bplans.com/writing-a-business-plan/

getting-started-on-your-busines-plan/26>. *Give URL if source is difficult to find.*

GLOSSARY

A

abstract   A summary of a report, specifying the recommendations and the reasons for them. Also called an executive summary.

acknowledgment responses   Nods, smiles, frowns, and words that let a speaker know you are listening.

active listening   Feeding back the literal meaning or the emotional content or both so that the speaker knows that the listener has heard and understood.

active voice   A verb that describes the action done by the grammatical subject of the sentence.

adjustment   A positive response to a claim letter. If the company agrees to grant a refund, the amount due will be adjusted.

agenda   A list of items to be considered or acted upon at a meeting.

alliteration   A sound pattern occurring when several words begin with the same sound.

alternating pattern (of organization)   Discussing the alternatives first as they relate to the first criterion, then as they relate to the second criterion, and so on: ABC, ABC, ABC. Compare *divided pattern*.

analytical report   A report that interprets information.

anchor effect   The tendency to rely on the first piece of information given (the anchor) when making decisions.

argument   The reasons or logic offered to persuade the audience.

assumptions   Statements that are not proved in a report, but on which the recommendations are based.

audience benefits   Benefits or advantages that the audience gets by using the communicator's services, buying the communicator's products, following the communicator's policies, or adopting the communicator's ideas. Audience benefits can exist for policies and ideas as well as for goods and services.

auxiliary audience   People who may encounter your message but will not have to interact with it. This audience includes "read only" people.

average   See *mean*.

B

backchannel   The practice of using online technology to hold conversations concurrent with another activity, such as a speaker.

ballpark figure   An estimate of what a number should be.

bar chart   A visual consisting of parallel bars or rectangles that represent specific sets of data.

behavioral economics   A branch of economics that uses social and psychological factors in understanding decision making. It is particularly concerned with the limits of rationality in those decisions.

behavioral interviews   Job interviews that ask candidates to describe actual behaviors they have used in the past in specific situations.

bias-free language   Language that does not discriminate against people on the basis of sex, physical condition, race, age, or any other category.

blind ads   Job listings that do not list the company's name.

blind copies   Copies sent to other recipients that are not listed on the original letter, memo, or e-mail.

block format   In letters, a format in which inside address, date, and signature block are lined up at the left margin; paragraphs are not indented. In résumés, a format in which dates are listed in one column and job titles and descriptions in another.

blocking   Disagreeing with every idea that is proposed.

body language   Nonverbal communication conveyed by posture and movement, eye contact, facial expressions, and gestures.

boilerplate   Language from a previous document that a writer includes in a new document. Writers use boilerplate both to save time and energy and to use language that has already been approved by the organization's legal staff.

boxhead   Used in tables, the boxhead is the variable whose label is at the top.

brainstorming   A method of generating ideas by recording everything people in a group think of, without judging or evaluating the ideas.

branching question   Question that sends respondents who answer differently to different parts of the questionnaire. Allows respondents to answer only those questions that are relevant to their experience.

bridge (in prospecting job letters)   A sentence that connects the attention-getter to the body of a letter.

brochure   Leaflet (often part of a direct mailing) that gives more information about a product or organization.

buffer   A neutral or positive statement designed to allow the writer to delay, or buffer, the negative message.

build goodwill   To create a good image of yourself and of your organization—the kind of image that makes people want to do business with you.

bullets   Small circles (filled or open) or squares that set off items in a list. When you are giving examples, but the number is not exact and the order does not matter, use bullets to set off items.

business plan   A document written to raise capital for a new business venture or to outline future actions for an established business.

businessese A kind of jargon including unnecessary words. Some words were common 200–300 years ago but are no longer part of spoken English. Some have never been used outside of business writing. All of these terms should be omitted.

buying time with limited agreement Agreeing with the small part of a criticism that one does accept as true.

bypassing Miscommunication that occurs when two people use the same language to mean different things.

C

case The grammatical role a noun or pronoun plays in a sentence. The nominative case is used for the subject of a clause, the possessive to show who or what something belongs to, the objective case for the object of a verb or a preposition.

central selling point A strong audience benefit, big enough to motivate people by itself, but also serving as an umbrella to cover other benefits and to unify the message.

channel The physical means by which a message is sent. Written channels include e-mails memos, letters, and billboards. Oral channels include phone calls, speeches, and face-to-face conversations.

channel overload The inability of a channel to carry effectively all the messages that are being sent.

chartjunk Decoration that is irrelevant to a visual and that may be misleading.

checking for feelings Identifying the emotions that the previous speaker seemed to be expressing verbally or nonverbally.

checking for inferences Trying to identify the unspoken content or feelings implied by what the previous speaker has actually said.

choice architecture A form of persuasion that involves changing the context in which people make decisions to encourage them to make specific choices.

chronological résumé A résumé that lists what you did in a dated order, starting with the most recent events and going backward in reverse chronology.

citation Attributing a quotation or other idea to a source in the body of the report.

claim The part of an argument that the speaker or writer wants the audience to agree with.

claim letter A letter seeking a replacement or refund.

clip art Predrawn images that you can import into your documents.

close The ending of a communication.

closed body position Includes keeping the arms and legs crossed and close to the body. Suggests physical and psychological discomfort, defending oneself, and shutting the other person out. Also called a defensive body position.

closed question Question with a limited number of possible responses.

closure report A report summarizing completed work that does not result in new action or a recommendation.

clowning Making unproductive jokes and diverting the group from its task.

cluster sample A sample of subjects at each of a random sample of locations. This method is usually faster and cheaper than random sampling when face-to-face interviews are required.

clustering A method of thinking up ideas by writing the central topic in the middle of the page, circling it, writing down the ideas that topic suggests, and circling them.

cognitive dissonance A theory positing that it is psychologically uncomfortable to hold two ideas that are dissonant or conflicting. The theory of cognitive dissonance explains that people will resolve dissonance by deciding that one of the ideas is less important, by rejecting one of the ideas, or by constructing a third idea that has room for both of the conflicting ideas.

cold list A list used in marketing of people with no prior connection to your group.

collaborative writing Working with other writers to produce a single document.

collection letter A letter asking a customer to pay for goods and services received.

collection series A series of letters asking customers to pay for goods and services they have already received. Early letters in the series assume that the reader intends to pay but final letters threaten legal action if the bill is not paid.

comma splice or comma fault Using a comma to join two independent clauses. To correct, use a semicolon, use a comma with a conjunction, subordinate one of the clauses, or use a period and start a new sentence.

common ground Values and goals that the communicator and audience share.

communication channel The means by which you convey your message.

communication theory A theory explaining what happens when we communicate and where miscommunication can occur.

competitive proposal A proposal that has to compete for limited resources.

complaint letter A letter that challenges a policy or tries to get a decision changed.

complex sentence Sentence with one main clause and one or more subordinate clauses.

complimentary close The words after the body of the letter and before the signature. *Sincerely* and *Yours truly* are the most commonly used complimentary closes in business letters.

compound sentence Sentence with two main clauses joined by a comma and conjunction.

conclusions Section of a report or other communication that restates the main points.

conflict resolution Strategies for getting at the real issue, keeping discussion open, and minimizing hurt feelings so that people can find a solution that seems good to everyone involved.

connotations The emotional colorings or associations that accompany a word.

consensus Group solidarity supporting a decision.

contact letter Letter written to keep in touch with a customer or donor.

convenience sample   A group of subjects to whom the researcher has easy access; not a random sample.

conventions   Widely accepted practices.

conversational style   Conversational patterns such as speed and volume of speaking, pauses between speakers, whether questions are direct or indirect. When different speakers assign different meanings to a specific pattern, miscommunication results.

coordination   The second stage in the life of a task group, when the group finds, organizes, and interprets information and examines alternatives and assumptions. This is the longest of the stages.

corporate culture   The values, beliefs, norms, history, and assumptions of an organization that shape behaviors and decisions of individual employees.

counterclaim   A statement whose truth would negate the truth of the main claim.

credibility   Ability to come across to the audience as believable.

criteria   The standards used to evaluate or weigh the factors in a decision.

critical activities (in a schedule)   Activities that must be done on time if a project is to be completed by its due date.

critical incident   An important event that illustrates behavior or a history.

crop   To trim a photograph to fit a specific space, typically to delete visual information that is unnecessary or unwanted.

culture   The patterns of behavior and beliefs that are common to a people, nation, or organization.

cutaway drawings   Line drawings that depict the hidden or interior portions of an object.

cycling   The process of sending a document from writer to superior to writer to yet another superior for several rounds of revisions before the document is approved.

D

dangling modifier   A phrase that modifies the wrong word or a word that is not actually in a sentence. To correct a dangling modifier, recast the modifier as a subordinate clause or revise the sentence so its subject or object can be modified by the dangling phrase.

decode   To extract meaning from symbols.

decorative visual   A visual that makes the speaker's points more memorable but that does not convey numerical data.

defensive body position   See *closed body position.*

demographic characteristics   Measurable features of an audience that can be counted objectively: age, education level, income, etc.

denotation   A word's literal or "dictionary" meaning. Most common words in English have more than one denotation. Context usually makes it clear which of several meanings is appropriate.

dependent clause   See *subordinate clause.*

descriptive abstract   A listing of the topics an article or report covers that does not summarize what is said about each topic.

deviation bar charts   Bar charts that identify positive and negative values, or winners and losers.

devil's advocate   Person who defends a less popular viewpoint so that it receives fuller consideration.

dingbats   Small symbols such as arrows, pointing fingers, and so forth that are part of a typeface.

direct mail   A form of direct marketing that asks for an order, inquiry, or contribution directly from the reader.

direct mail package   The outer envelope of a direct mail letter and everything that goes in it: the letter, brochures, samples, secondary letters, reply card, and reply envelope.

direct marketing   All advertisements that ask for an order, inquiry, or contribution directly from the audience. Includes direct mail, catalogs, telemarketing (telephone sales), and newspaper and TV ads with 800 numbers to place an order.

direct request pattern   A pattern of organization that makes the request directly in the first paragraph.

discourse community   A group of people who share assumptions about what channels, formats, and styles to use for communication, what topics to discuss and how to discuss them, and what constitutes evidence.

divided pattern (of organization)   Discussing each alternative completely, through all criteria, before going on to the next alternative: AAA, BBB, CCC. Compare *alternating pattern.*

document design   The process of writing, organizing, and laying out a document so that it can be easily used by the intended audience.

documentation   Full bibliographic information so that interested readers can go to the original source of material used in a report.

dominating (in groups)   Trying to run a group by ordering, shutting out others, and insisting on one's own way.

dot chart   A chart that shows correlations or other large data sets. Dot charts have labeled horizontal and vertical axes.

dot planning   A way for large groups to set priorities; involves assigning colored dots to ideas.

E

editing   Checking the draft to see that it satisfies the requirements of good English and the principles of business writing. Unlike revision, which can produce major changes in meaning, editing focuses on the surface of writing.

ego-involvement   The emotional commitment that people have to their positions.

elimination of alternatives   A pattern of organization for reports that discusses the problem and its causes, the impractical solutions and their weaknesses, and finally the solution the writer favors.

ellipsis   Spaced dots used in reports to indicate that words have been omitted from quoted material and in direct mail to give the effect of pauses in speech.

emotional appeal   A persuasive technique that uses the audience's emotions to make them want to do what the writer or speaker asks.

empathy The ability to put oneself in someone else's shoes, to feel with that person.

enclosure A document that accompanies a letter.

enunciate To voice all the sounds of each word while speaking.

evaluating Measuring something, such as a document draft or a group decision, against your goals and the requirements of the situation and audience.

evidence Data the audience already accepts.

exaggeration Making something sound bigger or more important than it really is.

executive summary See *abstract*.

expectancy theory A theory that argues that motivation is based on the expectation of being rewarded for performance and the importance of the reward.

external audiences Audiences who are not part of the writer's organization.

external documents Documents that go to people in another organization.

external report Report written by a consultant for an organization of which he or she is not a permanent employee.

extranets Web pages for customers and suppliers.

extrinsic motivators Benefits that are "added on"; they are not a necessary part of the product or action.

eye contact Looking another person directly in the eye.

F

fallacies Common errors in logic that weaken arguments.

feasibility report A report that evaluates a proposed action and shows whether or not it will work.

feedback The receiver's response to a message.

figure Any visual that is not a table.

filler sounds Syllables, such as *um* and *uh*, which some speakers use to fill silence as they mentally search for their next words.

five Ws and H Questions that must be answered early in a press release: who, what, when, where, why, and how.

fixed font A typeface in which each letter has the same width on the page. Sometimes called *typewriter typeface*.

flaming Sending out an angry e-mail message before thinking about the implications of venting one's anger.

focus groups Small groups who come in to talk with a skilled leader about a potential product or process.

font A unified style of type. Fonts come in various sizes.

forecast An overview statement that tells the audience what you will discuss in a section or an entire report.

form letter A prewritten, fill-in-the-blank letter designed to fit standard situations.

formal meetings Meetings run under strict rules, like the rules of parliamentary procedure summarized in *Robert's Rules of Order*.

formal report A report containing formal elements such as a title page, a transmittal, a table of contents, and an abstract.

formalization The third and last stage in the life of a task group, when the group makes its decision and seeks consensus.

format The parts of a document and the way they are arranged on a page.

formation The first stage in the life of a task group, when members choose a leader and define the problem they must solve.

freewriting A kind of writing uninhibited by any constraints. Freewriting may be useful in overcoming writer's block, among other things.

frozen evaluation An assessment that does not take into account the possibility of change.

full justification Making both right and left margins of a text even, as opposed to having a ragged right margin.

fused sentence The result when two or more sentences are joined without punctuation or conjunctions.

G

Gantt charts Bar charts used to show schedules. Gantt charts are most commonly used in proposals.

gatekeeper The audience with the power to decide whether your message is sent on to other audiences.

gathering data Physically getting the background data you need. It can include informal and formal research or simply getting the letter to which you're responding.

general semantics The study of the ways behavior is influenced by the words and other symbols used to communicate.

gerund The *-ing* form of a verb; grammatically, it is a verb used as a noun.

getting feedback Asking someone else to evaluate your work. Feedback is useful at every stage of the writing process, not just during composition of the final draft.

glossary A list of terms used in a document with their definitions.

good appeal An appeal in direct marketing that offers believable descriptions of benefits, links the benefits of the product or service to a need or desire that motivates the audience, and makes the audience act.

goodwill The value of a business beyond its tangible assets, including its reputation and patronage. Also, a favorable condition and overall atmosphere of trust that can be fostered between parties conducting business.

goodwill ending Shift of emphasis away from the message to the reader. A goodwill ending is positive, personal, and forward-looking and suggests that serving the reader is the real concern.

goodwill presentation A presentation that entertains and validates the audience.

grammar checker Software program that flags errors or doubtful usage.

grapevine An organization's informal informational network that carries gossip and rumors as well as accurate information.

grid system   A means of designing layout by imposing columns on a page and lining up graphic elements within the columns.

ground rules   Procedural rules adopted by groups to make meetings and processes run smoothly.

grouped bar chart   A bar chart that allows the viewer to compare several aspects of each item or several items over time.

groupthink   The tendency for a group to reward agreement and directly or indirectly punish dissent.

guided discussion   A presentation in which the speaker presents the questions or issues that both speaker and audience have agreed on in advance. Instead of functioning as an expert with all the answers, the speaker serves as a facilitator to help the audience tap its own knowledge.

H

headings   Words or short phrases that group points and divide your letter, memo, e-mail, or report into sections.

hearing   Perceiving sounds. (Not the same thing as listening.)

hidden job market   Jobs that are never advertised but that may be available or may be created for the right candidate.

hidden negatives   Words that are not negative in themselves, but become negative in context.

high-context culture   A culture in which most information is inferred from the context, rather than being spelled out explicitly in words.

histogram   A bar chart using pictures, asterisks, or points to represent a unit of the data.

hypothetical interview question   A question that asks what a person would do in an imaginary situation.

I

impersonal expression   A sentence that attributes actions to inanimate objects, designed to avoid placing blame on a reader.

indented format   A format for résumés in which items that are logically equivalent begin at the same horizontal space, with carryover lines indented.

independent clause   See *main clause.*

infinitive   The form of the verb that is preceded by *to.*

infographic   An informative graphic combining statistics, text, color, and visuals.

informal meetings   Loosely run meetings in which votes are not taken on every point.

informal report   A report using letter or memo format.

information interview   An interview in which you talk to someone who works in the area you hope to enter to find out what the day-to-day work involves and how you can best prepare to enter that field.

information overload   A condition in which a person cannot process all the messages he or she receives.

information report   A report that collects data for the reader but does not recommend action.

informational dimensions   Dimensions of group work focusing on the problem, data, and possible solutions.

informative message   Message giving information to which the reader's basic reaction will be neutral.

informative presentation   A presentation that informs or teaches the audience.

informative report   A report that provides information.

inside address   The reader's name and address; put below the date and above the salutation in most letter formats.

interactive presentation   A presentation that is a conversation between the speaker and the audience.

intercultural competence   The ability to communicate sensitively with people from other cultures and countries, based on an understanding of cultural differences.

internal audiences   Audiences in the communicator's organization.

internal document   Document written for other employees in the same organization.

internal documentation   Providing information about a source in the text itself rather than in footnotes or endnotes.

internal report   Reports written by employees for use only in their organization.

interpersonal communication   Communication between people.

interpersonal dimensions   In a group, efforts promoting friendliness, cooperation, and group loyalty.

interview   Structured conversation with someone who is able to give you useful information.

intranet   A web page just for employees.

intrapreneurs   Innovators who work within organizations.

intrinsic motivators   Benefits that come automatically from using a product or doing something.

introduction   The part of a report that states the purpose and scope of the report. The introduction may also include limitations, assumptions, methods, criteria, and definitions.

J

jargon   There are two kinds of jargon. The first kind is the specialized terminology of a technical field. The second is businessese, outdated words that do not have technical meanings and are not used in other forms of English.

judgment   See *opinion.*

judgment sample   A group of subjects whose views seem useful.

justification report   Report that justifies the need for a purchase, an investment, a new personnel line, or a change in procedure.

justified margins   Margins that end evenly on both sides of the page.

K

key words   Words used in (1) a résumé to summarize areas of expertise, qualifications, and (2) an article or report to describe the content. Key words facilitate computer searches.

L

letter   Short document using block, modified, or simplified letter format that goes to readers outside your organization.

letterhead   Stationery with the organization's name, logo, address, and telephone number printed on the page.

limitations   Problems or factors that constrain the validity of the recommendations of a report.

line graph   A visual consisting of lines that show trends or allow the viewer to interpolate values between the observed values.

logical fallacies   See *fallacies.*

low-context culture   A culture in which most information is conveyed explicitly in words rather than being inferred from context.

M

main clause   A group of words that can stand by itself as a complete sentence. Also called an independent clause.

Maslow's hierarchy of needs   Five levels of human need posited by Abraham H. Maslow. They include physical needs, the need for safety and security, for love and belonging, for esteem and recognition, and for self-actualization.

mean   The average of a group of numbers. Found by dividing the sum of a set of figures by the number of figures.

median   The middle number in a ranked set of numbers.

memo   Document using memo format sent to readers in your organization.

methods section   The section of a report or survey describing how the data were gathered.

minutes   Records of a meeting, listing the items discussed, the results of votes, and the persons responsible for carrying out follow-up steps.

mirror question   Question that paraphrases the content of the answer an interviewee gave to the last question.

misplaced modifier   A word or phrase that appears to modify another element of the sentence than the writer intended.

mixed punctuation   Using a colon after the salutation and a comma after the complimentary close in a letter.

mode   The most frequent number in a set of numbers.

modified block format   A letter format in which the inside address, date, and signature block are lined up with each other one-half or two-thirds of the way over on the page.

modifier   A word or phrase giving more information about another word in a sentence.

monochronic culture   Culture in which people do only one important activity at a time.

monologue presentation   A presentation in which the speaker talks without interruption. The presentation is planned and is delivered without deviation.

multiple graphs   Three or more simple stories told by graphs juxtaposed to create a more powerful story.

Myers-Briggs Type Indicator   A scale that categorizes people on four dimensions: introvert–extravert; sensing–intuitive; thinking–feeling; and perceiving–judging.

N

negative message   A message in which basic information conveyed is negative; the reader is expected to be disappointed or angry.

networking   Using your connections with other people to help you achieve a goal.

neutral subject line   A subject line that does not give away the writer's stance on an issue.

noise   Any physical or psychological interference in a message.

nominative case   The grammatical form used for the subject of a clause. *I, we, he, she,* and *they* are nominative pronouns.

nonageist   Refers to words, images, or behaviors that do not discriminate against people on the basis of age.

noncompetitive proposal   A proposal with no real competition and hence a high probability of acceptance.

nonracist   Refers to words, images, or behaviors that do not discriminate against people on the basis of race.

nonrestrictive clause   A clause giving extra but unessential information about a noun or pronoun. Because the information is extra, commas separate the clause from the word it modifies.

nonsexist language   Language that treats both sexes neutrally, that does not make assumptions about the proper gender for a job, and that does not imply that one sex is superior to or takes precedence over the other.

nonverbal communication   Communication that does not use words.

normal interview   A job interview with mostly expected questions.

noun–pronoun agreement   Having a pronoun be the same number (singular or plural) and the same person (first, second, or third) as the noun it refers to.

O

objective case   The grammatical form used for the object of a verb or preposition. *Me, us, him, her,* and *them* are objective pronouns.

omnibus motion   A motion that allows a group to vote on several related items in a single vote. Saves time in formal meetings with long agendas.

open body position   Includes keeping the arms and legs uncrossed and away from the body. Suggests physical and psychological comfort and openness.

open punctuation   Using no punctuation after the salutation and the complimentary close.

open question   Question with an unlimited number of possible responses.

opinion   A statement that can never be verified, since it includes terms that cannot be measured objectively. Also called a judgment.

organization (in messages)   The order in which ideas are arranged.

organizational culture   The values, attitudes, and philosophies shared by people in an organization that shape its behaviors and reward structure.

outsourcing   Going outside the company for products and services that once were made by the company's employees.

P

package   The outer envelope and everything that goes in it in a direct mailing.

paired bar chart   A bar chart that shows the correlation between two items.

parallel structure   Using the same grammatical and logical form for words, phrases, clauses, and ideas in a series.

paraphrase   To repeat in your own words the verbal content of another communication.

passive verb   A verb that describes action done to the grammatical subject of the sentence.

people-first language   Language that names the person first, then the condition: "people with mental retardation." Used to avoid implying that the condition defines the person's potential.

performance appraisals   Supervisors' written evaluations of their subordinates' work.

persona   The "author" or character who allegedly writes a document; the voice that a communicator assumes in creating a message.

personal brandings   A pop term for marketing yourself, including job searching. It includes an expectation that you will use various options, including social media such as LinkedIn, to market yourself.

personal space   The distance someone wants between him- or herself and other people in ordinary, nonintimate interchanges.

personalized   A message that is adapted to the individual reader by including the reader's name and address and perhaps other information.

persuade   To motivate and convince the audience to act or change a belief.

persuasive presentation   A presentation that motivates the audience to act or to believe.

phishing e-mails   E-mails that look like messages from official business but actually connect to private sites seeking to acquire data for fraud or identity theft.

pictogram   A bar chart using pictures or symbols to represent a unit of data.

pie chart   A circular chart whose sections represent percentages of a given quantity.

pitch   The highness or lowness of a sound.

plagiarism   Passing off the words or ideas of others as one's own.

planning   All the thinking done about a subject and the means of achieving your purposes. Planning takes place not only when devising strategies for the document as a whole, but also when generating "miniplans" that govern sentences or paragraphs.

polarization   A logical fallacy that argues there are only two possible positions, one of which is clearly unacceptable.

polychronic culture   Culture in which people do several things at once.

population   The group a researcher wants to make statements about.

positive emphasis   Focusing on the positive rather than the negative aspects of a situation.

positive or good news message   Message to which the reader's reaction will be positive.

positive psychology   A branch of psychology that studies how to help people thrive.

possessive case   The grammatical form used to indicate possession or ownership. *My, our, his, hers, its,* and *their* are possessive pronouns.

post office abbreviations   Two-letter abbreviations for states and provinces.

prepositions   Words that indicate relationships, for example, *with, in, under, at.*

presenting problem   The problem that surfaces as the subject of discord. The presenting problem is often not the real problem.

primary audience   The audience who will make a decision or act on the basis of a message.

primary research   Research that gathers new information.

pro-and-con pattern   A pattern of organization that presents all the arguments for an alternative and then all the arguments against it.

probe question   A follow-up question designed to get more information about an answer or to get at specific aspects of a topic.

problem-solving pattern   A pattern of organization that describes a problem before offering a solution to the problem.

procedural dimensions   Dimensions of group work focusing on methods: how the group makes decisions, who does what, when assignments are due.

process of writing   What people actually do when they write: planning, gathering, writing, evaluating, getting feedback, revising, editing, and proofreading.

progress report   A statement of the work done during a period of time and the work proposed for the next period.

proofreading   Checking the final copy to see that it's free from typographical errors.

proportional font   A font in which some letters are wider than other letters (for example, *w* is wider than *i*).

proposal   Document that suggests a method and personnel for finding information or solving a problem.

prospecting letter   A job application letter written to a company that has not announced openings but where you'd like to work.

psychographic characteristics   Human characteristics that are qualitative rather than quantitative: values, beliefs, goals, and lifestyles.

psychological description   Description of a product or service in terms of audience benefits.

psychological reactance   Phenomenon occurring when a person reacts to a negative message by asserting freedom in some other arena.

purpose statement   The statement in a proposal or a report specifying the organizational problem, the technical questions that must be answered to solve the problem, and the rhetorical purpose of the report (to explain, to recommend, to request, to propose).

Q

questionnaire   List of questions for people to answer in a survey.

R

ragged right margins   Margins that do not end evenly on the right side of the page.

random sample   A sample for which each member of the population has an equal chance of being chosen.

range   The difference between the highest and lowest numbers in a set of figures.

recommendation report   A report that evaluates two or more possible alternatives and recommends one of them. Doing nothing is always one alternative.

recommendations   Section of a report that specifies items for action.

reference line   A *subject line* that refers the reader to another document (usually a numbered one, such as an invoice).

referral interview   Interviews you schedule to learn about current job opportunities in your field and to get referrals to other people who may have the power to create a job for you. Useful for tapping into unadvertised jobs and the hidden job market.

reflexive pronoun   Refers to or emphasizes a noun or pronoun that has already appeared in the sentence. *Myself, herself,* and *themselves* are reflexive pronouns.

release date   Date a report will be made available to the public.

reply card   A card or form designed to make it easy for the reader to respond to a direct mail letter. A good reply card repeats the central selling point, basic product information, and price.

request for proposal (RFP)   A statement of the service or product that an agency wants; an invitation for proposals to provide that service or product.

respondents   The people who fill out a questionnaire; also called *subjects*.

response rate   The percentage of subjects receiving a questionnaire who answer the questions.

restrictive clause   A clause limiting or restricting the meaning of a noun or pronoun. Because its information is essential, no commas separate the clause from the word it restricts.

résumé   A persuasive summary of your qualifications for employment.

résumé blasting   Posting your résumé widely—usually by the hundreds—on the web.

reverse chronology   Starting with the most recent events, such as job or degree, and going backward in time. Pattern of organization used for chronological résumés.

revising   Making changes in the draft: adding, deleting, substituting, or rearranging. Revision can be changes in single words, but more often it means major additions, deletions, or substitutions, as the writer measures the draft against purpose and audience and reshapes the document to make it more effective.

RFP   See *request for proposal.*

rhetorical purpose   The effect the writer or speaker hopes to have on the audience (to inform, to persuade, to build goodwill).

rhythm   The repetition of a pattern of accented and unaccented syllables.

rival hypotheses   Alternate explanations for observed results.

rule of three   The rule noting a preference for three short parallel examples and explaining that the last will receive the most emphasis.

run-on sentence   A sentence containing two or more main clauses strung together with *and, but, or, so,* or *for.*

S

sales pattern   A pattern of persuasion that consists of an attention getting opener, a body with reasons and details, and an action close.

salutation   The greeting in a letter: "Dear Ms. Smith:"

sample (in marketing)   A product provided to the audience to whet their appetite for more.

sample (in research)   The portion of the population a researcher actually studies.

sampling frame   The list of all possible sampling units.

sampling units   Those items/people actually sampled.

sans serif   Literally, *without serifs.* Typeface whose letters lack bases or flicks. Helvetica and Geneva are examples of sans serif typefaces.

saves the reader's time   The result of a message whose style, organization, and visual impact help the reader to read, understand, and act on the information as quickly as possible.

schematic diagrams   Line drawings of objects and their parts.

scope statement   A statement in a proposal or report specifying the subjects the report covers and how broadly or deeply it covers them.

secondary audience   The audience who may be asked by the primary audience to comment on a message or to implement ideas after they've been approved.

secondary research   Research retrieving data someone else gathered. Includes library research.

segmented, subdivided, or stacked bars   Bars in a bar chart that sum components of an item.

semantics or general semantics   The study of the ways behavior is influenced by the words and other symbols used to communicate.

sentence fragment   Words that are not a complete sentence but that are punctuated as if they were a complete sentence.

sentence outline   An outline using complete sentences. It contains the thesis or recommendation plus all supporting points.

serif   The little extensions from the main strokes on letters. Times Roman and Courier are examples of serif typefaces.

signpost   An explicit statement of the place that a speaker or writer has reached: "Now we come to the third point."

simple sentence   Sentence with one main clause.

simplified format   A letter format that omits the salutation and complimentary close and lines everything up at the left margin.

situational interviews   Job interviews in which candidates are asked to describe what they would do in specific hypothetical situations.

skills résumé   A résumé organized around the skills you've used, rather than the date or the job in which you used them.

social signals   Nonverbal communications such as gestures, facial expressions, voice tone, and proximity.

solicited letter   A job letter written when you know that the company is hiring.

spot visuals   Informal visuals that are inserted directly into text. Spot visuals do not have numbers or titles.

stereotyping   Putting similar people or events into a single category, even though significant differences exist.

storyboard   A visual representation of the structure of a document, with a rectangle representing each page or unit. An alternative to outlining as a method of organizing material.

strategy   A plan for reaching your specific goals with a specific audience.

stratified random sample   A sample generated by first dividing the sample into subgroups in the population and then taking a random sample for each subgroup.

stress (in a communication)   Emphasis given to one or more words in a sentence, or one or more ideas in a message.

stress interview   A job interview that deliberately puts the applicant under stress, physical or psychological. Here it's important to change the conditions that create physical stress and to meet psychological stress by rephrasing questions in less inflammatory terms and treating them as requests for information.

structured interview   An interview that follows a detailed list of questions prepared in advance.

stub   The variable listed on the side in a table.

subject line   The title of the document, used to file and retrieve the document. A subject line tells readers why they need to read the document and provides a framework in which to set what you're about to say.

subordinate clause   A group of words containing a subject and a verb but that cannot stand by itself as a complete sentence. Also called a dependent clause.

summarizing   Restating and relating major points, pulling ideas together.

summary abstract   The logic skeleton of an article or report, containing the thesis or recommendation and its proof.

summary sentence or paragraph   A sentence or paragraph listing in order the topics that following sentences or paragraphs will discuss.

survey   A method of getting information from a group of people.

SWOT analysis   A method of evaluating a proposed action that examines both internal factors (Strengths, Weaknesses) and external factors (Opportunities, Threats).

T

table   Numbers or words arrayed in rows and columns.

talking heads   Headings that are detailed enough to provide an overview of the material in the sections they introduce.

template   A design or format that serves as a pattern.

10-K report   A report filed with the Securities and Exchange Commission summarizing the firm's financial performance.

thank-you note   A note thanking someone for helping you.

threat   A statement, explicit or implied, that someone will be punished if he or she does or doesn't do something.

360-degree feedback   A form of assessment in which an employee receives feedback from peers, managers, subordinates, customers, and suppliers.

tone   The implied attitude of the author toward the reader and the subject.

tone of voice   The rising or falling inflection that indicates whether a group of words is a question or a statement, whether the speaker is uncertain or confident, whether a statement is sincere or sarcastic.

topic heading   A heading that focuses on the structure of a report. Topic headings give little information.

topic outline   An outline listing the main points and the subpoints under each main point. A topic outline is the basis for the table of contents of a report.

topic sentence   A sentence that introduces or summarizes the main idea in a paragraph.

transitions   Words, phrases, or sentences that show the connections between ideas.

transmit   To send a message.

transmittal   A message explaining why something is being sent.

truncated code   Symbols such as asterisks that turn up other forms of a keyword in a computer search.

truncated graphs   Graphs with part of the scale missing.

two-margin format   A format for résumés in which dates are listed in one column and job titles and descriptions in another. This format emphasizes work history.

U

umbrella sentence or paragraph   A sentence or paragraph listing in order the topics that following sentences or paragraphs will discuss.

understatement   Downplaying or minimizing the size or features of something.

unity   Using only one idea or topic in a paragraph or other piece of writing.

unjustified margins   Margins that do not end evenly on the right side of the page.

unstructured interview An interview based on three or four main questions prepared in advance and other questions that build on what the interviewee says.

usability testing Testing a document with users to see that it functions as desired.

V

venting Expressing pent-up negative emotions.

verbal communication Communication that uses words; may be either oral or written.

vested interest The emotional stake readers have in something if they benefit from maintaining or influencing conditions or actions.

vicarious participation An emotional strategy in fund-raising letters based on the idea that by donating money, readers participate in work they are not able to do personally.

visual impact The visual "first impression" you get when you look at a page.

volume The loudness or softness of a voice or other sound.

W

watchdog audience An audience that has political, social, or economic power and that may base future actions on its evaluation of your message.

white space The empty space on the page. White space emphasizes material that it separates from the rest of the text.

widget A software program that can be dropped into social networking sites and other places.

wild card Symbols such as asterisks that turn up other forms of a keyword in a computer search. See also *truncated code.*

withdrawing Being silent, not contributing, not helping with the work, not attending meetings.

wordiness Taking more words than necessary to express an idea.

works cited The sources specifically referred to in a report.

works consulted Sources read during the research for a report but not mentioned specifically in the report.

Y

you-attitude A style of communicating that looks at things from the audience's point of view, emphasizes what the audience wants to know, respects the audience's intelligence, and protects the audience's ego. Using *you* generally increases you-attitude in positive situations. In negative situations or conflict, avoid *you* since that word will attack the audience.

PHOTO CREDITS

NAME INDEX

COMPANY INDEX

SUBJECT INDEX